A HISTORY OF CHILDREN

A HISTORY OF CHILDREN

A SOCIO-CULTURAL SURVEY ACROSS MILLENNIA

A. R. Colón,

with *P. A. Colón*

GREENWOOD PRESS
Westport, Connecticut • London

Library of Congress Cataloging-in-Publication Data

Colón, A. R.
    A history of children : a socio-cultural survey across millennia / A. R. Colón
with P. A. Colón.
        p.   cm.
    Includes bibliographical references and index.
    ISBN 0-313-31574-4 (alk. paper)
    1. Children—History.   2. Children, Prehistoric.   3. Children—Cross-cultural
studies.   4. Children—Social conditions.   I. Colón, P. A.   II. Title.
HQ767.85 .C65 2001
305.23′09—dc21
                                            00-042236

British Library Cataloguing in Publication Data is available.

Library of Congress Catalog Card Number: 00-042236
ISBN: 0-313-31574-4

First published in 2001

Greenwood Press, 88 Post Road West, Westport, CT 06881
An imprint of Greenwood Publishing Group, Inc.
www.greenwood.com

Printed in the United States of America

♾™ The paper used in this book complies with the
Permanent Paper Standard issued by the National
Information Standards Organization (Z39.48–1984).

10 9 8 7 6 5 4 3 2 1

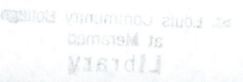

Copyright Acknowledgments

❑ ❑ ❑

For material reproduced in this book, the following publishers are gratefully acknowledged:

Figures

Figure 2.3 is reproduced by permission from the Egyptian Ministry of Culture, Supreme Council of Antiquities, Egyptian Museum.

Figures 2.4, 2.5, and 2.6 are reproduced by permission of the National Archaeological Museum, Athens.

Figure 2.10 is reproduced by permission of the British Library.

Figure 3.6 is reproduced by permission of the Louvre Museum, Paris.

Figure 3.7 is reproduced by permission of James Higginbotham.

Figure 4.3 is reproduced by permission of the Bibliothèque de Troyes, France.

Figure 5.1 is reproduced by permission of the American Museum of Natural History.

Figures 5.2 and 5.3 are reproduced from objects in the collections of the University of Pennsylvania Museum (Nos. NA 4322, 42-1-66, 45-15-749, NA 1079, NA 1089, NA 9973, 41973, 42306).

Figure 5.6 is from *Medicine in Mexico: From Aztec Herbs to Betatrons* by Gordon Schendel, written in collaboration with Dr. José Alvarez Amézquita and Dr. Miguel E. Bustamante. Copyright © 1968, renewed 1996. By permission of the University of Texas Press.

Figure 6.2 is reproduced by permission of the Bibliothèque nationale de France.

Figure 6.5 is reproduced by permission of the Istituto degli Innocenti, Florence.

Figure 6.8 is reproduced by permission of the National Gallery of Scotland, Edinburgh.

Figure 7.1 is reproduced by permission of the Kunsthistorisches Museum, Vienna.

Figure 7.2 is reproduced by permission of The Walters Art Gallery, Baltimore.

Figure 7.4 is reproduced by permission of The Art Museum, Princeton University.

Figure 8.3 is reproduced by permission of the Oxford University Press.

Figure 9.3 is reproduced by courtesy of the Simon Wiesenthal Center Beit HaShoah Museum of Tolerance Library/Archives, Los Angeles.

Text

Chapter 2: The Gortyn Code is from the *Civilization of Ancient Crete* by R. F. Willetts, reproduced by permission of the Chrysalis Books Group.

Chapter 2: The excerpts from *History Begins at Sumer* by S. N. Kramer are reproduced by permission of Random House, Inc.

Chapter 3: The excerpts from *Life in Egypt under Roman Rule* by N. Lewis, copyright © 1983, are reproduced by permission of Oxford University Press.

Chapter 4: Excerpts from *The Kindness of Strangers* by John Boswell, copyright © 1988 by John Boswell. Reprinted by permission of Pantheon Books, a division of Random House, Inc.

Chapter 7: The excerpts from *English Family Life, 1576–1716* by R. Houlbrooke are reproduced by permission of Blackwell Publishers.

Chapter 7: The excerpts from *When Fathers Ruled* by S. Ozment are reproduced by permission of Harvard University Press.

Chapter 8: Excerpts from *Children in Historical and Comparative Perspective: An International Handbook and Research Guide,* Joseph M. Hawes and N. Ray Hiner, editors (Greenwood Press, Westport, CT, 1991). Copyright © 1991 by Joseph M. Hawes and N. Ray Hiner. Reprinted with permission.

Chapter 8: The poem "Pediatric Profiles" appeared in the *Journal of Pediatrics* (1933, 2:391–92) and is reproduced by permission of Mosby, Inc.

Chapter 8: Excerpts from *Eighteenth-Century London Life* by Rosamond Bayne-Powell, copyright © 1938 by E. P. Dutton & Company, Inc., renewed 1966 by Robert Lane Bayne-Powell. Used by permission of Dutton, a division of Penguin Putnam Inc.

for

Joseph

Jeanette

Cecilie

Julian

Meghan

Anton

Felicia

Emerson

and other children in our history . . .

Contents

❑ ❑ ❑

Illustrations

❏　❏　❏

Preface

❏ ❏ ❏

The quality of children's lives throughout millennia is the material of this book. The multitudinous factors across the centuries that both hindered and advanced progress in human behavior are examined as they affected social attitudes and behaviors toward children.

The challenge has been edifying and instructive. It has been a delightful discovery to mark the striking global similarities of human behavior and the commonality of human experience despite the passage of time, sometimes measured in thousands of years, and the divergent cultures that comprise the human family. My aim in these pages is to provide the reader with a recognition of how we are bound together over millennia by experiences common to our species. Certainly, this work has left me with an enriched appreciation of my fellow human beings, adult and child.

My intention also has been to describe children's experience in the past as a prelude to understanding their condition in our present age and to do so worldwide, since I am convinced that mankind's concerns and efforts in the future will encompass the planet. It seems to me inevitable that all of us, who even now have instantaneous access to a large percentage of the world's people, will be more and more involved as witnesses to, as well as participants in, global events. I would like to hope that our interests and concerns regarding our fellow human beings—and especially regarding the world's children—will be generous and that this study of children the world over throughout the ages is a positive step in that direction.

The survey arbitrarily ends with the Second World War, because I believe that the voluminous happenings involving children in the twentieth century would mandate another, independent text. I am overwhelmed by a sense of the importance of the task when I consider the statistics: worldwide, five children are born every second and in the United States of America, one every nine seconds. Four hundred thousand children are born daily. The world population in 1999 was nearly six billion people and is projected to reach ten billion by the year 2025. By that time, more than 60 percent of this planet's people will be children. The pressing need to study children's issues is now.

My interest in the lives of children and how they have fared on our planet through the ages is rooted in my training as a scientist whose pediatric experience has taken him well beyond a single cultural milieu. My work in the Peace Corps, with Project Hope, with Cambodian and Honduran refugee children, and with the inner-city poor of Brazil, Colombia, Bolivia, Egypt, and the United States has developed in me a keen sensitivity regarding children's well-being and suffering that are traceable to social factors.

Curiosity and interest in history complemented my concerns for children, and I began to examine societies' behavior toward children, from human beginnings to the present, attempting to keep in mind the degree to which current thought, attitudes, and customs in various countries have evolved from the distant and not so distant past.

Children through the ages have been the conduits of their cultures, passing them on to subsequent generations while incorporating their own life experiences with prevalent rearing practices in their societies. In this way, cycles of acculturation are assured in perpetuity, albeit infused with and modified by singular and collective experiences, good and bad, in childhood and beyond.

The Child is father of the Man
—William Wordsworth[1]

Since time began, at the best of times parental efforts to nourish, discipline, train, and protect children harmonized with children's tears and laughter, joy and sadness, in order to promote sound growth and maturation. Conversely, the absence of parental love and affection and of societal approbation that encourages children's discovery of and wonder about the world has been and is a root cause of self-inflicted human misery.

The childhood shews the man
As morning shews the day.

—John Milton[2]

Some of the suffering of children has been at the hands of malevolent individuals. Often, however, it has been the inevitable consequence of simply hapless people being overwhelmed by the struggle to survive. Heroic characters often have emerged—in the guise of social reformers in the industrial age or of individuals and institutions moved to compassion by strong religious principles.

There is a significant amount of surviving evidence to support an interpretation that societies have behaved badly toward children. In the main, however, I mostly have been impressed that societies throughout the history of the world have striven in varying degrees to provide positive and nurturing parenting in stable environments.

The many references to injustices and inhumane treatment of children serve as reminders of such instances in our own time, but while this realization heightens my own personal sensibilities in this regard, it by no means dominates my thinking.

I set out to explore prevailing conditions that contributed to the specific cultural milieu of societies, both ancient and modern: the economic circumstances, mystic obsessions, religious fervor, superstitious fears, forced tribal migrations, and the vicissitudes of hunger, disease, aggression, and war. Like stealthily meandering glaciers or terrifying convulsive jolts of earthquakes, these influences formed whole civilizations—rules, expectations, and philosophy. These factors, in turn, determined the lives and destinies of children.

Too often it was clear that accepted mores of societies, which shaped and molded children in preparation for future roles in society, decreed for them a tragic destiny, such as the custom of Inca child sacrifice. Often too, with the commonweal cited as the rationale, whole cultures embraced and institutionalized child abuse.

The disposal of children has always been facile. Their voices are small and weak. Too often throughout the history of mankind theirs was an ignored cry of anguish, their lives little valued by their parents or their societies. With tacit and sometimes explicit acquiescence, the mores of many cultures facilitated the disposal or abuse of children. An example that comes to mind is that of Letahulozo, who was born in the nineteenth century in Papua, New Guinea. Her father approached his wife in the birthing hut, waiting outside, leaning over the fence around the hut until the mother's exhaustion from her parturition abated. When he was told the newborn was a girl, he said casually, "Break it and throw it away." Letahulozo's mother disobeyed her husband's edict, and Leta lived into the twentieth century to tell the tale of her beginnings.[3]

Like events have occurred throughout the millennia; they still do occur and not always with such a happy ending. Plutarch described the enforcement of a similar decree of Lykourgos in Sparta: "[I]f it was ill-born and unshapely they sent it away to the so-called *Apothetai*" (to die of exposure).[4] In 1 B.C. in Ptolemaic Egypt, a man named Hilarion wrote his wife: "If you are delivered of child, if it is a boy, keep it, if a girl, discard it."[5] In Phoenicia, unwanted infants were burned in tophets; the Romans abandoned newborns at the *columna lactaria*, and the Vikings tested the legitimacy of newborns by seashore exposure. Some American Plains Indians stuffed unwanted infants down badger holes. During the Middle Ages unwanted children were given to the church, where, without a choice in the matter, they were trained to serve as oblates. Well into the Renaissance, in Christian countries, rejected infants commonly were discarded to a watery grave. In eighteenth-century England, infants were put to a soporific death with opium cordials, and in the nineteenth century, childhood morbidity and mortality soared as a consequence of industrial abuses.

In our own century, ghettos, death camps, and "ethnic cleansing" squadrons have accounted for the deaths of millions of children. Starvation and trade boycotts used as political strategies have extinguished the lives of countless others. Currently, in the United States over two million cases of child abuse are reported annually, and it is believed that millions more go unreported.[6] Our newspapers routinely describe the violent deaths of infants and children, victims of uncontrolled rage, "drive-by" shootings, and drug-induced aggressions—this in a "child-centered" society.

The collective outrage expressed whenever accounts of crimes against children surface, suggests, however, that, although we may not always be able to act or are not prepared to act to rectify wrongdoing, the more commonly shared value is the moral imperative that desires protection for vulnerable and powerless children of the world.

This is not an academic treatise. To some degree the lapse is mine, but it is also the case that insufficient data for so mighty an undertaking as a scholarly history of children reflects the scant attention history has accorded children. Their lives and experiences barely have been alluded to in historical documents and treatises, sometimes meriting reference only as a footnote. Therefore, the gaps between eras and places may be ascribed to voids in data rather than merely an author's capriciousness:

At first glance, [the]lack of interest in the lives of children seems odd. Historians have been traditionally committed to explaining continuity and change over time, and ever since Plato it has been known that childhood is a key to this understanding. The importance of parent–child relations for social change was hardly discovered by Freud; St. Augustine's cry, "Give me other mothers and I will give you another world," has been echoed by major thinkers for fifteen centuries *without affecting historical writing.*[7] (Emphasis added)

In the text following, the great events of history are briefly summarized to place the reader in familiar historical territories. Each chapter begins with a historical overview to set the scene for each respective age. The historical information that advances understanding of the evolution of child care and of how the practices of respective cultures affected children and the nature of childhood receives closer attention. The birth, nurturing, acculturation, education, and place of children in societies that extend back to prehistory and forward to our modern world are examined. Legal decrees that affected children are examined, and extant records that amplify an understanding of childhood experience are liberally referred to, especially those that cite pedagogy and child-labor laws. The abundant references from ecclesiastical sources, especially in the patristic and medieval periods, reflect the preponderance of Western sources available. This also is true of the bulk of data pertaining to children in Arabic, Hebrew, and Oriental cultures, which likewise comes from records kept by religious bodies in, respectively, canons, the Talmud, and scrolls. Finally, there are some references to children in literature and in literature written for children. The format, replete with illustrations and quotes to complement the text, has been without doubt influenced by Lewis Carroll's whimsical query, "What is the use of a book without pictures and conversation?"[8]

In the fifteen years since I began this manuscript, I have referred to hundreds of books that have touched on the subject of child-rearing practices, ancient and modern. This entire endeavor could not have been possible without the original research and scholarship of social historians who generously publish and share their passions and interests with us. Their data have allowed me to compile, analyze, and hypothesize in order to present this timeline of the child. I have reveled in the wise and wonderful plasma of past times that they have suffused. I am beholden to scholars like Philippe Aries, Elisabeth Badinter, John Boswell, Robert Bremner, Roger Chartier, Sally Crawford, Lloyd de Mause, Georges Duby, Joan Evans, Valerie Fildes, Jean-Louis Flandrin, Robert Garland, Frances and Joseph Gies, Michael Golden, Barbara Hanawalt, David Herlihy, Margaret Hewitt, Colin Heywood, Ralph Houlbrooke, Steven Ozment, Ivy Pinchbeck, Linda Pollock, Lionel Rose, Marjorie

Rowling, John Ruhräh, Shulamith Shahar, John Sommerville, George Still, Thomas Wiedemann, Bernard Wishy, and many others. I am also grateful to the late Helen Bagdoyan for allowing me access to her wonderful archives of rare and old books at Georgetown University, Washington, D.C.

NOTES

1. "My Heart Leaps Up," in *Wordsworth Poetry and Prose* (Oxford: Clarendon Press, 1924), p. 93.

2. *Paradise Regained*, bk. 4, in *Poems of John Milton* (London: Thomas Nelson and Sons, 1937), p. 345.

3. Hausfater and Hrdy, 1984, p. 427.

4. Plutarch, 1950, p. 14.

5. Lewis, 1983, p. 43.

6. A. R. Colón and P. A. Colón, "The Health of America's Children," in *Caring for America's Children*. Edited by F. J. Macchiarola and A. Gartner (New York: Academy of Political Science, 1989), pp. 48–49.

7. De Mause, 1974, pp. 1–2.

8. L. Carroll, *Adventures in Wonderland*, 1865.

Prologue

❑　❑　❑

The union of male sperm with a female ovum in a dark and moist fallopian tube marks a fertilization process that progresses with multiplication, differentiation, and specialization over a period of ten lunar months. During that time a human organism is formed, composed of some 10^{14} cells, a treasure of DNA, comprising forty-six chromosomes, fifty to one hundred thousand genes, and three billion base pairs of nucleic acids—the human genome. It has been so since the human specie evolved, with genetic information and the resultant organisms experiencing only subtle mutation and change.

Thus, an apparently simple, easily and almost universally understood concept reveals on closer analysis an unequaled complexity. Unanswered scientific questions abound: how does the sperm enter the ovum? Upon penetration by one sperm, how does the ovum exclude all others? How does the ovum begin to replicate? Why isn't the sperm's foreign protein rejected by the ovum? Indeed, how does the mother carry such a large "foreign body" to term without rejection? What is the secret of the tiny sperm's capacity to carry an amount of genetic information equivalent to that of the larger ovum? How is the ovum endowed with its potential for plenipotency (i.e., the process of cell differentiation and development into heart, lungs, liver, bone, hair, etc.)? What mechanism stops the differentiation? Why are we all not one big ball of hair, or all bone, or all brain, or all heart? Some of these unanswered questions first were posed in antiquity, by Anaxagoras, for example, in the fifth century B.C.: "How can hair come from non-hair, and flesh from non-flesh?"[1]

Fundamental and mysterious questions. Meanwhile, we focus on what is known, and the phenomenon of human development is described in fetal months. By two months in utero, lips are formed. By two-and-one-half months, kidneys begin to function. By three months, lungs have shape, and bone marrow begins to form blood elements. The fetus is at this stage a mere three-and-one-half inches long, and is already covered with newly composed skin. The velocity as well as the complexity of the growth process continues, peaking at about the fifth month. At this point, the cranial capacity—that is, the size of the brain—and the neurological specialization that distinguishes the genus *Homo* are already in full stride of development, as brain commissures appear and spinal cord maturation, called myelination, begins.[2] Thereafter, fat tissue develops, and the fetus doubles its weight in the last two months of gestation. In the final weeks before birth, placental senescence, or aging, ensues, resulting in the limitation of fetal growth.

Once the biological alarm of faint contractions begins, with uterine walls tremoring a message of impending labor and birth, the *social* dynamics of parturition take hold, thereafter dominating the minds and behavior of the mother and of all the surrounding participants. The biological miracle, the complex process of embryonic growth and development, is upstaged totally, suppressed by the overriding power of collective behavioral and emotional reactions, found in distinct and variable forms in each of the world's cultures.

At the time of birth the maternal sighs, moans, and grimaces are the social semaphores for the family, friends, and community. The physiological phenomenon of labor and birth set into motion timeless yet ever-changing social responses—molded human behavior that more often than not has been dictated by societal mandates that extend even to the maternal position of parturition. Societal rules inform attitudes toward and treatment of infants and children. Ideas about nurturing and rituals of welcome or rejection arouse individual and collective emotions—from excitement, enthusiasm, pride, and love to alarm, fear, shame, or mere indifference. What had been a nine-month biological process, within hours, even minutes, is transformed into an intense and unending social phenomenon—birth. Once the astonishment and euphoria of receiving a newborn into life devolves into the emotionally neutral response to the necessities of everyday living, the complex business of life proceeds.

It has been so since the beginning of time.

NOTES

1. Garland, 1990, p. 17.
2. A. R. Colón and M. Ziai, 1985, pp. 3–9.

PART ONE

❑ ❑ ❑

Chapter 1

Prehistory:
The Turkana Boy

❑ ❑ ❑

FOSSIL TRACES OF HOMINID ANTECEDENTS of the human race—the plumeless genus of bipeds of Plato's* image—record the first six million years of man's existence on this planet. Of those fossil records, only a few and for the most part incomplete remains of early hominid children have been unearthed.[1] Most of these very early fossils are of the genus *Australopithecus*. There are so few remains that scientists have given names to them: the Taung child, the "First Family," "Lucy," and, leaping forward two million years to another species, the Turkana boy.

In retracing the prehistoric past for clues about child life, archaeological studies are our reference points. When health status is considered, bone signs of good health suggest good care and nurturing; when remains are found in groups and children are among them, as with the "First Family," inferences can be made that children were protected by the group and shared the group's work for survival, that elemental social skills were taught. Prepared and adorned burial sites attest to loving attachments and bereavement

---

*"Seeing that the human race falls into the same classification as the feathered creatures, we must divide the biped class into featherless and feathered." Plato, *The Statesman*, 266-E.

among members of the group. All of these conclusions serve to fit together the pieces of a vast puzzle.

Bechuanaland, 1924: here was uncovered the Taung child. The isolated skull of this three-year-old hominid was found in a remarkable state of preservation.[2] The Taung baby had a full set of deciduous teeth and an erupting second molar. There was an endocranial cast, or mold, of the brain and no evidence of disease in the skull bones or teeth or suggestion of any paleopathology. The Taung child gave origin to the designation *Australopithecus africanus*,[3] a hominid who roamed the African continent five million to two million years ago.[4] Apart from its antiquity, this fragment of a child, cast in limestone and frozen in time, is a direct evolutionary link, a prototype, of a member of the group of hominids from which evolved the Turkana boy.

In 1975 the remains of thirteen species descendants of (and the closest chronological relatives to) the Taung baby were found at a site called Hadar, in Ethiopia. Four were children under the age of five years. There were no other animal species present. The bones of the group were not mutilated. The nature of this clustered find suggests that they all died suddenly, together. They might have been a group traveling or hunting together that, in one catastrophic event such as a flash flood, met its demise by drowning.[5] Their being grouped together has led anthropologists to conjecture their relationship, and they have been labeled as a family—indeed, the "First Family." The presence of children in the group further implies that *Australopithecus* functioned in communal and biological familial units.

As a genus, *Australopithecus* had a small cranial capacity. The *africanus* and *afarensis* species were gracile, slender, and slight. They grew to four feet (1.2 m) and weighed about eighty-five pounds (40 kg). "Lucy" is the most renowned of the graciles to have been found.[6] Her delicate body was typical of her species, as was her small head, with its cranial capacity of about 400 cc. Her jaw was strong, and her teeth were thick, enabling her to grind vegetable and fruit fiber.[7] Her slender fingers and long arms suggested an arboreal existence, yet the configuration of her hips and knees bespoke bipedalism as well. She lived over three million years ago. Lucy was approximately twenty years old when she died, one of a species that evolved to *Homo habilis*.

The emergence of *Homo habilis*, a more complex hominid species, marked the beginning of the Stone Age. With its larger brain capacity (750 to 800 cc), this group was able to develop more variable stone tools, which in turn led to a change of diet to include meat. Refinement of paleoecology investigative techniques suggests an evolving rudimentary sophistication in this species. *Habilis* probably led a partially arboreal existence, as evidenced by longer arms than those of *Homo erectus* or *sapiens*. The cranial endocasts

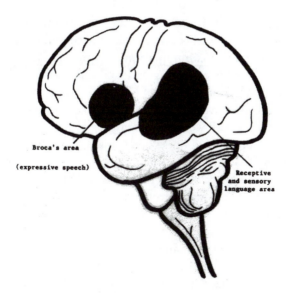

Figure 1.1 Broca's area and the receptive language area of the human brain.
DRAWING BY AUTHOR.

suggest a prominent Broca's area (figure 1.1). This part of the brain is associated with expressive speech and invokes the presumption of some vocal communication among *habilis* hominids. Study of dental ridges show a two-fold maturation rate in this species. *Habilis* children therefore probably matured faster than modern children do, reaching adolescence by twelve years of age and middle age by thirty years.[8]

There are few fossils of this species from which to derive developmental and behavioral extrapolations. Study of their stone litterings, however, give evidence of increasing skills in tool making and mark them as an advance guard of emerging *Homo erectus*. Thus, while no remains of children have been found, the place of *Homo habilis* is assured as an evolutionary link, for it leads directly to *Homo erectus* and the study of the Turkana boy.

He was found in an alluvial plain in Africa. The fossil records from the site, consisting of swamp snails, catfish, and pygmy hippopotamus, presume the place to have been a small swamp. The fossilized bones of this early male *Homo erectus*, field designation WT 15000, were found by Kamoya Kimeu during a Richard Leakey expedition in 1984. Although the Turkana boy is not the first or the oldest fossil of a child to have been found—the hominid ancestors of Taung and members of the "First Family" are among those who can claim these distinctions—the Turkana boy is the most complete pediatric paleoanthropological record to have been identified and studied to date.

By all appearances the Turkana boy had been well nourished and cared for. Judging by the boy's excellent overall physical condition, there must have been a nuclear family or communal unit to provide basic nutrition and health needs. His teeth were strong and well calcified. The degree of root development, the stages of eruption of his teeth, and his long bones indicate that he was about twelve years of age when he died. The calvarial sutures, or lines of fusion, in his skull were soft, and the epiphyseal ossification centers, or growth plates, of his long bones were intact, suggesting further growth potential. The boy had grown to five feet, six inches (1.7 m). Judging by his growth plates, another six inches (15 cm) of growth was possible.[9] Some bones had been fractured by herbivore trampling, but there were no signs of premortal injury or abuse, no bony or dental mutilations, and no osteomyelitis or smoldering bone infections. The articulation joint surfaces were clean and strong. The boy's remains showed no evidence of carnivore attack, and his death is shrouded in mystery. How he died and how his bones found their resting place near Lake Turkana, Kenya, 1.6 million years ago are unanswerable questions; however, it is possible to speculate somewhat on the social history of the child from general knowledge of the hominid group to which the boy belonged.

Homo erectus, dating from two million to one and a half million years ago, with its cranial vault capacity of 900 to 1100 cc in volume (over two-thirds that of modern man),[10] developed skills that ensured its survival as a species for well over a million years. The Turkana boy lived at a time when the savannas were temperate and posed little climatic threats to him or to the species. The ancient Tethys Sea of the Miocene epoch had retreated some 18 million to 3 million years earlier, forming the Black, the Caspian, and the Mediterranean Seas. The warm climate of the Pliocene epoch, 5 million to 2 million years ago, created the now-relic tropical forests and a temperate climate. As the grasslands expanded across Africa, Europe, and Asia, the vast savannas that resulted merged. The migratory routes that followed sought the sun and its bounty, as the earth's inhabitants searched for sources of food.[11]

At the time the Turkana Boy was alive, *Homo erectus* was experienced in making primitive tools, hunting in organized bands, sharing foods, and finding shelter in caves. As a young adolescent at the threshold of manhood, the twelve-year-old healthy Turkana boy would have been initiated to perform all the manly skills of the group. These skills would have included the use of spheroid stones as tools and the manufacture of bifacial stone cleavers. Millennia would pass before descendants of the Turkana Boy refined the Stone Age with more complex, multifaceted tools.

For a number of years he would have been shown the techniques developed by the group for hunting and been instructed about the cooperative attitudes of individuals that ensured the success of the hunt. He would have been taught to respect the need to share food with members of the group, thereby ensuring the survival of all. Learning how to protect himself and others from both the elements and from animal attack would have been a large feature of his education.

The Turkana boy's species knew how to tenderize and cook food. This knowledge in time would alter both tooth function and structural change. Molars would become smaller, with loss of grinding surface; jaws would become less powerful; and cranial bones would thin, leading to increased brain volume. These changes would become important to the survival of the group's descendants. By the time a new ice cycle started, cooling the planet and moving an ice line downward from the north, *Homo erectus* had learned to control fire to survive the cold, as well as to prepare food. The use of fire facilitated migration out of Africa. Groups learned to live with the harsher elements to the north and to the east, and they became nomadic, spreading the migratory pattern. The migration out of Africa was slow—extending over tens of millennia—but extensive. Fossilized remains of *Homo erectus* have been found in Europe, northwest Africa, eastern Africa, and Asia, along with traces of charcoal, ashes, hearths, and burned bones at multiple sites to testify to their presence.

In time *Homo erectus* also learned to build shelters and so moved from caves. They built oval huts made of posts with central hearths. Some, measuring twenty feet by forty feet (6×12 m), have been found, dating to about five hundred thousand years ago.[12] Litterings on the floors of these dwellings have been identified as limpet, mussel, and oyster shells and bones of deer, elephants, goats and boars, the variety adhering to the vagaries of seasonal supplies.

About four hundred thousand to two hundred thousand years ago, *Homo erectus* evolved into a new and distinct group called *archaic Homo sapiens*. The evolutionary process continued to alter the phenotype. The skull bones thinned further, a chin began to emerge as a feature, and the forehead became more vertical (figure 1.2). Brain volume increased and further neurophysiological evolutionary qualities developed. With greater encephalization,[13] maturation was delayed. Infant growth and development having slowed, maternalization increased. The postnatal altricial period therefore became prolonged, with continued cerebral growth and maturation (11 to 18 months), and a fixed mother–infant–child neurobiological interaction, characterizing *Homo sapiens*, emerged.[14]

Homo sapiens scattered over Europe, Asia, and Africa. The European member came to be called Neanderthal. The African member is believed to have evolved to *Homo sapiens sapiens*, or modern man. This view is not universally

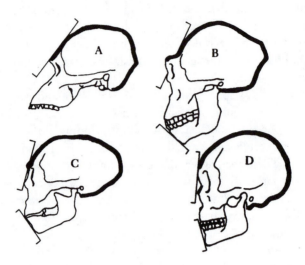

Figure 1.2 The gradual evolutionary appearance of a chin and a vertical fore-head: (A) *Australopithecus*, (B) *H. erectus*, (C) *H. Neanderthal*, (D) modern man. DRAWING BY AUTHOR.

accepted.[15] One view is that modern *Homo sapiens sapiens* evolved from *archaic Homo sapiens*, who in turn had evolved from *Homo erectus*. Another contends that there were three separate branches of species and that *archaic Homo sapiens* evolved sui generis. Finally, there is a theory that a parallel evolution of both the *archaic Homo sapiens* and the *Homo sapiens sapiens* occurred, with the archaic lineage dying out. There is evidence that during the last ice age, around forty thousand years ago, *archaic Homo sapiens* and *Homo sapiens sapiens* were in fact living alongside each other.[16] New support for this theory is lent by the recent find of a ten-month-old infant in a cave in Israel, named Baby Amud. This baby was ritually buried some sixty thousand years ago, within the time frame of *Homo sapiens sapiens'* presence. But more significant were the physical features of Baby Amud, which showed three classic and unique Neanderthal characteristics: a lack of chin, an oval foramen magnum, and a thick medial pterygoid insertion (a bony lip on the mandible where a chewing muscle, the pterygoid, attaches). These three features in the infant clearly were inherited and clearly separate it from *Homo sapiens sapiens*, further supporting the contention that the two species evolved along different lines.[17] By twenty thousand years ago modern man, apparently evolved from *Homo sapiens sapiens*, predominated and was by that time the inheritor of the earth. The temporal and geographical boundaries between these species, however, are often blurred, and a definitive time line is not absolutely possible.

The current molecular biological studies of the genetic material DNA have advanced theories of monumental importance on the subject of the origins of mankind and therefore warrant mention here. It has been posited that a common mitochondrial DNA links us all to prehistory and, specifically, to one female individual who lived in Africa two hundred thousand years ago, some ten thousand generations past.

Mitochondria, the energy dynamos of the cell, handle the oxidation, metabolism, and transformation of energy molecules for all of the body's biochemistry. Mitochondria number 300 to 600 per cell and are found in the cellular cytoplasm, existing as individual little packets of enzymes within the cell membrane and outside the nucleus. They are the only significant source of extranuclear DNA in humans, constituting about 1 percent of total body DNA. Each mitochondrion has four to ten double-stranded circular DNA bits that replicate separately from nuclear DNA.

Of the two cells, ovum and sperm, that create an individual, sperm is poor in cytoplasm and consists almost entirely of nucleus with a tail for propulsion. The sperm head is poor in mitochondria, which additionally is marked with a protein called ubiquitin, programming the organelles for destruction once fertilization is completed. Thus, when a sperm fertilizes an ovum, it remits genetic material ensconced in its nucleus but no mitochondrial DNA.* For all intents and purposes, the mitochondrial DNA found in an individual comes from the maternal ovum's cytoplasm. This fact, conjoined with the premise that we are all individually homogenous for our mitochondrial DNA, led researchers Cann and associates[18] to examine placental mitochondria DNA for distinctive types. Placental mitochondria, drawn from 145 individual women from five geographic populations, and two cell lines, derived from stored female tissues, were studied. Employing sensitive and sophisticated DNA mapping techniques, Cann and associates were able to conclude that the types of mitochondrial DNA that were isolated probably stemmed from one individual in Africa from prehistory. The hypothesis of the "African Eve" as the first *Homo sapiens sapiens*—the modern human being—received further molecular support in a study of Senegalese mitochondrial and Y chromosome DNA markers that reached the same conclusion as did Cann.[19]

More molecular evidence for the hypothesis that modern man evolved from a fairly recent species comes from an analysis of a Y chromosome intron. The examined sequence is part of a zinc finger Y gene handed down from father to son and apparently involved in sperm maturation. The sequence resides in a part of the Y chromosome that does not recombine,

---

*Recent data suggest extremely rare recombinations of maternal and paternal mtDNA, which are clinically unimportant but are nevertheless possible. *Lancet* 2000; 355:1290.

and none of the examined specimens had any sequence variation, suggesting a common ancestral modern human group that, by statistical modeling, is thought to have roamed the earth about 270,000 years ago.[20]

Just as mitochondrial DNA is of maternal origin, the Y chromosome is of paternal origin and thus can be studied to trace evolutionary polymorphic DNA changes in men. Several groups of researchers have sorted out these changes in men across the world and have plotted them out phylogenetically. Their findings have led them to an "African Adam" somewhere among the Khoisan of South Africa.[21] Thus, two different parts of the human genome suggest a recent common ancestor for modern man.*

All these studies collectively garner strong evidence for the origin of modern man to have been Africa. This becomes especially plausible in the region where the great civilizations of Egypt, Assyria, and the Fertile Crescent emerged.

But the theories of a single ancestral group have been challenged by a cadre of scientists who have found the artifacts of evolution and social anthropological progress more frequently in other lands, namely, Eurasia and the advancing fronts of the ice lines. A different hypothesis of modern human origin examines teeth and their secondary traits, such as crowns and roots. Turner and associates[22] examined twenty-eight secondary dental traits from twelve thousand individuals worldwide. Both archaeological and modern specimens were studied. Data based on these analyses placed the origin of *Homo sapiens sapiens* in southeast Asia.

While the roots of modern man's biological origins remain inconclusive, artifacts, particularly Neanderthal artifacts, continue to give valuable clues of the process and the quality of social evolution. *Homo sapiens neanderthalensis* inhabited the European landmass one hundred thousand to forty thousand years ago. The name derives from the region of western Germany called Neander Tal, where many fossils have been found. The *Neanderthals* were a large, muscular species with a brain volume of 1400 cc. They had heavy brow ridges, a long skull with sloping cheek bones, and large teeth. They were most probably nomadic, changing their habitats seasonally as they followed food sources. Paleopathology studies indicate that the sick and elderly were cared for; overall, the life expectancy was to the mid-forties. They evolved a social-spiritual presence and began to ceremonially bury their dead with artifacts and bones.

---

*Currently, based on conjoined mtDNA and Y chromosome studies, 28 lineages have been hypothesized: 10 for "Adam" and 18 for "Eve"—all beginning in the African continent and reaching Asia by about 65,000 years ago; Europe, 45,000 years ago; and the Americas, 20,000 years ago.

At the Le Mousteir site in France the remains of a young adolescent were found. Laid to rest in ceremonial fashion, he was curled on his right side with his head nestled in his arm. Flints had been decorously placed around his head. A stone ax and the bones of cattle that were found surrounding his fossilized remains suggest a belief that the dead required sustenance in the afterlife. A similar burial of a Neanderthal boy was found at Teshik Tash in central Asia. Another find at La Ferrassie near Le Bugue was that of a child's skull buried under a limestone slab marked with red ochre and eighteen pit-marks, suggestive of a memorial stone or a ritual stele. In Dederiyeh, near Aleppo, Syria, a two year old was buried some seventy thousand years ago with a limestone slab resting on top of its head and a small triangular flint over where the child's heart would have throbbed.[23] The meaning of the symbols is obscure.

Most remarkable of the Neanderthal findings was the burial site at Shanidar, where an array of pollen clusters surround the body of a man. The pollen was identified as cornflower, thistle, ragwort, hyacinth, hollyhock, and horsetail—a yellow, white, and blue floral burial bower. The image of the dead being lovingly and dolefully surrounded with beautiful fresh flowers is one familiar to all of us; it strengthens the impression that grief and mourning were commonly expressed and that the bonds of affection contributed to a sense of loss. The remains of infants and children that have been found have all yielded ritualistic artifacts of prepared burial sites.[24] Mysticism of some kind must have been an element involved in the practice, although none of the sites produced evidence that this would have been of a sacrificial nature.

The earthly inhabitants who followed the Neanderthals left many artifacts and trails as they walked the earth during their Ice Age existence some eighteen thousand years ago. They devised sophisticated throwing devices and hunting spears; they constructed complex homes made of varied materials such as wood, bones, skins, and tree fronds. Shelters were illuminated purposefully; light was extended beyond the hearth by burning animal fat in lamps. Needles of bone were fashioned and used to sew furs. All of these innovations combined to give them greater control over their environment. Their nomadic patterns consequently increased, allowing food supplies to become more varied. Caches of supplies that have been found imply that groups returned annually to prior encampment sites. The analysis of fossilized feces, called coproliths, disclose a pollen record that reflects seasonal variances[25] and patterns of parasitosis.[26] Some sites became burial grounds, with evidence of evolving more complex ritualized mysticism. Paleopathology information attest to sound health and increased longevity, with some individuals living to their mid-sixties. Yet bone and teeth show the effects of lean seasons with periods of malnutrition as food supplies dwindled. Tooth enamel dysplasia reveals cyclical patterns of this kind of deprivation.*

Along with this evidence of care and socialization there is recent disquieting forensic evidence suggesting that at least some groups practiced cannabalism. Some researchers believe that winter starvation periods may account for this practice, based on the observation that brains and marrows (both rich in fat) were primarily consumed.[27]

The coldest phase of the last Ice Age, about eighteen thousand years ago, covered the earth with ice from cyclical ice sheets that expanded down from the poles, so that the straits between landmasses were high and dry. As sea levels fell, by 450 feet (150 m), migratory routes expanded, enabling journeys worldwide. Diversity of people resulted as migratory routes spread and phenotypes intermingled, with a presumed common evolutionary thread remaining, traceable to DNA, the subsequent ten thousand years. The ice caps receded and the seas rose again, sea level increasing 0.5 to 1.0 meters per century. All the land bridges disappeared, halting migration.

By this time man's progress gave him the wherewithal to evolve a settled way of life, utilizing the tools and cunning that had been passed down from generation to generation. Tools developed for tasks such as fishing, hunting, and sewing, and defense evolved from simple faceted cutting-piercing stones to multifaceted specialized stones, bones, and horns used as needles, lamps, styluses, and projectiles. As man's groups grew in size and capabilities, ever widening common areas of protected dwelling places were defined. Crop cultivation and animal domestication, providing available food and clothing, enabled a settled lifestyle to evolve, making way for a community life, the harbinger of early civilization. The evolution from a migratory hunter-gatherer to a settled agrarian with a bent for community life was a slow process. It took six million years.

NOTES

1. The oldest fossilized fragment of an infant is from the Pliocene and early Pleistocene periods that date from five million to two million years ago. A mere baby molar attached to an immature mandibular fragment, the fossil has been dated as being 4.4 million years old. It was unearthed in Aramis, Ethiopia, a site fifty miles below Hadar, where "Lucy" was found. It appears to represent a new species, which has been called *Australopithecus ramidus*. Since few bones of this species have been

---

*In Northern Europe, tar resin findings suggest one other facet of childhood dentition—the apparent need to chew. Black lumps of tar with tooth marks have been found bearing dental impressions that suggest ages of 6 to 15 years. Prehistoric chewing gum? E. Aveling, *British Archaeology* 1997; 21:30.

found, conclusions regarding the species or its social evolution have been eschewed. At present it is a curiosity because of its age. T. White et al., *Nature* 1994; 371:306–12.

2. The skull was found among the remains of other animal bones but no other hominid fossils, leading researchers to conclude that the child was carried off by a large bird of prey into its den, which was littered with the remains of bats, rats, tortoises, crabs, and other meals. *Science* 1995; 269:1675.

3. Leakey, 1981, pp. 30–54.

4. Antiquity and sociobiological habits also dominate interest in the remains of two species of *Australopithecus* fated for extinction: *robustus* and *boisei*. Among the fossils studied, the teeth, jaws, and bones of these hominids indicate that they were predominately herbivores or vegetarians growing to some 5 feet (1.5 m). The grinding surfaces of their molars was large, their incisors were reduced, and their jaw lines were strong. They lived in the grasslands and savannas of Africa and shared the land with elephants, guinea fowls, giraffes, hares, ostriches, and other animals. In 1976, in the volcanic ash at Laetoli, Tanzania, footprints of stocky hominids, perhaps *robustus* and *boisei*, and other animal creatures were preserved for more than 3.75 million years. Although no remains of children from these species were found, their interest for us is in the additional evidence of social bands that relied on each other for sustenance and survival.

5. Johanson and Edey, 1981, pp. 213–16.

6. Ibid., pp. 16–25.

7. A new study examining carbon isotopes in the tooth enamel of *Australopithecus africanus* suggests that some carnivore activity may have occurred in their diet. M. Sponheimer and J. Lee-Thorpe, *Science* 1999; 283:368–70.

8. Beynon and Dean, 1988, pp. 509–14.

9. Brown et al., 1985, pp. 788–92.

10. Simons, 1989, pp. 1347–48.

11. Gowlett, 1984, pp. 70–92.

12. White, 1986, pp. 21–40.

13. Foley and Lee, 1989, p. 905.

14. Alan Walker, personal communications.

15. Lewin, 1987.

16. Some researchers contend that a skull found along the Solo River in Java is *H. erectus*. Confounding matters, they dated the fossil to 27,000 to 53,000 years ago, suggesting a tripartite coexistence of *H. erectus*, *sapiens*, and *sapiens sapiens*. C.C. Swisher et al., *Science* 1996; 274:1870–74.

17. B. Bowers, *Science News* 1994; 145:5.

18. Cann, 1987, pp. 31–36.

19. A. Gibbons, *Science* 1992; 257:873–75. Another study examining mtDNA reinforces this thinking. Geneticists Soodyall and Jenkins of the University of Witwatersrand in Johannesburg analyzed mtDNA from Khoisan (oldest indigenous people of South Africa) and sub-Saharan Africans and found that 84 percent of the mtDNA was unique to the Khoisan and dated to 120,000 years ago. *Science* 1999: 286:229.

20. R. L. Dorit et al., *Science* 1995; 268:1183–84.

21. A. Gibbon, *Science* 1997; 278:804–5.

22. Greenberg et al., 1986, pp. 480–85. Teeth also help in determining the sex of burial remains. Amelogenin in tooth enamel is coded differently between X and Y chromosomes. *Science* 2000; 287:34.

23. T. Akazawa et al., *Nature* 1995; 585–86.

24. New child burials continue to be discovered and reported. In the Nile Valley an 8–10-year-old "Taramasa child," ritually buried some 50,000 years ago, was found in a sitting position. More recently, in a site 140-km north of Lisbon a young child was found covered with red ochre, wrapped in a fur, and wearing a pendant. These bones are believed to be 28,000 years old. C. Holden, *Science* 1999; 283:169.

25. Harris, 1981, pp. 15–31.

26. Southwest Native American coprolithic analyses reveal a pattern of parasitic infections showing that hunter-gatherer groups had fewer infections than did agricultural groups. This is consistent with the common fecal-oral contamination cycles of most intestinal parasites. K. J. Reinhard et al., Helminth remains from prehistoric Indian coprolites on the Colorado Plateau, *J Parasitol* 1987; 73:630–39.

27. E. Culotta, *Science* 1999; 286:18–19.

Chapter 2

Early Civilizations: Sumerian School Son

❏ ❏ ❏

THE WORLD WAS FORMED BY EXPLOSIONS of matter in a time frame we refer to as eons, but the civilizations of modern man have been developing for only ten thousand years—a mere 0.2 percent of the time since man first appeared on earth. Yet there are sufficient data to suggest an exponential proliferation of language development, art, science, engineering, medicine, mysticism, and religion; and it apparently occurred concomitantly among the many tribes of *Homo sapiens sapiens*, which were by this time scattered over the "nine faces" of the world: Mesopotamia, the Indus Valley, the Orient, the Pacific Basin, Africa, Europe, North America, Mesoamerica, and South America.

The first four great civilizations are closely identified by historians with the giant rivers that sustained their growth: Mesopotamia, where the earliest writings appeared, with the Tigris and Euphrates Rivers; Egypt, with the Nile; Indus, where agriculture and ungulate domestication progressed, with the Hindus River; and China, where the earliest pottery and bronze appeared, with the Yellow River. These diverse geographic areas all reveal evidence of civilization patterns that began somewhere between 10,000 and 5000 B.C. Settlements evolved, growing in population from villages to towns. The populations growth resulted from social factors that included communal protection from enemies, shared agriculture, and barter interaction and from biological factors largely related to reproduction and enhanced nutrition, both of which resulted from positive changes in social patterns: Permanent settlements kept men at home more often; overall, there was less movement and exercise, and consequently, women maintained adiposity, facilitating more frequent ovulation. Food sources became more varied and reliable, leading to better nutrition and to less prolonged nursing, which in turn eliminated the ovulatory inhibition that nursing provides. With less migration there were fewer miscarriages. All of these factors contributed to increased fertility and birthrates.

These settlements and centers of population marked human evolution from prehistory into history and recorded thought. All, in different degrees and manner, left references to their children's growth and development and to their place in society.

THE FERTILE CRESCENT

The narrow band of land arching from Palestine to modern Iraq that is referred to as the Fertile Crescent owes its rich soil to the Tigris and Euphrates Rivers on the eastern arch and the fecund valleys luxuriating in a yearly twelve inches of rainfall (30 cm) on the western side. The crescent, part of the geographical pocket historians call the "Cradle of Civilization," ensured agricultural abundance to those who dwelt within its limits. The area became the site of many ancient Near Eastern cultures that touched on the crescent, such as Judah, Phoenicia, southeast Anatolia, and Assyria. Several Mesolithic settlements that date to 9000 B.C. have been found scattered throughout the area, but the world's earliest cities and towns are known to have evolved in Mesopotamia. Mesopotamia (from the Greek, "between the rivers") is located in what is now southeastern Iraq. The Sumerians first settled there around 5000 B.C., followed by the Semites, who founded Assyria and Babylonia around 2300 B.C. The Sumerians left the first written records of a full civilization. Initial attempts at written language (the pictograms) gradually evolved to cuneiform. Although this progression traditionally has been attributed to the Sumerians, recent studies indicate that pictograph and cuneiform writings may have had their roots in contiguous areas, where, as early as ten thousand years ago, clay counting tokens used by farmers and merchants for inventories and transactions have been described. This suggests that the Sumerians may have adopted and refined the innovation.[1]

Sumerian cuneiform had an initial grouping of some 350 ideograms. Over the centuries, as the influences of the Akkadian, Assyrian, Babylonian, and Chaldean dialects emerged, they grew to 600 ideograms. Cuneiform went on to become the "alphabet" for fifteen different languages, among them Elamite, Hittite, and old Persian. By around 3000 B.C. systematic cuneiform writing was established. Written records found in the region of ancient Mesopotamia, regarding business transactions and inventories, wills, laws, education, and diaries, number a quarter million tablets. One percent of the extant tablets pertain to literature.

The timeline between Sumer and Babylonia began to blur around 2500 to 2000 B.C., when the Semites migrated from Arabia into Mesopotamia, but already the deciphered cuneiform revealed extant law codes and social behavior from which images of family and child life in ancient Sumer can be appreciated. Beginning in the twentieth century B.C., the ruler of Isin in Sumer, named Lipit-Ishtar, left the earliest code of laws, predating Hammurabi by two centuries. The code's references to children are the first evidence we have that Sumerian society had a clearly recognized concept of parental responsibility toward their children:

. . . I, Lipit-Ishtar, the humble shepherd of Nippur . . . established justice in Sumer and Akkad. . . . I made the father support his children [and] I made the children [support their] father; I made the father [stand] by his children.[2]

This "humble shepherd of Nippur" explicitly extended these laws to legitimate and illegitimate children:

If a man's wife has not borne him children [but] a harlot [from] the public square has borne him children, he shall provide grain, oil, and clothing for that harlot; the child which the harlot has borne him shall be his heir.[3]

Several of the laws pertained to rights that could be expected among the three social classes in Sumer: the freeman; the poor, or *mushkinu*; and the slave. The code covered children of all three classes. Under the laws that pertained to slaves, children were considered slaves if they were the sons or daughters of slaves, if they or their mothers were war captives, or if they were sold into slavery to repay a debt. The code made redemption possible under various circumstances. Children who were being held as collateral had to be released after three years, and children of a slave-concubine were free at the death of the master. Physical branding was permitted, a practice that would, under Hammurabi's laws, be limited to wearing an identification tablet, such as a medallion, around the neck.

Hammurabi's fame derives from the comprehensive set of laws he compiled and administered, starting somewhere around 1792 B.C. He ruled Sumer for forty-three years from his court in Babylonia. The bulk of his

Figure 2.1 Black diorite stele with the code of Hammurabi. It was found in three fragments, and when fitted together, stood eight feet high. Shown in the front side with a relief of the sun-god Shamash presenting the laws to the king, Hammurabi. Sixteen columns of cuneiform line the front, and twenty-eight columns line the back. SMITHSONIAN AMERICAN MUSEUM OF NATURAL HISTORY.

famous code was found recorded on a large black stele (figure 2.1) uncovered during an excavation in Susa in 1901. The details of the codes were remarkably complex, with scrupulous attention given even to arcane human situations. Of the 282 clauses, 16 directly mention children and are documented in Appendix A to this chapter.[4]

Children born to governors, scribes, administrators, soldiers, priests, and slaves—all children—were protected as well as bound by the strictly enforced set of laws. Complex and comprehensive, the codes encompassed an extensive range of issues that, among other things, recognized and valued the family as a social and economic unit second only in importance to the state. The father was acknowledged as the supreme head of this unit. Codes 192, 193, and 195 are explicit regarding the harsh penalties that would befall any child who did not bestow appropriate honor and respect on the father who reared him. A son could lose a tongue, an eye, or fingers, depending on the circumstances of the offense. The father's absolute authority extended to a right to use his children as payment of or collateral for debts. He could sell them into slavery or servitude. Still, parental power was not unbridled. Code

117, for instance, as in the Lipit-Ishtar code, imposed a three-year limit to this slavery.

Although property rights and the conservation of property are recurring themes, they inclined to protect women and children as well, insofar as they were viewed as possessions, the property of the man. The laws tended to regard mothers as caretakers of the man's economic interests, which included both his property and the heirs to his property. Even in the event of a divorce, the material benefits for the woman would appear in the context of her duty to raise the children as heirs to the husband's property. The language of the codes that referred specifically to women's and children's issues, however, lead to a forceful conclusion that the vulnerability of women was recognized by the state and that the state provided laws specifically to protect women.

In these codes the welfare of all children and of women is the implied principle, with justice and equality the guiding precepts. Code 14, in which death is the penalty for abducting a minor child, clearly exemplifies this point of view, as do Codes 185 and 188, which protect the rights of adopted children. In the event that a man abandoned his wife, Code 137 decreed the return of her dowry to her, a significant parcel of a man's property, and custody of the children. Code 168 safeguarded a son's right to inherit his father's estate. This code clearly rejects a father's right to deny his son, capriciously or without just cause, his rightful inheritance. A formal court of inquiry would be convened to determine if a legitimate wrong against the father had been committed by the son. Even if such a misdeed had occurred, the law would leniently forgive a first offense. A second transgression, however, would, as stated in Code 169, mandate a decision in favor of the father.

In Hammurabi's Codes 28 and 29 the state evinced a special interest in those children whose fathers were captured or killed in the service of the country. In Code 28, an older son could assume control of his father's business and conduct his affairs, and in Code 29 the responsibility of raising young children would be given to the mother in the father's absence. She was additionally given control of one-third of the husband's property. Should a father regain his freedom to find his wife and children in the household of another man, however, Code 135 assured him the return of his wife and the children and, presumably, his property.

In the event of a mother's death, Code 162 decreed that children were to inherit her dowry. The code specifically states that the dowry did not revert to the mother's father. The laws relating to inheritance rights strongly favored the distribution to the children of all of the father's property in equal amounts. A favorite son's special bequest would be honored, but the residue of the estate would be divided among all of the brothers in equal shares

(Code 165). In a complex situation involving the death of a mother and a father's remarriage with additional progeny, code 167 protected each set of children. First, the children from each marriage were entitled to the dowries of their respective mothers. Thereafter, the equitable distribution of the father's property was ordained. While the codes do not say as much, it can be assumed that daughters could expect only dowries from fathers. The specifics of the endowments supposedly would depend on the wealth of the father, but this is conjecture, as is the assumption that customs existed that dictated the kind and amount of a woman's dowry.

Most information about the Babylonian and Sumerian child pertains to the upper classes. Records were kept by scribes of civic officials and other members of high-ranking families. Many of the references and letters that depict domestic situations have parallels in modern life. Even from grave excavation comes a poignant sense of the unchanging nature of childhood: Toys that were buried with their affluent young masters touchingly reveal the universal appeal of wheeled playthings—here in the guise of chariots as well as wagons. Other common play items—dolls, toy animals, balls—attest to childhood pursuits that are truly timeless.

Older children left written records of their times. Thousands of clay tablets with tutorial exercises (figure 2.2) tell a great deal, both about the structure of formal schools and about their young students. Since not a single reference to females as ambassadors, tax officials, archivists, accountants, teachers, and so on, was documented by scribes, it seems apparent that only boys were sent to school.

In Sumer, school was called *edubba* (tablet house). Most likely, boys were sent to these schools at an early age, remaining there as students until young adulthood. The traditional school nomenclature for its official hierarchy reinforces the impression of the importance in Sumer of family: a professor was called the "school father" of the "school son," or pupil. An assistant professor was called a "big brother" whose function correlated to the teaching assistants in our own colleges and universities. In addition to supervising students, he corrected examinations and the written exercises incised on the clay tablets and conducted oral measures of rote exercises. Specialized faculty, such as the "charge of drawing," the "charge of Sumerian," or, ominously, "charge of the whip," ensured a well-rounded education in a highly disciplined environment.

The curriculum fell into two core groups: scholarly and creative. Antecedent to study was learning not only how to write but how to make a tablet and to use a reed stylus. As the tablets show, a student practiced, over and over again, making wedge marks, called the *ge*—first the horizontal, then the vertical, then the slope. Once these were mastered, he progressed to a

Figure 2.2 Sumerian school tablet showing the practice and repetition of two basic sounds, the *ni* and the *ba*. SMITHSONIAN AMERICAN MUSEUM OF NATURAL HISTORY.

basic cuneiform ideogrammatic sign list. These encompassed language structure and dictionaries, mathematics, and catalogs of zoological, botanical, and mineralogical terms. Once all of these were mastered, he could proceed to the study of those topics and to the creative curriculum of drawing and poetry.

A student was expected to excel in his work or face the "charge of the whip." Judging by the number of exercise tablets that have survived four thousand years, students worked hard to avoid a caning. One essay, composed around 2000 B.C., unwittingly has provided vivid images of student life and feelings that bridge the ages. Written by a teacher, it was an allegory about a student written for students as a moral lesson on good and right behavior. A fictional student is employed to deliver the lesson, and although the dialogue is stiff and archaic, the theme is current. The essay is a wonderfully human portrait of boyhood in any time or place. The text sketches two days in a pupil's life, in which a student's best efforts obviously win praise and his misadventures bring woe:

Teacher: What did you do in school?

Pupil: I repeated my tablet, ate my lunch, prepared my [new] tablet, wrote it, finished it; then they assigned me my oral work, and in the afternoon they assigned me my written work. When school was dismissed, I went home, entered the house, and found my father sitting there. I told my father of my written work, then recited my tablet to him, and my father was delighted.[5]

The scenario of the following day tells a different tale. With a lunch prepared by the mother and "two rolls" as a treat, the student arrives late to school. "Afraid and with pounding heart," the boy makes a "respectful curtsy" to his teacher and takes his place in class. Several calamities follow: the teacher rejects the boy's written work as unsatisfactory, and the hapless pupil is caned. In an unabashedly self-serving manner, the teacher writes of an invitation to dinner and gifts, including a garment and a ring, from the boy's anxious parents. The "school father" is prepared to administer praise and promises of scholastic rewards to students such as this model boy:

Young man, because you did not neglect my word, did not forsake it, may you reach the pinnacle of the scribal art, maybe achieve it completely . . . of your brothers may you be their leader, of your friends may you be their chief, may you rank the highest of the schoolboys . . . you have carried out well the school's activities, you have become a man of learning.[6]

Another set of tablets—seventeen in all—describes a father's heartbreak. Written for him by a scribe, the father addresses his son with admonitions to behave well in and out of school. His pain and suffering become apparent as the tablets issue recriminations, self-recriminations, lectures imploring reform, pleading admonitions, and, finally, blessings from an anguished father whose love is greater than his despair:

Go to school, stand before your school father, recite your assignment, open your schoolbag, write your tablet, let your big brother write your new tablet for you. After you have finished your assignment and reported to your monitor, come to me, and do not wander about in the street.[7]

A long monologue follows as the father's angry emotions take hold:

Come now, be a man. Don't stand about in the public square, wander about the boulevard. When walking in the street, don't look all around. Be humble and show fear before your monitor. When you show terror, the monitor will like you. . . . Because my heart has been sated with weariness of you, I kept away from you and heeded not your fears and grumbling, no, I heeded not your fears and grumblings. Because of your clamorings, yes because of your clamorings—I was angry with you—yes, I was angry with you. Because you do not look to your humanity, my heart was carried off as if by an evil wind. Your grumblings have put an end to me, you have brought me to the point of death.[8]

His anger spent, the father reverts to appeals for filial reform. Finally, he is overcome by the love he feels for his son and offers his prayers and blessings:

From him who quarrels with you may Nanna, your god, save you,
From him who attacks you may Nanna, your god, save you,
May you find favor before your god,
May your humanity exalt you, neck and breast,
May you be the head of your city's sages,
May your city utter your name in favored places,
May your god call you by a good name,
May you find favor before your god, Nanna,
May you be regarded with favor by the goddess Ningal.[9]

The father's lament could be a metaphor of the Babylonian state's dwindling power. The greatness of Babylonian society began to wane by about 547 B.C., when Cyrus the Persian conquered the country and the Assyrian city-state began its ascendancy. Predictably, education declined and cuneiform writings along with it, as the civilization that had given the world the written word melted into history. By the first century A.D., the alphanumeric system had replaced cuneiform, rendering extinct a system of writing that had recorded life in the Near East for three thousand years.

Child-welfare laws became weak and unenforceable, and ultimately children lost most rights. Slavery became more prevalent, and abuse, in the form of the physical branding of slaves, was but one manifestation of the loss of respect for individuals. Children and adults were bartered into service for goods or traded as goods to businessmen from other countries. Redemption from slavery became more restrictive, if not impossible. The fundamental abrogation of human rights affected all and, assuredly, most of all affected the children.

THE NILE

The valley of the great river Nile is a land surrounded by desert on three sides and by the Mediterranean—the "middle earth sea"—on the fourth side. The six cataracts, interspersed along the river's two-thousand-mile length, have throughout history made invasion a logistical nightmare for covetous bands. This geographic protection provided centuries of sheltered security, allowing a great people to concentrate their energies and their genius on the creation of a civilization that endured for three thousand years[10] (table 2.1). Remnants of that civilization still inspire awe and reverence.

Near Thebes, north of the first Nile cataract, there are early burial

A History of Children

TABLE 2.1
THE THIRTY DYNASTIES OF EGYPT

Approximate Dates B.C.	Dynasties	Designation Periods
3100–2680	I, II	Archaic
2680–2180	III–VI	Old Kingdom
2180–1990	VII–XI	First Intermediate
1990–1790	XII	Middle Kingdom
1790–1570	XIII–XVII	Second Intermediate
1570–1080	XVIII–XX	New Kingdom
1080–400	XXI–XXX	Late

grounds at Nagada dating from about 4500 to 3100 B.C. All sexes and ages were interred in a fetal position surrounded by pottery, food, furniture, cosmetics and cosmetic implements, artistic decorations, jewelry, fishhooks, flints, toys, weapons, and deities—all of the paraphernalia used in this life and that would be needed to survive in the next. The site is a rudimentary example of the Egyptian tradition of preparing burial chambers for their dead that link them to the new life. Over time, during the New Kingdom, the rituals, arts and crafts of the Egyptians evolved to the highest levels of achievement. The bodies of the wealthy and of those with rank were mummified to forestall decay and to travel unmutated into another life. Premature infants and children of all ages were mummified (figure 2.3). Animal gods—cats, monkeys, birds—also were mummified and placed in the tombs. The practice continued for over four thousand years, well into the Roman era of Egyptian history.

The ritual constructions and supplies warehoused in the tombs from generation to generation increased in elaborate design and content, reaching grandiose levels during the New Kingdom (1570–1080 B.C.). King Tutankhamen's tomb (c.1350 B.C.) is one of our contemporary references to the magnificence and splendor with which the tombs were supplied. Tutankhamen was crowned at twelve years of age and was nineteen when he died. He was only a minor pharaoh, leaving us with the tantalizing thought that, had the tombs of the great pharaohs not been pillaged, the contents robbed, scattered, and destroyed, the grandeur that would have survived surely would overwhelm us.

Figure 2.3 Mummies of prematures, with miniature sarcophagi, measuring about forty-five centimeters. Note that the umbilicus is also mummified, in anticipation that in the next world the infant will resume his growth and nourishment through the cord. EGYPTIAN MUSEUM OF ANTIQUITIES.

The tombs were intended as way stations for the dead on their journey from our world into the next. The priests, artists, and artisans constructed a familiar and friendly environment that provided continuity for the dead, integrating wall paintings and dioramas of daily life with familiar objects used by the deceased. A tomb was outfitted as would be a home and included furniture, toys, deities, and implements of everyday use for personal adornment, entertainment, sustenance, and prayer. The colorful wall paintings that festoon the walls and ceilings of tombs and entry passages to the tombs depict life events of the deceased, great events of the country, and life at the royal courts. Many focus on everyday life in general: domestic scenes, agricultural and commercial endeavors, children at play. They are veritable snapshots of the times. The miniature dioramas of common events in village life and commerce were formed from clay and were intended to provide the dead with a continuity of reference, reminding them of family, friends, customs, and surroundings. The topics of the dioramas are so varied and the depictions so extensive in detail that we are able to form vivid images of ancient Egyptian life. Human warmth and delight in each other's presence are everywhere displayed, to be seen both in the humble clay figures of the common man found at home sites and in the great statues carved from stone that adorned great cities. Scenes of affection demonstrated between husband and wife and between parents and children touchingly reveal the strongly felt bonds of love that predominated.

The custom of burying mummified animals—deities to the Egyptians—
to accompany loved ones on their journey to a new life tells us about both
religious beliefs and love of family. Papyrus writings that have survived also
disclose a great deal about beliefs and feelings.

Through all of this treasure, the ancient civilization of Egypt comes alive,
exposing to view the hopes and dreams of families who aspired to share a
happy and productive life together, bear healthy and happy children, and
enjoy the bounty of a stable, affluent society in the comfort and joy of family and friends. The dioramas clearly indicate that children of all classes in
Egypt were similarly treated, at least until school age, when the wealthy and
the less fortunate followed separate paths. Studying the lives of Egyptian
children is especially intriguing as one contrasts the quality of their lives in
a highly developed society with that of neighbors in the immediate region
and, indeed, around the world.

To begin with the beginnings of life: the ancient Egyptians prayed to the
hippopotamus god Thoueris to ensure fertility and to provide a safe delivery.
The prospective parents turned also to the sages to prognosticate on issues
regarding a safe pregnancy or to reveal the sex of the fetus. The rituals were,
to say the least, curious:

You shall put the woman's excrement in bags of cloth with sand from the beach and
dates. She shall pass her water upon the bags daily . . . if they produce worms, she
will not give birth.

You shall put an onion on her vulva all night until dawn. If the smell passes to her
mouth she will give birth.

Watermelon, squeezed and mixed with the milk of a mother who bore a male child,
will be eaten by the woman. If she vomits she will give birth, if she has flatus, no.

You shall put wheat and barley into purses of cloth, the woman shall pass her water
on it, every day [it being mixed with dates and sand]. If both sprout, she will give
birth, if the wheat sprouts she will give birth to a boy, if the barley sprouts she will
give birth to a girl. If they do not sprout, she will not give birth at all. (Papyrus
Carlsberg VIII)[11]

At the accouchement of upper-class women, several midwives in attendance could be found. Birth was in a kneeling position either on bricks or
while sitting on heels. The goddess Maskonit was petitioned to watch over the
baby. A wet nurse would be in close attendance at the birth, and the goddess
Raninit was called upon to ensure proper nutrition for the infant. After the
infant was named and its birth noted in a legal registry, its horoscope was read.

Although boys were favored, all children were accepted with gladness. The family unit was strong and infanticide was rare. Although abandonment was known to occur, it also was a rare phenomenon. Egyptians, in fact, were known to rescue infants who had been abandoned by other cultures. The biblical story of Moses' rescue is a striking example. Unlike Moses, however, most abandoned children were relegated to a dungheap. Should such a child survive, its name would reflect its inauspicious entry into society—there are numerous Egyptian references to children named Copreus.

The child was carried about by the mother in a sling around her back until the age of three. The mild climate of the Nile basin allowed children to go unclothed. A common diet for children was bread, leeks, water, boiled papyrus shoots, and fish. During public holidays and festivals all children were treated to meats and fruit, but only children in upper-class families consumed meats on a regular basis.

Many of the tomb scenes depict children playing with pets, particularly dogs, cats, birds, and monkeys. Pottery, dolls, articulated toys, play jewelry, balls, and board games were available for play. Some games were common to all classes, including a type of tug-of-war played without a rope, leapfrog, and ball throwing. Playing with a hoop and stick, wrestling, and playing a balancing game in which semicircles were made on heels while counter-levered by playmates[12] were also popular pastimes. The sons of noble families were additionally initiated into running and chariotry through games.

Although no codices have been found that refer to the welfare of children, several documents attest to the existence of laws that protected both legitimate and illegitimate children and in some instances the unborn. A pregnant woman convicted of a crime could not be punished for that crime until the safe delivery of her child. A parent who had given life was not sentenced to penal servitude or death for taking that life, but the historical comments of Diodorus Siculus indicate that those found guilty were required to embrace the murdered children in their arms for three days and three nights, presumably to face the scorn and anger of the community.

There were laws of inheritance that extended to exposed children left on dungheaps. A Berlin papyrus makes clear that parents of abandoned children were still obligated by law to include such children in their estates. Such children received three-fourths of their rightful inheritance, with one-fourth confiscated by the state, but they could not become priests.

On the judgment day of the Egyptians, mistreatment of children, among other sins, would preclude entrance into the next life. The *Book of the Dead* lists thirty-six incantations of protestation—denial of malfeasance against man, beast, and children:

I have not committed evil against men.
I have not mistreated cattle.
I have not killed.
I have not had sexual relations with a boy.
I have not taken milk from the mouths of children.[13]

The average well-to-do Egyptian child progressed much as all children have progressed in civilized environments—they went to school. As in Sumer, school was not attended by peasant children. In contrast to the Sumerian culture, however, some girls were formally taught to read and write. The word for female scribe existed by the time of the Middle Kingdom (1990–1790 B.C.).[14] Moreover, in the archives of the Metropolitan Museum of Art in New York City there is a letter written by a seventeen-year-old girl around 2000 B.C. It reads: "Dear Mother, I am all right. Stop worrying about me." Apart from the contemporary tone of the entry, the letter exists as evidence that females were being educated in the scribal schools at an early date.

While the scribal schools specifically trained scribes, they also served as the entrance point for formal education. All disciplines began in scribal school. Mastery of the skill of writing was required before students could enter apprenticeships in medicine, engineering, art, architecture, or the priesthood. Geometry also was considered a particularly important subject for study. The annual Nile floods often destroyed property boundaries, and applied geometry frequently settled property disputes.

Boys entered scribal school at an early age. They spent years copying material over and over again, with reed and ink, on stones, potsherds, or writing boards. Papyrus was costly and was used only after well-practiced exercises. The temptation to romanticize the academic performance and behavior of ancient scribal students as universally disciplined and dedicated—infinitely superior to students of our day in every way—is tempered by one teacher's exasperated note to a delinquent charge:

I hear that you are neglecting your writing and spending all your time dancing, going from tavern to tavern, always reeking of beer . . . you sit in the house with the girls around you . . . you sit in front of the wench, sprinkled with perfume; your garland hangs around your neck and you drum on your paunch; you reel and fall on your belly and are filthed with dirt.[15]

Presumably, students for the priesthood kept to a higher standard. They were clean-shaven, circumcised, and dressed in white, with sandals made of papyrus, as the use of leather was taboo in the priesthood. There were no actual seminaries, and scribal schools were attached to temples.

The Egyptian child reached puberty at twelve years. At sixteen years a boy was officially considered to be a man, at which time he would begin a career. Professions generally were kept within families, with sons, nephews, sons-in-law, and cousins apprenticed to relatives. There were very few opportunities for young men to advance. This was especially true for the uneducated with aspirations. A military career was the exception, and all classes were encouraged to enlist. For those in the labor forces, it was particularly astute to volunteer for the military since they faced conscription in any case.

This was the record of preclassical Egypt and her attitudes toward children. With the end of the late dynasties, XXI through XXX, came the colonial kingdoms and a change in attitudes toward progeny. Greco-Roman Egypt behaved differently—and not as well—toward sons and daughters.

ANATOLIA

Another people—the Hittites—lived in what is modern-day Turkey. At the height of Hittite power, around 1400 B.C., the Egyptians had eased into a new and richer phase of their civilization, called by historians the New Kingdom, which lasted from 1570 to 1080 B.C. The Hittites serve as an interesting comparison to Egypt and even Sumer in that very little has survived that gives us insight about how children in Anatolia were regarded and treated. Since it was, nevertheless, a major civilization and one of the few ancient societies to leave written codes of law for us to examine, it should be mentioned here.

It is generally known that the Hittites were at the zenith of their power around 1400 B.C. and that their kingdom extended down toward the arc of the Fertile Crescent in modern Turkey. We can only deduce what kind of people they were from some codes that were discovered in their capital, Boghazkoy.

The codes,[16] indexed on two clay tablets, number two hundred clauses. They appear to have been interpreted differently from city to city, province to province. They fell into the following categories:

First Tablet

1–6	Homicide
7–18	Assault and battery
19–24	Ownership/rules regarding slaves
25	Sanitation
26–36	Marriage
37–38	Justifiable homicide
39–41	Feudal duties of land tenure
42	Hiring for a campaign

Second Tablet

Code 171, which gives the mother a right to disinherit and disown a son, is the only code that was specific to children. The codes on homicide (1–6) and on marriage (26–36) included references to children, who were considered as property and as inheritors of the father's estate. A woman also could will her dowry to her children but only in the event that her husband was dead.

Levirate marriages, in which a brother or closest male relative was bound to marry a widow and provide for her and her late husband's children, not uncommonly produced children whose names differed from those of their biological fathers. They inherited the property of the fathers who adopted them. Levirate marriages were common in many cultures throughout early civilizations, perhaps spreading with migrations, becoming autochthonous customs of the Athabascan and the Aztecs of the Americas.

Code 44 required a man to replace a child for one he had killed. No penalty was given for the original offense nor for any failure to comply with the law's mandate. According to the codes, there was a collective responsibility for any crime; therefore, the children of the perpetrator of a crime were given the same penalty as that imposed on their father. This was particularly true among slaves: "If ever he dies, he does not die alone but his family is included with him."[17]

Exquisite sculptures and carvings have survived that depict families in what can only be interpreted as caring and loving postures. Their beauty and their sentiment make them noteworthy, but little else is known about this ancient culture's treatment of children.

THE MEDITERRANEAN

The Mediterranean is an ancient relict sea some 2,300 miles long and 500 miles wide. Its composition is 20 percent rainwater, 5 percent river water, 2 percent from the Bosphorus (Black Sea), and nearly 75 percent from the Atlantic Ocean flowing in through the Gibraltar Straits. The "middle-earth-sea" is ten to thirty centimeters (4 to 12 in.) lower than the Atlantic; therefore, water flow is east into the basin, and it is surface water, warm and relatively hypotonic to the briny Mediterranean Sea. The Mediterranean basin became a magnet to civilization, because its water temperature averages eighteen degrees warmer than the Atlantic, thus creating more hospitable shorelines and a more temperate climate.[18]

The Mediterranean climate has produced a paradoxical landscape. Outcrops of rocks protrude through dry, gritty contours. Desert dunes stand next to sudden green patches of vegetation. Olive trees ubiquitously dot the basin. Palm trees grow alongside conifers, while littorals and contiguous fertile valleys encourage both farming and grazing.

The civilizations that plied its waters spread their roots, prospered, and shaped the course for the classical world. The people farmed the valleys, traded the sea routes, fished the waters, and lost souls in the boiling battle-filled waters while jealously guarding the navigation rights and secrets. Numbered among these preclassical civilizations were the Minoans, Mycenaeans, Cypriots, Phoenicians, Trojans, Etruscans, and Egyptians. A few left written records; others, only archaeological artifacts. But all left some evidence of the place of children in their society that provides an opportunity to note contrasts to Sumer and Egypt. Children are not featured either pictorially or in writings. It therefore seems likely that these societies were not as strongly child-centered as were those of Sumer and Egypt. Codes of law protecting rights of property and inheritance are the only clues we have of children's place in Minoan and Mycenaean cultures.

Knossos, the capital of Crete, was established about 2500 B.C. by people who may have originated in the north of Africa. Certainly their waistcoats and codpieces were similar to those worn in Libya and predynastic Egypt.

Some religious artifacts, particularly the double ax, suggest that they may have had origins in Caria. They were, at any rate, called Minoans, after the legendary King Minos. They became a major trading power, exerting strong cultural influences throughout the Aegean Cyclades and beyond. Even when invaders and settlers from Mycenae, in southern Greece, subdued them, significant aspects of the Minoan culture were incorporated into that of the Mycenaeans.* The Mycenaean civilization flourished in the late Bronze Age of Greece from about 1600 to 1200 B.C., and encompassed the surrounding Aegean area as far as Cyprus.

Cyprus was a Mycenaean island outpost with a history of many past occupations besides that of Mycenae. Anatolia, Phoenicia, Egypt, and Rome all, at one time or another, claimed Cyprus as domain. Cyprus, however, retained its indigenous character. Unaffected by the polycultural exposure were the rituals related to birth and the newborn. In Mesophilia, a Cyprus settlement of the same period as Knossos, excavations have yielded pottery figurines of women giving birth, the emerging infants painted red.[19] Curiously, two millennia later, in Lapithos, Cyprus, similar figures were found in a sanctuary: infants being born of women in five different birthing positions. They are reminiscent of the ex-votos that can be seen in Southern Europe and throughout South America today, where clay, metal, wooden, or painted terra-cotta body parts or whole figurines are left before a church or temple altar as a prayer of petition or of thanks. It is possible that these ancient figures, too, represented a prayer for a safe parturition and a healthy newborn. Or, buried as they were, their significance may pertain to a prepartum superstitious rite or a postpartum cleansing ritual. The speculations are not conclusive and do not give any insight into the attitudes of the people toward their offspring, but the figures themselves are fascinating.

Nor do the stone palaces and other dwellings left by the polycultural people of the Minoan-Mycenaean era make any statements about children. Full of artifacts and objects d'art, the life-size murals depict the nobility's luxurious lifestyles, occupations, sports, foods, sea life, and religious themes, with

---

*In Crete, the Mycenaean conquest was probably facilitated by what was believed to have been a spectacular eruption of the volcanic island Thera (modern-day Santorini). The whole western face of the volcano was blown off, spewing ashes for hundreds of miles. Cities and palaces were buried throughout the island of Crete. Earthquakes probably preceded and followed the eruption. Collapsed buildings have been uncovered in Knossos with contents preserved by the sudden calamity. One building in particular contained the bones of two apparently healthy children. Close examination of their bones revealed evidence of sacrifice and ritualistic cannibalism, perhaps appeasement to the gods for fear of further earthquakes. *Science News* 1990; 137:22. On top of the ashes, Minoans rebuilt their homes, but they were never to have the same glory they had had prior to the eruption.

Figure 2.4 A small (7.8 cm) ivory carving from Mycenae (13th century B.C.) depicting a child (believed to be Triptolemos) together with Demeter and her daughter Persephone. NATIONAL ARCHAEOLOGICAL MUSEUM, ATHENS.

flowers and hilly landscapes for decoration. Contrast these with the Egyptian tradition, which frequently and joyously featured children in their murals and wall reliefs.

Minoan-Mycenaean representations of children, such as the Demeter group, for the most part are rare (figure 2.4) and are limited to artifacts related to burials. Common people were buried in caves or under rock shelters. From what can be deduced, house burials of children were common. Infants in particular were entombed in jars resembling small *pithoi*, or amphoras. They were kept within the confines of the home, possibly with hopes and prayers that they would be reincarnated again in the same house and family. While it is difficult to know exactly what attitudes families were expressing about their children, the burials suggest more than a casual and thoughtless attempt to dispose of a corpse. This custom was observed not only on the mainland of Peloponnese and Crete but also among the Trojans.

The nobility and their children were entombed. Like the Egyptians, the Mycenaean aristocracy adorned their children in death. A magnificent gold costume covering a dead infant was found in a sixteenth-century-B.C. tomb (figure 2.5). The gold was finely hammered and tooled, and the fine delicacy of the garment and the attention to detail are reminiscent of the sarcophagi of Egyptian infants.

The early script of the Minoans, the undeciphered linear A, certainly reveals no clues about parental attitudes. The so-called linear B, common to all Mycenae and Cyprus, was finally deciphered in 1952, making possible

Figure 2.5
A gold funeral costume of an infant found in a
Mycenaean tomb from the sixteenth century B.C.
The costume is about fifty centimeters long.
NATIONAL ARCHAEOLOGICAL MUSEUM, ATHENS.

the translations of inscriptions on clay tablets and those painted across vases. Similar to if not the same as early Greek, the script was primarily used for record keeping. The multiple inventories, tallies of herds, records of payments and debts, and directories of personnel are the main sources of information pertaining to the lives of Mycenaeans.

A working census, naming an occupation and the number of individuals engaged in the work, can tell a great deal about Minoan society's customs and traditions. To illustrate: one particular job assignment required oarsmen. The record lists five young men and one boy. All were sons of the master rower. The inference is that skills were learned from the father, with "on-the-job" training, and occupations were, as much as possible, kept in the family.

Linear B ideograms for *man*, *woman*, *boy*, and *girl*, when matched with those of occupations, indicate that boys were trained to be gem cutters, carpenters, shipwrights, masons, farmers, and soldiers. The tools of those professions—knives, chisels, saws, borers, and tweezers—were all products of Bronze Age technology, which made possible the development of those occupations. The functional value of such tools has not diminished with time.

The occupations reserved for girls were those of weavers and spinners, flax workers, grain grinders, and public-bath attendants.

From food inventories it is possible to reconstruct common diets, although no direct information about children's fare can be deduced. The inventories of olive oil, wheat, figs, dates, honey, greens, grapes, pears, quinces, and fish suggest a healthy and abundant variety. Seafood was the predominant source of protein. Ungulates supplied milk and wool.

Figure 2.6
A fresco from Thera
depicting two children boxing.
NATIONAL ARCHAEOLOGICAL MUSEUM, ATHENS.

This highly cultivated society must have had schools, although no school tablets as such have been found. Formal schooling of scribes, accountants, general merchants, priests and priestesses can be assumed from the kinds of written records these people left behind. The tablets that have been uncovered attest to this likelihood.

The universal popularity of sport and athletics, major activities to which children early on were exposed, must have had a formal component of training and indoctrination. An early forerunner of bullfighting, called grappling, was particularly popular. It was essentially a gymnastic dance engaged in by both girls and boys, who had learned to leap nimbly over a charging bull! The sport is depicted in many sources but most dramatically among the ruins of the king's palace at Knossos, where a large mural depicting youth engaged in this extraordinary feat of daring has survived. Other, less hazardous pursuits included gymnastics, vaulting, wrestling, horsemanship, charioteering, and boxing. One of the earliest representations of child anatomy was uncovered among the earthquake deposits at Akrotiri, Thera. The very large fresco depicting two children boxing had been a wall decoration in the ancient civilization (figure 2.6).

The early Mycenaean classes of nobility, peasant, and slave predominated until a network of small city-states formed. As the classical period approached, four classes emerged: free citizen, *apetairoi*, serf, and slave. The *apetairoi* were a distinct group. Although they had no political rights, presumably other rights of freemen extended to them. The servile serfs cultivated the land, and slaves were either born into slavery or purchased.

The children from each of these classes looked to the law codes that assured them some protection. Although there probably were codes in some

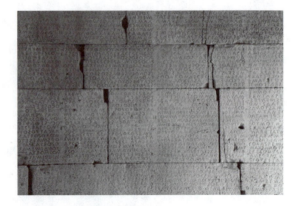

Figure 2.7 The Gortyn Code. It was discovered in Crete in 1884.

form from the beginning of the Minoan and Mycenaean civilizations, the version of the social codes that have come down to us, called the Gortyn Code, dates to around 500 B.C. The tablets were inscribed in early Dorian Greek, linear B having disappeared around 1200 B.C.* The code was found in Gortyn in central Crete inscribed in twelve columns on a stone wall that probably stood as part of a court of law (figure 2.7). Over six hundred lines long, the code overwhelmingly dealt with debt, property, and inheritance. While it resembled the code of Hammurabi (1792 B.C.), it was not as specific or codified. In one aspect, however, it was unique and singularly important historically: It documented legal acceptance of exposure—the abandonment of a newborn to the elements.[20]

If a wife who is separated [divorced] should bear a child, [they] are to bring it to the husband at his house in the presence of three witnesses; and if he should not receive it, the child shall be in the mother's power either to rear or expose. (Column III)

If a woman separated should expose her child before presenting it as written, if she is convicted, she shall pay, for a free child 50 staters, for a slave 25 staters. (Column IV)

Children's rights of inheritance and property were strongly protected, an inference that there was strong societal interest in children's well-being. If so,

---

*Dorian Greek introduced vowels into the language and was an adaptation of a Phoenician-like consonant alphabet. The Greeks used the Semitic flow of writing, from right to left, then pleated back and forth, "as the ox plows," in *boustrophedon*. Around 400 B.C. this custom was replaced by a left-to-right ionic script. By the time of the great Athenian writers the Attic dialect was favored, and it became the lingua franca of the Mediterranean basin. It was, of course, superseded by Latin in later centuries.

it is the sole indication of such interest that has come down to us from the Mycenaeans. A code in Column III, for example, describes a ruling whereby a dead man's widow may remarry and retain whatever property is left to her by her late husband. Should she take anything willed to the children, however, she would be prosecuted. The children's inheritance, moreover, extended to subsequent heirs:

When a man or woman dies, if there be children or children's children, or children's children's children they are to have the property. (Column V)

Both sexes received a share of the estate, but the females were dependent on their brothers for their share of the inheritance (Column XI). Children were accountable for parental debts of money and/or property but could not be fined for a parent's failure to settle any debts (Column XI). The rights and property of orphans were protected by the Judge of Orphan Affairs. It was his duty to administer the codes of law that applied to nonorphans. The judge also had the authority to arrange marriages for orphaned girls when they reached twelve years of age. The law protected the children's inheritance even from their father, who was prohibited from either selling or mortgaging his own or his children's property (Column VI). In the event of the mother's death, the father gained control of her property solely to protect it for the children when they came of age. If and when he remarried, the children at whatever age would assume control of their late mother's bequest (Column VI).

Social or class status, to be sure, affected the rights of children, and issues were settled along patriarchal lines. Men of property had authority to determine the fate of children born to serfs. For example, the child out of wedlock of a female serf either had to be accepted by "the master of the man who married her" or be subject to the power of his mother's master (Columns III– IV). If a male slave was accepted by a free woman in marriage, their children would be free; conversely, if a free woman sought a union with a male slave, their children would be slaves. In a household of free and slave children born to the same woman, any property would be inherited by the free children (Column VII).

Biological children and adopted children were given equal shares of the inheritance pie (Column XI). The legal status of adopted children, however, was subject to annulment. The adopter was required merely to renounce the adopted son in a "place of assembly" and pay a fine of 10 staters, to be given to the renounced child.

These are the only known, extant Mycenaean records pertaining to children. The Mycenaean expansion slowed and came to a halt around 1200

B.C., perhaps because of Dorian incursions from the northwest, a series of climatic cataclysms, or invasions by "Sea-People." (The same Sea-People, whose origins remain obscure, attacked Egypt in 1225 and 1191 B.C.) All three elements may have been factors in the culture's decline. What followed was the Iron Age and the gradual evolution of city-states into the Greek classical world. Greek influence blanketed the Mediterranean and by 550 B.C. had spread as far west as Spain and as far east as the distant Bosporus strait. It even left its mark in Latinum and Etruria, civilizations that were to form the seedling core of the Roman Empire.

THE ETRUSCANS

Between the Tiber and the Arno Rivers of modern Tuscany the Etruscan civilization of Etruria flourished between 1200 and 700 B.C. These Bronze Age people appear to have originated in Anatolian Lydia and northern Villanova, near Bologna. Their autochthonous roots were culturally infused by the Greeks, Phoenicians, and Asians. Although they had an alphabet similar to the Greek they left few written documents, and these are difficult to decipher. Ancient historians from other countries had a great deal to say about the Etruscans, mostly of an unflattering and damning nature: a materialistic people preoccupied by voluptuary affairs. This assessment, however, conflicts with impressions derived from their tomb artifacts and iconography, which yield a kindlier image of their society and their treatment of children.

The contemporary accounts are certainly salacious: Timaeus of Athens wrote that Etruscans were served by naked slaves. The Greek historian Theopompus gossiped that the Etruscan child seldom knew the identity of his or her father. Plautus added to this scandalous patter by writing that Etruscan girls amassed their dowries through prostitution.[21] Whatever the truth regarding behavior in Etruscan society, these sybaritic images of decadence and amorality are in stark contrast to the images depicted in sculptures, murals, burial monuments, and figurines, all of which suggest faithful husband–wife relationships and a society that cultivated family and home life.[22] One mural in Tarquinia illustrates the point: it shows husband and wife at a banquet, sharing wine, while their two children and the family dog sit by their side.

Domestic scenes in general depict women and men equally sharing daily life and activities in an affable and harmonious manner. Professional topics of several murals graced the walls of the tombs, implying that another kind of equality existed between the sexes. There is evidence that, in addition to running households, women were educated in languages, mathematics, and medicine and that their husbands consulted them for advice.

Figure 2.8 Ex voto: Etruscan head of a young boy. MUSEO ARQUEOLOGICO NACIONAL, MADRID.

Although the Etruscans cremated their dead, they buried the remains in tombs designed to resemble houses; the interior settings bore a close affinity to life. They were supplied with everyday clothing, furniture, food, and tools. Even burning lamps were carefully placed in the tombs to guide and comfort the dead and ease fearful thoughts as they made their way to the other life. In death women were honored with special sarcophagi that were particularly ornate, elaborate, and richly carved.[23]

Special attention in death also was given to small children. Images of children were carved into niches of maternal sarcophagi, with sculptured miniature pillows supporting their tiny heads. We must conclude that these expressions of tenderness and affection had their counterparts in life. Children frequently were depicted in terra-cotta statuary as swaddled and wearing good-luck lockets called *bullae*. Various gods were shown with children, further evidence of children's important status in society. In a temple in the Campana region, there were ex-votos dedicated to children, one of which depicts the head of a child (figure 2.8).

Wet nurses may have been commonly held in high esteem, since ex-votos dedicated to them and memorial stones commemorating them (figure 2.9) also have been found.

Although there was written language, no accounts of schools have survived to describe the education of Etruscans, who excelled in many areas of achievement. They traded widely along sea routes throughout the Mediterranean, and within Etruria itself they developed commercial ties with independent city-states. They maintained formal armies and were especially interested in the arts. All this supposes that education was formal. The Etrus-

Figure 2.9 Etruscan memorial stone with mother and children and wet nurse.
MUSEO ARQUEOLOGICO NACIONAL, MADRID.

cans gave great import to music, singing, and dancing. They were particularly skilled in the making and playing of wind instruments, occupations most likely learned early on by children.

The Etruscans, vulnerable to aggressors, were subject to repeated incursions by warring bands, and by 450 B.C. their civilization had declined. Their dominance of the famed seven hills of Rome yielded to the indigenous people, marking the beginnings of the Roman state, long after the legend had been established of two of history's most famous children, Romulus and Remus.* As the Roman state grew in size and ambition, it used military might to establish itself as the most formidable power of Italy. Borrowing heavily from Greek influences, the Romans gradually infused their society with their own customs and culture. By 295 B.C., Rome ruled all Italy; by the end of the Punic wars, the entire Mediterranean basin; and by the first century B.C. the Roman Empire was fully defined.

---

*The well-known Romulus and Remus fable recounts the story of twins born to Mars and the vestal virgin Rhea Sylvia. Having violated her vestal vows and raison d'etre, Rhea Sylvia was executed, and her children were thrown into the Tiber River. Following this watery abandonment, destiny washed them up onto the banks of the Tiber, where a wolf succored and nurtured them. When grown, the brothers founded the city (by tradition in 735 B.C.) that came to be called Rome—after fraternal quibbling led Romulus to kill Remus. This city around the Palatine Hill became the center of the region called Latium, south of the Tiber River, and of a loose federation of tribes with Etruscan cultural elements.

THE LEVANT

The treatment of children by the Phoenicians has been indicted summarily by both historical accounts contemporary to the times and by subsequent observers who have thoroughly examined the archaeological evidence that exposes the indifference, disrespect, and cruelty of the Phoenicians toward the young.

These Canaanite descendants occupied the Levant coast from Tartus to Mount Carmel in what are now Lebanon, Israel, and Syria. The height of their civilization extended from 1400 to 700 B.C. They were recognized as great seafarers of the Mediterranean and as traders and merchants. Their chief cities were Tyre, Sidon, and Byblos. They had colonies along their trade routes, the most famous of which was Carthage in what is now Tunis. They are best known for disseminating their twenty-two character alphabet, for crafted works of carved ivory and richly colored purple cloth, and for little else. Their art was not original, having been heavily borrowed from Egyptian and Assyrian elements, and their surviving written records were predominantly mercantile. Papyrus was used for the Phoenician archives, and unlike the dry desert climate of Egypt, the Phoenician climate was not amenable to preserving papyrus; hence, the paucity of written references to codices, societal standards, education, family life, and children. Nowhere in Phoenicia have dwellings been excavated or studied, and aside from funereal figures whose costumes and makeup are revealing, little of everyday life is known.

One form of worship that was alluded to over the centuries has been documented: the Phoenicians practiced infant sacrifice. The distinctions separating sacrifice from infanticide and from abandonment or exposure are real, even though all three acts generally result in the death of the infant. Infanticide and exposure have been common to many cultures for a variety of reasons. Child sacrifice has been rare. Some sacrifices of infants placed in foundations of dwellings have been mentioned in the Old Testament about Jericho (1 Kings 16:34). The Egyptians also have been cited as having performed foundation sacrifices. There are, however, no accounts that measure how common the practice was in either society.[24] The entombment of a body, not necessarily sacrificial, in the foundation of a new building was believed to assure its endurance.

Evidence of cremations of infants sacrificed to the god Moloch have been found in urns, called *tophets*, and temple pyres in the Phoenician colonies of Carthage (Tunis), Motya (Sicily), and Sulcis (Sardinia). There is a biblical reference to Moloch (2 Kings 23:10) that describes the defilement by Josiah of a temple in Jerusalem because there a man "might make his son or daughter . . . pass through the fire to Moloch." In hundreds of urns, burned remains of children, mostly under two years old but some as old as twelve years, have been found. Some urns were found with feeding bottles next to them, attesting to the age of the victims. There are inscriptions dedicating the sacrifice to the goddess Tanit or the Lord of Braziers, Baal Hammon.[25] There is no evidence that plant hallucinogens were given to the children to anesthetize them or that they were given soporifics prior to being burned. There is an extant stele depicting a temple priest carrying a child into a sacrificial chamber where the child is killed and cremated (Harden, 1962).

The unnatural ritual of newborn sacrifice also was practiced by Sabean priests in the ancient kingdom of Sheba, modern southwest Arabia. There the infants also were cannibalized. The sacrifices were made to the planet gods during cyclical periods of highest visibility. All ages and sexes were sacrificed. A postpartum girl was sacrificed to the sun; her three-day-old child would be sacrificed to Jupiter. A young brown-skinned scribe was proffered to Mercury; to Mars, a redheaded man. A chubby man was sacrificed to the moon, and a beautiful woman was offered to Venus. These prescribed horrors took place on the feast day of wine, celebrated (by our Gregorian calendar) on August 8th. The Sabeans pressed grapes and slaughtered a male newborn. The infant was boiled and deboned; the flesh was rolled in flour, oil, saffron, raisins, and spices and then oven-baked. It was eaten by the priests during the ceremony to Shemal.[26]

Whether the Phoenicians sacrificed their own children in their ritual killings or hostages from other countries is uncertain, although Josiah suggests that they willingly sent their children to sacrifice; and Plutarch in his *Moralia* unequivocally relates that the Phoenician wealthy sacrificed their own children or those purchased from the poor:

. . . with full knowledge and understanding they themselves offered up their own children, and those who had no children would buy little ones from poor people and cut their throats as if they were so many lambs or young birds. (*Moralia* 3.171.13)

Some of those sacrificed may have been abandoned infants, or they may have been abandoned boys who were victims of a fertility cult, being raised as "temple boys" or "sacred" prostitutes. These abhorrent practices were detested by many of the ancients, and they contributed to the overall disdain with which the Phoenicians were held, causing Plutarch to write:

. . . the character of the Carthaginian people; it is bitter, sullen, subservient to their magistrates, harsh to their subjects, most abject when afraid, most savage when enraged, stubborn in adhering to its decisions, disagreeable and hard in its attitude towards playfulness and urbanity. (*Moralia* 3.799.3)

Debilitated by repeated invasions of warring neighbors, the further deterioration of the Phoenician empire was precipitated by Alexander's conquest of Tyre in 332 B.C. The Punic wars that followed completed its demise. As part of the peace terms exacted by the Roman general, Agathocles, infant sacrifice was forbidden, and the nefarious practice, along with the Phoenicians, disappeared.

THE HEBREWS

The western arc of the Fertile Crescent was home to several cultural groups, the most prominent of which was the Hebrews. The Bible relates how Abraham led his nomadic Semite people out of Ur on the Euphrates and took them into Canaan. For a thousand years thereafter the children of Abraham suffered forced migrations, temporary encampments, battles and defeats, and a scattering of their people. They were battered and shifted around by Macedonians, Maccabeans, Egyptians, and Romans. Uniquely, the strength of the Hebrew people's relationship with their deity sustained a strong cultural identity, which endures to this day. They wrote extensively about their experience in the context of their spiritual beliefs and thus have left us an extensive record of their history. Their scriptures provide rich documentation, not only of the vicissitudes of the Hebrew people but of Hebraic attitudes toward and treatment of children. To be sure, the history of Hebrew children is fraught with turmoil and instability, as they suffered with their elders the effects of centuries of warfare, tumultuous upheavals, and aimless migration. Lamentations of their starvation, slaughter, and enslavement fill the pages of the Old Testament:

. . . her young children also were dashed in pieces at the top of all the streets. (Nah. 3:10)

. . . their infants shall be dashed in pieces and their women with child shall be ripped up. (Hos. 13:16)

. . . they took all the young men to grind and the children fell under the wood [carrying lumber]. (Lam. 5:13)

One inventory from the time of Tothmosis, 1504–1450 B.C., lists 84 children of 2,503 captives from Palestine destined for slavery and labor camps.[27]

Bible records reveal an uncomfortable similarity of the fate of Hebrew children with other cultures of the Middle East. Despite social codes that were written to protect them, a cultural tradition that esteemed children, and domestic life that fostered loving and caring family life, the children of Canaan too often fell into the hands of ignominious tribes with vile customs reminiscent of the Phoenicians—indeed, perhaps influenced by them. The Bible describes the sin of Ahaz who "made his son to pass through the fires according to the abominations of the heathens" (2 Kings 16:3). Like the Phoenicians, sons and daughters were sacrificed on burning pyres to Moloch by the people of the valley of the son of Hinnon (Jer. 32:35). The ignominious sacrifice of children and other heinous crimes against children were abhorrent to the Hebrews, who strongly condemned the practice as idolatrous worship of false gods (Ezek. 23:39). Josiah (639–609 B.C.) outlawed these practices throughout the Hebrew nation some three hundred years before the Roman edict to the Phoenicians prohibited them.

Not all child sacrifices were to Baal; other deplorable rituals were recorded in the Book of Kings. One was the construction offering. When the walls of Jericho were rebuilt, they were reconstructed over the slain firstborn son of the builder, and the gates were erected over the body of his second-born son (1 Kings 16:34). These were foundation sacrifices of healthy children, not house burials. In a house burial, a child dying of natural causes was interred within the house so that its spirit could be reincarnated.

Another deplorable indignity was the ritualized prostitution of boys, similar to the Phoenician practice, which entered Judea (during Rehoboam) under the influence of the Canaanites: "and also Sodomites were in the land" (1 Kings 14:24). This was detestable to the Hebrews, and the practice also was eliminated by Josiah (1 Kings 15:12, 22:47, and 2 Kings 23:7). Rather than a sexual crime, sodomy was considered a form of idolatry, a worship of the body. If the sodomized child was less than nine years of age, the punishment was flagellation; but if he was over nine, the sodomizer was stoned.

The average Hebrew child generally escaped these atrocious abuses. Their lives, however, were marked with hardships, little schooling, and early labor. Attitudes toward children were similar to surrounding cultures of the times, reflecting the common social mores, economic status, and tribal disputes.

The Old Testament, from the time of the exodus (1250 B.C.) to the fall of Jerusalem (586 B.C.), provides most of the information regarding the everyday life of Hebrew families and children. Archaeological excavations have revealed some evidence of household habits suggesting that most families lived in one room, and if coprolithic evidence is to be believed, with a sheep or two.

Children generally grew up in large families, often with many half brothers and half sisters. The father had two wives if he could afford to support them. His was a patriarchal household in which wives were subservient and could be disowned at will, and children were dealt with as property. To have many children was to have a great deal of property:

As arrows are in the hand of a mighty man; so are children of the youth. Happy is the man that hath his quiver full of them. (Ps. 127:4–5)

Sons in particular were wanted, both as help with labors and to perpetuate the family name. Should the head of a household die, a levirate union was expected, in which his widow married one of his brothers so that the firstborn of such a union would be given the name of the "brother which is dead, that his name be not put out of Israel" (Deut. 25:6).

Pregnancy was considered a gift of God, and biblical writers admonished against imbibing alcohol: "thou shall conceive and bear a son; and now drink no wine nor strong drink" (Judg. 13:7). The Old Testament describes a method of parturition similar to the Egyptian custom. Women gave birth with the assistance of midwives in a semikneeling position on bricks or stools (Exod. 1:16). There is some evidence that soporifics were used to ease labor. Recent excavations from a fourth-century A.D. tomb near Jerusalem uncovered skeletal remains of a fourteen-year-old girl who died during labor. Analysis of carbonized matter from the abdominal area of the skeleton documented that the substance was delta-THC, or cannabis.[28]

After a birth, an infant was washed, salted with soda ash, and swaddled. The salt acted as an astringent on the clouts and was bacteriostatic. The salting of infants was further propagated by the eminent ancient healers Galen and Soranus and was adopted by Christians for the baptism ritual. The custom persisted into the seventeenth century. In biblical times it may have had some religious significance, but it seems more likely that the custom evolved as a feature of cultural superiority, differentiating civilized and barbaric societies:

Thy birth and thy nativity is of the land of Canaan; thy father was an Amorite, and thy mother a Hittite. And as for thy nativity, in the day thou wast born thy naval was not cut, neither wast thou washed in water to supple thee; thou wast not salted at all, nor swaddled at all. (Ezek. 16:3–4)

Circumcision of the male was performed on the eighth day (Lev. 12:3), which is about the time the body stabilizes the vitamin K levels that are conducive to the normal coagulation of blood. Other Middle Eastern cultures (the Philistines were an exception) circumcised their sons at puberty.

The wealthy engaged wet nurses, who generally weaned their charges between the second and third year. Boys and girls were raised in a similar fashion until boys reached the age of five or seven, at which time the father assumed responsibility for a son's training for manhood.

No children's toys have survived, but funereal miniatures of houses, placed in tombs, depict furniture, whistles, rattles, animals, and dolls—evidence that playthings abounded. Gaming boards also were in use.

Discipline of children was, according to Old Testament descriptions, strict and corporeal:

Foolishness is bound in the heart of a child; but the rod of correction shall drive it far from him. (Prov. 22:15)

Withhold not correction from the child; for if thou beatest him with the rod, he shall not die. (Prov. 23:13)

Parents even had the authority to execute a difficult son perceived as incorrigible—a punishment far surpassing the severities of Hammurabi's mutilations:

If a man have a stubborn and rebellious son, which will not obey the voice of his father, or the voice of his mother, and that, when they have chastened him, will not hearken unto them:
    Then shall his father and his mother lay hold on him, and bring him out unto the elders of his city, and unto the gate of his place;
    And they shall say unto the elders of his city, This our son is stubborn and rebellious, he will not obey our voice; he is a glutton, and a drunkard.
    And all the men of his city shall stone him with stones, that he die. (Deut. 21:18–21)

Such psychic terror also was employed to coerce children into obedience—a cross-cultural tradition, it would seem, for thousands of years. The twentieth-century child is fearful of the generic "bogeyman." The Assyrians had the female demon Labartu. Mormo was said in Greece to eat "bad" children. The American Zuni tribe threatened with Shuyuku, who relished the taste of disobedient children. Among the Hebrews, Lilith was the ravisher of children, mercilessly devouring the undisciplined. In Hebrew lore, Lilith was the rejected first wife of Adam. In addition to cannibalizing children, she was thought to be responsible for miscarriages and the stealing of an infant's breath—what we moderns might call sudden infant death syndrome (SIDS). Only in the Indus Valley did a monster, Harti, become transformed into a child protector. The peaceable Buddha and the people he converted were the catalysts.

There were some common social threads seamlessly woven into the cultural fabric of several Middle Eastern countries during the third through the first millennia B.C. Laws related to property reflect similarities. In Hebrew law, as in that of several of its neighbors, property rights guaranteed some protection for children. The firstborn was recognized as the principal heir, and this right was guaranteed regardless of the father's domestic arrangements:

If a man have two wives, one beloved, and another hated; and they have borne him children, both the beloved and the hated; and if the firstborn son be hers that was hated:

Then it shall be, when he maketh his sons to inherit that which he hath, that he may not make the son of the beloved firstborn before the son of the hated, which is indeed the firstborn. (Deut. 21:15–16)

In contrast to the Hittite culture in which a man's family shared the same fate as the malefactor, punishment among the Hebrews was meted to individuals rather than collectively to entire families: "The father shall not be put to death for the children neither shall the children be put to death for the father" (Deut. 24:16). The exception was a defeated king and other members of royalty, whose families also were doomed to death.

As with the Sumerians and Babylonians, children of slaves also were slaves, and children could be used by the father to repay debts:

Behold, to me thou hast given no seed: and, lo, one [slave] born in my house is mine heir. (Gen. 15:3)

Thy servant my husband is dead; and thou knowest that thy servant did fear the Lord: and the creditor is come to take unto him my two sons to be bondmen. (2 Kings 4:1)

Unlike Sumer, Phoenicia, and other Near-Eastern lands where written language was used extensively to form contracts and record debt, the Israelites more commonly depended on a few scribes to record data, with nothing more than an *X* mark by a client sufficient to make documents legally binding. In the absence of a contract, a garment left by a client would serve as collateral for a loan. Royal scribes used papyrus to record the business of the king; one such is known to us: Baruch, secretary to Jeremiah (Jer. 36:4). There is evidence that this important profession was kept in the family (1 Chron. 2:55). While it appears that education apparently was not a priority for the Hebrews and children usually did not go to a school, there must have been formal training for scribes either in a school or within a family of scribes. Some business transactions were recorded on *ostraca* (pottery shards) by some literate, if informally educated, people. Literacy was sometimes found outside the circles of business and royalty—the ability to read having been passed along to children by literate parents.

One such illuminating example is a limestone tablet, dating from around 1000 B.C. A youth had reproduced the Gezer calendar, an almanac of agricultural cycles. From this simple writing exercise it can be deduced how young farm boys were taught to work the land, the kinds of crops that were grown, and when they were planted, weeded, harvested, and winnowed. A single year would reap olives for oil, grains for bread and to feed stock, grapes and other "summer" fruits, and fibers with which to make fabrics, rope, and twine; and harvest season was accompanied by community revels. Additionally, it indicates that village children, as well as the upper classes, received reading and writing instructions and that agriculture as well as trade and religion was recognized as vital to the economic life of the community:

> His two months are (olive) harvest
> His two months are planting (grain)
> His two months are late planting
> His month is hoeing up of flax
> His month is harvest of barley
> His month is harvest and festivity
> His two months are vine-tending
> His month is summer fruit.[29]

After the time of Jesus every town had a school attached to the synagogue, and an order from the high priest issued in 63 A.D. commanded all boys to attend.

The greatest legacy that has survived ancient Hebraic times is the wisdom of child care found in sections of the Mishnah, written from the time of Roman Judea and Galilee to the Patristic period and followed a few centuries later by the Talmud. From the sage pronouncements of the rabbis on a variety of topics, including agriculture, laws and liability, festivals, temple service and ritual, as well as human interaction, parents the world over were given aphorisms that remain shining pearls of wit and wisdom and useful guides in rearing children:

Never promise something to a child and not give it to him, because in that way he learns to lie. (Sukkah)

It is important for a growing child to be given things he can break: Rabbah often bought imperfect earthenware for his little ones to smash, should they want to. (Yomah)

Take care of the children of the poor, for they will be the ones who advance knowledge. (Nedarim)

A child is staff for the hand—and a hoe for the grave. (Yebamoth)

A child tells in the street what its father and mother say at home. (Succoth)

Don't threaten a child: either punish him or forgive him. (Yomah)

If you must beat a child, use a string. (Baba Bathra)

ELAM AND PERSIA

While there is little information about the status of children in ancient Persia and its cultural antecedent, Elam, the civilizations warrant mention. The Hammurabi stele was found in Elam's capital, Susa, firmly placing Elam on the historical map, for the Code of Hammurabi had a major impact on the rule of law in the entire Middle Eastern region of the world.

Located in what is now southwest Iran, Elam shared with Sumer long stretches of desert and marshland, making regular interaction difficult. Nevertheless, in the third millennium B.C. there were frequent raids between them, with periods of Sumerian rule and influence. Prior to 2300 B.C. hieroglyphic artifacts from Elam describe a matrilinear succession in which property was passed on from the mother or another female member of the family. A transition from hieroglyphic to cuneiform writing coincided with a shift in the laws of inheritance to conform to the Hammurabi model, in which property was left to heirs by the father. From 1900 to 1600 B.C. a paternalistic society evolved.

The few surviving artifacts allow interesting comparisons as well as striking contrasts with neighboring cultures in the area of family life. The family unit became male-dominated, with several related men living communally with their families. After a father's death, property was divided equally among his male children, after which they could elect to leave the household and found a new commune. The widow could not inherit her husband's property, but the new family head could give her an allotment.

Little else is known about the Elamites. The struggles with Sumerians and incursions into their land by the Hurrians and the Kassites produced, to be sure, cultural change as well as interaction. These people sustained a stable society of their own from 1300 B.C. to about 700 B.C. At that time, along with Lydia, Babylonia, Syria, and Palestine, Elam became an Achaemenid satrapy and was absorbed into the Persian empire.

A major political and societal force in the Middle East region, Persia also was clearly influenced by Sumerian and Akkadian mores and customs. The reigns of Cyrus II (559–530 B.C.); that of his son and successor, Cambyses II, who added Egypt to the empire; and of Darius, who established Persepolis, marked Persia's ascendancy. During the forceful reign of Achaemenid, issues pertaining to family and to the social structure in general were recorded and codified. Some were written and enforced directly by the "lawbearers," judges nominated for life by the king; others incorporated the mystical pronouncements on cosmology, the gods, and man found in the religious texts *Avesta* and *Videvdad*.

The *Avesta* was a compilation of liturgy, dogma, prayers, spells, lore, legend, and prescriptions from centuries-old oral tradition. The written text was set down around 500 B.C. It contained five archaic poems ascribed to Zarathrustra, known as Zoroaster (c.628–551 B.C.). The *Videvdad*, like the *Avesta*, had also been handed down orally but contemporaneously added new material. Both texts of proverbs and spells referred to social mores and individual behavior and to matters pertaining to the family. They mixed gods, humors, wisdom, mores, and medicine all into one. Water, moisture, or fluidity were thought to have mystical properties that influenced fecundity, parturition, and the formation of breast milk:

A woman rich in fat, in liquid, in milk, in oil, in marrow, and in progeny. I shall now wash the thousand well-springs which flow to the milk-vessels whereby the child is nourished.[30]

The reference suggests that breast feeding was thought to be more naturally a maternal obligation rather than the job of a wet nurse. There are no descriptions of midwifery techniques or suggestions that wet nurses were employed. In general there are few clues regarding conjugal life, save for references that indicate a fecund female hoped for a male child and, once pregnant, was forbidden intercourse, both to maintain purity and to prevent harm to the fetus.

Persians recognized five periods of life,[31] the first ending at five or seven years of age. During this period the child was strictly under the mother's care. The historian Herodotus offers the following explanation:

Up to the fifth year they are not allowed to come into the sight of their father, but pass their lives with the women. This is done that if the child die young, the father would not be afflicted with the loss. (*Histories* 1:136–38)

Education, limited to boys, began at about seven years of age. A boy could train for the priesthood instead of the military, but the warrior was held in great esteem. In the absence of formal schools, the father trained his son in the martial arts. Riding and archery were added to the curriculum of the elite. Other boys were trained as spear throwers or rock throwers.

Skeletons and artifacts uncovered in Sardis (now Turkey) reveal the detritus of battle subsequent to a Persian invasion in 547 B.C. Under centuries of sand and soil, slain helmeted soldiers were fixed in battle posture, including one twenty-year-old youth. His bone development indicated years of training to carry a heavy shield. In death his shield was grasped with one hand as the other prepared to fling a stone at the enemy.[32]

The second stage of Persian life ended at fifteen years of age. Intensive physical training, hunting, and endurance to enhance warrior skills became the focus for study. At this age, maturity of an elite male was recognized with initiation rites in which a sacred girdle, to be worn forever, was bestowed. At the age of twenty-five a man was considered to have completed the third season of life and was recognized as a full citizen of the state. The fourth cycle ended at fifty, and the final Persian stage of life terminated with death.

A girl from a privileged family was considered nubile at age fifteen and, trained to conform, would be eligible to contract a polygamous marriage with an affluent male. This culture went beyond the Egyptian practice of next-of-kin marriages between brothers and sisters. In Persia a man could marry a daughter or even his own mother.

The empire, which incorporated many aspects of the great classical civilizations of Sumer and Egypt and spread the long-lasting and far-reaching cult of Zoroastrianism, was conquered by Alexander in 331 B.C. It left great archaeological and architectural records but little information regarding its domestic life or the care of its children.

INDUS VALLEY

Around 2300 B.C. the Indus civilization, its principal centers located in the Indus River Valley (now Pakistan) extended west to Persia, east to Delhi, and south to the Gulf of Cambay. The most important centers were Harappa in the Punjab, Mohenjo-Daro in the Sind, and the port of Lothal to the far south. The civilization flourished for over five hundred years. Layouts of its cities are evidence of sophisticated urban planning, with housing for the rich, middle, and lower classes. Some areas of Mohenjo-Daro had two-story houses with running water, drains, and luxurious baths. The number of merchant and business documents, with seals incised into soapstone or steatite, that have survived suggest that commercial interaction was common. The nature of the seals, with ideogram similarities to Akkadian seals, suggests association with and influence from Akkadia.

In 1750 B.C. nomadic Indo-Aryans invaded the valley, destroying cities. It took centuries for the invaders to culturally assimilate and to produce a literature composed of detailed descriptions, religious hymns, and philosophical queries called the *Rigveda*, one of four Vedas that provided the eponym source for the Vedic period. During this period (c.1500–600 B.C.) the Aryans migrated to the Ganges Valley, establishing a pastoral economy. An urban-based economy evolved in the later Vedic age, from 1000 to 500 B.C., with merging tribes forming territorial kingdoms. A caste system, called *Varmas*, took root and would mold the society of India for the next millennium. There were *Kshatriyas* (warriors), *Brahmins* (priests), *Vaisyas* (craftsmen and traders), *Sudras* (laborers, hunters, and fishermen), and finally, untouchables (*Antyajas*), who scavenged and handled carrion.

The concepts of Hinduism, which regarded the cow as sacred, preached nonviolence and spiritual transmigration, or reincarnation, were formed during the last part of the Vedic period, called the Epic Age (c.600 B.C. to 200 A.D.) in recognition of the three great epics upon which Hinduism is based. The first, the *Ramayana*, concerns itself with religious duty and righteous behavior. The *Mahabharata* focuses on filial love, wifely virtue, duty, and devotion. The *Upanishads* is a philosophical discourse in the form of folktales. From these epics a picture emerges of a rural people living in fortified camps in a strictly observed caste system, where religion was the codifier of social behavior.

Although they worked bronze and gold and some of them were weavers of cloth, the very early Indo-Europeans who dwelled in the Indus Valley were predominantly farmers. They worshipped natural forces such as wind, fire, sun, and rain. Hymns, poems, precepts, and legends were woven into the Vedas; and still later, through the ritual treatises described in *Brahmanas*, more information was disclosed about this society and its ritualized approach to child rearing.

The baby born in the Vedic period underwent an initiation that followed a set prescription. Before the cord was cut, the newborn was given ablutions with ghee and rock salt and quickly enlisted into the *Samskaras*, or sacraments. Following the washing, he was given a mixture of honey, ghee, brahmi leaf juice, and gold dust on a golden spoon while pious words were whispered into his ear. The constellation under which he was born was recorded, and after ten days of life he was given two names: a daily familiar one and a secret one matched to his constellation. While awaiting the clearing of colostrum and appearance of breast milk, the newborn was fed ghee and honey on day 1, honey and lakshana root on day 2, and honey fortified with breast milk on day 3. These feeding recipes appeared in the *Caraka Samhita* (c.300 B.C.).[33] Only recently has honey as a recommended food for infants been questioned as a possible, if remote, vector for botulism.

Unlike any of the early civilizations, the Indus developed and accumulated a body of medical literature specific to pediatric care available to a physician, or *vaidya*.[34] By 200 A.D. a pediatric treatise, the Bowers manuscript, described an umbilical hernia as well as normal dentition. Observations about fetal life were recorded in the *Shatapatha Brahmana*: "A six months embryo is the last that lives when born, and the foetus becomes full-fledged in the tenth month."[35] By oral tradition, childhood ailments and a pediatric pharmacopeia were passed on and, over the centuries, were incorporated into Hindu medicine. These precepts, recorded in Sanskrit, blended the mystical with the organic. Newborn tetanus that appeared on the ninth day came from an evil spirit, and tears absent after the fourth month of life was the spirit of serious illness. In point of fact, both of these observations are pre-scient, grounded in acceptable modern pathophysiological premises. The incubation period of the tetanus spore is usually seven to ten days, with nine days being most common. The absence of tears after four months signifies at least a 5 to 7 percent dehydration in an infant. Only the *Brahmana's* con-clusions as to cause and effect are archaic.

Superstitious beliefs compelled parents to have their children's ears pierc-ed as a means to avert the influence of malignant stars. This had to be done on the sixth or seventh month under the proper alignment of stars and moon. Little boys had the right ear pierced first, then the left; vice versa for little girls. Oiled lint was threaded through with a needle; the lint was changed every three days, with thicker plugs used to enlarge the opening. Thus, the ear piercing assuaged parental anxieties but sometimes at the cost of the child's health, causing *káliká* (fever and pain) and *apatának* (tetanus). The infection would be blamed on the surgeon, not on omnipotent stars.

Given a healthy infancy and normal child development, childhood play was a predictable feature of the formative years. Marbles and a form of hop-scotch were popular games. Sophisticated mobile toys have been found, such as terra-cotta bulls with articulated mobile heads and monkeys that ascend up and down a string—a toy still being manufactured.

Children were tonsured between the ages of three and seven, and a formal education was delayed until the ages of eight to twelve years. Then, wrapped in antelope hides and offered the sacred cord of a free man, students were given the sacred Veda to commit to memory. Each book required twelve years of study. Dispensations from this rule were granted to boys who mar-ried, and often nuptials were prearranged in early childhood.

In addition to the study of sacred books, an education included courses in science, mythology, and legends. To inculcate humility, students were sent to beg for alms, following the directions set forth in the *Gopatha Brahmana*:

A student should overcome the various passions like sleep, lethargy, desire for name and fame, anger, greed, bragging, vanity and the like. He should avoid scents, devices to beautify himself, objects of luxury, the company of women and similar habits which hinder his spiritual, moral, and intellectual progress. He should wear an antelope's skin, serve the preceptor every day, overcome addiction for sleep, should not annoy anyone by angry words, must not take luxurious baths or glance at a naked woman, or smell the perfume of aromatic herbs by uprooting them. He should not frequent the cremation ground. He should sit low, lie down on the ground, walk and move about with humility. He should not lie on a cot, should not see or take part in music or dancing, and should not have bad habits, like spitting.[36]

Students left home to live with their teachers, where they were expected to perform household chores and to tend the cattle. A scholastic ritual attended the completion of students' courses of study, in which a symbolic final bath in the teacher's house was taken before a student could rejoin his family. Those boys who could not afford to leave home were educated by the *charakas*, wandering teachers who went from village to village.

While boys were trained to assume a leadership role in society, girls grew up with few, if any, rights. As agnatic families, their laws of inheritance of property were restricted to males. In the absence of male heirs, daughters and wives inherited by default. In theory, girls could expect only shelter and food, for any gifts given to them legally belonged to the father. In practice, however, relatives commonly gave presents and tokens of affection. Prepubescent girls were committed to husbands by the ages of eleven or twelve years. Upon maturity and marriage, the status of girls changed for the better, as they assumed defined roles with position, dignity, and power:[37]

> So rule and govern in your house
> over your husband's parents;
> His brother and sister too
> are likewise subject to you.
>
> (*Rigveda* 10.85.46)

Clearly, however, it was a patrilinear society, and, with males being the desired gender, women who produced sons in childbirth were highly regarded:

> O Indra bless this woman with worthy sons
> May she, with your blessing, have ten sons.
>
> (*Rigveda* 10.85.44)

Since marriage at an early age was the norm, females could be widowed as adolescents, should a husband succumb to a fatal childhood illness or accident. A levirate marriage was expected of widows of any age who had no children, cohabiting with a brother-in-law until a child of the union was born, at which time they formally married.

The esteem of the wifely status, with awe accorded to male-bearing mothers, persevered for several centuries. This respect was extended even in worship, when wives accompanied their husbands in the offering of sacrifices. However, these attitudes dwindled during the later Vedic period, when the caste system was firmly established and the priest became the co-sacrificer with the man. Thus, wives were displaced from this role and respect for women began to fade. The *Brahmana* now began describing females with disparagement:

Figure 2.10 Shang Chinese oracle bones. The pictogram for child is repeated.
BRITISH MUSEUM.

A daughter is the cause of sorrow
and a son, like the sun in heaven.
        (*Arsheya Brahmana* 7.31.1)

With the end of the Epic period, the civilization that started in the Indus Valley with urban sophistication, widespread trade, and a large body of traditional lore and legend had become imbued with immutable class distinctions and a subservient position for girls. These conditions, in effect, predestined the lives and future of children.

THE ORIENT

In one of China's large central plains, between the Huang Ho (Yellow) River to the north and the Yangtze River to the south, the ancient river civilization of Shang arose. It flourished between 1750 and 1000 B.C. Predominantly an agricultural society, it contributed to the evolution of fine bronzework and the erection of impressive civic buildings and tombs.

There is evidence to suggest that animal and human sacrifice were part of the commemoration rituals of important edifices. Carefully arranged beheaded bodies and entombed armed guards have been found surrounding royal tombs. No remains of sacrificed children, however, have been found.[38]

The Shang dynasty expanded trade, introduced the *cowrie* as monetary exchange, and compiled an accurate lunar calendar. It left behind a pictographic writing most commonly recorded on oracle bones (figure 2.10) and inscriptions of clan names. Little literature survived, but *Liki*, a code of civil-

TABLE 2.2
EARLY CHINESE DYNASTIES

Approximate Dates	Dynasties	Designation Periods
2360–2200 B.C.	3 sage rulers	Yao-Shun-Yu
2200–1750	Hsia	
1750–1000	Shang	Bronze
1000–600	Early Chou	
600–221	Late Chou	Classical
221–206	Ch'in	Warring states
206 B.C.–220 A.D.	Han	

life ceremonials, was compiled around 1145 B.C. during the reign of Emperor Tchin Ouang. The code gave supremacy to parents: "A son possesses nothing while his parents are living. He cannot even expose his life for a friend."[39]

Around 1000 B.C. the Shang dynasty was overthrown by tribesmen called the Chou (table 2.2). It was during the Chou dynasty (c.1000 to 221 B.C.) that the teachings of Confucius (K'ung Fu-Tzu, 551–479 B.C.), emphasizing the family and society, were adopted. His teachings, as recorded by his students in the *Analects*, marked the change from feudalism to Confucian political philosophy. During the Han dynasty that followed the short Ch'in dynasty (206 B.C. to 220 A.D.), district schools were built, and a university was established. The pictogram evolved to a more abstract and more easily written ideogram. Most important, paper made from fabric and bark was introduced. The combination produced a rich written history of a great civilization.

In China, as in other cultures of the times, the favored addition to a family was male, and the term "children" generally meant "sons." A passage from the Chou dynasty attests to this preference:

Sons shall be born to him. They will be put to sleep on couches: they will be clothed in robes; they will have scepters to play with. . . .

Daughters shall be born to him. They will be put to sleep on the ground. They will be clothed with wrappers. They will have spinning wheels to play with. It will be theirs neither to disobey nor to express opinions. Only about the spirit and the food will they have to think. And to cause no sorrow to their parents.[40]

In matters related to pregnancy and parturition, oracles and omens were studied and believed:

If delivery is on a *ting* day, it will be a boy.

If delivery is on a *keng* day, it will be a safe and easy delivery.

A boy born on the fifth day of the fifth month will kill his father; a girl born on the fifth day of the fifth month will kill her mother.[41]

The dire predictions of these omens influenced parental rejection of infants. Other factors leading parents to abandon or expose their children included the birth of triplets, an illegitimate birth, or a child who "cried" in utero. An infant born in the same month as the father was fated for exposure, unless an unusually caring and clever mother could conceal the birthdate in order to save the baby. During hard economic times or periods of starvation, the young were especially vulnerable.

Among patricians, the birth of a baby boy was announced to the neighborhood by placing a mulberry wood bow—symbol of the archer's military bow—on the left side of the door; for a girl a homemaker's symbol—a kerchief or napkin—was placed on the right side. The infant was not named at this time. For the first three days the baby was isolated, not even fed. If the infant displayed vitality and survived, a determination would be made to accept it into the family or to forsake it to the elements. If accepted, food was administered, and attention was given to bodily needs. Until three months of age, the baby, along with the mother, was concealed in a distant room before being presented to the father. Prior to the presentation, the male baby's hair was braided into two rows on either side of his head; the female's was woven into a cross on top of her head. An infant's acceptance was signaled by its being lifted up ceremoniously by the father.* Afterward, the child would be given a name. On the rare occasions when the father did not raise up the baby, it was abandoned.[42] There is a distinct Shang pictogram for "abandonment" showing a basket being held by two hands, ejecting a baby (figure 2.11). Abandonment supposed a predominantly passive demise precipitated by the elements, but on occasions infanticide per se was practiced. Stillborn or anomalous infants would be roasted, broiled, or cut up in the belief that this would eliminate an evil spirit, allowing a subsequent pregnancy to progress normally.

The *Record of Rituals* instructed parents on rearing principles for both boys and girls. These rules of conduct were compiled during the early Han dynasty but had their origins during the Shang and Chou eras:

When the child is able to take its own food, use the right hand.

When the child is able to speak, boys speak boldly, clearly, girls submissively and low.

---

*The Romans, who practiced a similar custom, had terms to describe the ritual of acceptance: *tollere* (to hold up) and *ingenuu* (to place on the knee).

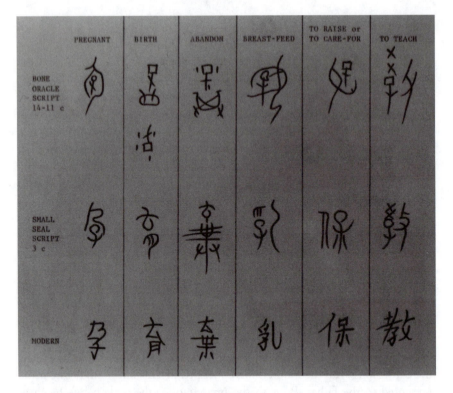

Figure 2.11 The evolution of six words in Chinese from the fourteenth century B.C. to the modern era. Note that the homunculus (stickman with a square head), central to all six words, represents a child. DRAWING BY AUTHOR, AFTER HSU, 1984.

Boys are fitted with a girdle of leather, girls with one of silk.

At six years the numbers and the cardinal points are taught.

At seven years boys and girls no longer eat together or occupy the same mat.

At eight years children follow behind their elders.

At nine years, children learn to number the days.

At ten boys go to a master teacher to learn reading, writing, calculations, conversation, dress, rituals and behavior.

At thirteen a boy learns music, poetry, dancing, archery, charioteering, and rope-tying.

At twenty a boy is capped.*

At thirty a man takes a wife.

---

*"Capping" refers to the symbolic deerskin reserved for marriageable males. This symbol was used in China from the third millennium.

At ten a girl ceases to go out. Her governess teaches her pleasant speech and manners, how to be docile and obedient,* how to handle hemp, cocoons, weave silk, how to cook and pickle, and how to make arrangements for ceremonies.

At fifteen a girl assumes the hairpin.

At twenty a girl is married.[43]

Punishment for infractions of the rules is not mentioned, but the pictograph for "to teach" depicts a child tying knots, a supervisory hand menacingly holding a whip (see figure 2.11). If the *Record of Rituals* was rigidly followed, it would appear that a great deal was expected of a child. Building and repair skills, whether for roads, bridges, or edifices, were the foci of a student's studies. This pragmatic training is reminiscent of Egyptian children's study of geometry in order to ascertain their property boundaries following the periodic flooding of the Nile. Emphasis was placed on learning rope tying and knotting, skills used in almost all civil engineering tasks. The handling of rope was taught to children of all classes, but the general curriculum, particularly with respect to literacy, was limited to the upper strata. Eighty-five percent of the population worked the fields and were not literate.

Those who use their hearts govern people, while those who use their physical strength are to be governed by people. (Mencius [Meng-tzu], 372–289 B.C.)[44]

This feudal dictum prevailed in neighboring Japan as well. In ancient China, however, the consequences for children were much more dire: children could be punished for parental crimes. Boys over the age of fifteen years shared the fate of a parent sentenced to death. Those under fifteen years were relegated to a relative's care, and at fifteen they would be banished. Girls of condemned parents, although exempted from death, could be sold as slaves.

Descriptive poetry of ancient Chinese peasant life documents the customs determined by the seasons of the year. In winter, families sensibly escaped the cold:

> In the tenth moon the cricket enters under our beds;
> we fill up the chinks, and smoke out the rats,
> we close the windows, we plaster over the doors.
> Ah! my wife and children!
> The change of year requires this.
> Let us enter and dwell here.

---

*The Confucian tradition spoke of "the three obediences of woman": as a girl, to her father; as a wife, to her husband; as a widow, to her son.

Spring's warmer weather readied the farmer for the planting, growing, and harvest seasons:

In the days of the third month we take our plough in hand. In the days of the fourth month we leave [the village] together with our wives and our children who bring us food to eat in these southern fields.[45]

While farmers toiled, youngsters reveled in the warm weather, singing and dancing in the fields. It was usual for nubile youths of fifteen to mate. If pregnancy resulted, by late autumn, at about the eighth month, a marriage was held.

Among courtiers, the regulations, rites, and rituals of marriage were more controlled. They even required a mediator. Marriage, however, did not prevent a man from purchasing concubines. The children of such arrangements assumed rank and seniority according to the mother's status. The eldest son of the prime, or favored, wife was considered senior and was acknowledged as heir.

The precept of filial piety, one of the major tenets of Confucius, was the cornerstone of all education dating back to the Chou dynasty. A child was taught at an early age to support and serve the parents and, after their death, to honor their wishes. This rule extended to all classes. The peasant father had total control over property and family. He could arrange his children's professions and marriages and could, if he wished, sell them off. If there were no sons in a family, a father could purchase one from a poorer family.

Among aristocratic families, decorous filial behavior was defined and imposed: children could visit their father once every ten days, but they could not sit, stand on one foot, or lean in his presence. Neither could they spit or clear their noses.

Mutilation of the feet, called foot binding, was forced on courtesans and daughters. Some sinologists date the custom of foot binding, or "lotus-foot," to the last empress of the Shang dynasty (c.1200 B.C.).[46] Thereafter, small feet were esteemed in China and the mutilating practice did not disappear until the beginning of this century. Little girls, through millennia, suffered the enduring pains of this practice. A nineteenth-century memoir poignantly relates an experience that was common to the author's ancestors and so elegantly describes the ancient foot-binding methodology that it is set down here:

It was in the first lunar month of my seventh year that my ears were pierced and fitted with gold earrings. I was told that a girl had to suffer twice, through ear piercing and foot binding. Binding started in the second lunar month; mother consulted references in order to select an auspicious day for it. I wept and hid in a neighbor's home, but mother found me, scolded me, and dragged me home. She shut the bedroom door, boiled water, and from a box withdrew binding, shoes, knife, needle, and thread. . . . She washed and placed alum on my feet and cut the toenails. She then bent my toes toward the plantar with a binding cloth ten feet long and two inches wide, doing the right foot first and then the left. She finished binding and ordered me to walk, but when I did the pain proved unbearable. . . . The feet were washed and rebound after three or four days, with alum added. After several months, all toes but the big one were pressed against the inner surface. Whenever I ate fish or freshly killed meat, my feet would swell, and the pus would drip. . . . Every two weeks, I changed to new shoes. Each new pair was one- to two-tenths of an inch smaller than the previous one. . . . After changing more than ten pairs of shoes, my feet were reduced to a little over four inches. I had been binding for a month when my younger sister started; when no one was around, we would weep together. In summer, my feet smelled offensively because of the pus and blood; in winter, my feet felt cold because of lack of circulation and hurt if they got too near the k'ang and were struck by warm air. Four of the toes were curled in like so many dead caterpillars . . . it took two years to achieve the three-inch model.[47]

APPENDIX A
CODICES FROM THE CODE OF HAMMURABI
THAT PERTAIN ESPECIALLY TO CHILDREN *

14. If a man steal a man's son, who is a minor, he shall be put to death.

28. If an officer or a constable, who is in a fortress of the king, be captured [and] his son be able to conduct the business, they shall give to him the field and garden and he shall conduct the business of his father.

29. If his son be too young and be not able to conduct the business of his father, they shall give one-third of the field and of the garden to his mother, and his mother shall rear him.

117. If a man be in debt and sell his wife, son or daughter, or bind them over to service, for three years they shall work in the house of their purchaser or master; in the fourth year they shall be given their freedom.

135. If a man be captured and there be no maintenance in his house, and his wife openly enter into another house and bear children; if later her husband return and arrive in his city, that woman shall return to her husband [and] the children shall go to their father.

137. If a man set his face to put away a concubine who has borne him children or a wife who has presented him with children, he shall return to that woman her dowry and shall give to her the income of field, garden, and goods and she shall bring up her children. . . .

*From the translations of R. F. Harper (1904).

162. If a man take a wife and she bear him children and that woman die, her father may not lay claim to her dowry. Her dowry belongs to her children.

165. If a man present field garden or house to his favorite son and write for him a sealed deed; after the father dies, when the brothers divide, he shall take the present which the father gave him, and over and above they shall divide the goods of the father's house equally.

167. If a man take a wife and she bear him children and that woman die, and after her [death] he take another wife and she bear him children and later the father die, the children of the mothers shall not divide [the estate]. They shall receive the dowries of their respective mothers and they shall divide equally the goods of the house of the father.

168. If a man set his face to disinherit his son and say to the judges: "I will disinherit my son," the judges shall inquire into his antecedents, and if the son have not committed a crime sufficiently grave to cut him off from sonship, the father may not cut off his son from sonship.

169. If he have committed a crime against his father sufficiently grave to cut him off from sonship, they shall condone his first [offense]. If he commit a grave crime a second time, the father may cut off his son from sonship.

185. If a man take in his name a young child as a son and rear him, one may not bring claim for that adopted son.

188. If an artisan take a son for adoption and teach him his handicraft, one may not bring claim for him.

192. If a son of a NER.SE.GA, or the son of a devotee, say to his father who has reared him, or his mother who has reared him: "My father thou art not," "My mother thou art not," they shall cut out his tongue.

193. If the son of a NER.SE.GA, or the son of a devotee, identify his own father's house and hate the father who has reared him and the mother who has reared him and go back to his father's house, they shall pluck out his eye.

195. If a son strike his father, they shall cut off his fingers.

APPENDIX B
CODICES FROM THE GORTYN CODE
PERTAINING SPECIFICALLY TO CHILDREN *

If a wife who is separated [divorced] should bear a child, [they] are to bring it to the husband at his house in the presence of three witnesses; and if he should not receive it, the child shall be in the mother's power either to rear or expose. (Column III)

---

*Translation of R. F. Willetts (1977).

If a man die leaving children, should the wife so desire, she may marry, holding her own property and whatever her husband might have given her according to what is written in the presence of three witnesses; but if she should take away anything belonging to the children, that becomes a matter for trial. (Column III)

If a female serf should bear a child while separated, [they] are to bring it to the master of the man who married her . . . if he does not receive it, the child shall be in the power of the master of the female serf. (Columns III–IV)

If a woman separated should expose her child before presenting it as written, if she is convicted, she shall pay, for a free child 50 staters, for a slave 25 staters. (Column IV)

When a man or woman dies, if there be children or children's children, or children's children's children they are to have the property. (Column V)

As long as the father lives, no one shall offer to purchase any of the paternal property from the son nor take out a mortgage on it . . . nor shall the father sell or mortgage the possessions of his children. (Column VI)

If a mother die leaving children, the father is to be in control of the mother's property, but he shall not sell or mortgage unless the children consent and are of age . . . and, if he should marry another woman, the children are to be in control of the mother's property. (Column VI)

If the slave goes to a free woman and marries her, their children shall be free; but if the free woman goes to a slave, their children shall be slaves. And if free and slave children should be born to the same mother, in a case where the mother dies, if there is property, the free children are to have it. (Column VII)

And if he [the adopted person] should receive all the property and there should be no legitimate children besides, he must fulfill all the obligations of the adopter towards gods and men . . . and if there should be legitimate children of the adopter, the adopted son shall receive with the males just as females receive from the brothers. (Column XI)

And if the adopter wishes, he may renounce [the adopted son] in the place of assembly when the citizens are gathered. (Column XI)

If a person die owing money or having lost a suit . . . the property shall belong to those who won the suit or those to whom he owes money, and the heirs shall not be liable to any further fine. (Column XI)

NOTES

1. Schmandt-Besserat, *Washington Post*, 6 December 1993.
2. Cottrell, 1965, pp. 143–44.
3. Ibid., p. 145.

4. All the citations from the Code of Hammurabi are from the translations of Harper, 1904.

5. Kramer, 1981, pp. 1–17.

6. Ibid., p. 15.

7. Ibid., p. 16.

8. Ibid.

9. Ibid., p. 17.

10. Romer, 1982, pp. 20–22.

11. Iversen, 1939, pp. 47–49.

12. Safway el-Alfy, 1981, pp. 12–14.

13. Casson, 1975, p. 105.

14. Aldred, 1961, p. 193.

15. Casson, 1975, p. 75.

16. Gurney, 1972, pp. 88–90.

17. Ibid., p. 99.

18. Grant, 1969, pp. 1–3.

19. *Science News* 1990; 137:5.

20. The translations of the Gortyn Code are all from Willetts, 1977, and appear in Appendix B at the end of this chapter.

21. Bloch, 1958, p. 40.

22. Heurgon, 1964, p. 135.

23. Strong, 1968, p. 89.

24. In this millennium, construction sacrifice has been observed among the Tlingit, who placed slave children into post holes prior to erecting an edifice.

25. Harden, 1962, p. 132. Researcher J. H. Schwartz notes that some of the cremated *tophet* bones are fetal in nature, suggesting that they may have been products of spontaneous abortions. *Skeleton Keys* (New York: Oxford University Press, 1995).

26. Payne, 1916, p. 170.

27. Heaton, 1956, p. 84.

28. J. Zias et al., Early medical use of cannabis, *Nature* 1993; 363:215.

29. Heaton, 1956, p. 154; Sommerville, 1990, p. 34.

30. Schwartz, 1985, p. 210.

31. Chrisman, 1920, pp. 164–66.

32. *Science News* 1990; 137:28.

33. Bahadur, 1979, pp. 92–95.

34. Manjo, 1975, pp. 261–66.

35. Sena, 1901, vol. 1.

36. Masson-Oursel, 1934, p. 147.

37. All of the passages from the *Rigveda* and other Vedic literature are from the translations of Bahadur, 1979.

38. Hsu and Ward, 1984, pp. 9–19.

39. Payne, 1916, p. 52.

40. Hsu and Ward, 1984, p. 404.

41. Ibid., pp. 408–9.

42. Ibid., p. 409.
43. Ibid., p. 49.
44. Tom, 1989, pp. 68–70.
45. Maspero, 1978, p. 71.
46. Levy, 1966, pp. 3–10.
47. Ibid., pp. 26–28.

Chapter 3

Classical Civilizations: The Ephebe

❑ ❑ ❑

GREECE

In the first millennium B.C., the Greek city-states were in constant competition for power and trade. Geographical hindrances—islands, peninsulas, mountains—discouraged communication and centralization, and the end result was three culturally distinct tribal groups with separate dialects and social mores. Aeolians inhabited Thessaly, Boeotia, and Aiolis (now Anatolia). Dorians lived in the eastern and southern Peloponnesus, Cyclades, Crete, Rhodes, and the Carian coast. Ionians occupied Attica and the Aegean and the Anatolian littoral. Athens was the largest and most powerful city-state, with Sparta in the Peloponnesus its main rival. Sifnos, famous for its gold and silver, Paros, known for its marble, and obsidian-rich Milos were among the other city-states. Only during periods of strife, when unity was essential to survival, did the city-states act in concordance. When the common threat was quelled, internecine jealousies and frictions resumed.

As the wealthiest and most influential of the maritime powers, Athens flourished. Unlike rigid, militaristic Sparta, Athens was a democratic society with extensive civil rights. Conflict between the two states was constant. The Olympiad every four years, however, declared a state of truce, honored as sacred, and for a few days political rivalries were played out in fiercely competitive athletic events.

The fundamental distrust harbored by these rivals culminated in the Peloponnesian War (431–404 B.C.). Sparta emerged dominant from the conflict, and the Greek city-states were fragmented and weakened. Philip of Macedonia (359–336 B.C.) unified the empire, and his son Alexander extended its domain to the Near East and to northern Africa. With the death of Alexander (323 B.C., from malaria at the age of thirty-three), a gradual dismantling of the empire ensued, and by the second century the Greek states were basically ruled from Rome.

The Spartan city-state contrasted with its rival, Athens, in every aspect of its society. In Sparta, education, customs, rituals, and laws had been devised to inculcate devotion to the concept of service to the state and to promotion of the state's welfare. At every level this idea was reinforced in the minds of its citizens. In Sparta, girls were valued in their maternal role as producers of warrior sons. Dance instruction was part of their curriculum, but the serious educational thrust was in the gymnasia, where they trained to become strong, self-sufficient competitors who would produce healthy offspring to loyally serve Sparta in peace and war. The arduous training was intended to ensure that

the root of what they have conceived should have a strong beginning in strong bodies and that they themselves by enduring labor with fortitude should struggle effectively and easily with labor pangs.[1]

Should a mother die giving birth to a son, the gravesite bore an inscription commending her sacrifice on behalf of the state. This same honor was uniquely extended to only one other, the slain warrior, and then only anonymously. Spartan law allowed no burial items in graves, mementos, or religious symbols on tombs. Only the soldier's red mantle of battle was permitted for display. Mourning was limited to twelve days, lest duties to the state be neglected.[2]

The Spartan concern for healthy offspring was so overpowering that the laws governing marriage and facilitating adoption were constructed and construed so as to assure this end:

It was permitted for an elderly husband of a young wife, if he liked and approved of some fine young gentleman, to bring him in to her, and filling her with good seed, to adopt the offspring as his own.[3]

In the state of Sparta, newborns were bathed in wine

. . . in order to test their constitution. For it is said that epileptic and sickly children experience convulsions as a result of contact with unmixed wine, whereas healthy ones are tempered and strengthened by it.[4]

Exposure was much more common among the Spartans, consistent with their disdain for flawed, weak physiques. Plutarch (46–120 A.D.) reported that Spartan fathers were required to have infant males inspected in order to receive the state's clean bill of health before receiving permission to keep their babies:

The father did not have authority to rear the baby, but he took it to a place called a *leskhe*, where the eldest members of the tribe sat and inspected the child. If it were well-built and strong, they ordered him to rear it, allocating to it one of the 9,000 lots; but if it was ill-born and unshapely, they sent it away to the so-called Apothetai, a place like a pit near Taygetos, believing that it was better both for itself and for the city that it should not live if it was not well-formed for health and strength right from the start.[5]

Plato, the paradigm of Greek moral thought, seems not to have objected to abandonment; in *The Theaetetus* (160) he had Socrates relate:

Then this child, however he may turn out, which you and I have with difficulty brought into the world. And now that he is born, we must run round the hearth with him, and see whether he is worth rearing, or is only a wind-egg and a sham. Is he to be reared in any case, and not exposed? or will you bear to see him rejected, and not get into a passion if I take away your first-born?

Once infants were taken to the place of abandonment, the *Apothetai*, it was illegal to rescue, sell, enslave, or prostitute them. Plutarch made no reference to Spartan female newborns. It can be presumed that the right to abandon and expose them was left to parents, since the inspection of girls by community elders was not mandatory. Moreover, a reference by Polybius of the declining Greek population indicates that throughout the Greek city-states abandonment became a frequent practice:

In our own time the whole of Greece has been subject to a low birth-rate and a general decrease in population, owing to which cities have been deserted and the land has ceased to yield fruit, although there have been neither continuous wars nor epidemics . . . as men had fallen into such a state of pretentiousness, avarice, and indolence that they did not wish to marry, or if they married to rear the children born to them, or at most as a rule but one or two of them, so as to leave them in affluence and bring them to waste their substance, the evil rapidly and insensibly grows. (*Histories* 36, 17.5–9)

Throughout Greece, only the *deme* of Ephesos and of Thebes forbade the practice. In Ephesos, abandonment was permitted only if an infant had signs of intrauterine malnutrition or hydrops (generalized swelling).[6] Of Thebes, Aelian wrote:

This is a Theban law most just and humane: that no Theban might expose his child or leave it in a wilderness, upon pain of death. But if the father were extremely poor, whether it were male or female, the law requires that as soon as it is born it be brought in the swaddling cloths to the magistrate, who, receiving it, delivers it to some other for some small reward, conditioning with him that he shall bring up the child, and when it is grown up take it into his service, man or maid, and have the benefit of its labor in requital for its education.[7]

The topic of abandoned babies being used as substitutes was a popular theme of many dramas of the times. Menander and Cratinus each wrote a play called *The Substituted Child*. *The Suppositious Child* was written by Alexis. Epinicus authored *The Suppositious Damsel*, and, finally, a variation on the theme, *The Pseudo-suppositious Child*, was written by Crobylus.[8] These plays may attest to an actual practice of deception, or perhaps they addressed the worst fears of their original audiences, or both.

Governed by Spartan law, boys left home at the age of seven years to live with other boys of the same age in companies and troops. Trainers, with the assistance of interested private citizens, strictly disciplined the groups. Granted "paternal" authority over the boys, they demanded from the boys the obedience and respect the law mandated. This period of training, the *agoge*, was segmented by age groups. The first segment occurred at about seven years, with the beginning of regimentation. The second began at twelve years, with austerity proscribing clothing and prescribing little food. At fourteen, the boy became an *ephebe* (the start of military training), and at twenty years he ceased being a boy and was called an *eiren*. Marriage would not be sanctioned until the final age group, beginning at thirty years. Clothing was scant in all seasons, with no concessions for a harsh winter. Food rations were meager. Baths were infrequent. In preadolescence, boys slept on straw; after fourteen, reeds were substituted to train boys to become indifferent to discomfort and pain. As a discipline to foster self-sufficiency, boys had to collect the reeds from the banks of the Eurotas River.[9] At the altar of Artemis Orthia, older, tested boys were publicly flogged to display their fortitude. Even thievery was condoned as long as it furthered the aims of the state:

On the other hand, so that they might not be too much oppressed by hunger, . . . he [the Lykourgos] permitted them to steal some things to relieve their hunger. . . . So clearly he educated the boys in this way because he wished to make them more resourceful at obtaining supplies, and more warlike. (Xenophon, *Lakedaimonion Politeia, Republic* bk. 2)

This was substantiated by Isokrates:

The Spartans send out their boys everyday, as soon as they get up, with whatever companions they each wish, allegedly to hunt, but in fact to steal from those who live in the country. The practice is that those who are caught are fined and beaten, but those who do most wrong and are able to escape detection have a higher reputation among the boys, and when they come to man's estate, if they keep to the habits which they adopted as boys, are in line for the highest offices. (*Panathenaicus* 211, 212)

Reading or writing was not part of the Spartan state's curriculum. Children who wished to learn these were left to their own devices. The state did teach arithmetic and instrumental and vocal music, but the principal purpose of a Spartan education was to train strong, healthy bodies with excellent military skills and bright minds for cleverness and stealth in battle. Consequently, no trade other than soldiering was taught. Merchandising was left to the Perioeci of Lacedaemon, and the trades to the Helots.

For most scholars, whether amateur or professional, the phrase *ancient Greece* evokes images of the Athens city-state and the ghosts of gleaming white marble edifices. The Acropolis—the apogee of classical architecture, planned by Pericles and built in the fifth century B.C.—endures in Athens as a visual reminder of the permanent impact on the Western world of the three hundred golden years of Greek civilization. The language, art and architecture, literature and drama, education, philosophy, and ethics of ancient Greece influenced Western cultures in perpetuity.

In ancient Athens, the *Akros-polis* (high city) was the economic, political, and philosophic center of the Golden Age of Greece, with the Parthenon its architectural jewel. The city below housed its citizens and slaves in tortuously narrow streets that often were cluttered with garbage disgorged from its houses. Shops of cobblers, potters, carpenters, metal workers, and the like, vying for trade, were grouped in districts by specialty on unnamed, unnumbered streets. Each *deme*, or district, of registration had its own name, and a young man assumed the name of his *deme* when, at the age of eighteen, he was registered. Athenians, therefore, could locate the homes of friend or family by referring to the pertinent *deme*. A business could be located in the same way, with reference to the kind of business further facilitating the search.[10]

Private homes in these quarters had few windows. They generally faced a central, open courtyard, called the *peristylon*. Parlors, dining rooms, store rooms, and bedrooms surrounded the court, with children and slaves rele-

gated to the upper levels of the house. Into this domestic scene children—
paides—were born. Various comments by Aeschuylus, Plato, Xenophon,
Aristotle, and Sophocles described them as physically weak, intellectually
wanting, fickle, amoral, noisy, wailing lispers with bad tempers. The majority of the populace thought of them as soft, desirable, sweet-smelling, innocent, unspoiled, and lovable creatures,[11] and they welcomed their young
with carefully planned and reverent ceremony. Athenians believed, however,
that too many children diluted family wealth. Hesiod (c.800 B.C.) advocated having only one male heir: "Let there be only one son to tend in his
father's house: for so shall wealth increase in the dwelling" (*Works and Days*,
422–23).

Expectations and rules for boys and girls were, not surprisingly, vastly different. Boys were educated for future careers. Girls were trained only to
assume the maternal role. There are traces of affection and regard, however,
for female progeny. A tombstone from the fifth century B.C., poignantly
depicting a grandmother affectionately offering food to her granddaughter,
illustrates the love families felt for girls as well as boys. The inscription on
the tomb of the ampharete leaves no doubt that daughters were treasured:
"Here I hold my daughter's child, my darling, whom once I held on my knee
when we both lived and saw the sunlight; now I am dead, and hold her, dead
too."[12]

Lives of girls were restricted, with few possibilities other than as heads of
households after marriage. There were no schools for girls, and education,
such as it was, was left to mothers and nurses. The lot of poor girls was even
more limited in scope. Girls were trained in housekeeping and cooking and
in skills related to making cloth—weaving, spinning, and the maintenance
and operation of a loom. They picked up some child-rearing principles and
some knowledge of herbal medicine within their households.

Foreign slave girls (called *hetairai*), on the other hand, received formal
education. Often obtained in infancy, sometimes as part of the spoils of war,
they formed a society of courtesans who, protected by the state, were highly
educated and cultivated. They were versed in literature, philosophy, music,
and mathematics. These girls lived alone or in small sorority groups and were
frequently hired to serve in symposia and family sacrifice ceremonies.[13]

In citizen families, fathers contracted betrothals for their daughters,
whose virginity was linked to the honor of the family. Solon, who otherwise
forbade the practice, advised parents to sell into servitude daughters who had
lost their virginity.[14]

Dowries were essential for girls' marital prospects, so the poor were helped
by friends, orphans by their guardians; in Sparta especially, the state
endowed daughters of citizens who had served the interest of the state.

Again, in Sparta, fathers deferred to the state's authority regarding marriage. Age and health criteria had to satisfy the state's interest in the progeny of marriage:

Lykourgos considered boys to be not the private property of their fathers, but the common property of the city. Hence he wanted the citizens to be produced not from any chance parents, but from the best.[15]

Elopement, called night of seizure, did occur, prearranged by Spartan fathers with little input from the daughters—although the rare elopement arranged without a father's knowledge also occurred. In Athens, contracted marriages were the norm but without the encumbrance of oppressive state laws. To enhance fertility, it was customary for girls to bathe in river water prior to marriage. Nuptial waters were considered magical and partially responsible for pregnancy and a smooth delivery. Sophocles pronounced the river Kephisos and the stream Kyllypera capable of hastening birth.[16]

Before marriage, Greek girls also made offerings of toys—symbols of childhood—to the goddess Artemis, and in prayer acknowledged the impending loss of virginal innocence:

Timareta before her wedding has dedicated to you, Artemis of the Lake, her tambourine, her pretty ball and the caul that upheld her hair, her dolls too, and their dresses: a virgin's gift, as is right to a virgin. Artemis, hold your hand above the girl and purely preserve her in purity.[17]

At an Athenian marriage, children were given special roles, particularly children with both parents living—*pais amphithales*. Such children were believed to carry good omens. On the night before the wedding, the bridegroom slept in the presence of a male *pais amphithales* at the bride's home. During wedding ceremonies, these children circulated among the guests, handing out bread from a basket in the shape of a cradle to symbolize the bride's readiness to conceive and bear her firstborn.

During the early months of marriage, girls refined their knowledge of herbal medicines that were used in pregnancy and at parturition. Root of peony helped with menses as well as with labor; myrtle prevented premature delivery, the galingale facilitated menses, and the lily checked menstruation. It was thought that pomegranates could stimulate libido, a botanical claim grounded more in superstition than in pharmacology. Supplication was made to Demeter, usually depicted holding a poppy or a pomegranate, for both euphoria and pregnancy. Before marriage, however, girls were taught to suppress libido by sleeping on a bed of withy, which also was believed to keep snakes away.[18]

Once pregnant, women anticipated the time and date of a birth with superstitious beliefs often encouraged by prevailing medical wisdom. Attributed to Hippocrates, *The Fleshes* anticipated no hope of survival for a child born in the eighth month.[19] The later writings of Galen promulgated this same belief among the Romans, and the Talmud described an eight-month baby as a "stone," doomed to be lifeless.[20]

Some days augured auspiciously; others were fraught with bad omens:

> The mid sixth is most unfavorable for plants,
> But is good for male births, though not favorable
> For a girl to be born, nor, therefore be married.
> Nor is the first sixth a proper day for a girl
> To be born, but is fitting for gelding kids and
> Sheep, good for the birth of boys; but such will be
> Fond of sharp speech, lies, cunning words, and
> Stealthy converse.
>
> (Hesiod, *Works and Days* 800)

At quickening, prayers were directed to many deities of parturition but primarily to Eileithyia, who personified a smooth, rapid, and safe delivery.[21] Pliny, in his *Natural History*, suggested tying to the mother's mons pubis

a stone voided by a sufferer from bladder trouble. . . . [T]he man by whom a woman has conceived unties his girdle and puts it around her waist and then unties it, with the ritual formula: "I bound, and I too will unloose," then taking his departure, childbirth is made more rapid.[22]

As the most private part of the house and a room reserved for use by women, it is supposed that women delivered their babies in the *gunaikeion*.[23] Newborns were bathed in a mixture of water and oil and then swaddled. The swaddle bands, *spargana*, were strips of cloth, saved exclusively for swaddling, that had been cut from garments worn by the parents at the annual Eleusian festival of sowing and fertility. Babies remained girdled for sixty days. They were bathed in the light of a full moon to ensure good health. To this day, lunar exposure is observed by several cultural groups, particularly the Bantu-root tribes of Africa. The newborn was adorned with amulets (*gnorismata*). Moonstone amulets were expected to prevent epilepsy, which was believed to be caused by the waxing and waning of the moon. In all, the *gnorismata* were distinct identifying talismans that children wore, even, it is thought, when abandoned. This latter notion has been disputed by at least one historian, who contends that these tokens were nothing more than dramatic devices used by playwrights to allow scenes of adult reconciliations—a dramatic tradition, it may be added, that has endured into our century. The ancients who abandoned their babies would most likely have removed any items that made identification possible.[24]

Births of welcomed babies were announced with adornments placed on the front door—wooden fillets for a girl, olive branches for a boy. Welcoming festivals, called the *amphidromia*, were held between five and ten days after birth, at which time children were given a name. By custom a firstborn male would receive the name of his paternal grandfather, followed by his father's name, and finally, the name of his *deme*.

Guests at these celebrations gave presents of good luck: charms and traditional gifts of cuttlefish and octopus. A ceremonial *amphidromia* (literally, "running around") was a traditional aspect of the festivities. Guests followed the mother, infant in arms, dancing several times about the family hearth, the sacred center of the home.[25] This symbolic binding to the hearth may have been an extension of the custom of house burials among the ancient Greeks, who entombed their dead newborns under fireplace stones.

Wealthy Greeks normally delivered their infants to a wet nurse, a *titthe*, for nutritional sustenance and general care during the formative years. Occasionally, loving attention and devotion were recognized and honored in writings and on tombstone dedications. Kallimalchos wrote in his *Epigrammata* about a *titthe*: "Mikkos provided for his good wet-nurse as long as she lived and even in her old age. When she died he set up a dedication to her for future generations to see."[26]

In caring for newborns, mothers applied knowledge of child-rearing practices, nutrition, and botanical medicine learned from mothers and nurses. Consultations with family and friends for norms of growth and development were adjunct sources of information, and physicians such as Hippocrates (460–370 B.C.), who for the first time had put order and sequence into their clinical observations, also could be consulted.

The weaning of children began when they were about a year old, with a watery gruel fed through a double-operculated bottle. Evidence of infant furniture—a kind of high chair—has been found on an Attic vase. The composition of the chair appears to be wood or reinforced terra cotta (figure 3.1). Sometimes, during the autumn *apaturia* festival, children three to seven years of age were initiated into a family fraternity, called a *phratry*. Parents entreated the fostering deities, *kourotrophoi*, to watch over their children as they matured.[27] For disciplinary purposes, other beings were invoked. Mormo, who ate children, or Empusa, a hobgoblin who could change shapes, were relied on to effect compliant behavior.

Apart from dress—little boys went about in the nude or wore open-fronted tunics, and girls wore long dresses—the early years of Greek childhood

Figure 3.1 High-chair (*cum* potty?) depiction on an Attic red-figure *chous*, c.440–430 B.C. BRITISH MUSEUM.

were similar for girls and boys. They played with noisemakers, carts, hoops, articulated dolls made of wax or clay, tops, balls, swords, kites, yoyos, and whizzing wheels. They engaged in group play on swings and seesaws and in games of hide-and-seek, tag, and blindman's buff.

At seven, girls and boys parted company. Girls were instructed in the domestic arts at home, and boys were sent off to school. In the Ionic states, parents were responsible for their children's education. The state was responsible in the Doric community. Old slaves (*paidagogos*) were charged to accompany boys to school and authorized to supervise their behavior (figure 3.2) until they were eighteen years old. The *paidagogos* attempted to inculcate his charge with *kalo kagathos*, a quality akin to good manners and comportment. *Kalo kagathos* addressed many behaviors, among them gait, eye movements, conversation, eating habits, even the length of the himation.[28] These lessons were crucial elements in latent Athenian childhood nurturing.

In classes that began early and ended late, boys studied literature, music, and gymnastics. Solon forbade classes before sunrise or after sunset. As interpreted by Aeschines, the ruling protected boys from sexual abuse:

He [Solon] forbids the teacher to open the schoolroom or the gymnastics trainer the wrestling school, before sunrise, and he commands them to close the doors before sunset; for he is exceeding suspicious of their being alone with a boy, or in the dark with him. (*Against Timarchus* 9–10)

Figure 3.2 Drawing reproduced from the shoulders of an Attic *kylix* (c.500 B.C.) in the Berlin Museum, showing the *pedagogus* overseeing a boy's education. Note, on the right shoulder, the *pedagogus* sits sideways, holding a caning stick, and observes instruction being given in flute and stylus-writing. On the left shoulder, he sits with his legs crossed and observes instruction in reading and recitation and in playing the lyre (Blumner, 1914).

Aristotle discouraged liaisons between young and older males (figure 3.3) by proposing that gymnasia be divided according to the *helikiai* (the periods of life).[29] Pederasty was frowned upon and was illegal to the extent that known pedophiles had their civil rights curtailed.[30] Male pedophilia and boy brothels were not uncommon in ancient Greece, giving rise to the impression that the open tunics little boys wore may have facilitated a more invidious practice than toiletry measures.

Writing exercises were practiced on wax diptychs or triptychs and were read aloud in recitation. A type of abacus was used for counting, but not until hand counting was mastered. The left hand marked units of ten; the right, hundreds and thousands. Although some instruction was given in singing and in flute, lyre, and citharas playing, boys focused on writing, reading, and arithmetic, with serious music study beginning in earnest at the age of twelve or thirteen. At sixteen, seventeen, and eighteen, geometry, astronomy, drawing, advanced music, and sophistry were added to the curriculum. These were taught in concordance with the period of gymnasia and in the same environs: therefore, Plato taught at Academy, Aristotle at Lyceum, and Antisthenes at Cynosarges.

Figure 3.3 The tondo of an Attic *kylix* (c.470 B.C.) in the Ashmolean Museum, depicting a homosexual encounter between an older man and a boy..

Beginning training when students were seven years old, the gymnasia prepared boys for four major panhellenic games: the Olympiad, the Isthmian, the Nemean, and the Pythian. The students were grouped by developmental age into teams of *paides* (boys), the "beardless" *ageneioi* (adolescents), and *andres* (men). Wrestling was the principal sport, followed by jumping, running, and discus and javelin throwing. In the Aegean empire, swimming, to be sure, was an important skill and was either self-taught or taught by fathers.

The age of maturity, *ephebus*, was celebrated at eighteen or nineteen, by family and state, in rites of passage signaling the end of childhood and the entry into manhood. Youth donned adult clothing and were given adult haircuts. After being registered in the *deme* book, the young men took the oath of Solon and were given spears and shields:

I swear by Zeus never to disgrace my holy arms, never to forsake my comrade in the ranks, but to fight for the holy temples and the common welfare, alone or with others: to leave my country, not in a worse, but in a better state than I found it: to obey the magistrates and the laws and defend them against attack: I swear to hold in honor the religion of my country.[31]

Only with marriage were girls recognized as adults. Except for a passage written by Aristophanes, there is scant evidence that they celebrated other occasions—rites of passage—to mark milestones:

As soon as I was in my seventh year I became an *arrhephoros*. Then in my tenth I was an *aletris* to the Archegetis. Then, wearing a saffron robe, I was an *arktos* (bear) at the festival of Artemis Brauronia. Next, on becoming a beautiful *pais*, I performed the function of *kanephoros*, wearing a string of figs.[32]

Yet, shortly after marriage, the ennui of domestic life must have settled in, perhaps accounting for the popularity of the Amazon legend among Greek girls.*

The Amazons were said to be strong, self-sufficient women from the north coast of Anatolia, who were farmers, horsewomen, and warriors. They purportedly mutilated their daughters in infancy by having one breast cauterized to facilitate the use of bow and arrow. The etymology of the name may relate to the Greek word "breastless" (*amazoi*), to reaping harvests (*amao*), or to work girdles (*zonai*).[33] The Amazons are mentioned throughout classical literature; in the works of Diodorus Siculus, Herodotus, and Strabo. Some contemporary authors think the repeated reference to Amazons may indicate that some matrilinear tribes of warrior women did exist. Strabo placed them out of Asia Minor in Caucasia. Diodorus was especially specific in his account of an Amazon nation in North Africa:

In the western parts of Libya, at the frontiers of the world, there is supposed to have been a nation ruled by women; they waged war, served for a defined period in the army during which period they had to exist without men. When their years of service were past, they got together with men in order to perpetuate their race. . . . Straight after birth, male offspring is handed over to the father, who feeds him milk and other foods according to his age. If the child is female, however, her breasts are burned so that they do not grow in puberty, for it is regarded as an encumbrance for the carrying of weapons if the breasts project from the body; for this reason they are called Amazons (breastless) by the Greeks.[34]

Finally, prehistoric rock drawings in the Sahara depict bow-carrying women warriors. As late as 1747 there was a report from Dahomey of a king who was guarded by an army of women five thousand strong.[35]

ROME

The classic civilizations of Greece and Rome have been among the most influential, visually beautiful, and enduring in the evolution of human history. The topography of the planet still reverberates with the architecture and

---

*Scholars have strong, sometimes passionate, opinions about the existence of the Amazons. Some consider them totally mythical: "The Amazon is a dream that men created, an image of a superlative female that men constructed to flatter themselves" (Kleinbaum, 1983, p. 1).

engineering of the period. The ubiquitous residues of the language roots, political and governing bodies, and judicial systems of these two cultures continue to influence societies globally. Yet the cultures were very different—in a facile phrase, the philosophic versus the pragmatic.[36]

These differences significantly influenced societal attitudes toward children. The Greeks taught boys basic learning skills of writing, reading, and arithmetic but additionally immersed them in music, literature, sophistry, and gymnasia. The muses were given the same import as the sciences. The Romans, on the other hand, taught the basics to both boys and girls but in the end thought of children as property. The *patria potestas*, the father's will and power, defined the role and course of children. But remarkably influential and beneficial was the prolonged period of relative peace the Romans sustained, the *Pax Romana*, which allowed for expansion of the cultural and educational horizons of children. The massacres and sustained periods of malnutrition, destruction, and poverty inherent in war were absent for centuries. Despite the Roman propensity to regard children as property, as *res vacantes*, or as paternal servants, early Roman law, in which children's rights were limited, gave way to the classical Roman period of more enlightened and nurturing concern for children.

Rome, from very early on, was the center of the empire, growing progressively larger until, by the second century A.D., it covered seven square miles and had well over a half-million citizens. The Tiber River that coursed through the city was a site for religious ritual as well as the main outflow vector for the extensive system of sewers and aqueducts. To honor Jupiter and pray for a propitious future, Roman mothers dipped their babies into the waters that also served the disposal needs of the city. The Roman house, like the Greek, generally had windowless rooms facing an inner court, or atrium. Niches and miniature altars to household spirits and gods—lares and penates—were found in various rooms throughout the house. Many of the spirits were dedicated to children. Levana blessed the *tollere* of a father accepting his newborn. Cunina guarded the cradle, and Nundina blessed the naming ceremony. Fabulina watched over the learning of speech and the first uttered words. Ossipago was believed to make bones grow straight and strong, and Interduca watched over children in school. The statues and figurines of these and other lesser gods would be honored by little crowns of myrtle and rosemary and miniature cakes baked in their behalf.[37]

Roman matrons managed their households with a great deal more freedom and with legal rights unheard of in Greece. For the most part, girls were trained to assume the role of mistress of the household, but, unlike the Greek customs, girls and boys were instructed in the basic subjects of reading, writing, and mathematics. Moreover, females could aspire to the professions. Roman women became physicians, scribes, and philosophers.

For all that, the majority opted for domestic careers and motherhood. The position of the Roman matron was imbued with prestige and status. Home was a woman's domain, in which women exercised authority as chief administrators and decision-makers, as spinners and weavers, and as hostesses. Roman matrons considered *cultus*[38]—the mystique of feminine demeanor and dress—important, and as an adolescent, the Roman girl learned the skills of concocting makeup and making wigs.*

In matters of property, women bowed only to the power of *patria potestas*, the unquestioned authority of the male head of household and family. This concept of male authority apparently had its origins in the Sabine law of *manus*, the sign of possession used by a ruler that all he laid hands on was his. When the Palatine tribes of Romulus united with the Capitoline Sabine tribes, the *manus* law prevailed and gradually evolved into the *patria potestas*.

The concept featured prominently in Roman law and was delineated clearly in the Twelve Tables (c.450 B.C.),[39] from which evolved Roman jurisprudence. Similar to the public display of the codes of Hammurabi and of Gortyn, bronze tablets were posted on the Roman Forum's tribune of the Comitum for citizens to read. The inviolability of *patria potestas* was acknowledged even in the outlying Roman colonies. The codes were posted in public forums where variations of the original Twelve Tables[40] (figure 3.4) were modified to incorporate civil codes relevant to each province.

Table 4 referred to the law of *patria potestas*. The fifth table established patrimony and made sons, daughters, and wives subject to paternal authority. Paternal control was absolute, affecting the actions and the destinies of all members of the family. Sons could not free slaves, sign contracts, make career choices, buy property, or make wills without the cognizance and consent of their fathers. Until the first century B.C., when it became a capital offense, fathers had the power to condemn recalcitrant offspring to death. Such sons could always, of course, be disinherited. Only when their fathers died were sons recognized as independent—*sui iuris*—at which time they inherited their fathers' estates and their fathers' status as *paterfamilias*.

Marriages were arranged by the fathers of both young men and young

---

*Eyelash liner, for example, was made by grinding bituminous coal into a fine powder and suspending it in oil. Eye shadow could be white from white lead oxide or chalk or gray from ashes or antimony. Malachite was obtained from Egypt to make green eye shadow and lapis lazuli from the Levant for blue color. Red plant dyes or red lead oxide was made into rouge, and mollusks from Phoenicia provided a purple hue. Ovid provided recipes for unguents, concocting a mixture of barley meal, eggs, ground antlers, narcissus bulb, gum, honey, and wheat. Wigs were made from purchased hair. Blond hair was obtained from captive German girls. Pearl earrings were the favored jewelry, followed by necklaces, bracelets, rings, and brooches.

Figure 3.4 Bronze tables with the Lex Coloniae Genetivae Juliae from the colony of Asuna in Spain. MUSEO ARQUEOLOGICO NACIONAL, MADRID.

women. The law required, nevertheless, the consent of both parties: *Nuptias consensus, non concubitus facit* (Consent, not coition, makes marriage). These arranged affairs often evolved into genuine connubial love, as a tombstone from Roman Lyon indicates:

To the eternal memory of Blandinia Martiola . . . his wife incomparable and most kind to him. . . . You who read this go bathe in the baths of Apollo as I used to do with my wife—I wish I still could.[41]

As a rule, girls married between the ages of thirteen and seventeen. Their property was given to them, only to be lost to the new *paterfamilias*, in deference to the long-recognized laws of *manus* marriages.

A Roman couple aimed to have three children,[42] a number approved by the state. Citizens of early Rome were enjoined to raise all healthy male children and at least one female. All children had to be allowed to live until they were three years old. The exception was the anomalous child. Lame or abnormal infants could be exposed after five witnesses approved the intention.[43] Violation of this law was punished by confiscation of one-half of the family fortune.

By the age of twelve, nubile girls had learned that woolen pessaries soaked in honey or olive oil served as safe, albeit not totally reliable, contraceptives. Considering that the rate of infant mortality, excluding deaths from abandonment, was as high as 33 percent and that childless couples were common, it is doubtful that contraception measures were taken in excess. To

Figure 3.5 A relief showing the trade sign of a Roman midwife. The midwife sits below the mother, who clings to a birthing chair. MUSEUM OF OSTIA ANTICA.

judge by tomb inscriptions, life expectancy in general was poor. Analyses of tomb inscriptions reveal that one-third of all children were dead by the age of two *lustra* (a *lustra* was approximately five years). The average life expectancy for men could have been as low as twenty-two and, for women, twenty years.[44] Adoption, therefore, was common and legal, with the laws of property and inheritance extended to adopted children.

Roman women who became pregnant prayed to, among others, the goddess Juno Lucina, for a safe delivery, and the goddess Carmenta, who was asked to watch over the newborn. Parturition occurred in a birthing chair, with a midwife prepared to catch the baby (figure 3.5). Soranus, in his book *Gynaecology*, listed all the paraphernalia a prepared midwife should have[45]:

. . . oil for injections and cleansing, hot water in order to wash the affected area, hot compresses to relieve the labor pains, sponges for sponging off, wool for covering the woman's body, and bandages to swaddle the baby in, a pillow so that the infant may be placed on it below the mother until the afterbirth has been taken away; scents . . . for the recovery of the mother's strength; a birthing stool. (1:10)

Generally, there were witnesses to the birth to prevent substitutions. To avoid legal disputes the Justinian *Digest* provided guidelines to be followed: Birth was to be in a home selected by the praetor. The birthing room had to have no fewer than three lights and could have only one entrance, guarded by three men and women who searched all who entered and left the room. At the delivery, five nonpregnant free women were expected to keep a watchful eye and, immediately after birth, inspect the child for vital signs or their absence.[46] Following delivery, invoking the tradition of *patria potestas*,

Figure 3.6 Relief from a Roman sarcophagus showing various stages of child-hood. The father can be seen observing his child suckle and holding up his child (*tollere*). The child plays with a toy chariot and in the last scene is observed in the posture and gesture of rhetoric, holding in his left hand the scroll of position. An admiring father looks on. LOUVRE MUSEUM, PARIS.

infants were placed at their fathers' feet. When held up (*tollere*, figure 3.6) or placed on the knee (*ingenuus*), an infant's acceptance into the family was complete. Rejected babies were exposed or abandoned, to be picked up by passers-by or left to die.

Roman infants, upon acceptance by the *paterfamilias*, were salted with astringent bicarbonate and swaddled. Swaddling even then was a millennia-old tradition. It was common wisdom that the bound baby is more passive and has less colic and irritability. It has a slower heart rate and sleeps more than an unswaddled baby does. Although swathing with bands and ritualistic wrappings is no longer done, the habit of caretakers in modern nurseries, who tightly envelope infants in cotton blankets and place them on their sides, still echoes the practice, and indeed, it has been shown that such babies sleep longer and more deeply.[47]

Cleansing was done with olive oil, since the Romans used no soap. This was lathered on, forming an emulsion of oil and dirt particles, then wiped off with *strigils*, or contoured blades made in variable sizes to accommodate different somatotypes (figure 3.7). The Romans, some scholars hold, believed the oil of the olive would not only cleanse the infant but strengthen the "marrow" of the brain, where the psyche took form.[48]

A festival of purification, called the *lustratio*, was held following a birth. For girls this fell on the eighth day; for boys, the ninth. On the eve of the

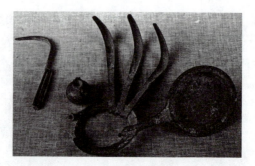

Figure 3.7 *Strigils*, oil jar and mirror. After applying oil to emulsify body dirt and detritus, these contoured bronze blades were run along the body to scrape off the cleansing oil. METROPOLITAN MUSEUM OF ART, NEW YORK CITY.

purification, the *dies lustricus*, the baby was protected by a vigil. Three men, respectively armed with an ax, a pestle, and a broom, approached the house, tapped at the threshold, and swept the floor. They symbolized the refinements of an agriculturally rich civilization that had emerged from the barbaric past of *silvanus*.[49] At the following dawn began the festival at which the baby received its name. Three names were traditional, and a sacrifice in the baby's name was offered. Guests gave the baby toys and charms. The gift of a *bulla* or locket containing some antiwitchcraft element always was given for a baby to wear until adulthood.

Wet Nurses

Parents of means entrusted infants to the care of wet nurses, whose responsibilities were those of a governess. Together with a pedagogue, a wet nurse supervised a child's education until puberty. Seneca's (4–65 A.D.) dour comments on child-rearing practices imply that severe and corporal punishments were the Roman norm:

Parents subject the still malleable characters of their children to what will do them good. Let them cry and struggle as they will, we swaddle them tightly lest their still-immature bodies become deformed rather than grow up straight and tall. Later we instill liberal culture by means of terror if they refuse to learn.[50]

The practice of employing wet nurses was lamented by Tacitus (55–120 A.D.):

In the good old days, every man's son, born in wedlock, was brought up not in the chamber of some hireling nurse, but in his mother's lap, and at her knee. And that mother could have no higher praise than that she managed the house and gave herself to her children. Again, some elderly relative would be selected in order that to her, as a person who had been tried and never found wanting, might be entrusted the care of all the youthful scions of the same house; in the presence of such a one no base word could be uttered without grave offence, and no wrong deed done. Religiously and with the utmost delicacy she regulated not only the serious tasks of her youthful charges, but their recreations also and their games. . . .

Nowadays, on the other hand, our children are handed over at their birth to some silly little Greek serving-maid, with a male slave, who may be anyone, to help her,— quite frequently the most worthless member of the whole establishment, incompetent for any serious service. It is from the foolish tittle-tattle of such persons that the children receive their earliest impressions, while their minds are still pliant and unformed; and there is not a soul in the whole house who cares a jot what he says or does in the presence of its lisping little lord. Yes, and the parents themselves make no effort to train their little ones in goodness and self-control; they grow up in an atmosphere of laxity and pertness, in which they come gradually to lose all sense of shame, and all respect both for themselves and for other people. (*Dialogus de Oratoribus* 28, 29)

The same sentiments were expressed by Vipstanus Messalla in 74 A.D.:

For in the early days every child born of a good mother was reared not in the dismal room of a mercenary nurse, but in the lap of its own mother, enfolded in her care. Such a woman took particular pride in being described as looking after her own home and devoting herself to her children.[51]

The cultural inheritance from Greece was so highly favored by the Romans that they often employed Greek nurses so that their children would be bilingual.[52] Quintilian (?33–100 A.D.), however, feared such nurses would teach a corrupted Latin:

It is the nurse that the child first hears, and her words that he will first attempt to imitate. And we are by nature most tenacious of childish impressions, just as the flavor first absorbed by vessels when new persists and the color imparted by dyes to the primitive whiteness of wool is indelible. Further, it is the worst impressions that are most durable. (*Institutio Oratoriae* 1.1.5)

Despite such criticism, the custom prevailed, with wet nurses frequently regarded as surrogate mothers, esteemed and loved by their charges.[53] Parental epitaphs to children often mentioned the wet nurse, or *nutrix*, by name, using the superlative *carissima* to describe her. Some wet nurses had more than one child to care for, *collactanei*, who themselves often would form close bonds of affection. Tomb inscriptions refer to departed companions as *collacticio dulcissimo* or *collactaneae pientissmae*.[54] These children were not always related, but almost always were from the same social class. Sometimes, as when a biological mother died, a child had a second nurse who served as a foster mother (*mammae* or *amita educans*).

Tomb inscriptions testify to the love Roman parents felt for their children. With epitaphs that described children as *dulcissima et amantissima*, the expressions of futility and waste, pride and sorrow felt at losing cherished ones to *mors immatura* are timeless:

What was the point of your enduring the rigors of learning literature and of having read words appropriate to the trumpet of rhetoric if relentless death snatched away your childish years.[55]

The loss of a seven-year-old daughter evoked the sentiment that "had your life been longer, no girl on earth would have been more learned."[56] Statius despaired over an adopted son:

> Shall I not mourn thee, darling boy? with whom,
> Childless I missed not children of my own;
> I, who first caught and pressed thee to my breast,
> And called thee mine.[57]

Quintilian lamented the death of his sons in a panegyric, *Institutio Oratoriae*, in which he remembered "those tiny sparks of brilliance" exhibited by his five-year-old and described the signs his nine-year-old son showed "not of budding, but of complete and well-formed fruit."[58] Both in words and in stone, children were immortalized. The hundreds of childhood sculptures from the Roman era elucidate even more than the writings the affection parents felt for their children.

Roman authors of the pre-Christian period evoked sentiments reflecting sensitive insights on the nature of children. Their writings gave expression to parents' intuitive awareness that patience and love are the vital components in nurturing. They greatly influenced and subtly altered for the better public perceptions about child rearing. Cicero (106–43 B.C.) and Lucretius (?94–55 B.C.) expressed—at times, amusingly—their understanding of the slow and sometimes exasperating stages of growth[59]:

Of all nature's gifts to the human race, what is sweeter to a man than his children. (Cicero, *Post Reditum*)

> We know that all things grow
> Little by little, as indeed they must
> From their essential nature.
>
>   (Lucretius, *De Rerum Natura*)

Kids wet the bed
Soaking not only sheets, but also spreads.
(Lucretius, *De Rerum Natura*)

Every society has its paradoxes, and Roman parents' normal and affectionate regard for children coexisted in a society that traditionally referred to children in callous or at least indifferent terms that contributed to a great deal of suffering and abuse. Protection under the law was a slow, tortuous process, made possible by enlightened writers, as cited, and by three great medical writers of classical Rome: Celsus (c.30 B.C.–45 A.D.), Soranus (?– 129 A.D.), and Galen (c.130–200 A.D.), who produced a pediatric literature that was referred to through the ages. The scope of their expertise suggests the growing and increasingly intense interest in the welfare of children. Although the profession of physician was not highly esteemed, Celsus, Soranus, and Galen were regarded as authorities in their own time and in fact were cited throughout Western cultures for over a millennium and a half. In our own time they continue to command respect for their early contributions to the medical care of children. Celsus was the first to state that "children require to be treated completely differently from adults" (*Et ex toto non sic pueri ut viri curari debent* [*De Medicina* 3.7]), an observation that should be obvious but that still manages to elude a vast number of people who are involved in health-management issues.

When Roman children became ill, mothers turned to both physicians and gods—probably not in that order. Prayers to Jupiter for a child's recovery would be followed by the recovered child's naked dip in the River Tiber on the subsequent feast day of Jupiter. Then, to protect the child from the birds of prey that hovered over the Tiber, the mother prayed to Carna. Medical superstitions and curious treatments were commonplace, despite the influence of the great Roman physicians. Cato the Elder suggested bathing children, to strengthen them, in the warm urine of a cabbage-eater. It was believed that a colicky baby could be calmed by placing goat dung in its diaper.[60] Pliny, in his *Natural History*, admonished nurses to spit on their charges three times at the approach of a stranger. This admonition most likely was an antidote to the evil eye, a malediction and peril considered so common that a special goddess of the cradle, Cunina, additionally was invoked to protect the infant. The spitting anti–*mal-occhio* remedy was promulgated throughout the centuries to protect children. It was practiced by the Greeks, Turks, Slavs, Poles, Persians, and Romanians, all of whom had an unshakable belief in the evil eye and its morbid consequences.[61]

A piece of liver from a slain gladiator was believed to cure epilepsy. Majno relates that children were known to step into the arena after major events and to stroll among the dead combatants, searching out eviscerated corpses to find exposed liver. He notes that children must have been inured to the spectacle and that a floor mosaic in a Roman Carthage villa suggests as much, with a depiction of eight children playing gladiator and spearing cats and rabbits.[62]

Roman children enjoyed toys such as marbles, balls, tiny bronze animals, soldiers, gladiators, and chariots. They played many games utilizing nuts as markers or tokens, and the phrase *nuces relinquere* (to give up the nuts) was used as serious schooltime approached and was interpreted to mean it was time to grow up and put away the things of childhood.

Children who survived both illness and ignorance followed expected patterns of development. The elementary levels of school were attended by girls and boys alike until their twelfth year. Their curriculum, the *ludi litterarii*, was composed of the three "R's"—reading, writing, and arithmetic—practiced on wax tablets. School generally was an outdoors affair, conducted amid the clamor of vendors, pedestrians, and cart traffic. Children first learned the alphabet—the *elementa*—forward and backward by recitation. Once memorized, the letters were shown to the children. When they were able to recognize them, words were introduced, the more difficult ones first, an achievement that made mastery of simple vocabulary easier, or so it was thought. Learning sentences followed, using the moral maxims of Cato's *Dicta Catonis* or Aesop's *Fables* as texts. Alas, frequent caning was the preferred method of discipline. There were several school holidays during the year, including one dedicated to the docents and celebrated on a day sacred to Minerva, our March 19th.

Girls older than twelve were considered nubile, although wealthy fathers could hire tutors to continue their daughters' education. As with the Greeks, a daughter's virginity was critical to family honor:

Your maidenhead is not all your own; partly it belongs to your parents, a third part is given to your father, a third part to your mother, only a third is yours; do not contend with two, who have given their rights to their son-in-law together with the dowry. (Catullus, 63)

A small, select group of girls coming from patrician families could enter the college of Vestals. These girls were chosen by the Pontifex Maximus to guard the sacred fire in the Temple of Vestas, as the Vestal Virgins.[63]

Only boys continued in school after the age of twelve, progressing to the *grammaticus*, where language and literature were learned. A son whose father had senatorial or equestrian status often hired a *paedagogus*, who functioned in loco parentis as a tutor in social skills and in the rudiments of reading and arithmetic. At fourteen or fifteen, boys were given adult garb to wear with great ceremony. The momentous occasion was likely celebrated on Liberalia, our March 17th, rather than on a boy's birthday. The festivities included a sacrifice, a ritualistic removal of the *bulla*, and the discarding of the purple-bordered toga of childhood (*toga praetexta*) in favor of the adult's white toga, the *toga virilis* or the *toga pura*. Boys and their families marched to the Tabularium in the Forum to register as adult citizens. With entry into adulthood, young males were expected to exercise newfound sexual freedom bought from servants or procured at brothels; or they were given libidinous instruction by older, experienced women. Only a select few boys advanced to the prestigious study of rhetoric and philosophy, equivalent to education at our modern universities. Special schools taught skills of rhetoric, which involved learning gestures, postures, phrases, expressions, logic, set arguments, and so on. Boys learned set speeches and became adroit at delivering these on command.

At sixteen or seventeen, well-born young men had to choose a public career and be apprenticed or enter the military. Those who chose the military signed on for twenty-five years, a major career decision. After passing a physical examination (minimum height was 172 cm), young men began rigorous training. In the years of peace—the *Pax Romana*—soldiers mainly served as engineers, building roads, bridges, canals, and aqueducts.

With luck, youths were trained as scribes and spared the physical hardships of life in the wilderness. The position of scribe placed ambitious young men where powerful superiors could advance them in political careers. As the following letter illustrates, this also was the case for those in the navy, for whom education and foreign assignment were important to career advancement. The letter was written about the second century A.D. by an Apion to his father and posted from Roman Egypt:

Dear Father,

First of all, I hope you are well and will always be well, and my sister and her daughter and my brother. I thank the God Serapis that when I was in danger on the sea he quickly came to the rescue. When I arrived in Misenum I received from the government three gold pieces for my traveling expenses. I am fine. Please write me, father, first to tell me that you are well, second that my sister and brother are well, and third so that I can kiss your hand because you gave me a good education and because of it I hope to get quick promotions if the gods are willing.[64]

Teaching, medicine, and law were not often selected as professions by the sons of the well-born. These professions had no prestige and commanded low income. Teachers collected fees from students, physicians were for the most part trained Greek slaves or freedmen, and lawyers were not commonly allowed to charge fees and often had to barter their services.

Delinquency seems always to have dogged societies. Gangs were common-place in Rome, and frankly malevolent groups of well-born adolescents wandered the streets at night, assaulting pedestrians, attacking women, and vandalizing shops. Young men had several mistresses and even male lovers. Excesses of drinking, eating, and sex were common at festivities. Tales of Roman excesses and orgies still have the power to scandalize. Such behavior, however, was expected to cease after marriage. By the second century A.D., Roman mores had become rigidly conservative, probably in reaction to the wanton excesses of its past. Celibacy as well as virginity until marriage became societal expectations and were thought to preserve health and energy. Sex had come to be considered enervating and dissipating; fidelity or morality were not the factors that informed the changes in attitude.

Abandonment

As noted, citizens of early Rome were by law required to raise all healthy male children and at least one female. Only lame or abnormal infants could be exposed once the approval of at least five witnesses was given, and violation of these laws meant state confiscation of one-half of a parent's fortune. Enforcement of these laws, however, was poor, and by the second century B.C. constraints on abandonment had disappeared.[65]

Given supreme power by the Roman senate in 27 B.C., Emperor Octavian Augustus decreed two laws of significance that amplified the code of the Twelve Tables. The *Lex Papia* measured a man's status in the community by his children. Unmarried men with no legitimate children forfeited their inheritance. If married but without children, a man's inheritance was cut by half. The *Lex Julia* favored public-office candidates who had many children and granted tax relief to Roman citizens with three or more children. There was tax relief with four children if the family lived in Italy, and with five children for those in the colonies. Both of these laws contributed substantially to a diminution of *expositi* (abandonment). Later, Emperor Augustus tried to persuade wealthy Romans to raise children:

Is it not a joy to acknowledge a child who possesses the qualities of both parents, to tend and educate a person who is both the physical and the mental mirror of yourself, so that, as he grows up, another self is created? Is it not a blessing, when we leave this life, to leave behind as our successor an heir both to our family and to our property, one that is our own, born of our own essence, so that only the mortal part of us passes away, while we live on in the child who succeeds us?[66]

In the late Republic, however, the *sine manus* marriage evolved, which allowed women to maintain control of their property after the contract, protected them from poverty, and facilitated female-initiated divorce.[67] Divorce became simple for man and wife, merely requiring a public utterance of "*Tuas res tibi habeto*" (keep what is yours for yourself). A woman could eschew the formality of a marriage contract in favor of a *matrimonium concubinatus*, our common-law marriage. It became more unrealistic to aspire to be an *univira* (singular lifetime wife), and fewer girls grew up with expectations that a marriage would last. These conditions reinforced the concept of *patria potestas*, weakened maternal rights, and led to an increased level of infant exposure and abandonment.

An infant could be abandoned without penalty or social stigma for many reasons, including an anomalous appearance, being an illegitimate child or grandchild or a child of infidelity, family poverty, parental conflict (*ob discordiam parentum*), or being one of too many children. Sometimes they were given to friends,[68] but more often than not they were abandoned to the elements, and death resulted from hypoglycemia and hypothermia. Sometimes the infant was devoured by the dogs that scavenged public places. It was likely, however, that the *expositi* were rescued from these fates and picked up by slavers. Abandonment generally occurred in a public place, where it was hoped that the infant could be taken up by some wealthy person. A well-traveled street called the Velabrum, where oil and cheese merchants worked, and the vegetable market in the Forum (Olitorium), with *columna lactaria*, or nursing columns,[69] were two favored locations for placing sucklings. Such an infant was considered a *res vacantes* (an unclaimed thing) and legally could be claimed.[70] If picked up by wealthy persons, the child could become a slave, a play companion for another child, a pet (*delicia*), or a prostitute; it could be sold for begging purposes after mutilation or become a truly adopted child, a treasured *alumnus*. Most adoptions, however, were not of abandoned infants but of a close relative, a *propinquus*, because adoption commonly was used for purposes of succession or inheritance, to keep wealth within a biological family.[71]

The population of slaves grew not only through *res vacantes* or buying the children of the poor but also by reproduction among slaves, since "house-born" slaves belonged to the master of the house. The vast majority of child slaves entered the service of the rescuer or the buyer. The selling of children was allowed according to the codes of the Twelve Tables, and under its sanction, a father could sell and repurchase a son up to three times, but thereafter a child was free (*Si pater filum ter venunduit, filius a patre liber esto*).[72] This custom endured for six centuries. By the third century A.D., the sale of children was forbidden.

Slaves also were war captives or were acquired from foreign slave traders. Children commonly were purchased from Thrace. The Thracians were thought to be insensitive with respect to children. Herodotus believed they sold their offspring with facility and aplomb, and he described their dour fatalism:

When a child is born, the kinsfolk sit round and lament for the tale of ills that it must endure, from its birth onward, recounting all the sorrows of men. But the dead they bury joyfully and gladly, since they reason that he is, after quitting so many ills, in perfect blessedness. (*Histories* 5.3–10)

Commonly, a slave who became a pet child did not work and was kept around the house for play purposes. Some of these children were genuinely loved and educated. Some were assigned a *mammae* or *tatae* to nurture them, but more often than not, they were simply for jester-like entertainment or pedophilic gratification.

Sometimes an abandoned male infant was made a eunuch. Castrated boys were favored for buggery, and castration commonly was done in infancy when the testicles were small and soft. Before Emperor Nerva (96–98 A.D.) passed a law forbidding infant castration, the procedure was practiced as described by Paulus Aegineta (c.670):

. . . children, still of a tender age, are placed in a vessel of hot water, and then when the parts are softened in the bath, the testicles are to be squeezed with the fingers until they disappear. (*The Seven Books* 6.68)

The hot water accomplished three things: it was a form of numbing anesthesia; it relaxed the testicles, allowing them to drop into the scrotum; and it softened the tissues.

The Romans were not alone in their custom of castration and male pedophilia. Other ancient cultures created catamites and engaged in these practices. The Egyptian disclaimer in the *Book of the Dead*—"I have not had sex relations with a boy"—suggests that such practices occurred. Greek men were stimulated during gymnasia by their charges, and Phoenician temple boys were depicted as chubby eunuchoids.

An *expositi*, or abandoned child, if recognized[73] years later and desired, could be reclaimed if the cost of rearing was repaid. Although exposure was common, not all Romans approved of it, and some, like Epictetus (writing in Greek), asserted with quiet passion about the proper care and nurturing of children:

A sheep will not abandon its young, nor a wolf, but a human should abandon his? Would you have us be as simple as sheep? (*Discourses* 1.23.7–9)

Doesn't one have to provide cloaks for his children? Doesn't he have to send them to school with tablets, writing tools, notebooks? Doesn't he have to turn down their beds and if he doesn't do all this, it would have been better to expose them at birth? (*Discourses* 3.22.72–74)

With the death of Augustus in 14 A.D., a succession of notorious and tragic rulers, for whom child welfare had little priority, sustained the atmosphere that tolerated the abuses children suffered.

The writer Juvenal (?60–130 A.D.) may have had substantial influence on moderating Roman society's acceptance of child mistreatment when he wrote: "Let nothing foul to either eye or ear reach those doors within which dwells a boy" (*Satires* 14.44) and "The utmost reverence is due to a child" (*Satires* 14.47).

The emperor Nerva, in his brief reign, began a series of initiatives to alleviate the plight of children. He prohibited castration. In a mostly futile effort to curtail the practice of abandonment, he ordered state subsidies for poor parents in a program called the *Alimenta*. When public-assistance programs were depleted, private and compassionate philanthropy sometimes intervened. A woman from Terracina left the following bequest:

. . . one million sesterces to the town of Terracina in memory of her son Macer, so that, out of the income from this money, child-assistance subsidies might be paid to 100 boys and 100 girls—to each citizen boy 5 denarii each month, and each citizen girl 3 denarii each month, the boys up to sixteen years, the girls up to fourteen years.[74]

Nerva's humanitarianism was adopted, expanded, and propagated by the emperors Trajan (98–117 A.D.) and Hadrian (117–138 A.D.), perhaps influenced by Quintilian's compassionate and loving regard for his children and his insightful recognition of the importance of nurturing and early education:

. . . boys commonly show promise of many accomplishments and when such promise dies away as they grow up this is plainly due not to the failure of the natural gifts but to lack of requisite care. (*Institutio Oratoriae* 1.1.2)

The emperor Trajan used the interest collected on loans to landowners to secure additional funds for the *Alimenta*, now administered by imperial officers for distribution. Paradoxically, during the reign of this emperor, who was committed to a public-welfare program, there is evidence that selective infanticide was not uncommon. An inventory lists public assistance[75] given to 179 legitimate children (145 boys and 34 girls) and 2 *spurii*, or bastards. The disproportionate figures cited for boys, on the one hand, and girls and illegitimate children on the other suggest that the unwanted were discarded.

Despite this bleak conclusion, Trajan's humane reforms prevailed, and they were amplified greatly by his successor, the emperor Hadrian. Hadrian appointed a *praefectus alimentorum*, a superintendent of child welfare, to end shameful embezzlement of funds from the *Alimenta*. Moreover, he presided over a new era of civil and social reform aimed at protecting children and the needy. Although it proved difficult to enforce the law, the so-called right for fathers to expose their children was for the first time unconditionally revoked, and the sale of children was deemed *res illicita et inhonesta*.[76] Hadrian made it a crime to sell slaves for immoral purposes and enforced the law prohibiting castration, extending its application to slave children, who were the most vulnerable. He funded secondary schools and their teachers and established and endowed professional schools of rhetoric, philosophy, and medicines.[77]

Emperor Antoninus Pius (138–161 A.D.) succeeded Hadrian, advancing the principle of state responsibility to protect children. In the name of his wife, Faustina, he started a foundation to protect girls—the *Puellae Alimentariae Faustinianae*, which in time assisted all children in need.[78]

ROMAN EGYPT

Roman culture under Trajan influenced disparate societies as the empire expanded, from Scotland and the entire Mediterranean basin to the Euphrates valley. The richest record of the cultural consequences of Roman occupation[79] comes from Egypt, where climate and environment favored the survival of documents written on papyrus. From these the impact of Rome on children's lives in the colonies can be traced, highlighting the shift from a child-centered Egyptian society to an environment in which children were less favored.

In Egypt, the narrow band of fertile land where life can be sustained forced crowding in cities. Extended families, uncommon in Rome, were the norm. It was not unusual to have three generations living in a small house. One census enumerated seventeen adults and seven children living in one small abode: a husband, fifty years old, and a wife-sister, fifty-four years; four sons, twenty-nine to nine years; one daughter, seven; the wife and two boys of the eldest son; the wife and two boys of the second son; three nephews and one wife; the maternal grandfather and his wife and his three brothers and their wives.[80]

To the Romans, ethnicity existed in two groups: Romans and others.[81] The diverse ethnic roots of settlers in Egypt—Ptolemaic, Greek, Macedonian, Hebrew, Minoan, and others—lost their cultural identities under the Romans who recognized them only as "Egyptians." The Romans viewed themselves as ethnically elite citizens of a superior society. Their laws, especially those of inheritance, reflect their interest in maintaining this bias.

Like the Greeks, Romans instituted mandatory registration of newborns. Children born to interethnic parents assumed the cognomens of both mother and father, facilitating ethnic identity that determined laws of legacy. Children born of Greek mothers and Egyptian fathers were legal heirs to both estates. Children of Roman-Greek or Roman-Egyptian parents were denied Roman citizenship. The inheritance laws that protected the estates of the Romans, therefore, did not apply to them.

The Greeks in Egypt, according to extant papyri, similarly strove to maintain a pure line of Hellenic lineage by manipulating laws to discourage their children from marrying non-Greeks. In townships like Oxyrhynchus and Hermopolis, formal registration, with genealogical information, was decreed for children by the age of fourteen. Incestuous unions of brother and sister became a socially acceptable, albeit uncommon, phenomenon. A papyrus bearing an illustrative invitation to a wedding read as follows: "Herais invites you to the marriage of her children, at home, tomorrow, the 5th, starting at the ninth hour."[82]

The following letter from a husband/brother exemplifies genuinely affectionate marital relationships in such unions.[83] It exhibits a nonchalant attitude about abandonment, particularly of girls, and reveals the prevailing mores of the time. It was written by a man named Hilarion on 17 June, 1 B.C., while he was on a business trip to Alexandria. A modern reader can identify with the paternal as well as spousal feelings of a lonely businessman far from home reassuring his wife on fiscal matters and husbandly devotion. (*Plus ça change, plus ça reste la même chose.*)

Know that I am still in Alexandria. And do not worry if they all come back and I remain in Alexandria. I ask and beg you to take good care of our baby son, and as soon as I receive payment I will send it up to you. If you are delivered of child, if it is a boy keep it, if a girl discard it. You have sent me word, "Don't forget me." How can I forget you? I beg you not to worry. (Oxyrhynchus papyrus)[84]

Some scholars argue that these marriages were not between biological brothers and sisters but rather that the use of "brother" as husband and "sister" as wife were terms of endearment.[85] It may be argued, however, that Greek couples contemplating marriage sacrificed to Zeus and Hera—the dieties of marriage—who were brother and sister, and therefore, biological brother–sister marriages were not necessarily considered wrong or culturally repulsive. Additionally, brother–sister marriages also occurred in other cultures and in other periods, particularly among Orientals, Persians, and Egyptian Ptolemies. However, in Egypt the governance began to frown on endogamous marriages, and the matches became anathema to the Romans. They were banned in 295 A.D. throughout the entire empire.

Children went to school at a later age than in Rome. Since there was a large Greek population, Greek studies were emphasized over Roman ones. Boys in Egypt entered school when they were ten years old. Advanced studies took place at boarding schools in Alexandria or, for children of wealthy parents, in the empire's capital, Rome. Children from the middle classes between the ages of ten and thirteen were apprenticed to the numerous trades, to skilled artisans, or to service businesses such as scribes. The arrangement was bound by formal contracts, and the children were called *discentes*. They could learn weaving, pottery, stonemasonry, cobbling, coppersmithing, shearing, baking, nail-making, brickmaking, carpentry, and papyrus-making.[86] Slaves sometimes were apprenticed, as the following two contracts illustrate:

. . . Platonis also known as Ophelia has apprenticed her female slave Thermouthion, a minor, to Lucius for four years from the first of next month of the current year to learn the weaver's trade, on the following terms: she will feed and clothe the girl, and will place her at the teacher's disposal every day from sunrise to sunset to perform all the orders given her by him relating to the aforesaid trade, wages for the first year being 8 drachmas a month, for the second year 12 drachmas a month, for the third year 16 drachmas a month, and for the fourth year 20 drachmas a month; the girl will take 18 days a year off for holidays, and for any days that she does not work or is sick she will remain with the teacher an equal number at the end of the period; the taxes on trades and apprenticeships are to be paid by the teacher.[87]

Panchotes also known as Panares, ex-kosmetes of Oxyrhynchus, represented by his friend Gemellus, to Apollonios, shorthand writer, greetings. I have placed with you my slave Chairammon, to learn the signs which your son Dionysios knows, for a period of two years, not counting holidays, from the present month Phamenoth of the 18th year of Antonius Caesar our Lord, at a fee agreed upon between us of 120 drachmas; of which sum you have received a first installment of 40 drachmas, and you will receive the second, another 40 drachmas, when the boy has memorized the whole syllabary, and you will receive the third, the remaining 40 drachmas, at the end of the period, when he can without error take down and read back prose of every kind.[88]

More often than not, slaves and lower-class children became common laborers in all of the colonies that provided Rome with raw materials. A tombstone in a Spanish colony depicts a mere four-year-old miner clutching the tools of his trade, a hammer and an ore basket* (figure 3.8).

---

*The child as miner has existed throughout human history. In the Bronze Age (3000–1100 B.C.), children were used to work the narrow shafts, just like the sad child miners of the nineteenth century (see chapter 8). Revelations continue and recent excavations in Kestel, Turkey have uncovered skeletons of children entombed in a tin mine shaft. *Washington Post*, 4 Janu-

Figure 3.8 Roman colony child miner. MUSEO ARQUEOLOGICO NACIONAL, MADRID.

Taxes annually were collected from the age of fourteen, regardless of status. The privileged were exempt from this poll tax, called the *laographia* or "populace registration." Apprentices, boys and girls, additionally paid a monthly handicraftsman's tax. In the above contract of Platonis, a clause shrewdly arranged for the teacher to pay the taxes.

For poor urban girls unable to enter apprenticeships, the two major professions left to them were wet nursing and prostitution. The high infant mortality supplied the populace with lactating mothers bereft of their own babies and in need of employment. A postpartum girl as young as thirteen could enter the wet-nurse market. A more mature nurser, however, was favored and more commonly engaged, bound by a contract that guaranteed employment for six to thirty-six months. The details of the contract in effect relieved biological mothers of all responsibility for their babies. Infants were taken to the wet nurses' homes to be fed, clothed, and nurtured there.

Prostitution, most often involuntary, was thrust on girls, inasmuch as they were *expositi* raised for the trade or were sold into it by impoverished parents. One record pertaining to an Alexandrian named Diodemos, on trial for the murder of a prostitute, is illustrative:

ary 1994. Further evidence of child laborers during this period is found in more paleopathology uncovered in first-century Herculaneum. The skeletons of three children, ages five, eight, and nine years, reveal syndesmopathic lesions of the clavicles. (Syndesmoses are osteopathic changes induced by forceful repeated stress, such as tilling or rowing.) *Lancet*, 1998; 352:1634.

The mother of the prostitute, one Theodora, a poor old woman, asked that Diodemos be compelled to provide her with means of support as some small consolation in her life. She said, "It was for this that I gave my daughter to a brothel-keep-
er, in order that I might have some means of support. Now since, with my daughter
dead, I have been deprived of my source of sustenance, I accordingly ask that some
modicum be given to me, a poor woman, for my support."[89]

Girls registered as prostitutes (*meretrix*) were not allowed to marry. Contraceptives were used, but in the event a pregnancy occurred, abortifacients
and abortionists were, for a fee, available. Bastard children (*spurii*) born to
prostitutes were either exposed or sold.

Despite high infant mortality, the frequency of abandonment, and the
general regard of children as property, there were families who felt and
expressed love for their children. Commiseration at their loss was a natural
corollary for many. The following letter of condolence to grieving parents
incidentally reveals that affection for slaves was not uncommon:

Mnesthianus to Apollonianus and Spartiate, be brave! The gods are witness and
when I learnt about my lord your son I was grieved and I lamented as I would my
own child. He was a person to be cherished. . . . Well, bear it nobly, for this rests
with the gods. . . . I too have had a loss, a houseborn slave worth two talents.[90]

❏   ❏   ❏

The golden years of the classical period lasted seven hundred years, from
about the fifth century B.C. to the second century A.D. It was a time that witnessed the expansion of the *trivarium curriculum*, the education of girls, the
evolution of a formal body of pediatric literature, and welfare laws for children. Above all, the gradual disintegration of the concepts of *patria potestas*
and *res vacantes* enriched the future prospects of children.

NOTES

1. Plutarch. *The Lycurgus*. From the Langhorne 1819 translation, Mentor Edition, 1950, p. 26. Some authorities hold that all of "Lycurgan" Sparta, as revealed
by Plutarch, was idealized and that the strict codes of society may not have existed
at all. Lacey, 1984, p. 194. Yet Plutarch's writing is concise and compelling.

2. Ibid., pp. 32–33.

3. Ibid., p. 23.

4. Ibid., p. 22.

5. Ibid., pp. 23–24.

6. Garland, 1990, p. 93. Hydrops fetalis—or the birth of a baby swollen with severe congestive heart failure—has multiple causes, but most common is the breakdown or hemolysis of red blood cells in utero.

7. Payne, 1916, p. 207.

8. Ibid., p. 205.

9. Plutarch, *The Lycurgus*, pp. 23–26.

10. Blumner, 1932, pp. 178–80.

11. Golden, 1990, pp. 1–22.

12. Lacey, 1984, p. 122.

13. Blumner, 1932, pp. 171–74.

14. Anderson and Zinsser, 1988, 1:34.

15. Plutarch, *The Lycurgus*, p. 23.

16. Garland, 1990, p. 68.

17. Anderson and Zinsser, 1988, 1:35. There was a male equivalent to this prayer, a dedication recited by a young man who had just completed his ephebic training:

> To you, Hermes, did Kalliteles hang up his felt hat made of well-carded sheep's wool, his two-pinned brooch, his strigil, his unstrung bow, his threadbare travelling cloak soaked in sweat, his javelins and his ever-spinning ball. Receive, I beseech you, friend of youth, this gift of a well-ordered adolescence. (Garland, 1990, p. 187)

18. The snake was at times considered the fertilizer. It is said that Philip came home one night and found Olympias, the mother of Alexander, in bed with a snake. In some parts of the world, such as the Andean plateau and West Africa, the snake is still held to be responsible for pregnancies.

19. Hippocrates, *The Fleshes*, 613.

20. Reiss and Ash, 1988, pp. 270–73.

21. Garland, 1990, pp. 66–67.

22. Pliny, *Natural History*, 28.9.42.

23. Garland, 1990, p. 61.

24. Ibid., p. 92.

25. Golden (1990) maintains that this task was performed by the father in a naked state, but the reason behind the nudity is unknown. Socrates refers to the ritual in *Theaetetus* (see p. 104).

26. Garland, 1990, p. 117.

27. Ibid., p. 111.

28. Stuart, 1926, p. 61.

29. Garland, 1990, pp. 9–10.

30. Lacey, 1984, pp. 157–58.

31. Blumner, 1932, pp. 117–18.

32. Garland, 1990, p. 188.

33. Anderson and Zinsser, 1988, 1:54–55.

34. Loth, 1987, p. 61.

35. Ibid., pp. 62–63.

36. Carrington, 1971, pp. 138–40.

37. Stuart, 1926, pp. 74–77.

38. Baldson, 1962, pp. 260–62.

39. Montanari, 1990, p. 7.

40. Heichelheim, 1962, p. 58.

41. Montanari, 1990, p. 37. Tributes such as this were not uncommon. A well-known first-century-B.C. eulogy, the *Laudatio Turiae*, similarly honors a wife but is too long to cite here. Amt, 1993, pp. 29–31.

42. Veyne, 1987, pp. 12–14.

43. Boswell, 1988, p. 59.

44. Wiedemann, 1989, p. 15.

45. Soranus, *Gynaecology*, 1:10–13.

46. Rawson, 1991, pp. 11–12.

47. E. L. Lipton et al., Swaddling, a child care practice. *Pediatrics* 1965; 35: 519–67.

48. Distasi, 1981, p. 47.

49. Rawson, 1991, p. 11.

50. Veyne, 1987, p. 16.

51. Dixon, 1988, p. 109.

52. Fildes, 1986, p. 29.

53. Ibid., pp. 30–32.

54. Bradley, 1991, pp. 149–54.

55. Wiedemann, 1989, pp. 52–59.

56. Ibid.

57. Scudder, 1895, pp. 33–34.

58. Wiedemann, 1989, pp. 52–59.

59. Colón, 1987, pp. 26–61.

60. C. W. Rucker, Folk medicine in the Roman Empire. *Mayo Alumnus* 1974; 10(1):26–30.

61. Dundes, 1992, pp. 12–38.

62. Majno, 1975, pp. 401–2.

63. Montanari, 1990, p. 21.

64. Casson, 1975, p. 71.

65. Payne, 1916, pp. 211–13.

66. Wiedemann, 1989, p. 25.

67. Gies and Gies, 1987, p. 21.

68. *Patria potestas* permitted the father to order abandonment, but a mother could fake the process and entrust the baby to a secret friend.

69. So called because wet nurses gathered there to sell their services. Payne, 1916, p. 242.

70. Boswell, 1988, p. 63.

71. Rawson, 1991, pp. 63–67.

72. Ulpian, cited in Boswell, 1988, p. 65.

73. Anecdotal evidence suggests that some of these infants were given lockets and charms that remained on them even in abandonment. Many of the charms were unique and thus easily recognizable.

74. Casson, 1975, p. 20.

75. Payne, 1916, p. 229.

76. Ibid., p. 247.

77. Heichelheim, 1962, pp. 354–55.

78. Payne, 1916, pp. 247–49.

79. It was under Roman colonization in Judea that one of history's great mass murders of children was recorded. Herod the Great ruled in Judea under Roman appointment from 37 to 4 B.C. Because of a prophecy regarding the birth of a king in Bethlehem, he had all male infants of Bethlehem under one year of age killed. Christians still refer to the deed as the massacre of the Holy Innocents. During the late medieval period and the Renaissance, the Holy Innocents became a major topos of church teaching and of hagiography representation. (See chapter 6.)

80. Lewis, 1983, p. 53.

81. Ibid., p. 19.

82. Ibid., p. 43.

83. The letter begins, "Hilarion to his sister Alis very many greetings." The salutation is not necessarily proof of a biological relationship.

84. Lewis, 1983, p. 54.

85. Boswell, 1995, pp. 41–47.

86. Bradley, 1991, pp. 107–15.

87. Lewis, 1983, p. 135.

88. Ibid., p. 136.

89. Ibid., p. 146.

90. Ibid., p. 81.

Chapter 4

Late Antiquity and Patristic Periods: The Oblate

❏   ❏   ❏

THE ENTIRE MEDITERRANEAN BASIN experienced profound cultural, social, and moral upheavals in the tumultuous centuries following the reign of Hadrian. The erosion of Roman culture and power was as slow and protracted as a fading light that lingers on. The mutation of Roman society into an amalgam of pagan and Christian, Eastern and Western cultures, was achieved over five hundred years. The Empire's ebbing glow finally was extinguished with the death of its last emperor, Justinian (527–565 A.D.).

The *Pax Romana* collapsed in the reign of Marcus Aurelius (161–180 A.D.), as the empire's frontiers intermittently were violated by Goths and other barbaric tribes and epidemics rampaged across the continent. Smallpox and measles from the East decimated populations between 165 and 180 A.D., and again from 251 to 266 A.D. There were periods of crop failure and famine as well as of disease that exacerbated suffering and poverty in the provinces, while in Rome, rich from the crippling and ever-increasing taxes collected from the outlying regions, depraved behavior increased. Unrest was followed by anarchy. In 193 A.D. Emperor Commodus was assassinated, inaugurating a convulsive social instability lasting seventy-five years and featuring twenty-seven emperors, twenty-three of whom died violently. Con-

Figure 4.1
The four tetrarchs as seen near the
entrance to St. Marks in Venice.

verts to the new religion of Christianity became scapegoats, with intolerance giving way to persecution on an ever-increasing scale. The spasmodic disarray temporarily ended under the auspices of Diocletian (284–305), who divided the empire into East and West, and appointed each a supreme leader, a *caesar* and an *augustus*. This tetrarch (figure 4.1) of rulers effected a short-lived stability. In 305 A.D. Diocletian and his co-augustus counterpart Maximian resigned their offices, and Roman society reverted to its former chaotic state.

In 312 A.D. Constantine ended a civil war with a decisive victory and assumed power. A pre-battle omen had persuaded Constantine to brandish a Christian symbol as a call to arms. Convinced of the Christian God's intervention, he inspired his army to victory, sending the enemy into the rain-swollen Tiber River in retreat. Christian suffrage was Constantine's reward to his people. When the Eastern emperor Licinius died in 324 A.D., Constantine reunited East and West and established his Holy Roman Empire's capital in Byzantium (later, Constantinople).

Upon his death in 337 A.D., Constantine's sons split the empire once more. It was briefly reunited under Julian (360–363), but by then the empire's political power was diminished forever. The West succumbed further to barbarian incursions and sway, while in the East, Christian philosophy and worship were in ascendancy; their influence was rivaled and ultimately overcome by Islam.

Rejected by cultures of the Levant, Christianity had gained a foothold in Rome and in other eastern countries, finally evolving into distinct factions:

Latinate Roman Catholicism in the West and Coptic Catholicism in the East. Its precepts attracted converts to the faith exponentially, so that by the fourth century the new religion had squeezed out and suffocated many pagan rites and beliefs.

Although laws that applied to children still were based on the Twelve Tables, the introduction of Christianity in the West collided with prevailing concepts of children as property. Christian attitudes about and treatment of children immeasurably changed society's entire attitude about the young, and in accepting the concept of a guardian angel watching over children, changed it to a revolutionary degree. In Matthew's Gospel, chapter 18, the synoptic author described how Christ turned to a child to illustrate to his disciples a fundamental point. He says to them that unless they become as this child, they may not enter the kingdom of heaven. Furthermore, he says:

And whosoever shall receive one such little child in my name receiveth me. . . . Take heed that ye despise not one of these little ones; for I say unto you, That in heaven their angels do always behold the face of my Father which is in heaven. (Matt. 18:5, 10)

Christians therefore were exhorted to love children and, to sustain God's love, to emulate the qualities of children that were favored so highly by Christ. The fourth-century Pope Leo wrote on the subject: "Christ loves childhood, for it is the teacher of humility, the rule of innocence, the model of sweetness."[1]

EXPOSURE

Children were perceived by Christians as gifts of God and innocents protected by angels. In time they were represented in art as angels and cherubs who adorned heaven and who attended the muses and the saints. Memorials to children, bearing Christian symbols, were carved with increasing frequency. Christian scholars, theologians, philosophers, and priests, in their writings and in regulations they devised, reinforced the divine interest in children and passionately repudiated infanticide and abandonment. One of the early church fathers, Justin (?100–?165 A.D.), disturbed by the persistence of infanticide and abandonment, lamented the abuses to which children were subject. Death by exposure was an act of murder, and procreation a primary marital duty in his view:

We fear to expose children, lest some of them be not picked up, but die, and we become murderers. But whether we marry, it is only that we may bring up children; or whether we decline marriage, we live continently. (Justin Martyr, *Apology* 1.29)

Athenagoras, a second-century Christian apologist, expressed these opinions as well:

. . . we who condemn as murder the use of drugs for abortion, and declare that those who even expose a child are chargeable with murder. (*Plea* xxxv)

. . . man cannot forbid the exposure of children, equating such exposure with child murder, and then slay a child that has found one to bring it up. (*Embassy* xxxv)

Other writers joined in. Clement of Alexandria (?150–?220), in *Paedagogus*, reiterated Justin's position on exposure and marriage: "What cause has a man for the exposing of a child? If disinclined to have children, he ought not to have married in the first place."[2]

In his *Institutes*, Lactantius (260–340), tutor to Constantine's eldest son, Crispus, offered conjugal abstinence as an alternative to abandonment: "If someone really cannot support children because of poverty, better he should abstain from relations with his wife than undo the work of God with guilty hands."[3]

The renowned theologian Augustine (354–430) reinforced the Christian viewpoint that children were divinely created:

In view of the encompassing network of the universe and the whole creation—a network that is perfectly ordered in time and place, where not one leaf of a tree is superfluous—it is not possible to create a superfluous man. (*On Free Choice of the Will* 3.23)

By implication, deliberate harm to a child was a violation of God's will. In addition to death and prostitution, abandoned children were vulnerable to incest, the universal taboo, and a particular fear of church authorities:

We have been taught that it is wrong to expose even the newborn . . . because we have observed that nearly all such children, boys as well as girls, will be used as prostitutes. (Justin Martyr, *Apology* 1.27)

How many fathers, forgetting the children they abandoned, unknowingly have sexual relations with a son who is a prostitute or a daughter become a harlot? (Clement of Alexandria, *Paedagogus*)[4]

The gods you worship have incestuous relations with a mother, a daughter, or a sister. No wonder then that among you cases of the same offence are often exposed, and constantly practised. Without knowing it you may incur the risk of illicit connexions; with promiscuous amours, with children begotten here or there; with frequent exposure of legitimate children to the mercy of strangers, you inevitably return upon your own tracks and go wrong with children of your own. Unwittingly you involve yourselves in a tragedy of guilt. (Minucius Felix, *Octavius* 31.4)

When the family is discarded, sometimes memory must be lost; and when once mistake strikes in, then a strain of incest will continue as stock and sin creep on together. Then, in the next instance, whatever the spot, at home, abroad, across the sea, lust goes with you, whose sallies may in every place beget you children without your knowing it; a very little of the seed will do it; so that a stock scattered through the range of human travel may fall in with its own source, and, all unaware, fail to recognize an incestuous union. (Tertullian, *Apology* 9.18)

Although the debate had ethical merit, reality was determined by the desperation and misery of the poor, who often saw no alternative to exposure of their young. Contemplating children's fates, Augustine was moved to comment: "Who would not shiver with dread and choose to die, if he were offered the choice of death or a second infancy? The fact that the babe begins his life not with laughter but with wailing is a kind of unconscious prophecy what a path of evils it has entered upon."[5] St. Basil of Caesarea (?330–?379) was eloquent on the subject:

How can I bring before your eyes the suffering of the poor man? He considers his finances: he has no gold and never will. He has some clothes and the sort of possessions the poor have, all worth only a few coins. What can he do? He turns his glance at length on his children: by selling them he might put off death. Imagine the struggle between the desperation of hunger and the bonds of parenthood. (*Destruam* bk. 4)[6]

Constantine, in 315 A.D., was the first of the Christian emperors to condemn and forbid exposure, offering at the same time an alternative to the poor:

Let a law be at once promulgated in all the towns of Italy, to turn parents from using a patricidal hand on their new-born children, and to dispose their hearts to the best sentiments. Watch with care over this, that, if a father brings his child, saying that he cannot support it, someone should supply him without delay with food and clothing; for the cares of the new-born suffer no delay, and we order that our revenue, as well as our treasure, aid in this expense. (*Codex Theodosianus*)[7]

The practice, however, persisted as poverty endured. Children were forsaken and also used as pawns in transactions to relieve debt, prompting Ambrose, bishop of Milan (374–397) to write contemptuously:

Such is the inhumanity of the creditor, such the stupidity of the debtor, that from children to whom he can leave no money he takes even their freedom, in place of a will he pays a debt, for their inheritance he leaves a contract of servitude. (*De Tobia*)[8]

Successive reigns of responsible emperors—Valentinian I (364–375), Valens (364–378), and Gratian (375–383)—legislated increasingly punitive measures for acts of exposure or sale of children. Valentinian II (378–392), Theodosius I (379–395), and Arcadius (394–408) each issued laws that allowed enslaved children to become freemen despite unpaid debts. Honorius (395–423) and Theodosius II (408–450) limited childhood slavery to five years. Valentinian III (423–455), recognizing poverty as the root cause of the problem, issued an injunction that nullified the sale of children, with reimbursement to the purchaser (*nutritor*) 20 percent beyond the purchase price.[9] One important legal edict prevented exposed newborns from being snatched from the place of their abandonment without a witness's signature on the local bishop's registration form. These regulations, along with Constantine's dictum, were codified to form the *Codex Theodosianus*.[10]

Christianity and its church were the driving forces propelling sweeping reforms. The late John Boswell described best the phenomenon:

In the chaos following Rome's demise, only her own foster child, Christianity, wielded enough power and influence in Europe to offset the increasingly haphazard and uncontrolled character of abandonment. It was she who composed and disseminated new rules for exposing, selling, and rearing children, she who undertook to facilitate the finding of new homes for *expositi* through churches and parish organization, and she who created—for the first and only time in European history—a system of caring for them [oblation] in which they were at no social, legal, or moral disadvantage because of their abandonment.[11]

Patristic councils of bishops and church leaders convened periodically to analyze pressing theological, liturgical, moral and social dilemmas. Their observations and conclusions often addressed issues related to abandonment. Asylums, called *Xenodocheion* (hotels), were ordered built by the Nicaea Council of 325 in all Christian villages, to care for the poor, sick, and abandoned. Asylums that provided for illegitimate children came to be called *Brephotrophia* (baby shelters).

The Council of 341 in Ancyra (modern Angora) barred women from the church for life as punishment for exposing their babies. (In 546 the banishment was limited to seven years.[12]) The Council of 442 in Vaison granted remorseful parents a ten-day grace period to reclaim their abandoned child but thereafter moved to prevent them from reclaiming the child:

Whoever takes up an abandoned child shall bring him to the Church where that fact will be certified. The following Sunday the priest will announce that a new-born child has been found and ten days will be allowed to the real parents to claim their infant. When these formalities have been complied with, if any one of them claims a child or in any way calumniates those who have received it, he will be punished according to the Church laws against homicide.[13]

A form letter in support of this decree is thought to reflect the casual and daily involvement of the church in dealing with the practice of abandonment. Further, the council members were largely composed of converted Roman aristocrats and undoubtedly were influenced by their cultural affinity with the old Roman laws and customs of rearing *alumni*:

In the name of God. Whereas, I, brother _____, one of the dependents of the parish of St. _____, whom Almighty God sustains there through the offerings of Christians, found there a newborn infant, not yet named, and was unable to find relatives of his among any of the populace, it was agreed to and permitted by the priest _____, that I could sell the child to _____ which I have done. And I received for him, as is our custom, a third plus food. And I wish to make clear that if the owner or parent of the child should try to take action counter to this document, in the first place Christ the Son of the living God . . . should strike him with an eternal penalty, terrible and terrifying, and that he should not be able to reclaim what he seeks, and that his deed should remain in force for all time.[14]

The legal reforms of Justinian (527–565) in the *Codex Justinianus* fused patristic and civil interests. The code remained the authoritative legal source throughout the Middle Ages, with church and state unified to protect children and their liberty. Abandoned or orphaned children could no longer be enslaved or sold, except in extreme cases of poverty, a provision that also allowed reclamation. At the Council of 592 in Constantinople—over four hundred years after Justin called it murder—abandonment officially was decreed an act of homicide punishable by death.[15]

Therefore, from the reigns of Trajan to Justinian, it took half a millennium to gradually soften attitudes toward children until they became gentler and more humane. The powers of *patria potestas* dissolved, and parental attention and devotion became an expectation that was equated with the attention and respect given to God. Marriage became a sacrament, a holy state in which children had a rightful place.

BYZANTIUM

When Diocletian established Byzantium in 285 as the eastern center of the Roman Empire, this conduit between Europe and Asia became a Greco-Roman bastion that flourished until 1453 A.D., when it was conquered by the Ottoman Turks of Constantinople. While the Western empire was preoccupied with "barbarian hordes" and shifts in territories and national boundaries, Byzantium was shaping its culture and power around Christianity, surviving frequent political and doctrinal conflicts that arose between East and West. Although Byzantium resisted the influence of various incursions by Arabs, Slavs, and Turks for over a thousand years, it experienced a diverse and complex cultural evolution. The many cycles of societal changes over so vast a period of time included, to be sure, changes in the nurturing and treatment of children. Byzantium's apogee, around 900 to 1100 A.D., however, produced a wealth of cultural data that is extant. Having survived the archetypal "end of the world" predicted for 1000 A.D.,* Byzantine life from this period in and around Constantinople can be examined with special clarity, particularly as it pertains to children.

At birth, the centuries-old custom of washing, salting, and swaddling was an infant's introduction to the world. Maternal milk or that of a wet nurse progressed to weaning on barley gruel with honey. Toddlers were fed white wine and vegetables and until adolescence very little meat. Toy paraphernalia included clay carts, horses, balls, whistles, flutes, house models, tops, hoops, and dolls.

For propriety and to preserve virtue, girls were relegated to quarters separate from the general household to live a life of "domestic monasticism." In wealthy homes a *gynaikonitis*, or women's apartment, was provided. On festive occasions other than a *symposia*, where debauchery was likely, daughters were permitted to sit at the dinner table. Marriages frequently were contracted for young children, particularly for daughters. Marriage ceremonies were delayed until girls were twelve years old and boys were fourteen.

Not all children in a household were biologically related. Many were slaves (*agouroi*, or houseboys) whose functions varied from servile to companionship. Although the church was opposed to slavery, it was commonplace. There were fixed prices in the trade. Children under ten fetched ten *nomismata* (one was equivalent to 4.48 grams of gold); adults, twenty; and physicians, up to sixty.[16]

Every aspect of living was influenced by church strictures. Abstinence from coition and restrictions in diet were mandated by events in the liturgical calendar, such as Lent and Advent. The Council of 692 decreed that spiritual relationships, such as between godparents and godchildren, were as much compelling impediments to marriage as were biological relationships.

---

*Although superstitions ran high in the medieval world, most historians contend that few people had the knowledge or instruments to know with any accuracy when the thousandth year would dawn. Yet there is no doubt that documentation and historical records more than trebled after 1000 A.D., suggesting that historical ennui attributed to the despair of the end of the millennium was real.

Society accepted eunuchs since the church commonly incorporated them in services at church functions. Considered a "third, or neutral sex," eunuchs even had their own monasteries. Families often favored eunuchs since they prevented large estates from being heavily diluted by the laws of inheritance.* (See chapter 3, page 92 for Paulus Aegineta and his method of infant castration.) The monasteries were looked on as symbolic households, consisting of *pater pneumatikos*, spiritual fathers who guided the brothers (*adelphoi*) and children, the *tenka* or oblates. Similar situations existed for women in convents. Sometimes widows and widowers who wished to take religious vows established monasteries or convents in their private homes.

Each parish or bishopric had a religious school or monastery classroom for day pupils and oblated children who were permanent boarders. In libraries and scriptoria, young children patiently began the lengthy process of learning calligraphy.

General schooling began in the women's quarters of the home, with the practice of clear, fluent speech and of the "good hand," or writing. Formal education started between the ages of five and six, with a pedagogical bias for rote memory. By the age of fourteen, children were expected to recite from memory the *Iliad* and Aesop's *Fables*, along with large portions of the Bible.

By the time of Alexius Comnenus in the eleventh century, free schools had been established for all children. The curriculum included gymnastics, grammar, and literature, with fifty lines of Homer to be memorized daily. Three forms of Greek were taught: a vernacular Romaine, a classical Greek for lofty conversations, and the elegant Attic Greek for writing. At fourteen, rhetoric, mathematics, science, and music were added to the syllabus.

As Christian attitudes were adopted, children more commonly were treated kindly and with consideration for psyche and soul. Attention to their medical needs became more commonplace, with physicians who specialized in their treatment. Most special was Oribasius (325–403), who in particular gave import to the child's mental well-being as well as physical. Oribasius wrote a seventy-volume treatise on medicine, named *Synopsis*. The table of contents of volume 5 suggest the close and detailed attention he gave to childhood ailments:

---

*Castration gradually fell into disuse during the medieval period but reappeared in Spain and Italy in the sixteenth century. Two factors prevailed: Pope Sixtus V in 1589 prohibited women on stage, and there was a need for postpubertal male sopranos for a genre of secular music that was popular. Since only the papal states enforced the proscription of female actors, the center of the states, Italy, gradually became the capital of castrati for both stage and chorus until, in 1903, Pius X banned them from the papal chapel. A. M. Smith, Eunuchs and castration. *JAMA* 1991; 266:655–66.

On the feeding of an infant
The qualities of a wet nurse
On milk
The correction of milk
On rashes which occur in an infant
On cough in an infant, and coryza
On itching
On teething
On aphthae
On excoriation of the thighs
On running of the ears
On seiriasis [meningitis?]
Regimen from infancy to maturity.[17]

But the most endearing aspect of Oribasius was his keen observations on the healthy rearing and nurturing of children, as appeared in chapter 14, volume 5 of *Synopsis*:

Infants who have just been weaned should be permitted to live at their ease and enjoy themselves: they should be habituated to repose of the mind and exercise in which little deceptions and gaiety play a part. . . . After the sixth or seventh year, little girls and boys should be confided to humane and gentle teachers: for those who attract children to themselves, who employ persuasion and exportation as a means of instruction and who praise their pupils often, will succeed better with them and will do more to incite their zeal to studies. . . . [Those who] are insistent in instruction, who resort to sharp reprimands, will make the children servile and timorous and will inspire them with an aversion for the objects of their instruction. . . . It is not necessary either to torment children just beginning to learn by trying to teach them something through the whole length of the day: on the contrary the greater part of the day should be devoted to their games. . . . Children of twelve years should already frequent the grammarians and geometers and exercise their bodies; but it is necessary that they should have preceptors and supervisors who are reasonable and not entirely devoid of experience, so that they may know the amount and proper time for meals, exercise, bathing, sleeping and other details of personal hygiene.[18]

BARBARIANS

Ostrogoths, Visigoths, Gephids, Longobards, Vandals, Burgundians, Franks, Sueves, Jutes, Angles, Alans, and Saxons at one time or another rampaged the Roman Empire, terrorizing the populace and, because of the destruction they wrought, catalyzing famine. To Romans, they were barbarians, as were all non-Romans or non-Greeks. To Christians, all were subjects for conversions:

To the Romans and their adopted allies it was a world of terror—to the Christians it was a friendly world, for the barbarians were known to the Church long before they were known to the soldiers who tried to repulse them.[19]

Thomas the apostle had been sent to Parthia, Andrew to Scythia, John to Asia, Peter to Cappadocia, Paul to Illyricum, and Matthew to Ethiopia. Among later patristic missionaries were Ulfilas, who in 325 A.D. had translated the Bible in Goth, John Chrysostom, who had sent missionaries among the Goths, and Honoratus, whose bishops had gone to south and western Gaul. The renowned Patrick had converted the Celts; Columba, the Picts and Scots; Aidan, the Saxons; Columbanus, the Burgundians; and Augustin, the English.

The barbarians began their forays across the Danube and Alps in about 167 A.D. Actual invasions took place during the fourth and fifth centuries. The conquering Visigoths established settlements across the Danube. The Vandals tore across France and Spain, finally settling in North Africa. Jutes, Angles, and Saxons raided Britain and made it their home; the Franks and Burgundians did the same in northern France, and the Ostrogoths settled in Italy.

Despite the presence and power of these marauding tribes, Roman governance in its erstwhile colonies prevailed at first. Only in Ireland and Scotland, where Roman influence had never been significant, did indigenous Celtic, Druid, and then Christian traditions endure. The Celts, like the other tribes, had no written language. Their culture, mythical tales, and rules and regulations were passed along by oral tradition until recorded, after 600 A.D., by literate Irish monks. What is known of early Celtic culture comes from Greek and Roman observations. Diodorus of Sicily (d.21 B.C.) called them drunkards: "The Gauls are exceedingly addicted to the use of wine . . . drinking it unmixed."[20] Strabo, the Greek historian and geographer (?63– ?24 B.C.), thought they were warmongers: "The entire race which goes by the name of Gallic or Galatic, is warlike, passionate, and always ready for fighting, both otherwise simple and not malacious."[21] He counted sixty tribes in Celtica (Roman Gaul). There were kings and warrior aristocrats in these tribes. Their Druid priests were a powerful governing force who passed down the rules of conduct that were recorded as the Brehon laws. After Patrick won them over to Christianity, the Celts looked to the church for their laws. Gradually, the conquering tribes absorbed the Christian culture and the societal codes of the host country. In time the communities in Ireland, like those throughout vanquished Europe, became amalgams of Christian ethics, autochthonous mores, and residual Roman codices, blended with the conquerors' cultures, mores, codes of civil conduct, and modes of governing.

There is little information on the barbarians' social life. They were all an illiterate population, and wars, famine, plague, and survival skills comprised their focus and concerns. Peace seemed to elude them. They grappled steadily with internecine frictions and external enemies, like the Huns.

Roman documents from the provinces chronicled enough information to deduce the milieu in which children were received. In tribes numbering twenty-five thousand to one hundred thousand, infant mortality ran at about 45 percent, and life expectancy averaged forty years. Farming was left to slaves while the men of the tribes soldiered. Early on, in 98 A.D., Tacitus noted in *Germania* with admiration that:

> . . . the children, in every house, filling out amid nakedness and squalor into that girth of limb and frame which is to our people a marvel. Its own mother suckle each at her breast; they are not passed on to nursemaids and wet-nurses. Nor can master be recognized from servant by any flummery in their respective upbringing. (*Germania* 20)

The Celts were equally spartan and casual with their young. They preferred not to swaddle them, leaving nature to shape them.[22] Giraldus Cambrensis, known as Gerald of Wales, deplored the custom, writing that infants were

> . . . abandoned to ruthless nature. They are not put in cradles, or swathed; nor are their tender limbs helped by frequent baths or formed by any useful art. The midwives do not use hot water to raise the nose, or press down the face, or lengthen the legs.[23]

The polygamous Celts commonly sent their children, at age seven, to foster families to be educated. Services were paid in livestock. A freeman paid six heifers or one-and-a-half milk cows for a son. Charges for daughters were higher—eight heifers or two milk cows.[24] Girls remained in these foster homes until they were fourteen; boys, until seventeen. Freemen farmers' girls learned domestic skills, while noblemen's daughters learned sewing and embroidery (*muliebria opera*). Only boys were taught the "unwomanlike" skills of battle.

It is probable that all of the tribes practiced infanticide in one form or another. Among the Frisians, infanticide was sanctioned for a variety of reasons unless an infant had been fed.[25] It is uncertain how common were the incidents. Emperor Julian recounted the custom of tribes living along the banks of the Danube River, who tested legitimacy by placing an infant along the river's shores. Those who drowned were deemed adulterous products.[26]

Most tribes, however, had codes to penalize those who abandoned their young, and some tribes, such as the Franks, viewed infanticide as a cowardly deed, subject to *wergeld*, large pecuniary fines. Their Salic laws (*Pactus Legis Salicae*), enforced by Clovis, Childbert, and Lothair, exacted four thousand deniers (one denier equaled twenty-five grains of silver) for killing an unnamed child under eight days old; twenty-four thousand deniers for a boy under ten years old or for a pregnant girl. The penalty for slaying a free, pre-pubertal girl was eight thousand deniers, with the same penalty amount for an abortion. After puberty the sum increased to twenty-four thousand. The fine for the murder of an adult was, in comparison, only eight thousand deniers.[27]

Parenthetically, the same *Pactus Legis Salicae* prescribed a stiff fine of 1,800 deniers for unlawfully cutting a child's hair. Long locks among the Franks was a mark of position and worth. The Merovingian kings were known as the *reges criniti* of whom Agathias (c.532–582) wrote: "It is the rule for Frankish kings never to be shorn; indeed their hair is never cut from childhood on."[28] Not surprisingly, the privilege of flowing hair was denied to serfs and slaves. The Romans, whom the Franks despised anyway, wore their hair short, invoking enhanced Frankish contempt.

The Angles' laws also imposed monetary penalties for murderous acts: twenty-four thousand deniers for a girl from the nobility; seventy-two thousand for a nubile maiden. The Burgundians from eastern Gaul invoked existing Roman codes. Sigismund's decree in 516 A.D. ruled in favor of rescuers of abandoned children to rear the young without fear of reclamation by biological parents.[29]

The Visigoths in Spain followed the Frank and Angle models of *wergeld* based on age and sex and specifically outlawed abandonment, selling, or bartering of children. The fines were incremental, beginning at sixty solidi for abuse to a free male baby. Thereafter, from two to nine years of age, the *wergeld* increased by $3\frac{3}{4}$ solidi per year, leveling off at 90 solidi for boys under ten. From ten to fifteen years, the solidi fine was increased by ten. Until the age of fifteen, the fines were halved if the victim was a girl; thereafter, the fines for both genders were fixed at the same rate. So from sixteen to twenty, penalties rose thirty solidi per child year. Punishment for harming a twenty-year-old Visigoth was three hundred solidi.

Rewards were given by the Visigoths to those who rescued and nurtured abandoned children; a slave was given as compensation for such kindness. The *nutritors* of children voluntarily given over by the parents were entitled to annual stipends until the children reached ten years.[30] Thereafter, through service, children earned their own keep. In Boswell's view, this was a common form of legal abandonment, as it cheaply absolved families from any responsibility regarding unwanted children.[31] Children's rightful claims to their inheritances, however, were protected by deterrent laws that prohibited parents from selling property unless the sums of the transactions were equally divided among their children, both boys and girls.

Anglo-Saxon King Ina of Wessex legislated monetary rewards for families raising abandoned children. Six sous (6,000 grains of silver) were paid the first year of care, twelve sous the second year, and thirty sous in the third. He also forbade the sale of children "over the sea," or into slavery. Under his reign a man could acknowledge an illegitimate child and provide for it. King Alfred required proof by the caretaker that the death of an abandoned child was from natural causes.

It was not until the eleventh century that King Cnut exonerated children from blame for the sins of their fathers:

Up till now it happened that the child which lay in the cradle, although it had never tasted food, was reckoned by avaricious folk as being guilty as though it had had discretion. But I earnestly forbid this henceforth.[32]

In the reigns of King Hlothaere and King Eadric, paternal kinsmen were appointed for children whose fathers had died, until the children reached ten years of age, in order to guard their patrimony.[33] Theodoric, king of the Ostrogoths in Italy, decreed that children sold by poor parents were not to be considered slaves and could not lose their liberty.[34] Nevertheless, they were sold and not necessarily by poor parents, as Theodoric's own secretary, Cassiodorus, noted in a description of a sale being conducted at a fair:

This fair, which according to the old superstition was named Leucothea from the extreme purity of the fountain at which it is held, is the greatest fair in all the surrounding country. Everything that industrious Campania, or opulent Bruittii, or cattle-breeding Calabria, or strong Apulia produces, is there to be found exposed for sale, on such reasonable terms that no buyer goes away dissatisfied. . . . There stand ready boys and girls; with the attractions which belong to their respective sexes and ages, whom not captivity but freedom sets a price upon. These are with good reason sold by their parents, since they themselves gain by their servitude. For one cannot doubt that they are benefited even as slaves by being transferred from the toil of the fields to the service of the cities.[35]

Boswell[36] opined that children were sold by one landowner to another in order to bypass inheritance laws that diluted estates. Farms, divided and redivided by heirs, after a few generations would be reduced to nonutilizable parcels of land. Children "sold" or traded between farmers allowed the dealers to circumvent the law and keep the estate in one piece.

Aside from these mentions of *wergeld*, abandonment, and fosterage, little is known regarding the acceptance or education of tribal children. Certain-

ly, some tribes practiced infanticide at one time or another. It is also possible that they practiced animal and human sacrifices. The find of a fourteen-
year-old girl's remains raises the question of human sacrifice. Found preserved since the first century A.D. in a bog in Schleswig,[37] the girl had been
blindfolded and drowned. She may have been a victim of execution for adul-
tery or some such taboo or a victim of ritual sacrifice.

The Vikings left no doubt that they practiced human sacrifice for ritual
purposes. A sacrifice was made to ascertain success in battle, as in the instance of the child of a Viking chief. Hakon Jarl killed his son circa 990:

He had son Erling, who was seven winters old, and a very promising youth. Thorg-
erd accepted [Jarl's] offer and chose Erling, his son. When the Jarl found that his
prayers and vows were heard, he thought matters were better, and thereupon gave
the boy to Skopti Kark, his thrall [commonly a prisoner of war], who put him to
death in Hakon's usual way as taught by him.[38]

A sacrifice was called for to ensure the sovereign's longevity:

When King Aun was sixty, he made a great sacrifice in order to secure long life; he
sacrificed his son to Odin. . . . Odin told him that he should live forever if he gave
him a son every tenth year . . . during ten winters after he had sacrificed seven of his
sons he was unable to walk and was carried on a stool. He sacrificed his eighth son
and lived ten winters more in bed.[39]

This mythical account from the *Ynglinga* saga probably had truthful roots.
Human sacrifice among the Vikings continued until Christianity gained a
foothold in Iceland.

The Vikings imbued events like the births of babies with mythical properties, rituals, and laws. The Northmen believed their lives were preordained
by the Nornir spirits at birth. There were three Nornir spirits, sisters who
dwelt about the mystic ashtree Yggdrasil—all night visitors who came after
the birth of the child: Urd, representing the past; Verdandi, the present; and
Skuld, the future. In Viking households, births by law had to be witnessed:

Housemaids and neighbouring women shall be at the bedjourney of every woman
until the child is born, and not leave it before they have laid it to the breast of the
mother. (Borgarthing Law)[40]

Newborns were placed on the floor and not touched until picked up by
the father and placed in his cloak, a gesture signifying legitimacy. Fathers had
the right to keep their infants or discard them. The exposure was called
utburd (carrying out). Most commonly, deformed or illegitimate infants

were exposed, but overwhelming family poverty could precipitate such a measure. A normal baby was abandoned with a piece of salt pork clasped in its fist to suck on, presumably to sustain it until rescued or claimed by the Nornir.[41] Adam of Bremen's account (c.1075) suggests that babies had been thrown into the sea prior to the Christian influence.[42] The following chronicles, written well into the Christian era, are evidence that, at least, badly deformed infants were abandoned and buried. The one text suggests that such infants were thought to have come from evil, and people reacted from fear, not malice:

Every child which is born into this world shall be raised baptized, and carried to the church, except that only which is born so deformed that the mother cannot give strength to it, whose heels are in the place of the toes, whose chin is between his shoulders, the neck on his breast, with the calves on his legs turning forward, his eyes on the back of his head, and seal's fins or a dog's head. It shall be carried to the beach and buried where neither men or cattle go; the beach of the evil one. Next is the child which is born with a skin-bag on its face; it can be seen by every one that it cannot get its food, though it might grow up; it shall be taken and carried to the church, be prime-signed, laid at the church door; the nearest kinsman shall watch it till breath is out of it; it shall be buried in the churchyard, and its soul shall be prayed for as well as is possible. (Frostathing's Law)[43]

Healthy, accepted children were sprinkled with water in a sacred rite pre-dating Christian baptism. Christian baptism spiritually cleansed souls, making them worthy to enter the "kingdom of heaven." The Vikings' older initiation rite of sprinkling served a more secular purpose—it welcomed infants as members of the human race. An anomalous newborn with an "animal" appearance was denied Christian baptism, just as in pagan times the sprinkling ritual would have been withheld. Once the child was baptized, or sprinkled, exposure was regarded as an act of murder.

Children were named at these rituals and given gifts called "name-fastenings," which were commonly symbols of a warring race such as miniature swords, axes, spears, and bows.[44] The eruption of first teeth marked the next occasion at which presents were bestowed.

Fostering for legitimate children was the norm. Children of nobles were reared in the homes of learned friends, where it was expected they would receive kind and supportive nurturing. Strong, affectionate bonds developed in these relationships. Foster children received the same care and affection as if they were biological progeny. Foster parents were rewarded with filial respect and trust, unsevered even in death. Boys' educations focused on physical development, martial training, and hunting. They learned swimming, running with snowshoes, rowing, wrestling, falconry, and dog han-

Figure 4.2
A Swedish runestone from Vallentuna, Sweden. The inscription reads in part: "Jarlabanke commissioned this stone and had it raised in his memory while he was still alive." (THANKS TO MARIA FUNSETH COLÓN)

dling. Some boys were more inclined to learn runic writing, the law, and art. Girls were taught household skills, but some, at least, learned runic writing, evidenced by eleventh-century runic rhymes written by women to commemorate husbands and sons. Unlike the Roman tabular stones, runic steles (figure 4.2) seldom gave complete names and almost never gave the age of the commemorated. They did provide small glimpses of family size, occupations, and even loving sentiments within families. One stone left by a bridge by a woman named Ragnegv to Anund, her son, reads: "There will not be a greater memorial mother made after her only son."[45]

Viking raiders were particularly active from 800 to 1050.[46] Plundering the whole of Europe, they captured and enslaved mostly women, to keep as concubines.* Children of these alliances could be legitimized at the discretion of masters. Slaves were sometimes permitted to marry other slaves. Some slaves were given freedom. Marrying other manumitted individuals, they created a new, low-caste stratum of society. An extant poem, "Rigspula Elder Edda" (c.900), about a bondsmaid named Thir married to a bondsman named Thrall, is indicative of Viking society's low opinion of this class. The personified names of their children—Stable Boy, Clumsy One, Brawler, Coarse, Slave, Foul Lump, and Laggard among the boys, and She-Lump, Thicklegs, Clumped, and Noise for the girls—does not flatter the breed.[47]

The Viking exploits that expanded their slave economy and their Nordic settlements also exposed them to the medieval advances being made in education that were evolving in several places. Harald the Fairhaired set the precedent in 930 when he sent his son to be educated in England.[48]

---

*Every Sunday, priests chanted a special litany: *a furore Normannorum, libera nos* (from the fury of the Norsemen, deliver us). Stuart, 1926, p. 95.

Education had flourished in England since the seventh century. There were formal schools, mostly attached to parishes or cathedrals. Educators, renowned for their erudition, had set down much of their wisdom in writing. Aldhelm (639–709) was a West Saxon abbot from Malmesbury who wrote, as a teaching aid, over one hundred riddles, or *aenigmata*, in a Latin hexameter. The Venerable Bede (672–735) wrote handbooks on natural science (*De Natura Rerum*), an ecclesiastical history, and a grammar book based on Donatus. Alcuin (732–804), headmaster of the cathedral school at York, then of Charlemagne's Palatine school, wrote about astronomy, natural science, scripture, and arithmetic, using a time-tested "word-problem" methodology:

A swallow invited a snail to dinner: He lives just one league from the spot, and the snail traveled at the rate of an inch a day. How long would it be before he dined?[49]

Alcuin was most enlightened and eloquent on the subject of the natural sciences. He wanted children taught about

. . . the harmony of the sky, the labor of the sun and moon, the five zones, the seven wondering planets; the laws, rising and setting of the stars, and the aerial motions of the sea; the nature of man, cattle, birds, and wild beasts, with their various kinds and forms; and the sacred Scripture. . . . Despise not human science, but make them a foundation; so teach children grammar and the doctrines of philosophy that, ascending the steps of wisdom, they may reach the summit, which is evangelical perfection.[50]

The monastic school of Ælfric, Abbot of Eynsham (c.950) had a formal course in Latin employing a *Grammar*. He apparently used traditional physical coercions judging by the examples in his *Grammar*. Accusative tense: *hos pueros flagello*. Imperative tense: *o pueri, cantate bene: flagellaistum puerum*.

Much of the educational focus was shaken with the Viking incursions of the tenth century, but when order was reestablished, a new scholasticism emerged under the leadership of Anselm of Canterbury (1033–1109). The renascent scholasticism, as in Anselm's book, *Elucidarium*, a general information book in question-and-answer format written for children, was to lead England out of the so-called Dark Ages.

❏ ❏ ❏

These were paradoxical times. Amid the influence of these educators, tribal warfare continued throughout many parts of Europe, and whereas one culture abandoned children, another took them as spoils of war. Captors often followed the tenet to execute "everyone who could piss against the wall," thus enslaving all women, infants, and toddlers. The compassion for children and the progress against infanticide that was engendered during one century was just as quickly forgotten in the next. Codices were written and rewritten, but for all the attempts to do away with infanticide, it continued to permeate European society, practiced even by nuns, according to Boniface, an eighth-century missionary:

. . . when these harlots, whether in the world or in convents, bear in sinfulness their ill-conceived offspring, they also for the most part kill them, not filling the churches of Christ with adopted children, but rather filling tombs with their bodies and hell with their pitiful souls.[51]

Exposure was so commonplace that in the ninth century St. Goar could describe a known site used to abandon infants—reminiscent of the ancient Roman location of the *columna lactaria*:

For it was then the custom at Trier that when a woman bore a child whose parent did not wish to be known, or whom they could not afford to rear because of poverty, she would expose the newborn infant in a certain marble basin designed for this . . . and when the exposed child was found, there would be someone who, moved by pity, would take him and rear him.[52]

Christian penitentials (formulary handbooks for dealing with sins) forgave abandonment only if a father had been motivated by poverty or if a mother's child was the product of rape. Rules, however, were not consistent, varying from handbook to handbook. Authoritative canonical decrees collected in 906 by Regino of Prum imposed strict penalties for infanticide. Mothers were encouraged to leave infants at church doors rather than risk a charge of murder,[53] and from this beginning the new, revolutionary social phenomenon of oblation was introduced.

OBLATION

A child given as a permanent gift to a monastery was called an oblate (figure 4.3). Monasteries were obliged to provide temporal as well as spiritual guardianship to its charges in their formative years. The bonds created were, ideally, similar to the relationships in households with *alumni* of ancient times and the fostering families of medieval times. Originating in the East, oblation soon gained popularity in Europe.

Depending on the era, oblation almost always was permanent and irrevocable, whereas children placed in monasteries to be educated were free to

Figure 4.3 Oblation. A father oblates a son as illustrated in a Cistercian manuscript. BIBLIOTHÈQUE DE TROYES.

return to their homes when schooling was completed. In some epochs, ten-year-old children were permitted to decide whether or not they wished to remain in religious service. At other times, parents were authorized to make these decisions for them. There were, however, hundreds of years in which oblated children were obliged to remain monastics, living servile lives subject to the authority and laws of monastic superiors.

The premise that oblation for both boys and girls was a permanent commitment was established at the Council of Orleans in 549, and reinforced at the Council of Macon in 583. The Council of Toledo in 633 formalized, in Canon 49, the process for boys:

Either parental desire or personal devotion can make a monk; both are binding. We deny henceforth any possibility of returning to the world for either category, and we forbid any resumption of secular life.[54]

Monastic authority was so pervasive that in the West the monastic code often was incorporated into the civil code. For example, oblated children who ran away from monasteries were returned by civil authorities. It took centuries for this authority to be questioned, but the issue was recognized as serious enough to be argued by a church council. The Council of Mainz in 829 ruled that one could not be forced to remain a monk against his will.[55] This edict was opposed by Abbott Rabanus Maurus (c.870), who in his treatise defended traditional rules of oblation, citing primarily biblical analogies to support his contentions:

We have undertaken to write against those who say that it is not right for parents to commit their freeborn children to the service of God, and against those who, counting as little the oath they swore to God, angrily reject the holy service they have professed, as if they could abandon it without sin: they detest and despise the monastic discipline ordained according to the rules of the holy fathers. . . . We will first show with the testimony of sacred scripture and the example of the holy fathers that it is licit to consecrate one's child to the service of God; then that a vow one has sworn to God cannot be abandoned without grave sin; finally, that monastic life was established not by human design but by divine authority.[56]

The Councils of Worms in 861 and of Tribur in 895 reaffirmed church authority and the permanency of oblated and monastic life: "If [the oblate] leaves, he is to be returned; if he has let his hair grow, he is to be tonsured again; if he has taken a wife, he is to be forced to dismiss her."[57]

For many parents, the motives were genuinely to oblate (offer up) their children to the service of the church for the greater honor and glory of God. It can be surmised that others, consciously or otherwise, chose this socially condoned, even exalted form of abandonment to rid families of unwanted children. Certainly it was a particularly convenient method of casting off defective children. Ulrich of Cluny in the eleventh century commented:

After they have a houseful . . . or if they have any who are lame and crippled, deaf and dumb, or blind, hump-back or leprous, or who have any defect which would make them less desirable in the secular world [parents] offer them as monks with the most pious of vows.[58]

Oblation was also a rational choice for children who were commonly orphaned by one or sometimes both parents or for those whose parents went off to the Crusades. Nunneries were favorite havens for families overly supplied with daughters.

Marriage among the clergy had been strongly discouraged by the church, although a celibate clergy was not a church mandate until the eleventh century. However much frowned upon—and it always was considered a disgrace to have children—such unions were not uncommon.[59] The Ninth Council of Toledo ruled, with stern rebuke, that children born of clerics belonged to the church, to be oblated:

The offspring produced by such pollution, moreover, shall not only have no share in their parents' estate, but shall remain in perpetual servitude to that church of whose priest or minister they were ignominiously born.[60]

The oblation of children in general became so widespread that monastic councils from many different bishoprics developed set regulations on procedure. As might be expected, the directives for nobles differed from those for the poor, as with the Rules of St. Benedict:

If anyone of the nobility offers his son to God in the monastery and the boy is very young, let his parents draw up the petition which we mentioned above; and at the oblation let them wrap the petition and the boy's hand in the altar cloth and so offer him.

As regards their property, they shall promise in the same petition under oath that they will never of themselves, or through an intermediary, or in any way whatever, give him anything or provide him with the opportunity of owning anything. Or else, if they are unwilling to do this, and if they want to offer something as an alms to the monastery for their advantage, let them make a donation of the property they wish to give to the monastery, reserving the income to themselves if they wish. And in this way let everything be barred, so that the boy may have no expectations whereby (which God forbid) he might be deceived and ruined, as we have learned by experience.

Let those who are less well-to-do make a similar offering. But those who have nothing at all shall simply draw up the petition and offer their son before witnesses at the oblation. (*Rules of Saint Benedict* 59)

Monasteries expected gifts of land or monetary compensation from parents as recompense for the cost of nurturing their children and to offset the expenses of children of the poor, who had no means to offer. There were no objections to payment for the service since the arrangement was not unlike those financial transactions made by families fostering their children to others. Moreover, it was a common practice for wealthy parents who openly abandoned children to leave significant sums with them as incentive to rescuers to treat the children well. Once a child was oblated, parents had no further financial obligation.[61] Oblation was therefore a wonderful device for the wealthy to bypass laws of patrimony and keep estates intact. This maneuver was not lost to either the aristocracy or the church, for as early as the fourth century, Basil had decried the practice:

Many are those whom parents or siblings or some relatives bring before the proper age, not having undertaken celibacy of their own accord, but disposed of for some material advantage to those who brought them.[62]

Since monks took vows of poverty, the problems attached to the child's patrimony were obviated by dividing the inheritance. One-third was given to the abbot to distribute to the poor, one-third was given to the monastery, and one-third stayed with the family. In theory, this distribution of inheritance also eliminated the temptation to "return to the outside world." Once oblated, it was possible for a child to remain in permanent ignorance of his origins.

As parents oblated their children into a life of servitude, the church assured the parents—not the children—of spiritual rewards. The following declaration of oblation is typical of these documents in context and tone. Many documents have survived, especially those written after the year 1000: "I herewith offer this my son to Almighty God and Holy Mary his mother, according to the Rule of Benedict for the good of my soul and those of my parents."[63]

Unconsulted, without the right to protest, newly weaned toddlers to youngsters up to ten years old were oblated to monasteries or convents. The intense, lonely, frightened feelings of all of these children poignantly were rendered in the recollections (c.1138) of a twelfth-century monk:

And I a mere boy, did not presume to oppose my father's wishes, but obeyed him in all things, for he promised me for his part that if I became a monk I should taste of the joys of Heaven with the Innocents after my death . . . and so a boy of ten, I crossed the English Channel came into Normandy as an exile, unknown to all, knowing no one . . . so weeping, my father gave me, a weeping child, into the care of the monk, Reginald, and sent me away into exile for love of Thee, and never saw me again. (Orderic Vitalis, *Ecclesiastical History*)[64]

The Japanese, Chinese, and other cultures oblated their children (ten was apparently the cut-off age in Japan as well as in Europe), and impressions of the practice have survived from both countries. From Japan, this haiku:

> A boy not ten years old
> they are giving to the temple!
>   Oh, it's cold!
> Masaoka Shiki, *The Apprentice Priestling*[65]

The medieval Chinese conceived ten different hells for various evils. In the second hell resided those priests who had lured innocent children into monasteries.[66]

The enforced servitude of the system, a monastic life forcibly imposed on those disinclined to the religious community, deprivation of inheritance, and so on, all count among the obvious abuses of oblated children. In the context of the times, however, oblation can be viewed as an improvement over the exposure to which children had been vulnerable. Children, unwanted for many reasons, were provided a temporal and spiritual home as a part of communities committed to care for them; and in the best of these communities, comfort and companionship were found in institutions dedicated to the highest morality. Oblates could also advance in the church to positions of high office and esteem. Further, not all oblates lost contact with their families, although, to be sure, there were those who had no idea of their family's identity. In time, some orders instituted reformations that addressed the concept of freedom of choice. Among the Cistercians, an oblate had to be at least fifteen years old, and for the Carthusians, boys had to be twenty years old. In the thirteenth century, Thomas Aquinas (1225–1274) (himself given at six years of age) spoke against oblation, declaring that it should not be imposed since religious commitment was not possible before the age of reason, which he ascertained to be fourteen years old for boys and twelve years for girls.[67]

Oblation, at its best, inspired a ninth-century innovation of familial bonds between children and guardians who became responsible for the children's spiritual and corporal needs. The church elevated the status of this relationship by naming the guardians "godparents." The kinship was created at baptism, when a child became a "godchild" to the godmother and godfather.* In many cultures these godparents were true guardians, *in loco parentis*. The relationship, a kinship considered intimate and sacred, prompted canon law to forbid marriages between godparents and godchildren. Laws were written imposing penalties for negligence of godparental duties. The thirteenth-century laws of Archbishop Rande in Scandinavia made it obligatory for godparents to ensure that godchildren learned the Credo, the Our Father, and the Ave Maria by the time they reached fifteen years of age. Thereafter, fines were imposed if children of normal intelligence could not recite these prayers.[68]

Children in monasteries followed a regimen similar to that of adults, in which four hours were given to liturgy, four to reading, six to work, and six hours to eight hours to sleep. The remaining two to four hours were time allowed for personal hygiene and eating. Like the adults, oblates were required to eat standing. In deference to their youth, meals were more frequent, with more meat. The need for special diets for growing children was widely acknowledged, as in one statement by a penitential: "Children brought up in a monastery shall eat flesh for 14 years."[69]

Lanfranc, the Canterbury archbishop under William the Conqueror, composed monastic rules that forbade abstinence from food or drink as a penance for children.[70]

The Rule of Benedict concluded that every ten boys should have three to four masters assigned to them. Anywhere from twelve to twenty-five boys could be quartered in dormitories, and in the inner, warmer rooms of a monastery.[71] Play was sparingly allowed once a week, and discipline was cor-

*Marcus (1996) contends that as the baptismal age changed from adulthood to infancy, the godparent's speaking in behalf of the baby became necessary (pp. 106–7).

poreal and severe. Beatings in some monasteries may have been very common, evidenced by the popularity and title of St. Dunstan, archbishop of Canterbury, as oblate protector from beatings.[72]

Although there were orders that rewarded good behavior and obedience, the general trend, as with St. Benigne of Dijon, was to enforce a strict code of discipline:

At Nocturns, and indeed at all the hours, if the boys commit any fault in the Psalmody or other singing, either by sleeping or such like transgression, let there be no sort of delay, but let them be stripped forthwith of frock and cowl, and be beaten in their shirt only . . . let the masters sleep between every two boys in the dormitory, and sit between every two at other times . . . when they lie down in bed, let a master always be among them with his rod . . . for children everywhere need custody with discipline and discipline with custody . . . when they wash, let masters stand between each pair . . . when they sit in cloister or chapter, let each have his own tree-trunk for a seat, and so far apart that none touch in any way even the skirt of the other's robe . . . let them wipe their hands as far as possible one from the other, that is at opposite corners of the towel . . . nor doth one ever speak to the other, except by his master's express leave, and in the hearing of all who are in school . . . one reporteth whatsoever he knoweth against the other; else, if he be found to have concealed aught of set purpose, both the concealer and the culprit are beaten.[73]

The homophobic attitudes implied in these rules was common in monasteries, to the extent that some institutions did not permit a traditional kiss of peace among the oblates. Concerns about clerical homosexuality were reflected in Peter Damian's *Liber Gomorrhianus*, which recommended a public beating, loss of tonsure, and six months imprisonment in chains for the seduction of an oblate.[74]

The numbers of oblated children, it is agreed, will never be known, since record keeping was erratic at best and that which has survived is incomplete. Attempts to keep track of the numbers were made, such as one Benedictine account that estimates that 25 percent of the Carolingian monastic population was oblates. The estimate does not give the total number of this community, nor does it suggest the number or percentage of oblates who were children. An eleventh-century registry in Winchester recorded that 85 percent of the monks were oblates; at Cluny it was about 25 percent.

❑   ❑   ❑

By the end of the first millennium A.D. in Europe, concepts of marriage, family, and childhood had progressed, subject to church definition, influence, and control. Marriage was deemed a sacrament, with procreation sanctioned as the *raison d'etre* of the union. Children, singled out by Matthew's Gospel 18 as being divinely protected, also were protected by the church and the guardian angels of God's heaven. Earthly protectors—godparents—saw to children's spiritual and temporal safety. Infanticide was condemned. Houses of asylum were provided for abandoned children, and medical attention, made cognizant by Oribasius's understanding of children's special needs, showed concern for those factors that facilitated normal growth and development. The pedagogy of the trivium—arts, grammar, logic, and rhetoric—was defined, and the quadrivium of arithmetic, music, geometry, and astronomy was soon to follow.

Oblation, an institution of children, evolved from an offering to God of a child to institutions of men and women who chose to dedicate their lives to the service of God and the church. Church power was to continue throughout the Middle Ages, into the Renaissance. Redefinition would await the Reformation.

NOTES

1. Herlihy, 1985, p. 27.
2. Boswell, 1988, p. 158.
3. Ibid., p. 161.
4. Ibid., p. 3.
5. Augustine, *City of God*, 21.14.
6. Boswell, 1988, pp. 165–66.
7. Payne, 1916, pp. 264–65.
8. Boswell, 1988, p. 169.
9. Ibid., p. 171.
10. Payne, 1916, pp. 266–67.
11. Boswell, 1988, p. 184.
12. Payne, 1916, pp. 266–69.
13. Ibid., p. 270.
14. Boswell, 1988, pp. 202–3.
15. Payne, 1916, pp. 268–69.
16. Rice, 1967, p. 162.
17. Oribasius, *Synopsis*, bk. 5.
18. Ibid., 5.14.
19. Payne, 1916, p. 273.
20. Diodorus, 5.26.
21. Strabo, 4.2.
22. Anderson and Zinsser, 1988, 1:109.
23. Gies and Gies, 1987, p. 199.
24. Markale, 1975, pp. 31–34.
25. Boswell, 1988, p. 211.

26. Payne, 1916, p. 278.
27. Ibid., pp. 279–80.
28. Coates, 1999, p. 7.
29. Ibid., p. 281.
30. Ibid., p. 282.
31. Boswell, 1988, pp. 201–2.
32. Gies and Gies, 1987, p. 110; Crawford, 1999, p. 65.
33. Gies and Gies, 1987, p. 111.
34. Payne, 1916, pp. 282–83.
35. Ibid.
36. Boswell, 1988, p. 202.
37. Glob, 1969, pp. 38–52.
38. DuChailler, 1889, p. 364. This passage suggests that sacrifice was common and ritualized.
39. Ibid.
40. Ibid., p. 36.
41. Stuart, 1926, p. 99.
42. Brondsted, 1960, p. 24.
43. Ibid.
44. Stuart, 1926, p. 100.
45. Jesch, 1991, pp. 61–68.
46. Martinson, 1992, p. 42.
47. Ibid., p. 41.
48. Ibid., p. 103.
49. Godfrey, 1907, p. 36.
50. Ibid., p. 37; Crawford, 1999, p. 152.
51. Boswell, 1988, p. 210.
52. Ibid., p. 218.
53. Ibid., p. 222.
54. Ibid., p. 233.
55. Ibid., p. 246.
56. Ibid., p. 439.
57. Ibid., p. 249.
58. Ibid., p. 298.
59. Ibid., p. 259.
60. Ibid.
61. Ibid., p. 236.
62. Ibid., p. 240.
63. Ibid., p. 237.
64. McLaughlin, 1974, pp. 123–29.
65. H. G. Henderson, *Haiku* (New York: Doubleday, 1958), p. 180.
66. Tom, 1989, p. 95.
67. *Summa Theologica*, 2.2, question 189, article 5.
68. Martinson, 1992, pp. 104–5.

69. Boswell, 1988, p. 250.
70. Gies and Gies, 1987, p. 211.
71. Ibid.
72. McLaughlin, 1974, pp. 172–73.
73. Evans, 1925, p. 155.
74. McLaughlin, 1974, p. 171.

Chapter 5

Late Civilizations: The Yanacona

❑   ❑   ❑

THE PACIFIC

The establishment of societies across the Pacific basin occurred over a period of four millennia (see table 5.1).

The South Pacific first was populated during the last Ice Age (40,000–20,000 years ago), when prehistoric groups crossed the Asian subcontinent in an easterly direction to New Guinea and Australia, prior to the warming cycle that flooded the land bridges between these many islands. The resultant cultures can be broadly examined in five geographic areas: Australia, Polynesia, Indonesia, Melanesia, and Micronesia.

Anthropological and social data acquired during the eighteenth and nineteenth centuries are the primary sources of information about these isolated people, because traditional archaeological and older anthropological artifacts are sparse and contribute little toward understanding these cultures. Cranial vaults have been found but no complete skeletal remains. There are ritualistic wood carvings and, mainly, domestic artifacts, such as fishhooks, adzes, shells, tattooing bone implements, and some pottery from coastal, sometimes valley, cluster dwellings. In general, the Pacific people had few metals,

TABLE 5.1

**APPROXIMATE CHRONOLOGY OF THE EASTWARD EXTENSION
OF SETTLEMENTS ACROSS THE PACIFIC**

Approximate Dates	Geographic Areas
B.C. 3000	New Guinea/Australia
1500	Lapita (New Caledonia)
500	Fiji, Tonga, Samoa
100	Marquesas
A.D. 250	Easter, Hawaii
300	Austral
500	Cook
700	New Zealand

and little pottery was made after 500 A.D. Best studied are the distinctive pottery shards of the coastal culture of Lapita, in New Caledonia, which flourished after c.1500 B.C.

Geographically isolated and ignorant of Eurasian cultures, the Pacific settlers were illiterate and therefore produced no pictograms or ideograms. Oral traditions and rituals of the Pacific cultures, however, were rich and enduring. Each generation took care to relate its lore and legends with precise fidelity, and consequently, there has been little change in the material over the course of millennia.[1] This is evidenced by the archaic words found in songs and legends from Polynesia that were handed down by countless priests who had memorized their cultural treasure.[2]

The Polynesian chain of islands numbers more than thirty thousand, extending over vast expanses. Purportedly, it took two millennia to settle the islands by people who managed to preserve some cultural similarities. Linguistic analyses suggest that Polynesia was mainly settled by emigrations from Fiji.[3] There are thirty closely related Austronesian languages and hundreds of dialects. Cultures can be glottically divided into western (Uvea, Samoa, Tonga), central (Society, Cook, Austral, Hawaii), and marginal (Marquesas, Easter, New Zealand) territories to facilitate classification and study. Vocabulary, with glottogenic roots extending back as far as 2500 B.C., refers to dietary staples that suggest little change in available foods over time, with taro, yams, breadfruit, coconut, rice, pigs, and fowl enduring as nutritional sources. The dog was domesticated.[4]

ABORIGINES

The Australian aborigines lived communally in groups consisting of several families headed by the eldest male. They were nomads with no permanent settlements, although temporary camps were set up to facilitate food gathering, such as nut and root collecting by the children. During periods of encampment, children were taught tribal rituals in song and dance. In their wanderings, women and children served as porters while the men hunted and formed an advance guard.

Boys and girls played and lived together until their seventh year, when preparation for their adult roles began in earnest. Little girls imitated the domestic role of their mothers and other females in the group. They kept "house," hunted for grubs, dug up tubers, and mourned at mock funerals of their imaginations. Throughout latency, females absorbed the tribal expectations of mature women. As adolescent girls neared marriage age, secret ceremonies conducted by the women of the commune initiated them in preparation for a betrothal. Faces were painted red, with white bands worn across the forehead. After a ritual washing in a stream, the nubile were presented to the commune, eligible for marriage.

Boys joined the men on hunting expeditions, learning every nuance of this essential activity. At fifteen or sixteen, boys were prepared for rites of passage, with decorative nose piercing and skin scarification as the preludes to initiation observances. Circular areas, separated by approximately a half kilometer, were arranged. Secret rites were conducted in the smaller of two circles; the larger was reserved for public ceremonies. Each boy was "sponsored," or guided, generally by a maternal uncle. First, red paint was lathered on the boys' faces, after which they engaged in cult dances. Boys then were admitted to the secret circle for initiation services, of which little is known except that sometimes a tooth was forcibly avulsed or hot coals were placed on a boy's head.[5] Other than presuming that these mutilations were tests of endurance and stamina, little of their significance is known. Boys spent a week in these inner circles to learn tribal legends and laws, after which they emerged, deemed ready for marriage.

In Papua, just to the north of Australia, children also were scarified. After three days of sleep deprivation had induced a kind of anesthetic apathy, facial scars were incised with a sharp talon of a flying fox.

PACIFIC ATOLLS

Beyond the large landmass of Australia, Pacific cultures flourished on small island outcrops. Children universally were desired and were treated as treasured possessions. On the Carolines, babies and toddlers were constantly handled, played with, hugged, kissed, and even smelled. Scoldings or corrections were rare. Toys were plentiful and readily provided. Coconut trees were used to make kites, balls, and tops.

Childless couples were pitied, and parents with more than one child often were expected to offer their next baby to a couple who had none.[6] Among the Maori, an orphaned child was adopted immediately and thereafter amply spoiled.

Although abandonment of infants was unheard of, paradoxically, infanticide, mostly rooted in superstitious beliefs, was known to occur. If one twin died, the other was killed. If an infant was born deformed, it was killed.[7] Both the Maori and the Polynesians practiced construction sacrifice; in a practice reminiscent of the foundation sacrifices of Jericho, the son of a chief was offered up prior to the construction of a sacred canoe or other significant structure.[8] Some island cultures controlled their populations. The Tokelaus of the Line Islands allowed four children per couple; after that number had been reached, infants were buried just after birth. The Vaitupu allowed two children, and the Nukufetau only one. The Tonga strangled sick babies. Moreover, if they perceived that the gods had been offended, a two-year-old was chosen for sacrifice and strangled. In Papua New Guinea, infanticide of girls was practiced as recently as this century, as this contemporary account suggests:

When I was born, and my mother was still in the birth hut, my father came and hung over the fence, and called out, asking what it was, a boy or a girl. My mother replied, "a girl." And my father said, "break it and throw it away." But my mother refused [and I was named] *Letahulozo*, which means break it and throw it away.[9]

Given the context of cultures in which children were revered, coddled, and spoiled, infanticide was a striking aberration. While acknowledging that infanticide occurred in times of famine, one nineteenth-century observer, the celebrated writer Robert Louis Stevenson, noted in his book about the Polynesians, *The South Seas*:

No people in the world are so fond or so long-suffering with children—children make mirth and the adornment of their homes, serving them for playthings and picture-galleries . . . the spoiling, and I may almost say the deification, of the child is nowhere carried so far as in the eastern islands.[10]

Micronesia, 2,141 islands scattered over an area the size of the continental United States, exhibited remarkable cultural similarities in rituals and living habits. As noted, the desire for children was paramount. In the Carolines, mothers expressed gender preferences before they conceived.[11] To have

Figure 5.1 An example of head molding among Pacific people from New Britain. AMERICAN MUSEUM OF NATURAL HISTORY, NEW YORK.

a boy, they drank coconut water; if a girl was wanted, they abstained from the liquid.

Babies were born in birthing huts with fifty-foot perimeters; they were taboo for men. Mothers delivered their infants alone. They knelt on birthing mats to extract their babies with their hands. Relatives were asked to assist only if complications occurred. Tiny white shells, called *giligins*, were used to cut umbilical cords, after which infants were washed in the ocean and fed coconut oil before breast feeding commenced. Impressively, the identical ritual was practiced in Samoa, four thousand kilometers away![12]

Babies remained with their mothers in birthing huts for ten days, after which mothers were welcomed home with community feasts. Sacred fires were kindled to serve exclusively their infants' needs. Fathers bowed to maternal supremacy by requesting permission from their wives just to hold their babies. Pampered and loved, infants were not given names until they survived three months. Babies also were introduced to solid foods at three months of age, such as prechewed taro root or fish, but nursing continued, and during these early months head wrapping was practiced.

Multiple cultures throughout the world have for millennia used head molding, or passive cranioplasty, to shape their infants' malleable skulls. So it was in Micronesia (figure 5.1). Boards were fixed to the head and wrapped for a prescribed period, generally three to six months, until the desired shape was achieved. Basically, there are five classes of molding: vertico-occipital, fronto-occipital, frontal, lambdoid, and annular.[13] Most cultures employed the fronto-occipital mold, flattening the front and back of the head.

First used at birth for washing and anointing and throughout infancy for making cradles of its wood and fiber, the coconut was an integral part of fertility rituals. For example, at menarche girls became the focus of tribal families, who assembled to celebrate the event, and the community offered them gifts of beads and coconut. Girls were painted in red from head to toe and led to the menstrual hut. On each of four days a coconut gift was given to each girl. On the fifth day the girls, now deemed nubile by the community, were allowed to emerge from the hut. Among their first responsibilities was to chew dried roots of *Piper methysticum*, used to make an intoxicating drink known as *kava-kava*. For ceremonial purposes during harvest liturgies, young men of the hamlet drank this potion prepared by marriageable virgins.[14] Curiously, there appears to have been no initiation rites for boys in this culture.[15]

Melanesian girls were tattooed at menarche, a ceremonial mutilation that marked the passage from childhood to nubility. At a festive celebration, skin was incised with a bat wingbone and vegetable stain applied. Girls were considered nubile when the tattoos healed.[16]

Maori children were educated to their future roles from the age of six. Girls learned to gather flax and firewood, to weave mats and baskets, to cook, and to garden. They learned to pound bark to make tapa cloth.* Boys learned how to farm, hunt, and fish. They were taught how to build houses and make canoes. Martial rituals and dances were learned, along with combat skills such as spearing and clubbing. Apparently unique among the Pacific cultures, the Maori valued formal education and sent the sons of nobles to schools when they were sixteen years old. There tribal priests taught them the legends, traditions, and sacred rites of their people.[17]

Legend and superstition were infused into child care and healing practices in all of the Pacific cultures. Among Melanesian Vanuatu, illness was thought to come from *tamate*, the spirit of the dead who wandered the forest in search of children. In the Solomons, children were believed to be particularly vulnerable to losing their souls when sneezing. "Ora," meaning life and soul, was hastily incanted to contravene such calamity.[18]

The Polynesian Tahitians treated specific childhood illnesses (table 5.2)[19] with straightforward botanical preparations, unlike the Cook Island Rarotongas, who dosed their children with botanicals only during specified lunar phases, convinced that the moon had power over sickness and health.

The death of a child occasioned inconsolable grief and superstitious burial rituals. Indonesian Keisar children were buried underneath the site where

---

*The pounding of plant pulp into thin pliable material was common throughout many early cultures. Egyptian papyrus was made by pounding strips of the reed into a pulpy material. Similarly, the Aztecs made paper from the bark of the fig tree. The inner bark was soaked in lime water and stone-pounded until it was a thin porous sheet. This was then glazed with chalk.

TABLE 5.2
PEDIATRIC ILLNESSES RECOGNIZED BY TAHITIANS

ira miti	Diurnal fever
ira ahure	Vulvitis in little girls
ira ute	Red, painful lips
ira ninamu	Lethargy, dark eyes/lips, fever
ira hitirere	Seizures
hua ira	Penile swelling
papa tui	Cervical adenitis (enlarged neck nodes)
tushe'a	Otitis media (ear infection)
he'a ha'amae	Anorexia and pica

their parents slept. Aaru dwellers hung their dead infants above the parents' sleeping mats. In Java, children who died unnamed were buried behind the family hut.

House burial of children was observed in other cultures. The Andaman Island natives disturbed the hearthstone fire to bury the child beneath the hearth, in the belief that the child's soul would enter the mother's body as she cooked and thus be reborn. The Vanuatu of New Hebrides, the Kois of southern India, and the Bishnois of the Punjab also practiced house burial. In northern India, children were not burned on a pyre, as were adults; they were buried at the threshold of a house, where, it was believed, the soul of a child would enter the body of a woman who crossed the threshold and be reincarnated in another child of her conception.[20]

THE AMERICAS

A recent study of mitochondrial DNA from South American Ticuna, Central American Maya, and North American Pima Indians concluded that Pan-American prototypes (excluding Eskimos, Navajos, and Apaches) evolved from one early migration of people who crossed the Asian-American land bridge over what is now the Bering Strait fifteen thousand to thirty thousand years ago. A second mitochondrial DNA analysis yielded conflicting data, dating the migratory journeys as far back as forty thousand to fifty thousand years.[21] It is a safe assumption to say that the major migrations took place about twenty-eight thousand years ago, because, by the time of the last warming cycle, when land bridges disappeared under rising sea levels, migratory routes already were established.

The Americas were populated from the Arctic regions progressively south to Cape Horn, bequeathing a rich diversity of culture and language similar in phenomenon to the glottic variations and variegations found across the Pacific basin. More than twenty-five major language groups evolved in the Americas, involving over 335 distinct cultural groups.[22]

Archaeological yields have been limited to circa 3000-B.C. pottery from the Andean regions, circa 2000–1000-B.C. hammered copper items found in the western Great Lakes region of North America, and a few ancient mummies from arid burial sites on both continents. Ancient cultures, such as the Adena-Hopewell of Ohio, Illinois, and Pennsylvania, the Mississippian, and the Olmec of Veracruz, Mexico, are known mostly from burial artifacts and mounds. Analyses of children's bones and teeth obtained from these inhumation sites revealed that growth, consistent with good health, had preceded sickness and death. The bones from children who had had a varied hunter-gatherer diet were longer and stronger than those who subsisted on a corn diet. Additionally, the former had fewer carbohydrate-induced caries.[23]

There is agroarchaeological evidence of early domestication of plants and animals that rendered nomadic ventures unnecessary and encouraged permanent settlements. Corn, squash, beans, peppers, and pumpkins were selectively grown. Wild cameloids, llamas, vicuñas, and alpacas were domesticated for food and fur.

The parasitoses diagnosed from coprolithic specimens of the Colorado plateau indicate that agricultural groups were more prey to infestations such as round and flat worms than were hunter-gatherer cultures. Migratory cultures left latrine areas that decreased the incidence of fecal-oral contamination.[24]

The major database for the study of early settlements and culture is derived from later civilizations that flourished in the first millennium A.D. and onward. With the presumption that the centuries little altered cultural patterns and behavior, a reasonable description of child life among the Eskimo, Plains, tropical, and Andean habitats from 500 B.C. to 1500 A.D. is possible. In all of these, the education of children centered on *enculturation* and survival skills.[25]

North America

Several Eskimo cultures are believed to have been among the first to people the Alaskan peninsula and Canada. Diverse in habits and customs, they were similar in diet, dress, and dwellings and especially in their ability to adapt to their frigid environment.

Among the Chukchi, pregnant women arose each morning to face the propitious rising sun, the dwelling place of all benevolent spirits. Koryak women burned pieces of fat, meat, and fur at shrines as sacrificial offerings to ensure a safe pregnancy and birth. Women of the Even tribe were forbidden to visit or even receive guests at home during pregnancies. They eschewed fatty foods and did not touch fishnets, which could invoke a knotted or tangled umbilical cord. To hasten delivery during labor, the tent's curtain ties were loosened and pots were unlidded to facilitate the baby's passage. At parturition, husbands staved off the humiliating couvade by desisting from making fishnets and from tying knots of any kind.

From life's beginning to its end, certain rituals separated the genders. For example, midwives severed the umbilical cord of a male baby with the father's knife and used the mother's knife to cut that of a girl. Midwives bathed all babies with grass soaked in maternal urine. Once "cleansed," infants were wiped with soft wood chips and swaddled with skins onto boards while the grass was burned.

Bridging the thermal extreme between intra- and extrauterine life,[26] Bering Sea Eskimo babies were wrapped at birth in diapers of soft seal skin lined with sphagnum moss.[27] In all of the Eskimo cultures, babies were sequestered with their mothers in birthing huts, kept warm with maternal contact and furs. In contrast, at the other frigid end of the earth, close to the South Pole, the inhabitants of Tierra del Fuego deliberately exposed their newborns to the cold, as did the Onas, Yahgans, and Fuegians, who dipped their newborns into the ocean or a stream to "toughen" them.[28]

For the most part, Eskimo babies were welcomed and sometimes shared with childless couples, who kept track of village pregnancies with adoption in mind. Babies of any paternity were recognized as family. Occasional abandonments occurred, with predictably swift, lethal consequences for those exposed in the severe cold. It must be added that infanticide of females happened with enough frequency to provoke wife-stealing raids by bands of young men from other clans.

The reindeer-herding Asiatic Eskimos, the Chukchi and Koryak, used a shaman's divinations to name a baby. Names were always those of deceased family members, since babies were believed to be ancestral reincarnations. Children never were struck, lest the soul of an offended ancestor depart the body, leaving behind a dead child.[29]

The Siberian Even actively imbued newborns with ancestral identities. A baby boy or girl would be pronounced a reincarnation with quiet certitude: "Father is back" or "Father is back as a woman."[30] Among the Kerek, male infants were named for reincarnated maternal grandfathers or great-grandfathers; girls, after maternal grandmothers. Bering Sea Eskimo infants were named after the last member of the community to have died. Multiple names were common, each name being associated with a specific food taboo. Violations of taboos were thought to cause illness.

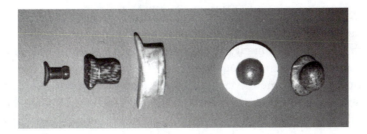

Figure 5.2 Labrets. UNIVERSITY OF PENNSYLVANIA MUSEUM, PHILADELPHIA.

Strictly defined gender roles separated men from women and, after the age of five, boys from girls. Boys lived with the men in large ceremonial houses, called the *qasgiq*, absorbing tribal history, customs, superstitions, and wisdom. They were tutored in the skills of hunting—the chief endeavor of adults. Ceremonials and ritual observances reinforced the hunt's importance to the community's survival, as indeed did children's games and toys such as toy bows and arrows and harpoons. Celebrations were extended to each hunting success: a boy's first bird kill was feted in the *qasgiq*, and a first seal kill, its meat shared with the community, commanded particular acclaim and festive rejoicing.

At puberty, boys were prepared for adult life and marriage in a lip-piercing ceremonial. Labrets, large collar-button-like ornaments made from carved ivory or bone, were inserted into the pierced lip to connote coming of age[31] (figure 5.2).

Preparation of the hunting paraphernalia was left to women, who taught their daughters to prepare foods, tailor garments, make boat covers and boots, and weave baskets, all the while reciting customs and taboos of the clan for their children's edification. Bering Sea girls had dolls whose garments were changed with the seasons. For fear the spring geese would bypass the hamlet without roosting, children were forbidden to play with their dolls inside the house during winter. Bearing Sea girls gave up their dolls at menarche, whereas Chukchi girls kept theirs to hasten conception. Since the aura or ethereal plasma of menses was said to make the hunter visible to his prey, menstruating girls were confined and isolated.[32] The only female puberty custom among the North Alaskan Eskimos was a chin tattoo to mark menarche and marriageability.

Girls were given a "storyknife" made by either the father or an uncle. It was used to draw pictures in the sand or mud in the course of storytelling. This knife was a like a spatula, made of wood or ivory and carved with motifs of fish or birds. Girls used standardized symbols to make drawings, symbols recognized by all children of the village. Children gathered around the little girl telling a story passed on to her (or made up), as she illustrated it on the ground, using her storyknife to draw the symbols.[33]

Each family of the Tlingit tribe was divided into two groups called Eagles and Ravens. All males in a household had to belong to the same clan, a rule not imposed on women. Marriage between two Eagles or between two Ravens was taboo. Descent in these families was matrilinear. Maternal uncles assumed the responsibility for the education of their nephews, teaching clan songs, ceremonial dances, legends, folklore, and taboos to spellbound charges.[34] They taught the boys to hunt and instructed them in constructing and maintaining paraphernalia pertaining to the hunt and to village life. When boys were ten years old, they were tested for endurance. At winter daybreak they were expected to wade into icy waters and stand, neck-deep, until summoned by their uncles to shore. Then, cold and wet in the glacial air, they were whipped by their uncles with alder branches.

Menarche of Tlingit girls was observed with ceremonious rituals in which girls spent eight days in menstrual huts, immobile save for intermittent rubbing of the face and lips with a stone. To avoid growing up as gossips, they performed this ritual eight times daily. To safeguard against becoming a gluttonous adult, they fasted eight days, with one break in the fast on the fourth day. On the ninth day and following, still isolated from their respective family, girls practiced domestic skills until they were mastered. When they returned to the village, girls were feasted by fathers, given a lower-lip labret, tattooed, and declared nubile.[35]

Tlingit babies remained in the birthing huts, isolated from their fathers for eight days. As in the Chukchi and Koryak tribes, infants were thought to be reincarnations of ancestors and accordingly were given names of dead relatives from the mothers' clan. The yearly "return to life" of upstream salmon migrations symbolized to the Tlingits their belief in reincarnation and the cycles of life and death.[36]

❏   ❏   ❏

More than twenty-five subarctic tribes of the Athabascans lived south of the Eskimo tundra in the conifer-bordered Yukon and MacKenzie watersheds of northwestern Canada. Although they were favored with a less-forbidding climate than that of the frozen Arctic, a more plentiful flora and fauna, and less extreme diurnal cycles, the cultural similarities between these tribes and those of the Eskimo are notable.

These were particularly matrilinear societies, in which husbands relocated to wives' villages and children were born into and grew up in uxorial homes. Nurturing practices did not differ significantly from those of the

Eskimos until puberty. Among the Sarcee, mentors were assigned by tribal leaders to preadolescent boys and charged to build their stamina and endurance. Bathing holes were kept open all winter so that boys periodically could be dipped into the icy water. In the absence of a water site, boys were rolled, naked, in the snow. If a camp site moved, boys were detained for hours and then had to run to the new encampment.[37]

Pubescent Naskapi girls of eastern Canada performed initiation rites similar to those of the Tlingit. Wearing caribou menstrual hoods decorated with porcupine quills and a fringe, girls were isolated for ten days in menstrual huts. Local folklore predicted sore eruptions and hair loss from the touch of a menstruating woman.[38] Preventive measures, such as gloves and scratching sticks, therefore were supplied so that girls could avoid directly touching their bodies. Taboos determined the diet. It was taboo for menstruating females to walk on a hunting trail,[39] and since the glance of a menstruating girl or woman was considered harmful to game, veils had to be worn during menstruation. Weapons lost potency if touched, and similarly, men were sapped of power. The condition was considered so forceful and debilitating that cloths dipped in menstrual flow were attached to cradle boards to weaken evil spirits that might attack infants.

❑ ❑ ❑

There were over thirty different cultures living along the coast from southeastern Alaska to northern California, many of them also matrilinear. Rank and wealth passed not to men's own sons but to their sisters' sons. At ten years of age boys were sent to live with their mothers' brothers, whose goods and possessions they would inherit. Girls therefore were the preferred gender because they added to both lineage and wealth.

Women passed on customs, taboos, and rituals. Many taboos, the origins of which are unknown, involved food. Eating foods gathered at low tide was forbidden during pregnancy. Yurok mothers, desiring small babies for easier parturition, thought working hard, sleeping little, and eating sparingly would achieve this goal.[40] To prevent convulsions, mothers and fathers did not eat deer or salmon until a newborn's navel had healed.

At the birth of a son, the father's sister was accorded the honors of cutting the umbilical cord, washing, wrapping, and cradling the infant. Mothers named their babies but only several days after their births. For the first ten days infants were fed a starchy nut gruel from a shell. Thereafter they were breast fed until they were about six months old. Revealingly, weaning in these cultures was called "forgetting the mother."[41]

The Yurok did not swaddle the lower extremities of their infants so that grandmothers could massage them with regularity, prompting early creeping. Babies never were allowed to fall asleep at dusk lest the setting sun permanently close their eyes. Animal fables were used to teach children virtues. The buzzard, for example, became bald after gluttonously putting his head into scalding soup. The eel gambled away his bones.[42]

When, at ten, boys went to their uncles, they were expected to honor, respect, and obey them as they did their fathers. A festive potlatch, or celebration, marked such occasions, at which, by tradition, the host was to give away some of his possessions or to free a slave.[43] Potlatches also were held as part of ritual puberty celebrations for boys and girls.

Yurok girls were, in fact, unique in that once their menarchial isolation ended, they were feted by the entire community. At puberty, girls had ears and lips pierced for earrings and labrets, and boys had their nasal septum pierced. Among the Haida, tattooing was a tradition.

❑ ❑ ❑

Over two hundred distinct tribal groups lived on the plains and foothills and in forests, deserts, swamps, and lowlands that stretched over continental North America. Topography, climate, and water for the most part determined the kinds of habitats they made, traditions and customs they evolved, and child-rearing practices they espoused. Prairie tribes of between one hundred to three hundred individuals, commonly divided into clusters of thirty to fifty persons, lived in villages or encampments near water sources and hunting grounds. Children were nurtured and protected by immediate family members as well as by the community at large.

The Plains buffalo provided the necessities of life for these people—food, clothing, shelter, and fire.[44] Recognition of this dependency was expressed in the many thematically buffalo-focused rituals. Newborns were wrapped in soft buffalo calfskin in teepees covered with buffalo hides. Buffalo hair was braided to make rope for cradle boards, moccasins, and even balls for games. Buffalo ribs were used for making sleds. Clothing was made from buffalo hides, and meals of buffalo meat were cooked by fires fueled by the dried dung of these animals.

Seneca children were taught to revere corn as Plains children revered the buffalo. Corn was central to survival, as it was for Mesoamerican natives.[45] At birth, a baby was dusted with cornmeal. Adults and children slept on cornhusk mats. Children played with cornhusk dolls that had cornsilk hair and played warrior games with weapons made from cornstalks. Corn also was used for magic and medicinal purposes. For nosebleeds, a ring of cornstalk was placed around a finger; a suspension of corn ashes was drunk to kill roundworms; a corncob scrubbing cleansed the body.

Seneca girls learned domestic chores from older clan women, not necessarily related. Boys were allowed to wander about alone, learning hunting skills at random. A first kill with a bow and arrow gave entry into adult hunting parties. Old tribal males assigned to boys at puberty took them into the woods or other isolated areas, where the boys tested their endurance by repeatedly striking themselves with a sharp rock until they bled.

Among the Mandan and the Sioux,[46] a rite of passage for the young was to demonstrate their strength in a grueling four-day endurance test held in the Okipa ritual.[47] Subjects fasted, and their backs, chests, and legs were slashed. They were skewered through the chest muscles and skin and suspended from the lodge's roof with long leather tongs. When they lost consciousness, they were considered receptive to visions and auguries.

The Sioux trained boys to regard bravery in battle as the highest virtue. The culmination of all aspirations was to earn the eagle feather that codes of bravery accorded warriors.[48] Games were competitive and geared to develop strength and mastery of hunting skills using bows and arrows. Boys wrestled, raced, played what is now called lacrosse, and raided wild beehives. Painful bee stings were worn proudly as badges of courage, and discomfort was suffered without complaint.

At the turn of the century, a Sioux tribesman named Ohiyesa amusingly described a boyhood adventure, the chronology of which is incidental to the image it evokes of like experiences in childhood since time began. While playing by a lakeshore, Ohiyesa and his playmates saw a huge moose swimming toward them:

We disappeared in an instant, like young prairie chickens, in the long grass. I was not more than eight years old, yet I tested the strength of my bow string and adjusted my sharpest and best arrow for immediate service. My heart leaped violently as the homely but imposing animal neared the shore. . . . I gathered myself into a bunch, all ready to spring. As the long-legged beast pulled himself dripping out of the water and shook off the drops from his long hair, I sprang to my feet. I felt some of the water in my face! I gave him my sharpest arrow with all the force I could muster, right among the floating ribs. Then I uttered my war whoop. The moose did not seem to mind the miniature weapon, but he was very much frightened by our shrill yelling. He took to his long legs, and in a minute was out of sight.[49]

Constantly challenged, adolescents developed stamina and learned how to endure hardships. Boys were sent off for two or even three days without food or water. They were made to run a day and a night without rest and without becoming lost. They were painted black to signify fasting, and villagers joined in teasing and tempting the boys with food and water. Tribesmen invaded the sleeping quarters of candidates, startling them with raucous war whoops. The future warriors were expected to leap up and grasp a weapon, ready to do battle. On moonless nights one boy would be selected to fetch water from a distant stream—to test skill in treading silently, to evaluate the proper disdain for darkness, and to observe courage in confronting the unknown.

Little Sioux girls were initiated to a domestic role with deerskin dolls and miniature teepees. They imitated their mothers, dressing puppies and carrying them like babies on their backs. As they matured, the serious business of life was introduced, and girls learned to do the complex work of a woodland environment that was needed to keep settlements thriving.[50]

They acquired skills in tanning skins and sewing resplendent beaded garments made from the tanned animal hides. They learned to sew furs and to weave cloth with distinctive tribal patterns. Their mothers taught them how to cure and store meats, to recognize special nuts, berries, and wild rice, and to prepare them all for meals and for storage. They were taught to recognize special herbs and to prepare medicinal concoctions from them.

Seasonal rituals, dictated by nature, determined the activities of men and women, boys and girls. March, for example, was the month to hunt for fur and to tap trees for sugar. While the men were hunting, women collected sap, boiled it, and condensed it to sugar. Maple sugar was made for general use as a sweetener; birch/ash bitter sugar was added to medicines; and white box elder sugar was reserved for ceremonial occasions. The better a girl learned these skills, the more desirable she was as a bride.

Not surprisingly, menarche marked the passage into womanhood, with ceremonious celebrations during which the sexual and reproductive mysteries of the female gender were disclosed. Each nubile girl was crowned with an eagle plume, proudly worn at the annual summer maidens' feast. Sioux tribesmen from many camps gathered for the occasion. Girls paraded before them in their finest beaded buckskin dresses, with cheeks touched with vermilion for color, displaying the eagle plume. Surrounded by chaperons, girls gathered in a circle, where their purity and nubility was publicly acclaimed. Girls chosen as brides went to live with their husbands in their camps. With them went the tribal knowledge and ritual heritage of the Sioux, especially that which pertained to pregnancy and birth. Taboos were strictly obeyed. For instance, pregnant women did not eat rabbit, lest a baby be born with a harelip.

To prepare for parturition, Sioux girls learned to make "beds" of sand with four pegs imbedded in the ground. Women pressed against two of the pegs with their feet, grasping the other two in order to push. Births were expected to occur quietly, without vocal expressions of discomfort. If a tribe migrated while a woman was in labor, it was left to her and a midwife to deliver the baby, perform the afterbirth ritual, and catch up with the others as quickly as possible. While praying, "May the child live and grow up to see you bear fruit many times," the midwife suspended the placenta from a fruit tree—a practice also observed by the Chiricahua.[51]

As parturition neared for mothers of Plains tribes, they were confined to birthing huts, whereas Dakota Tetons remained in their lodges to deliver, surrounded by kin.[52] The squatting-kneeling position of parturition was common to almost all North American groups. Generally, a pole or a rope provided an overhead grasp within easy reach to facilitate the pushing that would expel the infant from the birth canal.

The Omahas welcomed new babies with the invocation:

Ho! Ye Sun, Moon, Stars, all ye that move in the heavens.
I bid you hear me!
Into your midst has come a new life.
Consent ye, I implore!
Make its path smooth, that it may reach the brow of the first hill![53]

The Shoshone, from the Great Basin of Arizona and Utah, imposed myriad taboos on fathers, more so than on mothers.[54] At parturition, fathers could not make cords or arrows lest their infants be strangled by their umbilical cords. After births, as a form of couvade, fathers were not allowed to eat meat or grease, smoke, take a sweat bath, or gamble. Such measures were thought to strengthen paternal bonding. Deformed infants or twins were rejected and buried in badger holes.

Since the Paiutes of the Great Basin considered birth a voluntary process on the part of the infant,[55] it followed that, after the prescribed period of nine moons, infants would emerge only if hungry, just as hibernating mammals emerged seeking food. Mothers, therefore, fasted for several weeks prior to delivery. After birth, umbilical cords were carefully dried and preserved, placed inside buckskin pouches and used as cradle toys. These amulets, considered good-luck charms, were cherished and kept throughout life. The pouches were decorated with images of animals that were endowed with long life and were difficult to kill.[56] Lizards, who gave up their tails in order to escape, and turtles, who lived to very advanced ages, were considered suitable decorations for girls (figure 5.3). Snakes, rapid and difficult to catch, were selected for boys. Two umbilical pouches often were made, one kept empty as a decoy for evil spirits.

The Sioux term for a baby was "one who wears his navel," and the great spirits were invoked to protect the newborn. Brothers or even sisters of newborn Sioux males immersed themselves with bravado in cold water or rolled

Figure 5.3 Umbilical buckskin pouches decorated with beads. UNIVERSITY OF PENNSYLVANIA MUSEUM, PHILADELPHIA.

in the snow to welcome their new "warrior" siblings. Muskhogee newborns themselves were plunged into cold water, a portent of tribal expectations—winter or summer, Muskhogee children bathed in cold water four times upon arising.*

Among the Pawnee, unwanted babies were smothered. Otherwise, special papoose beds were lovingly prepared. First, cradle boards were fashioned from the center of freshly cut trees, symbolizing the desire that the "center of life" would be preserved.[57] Boards were decorated with a spirit of life, such as the morning star. In times of migratory hunts, in which facile mobility was expedient, lightweight and smaller cradles were made from skins, painted and decorated with symbols of life.

When Hupa babies of northwestern California were eight or ten days old, the stubs of their dried umbilicals were forced into a gash cut in young pine trees.[58] The gashes would be overgrown, and, in the process, the stubs would be sealed into the matrix. The Hupa believed this ritual ensured that children would grow straight and tall as the pines.

Newborns were not breast fed for the first few days but were given a gruel of mashed pine and hazel nuts. North American tribes commonly thought colostrum and early milk were fetid. As a first feeding, mashed berries gathered by Sioux families were funneled into a buffalo bladder that had been fashioned into a nursing bottle. Thereafter, mothers nursed babies for two to three years. A weaning gruel used by the Sioux consisted of wild rice, ground maize, venison broth, and pulverized dried venison, blended into a pap. It

---

*This curious custom, as we have seen, was common in many cultures through millennia, from the Stoics to the Celts, Vikings, Tierra del Fuego natives, and Plains natives of America. As we shall see, it was advocated even into the eighteenth century by Locke and others.

Figure 5.4
Muskogean infant burial jar from
Wilcox City, Alabama (Powell, 1903).

was the staple food for toddlers until the majority of their deciduous teeth erupted.

Sioux children were trained not to cry out at night, lest the sound attract predators. Children were habituated to awaken early, since game was most abundant at daybreak, and hostile attacks usually were plotted to begin in the early morning hours. Sioux children grew up in disciplined environments that all the same kept unfettered children's natural curiosity and sense of adventure. They were encouraged to meander through the camp and explore at leisure.[59] They never were shouted at or beaten.

Since infant and child mortality was high among all of the Natives, children were called generically "baby" or "little one" until such time as threatening childhood injuries, accidents, and illnesses had been survived. Then, at about five or even ten years old, children were accorded the personal identity of a given name.

Huron and Musquakie mothers buried deceased infants beside footpaths, firm in the belief that a baby's spirit could be reincarnated by entering the body of a woman passing.[60] Some ancient burials of Muskogean tribes were reminiscent of Mycenaean burials in *pithoi* (figure 5.4).

Pregnant women of the Pomos tribe of central California were forbidden to look at the sun or weave baskets. They delivered at home, not in birthing huts. While the significance of a so-called health-promoting ritual is not completely understood, Pomos children between five and ten years old had to lie on the ground and steel themselves unflinchingly while aged mentors etched their backs with shells until blood was drawn.[61]

Luiseno mothers, in coastal southern California, faced parturition in the family home. Unlike other cultures in which infanticide was the fate for twins, the Luiseno considered twins to be magical, with special powers. Consequently, Luiseno twins were lavished with gifts from those seeking favors and intervention from the great spirits.

Adolescent Luiseno, Yuroks of San Joaquin, and Anza-Borrego boys were given hallucinogens during initiation rituals. These rites were held only every few years and in four phases: the drinking of *toloache* made with jimsonweed, the challenge of the ant ordeal, sand painting, and the fire dance.[62] Village elders selected the boys to be initiated into the tribes as adults. Their fathers rehearsed ancient songs and legends with sons and left tribal leaders to give instructions in ceremonial dances. Shamans mixed the intoxicating *toloache* by grinding dried jimsonweed leaves mixed in water. Naked boys sipped the brew until hallucinations impassioned their dances around the central fire in the company of adults participating in the ritual. The next day, boys were introduced to secret and sacred canyons, where further tribal legends were narrated as they learned to paint rocks with tribal symbols.

The ant ordeal tested the courage and mettle of denuded boys who were plunged onto red ant hills to endure stinging bites of the ant colony, which later were extracted from the backs of the stalwart initiates with nettles. Sacred sand paintings full of symbols were created by the high priests or shamans as gifts for newly designated warriors. The same symbols were employed for girls in their initiation. The finale of the puberty rites was celebrated outside the ceremonial house by all of the community, performing a fire dance around a huge bonfire.

Luiseno boys engaged in a ritual that purportedly prophesied how long a life could be anticipated.[63] A pit resembling a burial site was dug, and in the floor of the pit a string outline of a body was laid out, bordered by three flat stones. Boys entered the pit and jumped from stone to stone without stumbling, lest the destiny of a shortened life be foretold. As part of their initiation rites, Luiseno girls were given tobacco in warm water to swallow. Should a girl vomit, her virtue was considered questionable.

The puberty rites of Anza-Borrego, Hupa, and Pomo girls involved a quasi-burial that took place in daytime.[64] In a ceremonial chamber called the *wamkic*, girls, with faces painted black and wearing basket caps and garlands of flowers entered a pit and were surrounded with sand. Two warm stones placed on abdomens and between legs were supposed to ease menstrual cramps and childbirth pain in the years to come. Postnatal women repeated the ceremonial pit ritual to diminish pain and compress the uterus. For the nubile girls, songs were sung about food, uxorial duties, maternity, parturition, and child care. After four days the girls left the pit, armed with a duty to abstain from meat, salt, and cold water for a prescribed period of time. Shamans made the girls distinctive circular sand paintings, two to three feet in diameter, to explain life's interrelationships. Colors—white for the Milky Way, red for the sky, and black for the spirit—were used to depict the elements of earth, sun, moon, mountains, and creatures. Sand paintings of the Pueblo, Luiseno, and Navaho served a similar instructive purpose. In all of the tribes these drawings were considered sacred and were destroyed at the end of the ceremony.[65]

❑   ❑   ❑

Tribal rearing practices generally were similar, with shared customs and rituals, across North America.[66] Weather permitting, children in most communities often went naked about the village until they were four or five years old. Weaning at around three years of age was the norm. The Tetons weaned their young at about five, with an ear-piercing ceremony commemorating the achievement. At an early age children commonly were taught to recognize and gather nonpoisonous nuts, berries, and fruit. Tattoos and decorative marks usually were incised with bone needles. Rituals of endurance were inflicted and tolerated. Some called for a plunge into an icy river or the painful stings of ants and centipedes. Boys in some tribes were given a mouthful of water and expected to run on hot, sunny days without swallowing the water. Play imitated life. Games of capture and fighting dominated. The Louisiana Creek even called their two-stick ball game "the little brother of war."[67] Blackfoot boys were given demeaning names prior to a first war party. The derogatory appellations were cast off only after an enemy had been captured or his horse had been stolen.[68]

Boys' puberty rituals commonly involved the forced avulsion of a tooth, piercing of lips and nose, or slitting nostrils. Girls were forced into menstrual huts, enduring days—sometimes weeks—of fasting. Teton fathers employed shamans to officiate at public ceremonies honoring daughters several weeks after menarche. Buffalo skulls were placed on an altar and sage burned as incense while the shamans' incantations listed desired virtues in young women. They painted the girls' foreheads and parts in their hair with red paint. Eagle feathers were tied to crowns as the following blessing was intoned: "The spirit of the eagle and the duck are with you. They will give you the influence of the sun and the south wind. They will give you many children."[69]

Pacific or Plains young men bought their brides, paid for with horses or furs. Prospective grooms from the east and north paid for their brides with a prescribed period of servitude in the households of the girls' parents, usually until the first child was born.

The Delaware, a northeastern Algonquian tribe, lived in river meadows, incorporating environment to complement custom. After purifying themselves in sweathouses twice a week to prevent illness, they sought relief from the steamheat by plunging into the river or rolling in snow. After bathing they painted their bodies with berry-juice vermilion.[70] Settlers had this exogenous color in mind when they began to refer generically to Native Americans as "redskins." The Powhatan of Virginia used red inkberry made from roots and hickory oil to paint their heads and shoulders.[71]

At puberty, Delaware boys were sent alone into the woods, where they fasted for several days. Raised to be hunters, Powhatan boys had to pass daily morning archery tests before their mothers gave them breakfast. In adolescence the initiation was fierce, lasting several grueling months. The pain from beatings and endurance tests was mitigated by the jimsonweed allotted them.[72]

Powhatan girls grew up in a matrilinear culture observing daily decisions on issues regarding property and clan responsibilities. At menarche they merely were isolated in compliance with the simple initiation requirements of the tribe.

The Eastern woodland tribes had over thirty different cultures. Among them, the Micmac culture was unusual because it assigned specific tribe members to children as "official watchers of young people." One of their responsibilities was to keep village chiefs informed about young marriageables.[73]

Southeastern tribes included the Natchez of the lower Mississippi valley, the Creek, Choctaw, Chickasaw, Apalachee, Timuca, Calusa, and Seminole. The last four tribes lived in what is now Florida.

The Natchez used Spanish moss to cradle newborns, head-molding straps, bison-wool garters for the legs, and bear oil to rub over the body. Village elders dispensed discipline. Marriage among the Natchez, in contrast to other North American tribes, was as late as twenty-five years of age.

Creek and Muskhogee cultures had similar nurturing attitudes, mores, and laws.[74] Matrilinear authority was supreme. Mothers were licensed to commit infanticide of children under one year; after one year the tribe punished offenders for murder. Discipline and punishment of children among the Creek were almost always physical. Children's legs were scratched with sharp items, such as garfish teeth, to the point of bleeding. Their care was left entirely to the mother. Each clan employed older uncles to provide male role models for boys, while the boys' fathers performed the same avuncular duties for their sisters' boys. Uncles taught games related to hunting, fishing, and the skills of battle. Boys in latency (four to seven years of age) were tattooed with elaborate tribal designs and were expected, of course, to tolerate stoically the painful procedures. Bravery or distinguished service in battle were the prerequisites to honor and a permanent name.

Muskhogee[75] boys slept on panther skins, girls on fawn skins, hoping that the attributes of the respective animals would transfer to them. Girls were given permanent names, but boys' names were temporary until they proved their prowess according to tribal standards, with each successful trial or test earning a new and stronger name.

Menses was considered unclean. At such times women and girls avoided being upwind or upstream from males and made their way to menstrual huts until menses ceased. While there, special containers were provided from which to eat. Following menses, they bathed and dressed in clean attire before returning to the community.

Clan women acted as matrimonial agents on behalf of smitten young men. Once informed of a suitor's intentions, it was up to the girl to accept or reject a young man's proposal. Acquiescence or refusal was both coquettish and subtle. In a charming ritual, a girl signaled acceptance by placing a bowl of hominy outside her door. A boy's request to sample the grits always was granted by the girl, and the betrothal was publicly recognized. The absence of the hominy bowl, however, indicated a girl's lack of interest, allowing a somewhat abashed but dignified retreat of the unfortunate fellow. Before capitulating, a courting couple had to demonstrate homemaking skills suitable in a marriage. A young man built a dwelling and killed and butchered an animal. The intended wife cooked a meal for the lad, perhaps of the slain animal. When the meal was over, the union was considered official by the community.

Cherokee[76] women who were pregnant drank a potion made of touch-me-nots to frighten the baby out of the womb, elm bark to make the vaginal passage smooth, speedwell for the baby's good health, and pine cones for longevity. Pregnant women could not eat spotted trout, which they thought caused birthmarks; salt, which caused swelling; rabbit, believed to cause deformed eyes; or squirrels, who climb up trees when frightened and therefore delay vaginal passage. No handkerchiefs could be worn or carried so that the umbilical cord would not strangle the infant.

In Florida, according to the journals of Jacques Le Moyne de Mourgues, Timucua natives regarded their chief as being a descendant of the sun. Their homage to him involved the sacrifice of a firstborn.[77] Sacrificial victims were placed on wooden stumps and slain in the presence of the king, while tribal women danced and mothers wept (figure 5.5). To accompany dead royalty to the afterlife, the Natchez sacrificed attendants or family members. Commoners on occasion showed their respect by sacrificing one of their children, throwing it at the feet of the pallbearer.

❏ ❏ ❏

The best-preserved North American aboriginal archaeological sites are located in the southwestern territories of Arizona and New Mexico, extending

Figure 5.5 A Florida woman sacrificing her firstborn to the king (Payne, 1916).

into southern Utah, Colorado, and northern Mexico. The ancient cultures of Anasazi, Hohokam, and Mogollon are the precursors of today's Pueblo, Zuni, Apache, Navaho, Hopi, Pima, and Papago people.

Anasazi—the Navaho term for "the ancient people who disappeared"— left many infant burial sites in the Canyon de Chelly (300–500 A.D.). In death they buried their babies with tender care as a testimony to the love and care they had extended to them in life. Infants were wrapped in yucca fibers, shrouded in fur, and interred in their cradles or on their cradle boards. Mortuary offerings of baskets, sandals, and beads were left by mourners at the burial sites.[78]

Pueblo babies were not acknowledged by the community until the nineteenth day of life, when their births were festively celebrated by guests, who gave the newborn gifts of cornmeal. In the early morning of the twentieth day, mothers bathed in juniper tea and washed their hair in a symbolic ritual of purification. Guests again were received to bathe and scrub the infants with ears of corn. Dusted with cornmeal and named by godmothers chosen by the parents, infants were strapped onto cradleboards, and, for the first time, taken out into the early morning to be presented to the rising sun.[79]

The matriarchal Zuni culture recognized only matrilinear descent. Women commonly resided in the places of their births throughout their lives, and men—husbands, sons, brothers—were regarded as outsiders; they enjoyed only ceremonial ties to their families' households. The men farmed property that belonged to the women, and crops were stored in warehouses communally owned by village women.

Menarchial girls had no puberty rites, but males, seven to eleven years old, were initiated every four years. Zuni girls were enculturated by their mothers and other women leaders of the tribe. They were instructed, for example, about two shrines sacred to pregnant women—one at which to pray for a healthy baby if a prior child had been aborted or had died, and one at which to request a preferred gender. Other rituals were enforced to fulfill maternal wishes: men were banned from the house when women wanted a girl baby. When they wanted to give birth to twins, they ate bread carried by husbands during a deer hunt, since twins were a common phenomenon with does.[80]

Twinning, endowed in many cultures with desirable mystical qualities, was feared by the California Pomo, who believed their power harmful to the family. To prevent having twins, the Pomo culture advocated side-to-side coitus. The Washington Quinault believed that twins could never be separated and that they would even die together. The Iroquois of New York credited twins with powers of divination, and the California Yumans imagined a special heaven for twins.

To prevent a stillbirth, Zuni women did not look at corpses. Piñon nuts were blamed for slow labor, and rapid-growing beans were swallowed for an accelerated labor. Babies would be born deaf as punishment to thieving mothers. Even a seemingly innocuous activity, such as scattering bran over an oven to test its temperature, was an ill omen that gave babies acne.

Zuni babies were bathed at birth in warm, slightly starchy and pasty yucca water and rubbed with wood ashes* to purify them. Ears of corn were placed by babies' sides, symbolizing life. Ears were pierced and adorned with turquoise. When eight days old, paternal grandfathers took their grandbabies outdoors and held them aloft before the rising sun. Only then, and for the first time, were infants placed in their cradles. Should an infant die, the cradle was burned.[81]

Girls were typically the preferred gender. At birth, infant boys' penises were sprinkled with water to "shrink" them, keep them small, while the vulvas of infant girls were covered with a gourd so that they would grow big.[82] Examples of rituals strictly adhered to in order to ensure healthy child development are listed in table 5.3.[83]

Zuni boys and girls grew up with different, gender-related vocabularies. For example, girls learned to say "Hia Atu!" for "Ouch!" Boys said, "Cha Kochi." Girls expressed fatigue by muttering "Hish Atu Ho Utechika"; boys said, "Hish Kochi Ho Utechika." When girls felt cold, they said, shivering, "Hish Itsu Tetse"; boys were taught to say "Cha Itsu Hish Tetse."[84] Lullabies also were gender-specific. Mothers soothed baby boys in song with references to turquoise, a male symbol:

---

*The practice is reminiscent of the Hebrew salting of newborns. The soda ash probably had astringent properties similar to the natron used by the Hebrews.

TABLE 5.3
ZUNI RITUALS FOR CHILD DEVELOPMENT

Function	Ritual	Reason
To walk	Held over smoke of burning deer hair	Deer are fleet-footed
To hear	Deer ear wax placed in baby's ears	Deer have keen hearing
Teething	Gums rubbed by someone who has been bitten by a snake	Snakes "like" biting
To talk	Tongue of a mockingbird is cut out for the baby to lick	Bird released to grow new, more vocal tongue
Hair	Cuttings are burned	Wind may scatter the baby's fortune
Fear	Moistened embers placed over the baby's heart	Not to be afraid of the dark

There, there, there,
Dear be quiet,
On a turquoise baby board
Hush, take care
On a turquoise baby board.

Girls were crooned to with references to moonlight and flowers:

There, there, there
Girl, why are you angry
Why are you captious, dear girl?
Here, here are wild roses
Here, here is moonlight.
The flowers, take them, dear.[85]

Zuni children were disciplined by the bogeyman, *Atoshle*, actually consisting of a couple. The old man and woman were assigned the role of punishing naughty children. The old woman carried a basket slung over her back to carry off miscreants, and the old man tripped misbehaving children with his crook.

Navaho infants were sprinkled with corn pollen at birth, and the afterbirth was buried secretly to keep witches from using any in their magic against children. As with virtually all other Southwestern tribes, babies were swaddled to a cradle board, but the Navaho did not swaddle until newborns were four weeks old. An easygoing and gentle nurturing also was characteristic of the Navaho, who were warm, nonpunitive, and above all, patient and forgiving with their children. Tantrums or aggressive behavior were ignored as passing phases.[86]

Hopi mothers[87] prepared for birth by avoiding all forms of knots during pregnancy, for these had the power to restrain, to tie up babies. Hair was worn loose, and clothing was never knotted. Women averted their eyes away from snakes, fearing their power to twist a baby inside the womb, causing a breech delivery. Those who had lost a child or children were given baby dolls, called *tihu*, for a safe pregnancy and a healthy baby. Husbands made parturition prayer-sticks during the winter solstice. When labor ensued, weasel skins were passed over mothers' abdomens. Clan women and mothers of birthing daughters assisted with births. Placenta—or a stillborn—always was thrown over the northeast cliff of the mesa. Girls' umbilical stumps were tied to stirring sticks for cornmeal, called a *silkuh*; boys' stumps were tied to arrows. The sticks or arrows then were wedged into the rafters of houses.

Fathers remained in *kivas* (sacred ceremonial rooms) without seeing their babies for twenty days. Both grandmothers took charge of infant toiletries. On the twenty-first day, fathers emerged from the *kivas* for the naming ceremony. Cornmeal was sprinkled on the ground along a path to the mesa's edge. There, infants were named and presented to the sun.

Children of Pueblo cultures were given kachina dolls that were widely used as instructional aids. They learned to recognize over three hundred kachinas, representing animals, plants, weather elements, insects, and "people." The dolls themselves were not sacred but personified sacred subjects, such as ceremonial divinities.[88] A basic elemental kachina, called a *puchtihu*, was flat and bare of details and was presented to babies. The detail complexity of the dolls increased as the child grew in years and sophistication. The *hololo* was friendly and represented the song of the kachina. Some dolls personified virtue; others, foolish behavior, such as the well-known "mudface." Hopi *wuyak-kuita* and long-beaked, buffalo-horned Zuni *nataschka* dolls evoked terror, for they were personifications of deities who ate unruly children.

Children were introduced at a young age to kachina impersonators—good deities dispensing gifts and the frightening ones who disciplined children. At the annual winter *powama* festival, Hopi boys and girls of eight years engaged in initiation ceremonies. Children descended into a *kiva* and sat on the floor—boys to one side, girls to the other. They were sprinkled with water and touched four times with ears of corn as a blessing, after which a startling howling noise ensued. Over the roof of the *kiva* an eerie rattling was heard and the ladder leading into the *kiva* began to tremble. Down the ladder appeared kachina impersonators bearing yucca whips. The first was called *Angwushahaii*, Mother Whipper, whose face was an inverted triangle with crow wings for ears. She was followed by two aides, the *Hu*, painted black with white spots, wearing red kilts and black masks with horns, and showing bared teeth and a long stripped beard. The giant kachina *Shuyuku* carried a knife, bow and arrow, and a basket on his back. Parents told children that the Shuyuku lived in fire, to discourage them from going near the hearth. At the ceremony, the children were admonished to obey their parents or the Shuyuku would carry them off in his basket and eat them. Ritual, nonpunitive whipping followed, and one by one the children were led to a sand painting of the kachinas to receive their four lashes. When all the children had been flogged, the kachinas whipped each other. The ritual ended with presents: the children were given cornmeal and sacred feathers. The following morning each child prayed to the sun and was given a ceremonial name. En masse they returned to the *kiva*, where, after more ceremony, the kachina impersonators unmasked themselves, revealing their identities to the astonished children. The children then were reminded that they in time would be responsible for teaching their children the kachina culture, and they were sworn to secrecy.

At sixteen to twenty years of age, Hopi girls were eligible to participate in the corn-grinding and hair-arranging ceremony.[89] Hair was braided into bilateral loops over the ears, forming large squash blossoms. This coiffure, called *nasumtah*, symbolized nubility. Boys engaged in mock battles, after which they were allowed to sleep in the *kiva* and were permitted to court marriageable girls.

Navaho girls experienced an intricate initiation at puberty, called the *kinalda*.[90] The ritual lasted four days and nights, with food taboos and "molding." Everyday older tribal females gave the girls massages to beautify the body. The girls ground corn every morning, had their hair washed, and ran to the east at dawn. Younger girls were invited to run along with them but were not allowed to pass the initiates or they would grow older before the initiates did. At the end of the four days the now-marriageable girls assumed their place in their matrilineal culture, in which all property, including the prized sheep, would be passed on to them by their mothers. Aware that brothers reared and nurtured sisters' offspring, husbands did not expect to assume responsibility for raising their own children.

Apache preadolescent girls were encouraged to compete with boys in all physical endeavors. In the absence of males, women were expected to guard the camps and therefore were taught how to fight. Girls also became skilled in hunting small game.[91] As each Apache girl approached adolescence, a four-day initiation ritual was held in her honor. On day 1, four spruce saplings were formed into a pyramid as a ritual teepee, and a buckskin carpet was placed on the floor. The maiden dressed in a yellow-dyed buckskin dress, symbolic of pollen, which was sacred. As a shaman chanted, she danced around the pyramid. During the subsequent three days, no smiling, laughing, or emoting of any kind was permitted. The girl was forbidden even to think of her future. At the termination of the ceremony, she was given a ritual wand made of yucca to plant in the ground. After her guests departed, the ritual tepee was dismantled. On the ninth day, the girl was cleansed ritually with yucca suds and declared nubile.[92] By tradition, these rituals always were chronologically timed to an individual's menarche. In the nineteenth century, however, the U.S. government restricted the celebration of puberty rituals of the Apache nation to the Fourth of July. The custom persists, with one common ceremony for all of the girls who have come of age during the year.

By the time Apache girls wed and were with child, their culture had prepared them to end the life of a twin or a feeble or abnormal infant. Healthy first babies were sprinkled with sacred corn pollen. They were wrapped with strips of buckskin onto a special cradle board with fur of a fawn or rabbit placed over crumpled grass as bedding. Soft shredded bark was placed between the legs as diapers, and the babies were tucked in with more fawn fur.[93] A baby who died was wrapped in its cradleboard and, hung on a tree, left swinging in the wind.[94]

Mesoamerica

The cultural antecedents of the Aztec can be traced to the Olmec (1500 B.C.), Monte Alban (500 B.C.), and Toltec (200 B.C.) cultures and various linguistically linked smaller tribes. While the Olmec stand out artistically, little is known of the culture or, indeed, the significance of their works of art. The huge stone head monuments, over two meters high, and the small man-child figures with phenotypic infantile obesity and fingers in the mouth remain, however, archaeological treasures of beauty and great interest.[95] Much, on the other hand, is known about the history of the Nahua-speaking people called the Aztec and the ways in which children fared in their culture. The topography and climate of their habitats in central and western Mexico varied, but the rich archaeological record they left, steeped in religion and mysticism, reflects a culturally homogeneous people.

The Aztecs consulted the deities about every detail of their lives and the lives of their children, beginning with pregnancy. Many of their customs, including those now viewed as gory and repugnant, were rooted in the belief that the gods had supreme power over mere mortals, and these gods constantly were either petitioned through prayer or appeased with sacrifices.

Figure 5.6
Tlazolteotl wearing her flayed skin,
crescent moons, and maggots, and
giving birth (Schendel, 1968).

Tlazolteotl was an exotic deity adorned with the flayed skin of sacrificial victims, signifying new vegetation and growth, and crescent moons, symbols of femininity and fertility. The maggots on her lips represented rejuvenation. This deity was always depicted giving birth[96] (figure 5.6). Aztec mothers prayed to Tlazolteotl for a safe parturition and healthy children. Babies were thought of as "gifts of Tlazolteotl." During labor, mothers invoked the spirit by drinking a potion of powdered ciuapatli root and ground opossum tail and had their vulvas packed with a mash of calabash root, soaptree roots, a bloodstone, and eagle's excrement. If a normal delivery was not possible and the mother's life was compromised, an embryotomy was performed to save the mother. An obsidian knife was inserted into the vagina, and the fetus was extracted piecemeal. A mother who died in childbirth was considered a heroine. If a mother gave birth to a deformed infant, the state assumed responsibility for its care in a state-owned and -operated refuge adjoining the zoo.[97] It was a unique culture for the times, indeed, that sanctioned abortion to save the life of the mother and had state assistance for the anomalous child.

Midwives ceremonially cleansed newborns' mouths, breasts, and heads to remove what were considered the evil forces of sexual appetite that had been acquired while passing through the birth canal. A few drops of water were placed in the mouth of the newborn with the incantation: "See with what you will live upon the earth, so that you might grow and flourish, receive it." As the head was sprinkled, the midwife incanted: "Receive and take the water of the lord of the world, that this clear blue celestial water might enter your body and live there."[98] The umbilical cords of males were dried and placed on battlefields as a dedication to battle and bravery. Girls' cords were buried under household hearths.

Most commoners simply named their babies without fanfare after the day of birth. Aristocrats engaged magicians from local temples to consult their babies' horoscopes for propitious names. Boys were given dynamic names like "smoking crest" or "speaking eagle" or were named after ancestors or animals. Girls received names of flowers, stars, or birds. Four days after birth, aristocratic families hosted festive events at which babies were formally named. Guests rubbed the infants' knees and joints with ashes from the fire, signifying their hope that they would be spared rheumatic conditions in the future. Sacred fires intended for the newborns' exclusive use were built and carefully guarded. Not a faggot could be removed from a fire unless it pertained to an infant's need.[99]

Mothers nursed their babies until they were three years old. Weaning began with a highly regimented, specific, and restricted diet of tortilla. One half of a flat, twelve-inch-diameter cake made from cornmeal mixed with lime and water was the daily allotment for three-year-old children. This was increased to one tortilla daily at five years of age. At nine, children were fed one-and-a-half tortillas, and at thirteen, two tortillas. Thereafter, the diet was supplemented with beans.[100]

There were specific remedies for childhood ailments.[101] Diarrhea was treated with pulverized avocado pit mixed with charcoal and plantain water. Asthmatic children had to inhale the smoke of burning jimsonweed. For parasites, children drank a mixture of papaya and artemisia or the emetic *Cephaelis ipecacuanha*. Fever was treated with aspirin-rich willow leaves soaked in water or with cold enemas. Tonsillectomies were performed for what were termed "spongy throat tumors."

Apparently common to both the Aztec and the Maya, many rituals were performed to assure normal child development and growth. There were, for example, preschool lip-piercing ceremonies for boys and breast and hip scarring for girls, to sharpen intelligence. A small stone, called a *tentetl*, was placed in a boy's incised lower lip, and, using an obsidian knife, a girl's breasts and hips were cut with small slits. Every four years, children were the focus of ceremonies in which they were lifted by the head to "stretch the neck," and limbs also were stretched to ensure growth. There was an annual ceremony in which children's fingers, legs, noses, and ears were pulled for the same purpose. Ixtlilton was the god who protected and healed Aztec children. Fray Shahagun described how the intercession of this god was invoked for a sick child:

This god had a temple made of painted wood, like a tabernacle, which contained his image. In this temple or tabernacle there were many bowls and tubs of water. . . . They called this water *tlilalt*, which means black water, and when a child sickened they took him to the tabernacle. . . . They gave the child to drink of the water, and he became whole.[102]

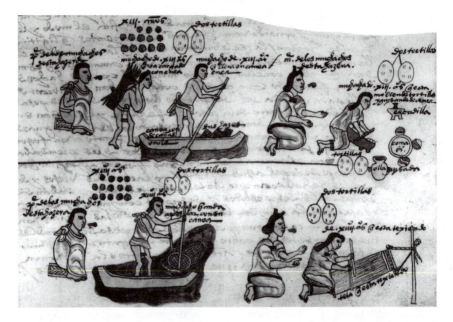

Figure 5.7 The Mendoza codex of 1541, showing boys being instructed by their fathers in gathering rushes and fishing. Girls are instructed by their mothers in the use of the *metate* and the making of tortillas and weaving.
BODLEIAN LIBRARY, UNIVERSITY OF OXFORD.

In imitation of their fathers, boys began to carry a small weighted bag around their necks when they were three years old. The weight gradually was increased until, by adolescence, boys were able to tolerate sixty pounds of weight, as did their fathers.

Boys learned fishing, canoe making, rush gathering, and sandal making (figure 5.7). Three-year-old girls were given domestic-related items of play, such as small looms or corn-grinding surfaces called *metates*. They also began to perform specific household chores at this age, learning how to weave and dye fabrics and how to stamp cloth with designs. At six years of age, these chores no longer were considered play.[103]

Aztec culture emphasized physical discipline, and children learned to endure various distinctly disagreeable experiences. Children were suspended over eye-stinging smoke of burning red peppers (figure 5.8). They were struck with the prickly maguey thorn leaf, exposed to the nocturnal elements, or detained in water-filled mudholes.[104]

Unlike the Maya, there were no elaborate puberty rites among the Nahua-speaking peoples. Physical changes of puberty were recognized in language: *Telpochtli*, referring to a young man, literally meant "he of the dark protu-

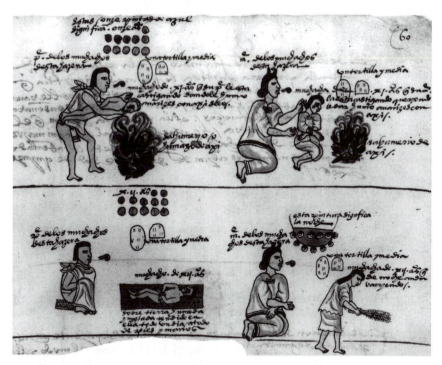

Figure 5.8 The Mendoza codex of 1541, showing smoke-and-pepper-fumes (Capiscum axi) discipline. Another boy is forced to lie in a mudhole with hands and feet bound. A disobedient girl is forced to work at night (the dark half-disk with "eyes" symbolizes night). BODLEIAN LIBRARY, UNIVERSITY OF OXFORD.

berance," and *ichpochtli*, which referred to a young woman, literally meant "she of the dark down." Save for a tuft of hair at the nape of the neck, boys' heads were shaved when they were ten years old. The tuft itself, called the *piochtli*, was cut when a boy captured his first enemy soldier.[105]

Boys and girls, aged twelve to fifteen, were sent to the *cuicacalli* at the temples, where they learned the music, singing, and dancing related to various religious ceremonies. Boys were sent off to schools within their *calpulli*, or ancestral group, when they were fifteen years old. They studied religion, citizenship, history, and most important, they learned military skills, the core of their training among these aggressive peoples. Every young man was expected to take at least one prisoner in battle during his lifetime. Priestly knowledge also was greatly respected, and boys from high-ranking families could qualify to study their religion further at the *calmecac*.

By the age of twenty, young men were considered ready for marriage to girls of at least sixteen.[106] Girls were strictly disciplined in preparation for their domestic wifely roles, with quiet decorum stressed. They were not permitted, for example, to speak at mealtimes. They were not permitted outdoors except, on rare occasions, for matters that were regarded as essential, at which times they were expected to keep their gaze downward.[107]

There were slaves in this society, but the children born of slaves were considered free citizens. Those children enslaved by parents to pay debts could not be harmed. This was an important point, since child sacrifice was practiced. It is not certain how victims were chosen. There is evidence that they were not slaves, although they may have been orphans or captives from some battle. Some children were drowned or decapitated in sacrifice to the rain god Tlaloc, their tears believed to ensure sufficient rain for the year. At Templo Mayor, a religious center in what is now Mexico City, a stone-lined pit once held the remains of children, ranging in ages from three months to eight years, who were sacrificed and dismembered in the name of Tlaloc.[108]

Each temple selected a youth for the questionable honor of representing the personified Aztec deity Tezacatlipoca.[109] For one year the boy was indulged with a luxurious life befitting a god on earth. No wants went unfulfilled. His only responsibility was to play the flute. When the year ended, he was readied for sacrifice. His pipes were dashed against the steps of the sacrificial pyramid as he was coaxed up to the ritual altar, where he was ceremoniously dismembered. His remains were disposed of—in contrast to adult war captives, who were offered to the gods in thanksgiving and when slain were cannibalized.

❏ ❏ ❏

Present-day Yucatan, Belize, Honduras, and Guatemala were the principal cultural centers of the Mayan civilization. Archaeological studies date pyramid remains as far back as 200 B.C.[110] and recognize three distinct periods of Mayan accomplishment: the early classic (300–600 A.D.), marked by the development of hieroglyphics and astronomy; the late classic (600–900), characterized by architectural and aesthetic evolution; and the postclassical (900–1500).

Women in this culture prayed fervently to Ix Chel, the goddess of childbirth, to become pregnant. Having children was a great joy in this culture. Women made pilgrimages in dugout canoes to the shrine of Ix Chel on the island of Cozumel. Incantations were intoned, and food sacrifices were offered to assure a safe pregnancy and delivery.[111]

When babies were born, midwives prayed and chanted while they severed umbilical cords with new obsidian blades over ears of corn. The bloodstained corn was smoke-dried, and the obsidian knife—used once only—was thrown into the river. The corn was planted in an auspicious season, and its harvest was shared with local priests. Seeds from each harvest were replanted yearly by family members. This responsibility was given over to every boy when old enough to do his own planting. Thus, it was said that he ate by the sweat of his brow and by his blood. In a murderous variation of this sanguine harvest ritual, the Pawnee yearly sacrificed a Sioux girl to sprinkle her blood over the corn crop.[112]

Head molding produced what is to modern eyes a deformity but was prized as handsome among many American cultures, including the Maya. The preferred molding was antero-posterior, resulting in a high, flat forehead. Mayan women waited five days after birth before attaching swaddling boards to the infant's forehead and occiput. Crossed eyes also was a desirable feature and was induced by tying a resin ball to the forelocks, forcing a child's eyes to focus on it. Ears, lips, and noses were pierced so that ornaments could be worn.

At about three months of age, babies were presented to priests to be named. Each baby was given four names: a formal given name, a surname, a conjoined lineage name from both mother and father, and a nickname. All had magical properties to the Maya, and each name was used with specificity—one for private use, one for public reference, one for illness, and one for love.[113]

Mothers cared for their children through latency. At the age of five, mothers tied one small white bead to the crown of a son's head. A string was tied around a girl's waist with a small red shell as a symbol of virginity. These adornments could not be removed prior to puberty rituals. The rituals were organized by a community-delegated sponsor and were celebrated communally. Many adolescents participated in each ritual—boys when they were fourteen and girls when they were twelve. The children gathered in a courtyard where a high priest and four assistant *chacs* placed pieces of white cloth on each of the children's heads. The priest sang an oblation and gave the sponsor a ceremonial bone, with which he tapped each child on the forehead nine times. Then he anointed with water the children's foreheads, faces, and interdigital spaces of fingers and toes, after which he removed the white cloth and cut off the white bead from each boy's crown. Mothers removed the red shells from their respective daughters' waists. The children were thenceforth considered nubile. The marriages that had been arranged by parents in childhood, typically took place during these puberty ceremonies.[114]

Marriageable young men without contractual obligations lived in a communal house set aside for them by village elders. The boys often painted themselves black to remind the community of their eligibility. During the day they worked with their fathers, learning by rote imitation how to farm maize, how to hunt, and how to weave cloth.[115] Girls spent their time with their mothers, learning home-economic skills and perfecting the complex art of making tortillas. This dietary staple was central to every home. Dried shelled corn was placed in a pot with water and lime and boiled until soft. Called *kuum*, the soft corn then was washed and the hulls removed. Then it was ground with *mano* and *metate*, until it became *zacan*, the cornmeal used to make tortillas over plantain leaves.

For the most part, children's lives were uneventful—agrarian and domestic in preparation for marriage and family. There were children, however, who were pressed into slavery and ritually sacrificed. A child could become a slave if born to a slave, if orphaned, or if purchased for that purpose. Orphans also could be purchased for sacrifice. A small boy would cost five to ten stone beads and could be sacrificed in two different ways: by cardioectomy or by drowning. Bows and arrows were reserved for the ceremonial sacrifice of adults.[116]

In the Mayan culture, a sacrifice by cardioectomy was the quintessential example of a ceremony by any standards, attended by ritual and costume, with dramatic processions of royalty, priests, and a corps of lesser luminaries, solemnly coursing through the main thoroughfare, slowing making their way up the broad steps of a pyramid that soared toward the sky. At the foot of the great pyramid, the hapless child was stripped, painted blue, and held down by four *chacs* with back arched over the sacrificial altar. The executioner, the *nacom*, thrust a stone knife between the ribs just under the left nipple, performing a deft and swift thoracotomy. He plunged his hand in, ripped out the pulsating heart, and held it aloft. The heart was placed on a ceremonial dish and given to the priest (*ahkin*), who quickly anointed the face of the Mayan idols with the blood of the slain child. When the blood had ceased flowing, the body was thrown down the steps of the pyramid to be flayed and the skin removed and worn by a priest for ritualistic dancing.[117]

Drowning sacrifices were held in the sacred well, the cenote of Chichen Itza. Children were hurled into this deep sinkhole of a sacrificial limestone pit (figure 5.9). The victim was thrown in at daybreak with hands and feet untied. At noon, if the child survived, a rope was lowered and the child was rescued and used for divination. Having survived this ordeal, the child was considered blessed, gifted, and capable of oracles. He would be queried about what the gods had planned for the future.

A third but uncommon form of childhood sacrifice was in vivo entombment, performed only for nobility. A young boy was sealed into the tomb of a dead king in order to join him in his royal sojourn to a reunion with ancestors.[118] The remarkable accounts of Maya child sacrifice are unique, both in ritual and in stark violence, and find no match in other American cultures.

Figure 5.9 Sacred cenote of Chichen Itza. COURTESY OF P. P. CECERE.

❑ ❑ ❑

The prehistory of the ancient Inca culture can be traced to around 8000 B.C., when crop and animal domestication began to evolve along the Andean plateaus of South America. Some of the mummies found in arid regions of Chile, suggest that a strong, religiously ritualistic culture existed early on. Elaborately mummified infants (c.3000 B.C.) have been found coated in clay, painted, and wrapped in leather casings with wigs made from human hair. One six-thousand-year-old infant mummy found in Peru had evidence of head swaddling and board molding.

It is thought that the Inca began to produce ceramic vessels around 2000 B.C. The remains of early religious ceremonial complexes date to around 500 B.C. The Mochica, Nazca, and Huari were Incan ancestral cultures that flourished between 200 B.C. and 1000 A.D. The classic Incan culture, centered in Cuzco, evolved from approximately 1200 to 1400 A.D., reaching the apex of its creativity in about 1438 and lasting until the Spanish conquest of 1532. The kingdom extended from southern Ecuador to northern Chile, across to Bolivia and into Argentina.

The Inca language expressed the clearly defined composition of their family units and the age-defined roles the culture recognized and expected in families and in the community as a whole.[119] As can be seen in table 5.4, the Incans referred to nine behavioral stages or milestones in the first twenty years of life, in contrast to a mere three for the subsequent forty years or longer.

Inca children were born into a closely related neighborhood group of clan members, called an *ayllu*, not unlike the *calpulli* groups of Aztec children or the *deme* of Greek children. Among the Inca, land was communally allocat-

TABLE 5.4
INCAN AGE GROUPS

Age	Name	Meaning
1–3 months	Antaguamarca	Sleeping child
4–8 months	Sompeguamarca	Swaddled child
9–12 months	Traguamarca	Defenseless child
1–2 years	Lloca	Child on all fours
2–4 years	Machapora	Frightened child
4–8 years	Tarariquea	Child with parents
8–12 years	Guamarca	Child
12–16 years	Cocopallac	Coca gatherer
16–20 years	Michoguayna	Messenger
20–40 years	Avcapora	Warrior
40–60 years	Chavpilco	Middle aged
over 60 years	Punoloco	Old sleeper

ed and expertly farmed, with terraced plains and rotated fields to ensure optimum crop yields. Each male baby entitled the family to an additional *tupu*, about an acre of land, whereas a family was credited with only one-half a tupu for a female baby. When people died, the land they had farmed was assigned to newborns for their future use. Babies, therefore, were a significant means of ensuring ample food and a livelihood. The average family size was five people, and not surprisingly, infanticide was rare. Abortion was punished by execution of both the mother and the abortionist. Twin births were considered a special gift from the deity, and mothers of twins were esteemed. Although there were no midwives and births generally were unassisted, a mother of twins would be summoned to help with a troubled delivery. At birth, umbilical cords were set aside to dry and be preserved. Infants' heads were molded with boards and swaddling bands, and until they learned to walk, babies were restrained in a four-legged cradle, either on the floor or tied to the mother's back with a shawl.[120]

Babies were nursed only three times a day. At feeding time, mothers placed their babies on the ground and bent over them. Once the cradle was outgrown, babies were transferred to a kind of playpen—a hole dug deep enough to keep them from mischief or harm in which rags and toys were placed.

There were commonly known remedies with which to treat sick children. Some of them were of dubious value but rooted in folklore, such as bathing

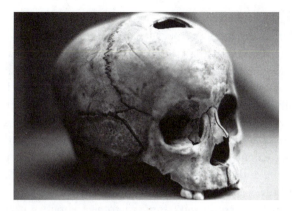

Figure 5.10 Skull of a trephined Peruvian child. Note the unfused suture lines.
SMITHSONIAN AMERICAN MUSEUM OF NATURAL HISTORY.

febrile babies in urine or giving the preserved umbilical cord to a sick infant to gnaw in hopes of restoring the baby to health and vigor. Other remedies, found in nature, in fact had healing features. Cocaine, a coca-leaf extract, can constipate and so was used to treat diarrhea. Quinua leaves, known for their antipyretic and antibacterial properties, were used to treat tonsillitis.

Some remedies were noxious. Trephining, an age-old practice of boring into the skull, purportedly to release the possessed of some evil, was practiced on children who most likely had seizure disorders[121] (figure 5.10). Cocaine sedation was probably used, either orally or by enema clysters, for anesthesia during prolonged procedures carried out with obsidian cutting instruments.

In the spring, the *situa* festival was celebrated to promote health. Children five to ten had the bridges of their noses scratched until they bled, and the blood was mixed with cornmeal. The paste this produced was smeared over the body, purportedly to protect the individual's health.[122]

Infants were left unnamed, generically referred to as a *huahua* (a baby). Once they were weaned, as toddlers two to three years of age, their survival was considered more probable, and the community recognized the occasion as a rite of passage with appropriate festive observances. The eldest uncle in a family was authorized to grant a niece or nephew a temporary name and to cut the infant's nails and hair, preserving them. A child received a permanent name at another ceremonial rite of passage at puberty.[123]

The Inca had no schools or written language. They learned cooking, weaving, farming, hunting, and all aspects of their culture and religion from their elders. Morality was summarized in one aphorism: *ama sua, ama llulla, ama cheklla* (do not steal, do not lie, do not be lazy).[124]

Selected girls, referred to as "chosen women," and sons of aristocrats, called the *Yanacona*, received special consideration from the community. Some authorities contend that the *Yanacona* was a servant class, since the Quechua word *yanay* means "to serve," and they theorize that these boys went to Cuzco to learn the trades of builders and miners.[125] It is believed more generally that *Yanacona* boys were sent to temples in the Cuzco valley for training by priest educators—to be taught the art of llama sacrifice and to learn to be administrators, to read ideograms, and to use the *quipus*, a knotted-string calculator. Like Egyptian boys, they learned geometry in order to measure and parcel land.

In this culture also families recognized festively a girl's coming of age. Each menarchial girl could look forward to a celebratory occasion of her own. A girl fasted for the better part of three days, at the end of which raw corn was served to her. On the fourth day the mother attended to her daughter's toiletries, bathing her and dressing her neatly in a white dress and sandals. Once again, an uncle was asked to preside as master of ceremonies. After presenting his niece to the family, who then presented their gifts to her, he conferred on her the permanent name with which she would be known for the rest of her life.

Boys had no individual rite of passage. Instead, a communally celebrated festival lasting three weeks was held yearly for all boys who had reached puberty.[126] Distinctive garments made from vicuña wool were fashioned by the boys' mothers. On the first day of the festival, a ritual sacrifice of a llama was made at the ceremony. Boys approached the shrine of Huanacauri, where high priests anointed their faces with the llama's blood. They solemnly were presented with a sling, a symbol of self-discipline and manhood as well as a tool used for hunting. They returned to Cuzco for the festivities that followed, at which the corn-liquor brew, *chicha* (still the favorite intoxicant of Andean people), was liberally drunk. At intervals during the celebration, parents ceremonially whipped their sons' legs in a symbolic assertion of their authority. On subsequent days there were races, dances, additional animal sacrifices, and athletic events that tested the endurance and courage the boys would need in wielding military might should the community need protection. The culmination of the annual celebration took place on the twenty-first day, with yet another communal gathering to ceremoniously drink *chicha* and to present each boy with the symbols of their newly-arrived-at maturity: a breech cloth and a gold ear-plug.

Yanacona boys were selected by the state to serve as pages or servants to aristocratic families, temple attendants, or as rewards for the valor of prominent nobles and warriors. These were desired positions, since most of these boys rose to positions of prominence as adults. The boys had four years of formal preparation for the various posts to which they would be assigned. In the first year they studied the Quechua language; in the second year they studied religion; using the *quipus* was practiced in the third; and in the fourth year they studied history. Corporal discipline was an integral part of boys' training, and routinely and daily they were administered ten beatings across the soles of the feet.

Representatives of the government periodically visited villages to select ten-year-old girls (generally the most beautiful) to serve the government's bidding as "chosen women."[127] They were sent to live with *mamacunas*, or teaching nuns, to receive a higher level of instruction in skills related to weaving, cooking, and other domestic activities. Some of these girls, called the *acllacuna*, were given by the emperor to nobles as second wives. Others were consecrated by high priests to serve as virgins of the sun. A few were destined to be sacrificed.

The state exercised supreme authority on the subject of marriage. Cyclically, it would be decreed that marriages would take place. All marriageable boys and girls were summoned before the governor. Prearranged betrothals were honored. Otherwise, boys and girls simply were lined up and paired. All of the couples then were married in a communal ceremony by the governor in the name of the emperor.

The religious rites of the Inca included sacrificial elements. Most commonly, however, the sacrifices were of food, coca, llamas, alpacas, guinea pigs, and figurines. Although human sacrifice did occur, it was infrequent—certainly not comparable to the staggering numbers of humans sacrificed by the Aztec, estimated at between fifteen thousand to twenty-five thousand a year.[128]

Human sacrifices were performed for the most sacred of the religious rites, such as a coronation, to appease the god of the mountains, or when ominous events generated widespread fear, such as a grave illness of one of their leaders or during times of famine or plague. Ten- to twelve-year-old children, boys and girls, were used for sacrifice. A number of preadolescents has been found preserved in ice at Andean altitudes of 20,000 feet, sacrifices to the mountain god who could bring snow, winds, condors, and rainclouds. Autopsies on these children have revealed intact organs with residual blood in the heart and lungs.[129] For other children, there is evidence that prior to the sacrificial ceremony they were feasted and given drink, presumably to induce a numbing stupor. They were ritualistically marched around the image of a deity several times and then strangled, bludgeoned, or had their throats slit. On occasions when children were cardioectomized, their blood was smeared on an effigy of a venerated idol. For the coronation of a new emperor, up to two hundred children might be sacrificed. If a person of importance became gravely ill, his son was sacrificed in the hope that the gods would accept the bloodline substitution.[130] Human sacrifices were executed among other South American cultures, such as the Guayaquil of Ecuador who annually sacrificed a hundred children to propitiate the gods and assure a good harvest.[131]

❑ ❑ ❑

The pre-Columbian civilizations[132] of the western and southern hemispheres, stretching from what is now called the Bering Strait to the Andean *cordillera* of Chile, flourished until the arrival of European explorers, who discovered and settled these territories in the fifteenth and sixteenth centuries. The appearance, cultures, and religions of the native people seemed strange, exotic, and primitive to the conquerors, who wrested from them their lore and legend, the cultural patterns of their lives, and their manners and mores. The threat of domination by the Europeans, however, was not as lethal as the alien germs they brought from the Old World to a continent of people who had no resistance to their diseases. Native Incan *quipo* records document population decimations from measles in 1531 and in 1557; from plague or typhus in 1547; and from smallpox in 1591. Twenty-five to 40 percent of the population died during those epidemics. Within seventy years of the first arrival of Euopeans, the Inca population dwindled from fourteen million to two million people.

Similar disasters took their toll on the Aztecs, the Caribbean Taino people, the Mississippian culture, and the Mohawks.[133] All of the Native populations were devastated by the introduction of germs against which their bodies had no defenses. Their vulnerability to newly introduced epidemic diseases extended well beyond the sixteenth century. The U.S. Congress passed the Indian Removal Bill in 1830, enabling the wholesale evacuation of the Choctaws, Cherokees, Chickasaws, Creeks, and Seminoles from their homelands. As late as 1839, forced to relocate to the west of the Mississippi River, they had to pass through cholera epidemics in Vicksburg, where large numbers succumbed to the disease. The Cherokee nation lost 25 percent of its people, and 45 percent of the Creek perished.[134]

AFRICA

The East

The great Nile civilization is the African culture best known and studied in the Western world. The splendor of ancient Egypt, with images of awesome pyramids, magnificent temples, and mighty pharaohs who ruled over

Nubians and tribes of Israel as well as Egyptians, overshadows other important and powerful African empires that flourished later on the continent. The
kingdoms of Ethiopia, the Noks of West Africa, the Congo, the Uganda in
East Africa, and the Monomotapa in South Africa all presided over sophisticated and advanced societies between the twelfth and nineteenth centuries.[135] Archaeological documentation, ancient cultural lore, written
chronicles of Arabic travelers—the most notable of which was written by Ibn
Battuta (1304–1377)—and diaries of Italian, Portuguese, Dutch, French,
and British explorers all testify to their considerable achievements.[136]

These African kingdoms began to evolve as far back as 1000 B.C., when
Egypt's New Kingdom faltered and, at Egypt's southern border, the territory of Kush and its capital, Meroe, were on the ascendancy. For over a thousand years, Kush advanced into an independent political state, with borders
extending as far south as Khartoum. This black empire thrived for more than
five hundred years, until the Axum empire of Ethiopia subdued it.

The Kush developed a form of writing that remains indecipherable. Azania, the name given in antiquity to Kenya and adjacent Somalia and Tan-
ganyika, was settled by megalithic Kush. It is known that this empire traded
with India and introduced Asian subcontinent botanicals into Africa, promoted a varied diet, the use of medicinals, and a more extensive hunter-gatherer toolkit. The Kush measured life in cycles that usually numbered eight
years. Societal expectations, skill levels, and community responsibilities were
incorporated into each age group, and children and adults were evaluated by
their accomplishments within these structured time frames. At eight, Kush
sons entered the first level of apprenticeship, while their fathers, after forty
years of work and practice, were considered to have completed the fifth level
in the lifecycle. Several of the eastern African cultures sustained and implemented this societal format. The Semitic-speaking Axum Empire of the
fourth century A.D. also left a script and architectural monuments and stone
art work as well. These people adopted orthodox Christianity, but little else
is known of the culture and mores of this society.

In the western part of Africa, about 200 A.D., the Nok culture, now
known as Nigeria, evolved into the kingdoms of Ghana and Hausa, important mercantile societies that controlled the caravan routes across the continent from Timbuktu to Nubia and Ethiopia. In East Africa, the empire of
Uganda was the most successful militarily. In South Africa, the kingdom of
Monomotapa, which had mastered smelting and the making of metal alloys,
peaked in power during about the sixteenth century. It gradually evolved
into the Zulu state.

In most of the early kingdoms matrilinear cultures prevailed. Children
belonged to and inherited from their mothers. The influences of both Chris-

TABLE 5.5
MARRYING AGE FOR GIRLS AMONG SOME
SEVENTEENTH-CENTURY AFRICAN REGIONS[137]

Region	Marriage Age
Sudan	12 to 14
North Guinea	10 to 12
Mandingo	14
Somali	13
Southeast Africa	12 to 14
Herero	12
Nama	8 to 9
San	7
Madagascar	10

tianity and Islam gradually shifted this bias to reflect patrilinear dominance and power. In a transition lasting centuries, privileges and rights that had been due to daughters were handed over to sons, radically redefining familial roles and relationships as well as property ownership. Child-nurturing patterns altered, influenced, as was the Congolese culture, by Christian doctrine and sentiment or by the tenets of Islam, the religion adopted by the majority of the African societies under discussion.

The positions in society of women and girls were especially affected by Islam. The birth of a girl no longer was considered good fortune. Marriage more and more was regarded as a means to ensure girls' economic security and personal protection. Contracted arrangements and early marriages began to occur at younger and younger ages. Eighteenth-century documents record marriages of seven-year-old girls (table 5.5).

Tribal custom amalgamated with Islamic and Christian traditions and widely different child-rearing practices throughout the continent evolved. By the end of the nineteenth century there were over five thousand indigenous African tribes and as many cultural notions of parental responsibilities. The traditions of the many cultures that lived in the southern Nile corridor survived virtually unchanged into the eighteenth and nineteenth centuries, when they were first described in print by Europeans.

Tribal variations along the Sudan were exemplified best in rituals and ceremonies attached to adolescent initiation. The Nuba, for example, expected their young men to master wrestling and thereby bestow honor on their villages. At puberty, boys were sent to live in wrestling training camps. The primary responsibility for boys was to develop into champion wrestlers. Curiously, with marriage, this vocation was abandoned altogether, and the more mundane but necessary tasks to sustain life became the manly focus.

Surgical alteration of the genitals were the most common initiation ritual. Some tribes practiced radical circumcision. The Nile Nubians circumcised both boys and girls. Girls were circumcised between nine and ten years of age with either a sunna or pharaonic type of procedure. Central Ethiopian groups performed the sunna ritual during infancy. The sunna resembled Moorish circumcision in that only the clitoral prepuce was removed. The pharaonic, however, was truly mutilating and invited recurrent medical problems. The clitoris, labia minora, and parts of the labia majora were removed. After applying raw egg and sugar, the vulva was infibulated and the lower extremities were bound together for fifteen to forty days until the vulva was fused. The unfortunate girls often had recurrent urinary tract and vaginal infections. Permanent kidney damage and infertility were not uncommon.* Some tribes practiced re-fusions after each parturition!

The suffering endured from this kind of mutilation compares to the excruciating pain associated with Chinese foot binding. The Chinese, however, abandoned the practice of footbinding in the early twentieth century. Pharaonic circumcision, on the other hand, is still practiced today. It is estimated that nearly 90 percent of Sudanese girls still are pharaonically circumcised.[138] Some twenty-six out of forty-three African nations still practice female circumcision, with high prevalences of 97 percent in Egypt, 94 percent in Eritrea, and 93 percent in Mali. All in all, across Africa and southern Asia, some two million girls are circumcised yearly.[139]

Large groups of health-care providers and mothers in many countries that continue the practice have joined in seeking broad, worldwide support to outlaw this cruel custom. In Kenya, an alternative called *ntanira na mugambo* (circumcision in words) is being introduced and popularized. During the weeklong ritual adolescent girls receive counseling and training in sexuality and conception, terminating in a community celebration of food, music, and dance.[140]

Some East African tribes eschewed circumcision but substituted nongenital mutilation as part of adolescent initiation rites. The Otoro, for example, forcibly avulsed the front incisors of boys and girls.[141]

One of the Abaluyia tribes, a Bantu people called the Tiriki, settled into an area called Azania, now Kenya. This group shared many common cus-

---

*Pharaonic circumcision has been called the "three feminine sorrows," bringing pain during the mutilation, at coition, and at parturition.

toms with several other East African tribes.[142] For example, in common
with the Ngoni, the Tirikis shaved the heads of newborns prior to naming
them. Older members of the Tiriki community cooperated in caring for
babies so that mothers could return to vital field work. When infants were
only six months old, they were handed over to seven- or eight-year-old girls
to be cared for and nurtured. While these Tiriki girls, themselves children,
were entrusted with the responsibility of child rearing, boys of the same age
began to learn how to herd and care for cattle.

Tiriki fathers made no attempt to bond with their young until they were
at least one year old, since it was believed that contact with the droolings of
babies caused severe itching of the skin. As far as is known, this curious
taboo of enigmatic origin did not exist in other cultures. In general, parental
involvement with children was limited. When children were six years old,
they were given over by their now-teenage caretakers to grandparents, whose
roles in the lives of children became the most influential and formative.

Adolescent Tiriki males were circumcised and ritually secluded with tribal elders for six months, during which time they were tutored in tribal lore
and legend. Dancing, singing, hunting, and learning the skills of warfare
were the focus of study. During this period, boys made costumes that were
worn in public at the end of the initiation. Tiriki boys advanced in their
communities according to the structured age-appropriate group, which
cycled every fifteen years.[143] Each age group had specific names and functions (see table 5.6).

The Ganda tribe of Uganda, which lived northeast of Lake Victoria, was
another of the Bantu-speaking groups. In this society, children were considered property, an unusual cultural attitude among African tribes.[144] Cesarean sections for complicated pregnancies suggest that both mother and child

TABLE 5.6
TIRIKI AGE GROUPS

Boys	0–10	yrs	Sawe
Initiated	11–25	yrs	Juma
Warriors	26–40	yrs	Mayina
Elder warriors	41–55	yrs	Nyonje
Judicial elders	56–70	yrs	Jiminigayi
Ritual elders	71–90	yrs	Golongolo
Elders	91–100	yrs	Kabalach

were important to the tribe. Nonetheless, children were commonly given away as presents to kinsman. Maternal uncles could claim 50 percent of sisters' children. Should a father balk, special payments might be accepted by an uncle in lieu of exercising his right to the children. Shortly after weaning, children were sent to live with a relative. Families, therefore, commonly were made up of other people's children, in the belief that the children would receive and benefit from a stricter upbringing. Exceptional boys were sent to the palace to learn tribal government. Detached as they were from children, it is not surprising that the Ganda did not consider adolescence any particular milestone and had no initiation rituals.

The Chagga of Tanzania raised their children collectively, separated by age groups. The young played, learned, and worked together under the guidance of village elders. Each group remained an intact unit until adolescence, when communal initiations recognized their manhood and the groups were disbanded.

The Somali, of the eastern Horn,[145] were a pastoral Cushite people who principally herded camel. Boys were sent at an early age to live in camel camps, and by the age of seven or eight they were skillful in all aspects of camel husbandry. Theirs was a harsh and lonely life, spent moving from pasture to pasture and sleeping in the open, with camel milk the almost-exclusive source of nourishment. Social contact with girls was limited to springtime, when, after the annual rainfall, pastureland could be found closer to their villages and hamlets. Nothing more than adolescent flirtations were tolerated, since virginity was highly regarded by the Somali and, as with the Nubians, was assured by infibulation or labial fusion.

The South

In Saharan Africa, proto–Bantu-speaking people started smelting iron about 2,500 years ago, significant of an accomplished early civilization. These people migrated southward toward equatorial Africa about 200 A.D., and to southern Africa about 300 A.D. Around 1000 A.D., origins uncertain, another round of migrations occurred. The Bantu-speaking black people evolved from these early migrants. Their cultural lifestyle did not begin to change until the Europeans arrived in the seventeenth and eighteenth centuries.

In south Africa a large number of separate tribes evolved. Although many customs and beliefs were held in common, significant differences emerged.[146] The Nguni and Sotho believed infants were formed from congealed menstrual blood abetted and strengthened by semen. Among the Zulu, dreams of green and black smoke or of buffalo foretold the birth of a boy, whereas dreams of a puff adder or a river crossing foretold a girl. Food taboos were common to all of the many tribes, although the specifics varied.

Zulu women, for example, avoided guinea fowl lest their babies resemble a bird head. Hot food also was avoided so that infants in utero would not be scalded.

In contrast to bush and savanna tribes that valued the self-sufficiency of unattended births, Zulu births were traditionally attended by midwives. Immediately after a birth, a fire of life was started, carefully tended and maintained during the period of maternal confinement. Zulu babies were made "hard and durable" by imbibing a mixture made from ground leopard whiskers, salamander skin, lion claw, and crushed meteorite. A castor-oil plant was inserted into the rectums of infants to the point of bleeding so that future lechery would be minimal. Babies were passed through the smoke of a medicinal fire to "immunize" them from disease. The Zulu, like the Sotho and Pedi, killed one of the infants of twin births. The Venda and Lobedu killed both twins. Other tribes, such as the Xhosa, Bomvana, Thembu, and Mfengu, considered all babies a blessing, including twins. Two euphorbia trees were planted so that the twins would grow with vigor and strength. Should one of the planted trees die, however, the corresponding child immediately was killed. Generally, as was the case among all early cultures, all deformed infants were killed. The one exception, as has been described, was the Aztec people in the western hemisphere who created institutions to care for surviving deformed newborns.

Like the !Kung, the Zulu mother believed that breast milk belonged to the baby in utero. Therefore, should she become pregnant, a currently nursing child was sent off to be nourished by the grandmother or someone else.[147]

The Zulu used their children in a ritual to promote rain. Anticipating that the gods would take pity on a crying child and spill forth needed rainwater, a child would be buried up to the neck and promptly retrieved at the end of the ceremony.[148]

Children commonly were named after ancestors. Long-awaited children born after prolonged barrenness or those considered particularly special for any reason were deliberately given odious names to confuse malevolent spirits, leaving them to think that these were children of scarce importance to the families. The Zulu named such children "vile" or "excrement,"* reminiscent of the medieval French eponym "ecreme" given newborns and "merdeux" for small children.[149] Likewise, the Zulu often gave boy heirs girls' names to confuse the enemy.

Childhood rituals that coincided with lunar phases abounded among

---

*Throughout Western Europe, Greece, and parts of Persia, it was not uncommon to give a child a coprogenic second name in order to ward off the *mal occhio*. Such a name was intended to make a child "unworthy" of attention from the evil eye.

Figure 5.11
The Tikoloshe child-eater.
COURTESY OF DR. WOLFGANG RENNERT.

Bantu-root cultures.[150] Venda infants were monthly held upside down and exposed to the full moon until first teeth erupted. In the light of the moon, vertical cuts were made in the cheeks of sick Bhaca, Xesibe, Mfengu, and Natal babies. The bile of sacrificed goats was rubbed into the wounds to effect the cure. The Khoi-khoi, Xhosa, and Thembu amputated the tip of the fourth left-hand digit* under moonlight in order to rectify failed toilet training.[151]

Little boys of four and five years learned herding, hunting, and warfare, while little girls learned to go to watering holes, to gather wood, cook, and tend infant siblings. All of the children were trained by example. Those who misbehaved were threatened with the child-eater, the Tikoloshe. The Zulu continue to refer to the Tikoloshe as the subordinate of the *sangoma*, or witch doctor. Abuse or mischief perpetrated on children is blamed on the Tikoloshe, exonerating the caregivers[152] (figure 5.11).

Like the Tiriki, Zulu adolescents entered initiation lodges where circumcision was performed and tribal lore and legend were taught. Menarchial girls were sent to isolation huts, where menstrual discharge had to be hidden to prevent witches from using it as an ingredient to do evil. They were not

---

*Ritualistic finger amputation was practiced in many cultures worldwide. Among the Dugum Dani of New Guinea, as recently as 1960, when a tribesman died in battle a consanguineous little girl, five to ten years old, was selected to have the first joint of a finger amputated. Such a sacrifice was believed to placate the ghost of the dead relative. The only anesthesia used was a rap to the elbow's ulnar nerve causing a tingling paresthesia. By adulthood, some Dani women had only stubs for fingers. Among the Bushman tribes, digits were amputated as a general measure for illness. Beginning with the little finger of the left hand, each significant episode of illness was addressed by removal of a joint. A lifetime of illness could leave an individual fingerless.

allowed to go near the cattle corral lest pregnant cows abort. While absorbing negative connotations associated with menses, girls nevertheless were welcomed as new adults and were bestowed with many gifts from the family when the isolation period ended. When Sotho girls married, they carried a magic beaded "name" doll. The name given to the doll would be used to name the first child.

Toward the northern fringe of the Kalahari desert in modern-day Tswana lived a Bantu-bush people, the !Kung. The "!" is the alveolar-palatal sound that resembles the pop of the tongue tip off the roof of the mouth. !Kung language today is still peppered with clicks, clucks, and tsks. The !Kung had taboos and customs[153] that resembled those of North American Eskimos. The !Kung considered an infant a true person only after it was introduced to the community. Births occurred in the bush away from the village. If children were wanted, they were taken into the village; unwanted children were buried immediately. Accepted infants were nursed for a prolonged period, often into the toddler stage. At any age, however, should a mother become newly pregnant, she smeared bitter botanical paste on her breast to force-wean the nursing child, since it was believed that the mother's milk now belonged to the new fetus.

Eleven-year-old boys were permitted to sleep around a so-called boy's fire, and girls at this age were sent to live with grandmothers. Boys were given toys that mimicked adult activities, such as small bows and arrows. At first, boys aimed their arrows at still targets. At twelve, their skills were considered adequately honed, and full-size bows and arrows were given to them for rabbit and bird hunting. A first big animal kill was celebrated by the tribe, and the hero was decorated with tattoos and small skin slits. These shallow skin cuts were filled with a paste of charred meat and fat to produce prominent cicatrices.

Initiation rites for boys did not involve genital mutilation but were held in secret places in long rituals lasting six weeks or more. They focused primarily on teaching tribal lore and legend. The most important traditions and taboos were related to the hunt. Like the Eskimos, the !Kung learned to keep their arrows from the sight and touch of menstruating females to preserve their weapons' potency. Similarly, coitus was avoided prior to a hunt so that male strength would not be sapped.[154]

At the ages of seven or eight years, the legs, thighs, buttocks, cheeks, and foreheads of girls were scarified in imitation of the gray antelope, thought to be a creature of great beauty and grace. !Kung girls were initiated at menarche in a special isolation hut. Menstruating girls covered their faces so that men would not lose their hunting prowess by the sight of them. While the girls remained in the isolation hut, the women of the village sang and danced for three to four days. Girls were not regarded as women until the end of the second menses, also celebrated. About this time, girls began to master the rituals related to trances. They were introduced to psychotropic roots, such as *gwa*, that induced a trance state thought to have mystical powers that aided the healing spirits evoked during times of family illness. There was recognition that these drugs had potentially damaging effects on fetuses, however, and during pregnancy trances were forbidden.[155]

In many African cultures it was important to free the souls of children who had died so that they could be reincarnated.[156] The Bageshu of Uganda buried their young in their houses, tending to the graves until the souls of the departed were infused into the bodies of siblings newly born. In such instances the buried children were thought to no longer possess their souls, and the bones were dug up and discarded. In the lower Congo, house burials of infants were thought to ensure future fecundity, with a single soul infusing itself again and again into the bodies of the newly conceived. Some West African tribes hid dead infants in bushes adjoining a path to allow the souls to leap into the bodies of passing women.

Midcontinent

Pygmy tribes of central Africa settled throughout the Bantu ethnic region. The Mbuti[157] occupied lands along the Ituri River. Their customs exemplified Pygmy society. At birth the umbilical cords of infants had to be severed with the fathers' arrows. Hydrophilic vines were cut, and the water was used to bathe newborns. A small piece of the vine was wrapped around a baby's wrist so that the vine's strength would be transmuted to the baby. One infant of a set of twins was killed. How the selection was made is unknown.

Babies were dressed in hammered bark cloth and passed around to members of the community to be held and fondled, and to be nursed as well. Men were encouraged to hold and admire infants. In direct contrast to Tiriki belief, Pygmy babies' drool was considered benign.

Parents could not eat meat until their babies had learned to crawl, at which time babies were free to wander throughout the village.[158] Infant and child care were communal, and all of the adults were considered responsible for keeping children out of harm's way. A wandering toddler who approached dangerously close to a fire, for example, simply was lifted by a passerby and dispatched in an opposite direction. After the age of three or four, children formally became the responsibility of the tribal band, and discipline and punishment were communal decisions.

Children had their own playgrounds, generally adjacent to a stream. Older children watched younger charges and initiated tribal education, teaching hunting skills, house building, cooking, and other group endeavors. Children cooked for one another, but little girls never cooked for a boy, because they had been taught that such a gesture was tantamount to a betrothal.

There were no age groups, and initiation for boys between nine and eleven years old was communal. Initiation ceremonies lasted three months and occurred every two to three years. Once girls were considered ready for marriage, a short menarche ritual was celebrated. During the ritual Elima period nubile girls were decorated with vines. Village women were enjoined to keep the girls away from adolescent boys. The boys, as part of their own initiation, were expected to reach the girls and claim them. Village women armed themselves with sticks and stones aimed at the boys running the gauntlet. Those that survived the beatings faced a further mock humiliation at the hands of the girls, who administered their own beatings in feigned resistance to their suitors.

The principal test for boys was a demonstration of hunting skills. Lads were not considered ready for marriage until they had killed an antelope or a buffalo. This accomplished, the kill was presented to future in-laws as affirmation of a suitor's manhood. The nonaffianced announced their first big-game hunting achievement by being tattooed with ash paste and marked on the forehead with three vertical slits made to form keloid scars.

Pygmy girls were considered a special commodity and were given in marriage only in exchange for a groom's sister. If the groom had no sister, then the bride could be purchased for highly valued items such as bows and arrows, arrow poison, knives, spears, bark cloth, and beads.

The central African Ngoni[159] traditionally built their villages in horseshoe shapes with a cattle kraal in the center. In these pastoral habitats, newborns were announced with the proclamation, "A new stranger has come!" Infants first were given millet gruel as a purgative to clear meconium. On approximately the eighth day, when the umbilical stump fell off, babies' heads were shaved, and they were presented for the first time to their fathers and to villagers. Paternal grandfathers gave infants their names. Babies were cared for by "nurse girls," unmarried adolescents selected by the grandmothers. Fathers made fresh kills of a large animal, extracted and washed the animal's esophagus, made it pliable with fat, and sealed one end to form a nursing "bottle." These pouches were used for supplemental feedings. Children grew up in cultures that rendered total obedience and honor to all adults. For example, in passing an adult, a child was taught to go in front— never behind—bowing and saying, "I am before your eyes." They were taught to serve adults' wishes in all respects and, among other things, acted as messengers between adults. Older children joined their elders in reinforcing these codes for the younger children.

Once boys' deciduous teeth were lost, they had their ears pierced and were sent off to live in dormitories until they married. With other members of the fraternity they learned herding, hunting, cow husbandry, warfare, and, above all, submission to authority. Young novices were initiated with one or two beatings. Despite moving to these "maturation huts," boys continued to receive affection and support from their families. Food from the home hearth, for example, was taken to them daily by a younger sibling.

Boys underwent two rituals. The first occurred after a first nocturnal emission, with a ceremonial cleansing at the river. The second occurred with pubertal voice changes, celebrated with a special herbal drink prepared for boys by their uncles.

Girls were secluded at menarche in the common tradition of isolation. When menstrual flow ceased, a cleansing ceremony took place in which girls marched to the river in procession with their fathers' sisters and other women of the village. At the river, the girls were undressed and seated in the water. It was necessary to sit facing southeast to be fully cleansed. Following this ceremony, girls returned to their villages, to their aunts' huts, to receive instructions on custom and propriety. They were informed of their duty to submit to bimonthly vaginal inspections by delegated senior village women, whose function was to ascertain virginity by examining the condition of girls' hymens. This system, while an invasion of privacy, was infinitely more humane than the pharaonic circumcision or infibulation practiced by other groups.

North and west of the Ngoni were the Ibo of Nigeria.[160] These people treated infants with respectful deference, as it was feared that, if offended, a baby would leave its body to return reincarnated in another. Infant death was therefore considered a sign of dissatisfaction with the parents or the quality of life. When they were about six years old, Ibo boys moved into all-male huts and began to learn farming and other adult responsibilities and tasks from their fathers. As in Ngoni society, respect for and submission to elders were norms, and boys acted as messengers for the adults. The communal initiations of adolescence required feats of courage to be performed. The girls suffered clitoridectomies and were tattooed in the homes of future mothers-in-law and under their supervision.

The Savanna and the West

The Sahara and savanna tribes, although generally nomadic, experienced periods in their history of great and rich empires. In the eleventh century, the Mali Empire became an Islamic center of such ardor that boys slow to memorize the Koran were put in chains. By the fourteenth century, Mali, including its capital, Timbuktu, was the wealthiest of western African territories. The empire boasted a university of great renown throughout Europe. It was a major center for the study of law and philosophy.

Further south in Nigeria, the kingdom of Benin had begun to grow in importance. From 1400 to 1900 it was a major force in the savanna, a center of bronze work and trade as well as of military might. Benin evolved societal strata in which the hunter was the most respected member of the community, second only to the king. As might be supposed, it was a highly select group of boys that entered the hunters' ranks. They attended special schools to learn oral tribal traditions and rituals that were believed to render them invisible to prey. Exceptionally skilled students of hunting were selected to train for the elephant hunt. They were taught unique skills related to stealthy tracking of the pachyderm, the use of poison-tipped blowguns, and the artful dismemberment of the carcass to claim the trophies of the kill.

In the kingdom of Bornu mothers believed in the magic of human–animal *animas* exchanges. An early nineteenth-century journal described the practices that had survived the centuries:

Married women are very superstitious and always make sure that their beds are covered with the skins of certain animals when their husbands come to them, and they like to believe that they can use the skins to determine what kind of child they will have. If the skin of a panther or a leopard is used as a blanket, it will either be a boy or there will be no child. If the father is a warrior and a leader, the boy will also be a soldier, brave but bloodthirsty. A lion skin actually prevents conception.[161]

The savanna nomadic ethnic groups included the Tuareg, Teda, Bedouin Arabs, and Fulani (Peul). The Fulani[162] were a primarily pastoral people of mixed Caucasian and Negro phenotype scattered across the savanna belt. Fulani babies were born in nomad tents. Their umbilical cords were cauterized with ashes and embers from the central hearth within the tents. The infants remained confined with their mothers for one week, after which time they were named in a ceremony in which their heads were shaved and an animal was sacrificed.

When Fulani boys were ten years old, they were tutored in herding and attending to the care of the cattle corral. Ritual circumcision was performed at this time. Thereafter boys were expected to herd cattle away from the villages. They could no longer eat or sleep in their mothers' huts but had to live at the edge of the cattle corral. Each boy's future herd was selected and placed in his care. Special staffs and Koranic charms were given to the boys to assist them in their work. Mothers gave their sons a gift of a special calabash water bottle. As puberty neared, boys learned singing and dancing from older boys in the corral, and used these newly learned skills, at an age considered appropriate, to flirt with girls at the market and at village festivals.

Fulani girls, expected to be virgins, were bartered for cattle in marriage contracts. In contrast to Teda girls, who received a lip tattoo at menarche, Fulani girls had no initiation rituals other than being groomed with a special coiffure that signaled they were of marriage age.

Bedouin newborns were salted and bathed in camel urine for the first seven days of life. Naming an infant was the mother's privilege.[163] Like the Fulani, Bedouin boys were trained to herd. During the circumcision rites, Bedouin boys had to eat a piece of bread smeared with camel dung so that they would attain the "endurance of a camel." The Tuareg were Caucasian descendants of the Berberians who had bartered in salt since the twelfth century. In this nomadic tribe, boys were circumcised in communal ceremonies between the ages of five and seven years.[164]

In tropical western Africa, today's Liberia, dwelled the Kpelle.[165] Kpelle babies were born in the bush or in birthing huts. Mothers returned home with infant girls after three days, or after four days when boys were born. This custom derived from a system of numerology practiced by the Kpelle in which three was the number designated to a female and four to a male. After weaning, grandmothers traditionally raised the firstborn progeny of their children.

Boys were given no responsibilities until they were twelve years old, when they were assigned predominantly agricultural duties. Girls, on the other hand, started lessons at a young age. Little girls were expected to know how to heat vats of water and to sweep the floor by the time they were six years old. By the time they were eight, they could hull and winnow rice, fetch water from rivers, and generally care for siblings. By ten, they could cook most dishes and apply the remedies for common illnesses that had been passed on from mother to daughter in perpetuity. Most of these remedies did no harm, such as the use of fresh ginger root for stomach pains or poultices of mustard and hogfat applied to a cut. Some were grounded in sound physiological logic only now understood. In Morocco, for example, girls learned to stop an infant's cough by blowing sharply in the infant's face. It is known now that this action invokes what is called the Santmeyer reflex, which induces swallowing[166] and subsequent cessation of the cough.

The Kpelle belief in numerology influenced the long initiation periods they established. These consisted of four years for boys and three years for girls. Boys were secluded and circumcised. They learned lore and legend, farming, crafts, dancing, skills of warfare, and general deportment. Hazing and ordeals were severe. After their initiation, boys were given new names and joined a fraternity, called *Poro* (girls had a sorority called *Sande*). Both met secretly and in seclusion in the bush. The Kpelle were unusual in this respect, for neither secret societies nor cults were common in African cultures.[167]

Twinning remained an enigmatic event depending on the tribe. Among the Yoruba a carved statue called the *ibeji* celebrated the birth of twins. The belief was that the *ibeji* would keep the twins spiritually together even if one of them died. Yet, in nearby Benin, twins were killed because all believed that the second twin was the result of adulterous superfetation.[168]

NOTES

1. Mead, 1953, pp. 153–64.
2. Whymant, 1958, 18:192–93.
3. Bellwood, 1987, pp. 2–30.
4. Ibid., pp. 32–60.
5. Elkins, 1938, pp. 188–219.
6. Burrows and Spiro, 1957, p. 245.
7. Hausfater and Hrdy, 1984, pp. 490–91.
8. Darlington, 1931, pp. 322–25.
9. Hausfater and Hrdy, 1984, p. 427.
10. Stevenson, 1919, pp. 38–39.
11. Burrows and Spiro, 1957, p. 246.
12. Parsons, 1985.
13. F. Adedonojo. *JAMA* 1991; 265:1178.
14. K. A. Frackelmann. *Science News* 1992; 141:424–25.
15. Burrows and Spiro, 1957, pp. 288–90.
16. Codrington, 1981, pp. 237–38.
17. Day, 1964, p. 40.
18. Parsons, 1985, pp. 105–7.
19. Ibid.
20. Darlington, 1931, pp. 186–89.
21. B. Bower. *Science News* 1990; 138:68.
22. Josephy, 1968, pp. 10–21.
23. Phieffer, 1977, p. 110.
24. K. Reinhard et al. *J Parasitol* 1987; 73:630.
25. Driver, 1961, p. 378.
26. Corlett, 1935, pp. 276–83.
27. Moss of varying species was used throughout many North American cultures as absorbent diaper material. Fitzhugh and Crowell, 1988, pp. 249–50.
28. Corlett, 1935, pp. 263–66.
29. Driver, 1961, p. 368.
30. Fitzhugh and Crowell, 1988, p. 249.
31. Fitzhugh and Kaplan, 1982, pp. 162–71.
32. Fitzhugh and Crowell, 1988, p. 263.
33. Fitzhugh and Kaplan, 1982, pp. 156–59.

34. Maxwell, 1978, pp. 302–5.
35. Ibid., pp. 305–6.
36. Ibid., p. 301.
37. Jenness, 1960, pp. 152–53.
38. Spencer et al., 1977, pp. 109–11.
39. Maxwell, 1978, pp. 346–47.
40. Corlett, 1935.
41. Erikson, 1950, p. 150.
42. Ibid., pp. 151–52.
43. Josephy, 1968, pp. 74–75. "Potlatch" derives from *patshatl*, which means "giving."
44. Maxwell, 1978, pp. 171–75.
45. Ibid., pp. 124–25.
46. Ibid., p. 191.
47. Spencer et al., 1977, p. 327.
48. Maxwell, 1978, p. 194.
49. Freedman, 1983, p. 42.
50. Erickson, 1950, pp. 129–31.
51. Stockel, 1991, p. 26.
52. Spencer et al., 1977, p. 352.
53. Maxwell, 1978, p. 181.
54. Spencer et al., 1977, pp. 197–98.
55. Corlett, 1935, p. 267.
56. Maxwell, 1978, p. 181.
57. Bancroft-Hunt, 1981, p. 42.
58. Spencer et al., 1977, p. 211.
59. Lowie, 1954, pp. 83–84.
60. Darlington, 1931, p. 187.
61. Spencer et al., 1977, p. 224.
62. Ibid., pp. 235–36.
63. Ibid.
64. Ibid., pp. 224–25.
65. Knaak, 1988, p. 66.
66. White, 1979, pp. 90–105.
67. Ibid., p. 130.
68. Driver, 1961, p. 384.
69. Spencer et al., 1977, p. 148.
70. Wissler, 1940, p. 83.
71. Rountree, 1989, p. 76.
72. Ibid., pp. 80–84.
73. Spencer et al., 1977, p. 370.
74. Ibid., pp. 432–34.
75. Tunis, 1959, p. 72.
76. Maxwell, 1978, p. 97.
77. Payne, 1916, pp. 144–46.

78. Cockburn and Cockburn, 1985, pp. 110–14.

79. Tunis, 1959, p. 126.

80. Driver, 1961, p. 368.

81. Spencer et al., 1977, pp. 285–86.

82. Babcock, 1991, p. 79.

83. Ibid., pp. 82–84.

84. Ibid., p. 40.

85. Ibid., p. 72.

86. Spencer et al., 1977, p. 304.

87. Babcock, 1991, pp. 107–8.

88. Maxwell, 1978, pp. 222–28.

89. Babcock, 1991, pp. 121–23.

90. Spencer et al., 1977, pp. 304–5.

91. Stockel, 1991, pp. 30–31.

92. Driver, 1961, pp. 372–73.

93. Stockel, 1991, pp. 26–27.

94. Ibid., p. 19.

95. Driver, 1961, pp. 12–14.

96. Schendel, 1968, pp. 29–31.

97. Ibid., pp. 45–48.

98. Shein, 1992, p. 30.

99. Spencer et al., 1977, pp. 487–88.

100. Ibid.

101. Lopez, 1988, pp. 286–90.

102. Shein, 1992, pp. 102–3.

103. Ross, 1978, pp. 69–85.

104. Ibid.

105. Shein, 1992, p. 67.

106. Spencer et al., 1977, pp. 487–88.

107. Shein, 1992, p. 69.

108. von Hagen, 1961, pp. 97–98.

109. Driver, 1961, pp. 404–5.

110. The civilization may be older since ceramics found in Copan, Honduras, date back to 600 B.C. B. Bower. *Science News* 1990; 137:56–58.

111. Morley, 1946, p. 163.

112. Frazier, 1951, p. 501.

113. Spencer et al., 1977, pp. 470–71.

114. Morley, 1946, pp. 164–67.

115. Ibid., p. 166.

116. Ibid., p. 159.

117. Spencer et al., 1977, pp. 490–91.

118. Morley, 1946, pp. 208–11.

119. Guidoni and Magni, 1977, p. 121.

120. von Hagen, 1961, pp. 435–36.

121. Ibid., pp. 482–89.

122. Frazier, 1951, p. 641.

123. Means, 1964, p. 366.

124. von Hagen, 1961, p. 439.

125. Guidoni and Magni, 1977, pp. 124–26.

126. Mason, 1966, pp. 151–52.

127. von Hagen, 1961, pp. 436–37.

128. Ibid., p. 161.

129. B. Bower. *Science News* 1999; 155:244.

130. Mason, 1966, p. 217.

131. Frazier, 1951, p. 500.

132. For a more detailed accounting of Mesoamerican and South American children, see Max Shein's *The Precolumbian Child* (1992).

133. L. Roberts. *Science* 1989; 246:1245.

134. Bosworth, 1967, pp. 20–23; Peavy and Smith, 1996, pp. 22–23.

135. Loth, 1987, pp. 21–25.

136. Anecdotally, mummies found in Libya predate Egyptian finds, suggesting early, forgotten civilizations. One infant mummy is estimated to be between 5,300 to 7,500 years old. Racially black, the thirty-month-old child had been eviscerated, mummified, and buried ritualistically. Cockburn and Cockburn, 1985, p. 43.

137. Loth, 1987, p. 94.

138. *Lancet* 1983; 1:569.

139. *Lancet* 1998; 325:126.

140. Ibid.

141. Murdock, 1959, p. 169.

142. Gibbs, 1988, pp. 59–62.

143. Ibid., pp. 69–72.

144. Ibid., pp. 106–8.

145. Ibid., pp. 335–40.

146. Tyrrell and Jurgens, 1983, pp. 145–60.

147. Baumslag and Michels, 1995, p. 9.

148. Frazier, 1951, pp. 86–87.

149. deMause, 1974, p. 39.

150. Tyrrell and Jurgens, 1983, pp. 145–60.

151. Majno, 1975, pp. 20–23.

152. G. P. Hadley et al. *Lancet* 1993; 342:1304.

153. Shostak, 1983, pp. 65–68.

154. Gibbs, 1965, pp. 264–67.

155. Ibid.

156. Darlington, 1931, pp. 180–88.

157. Gibbs, 1965, pp. 305–7.

158. Turnbull, 1965, p. 78.

159. Read, 1960, p. 90.

160. Murdock, 1959, pp. 245–48.

161. Loth, 1987, p. 98. "Maternal influences" were invoked as a cause of anomalies even into eighteenth-century Europe (see chapter 8).

162. Gibbs, 1965, pp. 390–95.

163. Musil, 1928, p. 243.

164. Ibid., pp. 244–46.

165. Gibbs, 1965, pp. 208–10.

166. S. R. Orenstein et al. *Lancet* 1988; 1:345–46.

167. Gibbs, 1965, pp. 219–20.

168. Shein, 1992, p. 3.

PART ONE

❑ ❑ ❑

summary and conclusions

In ending Part One of this survey of children's history with the late cultures of Africa, a comment should be made to the effect that, despite the absence of a considerable body of written accounts, enough pertinent material is available to illustrate children's familial and societal roles in the various African groups. If much of what they experienced appears to be similar to that which was experienced in other world cultures, including cultures thousands of miles and thousands of years apart, the fact serves to highlight the many aspects of the human experience that are truly universal. Even the archaeological evidence from prehistoric cultures suggests shared human experiences: affection, joy at birth, sorrow at death, the impetus to train new generations to sustain the culture of prior generations, the fear of the unknown, the belief in an afterlife, and so on. Three millennia of early and late civilizations that left a significant written record of their world further illustrate the many elements of childhood common to all and in all time.

Ideas of nurturing, nourishment, and weaning; of play and games; of acculturating initiation rituals, schooling, and work; of mischief tolerated and discipline meted; of bonding and rejection; and of religious beliefs and superstitions—all vary widely, certainly, and in many ways are determined by time and place. At some level, however, all of human behavior throughout time has been rooted firmly in a humanity we recognize as our own.* For example, filial love as it was known in these civilizations often was expressed in ways that are familiar to our own experience. The evidence is in the letters that have survived; in the murals that depict family life; in sculptures; in artistic depictions of children with toys, playing games, or fondling parents, siblings, and pets; in school records; and in parental concerns recorded on clay fragments and on parchment. Funereal scenes and artifacts testify to the grief that was felt by the loss of a child. Ceremonies and rituals and the gifts that accompanied them were testimonials of love, pride, and gladness expressed by families and friends for milestones successfully attained and also of societal support of the importance the community gave to life's milestones.

Education, "a great factor in extending the period of perceived childhood,"[1] was a fact of all children's lives. The kinds and forms of pedagogy were determined by each culture's philosophical and economic makeup, as well as by the degree of material sophistication achieved by individual societies. That is to say that the education and training of the young in Native American Hopi settlements that emphasized harmony with nature and tranquility among people had as much to do with philosophy and attitude as with place and time, as did education prevalent in Western civilizations such as ancient Rome that emphasized mercantile competition, conquest, and the acquisition of property. The one focused on the development of the inner self, and the other concentrated on the advantages of material gain and power. This duality is found in many different cultures to this day.

Education in the early societies often was provided by parental or sibling example and also was a communal endeavor involving nonfamily members. Formal schools in some societies existed for the most part for the offspring of the highly positioned and the well-off members of ranking families. Few cultures formally educated females.

Some of the societies that have been looked at left no record relating to formal education of the young. Yet, as with the Incas, the Mayas, and the

---

*Common cultural threads that emerged among disparate early cultures are summarized in Table A.

Aztecs, civilizations with great cities that incorporated astounding knowledge of engineering and architectural principles must have had institutions that taught the subjects required to understand and apply such principles.

The initiation rites marking nubility in Pacific, American, and African cultures, ranging from a simple change of dress to mutilation and scarification, may seem distant and alien to modern readers unless some connection is made between those cultures then and ours now, in which teenage behavior reflects budding sexuality. One of the differences may be that in the abovementioned cultures, elders in the society mandated the customs and behavior. In Western society today the young determine dress codes; the use of "cool" mind-altering substances, from beer to marijuana; and the makeup, tatoos, and even graffiti involved in "mating games."

The many laws regarding children in early civilizations generally were related to inheritance and property, and the protection of children was secondary to the protection of family wealth. Few were the cultures that emphasized specific rights to which children were entitled, and parental responsibilities related to those rights that the society mandated be fulfilled in all aspects of the formative years. In the evolving cultures of Western Europe, many of the rights and protections children did enjoy became lost, not to be regained until the nineteenth or twentieth century. The tendency to regard children as property may be viewed as having created an environment that encouraged physical chastisement, child sacrifice, prostitution, slavery, and abandonment, for child abuse was virtually ubiquitous in ancient cultures in one form or another. Since many of these abuses still occur in the modern world, one manner in which the difference may be explained is to point out that such abuses were institutionalized then, with laws specifying the rules and regulations permitting child slavery, abandonment, child sacrifice, and male and female prostitution. In today's global society, on the other hand, such abuse is collectively disdained.

It is, however, this author's view that throughout the entire process of societal evolution, fundamental maternal instincts worked steadily to preserve and nurture the young. The familiar story of Solomon's (1 Kings 3:16–28) reliance on natural maternal instinct to save the life of a child exemplifies this trust placed in maternal affections. Infanticide and abandonment, it can be said, were more often initiated by fathers confronted by cruel economic realities, to whom the survival of the family unity was the overriding consideration, than by mothers, who all too often had to execute the deed.

Fears and ignorance that spawned superstitious beliefs and behavior surely reflected the general sense of powerlessness felt in a hostile, unfriendly planet in which survival altogether was uncertain and disaster too often seemed arbitrary and unexplainable. Hence, some cultures imbued children at their births with powers to augur good or with powers of divination, or they decreed some as singularly blessed in one form or another, in which case they were welcomed by the family and the community. Some births were interpreted as portents of dire consequences, so such unwelcomed infants were slain and hastily discarded.

The concept that men's lives are structured into distinct periods of time was adopted by many cultures, for it contributed to a sense of control of life's rhythms and cycles, offered a framework within which societies could function, and most important, helped people to understand or at least accept life. Community rules, governance, and age-determined rituals facilitated authority and enhanced the sense of position and purpose of young and old. For the young, the rituals that pertained to "growing up" fostered pride in maturing and assuming adult responsibilities, such as in the Tiriki and aborigine cultures that viewed age groups as functional and practical means to measure such expectations.

For other cultures and in different times, the concept of age-group periods had semimagical, descriptive, and even medical significance. The Pythagoreans philosophically categorized "four ages of man" in a general way, giving to each a season: the *pais* for spring, *neos* for summer, *aner* for autumn, and *geron* for winter. Galen referred to these four ages and imbued them with "humours," making *pais* hot and moist, *neos* hot and dry, *aner* cold and dry, and *geron* cold and moist.[2]

Hippocrates used the concept of age groups to describe his astute medical insights:

In the different ages the following complaints occur: to little and newborn children, aphthae, vomit, coughs, sleeplessness, frights, inflammation of the navel, watery discharges from the ears.

At the approach of dentition, pruritus of the gums, fevers, convulsions, diarrhea, especially when cutting the canine teeth, and in those who are particularly fat, and have constipated bowels.

To persons somewhat older, affections of the tonsils, incurvation of the spine at the vertebra next to the occiput, asthma, calculus, round worms, ascarides, acrochordon, satyriasmus, struma, and other tubercles.

To persons of more advanced age, and now on the verge of manhood, the most of these diseases, and, moreover, more chronic fevers, and epistaxis.

Young people for the most part have a crisis in their complaints, some in forty days, some in seven months, some in seven years, some at the approach of puberty; and such complaints of children as remain, and do not pass away about puberty, or in females about the commencement of menstruation, usually become chronic.

To persons past boyhood, hemoptysis, phthisis, acute fevers, epilepsy, and other diseases, but especially the aforementioned.

To persons beyond that age, asthma, pleurisy, pneumonia, lethargy, phrenitis, ardent fevers, chronic diarrhea, cholera, dysentery, lientery, hemorrhoids.

To old people dyspnoea, catarrhs accompanied with coughs, dysuria, pains of the joints. nephritis, vertigo, apoplexy, cachexia, pruritus of the whole body, insomnolency, defluxions of the bowels, of the eyes, and of the nose, dimness of sight, cataract, and dullness of hearing. (*Aphorisms* part 3)

In the Mishnaic tradition, the numbers 5 and 10 mostly defined the cycles of life, which were forged and tempered by Scripture:

Five years of age, for the study of the Bible; ten years for the study of the Mishnah; thirteen years for the performance of the commandments; fifteen years for the study of the Talmud; eighteen years for marriage; twenty years for a vocation; thirty years for fullness of strength; forty years for understanding; fifty years for giving counsel; sixty years for old age; seventy years for the hoary head; eighty years for the grace of special vigor; ninety years for the bent back; at a hundred one is as if he were dead and gone from the world. (Mishnah Avot 5.24)

The ages of life as defined by the philosophers of the Byzantine empire were compiled in Latin and collated into one tome by medieval scholars during the thirteenth century. By that time the cult of numerology had been firmly established, with the number 7 thought to have semimagical properties. Thus, life's cycles were believed to advance in multiples of seven:

The first age is childhood when the teeth are planted, and this age begins when the child is born and lasts until seven, and in this age that which is born is called an infant, which is as good as saying not talking, because in this age it cannot talk well or form its words perfectly, for its teeth are not yet well arranged or firmly implanted, as Isidore says and Constantine. After infancy comes the second age. . . . It is called *pueritia* and is given this name because in this age the person is still like the pupil of the eye, as Isidore says, and this age lasts till fourteen.

Afterwards follows the third age, which is called adolescence, which ends according to Constantine in his viaticum in the twenty-first year, but according to Isidore it lasts till twenty-eight . . . and it can go on till thirty or thirty-five. This age is called adolescence because the person is big enough to beget children, says Isidore. In this age the limbs are soft and able to grow and receive strength and vigour from natural heat. And because the person grows in this age to the size allotted to him by Nature.

Afterwards follows youth, which occupies the central position among the ages, although the person in this age is in his greatest strength, and this age lasts until forty-five according to Isidore, or until fifty according to others. This age is called youth because of the strength in the person to help himself and others, according to Aristotle. Afterwards follows senectitude, according to Isidore, which is half-way

Figure A *The Seven Ages of Man.* From *Moralia super Bibliam* by Niccolo de Lyra, c.1450 (Jones, 1853). *Wheel center:* "Rota vita que fortuna vocatur" (The wheel of life which is called fortune). *Outer wheel:* "Sic ornata nascuntur in hoc mortali vita/Est velut aqua labuntur deficiens ita" (Thus adorned they are born into this mortal life, decaying they flow away like water). *Around the wheel clockwise, images of the seven ages:* "Infans ad vii annos, Puericia ad xv annos, Adolescenia

continued

between youth and old age, and Isidore calls it gravity, because the person is grave in his habits and bearing; and in this age the person is not old, but he has passed youth, as Isidore says. After this age follows old age, which according to some lasts until seventy and according to others has no end until death . . . old people have not such good sense as they had, and talk nonsense in their old age. . . . The last part of old age is called senies. . . . The old man is always coughing and spitting and dirtying until he returns to the ashes and dust from which he was taken. (*Le Grand Proprietaire de toutes choses, tres utile et profitable pour tenir le corps en sante,* 1556 edition)[3]

Shakespeare incorporated the mystical number 7 in his famous oration on the lifecycles of men:

> All the world's a stage,
> And all the men and women merely players:
> They have their exits and their entrances;
> And one man in his time plays many parts,
> His act being seven ages. At first the infant,
> Mewling and puking in the nurse's arms.
> Then the whining schoolboy, with his satchel
> And shining morning face, creeping like a snail
> Unwillingly to school. And then the lover,
> Sighing like a furnace, with a woeful ballad
> Made to his mistress' eyebrow. Then a soldier,
> Full of strange oaths, and bearded like the pard,
> Jealous in honor, sudden and quick in quarrel,
> Seeking the bubble reputation
> Even in the cannon's mouth. And then the justice,
> In fair round belly with good capon lined,
> With eyes severe and beard of formal cut,
> Full of wise saws and modern instances;
> And so he plays his part. The sixth age shifts
> Into the lean and slipper'd pantaloon,

---

ad xxv annos, Juventus ad xxxv annos, Virilitas ad l annos, Senectus ad lxx annos, Decrepitus usque ad mortem." *Bottom octet:* "Est hominis status in flore significatus/Flos cadit et periit, sice homo cinis erit/Si tu sentires quis esses et unde venires/Nunquam rideres, sed omni tempore fleres/Sunt triaq: vere que faciunt me sepe dolere/Est primum durum quod scio me moriturum/Secundum, timeo quia hos nescio quando/Hinc tertium flebo quod nescio ubi manebo" (The state of man is like a flower/The flower falls and withers, so shall man become ashes/If you could know who you are and where you come from/You would never smile, but always weep/There are three things which always make me sorrow/First, it is hard to know that I must die/Second, I fear I do not know where/Third, I weep because I do not know where I will come to be).

With spectacles on nose and pouch on sides;
His youthful hose, well saved, a world too wide
For his shrunk shank; and his big manly voice,
Turning again toward childish treble, pipes
And whistles in his sound. Last scene of all,
that ends this strange eventful history,
Is second childishness and mere oblivion,
Sans teeth, sans eyes, sans taste, sans everything.

As You Like It 2.7

The concept of age groups had metamorphosed from the functional societal units of tribal categorizations into a blend of spiritual and moral being encased in an all-too-human organism. By the early Renaissance, to speak about the ages of man was to refer to innocence, beauty, strength, physical and metaphysical weariness, and decomposition. By the Reformation, the physical posture of a child was believed to reveal spiritual posture. Age cycles became a topos for poetry, homilies, and even in paintings, all stemming from the original concepts of the *wheel of fortune* and the *seven ages of man* (figure A).

The expedient of early cultures to segment human life into defined stages gave order and comprehension to their societies. Once the philosophers, poets, and artists and the institutionalized church in Western civilizations borrowed the concept, the status and dignity of man were elevated and idealized. This shift in thinking applied to children as well and indeed to childhood itself. In the second millennium, learned great men, basking in the Renaissance—the rebirth—of learning and well versed in philosophical and ethical discourse, used their persuasive influence to champion the cause of children.

In the next part of this study the focus will be on the millennium it took to fundamentally alter the legal and ethical treatment of children and on societal attitudes that had such profound impact on children's lives.

NOTES

1. Crawford, 1999, p. xiii.
2. Garland, 1990, p. 6.
3. Aries, 1965, pp. 21–22.

TABLE A
A SUMMARY OF KNOWN SOCIAL MORES AND BEHAVIOR TOWARDS CHILDREN IN EARLY AND LATE CIVILIZATIONS

	SUM	EGY	HIT	PHO	HEB	PER	IND	ORI	GRE	ROM	PAC	NA	MA	SA	AFR
Child as birth omen	✓	✓						✓							
Child as property	✓	✓	✓					✓							
Formal school, boys	✓	✓			✓				✓	✓			✓	✓	
Formal school, girls	✓	✓							✓	✓				✓	
Codices for children	✓	✓	✓		✓	✓	✓	✓	✓	✓					
Physical discipline	✓				✓			✓	✓	✓		✓	✓	✓	
Mutilating discipline	✓				✓										
Evidence of toys, games	✓	✓			✓		✓		✓	✓	✓	✓	✓		
Health care	✓	✓					✓		✓	✓	✓				
Sacrifice				✓					✓	✓			✓	✓	
Prostitution				✓					✓	✓					
Abandonment	✓	✓			✓			✓	✓	✓	*	✓			*
House burials											✓				✓

Note the paucity of data with respect to the Hittite, Phoenician, Persian, African, and Pacific cultures where a written record was not extant, has not been deciphered, or did not survive climatic vicissitudes.

SUM = Sumer; EGY = Egypt; HIT = Hittite; PHO = Phoenician; HEB = Hebrew; PER = Persian; IND = Indus; ORI = Orient; GRE = Greek; ROM = Roman; PAC = Pacific; NA = North America; MA = Mesoamerica; SA = South America; AFR = Africa.

*Applicable to twins in some cultures.

PART TWO

❏ ❏ ❏

Chapter 6

The Medieval Period: The Clergon

❑   ❑   ❑

A LTHOUGH THERE ARE NO DISTINCT time lines that define when late antiquity in Europe ceased and the Middle Ages, preceding the Renaissance, began, the thousand years between 500 and 1500 A.D. are traditionally referred to as the medieval period. Christian philosophy and morality almost universally had been embraced in Europe during this period. The church and its patristic principles dominated the beliefs and controlled the behavior—at least in public—of both nobility and peasantry. Church influence was everywhere, in politics, economics, art, architecture, and music. Diverting attention from the hardship, struggle, and sorrow experienced on earth, the great themes of literature echoed the church's emphasis on salvation and celestial reward. One medieval scholar observed:

. . . cathedrals were the most impressive monuments of that era; its greatest poem was a description of Hell, Purgatory, and Paradise; crusades were the only collective enterprises which temporarily rallied all nations; there were heretics and infidels but agnosticism was nonexistent or cowed into silence; the clergy was more numerous and influential in politics, economics, philosophy, and other intellectual pursuits than it has ever been since.[1]

Figure 6.1 A walled medieval city, Avila, Spain.

The Latin used in high places and in print reluctantly yielded to vernacular tongues, stubbornly persisting only as the preferred language of law and liturgy. In 813, Charlemagne ordered all sermons and homilies be delivered in "lingua romana rustica" rather than in the "lingua latina" that had prevailed.

By the year 1000 A.D. the population of Europe had doubled from that of the seventh century, doubling again by the beginning of the thirteenth century.* Villages gradually grew into cities. Walls, guardhouses, and entry gates were erected to protect citizens from enemies and bandits. These cities became urban centers of learning, commerce, and government (figure 6.1), even though only 10 percent of the population resided in them. The remaining 90 percent, serfs and peasants, subsisted in the countryside to work the land.

For the first time in recorded history, significant numbers of children in these changing societies could aspire to grow up to become other than soldiers, clergymen, or peasants tilling fields. From expanded trade routes and commerce a new and burgeoning merchant class had begun to emerge. The need for lawyers and record keepers grew. Skilled artisans and other craftsmen were needed to build the new towns. To safeguard their jobs, craftsmen proudly established guilds particular to their professions. Specialized education and training had to be developed to provide the workers with the new kinds of skills, and this need created an entire system of vocational instruction. A complex number and variety of apprentice–master structures evolved, parish schools cum colleges and universities were founded, and formal foundling homes were established.

---

*The Black Death of the fourteenth century punctured this growth rate with a devastating loss of 25 to 50 percent of Europe's total population (Gottfried, 1983).

These changes were gradual, imperceptible at first, with small or no impact on the majority of the populace. Poll tax records, for example, continued to include entries that referred to a "daughter or slave." Nonbiological children of households were virtual slaves who labored for the lords of the household.[2] Peasants still endured meager returns for their back-breaking work in the fields, accustomed as they were to life's many vicissitudes while experiencing few of its pleasures. As late as the thirteenth century, the three traditional major classes of society—the *oratores*, *bellatores*, and *laboratores*—prevailed. A poem of the period, *Miserere*, described the duties and expectations of each:

It is the work of a cleric to pray to God and that of a knight to do justice. It is the laborer's to get their bread. This man labors, this one prays, and that defends. In the field, in the town, and in the church these three complement each other in beautiful harmony.[3]

Having acknowledged the languid pace of change, it remains true that the phenomena of expanding urban areas, increased kinds of specialized skills and trades, and the establishment of educational institutions by the end of the twelfth century had been ongoing in Europe for hundreds of years. Within this passage of time, concomitant, if gradual, changes in the structure of societies—some for better, some for worse—already had occurred. The framework of a new tapestry depicting European life had been finished and was ready for the weaving to begin.

The general populace was becoming aware that literacy had become a valuable tool for economic survival, that a merchant required reading and arithmetic to handle international commerce and accounts. Some nobles were literate; many merchants were.[4]

By the fifteenth century nearly one-third of the English population could read—clergy, aristocrats, tradesmen, and most significantly, farmers and peasants who were ambitious to improve their lot in life.

❏ ❏ ❏

The medieval world coped with life by embracing a duality of beliefs, Christian and magical in nature. Fairies, elves, and demons had facile coexistence with saints and angels in the minds of the populace. A pregnant woman prayed to St. Margaret for a safe delivery, and if she wanted a boy, she entreated St. Felicitas in her prayers. If a girl was wanted, she might just as casually consult the writings of the physician Trotula (c.1130), who had concocted a recipe that ensured the birth of a girl: The potion to be drunk contained ground-up desiccated testicle of rabbit.[5] The desire for a girl, however, would not have been a common wish. Dante (1265–1321) expressed the prevailing medieval attitude that "a daughter's birth brings fear upon a father."[6]

Throughout pregnancy, women were encouraged to wear a girdle made of sloughed snakeskin and to carry an eaglestone.[7] The canon of Canterbury, John Bargrave, described an eaglestone in 1662:

This is a kind of rough, dark, sandy-colour and about the bigness of a good walnut. It is rare and of good value, because of its excellent qualities and use, which is, by applying it to childbearing women to keep them from miscarriage.[8]

Eaglestones, he explained, were meant to be held in the left hand during labor. These hollow stones that rattled probably were geodes with loose crystals. Anne Boleyn, Bargrave noted, carried an eaglestone given to her by Henry VIII of England during her pregnancies.

Following parturition, the mother was "churched"—a blessing and repurification ritual started outside the church door. The priest chanted: "O God, who hast delivered this woman thy servant from the perils of childbirth. . . ." The woman was sprinkled with holy water as she invoked her own cleansing, saying, "Thou shalt purge me, O Lord, with hyssop," and thereafter was led by her right hand into the church.[9]

In the south of France, well-wishers gave newly delivered mothers four gifts symbolizing their aspirations for the newborn. It was hoped that a baby would be "wise as salt, good as bread, full as an egg, and straight as a match."[10] At parturition, midwives measured a four-finger length of umbilical cord, tied it, and severed it. They washed the infants, rubbed them with oil of rose or myrtle, and scrubbed the gums with honey. Then they salted and swaddled the babies and quickly dressed them in their baptismal garments.

Fathers chose godparents for the baptism. Two females and one male were selected for girls, the converse for boys. The church had incorporated into the ceremony of the sacrament of baptism the ancient and familiar ritual of salting, which was common to all of the Christianized cultures. Powerful symbolism was so imbued in these cultures that in 1234 the Council of Bordeaux further reinforced the importance of the ritual by declaring that infants to be abandoned should be salted to signify that they had been baptized.[11]

A child born on a Sunday was called a *sine-sal* (without salt), because it was the day the salt seller did not work. A *sine-sal* was thought to be unlucky, because baptism was not possible on its natal day. Salt sellers sold mined salt or sea salt. Therefore, sometime during the Middle Ages, salting changed from the use of sodium bicarbonate, or natron, to that of sodium chloride, or table salt. At baptisms, salt was placed by priests on the infants' tongues. Then the babies were anointed and immersed in baptismal fonts. An infant was named at baptism, traditionally given the name of the saint on whose feast day it had been born.

The local bishopric was an equivalent of the Greek *deme*, and children were registered at baptism at the local parish. The name, date of birth, parentage, and social status were inscribed in the church registry. This record often was the only written documentation indicating that an individual had existed.

Baptisms commonly took place in the first week of life before an all-too-common infant death could occur. According to the teaching of the church, when unbaptized babies died, their souls could not enter paradise. Centuries passed before church authority was questioned about the implications of this position. St. Augustine, in the fourth century, sagely observed, "If you admit that the little one cannot enter heaven, then you concede that he will be in everlasting fire."[12]

The church unwittingly had created a conundrum for itself, condemning to hell those whom Christ clearly favored and had regarded as pure and innocent beings:

And Jesus called a little child unto him, and set him in the midst of them. And said, Verily I say unto you, Except ye be converted, and become as little children, ye shall not enter into the kingdom of heaven. Whosoever therefore shall humble himself as this little child, the same is greatest in the kingdom of heaven. And whoso shall receive one such little child in my name receiveth me. (Matt. 18:2–5)

In time, the church was challenged on its position, which was viewed as fundamentally flawed and contradictory. Medieval scholars and philosophers Peter Abelard (?1079–1144) and Peter Lombard (1095–1160) argued that it was inconceivable that God would allow the innocent to suffer eternal damnation. Thomas Aquinas (1224–1274) pursued the issue and resolved it, finally, for the church. He suggested that the concept of *limbus antechristus* be applied to unbaptized infants who died. In early Christian theology, *limbus antechristus* had been defined as the resting place of those good souls born before Christ who could not enter heaven until redeemed by Christ's death and resurrection. The ninth-century Cappadocian topos of Christ's descent into limbo to rescue trapped souls illustrated the point.[13] Aquinas's description of *limbus*[14] as a place of quiet peace and tranquility, lacking only the vision of God, enabled the church and its members to consign unbaptized babies to a special and blessed place.

In Aquinas's centrist vision of heaven, there are concentric areas of existence. The beatific vision—God—is at the center. In the periphery is limbo, a neutral border in which no suffering occurs. Aquinas described purgatory as a peripheral zone further removed from the center, in which place atonement for unredeemed transgressions takes place until all stain of sin is removed and the soul can enter God's presence. On the extreme periphery is hell, from which there can be no redemption.

The concept of limbo, a *limbus puerorum*, resolved a theological and philosophical dilemma and additionally gave comfort to the grieving faithful anxious about the eternal fate of their unbaptized babies who died. The long-lasting debate about the innocence of the unbaptized and the innocence of children in general served as a catalyst in changing how an entire European society collectively perceived children and child care. Church thinking and teaching traditionally had focused on children as creatures of the dust of the earth, conceived in the womb and nurtured, as Galen insisted, from menstrual blood. At birth they were thought to have been spiritually contaminated by a vaginal sojourn. In the Judeo-Christian tradition, purification rituals for women who had given birth prevailed into the twentieth century. The Talmud exempted only women who had delivered by cesarean section from having to be "purified," since vaginal passage of the infant had not occurred.

From Augustine on, the church began to encourage the view of children as God's pure and holy innocents, albeit tainted by original sin. Christ himself had sanctioned this image. It took more than a millennium for the church and its followers to recognize and accept limbo as a secure and happy place provided by God for babies who died unbaptized. Once this transition in attitude took hold, it followed that God's earthly representatives were morally bound to instruct the faithful on the responsibility to provide well for their children and to see to their well-being. The church became the primary instrument of change in improving fundamental attitudes about infant and child care. Church teaching, however, was ignored in some quarters. Among the poor and desperate the practice of abandoning children continued. The church condemned the act, while accepting responsibility to care for the destitute. This special concern culminated in the establishment by church leaders of foundling homes.

The importance of baptizing infants remained constant in the popular mind, since it was church teaching that "original sin" was passed from generation to generation and could be eradicated only through baptism. Baptism was an unassailable necessity in order for a soul to enter heaven. In a calamitous pregnancy or parturition, it was emphatically urged that a cesarean section be performed, principally so that the infant could be baptized. Only the lone voice of Trotula expressed interest in saving the life of the mother: "Whan the woman is feble and the chyld may noght comyn out, then it is better that the childe be slayne than the moder of the child also die."[15]

For the most part, however, it was viewed as a Christian duty to baptize newborns, and some manuals instructed midwives to perform cesarean sections specifically to baptize the child[16]:

> And yef the wommon thenne dye
> For to undo hyre wyth a knyf
> And for to saue the chyldes lyf
> And hye that hyt crystened be
> For that ys a dede of charyte.[17]

In antiquity, cesarean sections on women who had died in childbirth often were required by law. In 715 B.C. the *Lex Regia* of Numa Pompilus stated that it was unlawful to bury an undelivered woman until the child was cut out. The same law was inscribed in the *Codex Justinian*, and in *Nidanasthana* the Indian doctor Susruta (c.150 A.D.) likewise recommended that this procedure be done. The Mishnah adopted this law and applied it to multiple births (i.e., twins). Twins delivered by cesarean section, however, were denied primogeniture.[18]

After christenings, with chrisom gowns removed, babies were reswaddled and placed in their cradles in their linen wraps, for the first and most precarious six months of life. Infants were susceptible to infectious diseases, to be sure, but there is evidence that accidents were a major factor in causing infant fatalities. The cradles to which infants were consigned and the linens in which they were swaddled were made of highly combustible materials, and fires were common accidents. Records in medieval England indicate that nearly 60 percent of deaths of children under one year of age were attributable to fire. Most of the accidents appear to have happened during the workday, when parents and siblings were busy and distracted by work. The months May to August were especially dangerous ones for the very young, when the primary focus of the family was on the vital tasks of planting and harvesting.[19]

Peasant children were nursed by their mothers for two years. Some were given supplemental feedings of animal milk poured into feeding horns. A pap of bread and milk was commonly used for weaning. Among the middle and upper classes, infants were sent to the homes of wet nurses, who generally provided babies' needs for the first two years of life. Only after weaning were children returned to the direct care of their mothers. After the eleventh century, wet nurses typically went to live in their employers' homes, where both mother and nurse could nourish the child and where nurses could be more closely supervised by the parents. By this time, over half of Europe's children under the age of two were nurtured by wet nurses.

The daughters of nobles and burghers, it must be remembered, often were betrothed at an early age. Unlike their peasant counterparts, who learned firsthand how to function as *nutritor, medicus,* and *pedagogus* to their children, aristocratic girls learned only how to be adept at selecting surrogates such as wet nurses to nurse their children, how to choose herbal potions and ointments to restore family members to health, and how to select parish or chapter schools to best educate their children. They knew little about the direct care of infants and had to rely on the surrogates they had chosen to nurture their children properly.

Like some of the early patristic fathers, there were those who voiced disdain for the practice of maternal surrogates for babies, among them a monk from Siena. Fra Bernadino preached:

You give your child to be suckled by a sow where he picks up the habits of his nurse . . . and when he comes home you cry, "I know not whom you are like; this is no son of ours!"[20]

Increasing criticism about wet nurses' care of and influence on their charges did not diminish the custom. Rather, closer care in their selection was given greater importance by parents.

Several sources published advice on the criteria for choosing a *balia, nordiza, nourrice, amme,* or wet nurse. Most concise was the Italian Francesco da Barberino (1264–1348) in his *Reggimento e costumi di donna.* He opined that a wet nurse should be a woman

. . . between twenty-five and thirty-five, as much like the mother as possible, and let her have good color and a strong neck and strong chest and ample flesh, firm and fat rather than lean, but by no means too much so, her breath not bad, her teeth clean. And as for her manners, guard against the proud and wrathful and gloomy, neither fearful, nor foolish, nor coarse.[21]

Peasant children's stark lives permitted little time for play, and the few toys that might be found in a household would have been crudely manufactured homespun items. The games and toys of childhood for the well-to-do were varied and plentiful. The universal appeal of these toys, spanning millennia, is an amazing example of how humanity's fundamental sensibilities are genetically connected to both the past and the future. There were dolls, doll carriages pulled by mice, toy knights and soldiers, miniature windmills, balls, and additionally, playground equipment such as swings, maypoles, and seesaws. Children of the manor, however, most likely had toys made by toy-makers, who began to appear, it seems, during the thirteenth century. By 1400 professional toy-makers had shops in Nuremberg and Augsburg and began to export their wares to Italy and France. Manor children also played chess and backgammon and learned falconry and fencing.

Much of the writing in medieval Europe regarding children was compiled in monasteries, predictably with widely varying opinions and philosophical attitudes. Thirteenth-century Franciscan Bartholomaeus Anglicus, in *De Proprietatibus Rerum*, wrote of children's natures realistically, yet with the warm and loving insight of a grandfather:

Children have soft flesh and lithe and pliant bodies, nimble and light of movement, and are easily trained. They live without thought or care. . . .They are easily angered and easily pleased and forgive easily. . . .

Children often have bad habits, and think only of the present, ignoring the future. They love games and vain pursuits, disregarding what is profitable and useful. They consider important matters of no significance and unimportant matters important. They desire what is contrary and harmful, and appreciate pictures of children more than those of adults. They cry and weep more over the loss of an apple than over the loss of an inheritance. They forget favors done for them. They desire everything they see, and call and reach for it.

They love talking to other children and avoid the company of old men. They keep no secrets but repeat all that they see and hear. Suddenly they laugh, suddenly they weep, and are continuously yelling, chattering, and laughing. They are scarcely silent when they are asleep. When they have been washed, they dirty themselves again. While they are being bathed or combed by their mothers they kick and sprawl and move their feet and hands and resist with all their might. They think only about their stomachs, always wanting to eat and drink. Scarcely have they risen from bed than they desire food. (*Proprietatibus Rerum* bk. 6, chap. 5)[22]

In contrast, Florentine Fra Giovanni Dominici's (1356–1420) guidelines for nurturing in *Regola del governo* (c.1400) were largely punitive and more preoccupied with repressing sexuality than with the business of understanding child behavior. His book was among the first of a genre of "books of urbanity" that were to become very popular in Reformation Europe and in many respects anticipates the ethos propounded by Erasmus and Brunfels (see chapter 7). Dominici's opinions revealed notable ignorance about the nature and healthy nurture of children. His idea that children should have no physical contact with people whatsoever after the age of three, not even with the mother, probably was a reflection of his life as monk with little exposure to childhood:

If it be possible from three years on he is to know no distinction between male and female other than dress and hair. From then on let him be a stranger to being petted, embraced and kissed by you until after the twenty-fifth year.[23]

Dominici envisaged children raised to be self-sufficient through strict discipline. He advised frequent yet tempered corporeal punishment:

They should also learn to wait on themselves, and to use as little as possible the services of maid or servant, setting and clearing the table, dressing and undressing themselves, putting on their own shoes and clothes and so forth. Because of the need to hold in check this age inclined to evil and not to good, often take occasion to discipline the little children, but not severely. Frequent yet not severe whippings do them good . . . and this should continue not only while they are three, four, or five years old but as long as they have need of it up to the age of twenty-five.[24]

Fra Dominici frowned upon the evolving public manners that were to be embraced fully during the Renaissance. He particularly was troubled by vanities inculcated in young girls by their caretakers:

How much time is wasted in the frequent combing of children's hair; in keeping the hair blond if they are girls or perhaps having it curled! How much care is taken to teach them how to have a good time, to make courtesies and bows; how much inanity and expense in the making of embroidered bonnets, ornamented capes, fancy petticoats, carved cradles, little colored shoes and fine hose![25]

In contrast to Dominici's depiction of the pampered life of wealthy children, peasant children were fated to harsh lifetimes of unremitting work. By seven years of age, sometimes as young as five, children were expected to share in the families' struggle to survive. As in other aspects of daily life, the church's influence was tacitly acknowledged, as workers, adults, and children followed the church clock in regulating and defining the time for work and the time for rest. Work began at prime, six o'clock in the morning, and work ended at compline, about nine in the evening. As *The Babee's Boke* relates, only seven hours of sleep were considered necessary for the growing child: "Seven hours for a child is temperate and good, If more, it offendeth and hurteth the blood."[26]

Small children helped work the land, breaking selion and furrowing sod, clearing rocks, gathering wood, herding sheep collectively with other village children, watering stock, harvesting, and seasonally gathering chestnuts, mushrooms, and berries. Accidents associated with these tasks contributed to the 17 percent death rate in the overall population. Parish registries and other records reported deaths by drowning while gathering reeds and fishing, scalding or burning while working in the kitchen, and ditch suffocation while digging for peat. The death rates changed little as children entered the workplace, remaining at about 16 percent.[27] There are no independent figures that give the percentage of children only who were killed in work-related accidents.

Children's protection under the law initially had derived from the predominant legislative influence rooted in the old Roman codices that had endured. In time, laws were adopted in new, emerging nations, towns, and rural areas that had been formulated to suit specific regions. In medieval courts of law, the question posed at the outset of a hearing—*sub qua legis vivis?*—awaited the answer before it could be determined which due process was appropriate to the case.

Allowing for regional variations, across the continent there generally were shared concepts of property and individual rights, with laws to protect them. The oldest codex of medieval Germany, the *Sachsenspiegel,* was compiled by the Saxon knight Ritter von Repkow sometime between 1220 and 1235,[28] and it serves as a good example of regional laws. The codex expressed concepts of common law, binding for children as well as for adults. Several of the codices protected children's rights. For example, physical punishment inflicted on pregnant women was curtailed to protect the unborn. Newborns were considered live-born if breath and cries were audible in all four corners of the house. Thereafter they were recognized as legal heirs. Half siblings were not entitled to succession. In matters pertaining to property, parents were liable for damages perpetrated by their offspring. Children of divorced parents remained with their mothers. The codex had no laws that referred to the education of children. Other examples of *legis franca* included thirteenth-century Norman laws specifically dictating care and attention to wards and orphans, controlling not only inheritance but also marriages. Similar laws were extant in Siciliy, the Constitutions of Melfi (1231), and in Spain—the *Siete Partidas* of Alfonso X of Leon and Castile.[29] Most regional laws included codices that at the very least protected the child's inheritance rights.

The church established parish schools in an effort to provide rudimentary educations for peasant children. The curriculum consisted of instruction in the Bible, some reading and arithmetic, and singing. In general, the parish school was the only formal education peasant children could hope for, and some were denied even this minimally basic schooling. Feudal lords imposed fines on peasants who requested permission to send their children to these schools on the grounds that the crop yield would be smaller in the absence of one of the workers.[30]

Bright peasant boys who showed promise were singled out by the church to become *clergons* (little clerics). Such children could progress from altar boys to rectory aides to scribes. They studied and mastered Latin in order to compete for scholarships to institutions of higher learning. They frequently studied for the priesthood and were ordained.

Most peasant boys simply became skilled in cultivating farms and mastering the numerous methods the *seigneurs* could use to impose taxes on their serfs. To marry, young men had to have accumulated the "betrothal tax" and "morning gift."

Young adolescent girls began in earnest at about twelve to fourteen years of age to train for their future roles as household managers. Women in the Middle Ages were all things to the family and greatly depended upon. One young woman lamented her work load:

I must serve the old women, I must learn to spin, to reke, to card, to knit, to wash buckes, and by hande, to brew, bake, make mault, reap, bind sheaves, weed in the garden, milke, serve hoggs, make cleane their houses, within doores make beddes, sweep filthy houses, rubbe dirty ragges, beat out old Coverlettes, draw up old holes: Then to the kitchen, turne the spit, although it was but seldome, for we did not eat meat often; then scour pottes, wash dishes, fetch in wood, make a fire, scalde milk Pannes, wash the Charne and butter dishes, ring out a Cheese clote, set everything in good order.[31]

Self-sufficient in all of those domestic chores, women additionally were the sole sources of care and comfort in matters pertaining to birth and death and every stage of life in between. Common lore to provide relief for all manner of ailments was passed from mother to daughter. Women knew how to use herbal medicines such as foxglove (digitalis) and willow bark (aspirin). They treated fever, headache, swelling, toothache, bleeding, and general neuralgia. Ferula species such as asafoetida, the artemisia species wormwood, and pennyroyal all were used as abortifacients during the Middle Ages.[32] Although their use was condemned by church authorities, women quietly prepared potions for themselves to imbibe following coitus. Since contraceptive pessaries were painful, the potions were favored for use. Their efficacy was at best uneven, and the admonition *si non caste, tamen caute* (if not chaste, take caution) remained an anecdotal truism. In the event that midwives were not available, girls were taught to attend themselves during labor.*

Skilled as they were in preparing for new life, women also were adept in their administrations to the dying. To ease pain and to quell the anxiety of one facing imminent death, women sedated patients with wine, poppy seed, mandrake root, and hemlock. After death, women prepared the bodies for burial—washing, anointing, and wrapping them in shrouds even as they mourned.

The view of marriage as an economic contract was not contested by the church, but the marriage state was elevated in status by church doctrine that decreed marriage a sacrament and therefore a holy union. The church dictated the conditions that constituted a valid marriage as well as the terms

---

*The risk of perinatal mortality was high among all groups, even the urban genre. In fourteenth-century Florence, a married woman had a cumulative 20 percent risk over the course of her married lifetime of dying from childbirth.

necessary before a marriage could take place. The church calendar forbade marriage ceremonies immediately preceding Christmas, Easter, or Pentecost. Dowries remained prerequisites for girls.[33] In medieval Florence middle-class girls typically were endowed with dowries of 2,500 florins.* Boys and girls had to be a minimum of fourteen years and twelve years of age, respectively, before they could marry. The consent of each of the couple officially was a requirement, although the countless numbers of children who were forced by their families to marry against their wills can only be conjectured. Betrothals were treated as solemn occasions and were blessed by parish priests. At the time of the betrothal, a young groom was required to pay a predetermined sum as a "deposit" for the bride. This sum quadrupled and was forfeited should the engagement be broken. Before a marriage ceremony, there was a forty-day waiting period, during which the intentions to marry, or the "banns of marriage," were announced from the altar at mass. On the morning after a marriage was consummated, a "morning gift," a *morgengabe*,[34] was expected from the groom for the gift of a wife's virginity.

Within marriage, the authority and control of the church were absolute under pain of sin, to the extent that sexual intercourse was proscribed by ecclesiastical whim. Young couples learned that the church forbade coitus during daylight hours; on Saturday nights before the Sabbath; on nights before holy days; as penance on Tuesday and Thursday nights; forty nights before Easter, before the feast of the Holy Cross, and before Christmas; ninety nights before parturition was expected; forty nights after parturition occurred; during lactation; and during menses. Couples who followed these mandates would have been able to anticipate approximately twenty days per year of sexual intimacy. The church warned that the consequences for violating these religious taboos could result in producing deformed children—changelings.[35] Gregory of Tours (538–594) wrote of just such a child, conceived on a Sunday and consequently born with multiple birth defects.[36] Considering the evidence of consistent population growth in Europe during the period when these church laws were in effect, it is safe to assume that the rules were broadly violated and ignored.

Ironically, given the significant constraints placed on couples with respect to coitus, the church taught that the primary purpose of marriage was procreative. Contraception and abortion were viewed as direct offenses against God's wishes and laws. The Christian church made no exceptions in this regard, whereas the Jewish faith provided an exception for lactating women.

---

*A florin (ducat) was worth 7 lire or 140 soldi. There were several kinds of florins, making it difficult to estimate a modern equivalent. However, for contrast, the going market rate at the time for a child slave was about 6 to 10 florins, and for a strong adult slave, about 75 to 90.

In the Talmud, contraceptive guidelines were given *only* to nursing mothers for the purpose of assuring infant nutrition.[37] The use of absorbent flax intravaginally (Niddah 45a) was permitted, or husbands could practice *coitus interruptus* (Yebamoth 34b). The prescripts of the Talmud certainly were superior to common lore passing as wisdom that prevailed at the time—even in the Jewish community. Ibn Ezra (1092–1167), a Spanish Jew and medical practitioner, recommended contraceptive measures that included hanging a boy's deciduous tooth or the dung of a hare around a woman's neck.[38]

Contraceptives and abortifacients were not topics about which young girls could learn openly. Sub rosa, however, Christian adolescent females learned a great deal about contraception from other females as well as from written materials. From the church was learned the penances for such offenses. Practicing contraception called for one unit of a class II penance. For the more serious act of abortion three units were imposed. A Rhenish bishop, Bourchard of Worms, in the book *Medicus* (c.1010), classified the three types of penance. A class I penance meant sexual abstinence and fasting for a prescribed unit of days. Class II limited the degree of fasting but extended its time to one year. Class III, the *carina*, was for a period of seven years.[39] Penalties for sinful infractions varied from jurisdiction to jurisdiction. In some parishes, an act of infanticide resulted in excommunication, whereas in others a sentence of twelve years of penance was decreed.

The general populace accepted church teaching that the primary purpose of marriage was to bear children, but often they viewed these children as burdens, seldom a cause for joy and often the source of sadness. Eustache desChamps (1346–1406) expressed this sullen viewpoint:

Happy is he who has no children, for babies mean nothing but crying and stench; they give only trouble and anxiety; they have to be clothed, shod, fed; they are always in danger of falling and hurting themselves; they contract some illness and die. When they grow up, they may go to the bad and be put in prison. Nothing but cares and sorrows; no happiness compensates us for our anxiety, for the trouble and expenses of their education. Is there a greater evil than to have deformed children?

> Que homs de membre contrefais
> Est en sa pensée meffais,
> Plains de pechiez et plains de vices.[40]

If these sentiments were widespread among the married, attitudes towards the *spurii*, the illegitimate children, can only have been far more negative.

The church condemned adulterous and unsanctioned sexual acts but extended compassion toward and acceptance of children of such unions. The position of the church reflected some ambivalence. In order for such children—universally referred to as bastards—to enter the service of God and the church, special dispensations were required. Depending on the country, bastards could assume either the paternal or maternal name. In many urban localities, legitimate and illegitimate children were entitled to identical legal rights. Records from fourteenth-century Ghent, for example, register the patrimony rights of all children, including bastards.[41]

Married parents had legal recourse to separate, and some parents did defy societal conventions and the church by filing for formal separations. In this event, the laws applied to both their legitimate and illegitimate children. The children of separated parents received one-third of parental property and were given the choice to remain with either of their biological parents. If no choice was made, the courts awarded custody to the fathers. Mothers could bypass their husbands and bequeath whatever estate they possessed to all of their children. If orphaned, children's rights were protected in the courts. Remaining family members were given forty days to catalog a list of the family estate and nominate to the court a guardian for the children. These court-appointed guardians were empowered to protect the children's interests, and they were monitored by the courts to ensure that this occurred. Severe fines were imposed for malfeasance or for malevolent treatment by a guardian of the children in their care.

In Spain, mothers cared for their illegitimate children for the first three years, during which time the fathers paid the costs of child support. After three years, fathers were legally entitled to raise their children. If the court, however, determined that a child would be more properly cared for by its mother, the father was compelled to continue financial support. In Scandinavia, similar concepts were incorporated into law. The thirteenth-century law of *Magnus Laboter* specified that "bastards" remain with their mothers until they were three years old, then with their fathers until they were seven years old. At eight, children were given the authority to decide with whom they wished to reside.[42]

EDUCATION AND APPRENTICESHIP

It was considered an honor to be accepted as a page in a great lord's household, especially in England and in France, where seven-year-old youths were sent to train in castles and manor houses of the nobility. In addition to general servitude, these boys learned horsemanship and swordsmanship, forming a class called the *laicus illiteratus* that left literacy to the upper classes, the bourgeoisie, and menial scribes. At twelve, training in fencing, archery, hand-to-hand combat, and target attack began in earnest for pages. For some boys, serving as a page was a prelude to becoming a "gentleman."[43] For others it was an early prerequiste of knighthood. At fourteen or fifteen, boys graduated to the status of squire to a knight. Squires dressed their masters, groomed their horses, polished their weapons, went hunting with them, and entertained them in games of chess. Squires accompanied knights into battles and attended to their horses during dismount engagements. Seneschals of the feudal estates taught squires how to safeguard both keys and purse, and the boys were entrusted to serve as confidential couriers. At some time between the ages of eighteen and twenty-one, these squires were ready to prepare for knighthood themselves.[44]

Upper-class children of the nobility and the bourgeoisie were given a substantially different education. These boys almost always learned to read, from texts as diverse as penitential psalters, Donatus's fourth-century *Minor Grammar*, Cato's *Moral Sayings*, and Priscian's sixth-century *Grammar*. Breeding good manners was given a great deal of importance in the education of the wellborn and was an essential aspect of an education. A thirteenth-century poem describes some of the expectations:

> A good child upright he must stand,
> Before his lord when he doth eat,
> Nor scratch his limbs with either hand,
> And if a great gift or a small is given,
> While kneeling he must render thanks.[45]

The school curriculum for these children followed the ancient traditions of the *trivium* and *quadrivium*. The study of grammar, rhetoric, and logic was followed by arithmetic, geometry, astronomy, and music. Writing was first practiced with styluses on wax tablets before going on to the more-expensive quill and parchment. Learning was predominantly by rote, tedious and numbing.

School authority probably reflected parental and societal attitudes about children, which, on examination, often appear to have been disinterested, with little warmth and affection demonstrated in the home. Or perhaps educators were influenced negatively by the austerity of communal life in monasteries. Schools were, in either case, inflexible, punitive, and tightly structured. Moreover, the usually physical discipline generally was supported by parents. Regarding her son Clement, Agnes Paston wrote to his teacher in 1457:

If he hath nought do well, nor wyll nought amend, pray hym that he wyll trewly belassch hym tyl he wyll amend; and so ded the last mastyr and the best ever he had att Caumbrege.[46]

The occasional parents disapproved of physical discipline. There are extant records of court proceedings in which parents sued teachers for abusing their charges.[47]

Generally, there were no grade levels to mark the degree of the subject-matter's difficulty, and there was no attempt to match classes by age levels commensurate with physiological maturation and development. Discipline, conduct, and class routine were strictly controlled. Reveille was at 4 A.M. Lessons ensued immediately and continued until Mass was said at 6 A.M. Following Mass, children were in class until 11 A.M., when the first meal of the day was served. From noon to three, children did their chores; at 3 P.M. lessons resumed and continued until dark, usually at 6 P.M.

Gerbert of Aurillac (945–1003), a French peasant who rose to the papacy in 999 as Pope Sylvester, significantly modified the educational curriculum of Europe. Following his own monastic education, he had traveled to Italy to enhance his skills in rhetoric and to Spain for further study in mathematics and music. There he was influenced by Moorish educational concepts and philosophy and became determined to apply much of what he had absorbed. When, in 972, he returned to France to assume the position of master of the Cathedral School in Reims, he introduced to the *quadrivium* Hindu-Arabic numerals as an alternative to the cumbersome numerals of the Romans, thus facilitating both the use of the abacus and the learning of arithmetic. Gerbert also gave greater emphasis to the study of logic, rhetoric, and music. The musical octave, derived from musical notes to the hymn to St. John (now used predominantly as a breviary absolution), is thought to have been devised by Gerbert[48]:

Ut queant laxis	Saint John, cleanse
*Re*sonare fibris	the guilty lips of
*Mi*ra gestorum	thy servant, so
*Fa*muli tuorum	that he may resound
*Sol*ve polluti	on soft strings
*La*bii reatum	the marvels
*Sa*ncte Johannes.	of your deeds.

The great cathedrals being built in the growing number of medieval towns founded cathedral schools. These schools typically flourished for many decades before the construction of the cathedrals themselves could be completed. In France, Italy, and England the schools encouraged children of both the bourgeoisie and the peasantry to attend, attracting ever-increasing numbers from these social classes. By the twelfth century the cathedral schools had

replaced the monasteries as major centers of education. At first the local bishops and canons governed cathedral schools. As they strengthened and proliferated, their administration became an issue, at the behest of Pope Innocent
III, for the Fourth Council of Latern in 1215. The council decreed that
henceforth the license to teach, the curriculum, and the administration of the
schools would be determined and enforced by the chancellor of each cathedral. These cathedral schools and to a lesser degree the parish schools in more
rural areas assumed responsibility for education. The social conditions that
had prompted the system of monastery *oblati* had disappeared and, with
them, the oblates themselves. The curriculum of the *trivium* and *quadrivium*
were no longer just for "freemen"—the *liberi* from which derives the term the
"seven liberal arts"—but for all classes of folk. Societies had begun to invest
in their children and their futures, a process that increased in momentum as
the years passed. In Florence, by 1330, for example, six- to twelve-year-old
boys and girls attending school numbered between eight thousand and ten
thousand. Based on Florence's fourteenth-century demographics, 50 percent
of its children at the time were becoming literate.[49]

❑ ❑ ❑

Historians are of two minds regarding the treatment of children in medieval
Europe. One position holds that a concept of childhood had not yet been
formulated:

In medieval society the idea of childhood did not exist; this is not to suggest that
children were neglected, forsaken or despised. The idea of childhood is not to be
confused with affection for children: it corresponds to an awareness of the particular nature of which distinguishes the child from the adult, even the young adult. In
medieval society this awareness was lacking.[50]

Data of other historians already set forth in this work modify, if not
negate, this point of view, at least with regard to children under seven. The
concern of the church as an institution; the writings of many of its philosophers, monks, and priests; and the manuscripts of physicians and herbalists
contemporary to the times all point to a great deal of interest in and recognition of the fragility and dependency of the stage we call "childhood." One
instance is the philosophical conceptualization of children as precious innocents watched over from heaven. In this scenario they were delivered to a
nonpunitive limbo in a quasi-state of salvation in the event that they died
without having been baptized.

Much thought and debate had been given to determine the age at which
children could be said to have attained the ability to know right from

wrong—"an age of reason." Before that age, children were not considered culpable of wrongdoing, because they were considered unable to form judgments and therefore were protected legally by society, morally by the church, and emotionally by the family. Having children and nurturing them properly were accepted by the majority as obligations. The general atmosphere of concern and often guilt strengthened intentions to improve the lives of small children. For the most part, families cared for their children, educated them when that was possible, and prepared them for life as adults. Institutions like the church assumed responsibility for the homeless and helpless children who were trying to survive in squalid, hostile urban environments. They established foundling hospitals all over Europe.

With regard to children over the age of seven, the thesis that a concept of childhood did not exist appears to have had considerable foundation in fact. In a changing world that was developing a new economy base within an evolving urban milieu, cruel realities of economic necessity had to be confronted by the general populace and its children. Among town families and among peasant and noble country stock, children's destinies were determined at an early age. The fortunate went to primary parish schools or to the new cathedral schools to begin an education. Others were forced to bypass school to prepare to make their own way and eke out a living. If lucky or well connected, these latter children trained to be pages and squires, prelates and teachers, or, as happened often in the towns, apprentices to guildsmen. Either scenario ended with childhood itself ending.

Throughout Europe, the cycles of plague epidemics periodically decimated populations, particularly children. The children who grew healthy and strong were put to farm labor and commonly excluded from schooling. In England, the Statute of 1388 declared that a child "which used to labour at the Plough or Cart or other Labour or Service of Husbandry till they be of Age of Twelve Years, then from thenceforth they shall abide by the same Labour without being put to any Mystery or Handicraft." This same sentiment was reinforced in the Statute of 1405. Yet at the same time, some advocated free schooling even for the poor. William Forrest petitioned the court of Henry VIII to educate children starting at the age of four years:

Leste some perhaps, at this might thus objecte, The poureman his child cannot so prefer: bycause hee hath not substance in effecte for so longe season to fynde his scholer, as (for his schoolinge) too paye his Maister: to which I answere, it must provyeded bee: in eaveye towne the Scoole too go free.[51]

Young boys of all classes commonly were packed off between the ages of seven and ten years to feudal manors, monasteries, or the homes of master guildsmen, where they were expected to imitate and live like the adults surrounding them. The hard work and the long hours left little time for child-hood play. In effect, the apprenticeship system halted childhood[52] and bypassed adolescence—a concept and term that in any case was centuries away from being conceived, expressed, or indulged.

Apprenticeships in various trades were such an important economic and social aspect of medieval life that examination of the system is warranted. In addition to being a vital component in successfully finding work in the cities, an apprenticeship was an obligatory step for anyone interested in becoming a guilded craftsman. Members of guilds could anticipate lifetime job security, as well as faring relatively well economically.

All craftsmen—bakers, tanners, stonecutters, cobblers, metalsmiths, and the like—had their own guilds, and apprenticeships were carefully con-trolled. Sons of freemen generally were accepted readily as apprentices; peas-ants had to pay a premium for one of their children to be considered for such a position and then only if a vacancy became available. An apprenticeship did not guarantee admittance to a guild. These memberships initially had been reserved for family members of guildsmen. It was only when cities grew in population and the demands for goods and services helped to create new jobs that new members began to be drafted from the ranks of the peasantry.

Some guilds permitted their members, called masters, to have up to five apprentices at one time. Parents paid the entrance fees to the guilds and con-tracted with guild members for the children's training, service, guidance, and sustenance. The masters agreed to clothe, shelter, and feed their charges and at times provide a small wage. Sometimes it was the parents who paid peri-odic sums to the masters as a kind of "tuition."

The following is a typical contract that appeared in the records of the English Merchant Guild in 1451:

John Harrietsham contracts with Robert Lucy to serve the said Robert as well in the craft and in all his other works and doings such as he does and shall do, from Christ-mas day next ensuing for the term of seven years. He is to receive 9s. 4d. at the end of the term, and he shall work one year after the seven at wages of 20s. Robert is to find his apprentice all necessaries, food, clothing, shoes, and bed and to teach him his craft in all its particulars without concealment. During the term the apprentice is to keep his master's secrets, to do him no injury and commit no excessive waste of his goods. He is not to frequent taverns, not to commit fornication in or out of his master's house, nor make any contract of matrimony nor affiance himself without his master's permission. He is not to play at dice, tables, or checkers or any other unlawful games but is to conduct himself soberly, justly, piously well, and honor-ably, and to be a faithful and good servant according to the use and custom of Lon-don. For all his obligations Robert binds himself, his heir and his executors, his goods and chattels, present, and future, wherever found.[53]

At first, novice apprentices were household servants and mere observers of the trades they had been contracted to learn. In time they were given simple tasks of the trade to do and, under the masters' watchful eyes, the tasks advanced in complexity and amplitude. An apprentice trained for four to twelve years. Some trades additionally required a period of internship for apprentices, and interns were known as journeymen. John Harrietsham's contract, for example, required that he serve Master Robert Lucy one year as a postapprentice.

Philippe of Navarre (1206–1260) felt that boys should begin their apprentice training as young as possible: "Those who early become and long remain apprentices ought to be the best masters."[54] Florentine Fra Giovanni Dominici admonished youths to choose a trade only after thoughtful and careful consideration: "Since nature aids art, and a skill chosen against nature will not be learned well."[55]

On completion of an apprenticeship, a test of skill specific to each guild, called the *chef d'oeuvre*, was required as proof of competency in the craft. Table 6.1 list examples of such tests. Apprentices demonstrated their proficiency before judges or guild wardens on whose approval depended their acceptance as members of the guilds. A satisfactory demonstration earned a certificate from the master attesting to his apprentice's skill and good moral character. After a swearing-in ceremony, in which the guild oath was repeated and the required fee was paid to the town lord, the erstwhile apprentice was acknowledged as a craftsman and member of his guild.

The few guilds for female apprentices were for makers of silk, gold embroidery, or *orfrois*, and purses or *aumonieres*. Most skilled work performed by women was not granted recognition as a craft, nor could women expect the remuneration of a craftsman. All the same, many of the crafts

TABLE 6.1
EXAMPLES OF MASTERPIECES

Trade	Chef d'Oeuvre
Saddler	A palfrey saddle, a burden saddle
Stonecutter	A statue one-meter high
Cobbler	Mending three pairs of shoes
Barber	Shave, beard trim, sharpening of razor and lancet, art of phlebotomy
Butcher	Dismembering a cow, sheep, pig

restricted to men were mastered by girls and women. Learned at home from fathers and then husbands, they received no formal acknowledgment of their expertise from the guilds. Both the fuller and leather guilds permitted members' daughters to practice the trade in their new homes after marriage, but these women could not teach the trade to their husbands or take on apprentices.[56] Most guilds also allowed widows to continue the work of what had been their husbands' craft as long as they did not teach apprentices the trade.

Not all apprentices honored their commitments. Some worked to buy themselves out of the contract, and some simply ran away. By the sixteenth century the commitment to the system had disintegrated to the degree that only 40 percent of apprentices honored their contracts to their completion;[57] for by that time, corruption within the guilds had become ingrained. Master guildsmen more and more selected family members or friends for admittance into the guilds, to the exclusion of increasing numbers of skilled, trained journeymen. Perfunctory tasks, impossible to fail, were given to the favored; others were challenged with exacting *chef d'oeuvres* designed to result in failure. In time the journeymen, denied membership in their guilds, turned their backs on them, moving forward to form a new "working class." It was from this group that the industrial working class of the eighteenth and nineteenth centuries emerged.

❑ ❑ ❑

Children who were able to attend primary schools probably began when they were between eight and ten years old. A more exact age is difficult to establish because records are sketchy, sometimes ambiguous, and customs varied from country to country. French historians, for instance, did not distinguish between the primary and secondary school experience, as did English historians. The age at which children advanced to secondary schools in France remains, therefore, vague.

Students in medieval Europe who could read and write qualified for entrance to universities, which were at first the equivalent of secondary schools. Matriculation at a university occurred most commonly at the age of fourteen years, although a twelve-year-old university student was not a rarity. As a consequence of newly established universities, the chapter schools disappeared along with the peripatetic teacher on whom they relied.

In order to protect their mutual scholastic interests and disciplines, a tradition evolved in which students and masters joined together into groups of guilds as craftsmen did. There were guilds composed of faculty and students who concentrated on the study of theology, law, and medicine. They called themselves *universitas vestra*. One of them, the University of Paris, at its

Figure 6.2
Seal of the University of Paris, reflecting church authority. Note that two professors are above the students but under the domain of the cathedral and its saints and hierarchy. BIBLIOTHÈQUE NATIONALE DE FRANCE.

inception in 1160, created a seal (figure 6.2) that reflected its allegiance to and the influence of the church that had inspired its founding and its status as an academic guild.[58]

In Italy, the members of the guilds (i.e., the students) hired and paid the teachers, determined the courses, and levied fines on incompetent teachers. Italian universities modeled their schools of rhetoric after the classical Roman model and were advanced beyond the rest of Europe in their secular curriculum, especially in law and medicine.

The forte of universities in England and France was theology. In these countries masters controlled the curriculum, the study calendar, and the students, reversing the Italian custom. They also determined dress regulations and disciplinary codes.

In Portugal, few students advanced beyond a bachelor's degree. After an additional seven to nine years of study, examinations, and fees, it was possible to be awarded the title *licentiate*. It was rare that a doctorate was conferred; it could be granted only by a bishop and only after a student had been named a *licentiate* and had passed additional public examinations.

A circa 1400 poem written by a young Eustache desChamps blessedly has survived to make possible the impression that not all of student life was as serious, even ponderous, as the extant records would have us believe:

Well beloved father, I have not a penny, nor can I get any save through you, for all things at the University are so dear; nor can I study in my Code or my Digest, for their leaves have the falling sickness. Moreover, I owe ten crowns in dues to the provost, and can find no man to lend them to me; I ask of you greetings and gold. The student has need of many things if he will profit here; his father and his kin must needs supply him freely, that he be not compelled to pawn his books, but have ready money in his purse, with gowns and furs and decent clothing; or he will be damned for a beggar; wherefore, that men may not take me for a beast, I ask of you greetings and gold. Wines are dear, and hostels and other good things; I owe in every street, and am hard bested to free myself from such snares. Dear father, deign to help me! I fear to be excommunicated; already I have been cited, and there is not even a dry dry bone in my larder. If I find not the money before this feast of Easter, the church door will be shut in my face; wherefore grant my supplication. I ask of you greetings and gold.

Envoi

Well beloved father, to ease my debts contracted at the tavern, at the baker's, with the professors and the beadles, to pay my subscriptions to the laundress and the barber, I ask of you greetings and gold.[59]

The poem also confirms for us the expense an education was then, as now. Bright students without money had some recourse in providing for their education. They could pay back an institution through service, an arrangement offered, for example, by the College of the Eighteen founded in Paris in 1180.[60] The scholarship students were lodged in the Hospice of Blessed Mary, provided with a bed and a small allowance; in return they assisted the clergy with anointing the sick and praying for the dead. Since they were poor, these students were allowed to borrow books on condition that they recite seven psalms for the repose of the souls of the donors of the manuscripts and offered a gratuity to the custodians of the tomes.

Some students abused the system, stealing food and gambling. In time, the institution devised several means to filter out the reprobates. They issued a series of weekly examinations that bona fide students, who had studied and prepared their lessons, would pass. Scholarships became one-year grants, renewable upon approval of student performance.

In England, endowed chantries provided free primary education in schools attached to the chapels. A form of scholarship, or at least subsidy, the endowments covered the costs of educating the poor.[61] These chantries, chapels, or chapters were buildings commissioned with large donations from members of an increasingly wealthy middle class, largely composed of merchants with a great deal of disposable money. Donors, preoccupied with and anxious about salvation, expected masses and prayers offered for their souls and for the souls of their families in exchange for their largesse. Some benefactors patronized artists with the understanding that the murals and paintings would feature the contributor in a pious pose before God, the angels, and the saints. The names of chantry donors (confratres) were registered into special prayer books, so that recognition of their generosity and the obligation to pray for their souls would be honored by all. Building chantries was a tradition that lasted several centuries. The custom was discontinued during the brief reign of Henry VIII's son, Edward VI, and with it disappeared the subsidized education the chantries provided.

Daughters of noble families had a different kind of education, although they too were sent off for training to castles and other great houses. Unlike their brothers, however, they were relegated to the ladies of the manors to be taught, above all, to behave demurely. From the middle of the medieval period to the late fifteenth century, girls wore topaz necklaces—the mineral believed to quell passions and libido. Under the tutelage of their *grand dames*, they learned to be laconic, courteous, and modest and to reflect their station in life in a regal carriage. Running and trotting were not allowed. When sitting, girls were to keep hands folded in laps, with eyes diverted downward. They were taught music, weaving, and the elegant gold and silver embroidery called *orfrois*. As a generalization, literacy was not encouraged, but learning to cook, to collect recipes, and to study herbal medicine were pursuits that were encouraged.

> If you wish to marry a wife,
> Think well, my dear son,
> Take none for her beauty,
> Nor for her book learning,
> for they are often deceitful.[62]

Rudimentary reading skills were considered sufficient for girls in order that they might read the Psalter. Some girls were sent off by their families to take the veil of the nunnery, while many followed them for the sole purpose of becoming completely literate. Literate girls, rich and poor alike, had available to them many manuscripts filled with advice for the female from which could be gleaned information useful in everyday life. The historian Barbara Tuchman cataloged the number of topics from which they could choose:

. . . etiquette, housewifery, deportment, home remedies, even phrase books of foreign vocabularies. A reader could find advice on washing hands and cleaning nails before a banquet, on eating fennel and anise in case of bad breath, on not spitting or picking teeth with a knife, not wiping hands on sleeves, or nose, or eyes on the tablecloth. A woman could learn how to make ink, poison for rats, sand for hourglasses; how to care for pet birds in cages and get them to breed; how to obtain character references for servants and make sure they extinguished their bed candles with fingers or breath, "not with their shirts"; how to grow peas and graft roses; how to rid the house of flies, how to remove grease stains with chicken feathers steeped in hot water; how to keep a husband happy by ensuring him a smokeless fire in winter and a bed free of fleas in summer. A young married woman would be advised on fasting and alms giving and saying prayers at the sound of the matins bell "before going to sleep again," and on walking with dignity and modesty in public. . . . She could find books on estate management for times when her husband was away at war, with advice on making budgets and withstanding sieges and on tenure and feudal law so that her husband's rights would not be invaded.[63]

Twelve was the average number of childbearing years that upper-class medieval women could anticipate. The average number of live births was five. Fifty percent of children throughout Europe died before the age of five years. In fourteenth-century England, it has been estimated, 15 percent of couples were childless. Malnutrition that caused hormonal dysfunction and/or venereal disease causing infertility could have been factors, or simply all of their offspring died. The constant awareness that small babies and children commonly died may have tempered bonding practices at every stratum of society, but ethnic differences also produced marked variations in parental attitudes toward children. Records illustrating the warm, social, and demonstrative interactions Italian parents enjoyed with their children and grandchildren probably also reflect the temperamental nature of an expressive people. Cosimo de' Medici (1389–1464), so goes an anecdote, interrupted his meeting with visiting foreign dignitaries so that he could make a toy whistle for his grandson. Happily whittling on a piece of wood, he said to the members of the group: "My lords, know you not the love of children and grandchildren? It is as well that he didn't ask me to play it, because I would have done that too!"[64]

Far fewer records substantiate the existence of this kind of emotional attachment in northern European families. A frequently cited diary entry from an Italian visiting England reads as follows:

The want of affection in the English is strongly manifested towards their children, for having kept them at home till they arrive at the age of seven or nine years at the utmost, they put them out, both males and females, to hard service in the houses of other people, binding them generally for another seven or nine years.[65]

Were it not for the documented evidence of the intentions of the English apprentice system and the important place the system had in English society, it could be—and indeed, has been—suggested that this practice was a form of child abandonment.[66] Families, however, did not sever ties with their children; conversely, they always maintained contact with them. English diaries further confirm this fact.[67]

Cultural differences in expressing affection *intrafamilia* between southern and northern European people are an inconsequential point when the two groups are compared on the issue of child abandonment. In the north, child slaves were uncommon, if not rare. In the wealthy, mercantile south, child slavery was common to many societies. Slaves from the Balkans, Serbia, Africa, and Romania were sold in Florence, Padua, Venice, Sicily, and Naples.

About 30 percent of these slaves were children.[68] In Seville many of the female slaves sold had infants who were sold along with their mothers. A foundling hospital in Genoa was established specifically to accommodate abandoned infants of slaves, highly suggestive of such abandonments being a common phenomenon. Francesco di Marco Datini (1335–1410) was a rich merchant of Prato, Italy, whose motto was "In the name of God and of profit." The casual references to child slaves that he made in his letters are revealing[69]:

I shall need a female slave or two, or a little slave-boy, as you prefer. (1385)

. . . a little slave-girl of 13 bought by Francesco. (1387)

Pray, buy me a little slave-girl, young and rustic, between 8 to 10 years old, and she must be of good stock, strong enough to bear much hard work, and of good health and temper, so that I may bring her up in my own way. I would have her only to wash the dishes and carry wood and bread to the oven, and work of that sort. (1393)

FOUNDLING HOMES

Many of the positive results of economic expansion and increased opportunities in trade and commerce, such as the new towns and cities of Europe and the schools and guild apprenticeships, have been discussed at the outset of this chapter. On the dark side of these influences, new social problems sprang up, and old ones predictably became exacerbated, with increasing numbers of poor, sick, disenfranchised people, many of whom were children, and ever-increasing numbers of orphaned and abandoned children. There were attempts from many quarters to mitigate suffering and misery. Throughout Europe money was donated specifically to establish houses for the dying. The patrons of these institutions came from the same new middle class that had built chantries in England, and the proviso that prayers for their souls, as well as for the souls of those dying, was an understood part of the arrangement. These so-called hospices usually were given over to religious orders to manage and control. In contrast to contemplative orders devoted to prayer, new religious orders were established for the expressed purpose of administering to the sick and dying and to otherwise needy people.

The hospices, already burdened by the needs of the dying, soon became repositories for increasing numbers of homeless children, further straining their resources. Overwhelmed by inundations of abandoned children, hospices were forced to develop policies specific to each institution. Some hospices accepted only exposed infants. Some pointedly excluded them but took in orphans. The Hotel-Dieu of Anger refused all abandoned children as did the Hospice de Troyes, which announced:

Figure 6.3
Ruota of Ospedali degli Innocenti in Florence.
The inscription reads: "Questa fu per quattro
secoli fino al 1875 la ruota degli innocenti
segreto rifugio di miserie e di colpe[.] Alle
quali perpetua soccorre quella carita che
non sera porte."

Abandoned children are not accepted at this institution because if we did accept
them there would be such a host of children that our resources would not be sufficient.[70]

The lack of facilities had become a serious problem. In attempts to ease
the crisis, the concept of establishing homes specifically devoted to the needs
of abandoned children became popular. It was not an entirely new concept;
the Byzantine world, around 400 A.D., had built the *brephotrophia* for
foundlings and orphans. Institutions founded in Constantinople—St. Paul's
in about 550 and St. Zoticos' in 600—were reserved for orphans. Efficient
central administrative offices, called *orphanotrophos*, were run by bishops.[71]
In the Western world the establishment of the first foundling home in 787
has been credited to Datheus, archbishop of Milan[72]:

... I, Datheus, for the welfare of my soul and the souls of my associates, do hereby
establish in the house that I have bought next to the church, a hospital for foundling
children.[73]

Foundling homes were built with small revolving doors so that, from the
street, infants could be placed unobserved in the doorway, safeguarding the
anonymity of mortified mothers or penitent fathers. In France this depository door was called the *tour*; in Germany, the *Drehlade*; and in Italy, the
ruota (figure 6.3).

In Florence, two major homes, Santa Maria della Scala and Santa Maria
de San Gallo, housed two hundred children. At that point, two other homes,
founded to relieve the overcrowding, were themselves overburdened. These
were the Loggia del Bigallo, located in the shadows of the Duomo (c.1358),

Figure 6.4 Ospedali Santa Maria degli Innocenti in Florence.

and the Santa Maria degli Innocenti. The architecture and artistic adornments of Innocenti are famous throughout the world. Designed by Filippo Brunelleschi (1377–1446), it features the prized Andrea della Robbia (1400–1482) enameled terra-cotta medallions of swaddled babies sitting above each Scamozzi capital (figure 6.4). The home had been founded by the silk guild for "those, who against natural laws have been deserted by their fathers or their mothers, that is, infants, who, in the vernacular, are called castaways (*gittatelli*)."[74] A painting from the workshop of Francesco Granacci (1477–1543) romanticizes the care these children were given (figure 6.5).

By the end of the fifteenth century nearly every major European city had a foundling home (table 6.2). One of the early orphanages was founded in

Figure 6.5
Mary Protects the Innocents, in the Ospedali degli Innocenti, Florence.

TABLE 6.2
MAJOR EXTANT FOUNDLING HOMES OF
THE FOURTEENTH CENTURY AND LATER

City	Hospital	Date
Marseille	Saint Esprit de Montpellier	1188
Rome	Santo Spirito de Sassia	1201
Embeck	Order of Saint Esprit	1274
Florence	Santa Maria de San Gallo	1294
Florence	Santa Maria della Scala	1316
Chartres	L'Aumone de Notre Dame	1349
Florence	Loggia del Bigallo	1352
Paris	Saint Esprit en Greves	1362
Florence	Santa Maria degli Innocenti	1445
Lyon	Hotel-Dieu de Notre Dame de Pitie	1523
London	Christ's Hospital	1552
Paris	La Couche	1636
Mexico City	La Cuna	1767
London	Eleemonsynary St. Katherine	?

England in 1146 by the mayor of Bristol, Robert Hardyng, for the descendants of Jews killed during an anti-Semitic pogrom.[75] Another, the Santo Spirito de Sassia in Rome, has a legend associated with it. Prompted by a dream, Pope Innocent III, in 1201, ordered fishermen to toss their nets into the Tiber River. When the nets were retrieved, they were laden with the bodies of 427 babies who had been drowned. The sorrowful pope thereupon founded Santo Spirito as a refuge for *expositi* in hopes of eradicating such wanton murder.*

The goals of foundling homes were threefold, and in implementing them, foundling homes often functioned as coordinating centers in which children were farmed out according to specific needs. Infants, for example, were assigned to wet nurses in either the foundling home itself or in private homes in the surrounding countryside. Boys were apprenticed as soon as they

---

*Santo Spirito was in fact a general hospital with a section dedicated to foundlings. In that section was a fresco depicting the legend of Innocent III first described by Jacob Twinger of Königshofen (c.1380). H. K. Mann, *Lives of the Popes* (St. Louis: Herder Book Company, 1925), 11:84–87.

reached latency, and girls were given small dowries and married off whenever possible. Florentine Gregorio Dati (1362–1436) was satisfied that his city's foundling homes, the three Santa Marias—de San Gallo, della Scala, and degli Innocenti—were successful in achieving their goals:

> . . . these will accept any children of either gender all of whom are given to nurses and cared for; and when the girls are grown they are all married off, and the males are taught a trade, which is a wonderful thing.[76]

Ambrogio Traversari (1386–1439) made similar optimistic observations, which probably were seldom realized:

> Boys are sent to learn their letters; Girls learn womanly things. When they later become adults, the boys learn a trade which will support them; the girls are married, with the institution providing the dowry.[77]

In fact, arranging marriages of female *expositi* was very difficult in societies that valued position and family ancestry. Moreover, funds for the dowries of orphan girls were hard to come by, and charity drives were depended upon to raise needed money. Even well-to-do Florentine fathers in 1425 Florence found it necessary to invest in a special dowry fund, called *il monte delle doti*. A timely investment would be made when daughters were five years old to ensure their future dowries, which would be handed over following the consummation of a marriage.[78] If a daughter died, the investment was lost. Fathers unable to invest in a fund or save money for a dowry contracted to send their daughters to the households of patrons, where they were housed, clothed, fed, and provided with dowries in exchange for a predetermined term of servitude.[79]

Overall, the goals of the foundling homes were successful in that they were focused, practical, and possible and, in the main, faithfully implemented. The greatest calamity that had to be dealt with in the homes, as in society generally, was infant mortality. Crowding and poor communal hygiene were the norm, and infectious diseases spread easily. In San Gallo, on the average, 20 percent of the children died within one month of arrival, and 50 percent of all infants were dead within one year. Approximately only one-third of the children lived to the age of five. In della Scala, the one-year mortality rate was 65 percent, and only 13 percent survived beyond five years. At Chartres, the mortality rate approached an appalling 100 percent! Sadly, the situation did not improve in succeeding centuries. Similar figures of mortality were recorded well into the eighteenth century.[80] Throughout all of those centuries, the popular thought in most places was that being sent to foundling homes presaged early death.

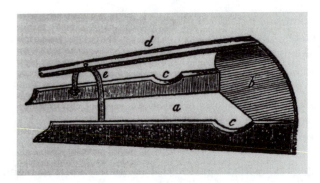

Figure 6.6 A Florentine breast-feeding cage, called an *arcutio*, to prevent "over-laying." *THE GENTLEMAN'S MAGAZINE, JANUARY 1746.*

Although far below those of the foundling homes, child-mortality rates in the general populace also were stupendous. With the exception of some geographic differences in mortality rates, the overall death rate for children under the age of fourteen years was nearly 50 percent. Perinatal mortality and premature deaths in Florence were well documented in the *Libri dei morti*. Premature infants, the *Nacque innazial tempo*, and those who died at birth, the *morti mal di trassinato*, accounted for the majority of infant deaths. Older children died of accidents, such as drowning, falls, or fires, or they died during crop failures or war famines.

They also were smothered to death. Although the majority of these deaths were reported as "accidental," due to the mother or nurse having rolled over the baby in bed, the suspicion was and is that these more likely were instances of infanticide. In fifteenth-century Canterbury, parish registries recorded "overlaying" as leading among all the causes of newborn deaths.[81] These incidents became so common that, by the early sixteenth century, to prevent sleepy mothers from smothering nursing infants, "cages" were manufactured that encased the baby, leaving an opening for breast feeding[82] (figure 6.6).

The legal and church supposition of malfeasance was widespread. A fourteenth-century English manual of penitence, for example, directed parish priests to query husbands: "Hast thou also by hyre I'layn And so by-twene you thy chyld I'slayn?"[83] Mothers, however, generally were held responsible for such deaths. After 1517, a mother was excommunicated from the church if it became known that a child was in bed with her at the time of its death.

Not all such deaths were deliberate; the converse, in fact, is probably true, since mothers have slept with their babies since the human race evolved. In the Middle Ages the commercial sales of popular nocturnal cages further suggest that most parents then were sincere in wanting to protect their sleeping babies from harm. Assuming parental goodwill, it may be supposed that in normal situations there is an unconscious maternal awareness of an infant's presence that restrains any physical movements during sleep and functions as a passive protective impulse. There are modern studies that support this concept.*

From all accounts, it appears that the vast majority of mothers and fathers throughout time fulfilled their obligations as responsible, caring parents to the extent that their respective cultures encouraged this behavior. This is, of course, true in the modern world. However, just as cruel or desperate parents resorted to infanticide in the past, there are current instances of deliberate infanticide. "Overlaying" of a baby was a particularly difficult murder to expose in the past, since there were rarely any witnesses to the act. Modern technology has developed video-recording devices that can be hidden from view in pediatric hospital rooms or pediatric chronic-care facilities, for example, and these have facilitated confirmation of criminal attempts by parents, with subsequent successful prosecutions and convictions. Pediatrician R. Meadow has recently reported twenty-eight attempted infant suffocations.[84]

In the Middle Ages, references to infanticide were recorded in England and throughout the European mainland. The reactions of authorities to suspected crimes reflected regional cultural biases. In Venice, verdicts of cases of *pochissimi* tended to favor a mother's protestation of innocence; whereas in another part of Italy, Fiesole, the courts were suspicious of mothers' claims. In Florence, San Bernadino assumed that *illegitimi* were subject to infanticide:

---

*In Third World countries, where new-technology incubators are not available or are too costly, premature babies' chances of survival are severely compromised. A unique program developed by neonatologists in these countries enlisted the participation of mothers who had given birth to very low-birth-weight infants. Called "marsupial babies," premature infants are wrapped to the mother's bosom all day for several weeks. They are unwrapped only for short periods of maternal toiletry and cleansing. Temperature, humidity, and infection are naturally controlled, and glucose homeostasis takes place by nippling on demand. The results of several studies have shown vast improvement in prognosis for these infants (*Lancet* 1985; 1:1206–9). Statistical data from the clinical study of Dr. Edgar Reyes, Hospital Materno Infantil in Bogota, Colombia, indicates that thousands of mothers and their premature infants have used the technique described above, with not one incident of "smothering" (personal communications).

One recent American study examined an eight-year mortality record and found 121 "overlaying" deaths (*Arch Pediatr Adolesc Med* 1999; 153:1019–23). These 15 deaths per year do not even come close to approximating the over 2,700 deaths per year from SIDS in the United States. Many authorities believe that the benefits of co-sleeping far outweigh the risk of "overlaying."

Figure 6.7
The *Kindlifresser*, ogre of Berne.

Go to the Ponte Vecchio, there by the Arno, and put your ear to the ground and listen [to] . . . the voices of the innocent babies thrown into your Arno and your privies or buried alive in your gardens and your stables, to avoid the world's shame, and sometimes without baptism.[85]

Infanticide in Germany was punished by legal and church authorities. In Metz, the mother who murdered her child was excommunicated and burned at the stake, to which one of her hands had been nailed. In Nuremburg, beheading was the penalty.

Acts of abandonment or infanticide could remain undetected if in childbirth the infant was reported to have been stillborn or to have died shortly thereafter. Such reports may have been widespread, and would account for skewed mortality figures. The usual male–female ratio is 105:100. In ninth-century Saint Germain des Pres the male–female ratio was approximately 116:100; in manorial fourteenth-century England the ratio was 133:100!

Parents sometimes cloaked their infanticide with feigned alarm at the "disappearance" of their toddlers or young children, a protestation that was difficult to contradict. The superstitions of the times supported well-crafted stories, ingenuously believed, of changelings who had been carried off by Satan or "murdering Jews"[86] or the *Kindlifresser* who devoured toddlers (figure 6.7). Jews also were accused of using Christian children's blood to make matzoh and for Passover rituals.

Occurrences of abandonment of children and outright infanticide were significant in the Middle Ages, but the loss of lives from those causes does not compare in scale to the number of children who succumbed to fatal infections due to poor hygiene, childhood diseases, epidemics, and the plague.

Relatively speaking, Europe had been spared plagues from the late eighth century to the mid-fourteenth century. The Black Death of 1347, from the bacillus *Yersinia pestis*, however, engulfed Europe as never before. The Black Death (or more accurately, the pestilence; the familiar term "Black Death" was not used until 1550) struck the most vulnerable—the young and the old. Whole families were lost. In Siena the chronicles of Agnolo de Tura dolefully summarized the horror:

... And it is impossible for the human tongue to recount the awful truth. Indeed, one who did not see such horribleness can be called blessed. And the victims died almost immediately. They would swell beneath the armpits and in their groins, and fall over while talking. Father abandoned child, wife husband, one brother another; for this illness seemed to strike through breath and sight. And so they died. And none could be found to bury the dead for money or friendship. Members of a household brought their dead to a ditch as best they could, without priest, without divine offices. Nor did the death bell sound. And in many places in Siena great pits were dug and piled deep with the multitude of dead. And they died by the hundreds, both day and night, and all were thrown in those ditches and covered with earth. And as soon as those ditches were filled, more were dug. And I, Agnolo de Tura ... buried my five children with my own hands.[87]

In France, Jean de Venette sadly wrote his own account of events that history has never forgotten:

In AD 1348, the people of France and of almost the whole world were struck by a blow other than war. For in addition to the famine ... and to the wars ... pestilence and its attendant tribulations appeared again. .... All this year and the next, the mortality of men and women, of the young even more than the old, in Paris and in the kingdom of France and also, it is said, in other parts of the world, was so great that it was almost impossible to bury the dead.[88]

The demographic records of Halesowen parish in central England, from 1270 to 1400, indicate that childhood mortality among the peasantry was an astronomical 60 percent. Specifically, registry data from the year 1393 reflected the toll the plague had taken on children in the preceding years.[89] Anthropological studies a little farther north, in a York parish graveyard, showed that, from 1389 to 1549, 31 percent of the dead were children, not including babies buried with their mothers or graves in which multiple siblings had been placed. This geographical variation of childhood mortality within England is difficult to explain.[90] Perhaps local crop failures, mini-epidemics, or environmental toxins (for example, peanut aflatoxin or potato blight) were responsible for the disparity in the rates of fatalities.

The losses in Ghent over a period of forty years were particularly well documented in families of the propertied, who were mandated by law to record births and deaths. Although the figures represent only the deaths of children from wealthy homes, a good idea of overall childhood mortality during times of plague can be gleaned from them. Peak rates of mortality were evident in 1350, a year of crop failure and famine during which twelve children died. From 1359 to 1364 and 1368 to 1372, all of which were full-blown plague years, thirty-two and seventy children, respectively, died. Finally, 1381 to 1386, which were years of civil unrest, saw seventy-five die.[91]

The pestilence affected survivor children in that educational institutions suffered devastating losses of the manpower needed to provide adequate educational programs. Across the European mainland 10 percent of university faculty died and 30 percent of the students. In 1361, students in Avignon petitioned Pope Innocent VI to send more faculty:

Most Holy Father, at a time when the university body of your studium at Avignon is deprived of all lectures, since the whole number has been left desolate by the death of pestilence of doctors, licentiates, bachelors, and students.[92]

In the four years subsequent to 1347, bubonic, pneumonic, and septicemic forms of the infection killed an estimated 25 percent to 50 percent of Europe's entire population. Half of those deaths were children. Another devastating outbreak of plague in 1363 was called the "children's plague" because it struck infants and toddlers with particular virulence.[93] Perhaps it was a second round of a strain for which older children and adults still had circulating antibodies, or perhaps that particular strain of plague had a propensity to strike immature immune systems. For whatever reason, it robbed the populace of all of its very young.

In the wake of these disasters and the catastrophic loss of children who might have replenished a wasted population, Europe's population in fact continued to decrease for the following hundred years, a bleak reminder of almost two generations of the young eliminated by disease. For the next three centuries the plague was to return sporadically but with diminishing intensity and virulence. In 1599, Valladolid, Spain, lost 20 percent of its populace, and London lost 25 percent in 1665. Marseilles witnessed the last great epidemic in 1720.[94]

ASPECTS OF EUROPEAN MEDIEVAL CHILDHOOD

Honey, Cake, and Eggs

Jewish parents in medieval Europe were formed by biblical precepts to welcome progeny:

Happy is the man who has a quiver full of them [children]. (Ps. 127:5)

A man without children is as if he were dead. (Talmud, Nedarim 64b)

The arrival of a child was an occasion for rejoicing, and beginning with birth, Jewish families incorporated each milestone of a child's life with the timeless rituals and traditions rooted in scripture that sustained their spiritual and group identities.

The first reading of the Torah after an infant female's birth was the occasion on which the father carried his newborn daughter to the temple, where blessings for the infant and mother would be offered and the child given a name.

The birth of a boy, an even more special event, was marked by the ritual of circumcision on the eighth day of life at a ceremony at which, by tradition, a quorum of ten was required but in fact was attended by all of the family and friends. In front of the *mohel*, a man skilled in the technique of circumcising, were placed two chairs: one for the infant's paternal grandfather (or uncle), on whom was bestowed the honor of holding the child during the circumcision, and an empty chair placed symbolically for the prophet Elijah, Israel's keeper of the covenant. The paternal grandmother ushered the swaddled infant into the room and onto the grandfather's lap amid general prayerful acclamation. Blessings and incantations by the *mohel* preceded the operation and were continued by the father while the *mohel* deftly performed the surgery. The infant was then pronounced to be a member of the covenant. Once the wound was dressed, the *mohel* raised a cup of wine and, placing a drop of wine on the baby's lips, named him. The wine cup was passed to the father to drink, and the baby was returned to the mother. The grandparents cum godparents usually gave the wine cup to the infant as a gift, to be used throughout his life for important rites of passage.

At the age of one year a boy was taken to the temple to offer a brief prayer, bearing his wimpel, a piece of the swaddling clothing from his circumcision. The wimpel, embroidered with his name, birth date, and petitions that he grow to honor the Torah, marry, and live a virtuous life, was wrapped around a Torah scroll, thereby symbolically linking forever the child to the sacred scripture.

Education of the Jewish child began at five years of age. Girls were educated at home: boys were sent off to school. Wearing a shawl called the talith on the festival Shavuot, a boy would be ritually accepted into the classroom by the teacher, who recited the Hebrew alphabet from a tablet—forward, backward, and in paired couplets—in the manner of classical Greco-Roman schoolboys. The boy would be encouraged to mimic the teacher's recitation. Honey then was smeared on the tablet as a sweet inducement to learning, and the child was obliged to lick it all off. Cakes (ritually prepared by a virgin) and eggs, decorated with biblical verses, were read by the teacher to the boy, who again mimicked the teacher's oration. Eating the cakes and eggs—and their sweet words—were his reward for his efforts. After swaying and chanting his lessons and incantations against that cohort of forgetfulness, *Potah*, the boy and company feasted on fruits and nuts. Finally, a walk to the riverbank concluded the schoolboy's initiation rites. There the teacher metaphorically compared the endlessly flowing river with the lifelong task of studying the Torah[95] and added this admonition:

Close your eyes, little child, to all that is around, the trials and the humiliations, but also all your earthly goods. All this, truly is not yours. Your heritage is within the Torah; it is your only assured heritage, no one can take it from you.

Although there were provincial variations on the written textual quotes on the cakes and eggs, the ritual, common to eastern and western Europe, was the same,[96] and the formula was as follows:

Food	*Text*
Tablet with honey	Hebraic alphabet; Lev. 1:1
	Deut. 33:4*
	Ps. 119:9, 12, 17, 125, 140
Cake	Hebraic alphabet; Ezek. 3:3
	Isa. 50:4, 5, 7
Egg	Ps. 19:8, 11

The symbolism of ingesting God's wisdom by consuming God's words was grounded in several Old Testament passages: Jer. 1:9, Ezek. 3:1, Prov. 24:13, and Ps. 119:103. The most literal reference is found in Ezek. 3:1–3:

Moreover he said unto me, Son of man, eat that thou findest, eat this scroll, and go speak unto the House of Israel.

So I opened my mouth, and he caused me to eat that scroll.

And he said unto me Son of man, cause thy belly to eat, and fill thy bowels with this scroll that I give thee. Then did I eat it; and it was in my mouth as honey for sweetness.

The religious and scholastic calendars were integrated and the curricula interwoven seamlessly so that secular subjects were learned in an atmosphere

---

*The responsibility to learn the entire Torah was invoked in this passage, which begins: "When Moses charged us with the Torah as the heritage of the congregation of Jacob, . . ."

of ritual and the celebration of holy days. Then, as now, the symbols and games of Hanukah, the festival of light, were observed and played. Sweet treats were offered, and an ancient spinning game was played with a four-sided dreidel top carved with the first letters of *Nes Gadol Haya Shom* (a great miracle happened there). It commemorated the phenomenon in the Maccabee temple, where the menorah, supplied with only one day's oil, was said to have burned for eight days and nights. Then, as now, children learned the Haggadah at Passover, during the Seder meal, ceremonially asking those present the meaning of the Seder symbols—the matzoth, shankbone, egg, parsley, salt water, bitter herbs, and haroset. The history of an enduring culture is embedded in the responses to even just one of the questions:

> Why is this night different from all other nights?
> Tonight we eat no bread, only matzoth, symbol of enslavement.
> Tonight we eat bitter herbs, symbol of enslavement.
> Yet tonight also, we dip our herbs in condiments, symbols of freedom.

The spiritual and cultural experiences of the Jewish people, spanning millennia; the prescribed rituals; the recitations and incantations; and the rewards of sweets and treats were, in sum, the center of medieval Jewish children's lives, as they were for their predecessors and are now for their descendants.

The Children's Crusade

Distant Palestine, as the homeland of Christ, was considered by the church a Holy Land and was a place to which Christian pilgrims traveled. When the Seljuk Turks began to hinder travel to Jerusalem, Pope Urban II rallied the faithful, pronouncing a holy war to liberate the Holy Land from the Saracens in a series of bloody, brutal wars, spanning almost two hundred years.

There were a total of eight major crusades from 1096 to nearly 1300 (table 6.3). History has sometimes romantically recalled images of kings, knights, and templars marching to the Holy Land to fight the "infidels." Seldom discussed is the Fifth Crusade—the Children's Crusade—in which the lives of thousands of children were sacrificed.[97]

Pope Innocent III in the early thirteenth century pleaded with the war-weary faithful to organize a fifth crusade to recapture Jerusalem. He was ignored by all, except for an impressionable adolescent shepherd, Stephen of Cloyes. Stephen had been approached by a priest, perhaps a refugee from Palestine or, as has been rumored, one claiming to be Christ. Certainly, Stephen believed it had been Christ who had enjoined him to organize an unarmed army of youths.[98] Stephen began, in May of 1212, to preach in the

TABLE 6.3
THE MAJOR CRUSADES

Crusade	Date	Notes
I	1096	Captured Palestine for several years
II	1147	Led by Bernard of Clairvaux
III	1189	Led by Frederick Barbarossa, Philip of France, Richard of England
IV	1202	Sacking of Constantinople to repay Venice for support of trip home
V	1212	Children's Crusade
VI	1228	Frederick II recaptures Jerusalem
VII	1248	Led by Louis IX
VIII	1270	Last crusade, ending 1290

parish of St. Denys, located five miles north of Paris, recruiting the young to join him in a children's crusade. He envisaged a nonviolent campaign in which his flock would convert "Mohammedans" to Christianity and thereby liberate Jerusalem. Mesmerized by his charisma, the young audience was convinced that the Mediterranean Sea would part, unimpeding the noble trek to the Holy Land.

Stephen's plan was received with wild enthusiasm, and word of it spread rapidly. Inspired with zealous conviction, a ten-year-old boy named Nicholas, in Cologne, Germany, organized his own march to Jerusalem. Rapidly, he was able to assemble an army of children, some of whom were selected "officers" to lead the throng. A visually impressive uniform, consisting of a long gray coat with a red cross on the breast, was adopted as a means of maintaining order and enhancing the concept of a disciplined army on the march. Each child carried a palmer's staff and wore a broad-brimmed hat. Two armies ultimately were assembled by Nicholas. One may have numbered twenty thousand children, although this figure has been disputed.[99] The boys ranged in age from eight to sixteen years. Marching in procession along the Rhine River, wearing their uniforms adorned with the bold Christian symbol, they carried banners and sang songs, touching the hearts of the people who watched them as they passed by. One song, from Westphalia, has survived:

> Fairest Lord Jesus,
> Ruler of all nature,
> Thou of Mary and of God the Son!

> Thee will I cherish,
> Thee will I honor,
> Thee my soul's glory, joy, and crown!
>
> Fair are the meadows,
> Fairer still the woodlands,
> Robed in the blooming garb of spring;
> Jesus is fairer,
> Jesus is purer,
> Who makes our saddened heart to sing.
>
> Fair is the sunshine,
> Fairer still the moonlight,
> And the sparkling, starry host;
> Jesus shines brighter,
> Jesus shines purer,
> Than all the angels heaven can boast.[100]

The journey of the innocents that had begun with inspiring religious commitment and belief quickly turned sour, bringing unimaginable suffering on naive and unsuspecting children. Many children were robbed, sodomized, prostituted, or enslaved. Dispirited, many turned back. Nearly half of the pathetic ensemble, however, continued their quest onward toward the Alps, succumbing to cold, starvation, and exhaustion as they crossed the formidable land barrier. As their ranks thinned, the fallen were buried along the roadside. By the time they reached the zenith of their crossing at the pass of Mont Cenis, their legions had been reduced to less than ten thousand children. At Mont Cenis they took refuge in a monastery to muster strength and moral fortitude before continuing their hapless journey. When they arrived in Genoa on August 25, 1212, Nicholas could count only seven thousand survivors in his group. The people of Genoa feared that the children might decide to settle among them and sent them out of the town gates on August 26, the very next day after the beleaguered band had arrived.

Disheartened, the children nevertheless directed their way toward Rome but without Nicholas among the group. He was never heard from again, and there is no record of what happened to him. It has been speculated that, disillusioned with his leadership, the sullen and embittered children broke ranks with him and abandoned him. Possibly he died. Despite his disappearance, the ragged company continued on, making one stop in Pisa. There, two boatloads of children set sail for the Holy Land, at which point they, too, disappeared. There was speculation that they had reached Ptolemais, but their whereabouts never were ascertained and they never returned to Germany. Enraged by the loss of their children, parents accused Nicholas's father of encouraging his son's folly. He was arrested, convicted of entrapping children, and hanged.

Those children who had stayed behind in Pisa formed several different bands, each taking separate routes to Rome. Some of them—not all—reached Rome, where Pope Innocent III, moved by the sight of the tattered, shoeless, hungry, and exhausted throng of children, beseeched them to return to their homes. He emphasized that he did not support their wish to embark abroad, but there were zealots who continued to sponsor the children, as well as slave traders who had other motives.

At about the same time that Nicholas's army had left Germany, another contingent of children, equal in number to Nicholas's army, rallied to the call of a leader (whose identify remains unknown) to crusade for souls in the Holy Land. This group crossed the Alps over a different route than the one taken by Nicholas and his group. They reached Brindisi after a long, arduous trip across Switzerland. How many survived the crossing is unknown, but eyewitnesses described them as looking exhausted, malnourished, clotheless, shoeless, and downtrodden. This ensemble apparently remained in Brindisi looking for financial support so that they could sail over the Aegean. It is known that several ships did leave the port in the months that followed, but the children were not seen again. One source contended that a Norwegian named Friso sold the children into slavery:

> To the sea of fools
> Led the path of the children.[101]

Well after the children from Germany had reached Italy, Stephen's army left France. Recruits had been gathered from many provinces. Thirty thousand children, averaging twelve years of age, departed from Vendôme on their holy crusade.[102] They traveled to Marseilles singing hymns and crying "Dieu le volt!" In Marseilles, King Philip Augustus prohibited the crusade. The king's decree was ignored. The populace, full of religious ardor and zeal, fully supported the children and the endeavor they had undertaken. Vessels were sought that would take the children to the Holy Land.

The story of that voyage is said to be the origin of the tale of the Pied Piper. Seven ships in all were provided for the journey by two villainous merchants, Hugo Ferreus and William Porcus. It is believed the Latin forms of their last names were probably given to them many years later, since their French surnames were not known. Five thousand children were crammed aboard the ships, and in August 1212 they set sail. As they neared Sardinia, two of the ships were wrecked on Hermit's Rock during a severe storm. More than a thousand children perished. The other five ships reached Bujeiah

(Bougie), one hundred miles east of Algiers. Waiting for them were slave dealers who previously had been contracted by Ferreus and Porcus to seize the children as they disembarked and deliver them as slaves to Muslim masters. Seven hundred children were sent to Alexandria and were purchased by Maschemuth, the governor. The majority of the children were dispatched and sold as they made their way to Baghdad. In Baghdad, purportedly eighteen children were executed because they refused to renounce Christianity and embrace Islam. Eighteen years passed before the children's fate became known in Europe, when the priest who had accompanied them on the voyage finally returned to Marseilles.

Shocked and saddened, the pope, Gregory IX, established a memorial to the children on the island of San Pietro, the site where the ships sank and where many of the children's bodies had been washed ashore. He ordered a church erected and named it the Ecclesia Novorum Innocentium, clearly identifying the lost children with the original "Holy Innocents" of the New Testament.*

Twelve prebendal locations were established for the purpose of constant prayer and the island became a popular site for pilgrimages. Gradually, the place and its meaning were forgotten. Five hundred years elapsed before a band of escaped slaves from Tabarca in 1737 sailed north from the African coast and rediscovered the island. Only the ruins of the church were to be seen—an unrecognized relic of a long-forgotten edifice, of which only a foundation remained.

Two further episodes reminiscent of the Children's Crusade occurred later. In July 1237 in Erfurt, over a thousand children assembled and marched to Armstadt. The reason the group gathered is for the most part unknown. The speculation associates it with the canonization of St. Elizabeth of Thuringia. The other episode occurred in 1458. In honor of the Archangel Michael and to commemorate his feast day, a hundred children marched to Mont St. Michel in Normandy. These assemblies did not match the Children's Crusade either in numbers or in pathos.

More than thirty historians have researched and written about the Children's Crusade. Figures and statistical data differ among them, but all are in agreement about the basic events that occurred.[103] None, however, quite

---

*There was one other group of slain "innocents," in the First Crusade. They were Jewish children, killed by their parents in family suicides to avoid forced baptism at the hands of crusaders during pogroms in the Rhineland. Billings, 1987, pp. 15–22. These events were recorded at Speyer, Worms, Mainz, Cologne, and Trier, despite the attempts of local bishops, who recognized the hysteria and injustice of crowd psychology, to shelter these Jews. Amt, 1993, pp. 279–85.

approaches the poignancy of the lamentable saga as does the rhythmical chronicle written about 1215 and attributed to Joseph Benedictus Gentilotus:

Here you will learn of the long wanderings of boys and how they were deceived
    through charms and imprecations.
It is amazing what they believed in those times.
And the staggering slaughter that grew out of it throughout the land.
For to such fine youth great evil did befall.
Indeed they were lured away with secret magic art.
Here is a song that was sung everywhere:
"Nicholas chosen by Christ will be transfixed
And he will travel to Jerusalem with the innocents,
Fearless, he will tread upon the sea with dry feet.
Young men and women will unite chastely.
For the honor of God, Nicholas will perform great deeds.
What peace and praise will resound to a jubilant God!
Pagans and infidels will all be baptized.
Everyone will sing this song in Jerusalem.
Christ will proclaim peace now to Christians.
And His light will shine wonderfully on those redeemed in blood.
And He will crown the boys of Nicholas."
Such dedication had never been heard of before this.
All ears were astounded that young girls were included.
Those who were converted were under sixteen years of age.
Boys traveling together contended that they might follow.
And they raised such loud cries that it was useless to comfort them.
Children from all over France and Germany joined together in this undertaking.
All the children were brought together by Friso the Norwegian.
He mutilated the eyes and feet of the boys who were sold.
The maidens were defiled in Brindisi.
And sold far and wide to the most evil money grubbers.
The crying children whom he seized with jeering laughter were justly mourned.
Mothers wept that the daughters born to them were given to death.
The fruitless venture of the children who were deceived drew mighty sighs.[104]

Gilles de Rais

An account of a fifteenth-century scandal of a young aristocrat, Gilles de Rais, and his fiendish companions is included here as further evidence of children's vulnerability in medieval Europe and the degree of suffering that many endured.[105]

Gilles de Rais (1404–1440) was raised in the duchy of Anjou by his maternal grandfather, Jean de Caron. A malevolent influence, de Caron inculcated into his ward an overweening arrogance and a strong sense of entitlement. When de Rais was sixteen years old, his grandfather goaded him to abduct a bride and to seize others' lands and castles. In 1429, Gilles, baron of Rais, fought alongside Joan of Arc (1412–1431) as one of her commanders in the liberation of Orleans. Thereafter he was honored by Charles VII, who named him a marshall of France and gave him the privilege to add the royal fleur-de-lis to his coat of arms.

As a young adult with many estates and properties and endowed with strong political ambitions and aspirations, de Rais mutated into a pedophile and necrophile. The owner of vast territories and many castles, de Rais, despite his arrogance and evil nature, surprisingly was regarded as a generous lord by his serfs and vassals. History does not remember him, however, for the public life in which he exhibited some chivalry but for his darker, demonic private life of sorcery, debauchery, and murder that were exposed in a dramatic trial in 1440.

In the medieval milieu in which spirituality and superstition coexisted without conflict, in which attendance at daily mass did not appear to be incongruous or in conflict with the practice of alchemy, magic, and geomancy, Gilles de Rais added another dimension—satanic ritual—to the curious melange of beliefs. After his grandfather died in 1432 and he inherited more than twenty castles and estates, he formed a cadre of followers to join him in demonic practices. His various castles and households became centers for witchery and satanism.

He and his cohorts began to gather children to use in their diabolical orgies. Some were purchased from poor peasants. At the trial, depositions of witnesses indicated that some children were bought for the price of a dress or a loaf of bread. Abandoned urchins were snatched from the streets and alleys. Some of the children were beggars, abducted while seeking alms at the doors of his various estates. Even children who had been entrusted by the unsuspecting to de Rais's protection and care in exchange for service in his choirs or as pages became his victims.

Although there were sporadic rumors, as far as the townfolk knew, the children simply had vanished. The horror of their fate was disclosed at the trial of Gilles de Rais and his colleagues. For crimes against the church, they were charged with heresy and apostasy, satanic rituals, and invocations of the devil. For crimes against humanity, they were charged with sodomy and murder committed in conjunction with voyeurism, sadism, and mutilation.

At the trial it was revealed that de Rais liked to watch as his victims struggled in panicked distress. The children were hanged—but just partially, enough to damage their larynges and vocal cords and thereby silence them. He sodomized some of the children as they were dying and sodomized some of those who were dead. Most of the children were brutally murdered by having their throats slit. During his trial, de Rais described sitting on the abdomens of some children as he watched them die from exsanguination and suffocation. He had some decapitated, after which, in a macabre ritual, he and his base companions, delirious with alcohol, lined up their severed heads and kissed them all. In the satanic rituals, Gilles and his men used the hearts, eyes, and blood of infants as sacrificial offerings. When finished with their gruesome business, they disposed of most of the bodies by burning them and burying the ashes.

One hundred forty children were identified as victims of Gilles; they had been abused, tortured, mutilated, and killed. The court adjusted the number to greater than two hundred victims on the strength of strong testimony from witnesses and after forty bodies at his castle in Machecoul and forty-six at Champtuce had been exhumed. These bodies were mostly of boys, although some found were the remains of girls. They were between the ages of seven and twelve years.

Astonishingly, the murders committed by Gilles de Rais were perpetrated over a span of eighteen years. The rumors that had circulated were given short shrift by incredulous authorities who considered that de Rais's exalted position and influence completely discounted the possibility of such devilish acts.

Moreover, as told to the court at the trial, some parents were cowed into silence, fearing reprisals from de Rais's men and therefore they failed to report their missing children. Others, realizing that there was no proof of wrongdoing to submit to the authorities, were afraid to make accusations and by so doing reveal their identities to the culprits. Finally, the rumors evolved into a public outcry and an indignation so great that the authorities had to react. The evidence of the heinous slaughter was not difficult to uncover.

On 13 October 1440, forty-nine counts of criminal conduct were charged against Gilles de Rais and his wicked retainers. Count 15 offers a concise summary of all of the accusations made by the court that day:

XV. Item, that because of the public rumor at first and in light of the secret inquiries made by His Reverend Father, the Bishop of Nantes, while visiting his city and diocese, by his agents deputized by apostolic authority and by the prosecutor in the ecclesiastical court in Nantes whom His Reverend Father had appointed in respect to crimes and transgressions pertaining to the ecclesiastical court; moreover, in consideration of the previous vehement, lamentable, tearful and very grievous public accusation made by several persons of both sexes, as from the city of Nantes as from its diocese, who wailed, complained and lamented about the disappearance and murder of their innocent sons and daughters and asserted that these sons and daughters had been seized, had had their throats slit in a cruel manner, had been butchered, then dismembered and cremated and had been otherwise treated cruelly and shamefully by Gilles de Rais, the defendant, by Gilles de Sille, Roger de Brique-ville, Henriet Griart, Etienne Corrillaut, alias Poitou, Andre Buchet, Jean Rossignol, Robin Romulart, by one named Spading and Hicquet de Bremont, all servants and followers of Gilles de Rais; and they said that Gilles de Rais, the accused, had damnably sacrificed the bodies of these innocents to demons while many others claimed that Gilles de Rais had evoked demons and made sacrifices to evil spirits, that he had horribly and vilely committed the unnatural sin of sodomy with these children, as many boys as girls sometimes while they were living, and others after the death of these innocent children and sometimes while they were expiring, and that he abused both sexes.

The trial was swift and the conviction certain. On October 26, 1440, Gilles de Rais was hanged and burned at the stake. Having expressed contrition for his vile deeds, the authorities spared his body the final dishonor of disembowelment by flames and permitted it to be buried in a casket and entombed in Nantes.

Changelings

In the medieval world, anxiety, fear, and ignorance were manifested in the majority belief in magic, sorcery, charms, spells, superstitions, witchery, and demonic possession. In this environment of thinking, to have a change-ling—an anomalous child—was believed to be the consequence for viola-tions of taboos or to derive from mysterious, malevolent forces beyond the control of mortals.

As mentioned elsewhere in this text, a broken religious taboo, such as coitus and conception on a Sunday or Good Friday, was thought invariably to result in the birth of a sickly, malformed infant. Likewise, a child con-ceived during a period of parental emotional or psychic distress—caused, for example, by bad dreams or omens—produced a changeling. Albertus Mag-nus (?1206–1280) recounted such a story of a king and queen who experi-enced such ill luck. The king, while making love to his queen, told her of the visions he had had of a dark monster. The queen gave birth, subsequently, to a deformed, dark infant—"proof" of the power of menacing influences.[106] People were fearful of ill-disposed fairies, demons, or evil spirits who had power to change infants—hence, *changelings*—in utero, at birth, or as suck-lings. The Scandinavian *huldrer*, for example, was a beautiful and alluring siren with a long tail who was believed to exchange her deformed offspring for human babies.[107]

The anomalies of changelings ranged from the obvious—a missing limb, a large nevus, or a deformed head—to an anomaly more gradual in being recognized, such as a child who failed to grow or an infant who became wasted and cachectic. The appellation applied to phenotypically normal children as well as to those who were perceived as weak, sickly, colicky, or irritable. It was thought that parents could employ several modalities that would "change" their little ones back to their "normal" selves. Enlisting the powers of the netherworld, all of the "remedies" appear strange to the modern mind, and since the initial premise was false, none of them was curative.

Parents believed they could force a malevolent spirit to return an exchanged normal baby by making the changeling cry incessantly.[108] The infant's wails, it was thought, attracted the attention of the demon, who would snatch the changeling and leave in its place the healthy child. It followed that changelings were stimulated to cry by whatever means, through beatings, threats, or abandonment. Sometimes unfortunate children were touched by hot coals, dunked in a stream, or forced to drink bushmore (digitalis).[109] Numerology and the mystical properties with which the cult had been imbued were enlisted in acts of abandonment. Children were placed at the junction of three roads or three streams, the number 3 being symbolic of the omnipotent and beneficent deity. When a child uttered an audible cry it was retrieved by its mother, who was hopeful that the cry signified that an exchange had taken place. Similarly, a mother cut her child's hair and stuck the hair on buttered bread and forced a dog to swallow the bread. If the animal coughed or gagged, it was believed that the child's illness had been transferred to the dog.[110]

One dog, Guinefort, became an object of veneration, endowed by people with curative powers. The legendary dog, a greyhound, apparently lived in Lyons in the home of an aristocratic family.[111] The dog was left one day, so the story goes, in the sole company of the infant of the house, whose parents and wet nurse were away. A snake made its way into the manor and approached the infant's cradle, whereupon the vigilant dog attacked it. During the ensuing melee, the cradle was upset and the baby fell to the floor and crawled to hidden safety. The dog killed the snake but was itself injured, weakened, and bloodied. When the lord and lady returned to the nursery, alarmed by the disordered scene and finding the baby missing, they assumed the simpering, bloodstained Guinefort had devoured their infant and ordered the dog killed. When the baby was safely found and the remains of the slain serpent uncovered, they realized Guinefort had been wrongly accused and punished.

Saddened and filled with remorse, the master had the dog buried at a special site with a monument stone. In time, Guinefort came to be regarded as a "martyr" who had mystical powers to protect and to cure children, and the place where Guinefort was buried became a shrine for pilgrims who had changelings. Incantations and rituals were performed at the shrine, as parents beseeched the blessed Guinefort to cure their children. Stephen of Bourbon, a Dominican monk and an inquisitor appointed by the church, described the wizardry in which mothers seeking cures carried their sick children to an old lady who lived near Guinefort's burial site (presumed by Stephen of Bourbon to be a witch). To elicit a cure, the old lady made an offering of salt, hammered a nail into a tree, and hung the afflicted baby's clothing on the nail. Nine times, during which the spirits were enjoined to "change" the baby, the naked child was passed back and forth between two trees. After the final pass, the "witch" lit two candles and left them and the baby at the foot of one of the trees. After a period of time, the parent recovered the child and dipped it into the river nine times. While it was probable that most of these infants died of exposure, parents were convinced that their children had been wrested from the demon's grip and transported at least to limbo, if not heaven.

The concept of a changeling was to endure even into the eighteenth century, where learned men continued to consider transmutation of species as a plausible explanation for anomalous human infants.

Boy Bishops

Sometime during the tenth century an ecclesiastical ritual in commemoration of the Holy Innocents on December 28th became institutionalized. The earliest records of child participation in the memorial procession can be found circa 867 in the monastery of St. Gall.[112] The celebration was a recognition of the first "martyrs" of Christendom, and it marked the beginnings of children's engagement in a liturgical ceremony. In the century that followed it was conjoined with the feast of St. Nicholas of Myra on December 6th. St. Nicholas was considered a patron saint of child scholars, and his memorial day therefore was the ideal one on which to elect the "boy bishop." His patronage of students was based on a legend of two boys who went to Athens for study. They had been asked to present themselves to Bishop Nicholas upon arrival but they postponed their visit, choosing instead to check on the delivery of their goods. Their valuable goods betrayed their wealth and they were killed, dismembered, and pickled for sale. The sorrowful Nicholas saw all this in a vision and confronted the murdering innkeeper. Nicholas prayed and obtained divine intercession, after which the boys were miraculously reassembled; they emerged from the pickling vat and went off to study[113] (figure 6.8).

The church's decision to annually select an *episcopus puerorum*—a boy bishop—on the feast of St. Nicholas and for one day reverse the roles of students and church authorities became a popular custom. In England, the ear-

Figure 6.8
St. Nicholas and the Boys, by Gerard David,
circa 1484. NATIONAL GALLERY OF SCOTLAND.

liest documentation of this event is recorded in the register of 1221 in York Cathedral.[114] Youths elected as boy bishops were usually thirteen to eighteen years of age. The church authorized them to be adorned with the robes of a bishop and to act with the authority of that position on the feast of the Holy Innocents, to be called Childermas. Other young schoolboys also were permitted to don the garb of ecclesiastics and engage in church duties and perform church services.

The festival itself began on 27 December, the eve of the feast of the Holy Innocents, when the schoolboys adopted the characters of their ecclesiastical elders. The designated boy bishop, followed by his entourage, progressed either to the altar of St. Nicholas or to that of the Holy Innocents, where the bishop extended his blessing to the group and transferred to them church power and authority for one day. On Childermas morning, the feast of the Holy Innocents, it was traditional for the boy bishop, suited in full bishopric regalia made to size, to deliver a sermon to the townspeople.[115] Only three complete homilies, all from the sixteenth century, have survived. One was called the Gloucester sermon. Two others were printed by Wynkyn de Worde and by Erasmus. All the sermons memorialized the Holy Innocents, and all spoke to the admonition of being "childlike" to enter the kingdom of heaven.

With the exception of Holland,[116] the custom became wildly popular throughout Europe, particularly in England and France, and by the late fifteenth century almost every parish had its own candidate. In England, some nunneries elected child abbesses, but this practice was mostly condemned by local bishops.[117] Some dioceses gave full church power to youthful boy bishops, with authority to deliver blessings, say vespers, and even fill vacant offices with appointees of their choosing.[118] Many dioceses extended the power of boy bishops and their attendants until Candlemas day, February 2nd, giving free reign to these "clerics" for over one month of the year. The feast was observed with street celebrations, plays, dancing, and costumes and became a major annual event. Increasingly, it evolved into a veritable saturnalia, with licentious and raucous behavior, much drinking, and open mockery of authority. A registry entry in St. Paul's Cathedral in London records at least one disgusted reaction to the practices:

. . . what had been invented for the praise of sucklings had been converted into a disgrace, and to the derision of the decency of the House of God, on account of the unruly crowd which followed it, and the riotous mob which disturbed the Bishop's peace.[119]

Offended and alarmed church officials attempted to suppress the festival, with little success. The custom in England, however, was abruptly discontinued with the Royal Proclamation of 1541 by Henry VIII forbidding the celebration of Childermas:

Whereas heretofore dyvers and many superstitions and chyldysh obseruances have ben vsed, and yet to this day are observed and kept, in many and sundry parts of this realm, as vpon Saint Nicholas, Saint Catherine, Saint Clement, the Holy Innocents, and such like, children strangelie decked and apparayled to counterfeit priestes, bishoppes, and women, and so be ledde with songes and daunces from house to house, blessing the people and gatheryng of money; and boyes do singe masse and preche in the pulpitt, with syche other vnfittinge and inconuenient vsages, rather to the derysyon than any true glory of God, or honor of his sayntes: the Kynges Maiestie therefore, myndinge nothinge so moche as to aduance the true glory of God without vaine superstition, wylleth and commandeth that from henceforth all svch superstitious obseruations be left and clerely extinguished throwout his realmes and dominions, for asmvch as the same doth resemble rather the vnlawfull superstition of gentilitie, than the pure and sincere religion of Christe.[120]

In the five-year reign of Mary Tudor, the custom enjoyed a brief revival. With the influence of John Calvin's belief that even infants were tainted with sin, the celebration of the festival of the boy bishop finally ended.

THE EASTERN WORLD IN MEDIEVAL TIMES

Islam

When Muhammad (570–632) was about forty years old, he had a vision in which he was commanded by the Archangel Gabriel to proclaim the glories of Allah. While he was in Mecca, from 610 to 622, and in Medina, from 622 to 632, Muhammad's revelations were recorded by scribes, and these documents formed the corpus of the Quran, or the Koran, the governing code of social and moral conduct for Muslims. By the year 1000, the nations of Islam and the Koran's influence reached from Spain and North Africa to Afghanistan.

Early Islam made no distinction between religion and law, since it was viewed that God's will encompassed all of life. The Koran was used to reveal this will, and (as in the *Fattiha*, the opening sura of the Koran) to provide prayers of petition for strength and guidance in all earthly matters:

> In the name of God, the Merciful, the Compassionate.
> Praise be to God, the Lord of the Worlds,
> The Merciful One, the Compassionate One,
> Master of the Day of Doom.
> Thee alone we serve, to Thee alone we cry for help.
> Guide us in the straight path
> The path of them Thou hast blessed.
> Not of those with whom Thou art angry
> Nor of those who go astray.[121]

The Koran, together with the *Shariah*, emphasized the duty of parents toward their children, and many of the prayers reflect the hopes and concerns of parents for healthy and moral offspring, beginning with the prayer of the Sura 3,39: "Lord, grant me from Thyself pure offspring." Sura 25,74 petitioned that children be righteous: "Lord, grant us of our spouses and our offspring the delight of our eyes, and make us a model for the righteous."

To ensure that children would be faithful to the principles of Islam, the opening of the prayer, *Igama*, was whispered into the ears of newborns. The *tahnik* was performed, in which infants' palates were rubbed with premasticated dates. This ceremony was thought to transfer blessings and traditions passed down from the prophet Muhammad:

Then I brought the child to Allah's Apostle and placed him [in his lap]. He asked for a date, chewed it, and put his saliva in the mouth of the child. Thus the first substance to enter his stomach was the saliva of Allah's Apostle. Then he did his *tahnik* with the date and invoked Allah to bless him.[122]

Traditionally, when firstborn sons were seven days old, their hair was cut, and *aqiqa*, the sacrificial slaughter of a sheep, was made. These rituals signified fathers' official recognition of their children and acceptance of fatherhood.

Several verses of the Koran identified and condemned infanticide, an indication that, while such acts were committed, they were not condoned. An examination of Sura 8,81 suggests that girls were more commonly victims of infanticide: "And when the girl-child that was buried alive is asked, for what sin she was slain. . . ." Several exegetes elaborate on *hadith* reports that cite multiple incidences of female infanticide, such as those ordered by Asim al-Tamimi, who said to the Prophet: "I buried alive eight daughters."[123] There was a passive form of infanticide recorded in which exsanguination resulted by neglecting to tie the umbilical cord. Such acts were unequivocal defiance of Koranic law:

Do not destroy your offspring for fear of poverty; it is We who provide for them and for you. Surely, destroying them is a great sin. . . . Do not destroy the life that Allah has declared sacred save for just cause. The heir of one who is killed wrongfully has Our authority to demand retribution. (Sura 17,32)

The prolific number of authoritative volumes related to pediatric health care that were produced in the Islamic world more accurately measure the degree of the Koran's influence in inculcating concern in its followers for the well-being of children. Ibn al-Jazzar, who wrote *The Book of Child-Rearing* in the tenth century, wrote extensively on the hygienic care of the newborn and on the nutritional benefits of nursing, as well as on diseases of infants. There were four other significant treatises written on the infant and the first year of life during the tenth and eleventh centuries. These were complemented by the most influential child-rearing manual, *Tuhfat al-Mawdud*, written in the early fourteenth century by Ibn Qayyim al-Jawziyya (1292–1350). Ibn Qayyim mixed popular folklore and superstition, Islamic theology, and behavioral modification into a unified approach to raising children. For example, Ibn Qayyim attributed an infant's cry to both physiological stimuli and a "poke" by the devil. He opined that smiles did not occur until a baby was forty days old, and dreaming commenced when babies were sixty days old.[124] Ibn Qayyim discussed a range of topics, including feeding, swaddling, walking, teething, first words, and education. He suggested that each child be individually assessed with respect to interests and aptitudes so that an appropriate plan for his educational future might be developed.*

---

*Boys started school at the age of six, primarily to memorize the Koran, but arithmetic and vocational skills were also taught. A school was commonly supported by a *waqf*, a charitable

❑ ❑ ❑

The Koran specified guidelines for the care of infants caught in the disharmony of a divorce:

In cases of divorce, mothers shall give suck to their children for two whole years, where it is desired to complete the suckling, and the father of the child shall be responsible for the maintenance of the mother during that period. (Sura 2,234)

The rights of orphans were protected by the Koran and are referred to several times:

Do not approach the property of the orphan during his minority, except for the most beneficent purpose, and fulfil every covenant, for you will be called to account for it. (Sura 17,34)

Give the orphans their substance, and render them not bad in exchange for good; and devour not their substance together with your own. Verily, that is a great sin. (Sura 4,2)

Meddle not with the substance of an orphan, otherwise than for the improvement thereof, until he attain maturity. (Sura 6,153)

Sura 4,47 addressed with specific detail the treatment and care of orphaned children and safeguarded their rights of inheritance:

Give not unto those who are weak of understanding the substance which God had appointed you to preserve for them; but maintain them thereout, and clothe them, and speak kindly unto them. And examine the orphans until they attain the age of marriage. And if ye perceive that they are able to manage their affairs well, deliver their substance unto them; and waste it not extravagantly or hastily before they grow up. Let him who is rich abstain, and let him who is poor take according to what shall be reasonable. And when ye deliver their substance unto them, bring forward witnesses thereof. But God is sufficient as reckoner.

trust where obligatory giving (*zakat*) by the faithful could be routed. Some *waqfs* were endowed by sultans, others by merchants or the military, and still others by the general citizenry. Some *waqfs* sponsored schools, while others supported poor *hajj* pilgrims, provided dowries, aided travelers, sheltered the sick, gave hospice to the incurables, or provided general charity. In his memoirs, Ibn Battuta (1304–1369) relates the story of a boy servant who dropped and shattered a Chinese porcelain dish. "A number of people collected around him and suggested, 'Gather up the pieces and take them to the custodian of the endowment for utensils.' He did so and when the endowment custodian saw the broken pieces, he gave the boy money to buy a new plate" (Bullis, 2000, pp. 3–38).

The fundamentals that guided the nurturing and the education of the Muslim child in early childhood were encoded in the five pillars of Islam: affirmation of belief in One God and the prophet Muhammad, daily prayers, the tithing of 2.5 percent, the fasting during Ramadan, and the pilgrimage to Makkah called the *hajj*. The memorization of the Koran was expected.

Few Islamic scholars wrote for children,[125] the exception being Arabian theologian Abu Hamid Muhammad al-Ghazali (1059–1111) who taught at the University in Baghdad. He wrote in the form of parables at a high level of linguistic sophistication, difficult for children to comprehend. His essay entitled "My Child" nevertheless is representative of the emphasis given in the medieval Islamic world to the spiritual education of children. In the essay, children are exhorted to be virtuous, to study the Koran, and to learn the eight insights that address human interrelationships and love of the Almighty. Insight number 6 is illustrative:

I have seen that people make enemies for many causes and intentions. Then I thought of the word of God the Highest: Satan is your enemy and hold him for such. And I knew that I was not permitted to make enemies except Satan.[126]

Al-Ghazali's writing exemplifies the emphasis on religious education. *Kitab Riyadat al-Nafs*, written sometime between 1095 and 1106, asserts that children do not belong to their parents but are entrusted to them to learn the way of Islam:

The child is by way of being "on loan" in the care of his parents. If he is made accustomed to good and is so taught, he will grow up in goodness, he will win happiness in this world and the next, and his parents and teachers will have a share of his reward. . . . As much as the father shields his son from fire in this world, it is more meet for him to shield him from the fire of the world to come.[127]

Moreover, al-Ghazali believed that religious education of children should begin at a young age, when minds are most impressionable. He directed that children fast for several days during Ramadan by the age of seven in order to inculcate the lifelong, obligatory practice, and that sections of the Koran be memorized, since, he explained,

[g]aining "acquired knowledge" in order to obtain a quality which will be permanently present in the spirit is difficult and is not possible except at a young age. At this age learning is like engraving on a stone, while the teaching of an elderly person is arduous and troublesome.[128]

Corporal punishment was permitted only to encourage learning and was to be meted out in a controlled, dispassionate fashion, according to prescribed rules. The number of lashes, the width of thong to be used, the parts of the body that could not be struck (head, face, hands, etc.)—all were ordained for the father to consult before administering discipline.[129]

A unique genre of writing emerged in medieval Islam. Addressed to bereaved parents, these were manuals of consolation for a dead child. They were written in Egypt and Syria between the thirteenth and sixteenth centuries. Although there are other sporadic and scattered examples of bereavement literature in the West, the large corpus of consolation books produced in the Arabic world is notable. More than twenty such treatises were written, the most prominent of which were Jalal al-Din al-Suyuti's *Book of Anxiety about Children's Death, Consolation for the Steadfast Person on the Loss of a Child*, coauthored by Sulayman, Banin, and Khalaf al-Daqiqi, and Muhammad al-Manbiji's work, *Consolation for Those in Distress on the Death of Children and Relatives*.[130]

The sequence of consolation books is remarkable and unusual and invites speculation. Was there a surge in childhood deaths or some catastrophic event that singled out children? Certainly, we know that the plague touched the East during the fourteenth century, and perhaps that was the catalyst that produced the cascade of consolation manuals that followed. Could there have been a change in the perception of children, a new appreciation about the nature of childhood? Perhaps, but the literature speaks to no such phenomenon, and in the Koran both law and the spirit of Islam remained immutable. No new revelations about children appeared.[131] The impetus behind this consolation sequence may never be known, but twentieth-century students of Elisabeth Kübler-Ross will find it noteworthy.

The fundamental principles imbued in the nurturing of medieval Islamic children remained unchanged for hundreds of years. Western influences, such as the influx of Christians during the Crusades or the travels of Marco Polo (?1254–?1324) and his crew, did not influence or alter the pattern of the strict upbringing of Islamic children.

As one moved eastward into Caucasia, however, Islamic influences became more diluted and less controlling. The people of Caucasia, a land between the Black and Caspian Seas, had a mosaic lineage—the Abkhar to the northwest, the Chechens to the northeast, and the Georgians to the south—with amalgamated cultures influenced by tribal lore, Islam, Christianity, and Avesta. Little of the medieval social or tribal data were recorded, but oral tradition preserved some of the customs regarding children.

Young women on their way to a bridal shrine were accompanied by children who incanted Christian prayers for male heirs: "So many boys and one blue-eyed girl grant thou, Mairem, to this our dear bride."[132]

Boys were raised in the Spartan manner in a mixture of Byzantine Christian tradition blended with tribal custom. A public display of affection for children was prohibited, so fathers were never even seen carrying a child.[133] Thievery was viewed as an "honorable" profession and had its own patron saint—St. Geagers, the saint of the Black Horseman. Boys were taught to rob without being caught. Chechen boys received their first arms ceremoniously, as their elders prayed "May they serve you on the right and wrong paths, in theft and in war."[134]

The sharply defined domestic roles for girls reflected rigid tribal traditions and regulations to which girls were strictly bound. At puberty girls were taught contraceptive and abortifacient skills because all of the tribal groups prohibited couples from having children until the fourth year of marriage.[135] When nubile, a girl could reject any suitor who did not prove his bravery satisfactorily. Young men learned early on that a display of bravery by killing an animal or stealing a cow was a necessary step to wooing and winning a bride.[136]

Although the child-rearing customs of these people resembled those of the Spartan, Celtic, Hun, and Avar cultures, the Caucasian people paradoxically appear to have been isolated from the medieval sociocultural changes that were crossing continents. In the main, they retained their own tribal lore and mores and passed these on to their children, of whom little else is known.

India

With pressure from the Islamic influence to the west and Buddhist concepts to the east, medieval India took refuge in Hindu predeterminist tenets. As the practice of Buddhism declined and the influence of Hinduism surged in India, the caste system, a concept that definitively determined the destiny of Indian children, became an ingrained feature of the culture. There were five major and fixed societal positions: the *Brahmanas*, thought to have been created from the head of Brahma, exercised spiritual powers in society; the *Kshatriyas*, formed from Brahma's shoulders and hands, controlled secular powers; the *Vaisyas*, who came from Brahma's thighs, mediated economic matters; and the *Sudras*, who evolved from his feet, were the serfs of the system. The remainder were the *Antyajas*, the untouchables, relegated to be society's outcasts.

There were "impurities" associated with childbearing in this rigidly stratified society, the degree of which varied, according to caste:

As long as the woman is in the child-bed, she does not touch any vessel, and nothing is eaten in her house, nor does the Brahmana light there a fire. These days are eight for the Brahmana, twelve for the Ksatriya, fifteen for the Vaisya, and thirty for the Sudra. For the low-caste people which are not reckoned among any caste, no term is fixed.[137]

Samskaras were pregnancy and birth rituals performed at prescribed times to ward off evil spirits and ordain propitious outcomes. The *garbhadhana* promoted conception; *pumsavana* ensured the birth of a male. Husbands engaged in the *simantonayana*, grooming their wives' hair in the fourth, sixth, and eighth months of pregnancy to ensure a safe delivery. In this ritual, the hair was parted in the middle, symbolic of the widening of the pudendal labia at birth.[138]

Birth ceremonies were common in all sub-Asia. To the north, Tibetan Buddhism taught that the birth of a baby was not a random happening, but a conscious reincarnation of a life. All newborn rituals, therefore, reflected respect for the rebirth of a human being. In Tibet, at birth, infants were painted with saffron, the symbol for wisdom. Butter was touched to their noses, after which infants were cleansed and robed. Their placenta was buried, but umbilical cord stumps were preserved. A lama was consulted for naming, and on the fourth day of life, friends and relatives visited, bearing gifts. Should an infant become sick, a barley flour dough was made to roll over the baby to pick up the sick humors. The lama baked the dough for the offending spirits to eat and satisfy their hunger so that they would no longer disturb the infant.[139] Food and oral anointments also were part of Indian *jatakarman* birth ceremonies.

Mantras were whispered in babies' ears as a mixture of ghee and honey was placed in their mouths. Sacrifices were then offered before the umbilical cords were severed or nursing was initiated.[140] Children were given their names on the tenth day of life in a ceremony called *namakarana*. The *niskramana* celebrated an infant's first exposure to the sun, and the *annaprasana* commemorated the introduction, at six months, to solid food—a rice gruel mixed with curds, honey, and ghee. Children continued to be nursed until they were three years old, at which time they also experienced their first haircut, which left only a topknot of hair. A ritual offering was made in a ceremony called the *cudakarana*. Ears were pierced when babies were seven or eight months old in a ceremony called the *karnavedha*.

For boys, there was one final *samskara* of childhood—the wearing of the sacred thread. It was called the *yajñopavitia* and was performed when vedic studies began.

Demons or malignant stars (*graha*) were believed to cause any of the nine categories of illness to which children were vulnerable. The treatment for all was the same and primitive: the sufferer of *skanda graha* (encephalopathies, seizures), *sakuni graha* (chicken pox and erysipelas), *revati graha* (dysentery), or *putana graha* (cholera), for example, simply was kept in a clean room and rubbed with old ghee. Mustard was strewn on the floor, and mustard oil was burned.[141] How these children fared is unknown.

Indian children grew up in large extended families along the lines of patrilinear inheritance. The medieval law of *mitaksara* consigned the paterfamilias only to the role of steward of the property. All of the domains of childhood were a shared responsibility within the family. Besides parents, children, grandchildren, uncles, and other male collateral members of a family, there might be adopted children. These families grew to an unmanageable size and upon the death of the paterfamilias, the property was divided among the sons and new family units were formed. The rite of *sraddha* taught boys at a young age to commemorate ancestors with offerings of rice, called *pinda*. Sons, grandsons, and great-grandsons of the dead made these offerings to unite their souls with those of the dead. In this way, elders promoted family unity for the young, and moreover, helped growing boys to recognize and identify members of their families, alive and dead.

Children's lives within castes were complex and ritualized, beginning with the highest order, the *Brahmana*. All males were taught that life was composed of four idealized stages that had to be studied and mastered. For *Brahmana* boys, the first stage, the *brahmacarin*, commenced at the age of eight years with the rebirth ceremony of *upanayana*. *Kshatriya* boys had to wait until they were eleven (*Vaisya* boys, twelve) before they could begin to master the first stage. *Sudras* and untouchables were excluded from these rites of passage.

In the *upanayana* ceremony, the sacred thread, *yajñopavitia*, was hung over a boy's right shoulder and under the left arm. The cord, three threads each of nine strands, had to be worn for life.[142] This first stage, lasting until *Brahmana* boys were in their twenty-fifth year, was years of preparation and training for what were the primary occupations of the brahmana—teachers or priests. At eight years of age boys went to live with masters and teachers, where they worked as servants and began the long process of learning the Vedas. They were allowed to leave the house only to beg. All collections were turned over to their masters. They practiced fasting by having meals every other day and by eschewing meat. As boys matured into adolescence they were taught to live the celibate life, with the understanding that each would have a bride selected for him by his master at an appropriate age. Unlike members of other castes, *Brahmana* males could marry outside their caste. The ideal age of a bride was considered to be one-third that of the groom, so a girl of eight could be selected to marry a man of twenty-four. In actuality, girls commonly were married at menarche and only rarely before thelarche, or breast development.[143]

In the second stage of life, the *grhastha*, *Brahmana* men were permitted to return home, marry, and assume the role of head of household. The second stage did not end until grandsons were born, at which time they eased into the third stage of life, the *vanaprastha*, a time of contemplation in an isolated hermitage. Albeit rarely attained, in life's final stage, the *sannyasin*, men became wanderers, breaking all earthly ties in preparation for death.[144]

The special prominence of *Brahmanas* exempted them from taxes or capital punishment for a crime committed. In all other ways, however, they were subject to the authority of the ruling and administrative caste, the *Kshatriyas*, who also comprised the military leadership. Services were rendered by the *Sudras*. The *Vaisyas*—merchants, farmers, and cattle raisers—supplied food and other commodities. Marco Polo related that, among the *Vaisyas*, sons were turned out of their homes when they were thirteen years old to fend for themselves and thereby learn to survive. Fathers looked on this as an integral part of their sons' training and gave them "twenty or twenty-four groats to trade and profit from":

In this way they became very clever and astute traders. They may take foodstuff home for their mothers to cook and dress for them, but not so that they eat at their father's expense. (*Travels* bk. 3, chap. 17)

Children born into the group of untouchables, the *Antyajas*, were no better off than slaves. As youngsters, children quickly learned their place, even to walking the streets with care, to ensure that not even a shadow touched another Hindu. Untouchables provided essential services for the urban society. They were indispensable in their work as fullers, weavers, shoemakers, fishermen, hunters, sailors, cleaners, basketweavers, and so forth. Children learned these trades from their fathers and learned, too, that their value outside the family was worthless. They and their families were prohibited from living in the city. They could even be murdered with little penalty imposed on the murderer.

Girls from any of the castes led even more constricted lives. Considered burdens and unpopular from birth, girls of all castes had few choices in life. Marriages were arranged and performed when they were between the ages of seven and twelve years. One advantage girls had over boys was the right to marry into a superior caste. Girls and women were subservient to their husbands in all ways, bowing, for example, to conjugal advances that were as often as not timed to coincide with the medieval belief in numerology that augured the conception of males on even-numbered nights. The fourth day after menses ceased was deemed the fertile period for conception. As in other cultures, girls and women were isolated at menses, being considered impure.

Girls also could be dedicated to the temple by her parents, a vocation reminiscent of the Phoenician temple boys who were exploited for erotic purposes. As temple dancing girls (*devadasi*), girls were taught to sing and dance ceremonially for the rituals of worship. They also were trained as courtesans to serve priestly and nonsectarian strangers, with the profits of such liaisons going to the temple priests. In some temples, an additional tax was imposed on the courtesans' fees to support the army treasury. Marco Polo, in writing about these maidens of the temples, mentioned only the innocent services they performed as cooks and as dancers and singers honoring temple gods and goddesses.[145]

Girls retained control over their own property, particularly gifts received from the family. They could inherit property only as daughters, not as wives, and were entitled to only one-quarter the valued amount given to sons.

Purdah was not practiced in medieval India, but *sati* or *suttee*, self-immolation on a dead husband's funeral pyre, was expected, particularly among *Kshatriyas* women. *Sati* was never compulsory, but widows were so severely stigmatized that many women, even child brides, chose *sati*.* *Sati* was declared illegal in colonial India in 1829 by Lord William Bentinck.

In general, the dead were considered polluted, and all those who touched the dead had to be cleansed with ritual ablutions. Children under three were considered "too innocent to require purification,"[146] so instead of being buried or their bodies being immolated, they were accorded a ceremonial water burial.

India's caste system, woven into the fabric of its society in medieval times, remained life's major determinant for children until well into this century.

China

From the seventh to the tenth centuries—the Western world's Dark Ages—the Chinese empire experienced dynamic periods of progressive change. A warring and erratic society evolved into a materialistic and mercantile one, reaching out on the Caspian Sea to sail to and trade with India, Persia, and Byzantium. China's influence was not limited to these western

---

*About *suttee* (Sanskrit meaning "virtuous wife"), Marco Polo relates:

[At the husband's funeral] his relations proceed, with great triumph and rejoicing, to burn the body; and his wife, from motives of pious regard for her husband, throws herself upon the pile, and is consumed with him. Women who display this resolution are much applauded by the community, as, on the other hand, those who shrink from it are despised and reviled. (*Travels* bk. 3, chap. 17)

countries and cultures but extended well beyond, to Japan in the east. China called itself the Middle Kingdom.* Over the next two hundred years its capital, Ch'ang-an, grew into the world's largest city, with a population of over a million people. The country flourished as a prosperous nation, with maritime powers, urban craft centers, and scholarly endeavors until the Mongolian invasion that ended in 1276 brought to a close the extraordinary medieval Sung era (907–1279).

The Sung era's economic and political stability promoted the evolution of the extended, multigenerational Chinese family. Grandparents, parents, children, married children, grandchildren, and family-owned slaves all lived in one household. A rigid and formalized hierarchy served to maintain order and control. Obedience and respect, based upon age and genealogy, were highly regarded and, in any case, mandated. In the T'ang code, for example, the penalty for a son who struck his parent or grandparent was execution by decapitation. If an older sibling was struck, the sentence was two-and-one-half years of hard labor. Striking an older cousin was considered far less serious and was penalized by a mere one hundred whips of the lash.

Filial duties and deference toward older family members, however, did not necessarily result in greater affection among the family members. A formalized and civilized peace within families and a community code of moral, ethical, and social behavior were instead the end results:

The respect owed to parents was not given to them as individuals: it was part of a kind of cult that made them into abstract figures and foreshadowed, in their lifetime, the cult of the ancestors. It was an anonymous feeling, impersonal and eminently transferable.[147]

In a society encoded to venerate its oldest members, the newest often were considered expendable. Among the poor, infanticide was common, as documented in a report sent to the emperor from Fukien in 1109, and in another report in the same city, stating:

... if a man have numerous sons he brings up no more than four and keeps no more than three daughters, if he claims that he has not the means for bringing up more.[148]

It became a common custom to keep a drowning bucket at the parturition site so that this formula could be enforced. The first official edict against infanticide, rendered by Choen Tche, did not appear until 1659:

---

*The Chinese had no ideogram for *China*. Their country was the Middle Kingdom. *China* may derive from *Qin*, a state near the western frontier.

I have heard that the sad cry uttered by these girl babies as they are plunged into a vase of water and drowned is inexpressible. Alas! that the heart of a father or mother should be so cruel.[149]

Children born late to a couple fared the worst, for often the family patrimony already had been assigned and divided. In these instances the "harrowing of progeny" occurred. In cities, abandonment in the street was more common than infanticide, and it became so widespread that, in Hangchow, a foundling hospital was established to rescue these infants. Gradually, community offices were opened in all of the provinces to handle the numbers of abandoned children. Poor families were encouraged to submit unwanted children to these offices, which assigned them nurses or sent them to foundling homes. Likewise, couples seeking adoption could file a petition in the community offices. Marco Polo commented:

[Facfur] was religious, and charitable to the poor and needy. Children whom their wretched mothers exposed in consequence of their inability to rear them, he caused to be saved and taken care of, to the number of twenty thousand annually. When the boys attained a sufficient age, he had them instructed in some handicraft, and afterwards married them to young women who were brought up in the same manner. (*Travels* bk. 2, chap. 65)

During periods of crop failure, poor couples often tried to keep their families together by seeking economic help. Facing interest rate charges of 20 percent per month on loans, or a contract in which 50 percent of the crop yield had to be given in payment, most were forced to sell their children or place them into service as options to abandonment. Selling children into servitude under these circumstances was not viewed a disgrace, but accepted by all as the best solutions to bad situations in a cruel and indifferent world.

The medieval Chinese engaged in slave trading with Arab countries. One fourteenth-century Arab writer commented:

[Y]oung slave girls are very cheap in China; and, indeed, all the Chinese will sell their sons as slaves equally with their daughters . . . those who are purchased cannot be forced against their will to go abroad with the purchaser; neither, however, are they hindered if they choose to do so.[150]

Rural peasant children were employed as soon as physically able. They were given chores to feed animals, collect faggots, fetch water, and tend buffalos. Some villages had winter schools to teach children the rudiments of writing and arithmetic. The poor who migrated to the city applied the same "beast of burden" psychology to their children, expecting them to serve the family as water bearers, scavengers, and porters.

A strikingly different spectrum of experience was enjoyed, of course, by babies born into the wealthy upper class, the *shin-ta-fu*, or literati/scholars. Typically, the families were propertied, classically educated in Confucian philosophy, and given leadership roles. Expectant mothers in these households were sent good wishes for the birth of a male and traditional gifts of rice-straw–covered silver dishes, with flowers, chestnuts, dates, and clothing for the baby. While pregnant, they practiced "placental instructions" (*t'ai chiao*) to shape the character of the fetus by regimenting their activities, avoiding specific foods, and listening to music and moral lectures.[151]

Births were registered immediately so that accurate astrological readings with respect to the stars, planets, time, and date could be made. After parturition, mothers were given rice, coal, and vinegar at the end of the first, second, and third weeks. When babies were one month old, silver bowls containing gifts of pins of silver and gold and jujubes and dates were filled with warm water for a ceremonial bath. The dates and jujubes were avidly eaten by the young women attending the ablutions in the belief these fruits could generate fecundity of male offspring. Following the baths, the babies were given haircuts, and the locks were sealed in precious boxes. Next, they were dressed in red gowns and carried to the temple to be presented to the spirits of their ancestors.

At this time children were given a "milk name" to be used by family and friends. Boys received names of good health, longevity, and virtues such as loyalty or patriotism. Girls were named after flowers, birds, and jewels as well as virtues. Sometimes girls were given numerical names such as "oldest," "second," "third," and so forth. Another naming device was to assign to fortune tellers the study of astrological data surrounding a birth, with respect to the five elements: metal, wood, fire, earth, and water. Should the soothsayer believe an infant to be deficient in any of the elements, the infant was given a compensatory name, such as "iron," "ocean," or "pine."[152] Children were never named after relatives, since each child was considered a new and unique person.

Landmarks at one hundred days of age and at one year were marked with ceremonies and celebrations. In China, the first birthday is called the second *sui*[153] and is considered particularly auspicious. The planetary influences on an infant were assessed at this time in conjunction with the evaluation of the baby's visual attention and grasp.

Parents surrounded their infants with books, measures, scales, clothes, flowers, and other objects. It was believed that whichever one a child grasped first was conjoined with the star under which he was born and the day of the lunar phase to prognosticate the child's future vocation. A baby born on the fifth day of the fifth moon was considered to have the bad influence of the scorpion, wasp, snake, and centipede and was believed to be predestined to suicide.*

Multiple deities also were believed to influence, for good or ill, the course of a child's life. The god Chang Hsien was the "Provider of Children," who protected families from the menacing "Celestial Dog." He often was depicted as a white-bearded man carrying a bow and arrow to fend off the Celestial Dog, accompanied by a little boy. The goddess of the Golden Flower protected children from smallpox and sores, and she was worshiped whenever a child became ill. There was a specific goddess, the Spirit of Scarlet Fever, to appeal to whenever a suspicious-looking rash appeared.[154]

Child-rearing practices were rigid, designed to minimize individuality and inculcate uniform and socially acceptable manners. Children were required to respect and yield to the authority of elders and exhibit politeness and passivity, with no display of aggression permitted, even among themselves. Adults served as the principal role models in this regard, as they never struck their children. Teaching respect and obedience was employed as a verbal discipline and reinforced with threats of various bogeymen, such as warnings about the Celestial Dog who devoured children who misbehaved.

There were a surfeit of toy vendors, sweets sellers, and entertainments to please the children of urban aristocrats, who undoubtedly led a pampered life. They also were incorporated as needed participants in the rituals of their society's folklore. Children, for example, joined their families for new year festivities, since all believed that their wakeful presence ensured longevity for their elders. On the other hand, they were forbidden to enter the kitchen during the twelfth lunar month of the new year because it was thought that rice cakes should absorb only the mature influences of adults. During the fifth moon festival for the living, children had vermilion symbols painted on their foreheads and cheeks—ideograms for the Wang, or sovereign, and for the tiger who provided protection from wild and evil spirits. Sulfur and cinnabar were smeared on children's noses and ears to prevent scars, furuncles, and ulcers. At the mid-autumn festival of life, children were treated to candies in the shapes of hares, butterflies, and carp.[155]

In the city, a six-year formal education began when children were seven years old. Upon entering school, children were given the "school names" their teachers and classmates called them: names like "strong reader" and

---

*The Chinese in the modern world continue to attribute great import to the cyclic calendar. The Year of the Sheep (1991) was believed to presage a bitter life for those born in that distinctly inauspicious time, particularly so for girls. That year the Chinese birthrate fell by 25 percent and the number of abortions increased by 60 percent. *Washington Post*, 13 May 1991, p. A20.

"bright star" that reinforced positive virtues of scholastic life. Children memorized and learned to write twenty ideograms a day and practiced using the abacus to solve mathematical problems. Girls were not necessarily excluded from formal education but could anticipate a much more curtailed curriculum. They particularly were held back in reading and writing:

Women should just learn to recognize a few characters, like those for fuel, rice, fish, meat, and the like; to learn more is of no benefit, and may even be harmful. (Madame Wen) [156]

[Girls] are to be allowed only to recognize written characters, and are to be taught filial behavior and ritual restraint. They needn't read a lot of books. (Yao Shun-mu) [157]

Higher education for boys normally was provided by private tutors. By the end of the eleventh century, the state schools opening all over urbanized China and the professional schools for pedagogy, military arts, and medicine contributed to the demise of the medieval system of education.

Educational philosophy expressed Confucian pedagogy, which taught that family and education were subjugate to the state. Examples from family-life experiences were used to emphasize duty to the state, a concept well stated by Lu Pen-chung (1048–1145) in *Instruction for Children*:

Serving the ruler is like serving one's parents. Serving one's official superiors is like serving one's older brothers. Associating with official colleagues is like associating with all the members of one's family. [158]

Huo T'ao (1487–1540) was an extreme example of a strict Confucian pedagogue, who, with others like him, echoed the severity of the Reformation pedagogy of Erasmus and Brunfels. He insisted that formal instruction should begin as soon as children were able to walk. He segregated the genders, providing separate living, eating, and learning areas. He taught that submissive deportment with peers, as well as with elders, was the only means by which children could achieve public virtue:

As for families with children, as soon as a child is able to walk and talk, it must be taught not to play with other children. When [children] see each other in the morning, they must be taught to bow solemnly to each other. When they enter primary school, they must be taught to order themselves by age-rank. When they see each other do good, they must increase their respect for each other. They must not gang-together to make jokes, laugh, or cavort. They must learn good from each other, and warn each other against evil. They must not slander each other, or compete with each other. [159]

Hsu Hsiang-ch'ing (1479–1557) offered similar advice:

. . . as soon as a child can walk and talk and eat, he will begin to show traces of good conscience. This is the right time to ensure that he does not become willful and unrestrained. Confucius said that the road to sagehood begins with the nourishing of uprightness in childhood. This means that the child must constantly be taught not to engage in silly behavior, that he must eat after his elders, that he should always yield the nicer and accept the poorer, and that, as for clothes, he should always be taught to take the plain and spurn the fancy.[160]

Chen Te-Hsiu (1175–1235) dictated postural as well as behaviorial controls, offering instructions on how to sit, walk, stand, bow, speak, recite, and write. He admonished children to

walk slowly with arms held within the sleeves, with no waving of arms or jumping. . . . [Recite] with the undivided mind upon the words, enunciating the phrases slowly, so each word is distinct and clear; don't look about you or play with things in your hands.[161]

Many city boys of the working classes were able to enter apprenticeships, with aspirations to become guild members. Chinese trades and skills were often more subspecialized and complex than their European counterparts. Whereas in Europe there was a guild for general consumable products, in China there were different guilds for specific food commodities. The rice guild serves as the example, and the varieties of rice available explain the need for the specialized organization. Young apprentices had to learn about new-milled rice, husked winter rice, first-class white rice, regular rice, yellow rice, unhusked rice, glutinous rice, pink rice, old rice, lotus rice, early rice, late rice, chipped rice, spotted rice, and powdered rice, among other kinds! There were also guilds for pork sellers, fish sellers, fruit sellers, crab vendors, olive merchants, ginger diggers, to name but a few, as well as highly subspecialized guilds for furniture, clothing, jewelry, and other commodities. Once the decision was made to become an apprentice, boys knew that they had no choice except to remain with their trade for the rest of their lives. No matter how well educated they became or how literate in reading and with numbers, tradesmen never were permitted to aspire to a middle-class position such as, for example, civil service. They were not permitted even to take the civil-service examination.

A coming-of-age ceremony was conducted at the beginning of April for twenty-year-old boys. If they had passed the examinations on the *Four Books* and on one of the *Five Classics* of Confucius, they were awarded a commemorative cap.[162] In a ceremony with a similar theme, girls received com-

memorative hairpins when they were fifteen years old. Thereafter they went
to live in their own rooms, away from parental quarters:

As for unmarried daughters, their housing must be especially secluded and quiet.
They must not visit the rooms of their parents, or those of their brothers' wives, for
fear they'll witness common or intimate goings-on, which would be most inappropriate.[163]

After passing these milestones, urban children were regarded as nubile,
and parents arranged their marriages, marked by the custom of appointing
the groom with a new, marital, third name. Marriages were intended for
political purposes and to merge estates and extend family alliances. Marco
Polo described an extreme example of this latter kind of marriage in which
dead children were wedded posthumously in order that their families could
be united:

. . . when there are two men of whom one has had a male child who had died at the
age of four, or what you will, and the other has had a female child who has also died,
they arrange a marriage between them. They give the dead girl to the dead boy as a
wife and draw up a deed of matrimony. Then they burn this deed, and declare that
the smoke that rises into the air goes to their children in the other world and that
they get wind of it and regard themselves as husband and wife. They hold a great
wedding feast and scatter some of the food here and there and declare that too goes
to their children in the other world. And here is something else that they do. They
draw pictures on paper of men in the guise of slaves, and of horses, clothes, coins,
and furniture and then burn them; and they declare that all these become the possessions of their children in the next world. When they have done this, they consider themselves to be kinsfolk and uphold their kinship just as firmly as if the children
were alive. (*Travels* bk. 1, chap. 55)

Among the poor, parents contracted marriages as insurance that they would
be looked after by their children. Once the horoscopic and astrological conditions were deemed favorable for the bride and groom, the parents ensued with
arrangments for an elaborate marriage celebration. When all of the children
were married and there were grandchildren and promises of more grandchildren, parents retired from their positions as head of the family, content in
knowing that their old age was assured of respect and support from their
young, all of whom had been trained to sustain this time-honored tradition.

Japan

Japan long had remained an isolated island culture until its more
advanced neighbor, China, breaching the Sea of Japan, broadened its cul-

tural and technological base. Early Chinese bronze culture had reached Japan at around 200 B.C. The first formal Chinese envoy arrived later, in 57 A.D. The first records of early Japanese culture can be found in Han documents of the first century and the Wei records of the third. At a time during late antiquity and the early Middle Ages, when Christianity was affirming its foothold in Europe, Japan was only beginning to respond to the presence and influence of China. Chinese script had introduced literacy, and scholars from China had carried written classics to Japan for its edification. In 552 the Korean king of Paekche sent to the court of Japan a large bronze idol of Buddha and a copy of his holy scripture. Buddhist doctrine was absorbed readily by the newly literate Japanese people, successfully competing with existing Shintô tenets. Buddhism at one point approached being named the state religion. Very gradually, between the sixth and sixteenth centuries, an amalgam of Buddhist, Confucian, and Shintô philosophies emerged. An eighth-century monk named Gyoki had influenced the eventual blending of the religions. Around 740 A.D. he traveled to Ise and prayed at length before the sun goddess's shrine in the main Shintô temple, asking her to intercede in the ongoing discussion about the merits of Buddhism and Shintô philosophies.[164] The sun goddess personally answered his prayers in Chinese verse, assuring all that the Buddhist and Shintô religions were in essence the same.*

From the amalgam of these spiritual doctrines, the cycles of life were viewed as confluent with a variety of fluid spirits—some good, some malevolent—and therefore all aspects of life were influenced by these forces. Diviners and exorcists became indispensable to worshipers who sought to manipulate even the most mundane of life's cycles to ensure the attendance of only the most propitious spirits.

Some aspects of life were thought to be pollutions that required cleansing. This could occur only if the evil spirits were exorcised from the scene. Disease, menstruation, wounds, death, and even the birth of children all were considered to be tainted. The bad spirit, moreover, possessed the person involved in the event as well as the surrounding participants, so exorcism had to be both general and specific.

For example, exorcists attended the accouchements of young mothers. These occurred in the center of a specially designated room where white linen cloths were spread out on the floor. Mothers dressed in white robes squatted over the cloths supported on either side by assistants, on whose shoulders her arms rested. During labor, exorcists twanged a bow string

---

*Further amalgamation was to be seen in medicine. The *Ishimpo*, the oldest known Japanese medical treatise (984 A.D.), called medical care *taijisokuin*, deriving from *taiji* (the great mercy of Buddha) and *sokuin* (Confucian sympathy and benevolence).

loudly, warding off the evil spirits, while monks audibly recited prayers. A diary, written in 1025, gives an account of the Empress Akiko, who had not expelled the placenta after she gave birth and was in danger of hemorrhaging. Exorcists shouted, wailed, and objurgated the evil spirits, conjuring them to enter substitute bodies and do their harm there. The substitutes singled out were the court ladies who, while dutiful to the needs of the empress, nevertheless registered significant dismay as they resisted being chosen as scapegoats.[165]

At normal births, umbilical cords were severed with a bamboo knife like the one used for the same purpose at the birth of the god No Mikoto.[166] Aural distractions of all forms were used to protect infants from bad spirits. Poems were read in loud voices, and archers contributed to the noise making by twanging heavy bow strings. Nobility and peasantry alike followed this ritual, but if a peasant had no access to a literate person for poetry readings, monks were enlisted to beat monastery drums or children were hired to beat gongs.

Newborns were given their first baths during the ceremonial called *ubuyu*. Among the upper classes, the bath water contained jewels to symbolize future prosperity. An image of a dog or a tiger was reflected over the surface of the bath water, as these were believed to safeguard the spirit and health of children.

The souls of newborns were believed to be loosely attached to the body, and lest a soul wander off, for the first month of life babies were not allowed to leave the home. On the third day of life, babies were fed for the first time and named. Boys often were given numbers for names, so that a firstborn would be named Ichirô, the second, Jirô, and so on. Girls frequently were named after an object or quality, such as Take (bamboo), Haru (spring), Toshi (goodness), or Sei (purity), not unlike the Heather, Rose, or Faith, Hope, or Charity with which we are culturally familiar.

Children were given first haircuts soon after their naming day, generally when they were seven days old. The locks were sealed in boxes and buried in a village shrine as a symbol that children's lives were being entrusted to the good spirit *kami*. Abandonment was almost unheard of, since children always were welcomed by families. This attitude was reinforced in folk literature. In *Yoshitsune*, a chronicle from the fifteenth century, an outlaw wishes his helpless infant dead:

Poor helpless child! Will he ever grow up? . . . It would be better to abandon him in these mountains while he is still too young to be aware of it.

To which his wife angrily replies:

Shame on you for saying such a thing! Now that he has been fortunate enough to enter the land of the living, how dare you speak of killing him before he has even had time to set eyes on the moon and the sun![167]

Infants and their mothers were isolated for one month, after which they, with their family and friends, went to a Shintô shrine for the presentation of the newborns to a priest. Mothers clapped loudly to attract the attention of the shrine's *kami* and lit a light as an offering. After this ceremonial, each infant was considered an official member of the family and a celebration was held in the home to commemorate the event.

Growing infants were nourished with breast milk and rice pap and were carried on their mothers' backs. At the beginning of the fifth month, weaning was initiated in a ceremony called *tabezome*. A small table with small eating utensils was prepared for a baby—black for a boy and red for a girl. With these delicate chopsticks a baby was fed a grain of rice. This ritual marked the beginning of progressive weaning.

As in China, gestation was looked on as the first year of life, and at the celebration of the first birthday, *tanjôbi*, a child was considered two years old and given its first toys. The next formal ceremony was the hair-cutting *kamisogi* in which children's hair was trimmed only, the hair left long for aesthetic and symbolic reasons. Children had their hair cut short only if it were infested with lice. Short hair in adults symbolized a lifestyle renounced or a criminal penalty imposed. Boys ran about in short kimonos with shoulder-length hair gathered and tied at the crown. Girls wore long kimonos and simply kept their hair away from the face with ribbons.

Early childhood ended for girls when they were six and for boys when they were seven. Ceremonies were held to mark the passage. Girls were given their first long kimono, and boys were given their first breeches. Thereafter there were almost no restrictions on children's behavior. Discipline was never corporeal; a simple scolding or an expression of parental displeasure were the only forms of control children suffered. The exception to this rule occurred in times of war, during which the barbarities associated with this inexplicable form of human behavior were committed against children. In the twelfth century, for example, during the rise of the samurai, the power struggle between the warrior leagues—the Minamoto and Taira factions—increased. At this time there was no imperial family or concept of Japan as a nation, and these leagues were the law-making and law-enforcing bodies of Japan. The struggle was a five-year war, which, in 1185, witnessed the execution of Taira refugees. All of the children were drowned, buried alive, or decapitated.[168]

Childhood pastimes in the East shared marked similarities with those of children in the Western world. Ball games, wrestling, dance, and songs were favored pursuits. Japanese children, however, had a special fondness for hunting and capturing insects. Girls collected fireflies in little cages. Fireflies were never killed, for it was thought that they harbored the souls of the dead.

Boys were especially interested in dragonflies. Dragonflies were considered a warrior insect, and knots of samurai costumes were tied to resemble their wings. A well-known poet of the eighteenth century, Chiyo (1703–1775), evocatively used the image of a child in pursuit of a dragonfly as a metaphor for childhood itself in a poem in which he lamented the death of his son.[169] The delicate haiku is entitled "My Little Son":

> I wonder in what fields today
> He chases dragon flies in play
> My little boy—who ran away.

Special festivals were celebrated for children. The Shichi-go-san (7-5-3) on the fifteenth of November honored all children aged three, five, and seven years. During this holiday, the child was dressed in finery and attended the local shrine to ring a bell, clap hands, and pray for good health and fortune. The fifth day of the fifth month, the Tango-no-sekku was dedicated to boys. Streamers were flown depicting huge carp, symbols of the virtue of endurance. Tasty rice cakes, *chimkai*, were eaten. Iris leaves, symbols of the samuri sword, were placed in the eaves of the house to protect the boy from evil. In honor of girls, on the third day of the third month the Hina matsuri, a dolls' day, was held.[170]

The sons of the nobility mostly went to monastery schools in which monks taught writing, Chinese classics, and the collected Vedic precepts, the *Sûtra*. Boys served as pages, *chigo*, to the monks in exchange for their education. A form of indenture resembling Western oblation, being a *chigo* was not meant as a permanent position. Some *chigo*, however, took vows on reaching their majority and remained in the monastery for their lifetime. Most, however, graduated to an institution of higher learning, known as the Daigaku, prominent from 700 to 1000 A.D. The Daigaku was a Confucian college where Confucian classics, history, composition, and law were taught to train young men for official careers. Unlike European universities, it operated with strict discipline as the rule. Students were examined frequently, and those who failed the examinations were dismissed. Successful completion of the college courses entitled students to take the civil-service examinations that conferred five distinct classes of degrees. The *Shusai*, the "exceptional talent," was the first degree. The second, for the "classicist," was the *Myokyo*. Knowledge of government, the *Shinshi*, was the third degree, and the fourth degree, for being learned in law, was the *Myobo*. Finally, the fifth degree was the *San*, for calculation.

Sons of warriors and their fathers formed a knight–squire relationship. An overseer delivered further specialized training on the subject of arms and battle skills, one of the two essential prerequisites for the samurai. Literature was the other, and boys began to study this subject at ten, when they entered the monastery schools. They remained in these schools for five years, studying the *Sûtra*, calligraphy, music, poetry, history, chronicles of war, and a collection of aphorisms called the *Dôjikyô*, or "Precepts for the use of children." When, at the age of fifteen, the young samurai was prepared to assume the responsibilities of adulthood, he was given his *mon*, a personal symbol that he used as his signature or mark and that his vassals and warriors displayed on his behalf.* He also was given his sword to carry and use, at a highly celebrated rite-of-passage ceremony called the *gempuku*.

During the Kamakura era (1185–1333), samurai and warrior romances dominated the literature. Legends of fierce and fearless warriors were recounted, influencing all classes of children. Warriors were glorified, and children were encouraged to mimic the valor and virtue depicted in the tales. In their play, boys often reenacted warrior scenes with wooden swords.

Girls also were expected to revere the values of the samurai, and celebrated in particular the feats of one heroine named Tomoe:

Tomoe had long black hair and a fair complexion, and her face was very lovely; moreover she was a fearless rider whom neither the fiercest horse nor the roughest ground could dismay, and so dexterously did she handle sword and bow that she was a match for a thousand warriors and fit to meet either god or devil. Many times had she taken the field, armed at all points, and won matchless renown in encounters with the bravest captains, and so in this last fight, when all the others had been slain or had fled, among the last seven there rode Tomoe.[171]

Girls did not have specific initiation ceremonies, but daughters of the nobility marked their entry into adolescence by plucking their eyebrows. Thereafter, eyebrows always had to be applied with facial paints. Peasant girls kept their eyebrows, but painted their teeth black at adolescence. Adolescent peasant girls polished their domestic skills and learned how to raise silkworms, to weave, and to cultivate the soil for different kinds of crops.

Girls of every class had their marriages arranged by their parents. After a marriage was arranged, a trial period was allowed wherein the bride went to her future in-laws' home to work on the farm and in the house, and the intended groom spent the night with his bride in her home. The probationary period granted the girl the right of refusal. If she agreed to the marriage,

---

*A *mon* was a simple circle or square with an ideogram in the center. The lower classes were not entitled to such a symbol but could "sign" with their right thumbprint.

a girl would go to the local shrine and pray to the *kami* in residence. She hung votive scrolls inscribed with her name and her intended's name on the sacred tree so that the *kami* would become familiar with them and be informed of their impending marriage. There was a ceremony that formalized their marriage, but the validity of the union was given by the family and the community only at the birth of the first child.

Unless they were training to be samurai, sons of noble families were initiated at the age of thirteen by being presented new breeches. They were then entitled to wear their hair coiled atop their heads. They also were given a man's headdress, and their godparents named them with a two-character *cognomen*, part hereditary and part personal. Outside the nobility there were no family names in medieval Japan. Naming, however, was important, and unique and convoluted combinations of names were common. Peasants, for example, were called *hyakushônin*, meaning "people with 100 names," yet they were identified only by nicknames combined with their professed skills, such as "Jiro the painter."

The rite of passage, *gempuku*, for city boys usually occurred at an early age, at ten or twelve, so that they could begin their apprenticeships. A father–son apprenticeship system existed in the cities—an urban phenomenon, much as it was in Europe. Peasant children remained ignorant and unskilled, simply learning domestic and farm skills and preparing for an early marriage. There were no schools for the lower classes until the fourteenth century, when Zen monks founded schools specifically to educate children of the poor.

A part of all childrens' cultural education, however, was to learn about life's inauspicious cycles. Adolescents learned about auspicious times, identified by adults, when it was safe to make important decisions. Dangerous times were called *yakudoshi*, when precautionary rituals were performed and caution was taken before decisions were made. Twenty-five, forty-two, and sixty years were inauspicious ages for men; for women, they were nineteen and thiry-three. During each of these times men and women threw a personal garment into the river to wash downstream, carrying with it all personal evils. The good periods were called *nenga*, when momentous decisions were safe to make and people could anticipate great personal happiness. These times occurred when men and women were forty, fifty, seventy, eighty, and ninety years old.

The codex *Jôei Shikimoku* controlled the laws regarding children's patrimonies.[172] Firstborn children could not be totally disinherited and were entitled to a minimum of 20 percent of the family inheritance. This was particularly important among the samurai, who chose the best warriors as their heirs, not necessarily their firstborn. Family rivalries during the fourteenth century encouraged fathers to disinherit their daughters for fear that property would go as dowry to a rival family. Another factor discrediting daughters and disinheriting them was the widely held belief that they could not fight to protect their families' rights and property. Therefore, to protect family wealth and property, heads of households with no male heirs resorted to male adoptions.

The system of adoption had a name—*yôshi*—and was a long-standing Japanese tradition. Japanese family heirs—always males—performed rituals honoring the spirits of ancestors, and childless couples or families without male heirs frequently adopted boys to fulfill what in Japan was an obligation. Rules of adoption specified that a father could not have a legitimate heir, that he was over thirty years of age, and that the child to be adopted belonged to a branch of the same family. Among the samurai, the shôgun's permission was needed before there could be an adoption.

Overall, the people of medieval Japan were most kind to their children, and even in death children were given special recognition reflecting familial and societal regard. The Japanese prayed to *Jizo*, the Buddhist guardian for the souls of dead children, and often wrote short but touching poems to their dead children[173]:

> Silver, gold, and precious stone
> What are they in comparison
> With a daughter and a son?
>
> *Eighth-century poem*

NOTES

1. Fremantle, 1965, p. 6.
2. Hanawalt, 1986, p. 156.
3. Labours de clerc est Dieu prier
   Et justice de chevalier.
   Pain lor truevent li laborier
   Chil paist, chil prie, et chil deffent.
   Au camp, a le vile, au moustier
   S'entreaident de lor mestier
   Chil troi par bel ordenement.
                    Evans, 1925, p. 16.
4. Wood, 1970, p. 90.
5. Gottlieb, 1993, p. 125; Anderson and Zinsser, 1988, 1:421.
6. Faceva, nascendo, ancor paura
   La figlia al padre.
                    King, 1991, p. 24.

7. Johann Schröder in *Pharmacopoeia medicochymica* (Ulm, 1641) catalogs the eaglestone as *aetites*. He further recommends *ceraunia*, or the thunderstone, to promote lactation.

8. Tucker, 1988, pp. 235–36.

9. Amt, 1993, p. 98.

10. Sage comme le sal, bon comme le pain, plein comme oeuf, et droit comme allumette.

11. Boswell, 1988, p. 324.

12. Herlihy, 1985, p. 27.

13. Boyle, 1989, p. 58.

14. Herlihy, 1978, p. 126.

15. Blumenfeld-Kosinski, 1990, pp. 21–27.

16. Hanawalt, 1993, p. 44.

17. Rowland, 1981, p. 32.

18. J. E. Sewell, *Cesarean Section: A Brief History* (Washington, DC: National Library of Medicine, 1993).

19. Hanawalt, 1986, pp. 175–76. Late-medieval hagiographical catalogs of cures (miraculous healings attributed to the intervention of a saint) portray hundreds of childhood injuries, many described in great detail before inquisitorial committees meeting for canonization proceedings. Fire, near-drownings, concussions, chokings, as well as feverish illnesses, anomalies, and "demonic" possessions can be found in these sources. See E. C. Gordon, *Medical History* 1991; 35:145–63; and R. C. Finucane, *The Rescue of the Innocents* (New York: St. Martin's Press, 2000).

20. Gies and Gies, 1987, p. 285.

21. Ross, 1974, p. 190.

22. Bartholomaeus Anglicus, translation of John of Trevisa (1326–1402) and transcribed into modern English by Gies and Gies, 1987, pp. 196–97.

23. Dominici, 4.3.2.

24. Ibid., 4.5.1.

25. Ibid., 4.4.7.

26. Hanawalt, 1993, p. 72.

27. Hanawalt, 1986, pp. 156–61.

28. Hinckeldey, 1985, pp. 3–13.

29. Amt, 1993, pp. 55–70.

30. Hanawalt, 1986, p. 161.

31. Ibid., p. 162.

32. J. M. Riddle and J. W. Estes. *Amer Scientist* 1992; 80:226–33.

33. Lucas-Dubreton, 1961, p. 101.

34. Delcort, 1972, p. 109.

35. Duby, 1983, pp. 28–29.

36. C. W. Atkinson, *The Oldest Vocation* (Ithaca, N.Y.: Cornell University Press, 1991), p. 91.

37. Shahar, 1990, pp. 71–72.

38. Leibowitz and Marcus, 1984, p. 229.

39. Duby, 1983, pp. 59–72.

40. That a man with deformed limbs is misshappen of mind, full of sins, and full of vices. Huizinga, 1924, pp. 25–26.

41. Nicholas, 1985, pp. 154–72.

42. Boswell, 1988, pp. 327–30; and Martinson, 1992, pp. 185–86.

43. Gottlieb, 1993, p. 11.

44. Shahar, 1990, pp. 210–14.

45. Rowling, 1968, p. 137.

46. Earle, 1899, 1993, p. 192.

47. Shahar, 1990, pp. 178–79.

48. Other sources credit this achievement to a thirteenth-century Benedictine called Guy of Arezzo. Evans, 1925, pp. 120–21.

49. Lucas-Dubreton, 1961, p. 110.

50. Aries, 1965, p. 128.

51. Pinchbeck and Hewitt, 1973, 1:23.

52. Aries and Duby, 1989, 3:484.

53. Hanawalt, 1993, p. 134.

54. McLaughlin, 1974, p. 138.

55. Herlihy, 1978, p. 110.

56. King, 1991, p. 66; Amt, 1993, p. 196.

57. Hanawalt, 1993, p. 138.

58. Fremantle, 1965, pp. 93–97.

59. Evans, 1925, pp. 132–33.

60. Rowling, 1968, p. 148.

61. Bagley, 1960, pp. 96–97.

62. Si femme volez esposer
    Pensez de tei, mon fils chier
    Pernez nule por sa beaute
    Ni ki soit en livre lettrie
    Car sovent sunt decevables.
           Evans, 1925, p. 120.

63. Tuchman, 1978, p. 51.

64. Gies and Gies, 1987, p. 298.

65. Hanawalt, 1986, p. 157.

66. Hanawalt, 1993, pp. 146–49.

67. Houlbrooke, 1988.

68. Boswell, 1988, pp. 406–8.

69. Origo, 1957, pp. 192–97.

70. Boswell, 1988, p. 361.

71. The first such bishop was St. Zoticos himself (c.350). Constantelos, 1968, pp. 241–56.

72. Payne, 1916, pp. 293–94; Herlihy, 1978, p. 122.

73. The historian Boswell (1988) disputes the validity of the above-quoted citation from L. Muratori's *Antiquitates Italicae Medii Aevi*, calling it "bogus," on the grounds that it was written in anachronistic Latin (p. 225).

74. Ross, 1974, p. 218.

75. Dunn, 1920, p. 133.

76. Boswell, 1988, p. 425. Seventeenth-century Venice developed a different approach to the problem of the vagabond—a musical one. Street urchins could seek shelter in the *Dereliti Ospedaletto* and there study violin. Those with disabling diseases could find hospice in the *Incurabili*, where violin and harpsichord were taught. Beggars could also learn violin in the *Ospedale dei Mendicanti* (S. Lazzaro). Abandoned infants and foundlings placed in the basket of the *Ospedale della Pieta* were fed, clothed, nurtured, and educated; eventually they studied music and it was said of *della Pieta* that it became the finest school of music in the eighteenth century, producing exceptional voices, instrumentalists, and orchestra. Stevens, 2000, pp. 23–27.

77. King, 1991, pp. 11–12.

78. Gies and Gies, 1987, p. 279.

79. King, 1991, pp. 27–28.

80. Pinchbeck and Hewitt, 1973, 2:349.

81. Nicholas, 1991, p. 38.

82. Carmichael, 1986, pp. 52–53.

83. King, 1991, p. 8.

84. *J Pediatr* 1990; 117:351.

85. King, 1991, pp. 9–10.

86. Shahar, 1990, p. 135.

87. Gottfried, 1983, p. 45.

88. Ibid., p. 56.

89. Razi, 1980, pp. 30–90.

90. Dawes and Magilton, 1984, pp. 12–40.

91. Nicholas, 1985, p. 150.

92. Gottfried, 1983, p. 154.

93. Gies and Gies, 1987, pp. 223–24.

94. Gottlieb, 1993, pp. 129–30.

95. Marcus, 1996, pp. 1–2; Trepp, 1973, pp. 157, 202, 211.

96. Ibid., pp. 30–32.

97. Gray, 1872, pp. 3–78.

98. Sources differ with regard to the priest's identity and Stephen's age, which was in any case between 12 and 15 years. Payne, 1984, p. 288.

99. These are Gray's (1872) figures, but Payne (1984) puts the number at 7,000 children (p. 288).

100. Gray, 1872, p. 73:

> Schonster Herr Jesus,
> Herrscher aller Erden,
> Gottes und Maria Sohn;
> > Dich will ich heben,
> > Dich will ich erhen,
> Du, meiner Seeke Fruend' und Kron!
>
> Schon sind die Felder,
> Noch schoner sind die Walder, Monde,

In der schonen Fruhlingszeit
> Jesus ist schoner,
> Jesus ist reiner,

Der unser traurig Herz erfreut.

Schon leuchtet die Sonne,
Noch schoner leuchtet der
Und die Sternlein allzumal;
> Jesus leuchtet schoner,
> Jesus leuchtet reiner,

Als all' die Engel in Himmelsaal.

101. Ad mare stultorum/Tendebat iter puerorum (contemporary epigram of unknown authorship). Gray, 1872, p. 52.

102. Payne (1984) estimates a band of 9,000 children (p. 288).

103. Ibid., p. 289.

104. Hic vide perigrinacionem puerorum et
qualiter per incantaciones sunt decepti.
Illis temporibus stupendum quid crevit.
Mundoque mirabilis truffa inolevit.
Nam sub boni specie malum sic succrevit.
Arte quidem magica ista late sevit.

Hic est carmen quod ubique cantabatur
Nycolaus famulus Christi transfretabit.
Et cum innocentibus Ierusalem intrabit.
Mare siccis pedibus securus calcabit.
Juvenes et virgines caste copulabit.
Ad honorem Domini tanta perpetrabit.
Quod pax jubilacio Deo laus sonabit
Paganos et perfidos omnes baptizabit.
Omnis in Jerusalem carmen hoc cantabit.
Pax nunc christicolic Christus proximabit.
Et redemptos sanguine mire collustrabit.
Nycolaie pueros omnes coronabit.

Talis devocio ante hec non est audita.
Aures cunctis pruriunt virgines ornantur.
Annos infra sedecim evangelizantur.
Concurrentes pueri certant ut sequantur.
Et rumare viderant casso consolantur.
Ungarus Theutunicus Francus sociantur.
Boemus Lombardicus Brittoque conantur.
Flandria Vestfalia omnes federantur.

Friso cum Norwagia cuncti conglobantus.
Prurit pes et oculus pueros venantur.
Illi de Brundusio virgines stuprantur.
Et in arcum pessimum passim venumdantur.

Risum luctus occopat digne lamentantur.

Plorant matres ut Rachel nati morti dantur.

Vanitates hauriunt pueri fraudantur.

(Gray, 1872, Appendix)

105. The factual account of Gilles de Rais's life and crimes is based on the transcripts of his trial, translated by Hyatte (1984) in *Laughter for the Devil*.

These atrocities are still recorded sporadically. A recent case coming out of Pakistan accuses a 38-year-old man of organizing a gang that raped, suffocated, and acid-dissolved the bodies of over a hundred runaway boys. *Lancet* 1999; 354:2144.

106. Albertus Magnus, 1987, p. 63.

107. Martinson, 1992, p. 16.

108. Shahar, 1990, pp. 132–33.

109. Dunn, 1920, p. 74.

110. Ibid., p. 77.

111. Shahar, 1990, pp. 132–34.

112. Dunn, 1920, p. 228.

113. Hanawalt, 1993, p. 79.

114. Wooden, 1986, p. 25.

115. Godfrey, 1907, pp. 42–43.

116. In Holland, only the feast of St. Nicholas was set aside by the church to honor children. The Dutch Reform Church tried to curb the celebration, being of the opinion that it invited and encouraged greed in children. Durantini, 1983, p. 80.

117. Wooden, 1986, p. 27.

118. Dunn, 1920, p. 229.

119. Wooden, 1986, p. 28.

120. Ibid., p. 28.

121. All the quotations from the Quran are from the translation of Khan, 1981.

122. Gil'adi, 1992, pp. 36–37.

123. Ibid., p. 108.

124. Ibid., p. 115.

125. Although he did not write for or about children, Ibn Khaldoun (1332–1406) is often cited as a great Islamic intellect and pedagogue. He was noted for his *Universal History*, in which he analyzed the evolution of civilizations.

126. Ulich, 1975, p. 197.

127. Gil'adi, 1992, p. 50.

128. Ibid., pp. 53–54.

129. Ibid., pp. 61–66.

130. Ibid., pp. 11–12.

131. Professor Judith Tucker, Georgetown University, personal communications.

132. Luzbetak, 1951, pp. 122–23.

133. Ibid., pp. 149–51.

134. Ibid., pp. 147–48.

135. Ibid., pp. 189–91.

136. Ibid., pp. 141–42.

137. Singh, 1981, p. 130.

138. Ibid., pp. 258–59.

139. E. Farwell and A. H. Maiden, The wisdom of Tibetan childbirth, *In Context* 1992; 31:26–31.

140. Bhagvat Sinh Jee, 1927, pp. 51–55.

141. Kutumbiah, 1962, pp. 198–201.

142. Basham, 1954, pp. 161–64.

143. Ibid., pp. 165–70.

144. Ibid., pp. 158–59.

145. Marco Polo, 1818/1926, bk. 3, chap. 17.

146. Singh, 1981, p. 199.

147. Gernet, 1962, pp. 145–47.

148. Ibid., p. 149.

149. Abt, 1965, p. 4.

150. Latham, 1982, p. 192.

151. Dardess, 1991, p. 75.

152. Tom, 1989, p. 13.

153. At birth an infant was one *sui* of age. A child began to be legally liable at seven *sui* and was fully liable by sixteen *sui*. Dardess, 1991, p. 73.

154. Tom, 1989, p. 80.

155. Ibid., pp. 19–43.

156. Dardess, 1991, p. 83.

157. Ibid.

158. Ibid., p. 74.

159. Ibid., pp. 76–77.

160. Ibid., pp. 77–78.

161. Ibid., p. 79.

162. Ibid., p. 82.

163. Ibid., p. 85.

164. Leonard, 1968, p. 17; and R. Kimura, *Hastings Center Report*, August 1986, p. 22.

165. Sansom, 1958, p. 217.

166. Aston, 1972, p. 85.

167. Frederic, 1972, p. 33.

168. Leonard, 1968, pp. 58–59. Wartime atrocities against children were universal. Simeon of Durham (11th century) described the gaming custom of "piking," whereby infants and toddlers were torn from their mothers, tossed into the air, and impaled on a pike as they came down (Amt, 1993, p. 95). During the First Crusade, stories were told of Nicaean infants roasted on spits (Billings, 1987, p. 27). In this century, during the Japanese invasion of China, "piking" was reintroduced, on rifle bayonnets.

169. H. G. Henderson, *Haiku* (New York: Doubleday, 1958), p. 160.

170. Chamberlain, 1971, pp. 92–93.

171. Leonard, 1968, p. 77.

172. Sansom, 1958, pp. 394–99.

173. Uno, 1991, p. 389.

Chapter 7

The Reformation and Humanism: The Apprentice

❏ ❏ ❏

HISTORIANS TRADITIONALLY CITE the fall of Constantinople to the Ottoman Turks in 1453 as the beginning of the Renaissance. During this period, Byzantine scholars fled from the crumbling empire into Europe, fueling the scholastic fever of renascent Europe. Their influx stimulated interest in reexamining classical principles in art, architecture, education, and letters, with astounding consequences. Moreover, the development of the printing press increased the number of books that could be published, providing the means to explore new ideas and test ancient philosophical and aesthetic thinking. New and bigger ships and skilled navigators provided the means for global exploration that expanded world vision and commerce. The monarchy, affirmed by scholars and statesmen, grew in importance and in power, leading to a "Golden Age of Kings." By about 1600, monarchs autocratically controlled England, France, Spain, and Russia. This newly wielded power in turn led to the evolution of concepts of the modern state.

The church's influence waned concomitantly. No longer did the church control learning. Intellectual thought was becoming humanistic, relegating to far lesser importance the church's primary concerns of spirituality, salvation, and life after death.

Revisionist scholasticism also had been facilitated by the printing press, and as the written word became more widely available to masses of people for the first time in history, a veritable philosophic, moral and theological, aesthetic, and educational revolution occurred. Armed with their books in the forums of the new universities, philosophers and theologians explored new ideas and tested ancient thinking. The questions posed and their responses challenged established ecclesiastical order and authority.

Exposure of corruption and simony in the church evoked outrage, and the foundation of the church shook from the weight of reform. The schism that resulted altered the spiritual and social map of the world thereafter. A new social order was introduced, with state sanction and support, in which a code of manners, public decorum, and norms of behavior were adopted, along with a new fashion code in dress. Reformation morality attempted to exert a viewpoint of its own on the body politic with a barrage of dour pronouncements on behavior and public comportment.

The most enduring aesthetic legacy of the Renaissance was in its art. A balance of state-imposed concepts of public deportment blended with humanistic refinement in thematic depictions, and the results echoed the elegance and grace of Greek and Roman art. The human figure once more was portrayed with anatomic correctness, in postures that expressed a range of human emotions and an almost haughty display of pride in being *human*.

Protestant worship became viewed as a very private matter, an introspective retreat into the individual conscience, with the discipline of silent meditation. It was the role of churches, as it was succinctly summarized by Roger Chartier,

> . . . to articulate within the context of a revitalized Christianity, the disciplines necessary to the faith, coupled with a credo invariably uttered in the first-person singular.[1]

Protestant theology altered in a major way the Christian concept of baptism as it pertained to children. The Protestant Church, in viewing religion to be a private matter, a personal dialogue between a rational human and God, grappled with the dilemma of infants' inability to make informed decisions to be baptized. Some sects resolved the issue by performing "dry" baptisms, in which infants were dedicated in the church and officially registered and baptisms by water were postponed until the children could avow the sacrament.[2]

NURTURE AND DISCIPLINE

Reformation idealists formed distinct guidelines for the rearing and nurturing of children that applied to all children, regardless of position, wealth, or number within a family. Parish registers[3] of the time kept records indicating that the average village household numbered 4.47 people (rich households averaged 6.2; the poor, 2.1 people). There were several reasons for smaller families among the poor. It took poor women ten to fifteen years to accumulate a dowry that would attract a marriage offer, and their reproductive span was considerably shorter than that of their middle-class counterparts. Poor mothers nursed their young for longer periods or hired themselves out as wet nurses and therefore experienced longer anovulatory periods. Finally, higher infant-mortality rates related to malnutrition and scanty hygiene prevailed among the poor.

Vigorous attempts were made to inculcate among the rich and poor alike a belief in pious discipline and a sense in parents of their responsibility to promote the *potential* of their children, thereby contributing to their development into worthy persons. Wittenburg's own Martin Luther (1483–1546) succinctly reinforced the belief in the importance of the parental role and influence: "There is no power on earth that is nobler or greater than that of a parent's."[4]

A colleague, Viet Dietrich (1506–1549), who was a reformer from Nuremberg, rhetorically asked: "Is there anything on earth more precious, friendly, and lovable, than a pious, disciplined, obedient, and teachable child?"[5]

The reformers of Protestant Europe insisted that parental duty was to produce good Christian souls, along with good, healthy human beings of limitless potential. The importance of baptism and salvation and of physical well-being and character were inseparable values to them. Yet in the midst of the torrent of new pious, more worldly ideas generated by the Reformation, people sustained their belief in age-old superstitions and magic. This was especially the case in relation to babies. After baptisms, when priests were no longer in view, it was common practice to roll babies on the altar to prevent rickets. Babies' mouths were washed with holy water to hinder tooth decay in the future.[6] To safeguard children from becoming mute, godparents kissed the baby as they passed under the belfry leaving the church. To protect children from deafness, village children followed infants out of the church beating drums and rattles.

Moral development began to be equated with good manners and general comportment, and these were expected to be the primary focus of training in families. In conforming households, children's private and public expression of good manners was inculcated with rigidly imposed discipline, consistent with the belief that indulging children was a cardinal sin.

All the same, several of the most influential reformists' admonishments to parents easily sound like contemporary observations on youth-related social problems in our own age. Conrad Sam (1483–1533), for instance, wrote:

. . . if you want to know joy in your children, take care you teach them virtue. Do not do as is done in the world, where children are taught to rule, but not to serve; to curse and insult, but not to pray; to ride, but not to speak properly. Children today are badly raised; not only do parents permit them their every selfish wish, but they even show them the way to do it.[7]

Juan Luis Vives (1492–1540) concurred with this view, and went further, ascribing the ills of society to indulgent mothers, who were ultimately (and not too subtly) responsible for the morality of children or the lack thereof:

. . . and so mothers damn their children when they nurse them voluptuously. Love as you should, in such a way that love does not prevent steering the young away from vice and instilling them with fear by mild verberations, castigations, and tears, so that the body and the understanding are made better, by the strictness of sobriety and food. Mothers, understand that the greater part of the malice of men is to be ascribed to you.[8]

Viet Dietrich made the same observation and believed that the indulgence of children was pervasive in all strata of society:

Today you find few parents who once mention study or work to their children. They let them creep about idly, eating and drinking whenever they please, casually dressed in ragged pants and jackets . . . children learn to curse and swear . . . stay out dancing till midnight or carouse around the public house.[9]

Books of Comportment

Disparaging imagery of animal behavior often was used by reformists as contrasts to ideal concepts of public manners and decorum and private morality. In time, their zealous preoccupation with public and private morality, a rigid code of behavior and the will in families to implement it, prevailed. In the sixteenth and seventeenth centuries, Reformation moral edicts and guidance proliferated from church pulpits and from secular printing presses. Literacy had created an insatiable appetite for the written word. Pedagogical sources of the times were delighted to comply with the demand and supplied parents with an endless stream of advice on how children should be raised. These treatises were found in most of Europe; known as "books of urbanity," they almost exclusively taught comportment to children. Several English versions were published, among them *The Boke of Nurture* by Hugh Rhodes in 1545, *A School of Vertue* written in doggerel rhyme (1557) by Francis Seager, and *Lessons of Wysedom for All Manner of Chyldren* by Symon. There had been earlier versions on the theme, written with aristocratic children in mind. Richart's *The Babee's Boke* (c.1475) was written for the court of Edward IV. Much later, *Stans Puer ad Mensam* (The boy at the table) was written for the court of Henry VIII.[10]

One of the books, Thomas Elyot's (?1490–1546) *The Governour*, written in 1531, gave advice on raising boys who were destined to rule. Elyot advocated molding the sons of the nobility, using conniving and manipulative tactics to achieve a dubious end. He urged that boys be sequestered to prevent them from adopting common habits. His thesis in general is riddled with an arrogant disdain for the common man, and the book's tone is replete with a droit du seigneur affirmation. Elyot's language thinly veiled an aristocratic hauteur that dismissed, if not ignored, the human rights of what were then socially inferior attendants. Autocratic will and insensitivity were portrayed as aristocratic virtues such as "courage" or "gentle wit." Elyot fostered contrived outcomes of contests between noble children and the riffraff. He instructed that orders be given that boys feign defeat at the hands of their noble competitors from time to time, since, he thought, in this way self-esteem and "self-assertion" would be enhanced among the upper-class children.[11]

Italian books of urbanity were popular with the public and were translated into both English and Dutch. Giovanni della Casa's *Galateo*, Guazzo's *Civile Conseration*, and Baldassare Castiglione's *The Courtier* were among those widely circulated.[12] *The Courtier* was the most popular of all the Italian works. Castiglione's (1478–1529) text was extolled as a general model for maturing young men to imitate, but, in fact, the book was directed only to youths from families of influence and political importance and defined for them the qualities Castiglione thought gentleman of the court should possess.[13] Books of courtesy specifically written for girls were published much later by Puritan writers. Dorothy Leigh wrote *The Mother's Blessing* in 1616; Elizabeth Joceline, *The Mother's Legacy* in 1624. Both of these books assumed that all girls believed that goodness was centered on the preservation of virtue.[14]

Most of these books, however, were written for adults' edification.[15] Exceptions were the books already mentioned, *The Babee's Boke* and Chaucer's *Treatise on the Astrolabe*, written for his ten-year-old son Lewis. When William Caxton set up his Red Pole Press in Westminster during the second half of the fifteenth century, however, he began to publish books on comportment specifically for children. William Sloane's *The Book of Curtesye* (1477) instructed boys on noble behavior, and *Knight of the Tower* (1484) did the same for girls. Unlike these books, which were well received, the chivalric romances published by Caxton and his colleagues (*A Lytell Geste of Robin Hode* [c.1500] and *Guy of Warwick*) were condemned by moralists like

Roger Ascham (1515–1568), Zachary Boyd (?1585–1653), and Hugh Rhodes (fl.1535) who complained that they and books like them encouraged inappropriate, vivid imaginations among the young. Rhodes, in his *Boke of Nurture* (1545), admonished parents:

Take hede [your children] speake no wordes of villany, for it causeth much corruption to ingender in them, nor shew them muche familiaritye, and see that they use honest sportes and games. Marke well what vice they are specially inclined unto, and breake it betymes. Take them often with you to heare Gods word preached, and then enquire of them what they heard, and use them to reade in the Bible and other Godly Bokes, but especyally keepe them from reading of fayned fables, vayne fantasyes, and wanton stories, and songs of love, which bring much mischiefe to youth. For if they learne pure and cleane doctryne in youth, they poure out plentye of good workes in age.[16]

Ascham expressed similar sentiments in *The Scholemaster* (1570):

In our forefathers tyme, whan Papistrie, as a standyng poole, covered and overflowed all England, fewe bookes were read in our tong, savyng certaine bookes of Chivalrie, as they sayd, for pastime and pleasure, which, as some say, were made in monasteries by idle Monkes or wanton Chanons: as one for example, *Morte Arthure*: the whole pleasure of which booke standeth in two speciall pointes, in open mans slaughter and bold bawdrye. . . . What toyes the dayly readyng of such a booke may worke in the will of a yong gentleman or a yong mayde, that liveth wealthilie and idlelie, wise men can judge and honest men do pitie.[17]

William Caxton popularized a genre of instructional book using bestial characters, most notably *Aesop's Fables* (1483) and an English translation of *Reynard the Fox* (1481). These were believed also to facilitate learning Greek and Latin and were widely read. The popularity of the genre endured for more than a century, culminating in the publication of John Taylor's *A Dogge of Warre* (1628), whose protagonist is sometimes heralded as the ancestor of the great dog hero, Lassie.[18]

Two of the leading manuscripts among the books of urbanity were Desiderius Erasmus's *De Civilitate Morum Puerilium* (Manners for children [1530]) and Otto Brunfels's *On Disciplining and Instructing Children* (1525). "Manners for Children" proved so popular that within two years it was reprinted in eight cities throughout Europe, and by 1537 it had been translated into English, French, German, Czech, and Dutch.[19] Believing that all inner peace and character were reflected in a myriad of behavioral manifestations that evinced inner qualities, both authors emphasized severe regimentation of the young.

Erasmus believed passionately that a child's education could not start too early—even as speech was evolving. In *De Pueris Statim ac Liberalites Insti-tuendis Declamatio* (The early liberal education of children [1529]) he declared, "Do not follow common fashion and opinion by allowing your son's first years to pass by without the benefit of instruction."[20] But education was to be gentle, persuasive: "Nothing is more damaging to young children than constant exposure to beatings."[21]

Erasmus (1466–1536) urged parents to control all gestures, manners, postures, clothing, and speech. He was particularly emphatic on the subject of what may be called the language of the eyes:

If a child's natural goodness is to reveal itself everywhere (and it glows especially in the face), his gaze should be gentle, respectful, and decent. Wild eyes are a sign of violence; a fixed stare is a sign of effrontery; wandering, distracted eyes are a sign of madness. The glance should not be sidelong, which is a sign of cunning, of a person contemplating a wicked deed. The eyes must not be opened too wide, for this is a mark of an imbecile. To lower and blink the eyelids is a sign of frivolousness. To hold the eyes steady is the stamp of a lazy mind, and Socrates was reproached for it. Piercing eyes signify irascibility. Too keen and eloquent eyes denote a lascivious temperament. It is important that the eyes signify a calm and respectfully affectionate spirit. It is no accident that the ancient sages said: the eyes are the seat of the soul. (*De Civilitate*, "On the Body")

The bestiality he perceived in children's natures, he thought, could be eradicated or at least controlled, allowing human elements to emerge, and his all-encompassing view was that a "well-natured child, whether at table or at play always maintains a singular temperament."[22]

His advice to parents, however, advocated rigid, demanding, and excessive discipline. Children were expected to keep their noses clean and free of mucus. Biting or licking lips was prohibited, since both of these habits mimicked animal behavior. Speech interrupted by frequent coughing was considered a liar's tic used as a delaying tactic. Yawning and excessive laughter were deemed impolite. Erasmus instructed that the face be covered by hand or with a handkerchief in the event of uncontrollable laughter, so that the contorted face remained unexposed. Spitting was anathema, but if unavoidable, the sputum was to be rubbed into the ground by a shoe.

Erasmus believed that a clean mouth was a disciplined mouth, and he advocated mouth care with frequent rinsing. Hair had to be neatly combed at all times to avoid the unkempt appearance of a wild horse or ox. He opined that neat dress bespoke good character—sloppiness and pompous dress, the converse—and that erect posture with even shoulders and head upright indicated an inner alignment and honesty.[23]

He issued sweeping guidelines regarding the rituals of the dining table. Children were directed to sit silently during meals. They were to be served only after their elders. Noting the short attention-spans of young children, Erasmus admonished parents to excuse them promptly from the dining table, adding, "Those parents hate their children, when they force them while still young to sit patiently at the table into the night."[24]

He attitudinized that only ill-mannered children engaged in games of fierce competition, and he advised that these be forbidden. By the time of the Counter-Reformation it was thought, however, that adults could moderate this danger by establishing and controlling the rules, rather than by prohibiting games altogether.

Erasmus regarded parents' example as the key to producing well-bred children. He often cited the Latin maxim *"A vicinis exemplum habent,"* as well as its vernacular equivalent, *"So de oude songen so pepe de ionghen."*[25] Both have modern counterparts in the adage "The apple does not fall far from the tree."*

Otto Brunfels (1488–1534) was a Carthusian who became a reformist in 1521. His upbringing as a monk colored his attitude regarding children, and he believed their day should be controlled from awakening until retirement:

Sleep neither too little nor too much. Begin each day by blessing it in God's name and saying the Lord's Prayer. Thank God for keeping you through the night and ask his help for the new day. Greet your parents. Comb your hair and wash your face and hands. Before departing for school, ask Christ to send his spirit, without whom there is no true understanding, remembering also, however, that the Spirit only helps those who help themselves. . . . At school be happily obedient; do everything wholeheartedly. When called on, answer quickly and modestly. Expect disgusting behavior not only to be rebuked with sarcasm, but punished firmly. Above all, do not let the teacher strike you with cause. Harm neither your teachers nor your peers in either word or deed. Try to learn from those who criticize you rather than simply turn them aside.

. . . Read something specific from Scripture every day; do not go to sleep until you have memorized a few new verses. Punish yourself when you have neglected your readings. . . .

After school go directly home; do not tarry in the streets. If your parents need help when you arrive, obey their requests without question. If you have time after your chores, use it to review and reflect on what you have read at school, remembering that nothing in this life is more precious than time, for once time is lost, it is lost forever.[26]

---

*"They [children] have example nearby"; "As the old sing, so pipe the young."

Brunfels's expectations of children required extraordinary self-discipline, as well as an unnatural degree of conformity. His expectations, moreover, of meditative skills would have daunted seasoned contemplatives. Even meal-time was imbued with moral overtones:

Make sure your nails are cut and your hands washed. Sit up straight, comply with the requests of those around you, do not drink too much wine, and be mindful of what is fitting for one your age. Serve yourself only after others have been served. If seconds are placed on the table, politely refuse; if you are not permitted to say no, take a modest portion, expressing thanks. . . .

Listen attentively to all who speak, but say nothing yourself unless you are addressed. If someone says something improper or shameful at table, do not laugh, but look puzzled, as if you do not understand what has been said. Let no insults, slanders, or idle gossip cross your lips. Do not belittle others or brag on yourself. . . .

Do not cut bread on your chest or in your hands. Eat directly in front of yourself. If you want something from a serving plate, take it with your knife. Do not fall upon your plate like a pig upon a trough. Do not mix food together. Do not eat with your fingers. When eating a soft-boiled egg, first cut a piece of bread for a sop. Take care not to drip the egg on the table or your chest. Eat it quickly, laying the shell, uncrushed, on your plate.

Do not put candles out with your fingers . . . do not poke your fingers into salt dishes . . . take modest bites. Do not spit chewed food out of your mouth onto your plate. Do not scratch your head while eating. Expect punishment for incessant giggling at table and ridicule if you dunk bread in your wine. After drinking, wipe your lips with two fingers. Permit no morsel of fat to swim about in your glass. Do not eat and speak at the same time, or recline on your elbows, or lean back in your chair. Do not throw bones under the table. If the meal goes on too long and you become tired, ask permission to leave and politely excuse yourself.[27]

Brunfels's mandates extended even to how children slept:

. . . lie neither on your face nor on your back, but first on your right side, your arms in the figure of a cross protecting your heart, stretching your right hand to your left shoulder and your left hand to your right.[28]

Like Erasmus, Brunfels opined about children's play and games, considering these activities to be sources for character building. Group activities, such as ball playing, dancing, singing, and gymnastics were encouraged. Individual or self-driven sports or games, such as swimming or top spinning, on the other hand, were discouraged, and certainly, activities related to gambling such as dice, cards or chess, were prohibited. Pieter Brueghel's (?1520–1569) well-known painting *Kinderspiel* (*Children's Games*) (figure 7.1) was contemporary to the moralistic writings of Erasmus and Brunfels. If the artist's depiction was typical of child play during those times, it must be con-

Figure 7.1 Pieter Brueghel's *Kinderspiel*. KUNSTHISTORICHE MUSEUM, VIENNA.

cluded that the painting serves as an ironic statement on the contrast between idealism and reality.*

Contemporary to Erasmus and Brunfels was Thomas More (1478–1535),
who thought play a wonderful and important pastime for children. In his
poem "Childhood," he characterized disdain of school and the love of games
as personifications of childhood itself:

> I am called Childhood, in play is all my mind,
> To cast a quoit, a cockshy, and a ball.
> A top can I set, and drive it in his kind.
> But would to god these hateful books all,
> Were in a fire burnt to powder small.
> Then might I lead my life always in play:
> Which life god send me to mine ending day.[29]

Catechisms

Complementing the social-moral indoctrination was a thorough, somber
religious education, using catechisms. The question-and-answer format of
the catechism lent itself to home use, and the movable-type printing press
made possible a catechism in virtually every home. One such text was written in 1550 by Erasmus Alberus (1500–1553) for children, with their small

---

*Sandra Hindman's well-researched study *Children's Games* reveals how Brueghel used the
allegorical themes of the Ages of Man and the Calendar of Seasons to explore the elements of
chance, folly, and fate in the human condition. *Art Bulletin* 1981; 63:447–75.

Figure 7.2 *Massacre of the Innocents* (1367), by Bartolo di Fredi, tempera on wood. WALTERS ART GALLERY, BALTIMORE.

hands in mind. The book, titled *Ten Dialogues for Children Who Have Begun to Speak*, measured a mere two by two inches. It was dedicated to the Holy Innocents, a topic of singular interest in the medieval period. Indeed, the cult of the Holy Innocents continued through the Renaissance. "Innocents' Day" or "Childermas" evolved into an elaborate festival for children celebrated on December 28th. Plays such as *Ordo Rachelis* and poems such as Peter Abelard's "Rachel's Lament" were written on the theme. The slaughter was portrayed in every art medium, such as murals, paintings (figure 7.2), sculptures, marble mosaics, and even on capitals (figure 7.3).

The catechism *Ten Dialogues* used a question-and-answer format, simple language, and short phrases, as in a dialogue between Alberus and his three-year-old daughter, Gertrude:

> A: Do you love Jesus?
>
> G: Yes, father.
>
> A: Who is the Lord Jesus?
>
> G: God and Mary's son.
>
> A: How is his dear Mother called?
>
> G: Mary.
>
> A: Why do you love Jesus? What has he done to make you love him?
>
> G: He has shed his blood for me.
>
> A: He has shed his blood for you?
>
> G: Yes, father.[30]

Figure 7.3
Capital from the monastery
Santa Maria Real de Aquilas de Campo
in Spain, showing the Innocents.
MUSEO ARQUEOLOGICO NACIONAL, MADRID.

The decorous and respectful tones of the daughter's answers reflect Reformist concern to teach respect for parents and for authority as well as the tenets and dogma of religion. In molding children, three basic principles were inculcated and taught: honor parents, obey parents, and protect parents in old age. The admonitions to children made by Johann Moeckard in 1550 exemplify the instructional emphasis generally adopted:

O you children! It should make no difference to you whether your parents are wise, learned, rich, and powerful, or simple, unimportant, poor, and despised; think first what a great thing it is that you have parents through whom God has given you life.[31]

A century later, in 1647, Le Brun de la Rochette echoed Reformist thought when he wrote: "The father and mother [are] like images of God for children."[32]

The colonial, Thomas Cobbett (1608–1685), also wrote on the topic in *A Fruitfull and Usefull Discourse Touching on the Honor Due from Children to Parents, and the Duty of Parents Towards Their Children* (1656). The book quickly reached England, where, despite its verbosity, it was praised as the most thorough exposition of the Fourth Commandment. Cobbett admonished children that "gabling, laughing, and flouting" were a show of irreverence in or out of their parents' presence and advised them to heed the old aphorism, "Children should be seen and not heard."[33]

Many of the numerous catechisms of religious instruction of the times were linguistically and theologically complex and intricate. The Strasbourg catechism of 1534, for example, clearly taxed the comprehension skills of children:

Father: What does it mean to know that all things are in God's hands?

Child: That I hold God above all things and desire his grace . . . and trust in his protection and fatherly favor in all adversity.

Father: What does it mean to you that Christ sits at the right hand of God in heaven?

Child: That I can trust completely in my Lord Jesus to whom the Father has given all power in heaven and earth and have no doubt that he will in the end save me from all sin and misfortune and let me dwell with him in heaven in eternal blessedness.[34]

Johann Agricola's (1492–1566) catechism, *One Hundred and Fifty-six Questions of Young Children in the German School for Girls in Eisleben* (1528), was more extreme, making saintly demands of young souls:

Child: If I live by faith alone, will tyrants drive me from the land and take all that I have?

Answer: That is the risk you must take; for as soon as you embrace the gospel and Christ, you must think to yourself: "Now I deprive myself of body and life . . ."

Child: Why do I do that?

Answer: So that when it actually happens to you, you can take it in stride and say: "This is nothing new; I have known all along that this would come about."

Child: Will it really cost me my life?

Answer: You must obey God more than man.[35]

Religious instruction also was delivered through the genre of stories. One of the most prominent and popular books of the times, *The Book of Martyrs* (1563) by John Foxe (1516–1587), also focused on the theme of child martyrs. Written in a narrative memorable for its imagery and use of language, Foxe recounted brutal stories, full of blood and gore, of small children who suffered unimaginable atrocities. The young heroes and heroines of these stories were clubbed, whipped, burned, flayed, scalped, and beheaded, all the while persisting in their affirmation of faith and trust in God.

Turks, Jews, assorted heathens, minions of the Antichrist and ministers of the pope were portrayed as the villainous perpetrators of these crimes against children. Interestingly, in spite of the fact that her successors condemned martyrs to death in equal or greater numbers, the soubriquet "Bloody Mary," coined by Foxe, endures, familiar to all.

Not all of the martyrs Foxe wrote about so stirringly were children, as in the instances of Hugh Latimer (1490–1555) and Nicholas Ridley (1500–1555) (figure 7.4). Foxe infused their inspirational story of courage and grace in language of such singular eloquence and religious fervor that

Figure 7.4 *Martyrdom of Ridley and Latimer* (1855), by George Hayter (1792–1876). PRINCETON UNIVERSITY MUSEUM.

Latimer's remarks to Ridley are still quoted. As they were led to the stake, Latimer turned to his comrade and said:

Be of good comfort Master Ridley, and play the man. We shall this day light such a candle, by God's grace in England, as I trust shall never be put out.[36]

Children's reactions to these stories of martyrs—child or adult—or the attention they gave to Foxe's stories cannot be known. The 160 woodcuts illustrating the book ensured that it was at least leafed through by children. A canon decree of 1571 required that a chained copy of *The Book of Martyrs* be placed in all English cathedral vestibules, indicative, certainly, of the import the book was given by church authorities. There were two editions of the book in Latin; the third and those that followed were published in English. Protestant children in Europe and in the American colonies were given the book for their edification for the next three centuries.

Death of Children

Protestant stoicism was expected of parents and children in all aspects of life and in death. Fear of death or grief in reaction to a bereavement were considered inconsistent with the belief in God's grace and the assurance of an afterlife in heaven. Reformists even preached that it was not appropriate to grieve for children who died. Conrad Sam pointed out in the early sixteenth century, moreover, that "it serves no useful purpose to sorrow for the dead, while to be concerned for the living is not in vain," and Ralph Josselin (1617–1683) reminded his congregation in a sermon in 1652 that "Christians should . . . think about the dead without too much sorrow . . . when others go to the tombs and graves to mourn, Christians go to rejoyce."[37]

Yet the very founder of the Reformist movement, Martin Luther, was unable to contain his grief when his daughter Elizabeth died at eight months of age:

I so lamented her death that I was exquisitely sick, my heart rendered soft and weak; never had I thought that a father's heart could be so broken for his children's sake.[38]

The death of yet another daughter, Magdalena, at age thirteen in 1542, prompted Luther to express the unbearable struggle it was to sustain the Christian concept that death be accepted with joy in the knowledge of the soul's passage into eternal life:

The force of our natural love is so great. . . . The features, the words, and the movement of our living and dying daughter, who was so very obedient and respectful, remain engraved in our hearts; even the death of Christ . . . is unable to take all this away as it should.[39]

Josselin's entry in his diary on 21 February 1648, while consistent with the admonitions he gave in his sermon four years later, more closely reflects the understanding Luther had when he wrote, "The force of our natural love is so great . . .":

This day my dear babe Ralph [10 days old] quietly fell asleep, and is at rest with the Lord. The Lord in mercy sanctify his hand unto me and do me good by it, and teach me how to walk more closely with him.

Josselin took some comfort forty-two days later (May 5th) with the birth of his third son:

My deare wife . . . was delivered before nine of the clocke of her 5t child, and third sonne, God giving us another sonne in stead of my deare Ralph whom he tooke away.[40]

Many diary entries suggest that no Christian comfort was found to mitigate the initial pain and grief experienced at the loss of a beloved child:

. . . and then my sweet child died at four o'clock in the morning, being the eleventh day of October, and was buried that day at night. The grief for this child was so great that I forgot myself so much that I did offend God in it. (Nehemiah Wallington, 11 October 1625)[41]

On Maunday Thursday my child [Mary, his firstborn, aged one year] died at 10 of the clock in the forenoon in its mother's lap . . . taken with vomiting fits, which would make it ready to die; and that was the beginning of our sorrow. Oh what grief was it to me to hear it groan, to see its sprightly eyes turn to me for help in vain! (Isaac Archer, 31 March 1670)[42]

A continental, perhaps Catholic, reference to a child's death, although controlled in its expression of sorrow, reveals in its constraint an overwhelming sense of loss felt by the child's father:

I loved her with a tenderness that I cannot express. . . . I spent my time at home very agreeably playing with my daughter [Louise-Anne], who, despite her tender age [four years] was so amusing to those who saw her. (Henri de Campion, 10 May 1653)[43]

Michel de Montaigne (1533–1592) has been frequently cited as representing the common sentiments of his age in a decidedly offhand comment he made about the deaths of his children in one of his essays:

I cannot accept the ardour with which some people caress children scarsely born, who have neither any mental action nor any distinguishable bodily shape whereby they can make themselves loveable . . . [of] the children I have had; they all die on me at nurse. (*Essays* 2:8)

Montaigne's cavalier tone, in this author's opinion, is an idiosyncratic attitude of a renowned rationalist and unreflective of common sentiment. Extant diaries typically described inconsolable grief and deep mourning, and funeral records bolster this view. Those parents who could afford it, ceremoniously buried their children symbolically garbed in white, the color of innocence, and in white caskets, surrounded by attendants dressed in white. Children under the age of one month were buried in the swaddling bands and chrisom gowns of their baptisms.

A diary entry that more closely exhibits the orthodox Reformist doctrine is one by Johannes Beringer in his *Hauschronik* in 1525: "Through God's will, [Theophilus was] taken from this world."[44]

Another such example was written by a woman named Alice Thornton:

It please God to take from me my dear Betty, which had been long in the rickets and consumption, gotten at first by an ague, and much gone in the rickets, which I conceive was caused by ill milk at two nurses. (Alice Thornton, 14 February 1655)[45]

In blaming wet nurses for young Betty's illness, Alice Thornton's entry is illustrative of the imputation of responsibility that children's nurses faced when illness or death—or both—affected their charges. Nurses also were scapegoated for children's bad manners or ill-humor. Thomas Becon (1512–1567) wrote, "For children by drinking in strange milk, drink in also strange manners and another nature." This thinking had been pervasive for a long time on the Continent and was voiced frequently. An earlier writer, the Florentine Leon Battista Alberti (1404–1472), expressed in *Della Famiglia* forceful concern about the dangerous influence bad nurses' milk had on children's characters and virtue:

. . . a dishonest and immoral nurse will corrupt a child, predispose him to vice and fill his spirit with bestial and wild passions, such as wrath, fear, and similar evils.[46]

Most diaries, however, indicate that parents ascribed their children's deaths, appropriately, to plague, diphtheria, smallpox, or childhood infectious diseases. Joost van Heemskerck's death in 1647 at the age of three years prompted his father to write:

He'd had a high fever for days, and was completely covered with the chicken pox and although most of these had in fact dried up still his fever didn't diminish. Finally his body was worn out, and the fever claimed his life.[47]

Nehemiah Wallington entered in his diary:

That in the year of our Lord 1625, it pleased God to send among us in the city and the suburbs such a plague . . . we did hear of three score children died out of one alley and thirty out of another alley, and many more out of other places.[48]

Similar statistics from epidemics were cited in multiple European urban centers, but accidents also claimed many lives or otherwise produced a residue of misery. Trauma was responsible for high morbidity among children, some of which was environmental, such as frequent near-drownings in sites ribboned by canals. Spills and falls often had dire consequences:

. . . Michael going childishly with a sharp stick of eight inches long and a little wax candle light on the top of it, did fall upon the plain boards in Mary's chamber, and the sharp point of the stick entered through the lid of his left eye towards the corner next to the nose. . . . God speed the rest of the cure. (John Dee, 1 January 1588)[49]

Burns frequently were incurred by children playing near hearths, resulting in permanently maimed bodies:

. . . then did the child stumble on the hearth and fell into the fire on the range with one of her hands, and burned her right hand three fingers of it, and by God's help I did pull her out of the fire by her clothes. I catched her out of it before she was exceedingly burned; only three of her fingers sore burned to the bone. (Alice Thornton, 1659)[50]

Some of the accidents were just that and truly unavoidable:

. . . my little son Richard, now about two years old, as he was fed with broth in the morning, a square but broad and pointed bone of some part of a ract of mutton stuck so fast in the child's throat and cross his weas and . . . the eyes and face were swollen and closed, the mouth full of froth and gore, the face black. . . . It please God that one then sudden effort, and as it were struggling his last for life he cast forth a bone of this shape and form. (John Evelyn, 1654)[51]

Some children assuredly were victims of habitual child abuse, while others simply suffered the consequences of overheated tempers infused into corporal punishment:

Katherine by a blow on th'ear given by her mother did bleed at the nose very much, which did stay for an hour and more. (John Dee, 21 May 1589)[52]

Judging by the frequency with which anecdotes appear in diaries, blows to the head, disciplinary and otherwise, commonly produced morbidity. In his autobiography, William Bedell (c.1571) described what happened to his brother John:

. . . he received such a blow from his cholerick Master, that he was beaten off a pair of stairs, and had one side his head so bruised that the bloud gush'd out of his ear, and his hearing was in consequence so impair'd.[53]

EDUCATION

On the Continent of Europe, monastic and chapter schools were gradually replaced, although catechetical instruction, as well as Latin, music, and arithmetic, continued to be taught routinely. Discipline, coercion, and group conformity, however, were given stronger emphasis in the evolving educational milieux. These factors particularly were apparent in Reformation England, which developed seven types of schools that had distinctly different administrative structures (table 7.1). The most common schools were the elementary, called ABC or "petty" schools, and grammar schools.

Children started *abecedary* instruction conjoined with catechetical studies at four years of age. The alphabet was assembled with prayers such as the

TABLE 7.1
REFORMATION ENGLISH SCHOOLS

Schools	Administration
Cathedral (chapter)	Rector overseeing secular monastics
Collegiate	Secular teaching clergy (Eton, Winchester)
Monastic (almonry)	Teaching monks (charity schools)
Hospital school	Connected with almshouses (Banbury)
Guild school	For crafts and merchant guilds
Chantry	Chapel grammar schools
Grammar	Attached to universities (Magdalen)

Pater Noster, Ave Maria, Credo, and the Ten Commandments, and all were learned together. Then a primer, a psalter-cum-litanies, was introduced for study. Three years were spent in petty school mastering the two basic texts. At seven, children began serious study in grammar schools. Free, except for a small entrance fee, these schools maintained only industrious students who wished to extend their studies until their fifteenth year.

Students' tutors were church-appointed, an arrangement mandated by the Canon of 1571:

It shall not be lawful for any to teach the Latin tongue or to instruct children, neither openly in the schools neither privately in any man's house, but whom the Bishop of that diocese hath allowed and to whom he hath given license to teach under the seal of his office.[54]

As tutors were licensed, they were given authority *in loco parentis*. They were charged by bishops and parents to emphasize Latin in the classroom and in the dormitory. Roger Ascham in *The Scholemaster* (1570) wrote: "All men covet to have their children speake Latin and so do I verie earnestlie too."[55] The works of Latin writers Terence and Cicero were used to teach conversational Latin, followed by *vulgarias*—books that translated common English phrases into Latin. John Stanbridge (c.1508) of the Magdalen School provided these examples:

> Scholars must live hardily at Oxford.
> *Scholasticos oxonii parce vivere oportet.*
>
> Sayest thou this in earnest or in game?
> *Ioco an serio loqueris?*

The master hath beat me.
Preceptor a me sumpsit poenas.[56]

The last expression would have been recited often, since caning was the common modality of discipline. Neither rancor nor bitterness was associated with the practice, however, as strict and corporal discipline had positive associations. The expression *educatus erat sub ferula* (he was educated under the rod) ordinarily was spoken in prideful tones.[57] The commonly employed aphorism *Ubi nulla disciplina, ibi nulla spes* (Where there is no discipline, there is no hope) evokes the general sentiment. Once boys mastered Latin, they were introduced to Greek and Hebrew so as to study the Old Testament. Mastery of the vulgar language, English, was a strong priority for many educators. Richard Mulcaster (1530–1611) wrote two essays—"Positions" and "Elementary"—in 1582 in which he argued:

While our religion was restrained to the Latin, it was either the only or the oneliest principle in learning, to learn to read Latin. But now that we are returned home to our English ABC, as most natural to our soil and most proper to our faith . . . we are to be directed by Nature and property to read that first which we speak first, and to care for that most which we ever use most.[58]

The educational goals of secular education in Protestant Europe were not modified dramatically by the Reformation. If anything, the theme of universal education was bolstered, since the two great reformers, Luther and Calvin, championed the idea. John Calvin (1509–1564) wrote in the *Ordinances* of 1541:

. . . it is necessary to raise offspring for the time to come, in order not to leave the Church deserted for our children, it is imperative that we establish a college to instruct the children and to prepare them for both the ministry and civil government. ("Concerning the Doctors")[59]

In a somber, admonitionary tone, Martin Luther emphasized directly to parents their duty to educate their children:

If now you have a son who is able to learn; if you can send him to school, but do not do it and go your way asking nothing of the worldly government, law, peace, and so on; you are, to the extent of your ability, opposing civil authority like the Turk, indeed, like the devil himself. . . . Therefore go ahead and have your son study. And even if he has to beg bread for a time, you are nonetheless giving to our Lord God a fine bit of wood out of which he can carve you a lord. (*Sermon on Keeping Children in School* pt. 2)[60]

Tapping a centuries-old tradition of church educational aid for the poor, Luther enjoined the government to identify boys with intellectual promise and encouraged the rich in their charity to establish scholarships for education through the church:

Therefore, let everyone be on guard; and wherever the government sees a promising boy, let him be sent to school. If the father is poor, the resources of the Church should be used to assist. The rich should make bequests to such objects, as some have done, who have founded scholarships; that is giving money to the Church in a proper way. (*Sermon on Keeping Children in School* pt. 2)[61]

In Scotland, Calvinists (called Presbyterians) firmly grasped and embraced the importance of education. Schools were established in every village, and in each was placed a university-trained *dominie* of learning.[62] Reformists, however, had difficulty attracting dedicated pedagogues since little prestige and small remuneration were given to those in the teaching profession. It therefore was seldom a full-time vocation. The advice of seventeenth-century educator Charles Hoole (1610–1660) was given with a warning:

. . . more encouragement should be given to the teacher of it [*sic*] than should be left as a work of poor women or others whose necessities compel them to undertake it as a mere shelter from beggary.[63]

The Puritan divine John Brinsley (1600–1665) decried in a letter the poor education his own son had received at the hand of a part-time, inept, and indifferent teacher:

My sonne hath been under you six or seven yeares, and yet is not able so much as to reade English well; much lesse to construe or understand a peece of Latin, or to write true Latin, or to speake in Latin in any tolerable sort. . . . Another shall complaine: my sonne comes on never a whit in his writing. Besides that his hand is such, that it can hardly be read; also he writes so false English, that he is neither fit for trade, nor any employment wherein to use his pen.[64]

Thomas Fuller (1608–1661), in *The Holy State and the Profane State* (1642), thoughtfully analyzed this problem, which was common in all of Europe and in the colonies as well. In his belief that teaching was perceived as a "stepping-stone" toward a more rewarding career, Fuller anticipated the views of many educators of the present day:

There is scarce any profession in the Commonwealth more necessary, which is so slightly performed. The reasons whereof I conceive to be these: first, young scholars make this calling their refuge, yea perchance before they have any degree in the University, commence Schoolmasters in the country, as if nothing else was required to set up this profession but only a rod and a ferula. Secondly, others who are able to use it as a passage to better preferment, to patch the rents in their present fortune, till they can provide a new one, and betake themselves to some more gainful calling. Thirdly, they are disheartened from doing their best with the miserable reward which in some places they receive, being Masters to the children, and slaves to their parents. Fourthly, being grown rich, they grow negligent, and scorn to touch the school, but by the proxy of an Usher. (*The Holy State* bk. 2, chap. 16)

Church leaders nevertheless pondered the means by which dignity and honor might be conferred on the profession of teaching. Its value and the importance of education repeatedly were emphasized from the pulpit. Gradually, the persistence altered perceptions and pedagogues in time were accredited with a great deal of prestige. Although the goal of universal education was not achieved, the Reformation did succeed in inculcating pride in teaching; in fact, the profession became regarded as a divine vocation, a *negotium cum Deo*, embraced with reverence.

The Jesuits

The increased number and influence of Protestant schools and methodology were factors in promoting the Counter-Reformation movement. In 1540 the Spaniard Ignatius of Loyola founded the Jesuit Order, naming it the Society of Jesus. In its charter, he described the Jesuit mission as "the propagation of the faith by the ministry of the Word, by spiritual exercises, and by works of charity . . . teaching Christianity to children and the uneducated."[65] Jesuit pedagogy encouraged children to learn, not by the rod but by competition and self-motivation and frequent assessment of individual students' progress.

The six-year curriculum offered by the Jesuits began when boys were ten years old. Four years of grammar studies were followed by one year of the humanities, which focused on poetry and history, and a subsequent year of the study of oratory, in which students' trilingual skills in the classical languages of Latin, Greek, and Hebrew were exercised. Students were grouped according to individual progress and mastery of subjects, in the *modus parisiensis*, allowing brighter students to move ahead. Jesuit "scholastics," young men training to be Jesuit priests, also taught, much as do our modern-day teaching assistants and postdoctoral fellows.[66]

Jesuits promoted a cooperative spirit between teacher and student and interclass rivalries, challenging student teams in both scholarly and physical pursuits. They reintroduced competitive games such as football, gymnastics, and tennis, which had been banned by many schools because they were thought to be a source of fermenting conflict between adult and child. By incorporating sports into the general curriculum and emphasizing the positive role they have in educating youths, the Jesuits controlled the issue and legitimized the function of sports in education. Greek (Platonian) principles of education were in many ways adopted, for the Jesuits introduced dancing to teach balance, drama to teach language, and gymnasia to foster physical hygiene:

Do not, then, my friend, keep children to their studies by compulsion but by play. That will also better enable you to discern the natural capacities of each. (Plato, *Republic* 7.16)

The successful Jesuit formula for educational acheivement has been ascribed to several factors.[67] The schools were free and welcomed all social classes. They supported the Reformation effort to build character. The curriculum presumed the compatibility of the study of both science and theology. Clear and pragmatic curricular goals were established. Jesuit scholastic teaching, which emphasized influencing students by example, was uniform, and the network of international schools ensured their wide recognition as leaders in education. Marian confraternities (devotional groups) were established and further enhanced group solidarity. These aspects of a Jesuit education—promoting as they did honor, loyalty, and camaraderie—echoed throughout their schools in this country and abroad and through the centuries until today.

The Jesuit influence was profound. After 1551, schools opened at a rate of four a year. In Italy, the wealthy frequently employed Jesuit tutors to teach their sons, and the general populace sent their boys to Jesuit schools. Colleges were founded in Messina (1548), Palermo (1549), and Bologna (1551). Their educational renown having reached Austria and Germany, schools were founded there in Vienna in 1545, and in Cologne and in Ingolstadt in 1556. A Jesuit school was founded in Prague in 1555. Jesuit education was not introduced into England for almost another century, however; St. Omer's school was established there in 1649. The schools encouraged attendance by Protestants as well as Catholics. In Prague, for example, Lutheran and Hussite boys were admitted to Jesuit schools. All, however, were expected to study the religious curriculum of the colleges.

The *Ratio Studiorum* of 1599 had been the result of a committee of Jesuit educators who had coalesced their most positive pedagogic experiences. In addition to expounding general principles of education and rules for theology, philosophy, ethics, rhetoric, and the humanities, it detailed the curriculum, schedule, and syllabus for students, as well as the duties and responsibilities of the teachers. The work was so thorough and complete an exposition of the Jesuit program that it continues to serve educators as an operant document to follow.

By the beginning of the seventeenth century, some Jesuit schools had huge enrollments. In 1603 the college at Rouen had 1,800 students grouped into only seven classes. By midcentury, the Society of Jesus was operating 520 colleges throughout Europe, in which over 150,000 boys per year were being taught.[68] Nearly half of these boys were nonpaying children of local peasants and artisans. The inscription over the door of the Collegio Romano boasted "Schola di Grammatica, d'Humanita e Dottrina Christiana, Gratis."[69] Similarly, in England, 50 percent of the students at Oxford were plebeians. In all, the number of Jesuit schools in Europe numbered over eight hundred colleges, and they flourished until the order was suppressed in 1773. (Pope Clement XIV issued a Brief of Suppression entitled *Dominus ac Redemptor Noster* citing complaints against the Society, which, although various, mostly were political. The society was not restored until 1814 under Pope Pius VII.)

Other Catholic orders joined the maturing and expanding Counter-Reformation movement. In the 1670s, Jean Baptiste de la Salle (1651–1719) of the Christian Brothers founded charity schools to educate poor urban children. He followed Erasmian principles and expounded on them in *Rules of Propriety and Christian Civility*. La Salle embraced Erasmus's notion that while demeanor, gesture, and posture were important, they should not be obvious: "Although there should be nothing studied about one's external appearance, one must learn to measure every action and attend to the carriage of every part of the body."[70]

The Jesuit success with boys' education in part inspired alterations in the curricula in schools for girls in the seventeenth century. Schools for *jeune filles* began to appear in France under the auspices of new Catholic teaching orders, among them the Ursulines, who also established schools for young girls in the French-American colonies.

Forward-looking educators ironically reached back in time to the second century, endorsing Plutarch's pedagogical concepts. On the whole, however, most communities relied on sequential, rote learning, conforming to traditional concepts in both instruction and in corporal punishment. Only gradually did educators, influenced by the Jesuits—who had been influenced by Plutarch—begin to espouse learning as the charge of youth, rather than its burden. These new pedagogues studied Plutarch's essay "The Education of Children" and adopted his viewpoint:

For youth is impressionable and plastic, and while such minds are still tender lessons are infused deeply into them; but any thing which has become hard is with difficulty softened. For just as seals leave impressions in soft wax, so are lessons impressed upon the minds of children while they are young.[71]

The Governour by Thomas Elyot was a restatement of Plutarchian thought:

And I verily do suppose that in the braynes and hertes of children, whiche be membres spirituall, whiles they be tender, and the litle slippes of reason begunne in them to burgine, ther may happe by ivel custome some pestiferous dewe of vice to perse the sayde membres and infecte and corrupt the softe and tender buddes, wherby the frute may growe wylde, and some tyme conteine in it fervent and mortal poyson, to the utter destruction of a realme. (First Book iv)[72]

Further, unlike his Reformation colleagues, Elyot decried corporal punishment:

Also by a cruell and irous maister the wittes of children be dulled: and that thinge for the whiche children be oftentimes beaten is to them ever after fastidious. (First Book ix)[73]

Roger Ascham in *The Scholemaster* concurred:

I have now wished, twise or thrice, this gentle nature, to be in a Scholemaster; and that I have done so neither by chance, nor without some reason, I will now declare at large . . . love is fitter than feare, gentleness better than beating, to bring up a childe rightlie in learninge.[74]

Ascham's ideas of an essential education for young courtiers in Elizabeth's court were quite elitist. The well-bred gentlemen, according to Ascham, should be fluent in Latin, French, and English grammar and excel in accomplishments requiring manly prowess and combat skills as well as in all of the courtly arts:

Therefore, I would wishe, that, beside some good time, fitlie appointed, and constantlie kepte, to encrease by readinge, the knowledge of the tonges and learning yong gentlemen shold use, and delite in all Courtelie exercises, and Gentlemanlike pastimes.

Therefore, to ride cumlie, to run faire at the tilte of ring: to plaie at weapones, to shote faire in bow or surelie in gon, to vaut lustely, to runne, to leape to wrestle, to swimme; to daunce cumlie, to sing and playe of instrumentes cunnyngly; to Hawke, to hunte, to playe at tennes and all pastimes generally which be joined with labour, used in open place and by the daylight, conteining either some fitte exercise for warre, or some pleasant pastime for peace, be not onelie cumlie and decent, but also verie necessarie for a Courtly Gentleman to use.[75]

Comenius and Other Pedagogues

In England, pedagogues came under the influence of a Moravian bishop, John Komensky (1592–1670), who was known by his Latinized name, Comenius. He believed that the natural instincts and talents of a child should be utilized in learning and reasoned that, since a child learned his own vulgar tongue* with such facility, other languages should be taught in the same way.

Comenius's work *Janua Linguarum Reserta* (The gates of tongues unclosed) (1631) ponderously outlined common phrases and names in progressive and increasing difficulty in parallel columns of English, French, and Latin. As students learned to speak the phrases in the foreign tongues, the grammar of each was introduced. Believing, like John Foxe, that the senses reinforced learning, Comenius supplied illustrations supportive to his texts, such as in *Orbis Sensualium Pictus* (1658) in which pictures accompanied the Latin words and phrases. The Aristotleian aphorism *Nihil est in intellectu, quod no prius fuit in sensu* (Nothing is in the mind which first was not experienced by the senses) embellished the title page, and the opening lines of the book—"The lamb bleateth, the grasshopper chirpeth, the infant crieth, and the chicken peepeth"—are complemented by both a Latin equivalent of the text and a small woodcut of each mentioned creature. This format was replicated throughout the book, with phrases about and illustrations of flowers, trees, birds, fishes, the seven ages of man, and fantastic creatures presented for the edification of young students. Occupations, trades, games, and religions also were depicted. Comenius even used pictures to convey theological principles.[76] Despite the innovations, it would seem that the key to learning the material depended on a great deal of memorization by the students—in other words, rote learning.

Comenius's other major text was the *Magna Didactica*, in which he coherently formulated and outlined principles he thought were essential to the

---

*Children's native, common, everyday language is referred to here, as distinct from the inventive "play language" of children about which Dunn (1920) wrote:

> Language, it is said, was given to man to conceal his thoughts. Perhaps this explains why young children when living together, and if not otherwise prevented, invent a language of their own . . . which, although perfectly understood by themselves, as a rule defies in toto the deepest philologists to interpret . . . and often forms a habit very troublesome to cure. (p. 99)

discipline of learning. He defined the psychology of learning, the role of education in a civil society, and the goals of education. The introduction to the text expounded on the physical facilities, curriculum, and curriculum schedules of schools. Most interestingly, he advanced his belief that girls as well as boys should be educated and in coeducational classes. In this regard, Comenius was at the vanguard of what has become commonplace thinking in modern education. He envisaged quiet, agreeable settings that had structured periods of time, delineated lesson plans, and defined goals[77]:

The Great Didactic in which is presented a generally valid art of teaching everything to everyone, or, reliable and perfect directions for erecting schools in all communities, towns, and villages of any Christian state. In these schools all youth of both sexes, without exception, can be instructed in the sciences, improved in their morals, filled with piety, and, in suchwise, be equipped in early years for all that belongs to the life here and beyond. This will be done by a concise, agreeable, and thorough form of instruction which: derives its reasons from the genuine nature of things, proves its truth by dint of adequate examples taken from the mechanical arts, arranges the sequence of instruction by years, months, days, hours, and finally, shows an easy and safe way for the happy pursuit of all these suggestions. (*Magna Didactica* introduction)

Comenius's philosophy of education, as expounded in chapter 12 of his book, was imbued with an idealism so great that its realization remains elusive; although, notably, some societies have made the attempt and continue to strive for the pedagogical goals Comenius articulated:

Schools can be improved. I promise a kind of school in which: 1. The whole youth is being educated (except those whom God has denied reason). 2. There should be taught all that can make men wise, honest, and pious. 3. Education, which is preparation for life, should be finished before adulthood. 4. Education should be carried out not with beating, severity and any kind of coercion, but easily, pleasantly, and, so to speak, by its own momentum. 5. Not a semblance of education ought to be provided, but genuine education, not superficial but thorough education; that means the rational animal man should be led by his own rather than a foreign reason. He should get accustomed to penetrating to the real roots of things and to take into himself their true meaning and usage, rather than read, perceive, memorize, and relate other people's opinions. The same ought to be the case with respect to morality and piety. 6. Education ought not to be painful but as easy as possible, everyday only four hours ought to be spent for public instruction, and this in such a way that one teacher should suffice for the simultaneous instruction of a hundred pupils. And he should do that ten times more easily than is now done with one pupil. (*Magna Didactica* 12.2)[78]

In Germany, the educator Georg Maler (b.1500) focused more on his theories of the ideal teacher in his work *De Instituendis Pueris* (1563).[79] The teacher, he believed, had to set the example, be faithful to his charges, and be a true in loco parentis. Good teachers, he continued, were honest about their fund of knowledge and acknowledged ignorance instead of feigning knowledge not possessed, or inventing answers. Nor were they conceited about what they did know, nor strove to demonstrate their superior erudition. Maler added that good teachers provided frequent intervals of recess and play for children during the school day. In all of these respects, Maler's beliefs were opposite to those of his contemporary, Otto Brunfels.

In France, Michel de Montaigne published "On the Education of Children," which also focused on teachers' roles and additionally suggested modifications to extant syllabuses. Montaigne's major contribution to pedagogy was to stress the importance of inculcating thirst for learning and scholarship and to do this without burdening students with anything more than a moderate workload—points of view similar to those of Comenius:

I would have the tutor make the child examine and thoroughly sift all things, and harbour nothing in his head by mere authority or upon trust. . . . Let different judgments be submitted to him; he may be able to distinguish truth from falsehood; if not, he may remain in doubt. . . . If by his own thinking he embraces the opinions of Xenophone or of Plato, the opinions will be no longer theirs, but will become his own. He that merely follows another, seeks nothing, finds nothing. . . .

I would have a boy sent abroad very young . . . for unless a man's tongue be formed to them in his youth he can never acquire true pronunciation. . . . I would not have this pupil of ours imprisoned and made a slave to his book, nor have him acquire the morose and melancholy disposition of a sour, ill-natured pedant . . . too much study diverts him from better employment and rends him unfit for the society of men. (*Essays* 1:26)

Two English pedagogues of the seventeenth century, William Petty and John Locke, elucidated educational philosophies that had major impact on future educational giants such as Rousseau, Pestalozzi, Herbart, Froebel, and Dewey.

William Petty (1623–1687) was educated in France by the Jesuits and studied medicine at Oxford University in England. In 1648 he printed a booklet entitled *The Advice of W.P. to Mr. Samuel Hartlib for the Advancement of Some Particular Parts of Learning*. In it he expressed his belief that *all* children should be educated, even if the state provided no scholarships or other means for this end. Inspired by the system of apprenticeships he had admired in France, he proposed that children pay back with labor or service the costs of their education. Today's students who take advantage of just such systems are referred to as work-study students or teaching assistants or even resident assistants:

That there be instituted *Ergastula Literaria*, Literary workhouses, where Children may be taught as well to do something towards their living as to Read and Write. That the businesse of Education be not (as now) committed to the worst and unworthiest of men, but that it be seriously studied and practised by the best and abler persons.

That all Children of above seven years old may be presented to this kind of Education, none being excluded by reason of the poverty and unability of their Parents, for hereby it hath come to passe that many are now holding the Plough which might have been made fit to steere the State.

Wherefore let such poor children be employed on works whereby they may earne their living, equall to their strength and understanding and such as they may performe as well as elder and abler persons . . . and if they cannot get their whole living and their Parents can contribute nothing at all to make it up, let them stay somewhat longer in the Work-house.[80]

His utilitarian ideas about education, encompassing rich and poor, were progressive and bold, but they could not have been advanced at a worse time. Education of the masses during the oppressive Puritan regime of Oliver Cromwell was perceived as a political danger, and once again education reverted to an opportunity available only to the children of the privileged classes. This regression endured for the subsequent two hundred years.

John Locke (1632–1704) was, like Petty, an Oxford physician. His views on education, however, were not as egalitarian as those of Petty. Having lived abroad extensively and being strongly colored by this experience, he recommended, as did Montaigne, travel as an informative and instructional activity, particularly for the young. One of his principal works, *Some Thoughts Concerning Education*, published in 1693, was a compilation of letters written to his friend Edward Clarke on how to raise his son. In it his pedagogical advice ranged from nutrition and dress to bowel training and education:

. . . most Children's Constitutions are either spoil'd or at least harm'd, by Cockering and Tenderness.

The first Thing to be taken care of is that Children be not too warmly clad or cover'd, Winter or Summer. . . . I will also advise his Feet to be wash'd every Day in cold Water, and to have his Shooes so thin that they might leak and let in Water whenever he comes near it. . . . [Y]our Sons Cloths be never made strait, especially about the Breast. . . .

Narrow Breasts, short and stinking Breath, ill Lungs, and Crookedness, are the Natural and almost constant Effects of hard Bodice, and Cloths that pinch. . . .

As for his Diet, it ought to be very plain and simple; and, if I might advise, Flesh should be forborn as long as he was in Coats, or at least till he was two or three Years old. . . . I would have no Time kept constantly for his Breakfast, Dinner and Supper, but rather vary'd almost every Day. . . .

His Drink should be only Small Beer; and that too he should never be suffered to have between Meals, but after he had eat a piece of Bread. . . .

Above all, Take great Care that he seldom, if ever, taste any Wine, or Strong drink. . . .

Of all that looks soft and effeminate nothing is more to be indulg'd Children than Sleep. In this alone they are to be permitted to have their full Satisfaction; nothing contributing more to the Growth and Health of Children than Sleep. . . .

Let his Bed be Hard, and rather Quilts than feathers. Hard Lodgings strengthens the Parts; whereas being buried every Night in Feathers, melts and dissolves the Body. . . . [T]his Course should be taken with a Child every day, presently after he has eaten his Break-fast. Let him be set upon the Stool, as if disburthening were as much in his power, as filling his Belly. . . .[81]

The last Part usually in Education is Travel which is commonly thought to finish the Work, and complete the Gentleman. I confess Travel into Foreign Countries has great Advantages; but the time usually chosen to send young Men abroad, is, I think, of all other, that which renders them least capable of reaping those Advantages . . . from Sixteen to One-and-Twenty, which is the ordinary time of Travel, men are, of all their Lives, the least suited to these Improvements. The first Season to get Foreign Languages, and form the Tongue to their true Accents, I should think, should be from Seven to Fourteen or Sixteen.[82]

Locke's endorsement of the "Grand Tour" as an ancillary educational tool would have been a costly venture—as was formal instruction at universities. In either case, these educational notions then would have been relevant only to the well-to-do. In our quasi-egalitarian and debt-tolerant society, such benefits for the young now are widely available and availed of. The following letter describing parental worry and anxiety illustrates a bond between parents of the past and the present:

I have within this week met with more fears about my two sons abroad at learning, and sustained more bitter agonies of soul than ever I did in all my life that I remember upon any account, occasioned upon some reports that I heard concerning them, which multiplied in my imaginations, and exceedingly aggravated by my own jealousies and suspicions so that I was almost distracted, could not sleep quietly, nor take content in anything, though I concealed it so from my wife and family that nothing was discerned; however God made good use of it to humble my heart more effectually for mine own sins, to be importunate with God for mercy. (Oliver Heywood, 14 January 1676)[83]

Another carryover from the past—schoolboy mischief—has been extensively documented. This example, provided by Claudine Hollyband in *The French Schoolmaister* (c.1590) refers to Elizabethan schoolboys of the sixteenth century. The litany of offenses will be recognizable to current readers, and in some parts of the globe, even the schoolmasters' punishment will not seem outmoded:

Nicholas (the tell-tale): Maister, John Nothing-worth hath sworne by God, plaid by the way, sold his poyntes, chaunges his booke, stollen a knife, lied twise, lost his cappe.

John (the Black Sheep): Nicholas doth mocke me, plucketh me by the heare, by the eares; hath stoken me: hath made me bleede.

Francis: Maister, I met him by the way which did leape, did slide upon the ice, which did cast snow: which fought with his fist, and balles of snow: which did scourge his top: which played for pointes, pinnes, cheries stones, counters, dice, cardes.

Nicholas: William hath spitted on my paper: torne my booke: put out my theme: broken my girdle: trod my hat under his feet: marred my copie: spoken English.

Master: Ah littell fellow, you prattell, brabell, cakell, play the vice. Geve me my roddes: stretch your hand.[84]

Other notorious elements of boys' schooling such as truancy, beer drinking, hazing, fighting, and indiscriminate spending of allowances were as true then as now. The letters[85] of a fourteen-year-old German boy, Friederich Behaim (c.1578), as well as the school ordinances,[86] were very revealing:

Dear Mother, know that although the first quarter is not yet over, I have been unable to get by on the gulden you gave me. . . . I need many things for which I must spend money. . . .

Dear Mother, . . . I owe Herr Oertel for beer and laundry. It came to one gulden, two pounds, three pfennigs. But know that I drink no more than a half-measure of beer, occasionally a full, each day.

❏ ❏ ❏

Reformist insistence that Scriptures be read generated and then accelerated the opening of catechetical schools in which reading was a prime focus. Literacy in the general population became the single most-important secular consequence to this turn of events. Presuming signatures in registries, on contracts, probates, and petitions as a measure of literacy, extrapolations can

TABLE 7.2
EXTRAPOLATED LITERACY RATES DURING
THE SEVENTEENTH AND EIGHTEENTH CENTURIES

| | Circa 1650–1700 | | Circa 1750–1790 | |
	% Male	% Female	% Male	% Female
Scotland	25	—	65	15
England	30	—	60	35
France	30	14	48	27
Amsterdam	57	32	85	64
Turin	70	43	83	63
New Castile	49	—	76	—
American colonies	61	31	84	46

be made regarding overall literacy during and after the Reformation. Around 1640 in Scotland, 25 percent of males were literate. A century later this rate had increased to 65 percent for men and 15 percent for women. Comparative numbers for other regions are noted in table 7.2.[87]

Children learned to read and write in Protestant and Catholic countries. The common wisdom prevailed, however, that women should be able to read so as to know Scripture but had no need to know how to write, for, it was thought, the world of contracts, business, or even of journals, diaries, and commonplace books was an exclusively male domain.

Although not every European country supported education for the general population, the Netherlands can boast of its success in enforcing a system of universal education for girls and boys. Francesco Guicciardini noted in 1566 that "the common [Dutch] people have mostly a beginning knowledge of grammar and just about all of them . . . know at least reading and writing."[88] In Germany, only 10 percent to 20 percent of the students came from the peasantry. In Spain, a fraction of a percent of the poor attended school. A report delivered to Philip IV typified the predominant attitude:

It would also help to close down some grammar schools newly founded in villages and small towns because with the opportunity of having them so near, the peasants divert their sons from the jobs and occupations in which they were born and raised and put them to study, from which they benefit little, and leave for the most part ignorant because the preceptors are not much better.[89]

By 1623, Philip had ordered closed all nonendowed grammar schools not under state control. Indeed, during the reign of Philip III (1598–1621), so many of the aristocracy went on to university that a neo–anti-intellectualism surfaced even among the nobility.

Printed books and tools of learning in general were expensive commodities and as such, were available almost exclusively to churchmen and the wealthy. The printing press, it should be added, was not a universally welcomed innovation and initially was received with reserve and viewed with suspicion. A Dominican, Filippo diStrata, convinced the Venetian senate that the printing device invited ecclesiastical error, facilitated corruption through distribution of heretical works, and debased knowledge by making it available to the masses. *Est virgo hec penna, meretrix est stampificata* (The pen is a virgin, the printing press a whore) barely expressed the prevailing sentiment, shared by, among others, Lope de Vega.[90] However, for those who owned printed books, the invention was welcomed enthusiastically and appreciated. Books were treasured for their monetary value as well as for their intellectual worth and they were carefully guarded. Students, proud to be book owners, commonly proclaimed ownership with penned verses and riddles in the flyleaves. Such an example was written by John Slie, who in 1589 wrote in his book *Caesar*:

> My father to me—this booke did give;
> And I will kep it as long as I live.
> Whose booke it is if you will knowe,
> By letters twaine—I will you showe.
> The one is I in all men's sight,
> The other S and full of might,
> Joyne these to letters—presently
> And you shall know—my name by and by.
> John Slye—is my name.[91]

An early tome written in England by John Holt (fl.1495) as a teaching guide for young children was printed around 1497. *Lac Puerorum*, or *The Mylke for Chyldrene* was designed to teach grammar. Illustrated with the woodcut print of a hand, the fingers served as memory aids, illustrating, as they did, a grammar case or declension.[92] However, the hornbook became the most popular primer for children in England and later in America (figure 7.5). This teaching tool remained popular until the late seventeenth century, when gradually it was replaced by the cardboard "battledore." Typically, a hornbook was composed of a piece of parchment or vellum (later, paper) mounted on a board covered with a protective lamina of transparent horn and bound with a band of brass for strength. The board had a handle

Figure 7.5
A hornbook (Tuer, 1887).

with a string running through a hole in it so that students could dangle the board around their necks. All hornbooks had the Lord's Prayer, the alphabet, and some rules of grammar written on the parchment. At the beginning and at the end of the alphabet was a cross and often the rhyme: "Christes Cross be my speede / In all vertue to proceede." Once its material was mastered, students passed their hornbooks on to the next batch of novices.

In England, the wealthy favored hornbooks carved from wood or made from ivory or silver.[93] There was an assuredly popular hornbook found in England made of gingerbread and meant to be eaten.*

To emphasize the educational purpose, hornbooks were embellished with the slogan "All the letters are digested / Hateful ignorance detested."[94] Shakespeare refers to the hornbook in jest in *Love's Labor Lost* (4.1): "Yes, yes, he teaches boys the Horne-booke: what is Ab speld backward with the horn on its head."

Vagabond Children

Habitually vagrant children were typically managed by being contracted as apprentices. An English law written in 1536 authorized parishes to collect beggar children between the ages of five to fourteen for placement in apprenticeships and to provide them with the appropriate clothing they would need

---

*This is reminiscent of the Jewish tradition of biblical cake and eggs to teach the alphabet and Torah verses (see chapter 6).

in their training. The aim was to redress a situation in which adult vagrants had "to procure ther livying by open beggyng euen from childehod, so that they nuer knewe any other waie of livyng but onely by beggyng," and to eliminate beggars, young and adult, from the streets.[95] Parishes were empowered to publicly whip children over twelve who refused without just cause to continue in their apprenticeships and who returned to the streets as beggars and vagrants.

Despite the well-intentioned efforts to train waifs in various trades, the problems associated with street urchins and vagabonds became exacerbated in the economically tempestuous and plague-ridden mid-sixteenth century in which the number of available apprenticeships became fewer and fewer. In England, the Act of 1547 was a harsh response to the problem. It decreed that young children of the streets were to be enslaved for two years and branded. Children called before the magistrate a second time for the same offense were put in chains. The legislation, hastily conceived and impetuously enacted, generally was considered extreme, and within two years it was modified significantly. The Act of 1549 eliminated corporal punishment of children but upheld the original intention to control vagrancy by mandating additional constraining conditions in apprenticeship contracts involving homeless children.

The Poor Law Act of 1572, reflecting the enduring economic hardship of the period, recognized the principle of a poverty baseline[96] and formulated a legal liability of children who had reached adolescence. Beyond fourteen years of age, vagabond children were tried and imprisoned as adults. The Act was amended in 1576 to permit parishes and larger jurisdictions to purchase specially discounted materials in order to create work for these poor young people:

To the Intente Yowthe maybe accustomed and brought up in laboure and worke, and then not lyke to growe to be ydle Roges, and to the Entente also that suche as bee alredye growen up in Ydlenes and so Roges at this present, maye not have any juste Excuse in sayeng that they cannot get any Service or Worke.[97]

During the reigns of England's Henry VIII and his son Edward VI, several London infirmaries attached to monasteries became by law reserved for the destitute and beggars. The growing poverty rate in England was occasioned by increasing population coupled with fluctuations in agricultural production. Between 1500 and 1700 the population of England doubled, and citizens flooded London to escape the countryside poverty. The result was a swelling of the poor in a city whose monastic houses of charity had been dissolved between 1536 and 1540.[98] Thus, it fell to Edward VI to re-establish charitable houses, and he chartered three royal hospitals: Christ's Hospital, St. Thomas Hospital, and Bridewell. A fourth hospital, St. Bartholomew, was recommissioned sometime after 1553.

In 1552 the Franciscan House of Grey Friars was renamed Christ's Hospital for orphaned children and was dedicated "to take oute of the streates all the fatherless children and other poor mens children that were not able to kepe them."[99] Bridewell became a workhouse for vagrant children-cum-house of correction. The volume of orphaned, destitute, and bastard children in London soon overwhelmed the resources of these institutions, and measures were taken in the Act of 1576 to restrict these establishments to children born legitimately, except in emergency situations. Christ's Hospital had originally been intended to house orphans over four years of age, who were clothed in a uniform of a blue coat with yellow stockings, and to accommodate 250 children. It quickly came to house over 600, including infants. Wet nurses had to be contracted, further stretching the budget. Nevertheless, the children were clothed, nourished and educated, receiving a traditional petty-school education.

The third hospital, St. Thomas* in Southwark, across the Thames,[100] functioned as a true hospital, where surgeons and "physiks" were in attendance. Through its benefactor, Rycharde Whytyngdon, the hospital established a small haven for unwed pregnant adolescent girls. He ordered and

made a new chambyre with viii beddys for young wemem that have done a-myss, in trust for good mendement . . . that alle the thynges that had ben don in that chambyre shoulde be kepte secrete . . . for he wolde not shame no yonge woman in noo wyse.[101]

The fourth hospital, St. Bartholomew's, just north of the city walls in Smithfield, also created an endowment for unwed mothers and their offspring.[102]

Despite the services the city of London offered, masses of children wandered the streets, particularly around St. Paul's Cathedral, sleeping at night under hedges and stalls. Not all of these were orphans. To alleviate crowded family conditions, some children were contracted by their parents for labor and taken to the city, where, when the work was completed, they were set adrift by their employers, left to wander aimlessly without sustenance or shelter. Each Sunday, the beadle of Christ's Hospital was responsible for rounding up children in the streets around St. Paul's for delivery to Bride-

*This hospital had originally been founded in 1106 and named St. Thomas the Martyr, after Becket. It was dissolved in 1540 and reopened in 1552 under the name of St. Thomas Apostle.

well, decreed an institutional workhouse by the Act of 1576; there they were given work-training and shelter.[103] The system of providing work within a house of correction endured in England until the mid-nineteenth century.

Those English parishes not overwhelmed by numbers assumed responsibility for orphans from infancy to adolescence. Parishes assigned infants to wet nurses and contracted apprenticeships at latency for those who survived the perils of childhood. Little interest and no advocacy were provided these children, and physical abuse was common. Moreover, many of the apprenticeships were little more than permanent indentureships, until the Act of 1601 sought both to curtail the practice and mitigate the instances of abuse. Some townships used apprenticeships as a pretext to control male adolescent behavior and prevent the formation of vandalizing gangs.[104] Child vagrants also were prey to criminal elements that provided their own unique apprenticeships to hapless youths, who were carefully molded into juvenile delinquents with exceptional skills for picking pockets and stealing in general. Like Charles Dickens's character Fagan, the Londoner Mr. Wotton in 1585 operated a "school" in which

[he] procured all the Cuttpurses abowt this Cittie to repaire to his said Howse. There was a schole howse sett upp to learne younge boyes to cutt purses. There was hung up two devises, the one was a pockett, the other was a purse. The pocket had in yt certen cownters and was hunge abowte with hawkes bells, and over the toppe did hange a little sacring bell; and he that could take a cownter without any noyse was allowed to be a *publique Foyster*; and he that could take a peece of sylver owt of the purse without the noyse of any bells, he was adjudged a *Judicicall Nypper.*[105]

Although the statute was not implemented often, the punishment for theft was death. In theory, children over seven years could be executed. Until 1780 there were over two hundred offenses that were punishable by hanging. In 1609 a boy of sixteen was publicly hanged, as was an eight-year-old in 1629.[106] During the reign of George II (1727–1760), ten children were strung up together on the same gallows as a spectacle of admonition against thievery.[107] Following the Gordon Riots of June 1780,* the number of children publicly hanged moved George Selwyn to comment, "I never saw boys cry so much."[108] Instances of the execution of children by hanging prevailed into the nineteenth century. Michael Hammond, aged eleven years, and his

---

*Lord George Gordon (1751–1793) led the Protestant Association to secure the repeal of the Catholic Relief Act of 1778. Gordon and his mob marched to the Houses of Parliament to petition against the Act. Days of rioting ensued during which Catholic chapels and homes were pillaged, prisons broken into, and the Bank of England attacked. The riot ended when the army intervened but not before 450 lay dead.

sister, aged seven, were hanged in 1808 for stealing. In the registry of the English court, the Old Bailey, are entries made in February 1814 of hangings for burglary of the boys Morris, eight years old, Solomons, nine years old, and Fusler and Wolfe, both twelve years old. A lad named Burrell, age eleven, was hanged for stealing a pair of shoes.[109] At Chelmsford in 1831, a nine-year-old boy was hanged for setting a fire.[110]

By the early seventeenth century, frustrated lawmakers, unable to correct the behavioral consequences of poverty and vagrancy, began to ship out many of the children to the new American colonies. Since the numbers of such children were high, all could not be accommodated in colonial settlements. Angry citizens, sated with the problem, continued, nevertheless, to demand the "placement" of these street urchins and vagabonds. The Act of 1703 was a response to public pressure, and boys of ten years or older were put to sea, where they had to serve as merchant seamen until the age of twenty-one. St. John Fielding commissioned a group of merchants, bankers, and shippers who gathered up nearly ten thousand of these strays, outfitted them, and sent them off to sea. Fielding's popular achievement prompted him to propose reforms for female youths who were street vagabonds and prostitutes. He advocated the establishment of asylums where girls could be taught domestic skills and through a placement service become domestics in private homes.[111]

Unlike apprentices during the medieval period, who were commonly contracted before having had any schooling, most trainees in the sixteenth and seventeenth centuries had learned the rudiments of reading and arithmetic. Only thereafter did parents strive to get their boys apprenticed. The most highly prized apprenticeships cost the parents large sums of money and indentured their children for a number of years. James Jackson's memorandum in 1675 is representative of contractual arrangements of the times:

Memorandum March 21th, 1675, did I send to Mr Gawin Chamber per John Stamper ten pounds and four crowns for his wife upon promise for my son John's apprenticeship and an acquittance for the same. Witness John Stamper younger and my son John Jackson.[112]

Girls

As a generalization, societal attention during the Renaissance continued to be directed at boys. Males remained the preferred gender. Despite some modest gains in education and status, women's roles in society did not substantially alter. This, of course, was most especially true for the poor and middle classes. From the pulpit, girls constantly were reminded that they were subordinate at home to husbands and second-class citizens in the community. Aphorisms and proverbs reinforced these viewpoints, as these fifteenth-century French examples illustrate:

> A good horse and a bad horse need the spur
> A good woman and a bad woman need the stick.

> A woman who talks like a man and a hen that crows like a cock
> are not worth keeping.

As a birth impended, women were wished health and, in France, "un beau fils." The birth of a girl was rationalized in the expression "she may in time bring forth a boy."

Domestic household "apprenticeships" that emphasized spinning, sewing, and cooking remained the educational lot of the average daughter. Since physicians seldom were proximate, most girls also learned the rudiments of midwifery and the mixing of medicines.

The Protestant culture argued that literacy was essential as a means to speak directly to God through Scripture, and this had significant and favorable repercussions for women and their education, especially for those from propertied families. The increase in the number of publications examining appropriate curricula for girls served as a catalyst for the growth in both the number of girls' schools and in the enrollment.

In Richard Mulcaster's "Positions," the essential elements of a refined young lady's education were given—reading, music, and language skills:

A young gentlewoman is thoroughly furnished which can read plainly and distinctly, write fair and swiftly, sing clear and sweetly, play well and finely, understand and speak the learned languages and those tongues also which the time most embraceth, with some logical help to chop, and some rhetorick to brave.[113]

His confining views on education for females followed accepted thinking of his times; yet at the same time, Mulcaster was a perspicacious pedagogue who recommended that teachers be given specialized university training, as was required for physicians, lawyers, and theologians. He recognized individual differences in children, including those among children of approximate chronological age, and advocated adjustments in curricula that acknowledged these differences.

Spain's Juan Luis Vives's curriculum for girls, called the *Instruction of a Christian Woman*, published in 1523, also reflected the general climate of opinion regarding training for girls. The book quickly became a popular resource text for the rest of the century, with over forty editions and translations into six languages. Vives recommended the inclusion of reading instruction to facilitate spiritual reading—the gospels, the saints, and philosophers—with the teaching of domestic skills.[114] The purpose of reading skills for girls was to enrich their spiritual lives; domestic skills perfected their earthly lives.

Upper-class females and daughters of merchants could anticipate a convent-school education with no oblation—an obsolete practice by the sixteenth century. In England, schools of renown for girls were the Carow Nunnery near Norwich, founded in 1146, the Dartford Nunnery in Kent, founded in 1355, and St. Mary's in Winchester, which had been suppressed in 1539 in the reign of Henry VIII. Boarder pupils at Winchester wore white veils after the archbishop of York (c.1513) decreed that "young gentlewomen who come to the nunneries either for piety or breeding should wear white veils to distinguish them from the professed who wear black ones."[115]

In Renaissance Florence, between 37 percent and 45 percent of *all* children went to school. In Paris, London, and Lyon, "little dame schools" were established to teach reading, scripture, and sewing. Many schools for the education of girls were founded in Germany. By 1600, Frankfurt alone had over ten schools for girls.[116]

Several books preparing girls for marriage were published, beginning, in England, with Becon's *Boke of Matrimony* (1543). It exhorted a girl to "love, beget children, and live chaste" and "to serve him [the husband] in subjection, to be modest in speech and apparel, to have charge of the house and its management." Advisors like Henry Smith did not express the prevailing attitude; in *A Preparation for Marriage* (1591), Smith admonished "Husbands must holde their hands and wives their tungs."[117] The common wisdom regarded a well-delivered blow as the way to keep a wife properly in her place.

In the Netherlands in 1625, Jacob Cats (1577–1660) published *Houwelick*, a rhyming dialogue expounding the virtues and responsibilities of being female. Cats divided a woman's life into six phases: *Maecht, Vuyster, Bruyt, Vrouwe, Moeder, Weduwe* (young girl, sweetheart, newlywed, wife, mother, widow). The book detailed the moral, social, and biological duties for each stage. It was immensely popular and by 1655 there were fifty thousand copies in circulation.[118]

The introduction of formal schools for girls did not broaden the number of career choices for young women. For the most part, girls continued to be prepared for their roles as homemakers. As in the medieval period, female apprenticeships were few and generally limited to those professions that traditionally had been open to women:

. . . I had occasion to go to Chesterfield, where I met with a bone-lace-weaver, with whom I bargained to take a daughter of mine apprenticed, Elizabeth by name. So for three pounds, ten shillings we agreed, and bound she was, September 14 . . . for four years. (Leonard Wheatcroft, 5 September 1681)[119]

Fostering of girls was not uncommon, particularly among the English gentry. A girl might be sent off to another family member or abroad to learn a second language.

Among the poor and even among the middle class, girls could be contracted out as domestics. Some families made sharecropping agreements that indentured both boys and girls to domestic service, exchanging them, for example, for hemp gardens, four to six sheep, and twelve livres in cash. Children generally were twelve years old when they began domestic service, and by fourteen years of age such children were expected to pay a poll tax.[120]

The marriage state usually defined who women were, and adolescent girls as they approached nubility sometimes had to endure the indignities of some local customs. In the northern countries of the Continent, it was traditional on the night of the thirtieth of April for young men to erect a maypole in front of the house of any girl considered marriageable, and decorate it. The fortunate maiden had beautiful wild flowers or fresh greens hung on the tree signifying her attractiveness as well as her availability. For others, the symbols—their meaning known to all—that were hung could be rife with malice and cruelty. Prickly plants denoted pride, elder signified debauchery. Urine, feces, grease, and even animal carcasses could be left at the foot of the maypole—symbols alluding to prudery, fickleness, or questioning a girl's virginity, dress, language, or even her femininity. If the community acknowledged the veracity of a symbol bearing charges of licentious behavior, a young woman would be forced to adorn herself with the symbols of a fallen maiden. A straw wreath was one such emblem.

ABANDONMENT

The indignities of city life for the poor and middle class were of a different nature. Urban children grew up in severely crowded quarters. Nearly half of the homes of craftsmen had only one room. To make more room, infants and toddlers would be sent out to wet nurses and latent children to schools, and adolescents were apprenticed. Since probate inventories almost exclusively were made by the propertied, few comments can be made regarding the goods and possessions these families owned. Only 8 percent of inventories derived from the working middle class in seventeenth-century England. The few records catalog a typical one-room home as having a cupboard, a chair, and some couches. There was no space in which to fit a table.

The plight of orphans and abandoned children can be imagined. The reforms of the Reformation ironically exacerbated the numbers of foundlings left to chance or to perish as, from the pulpit, out-of-wedlock and adulterous sexual behavior were condemned in the strongest terms. Known offenders were ostracized from the community, and instead of the reform that churchmen prayed for, adults resorted to concealing the consequences of their behavior, abandoning their illicit young in droves. Those who were caught abandoning a child were punished. In December 1556 a woman named Morton, who had abandoned her infant in a London street, was flogged and pilloried. A sign was placed on her head that read: "Whipped in Bridewell for having forsaken her child in the streets."[121]

In large urban areas the police found a dead child in the street or sewer almost daily. Parish records have provided chronicles of the numbers of nearly dead and starving exposed children, victims of hunger and infectious diseases. Some children were collected and mutilated by mountebanks and forced by them to act as deformed beggars. Alice de Salisbury was also pilloried, for "she had taken one Margaret, daughter of John Oxwyke, grocer, in the Ropery, in London, and has carried her away, and stripped her of her clothes . . . so that she might go begging with the same Alice."[122]

In Paris the numbers of abandoned children in the streets induced Vincent de Paul (1581–1660) to found a home for these orphans. He inspired a cadre of aristocratic women, most notably Madame le Gras, the niece of Lord Chancellor Marillac, to undertake the endeavor. Under her guidance was founded a religious order, the Dames de Charité (Sisters of Charity), and in 1638 she enlarged her home in the Faubourg Saint-Lazare to accommodate the foundlings. By 1643 the overcrowded Maison de la Couche was replaced by new, larger quarters in St. Denis.[123]

The commitment of Madame le Gras and her Sisters of Charity to the homeless, abandoned waifs received wide attention and support. Money and increased numbers of volunteer workers enabled the Maison de la Couche to serve greater numbers of those in need. Their work culminated in a show of interest at the highest levels. Louis XIII donated four thousand francs per year from his treasury in support of this work. The excerpt following, from a decree issued by the king, expresses the tenor of his concern:

Having been informed by persons of great piety, that the little attention which has been given up to the present to the nourishing and care of the parentless children exposed in the city and outskirts of Paris has been the cause of death, and even has it been known that they have been sold for evil purposes, and this having brought many ladies to take care of these children, who have worked with so much zeal and charitable affection that their zeal is spreading, and wishing so much to do what is possible under the present circumstances.[124]

Between 1670 and 1790 the number of foundlings admitted to the Hotel-Dieu in Paris increased over tenfold from 700 per year to 7,500 per year. Between 1771 and 1773 the Hotel-Dieu recorded mortality rates between 62 percent to 75 percent. French church registries of the same period show that in the private sector the death rate among infants was only 18 percent. The Hotel-Dieu policy of contracting infants outside the hospice to wet nurses additionally contributed to infant morbidity and mortality. This kind of arrangement historically had been associated with poor care, even neglect, from nurses, many of whom were unscrupulous and viewed their charges as mere sources of revenue. One wet nurse was given twelve infants to care for over a twenty-year period. Not one survived. French authorities made efforts to legislate the quality of wet nursing, and an actual Bureau of Wet Nurses was created as a kind of licensing agency to issue certificates of competence, experience, and recommendation.[125] Certified nurses were instructed to refer sick charges to local surgeons, who, in turn, billed the Hôpital des Enfants Trouvés. Only infants qualified for this service.

In order to raise sums to support older children, the hospices depended on revenues raised from "renting out" their charges to participate in funeral processions. It seems that status commonly was measured by the numbers in a funeral cortege. Wealthy families were willing to pay to have a train of children, dressed in the uniforms of their hospices, follow the coffins of their deceased. The children of the Hôpital Enfants Rouge wore red, those of Saint-Espirit wore blue, and those of the Hôpital des Orphelins wore gray.[126]

Continuing economic hardship prompted increased instances of abandonment. At Vincent de Paul's Hôpital des Enfants Trouvés,* admissions of abandoned infants rose twenty-five-fold between 1670 and 1772. Of these, nearly 75 percent were illegitimate.[127] As in all of Europe, in years in which there were grain-crop failures, a proportionate increase in abandonment of legitimate offspring of the destitute was noted. In Spain, for example, when the price of grain increased, the rates of abandonment increased, and the numbers of infants deposited at the door of the Inclusa of Madrid soared. At least one-half of the infants was illegitimate. A royal inquiry into the problem of abandonment in 1790 elicited a deposition from the rector of the Inclusa, Pedro de la Vega:

Many of these [infants] belong to poor mothers who have been delivered in the Pasión [La Sagrada Pasión was the women's section of the General Hospital of Madrid]. . . . Others are the infants of poor widows who leave them so that they can find work as servants or earn their living some other way. Another group belongs to

---

*The physician Charles-Michel Billard (1800–1832) did an internship there. Between 1826 and 1828 he performed autopsies on infants and, in the first pediatric treatise of its kind, *Traité des maladies des enfans nouveaux-nes é a la mamelle*, correlated the classification of disease with observed pathology, not, as was the norm, merely with symptoms. It was the beginning of modern pediatrics.

poor married women who, only seven or eight months after having had one child, find themselves pregnant again and so expose the nurseling in this Inclusa. These infants are the worse for having been weaned at such an early age on soups of milk and wine and they have become so weak that it is impossible to save them. In such cases, it is commonly asserted that these people bring their infants to the house of God and of the King because they cannot bear to see them suffer and die in their own homes. The same reason is given for abandoning infants sick with smallpox, syphilis, skin ailments, and ulcers—they have even brought us dead infants.[128]

Unlike other asylums of the times, the operating funds of the Inclusa were not donated by charities or the government. The home charged twenty-two reales per month per infant to the various districts from which the infants came.[129] Abandoned infants were taken to the Inclusa's admissions office, registered, and had a lead identification tag placed around the neck, an improvement on the procedure at an asylum in Santiago in which an incised identifying mark was made on an infant's arm.[130] At the Inclusa, infants were assigned a community bed and a wet nurse. The large beds accommodated fourteen to twenty infants, greatly facilitating epidemics of disease. As the numbers of abandoned increased, so did the mortality figures. In 1700, 58 percent of infants died. In 1790 it was 87 percent.[131] These conditions prompted every attempt to farm out babies to countryside wet nurses as soon as was possible. It was to no avail, since abandoned infants continued to be deposited at the Inclusa and other like asylums.

In France the disposition of infants was mostly from the countryside to the cities, and their volume created the need for a new profession, simply called the *meneur* or "driver," men who regularly transported infants from their rural abodes to city asylums. On their journey they encountered infants from well-to-do families (a reversal of the situation in Spain) as they were being transported to countryside wet nurses. Of twenty-one thousand Parisian newborns in 1780, nineteen thousand were sent out of the city to *nourrices*.[132]

Meneurs ferried three to five infants in baskets hitched to the backs of donkeys. These trips sometimes took up to a week. There was no nutrition for the infants, except for a rag soaked in watered wine for hydration. Infants were known to fall out of the bottoms of baskets; many died and casually were discarded on the roadside. Empty slots in the baskets quickly were filled in the next town en route, since *meneurs* were paid by the number of infants delivered to the hospices. Finally the state, pressured by scandalized citizens, was forced to act. A law in 1773, however, did not outlaw such trade. Instead, *meneurs* were ordered to use plank-bottomed wagons lined with straw and covered in canvas and to assign an accompanying nurse, both to nourish infants and to ensure that none fell out of the wagons. The *meneurs* did recruit wet nurses into what they called a *chambres des nourrices*—not to be confused with the Bureau des nourrices that registered and certified wet nurses. The bureau required proper attestations of character from parish curates before they would make a recommendation to their middle- and upper-class clients.[133]

In spite of the governmental intervention, the mortality of infants carried on these journeys by the *meneurs* ranged from 5 percent to 15 percent.[134] Finally, after public outrage and the inability of overwhelmed hospices to provide for the ever-increasing numbers of infants arriving from the countryside, the government acted in 1779 to criminalize the transport of children.[135]

One of the factors contributing to infant mortality in the private sector was ignorance. For example, a large percentage of the population thought coitus soured breast milk. This firmly held belief gave rise to the practice of denying breast milk to infants on those occasions when granting husbands their conjugal rights superseded the rights of infants. Infants commonly were denied maternal feedings and often suffered cachexia until they were old enough to be weaned to solid food. Jacques Guillemeau, in *De la Norriture et Governement des Enfants* (1600), bluntly stated that "there is no difference between a woman who refuses to nurse her own children and one that kills her child as soon as she has conceived."[136] Attempts were made to discredit the notion that breast milk was spoiled by intercourse with quasi-scientific contrary evidence, notably by theologian Thomas Sanchez in *Disputationum de sancto matrimonii sacromento* (1607):

When parents are poor, experience shows that they do not observe any period of delay during which they abstain from intercourse, and neither do they put the child out to nurse. Despite this, we see no serious damage to the child.[137]

François Mauriceau (1637–1709), in *Diseases of Women with Child* (c.1668), further affirmed the same sentiments, "founded upon the experience of all poor Women who bring up their children very well, notwithstanding they lie every Night with their Husbands."[138]

This concern about infant nutrition and the dismay regarding abusive wet nurses prompted the Dutchman Jacob Cats to propagandize the virtues of breast feeding, equating maternal nursing with godliness. In the *Houwelick*, Cats commented:

> One who bears her children is mother in part
> But she who nurses her children is a mother completely.[139]
>
> Employ O young wife, your precious gifts
> Give the noble suck to refresh your little fruit
> There is nothing an upright man would rather see

Than his dear wife bid the child to the teat
This bosom that you carry, so swollen up with life
So finely wrought, as if't were ivory orbs.[140]

The efforts of a few not widely read reformists and physicians would have been trickles in a vast ocean of superstition, as were the efforts of those who grappled with the volume of urchins and vagrants throughout the European Continent. In France, among those abandoned infants who reached adolescence, about 10 percent became the homeless ragamuffins of Paris. Claude Piarron de Chamousset, in his *Memoire politique sur les enfants* (1756), commented, "And what becomes of this expensive tenth, if one divides among those who remain the expense incurred for those who die? Very few learn a trade; the others leave the hospital only to become beggars and tramps."[141] Like reformers in England and other nations seeking to provide a livelihood to the large numbers of *gamins*, de Chamousset devised a plan to send these children to the French colonies in Louisiana to work in silkworm factories. The diversity of the European settlers in the New World may be said to have begun with the implementation of these emigration policies.

THE AMERICAN COLONIAL CHILD

By the middle of the seventeenth century, European and particularly English values pertaining to family, religion, and education had been transported to the American colonies by the many groups of settlers who had been molded by them in the Old World. Ethnically and religiously diverse immigrants who had been liberated from governmental and societal restraints of their native countries gradually combined to produce a unique common culture. At the same time, each group retained its religious, moral, and family-rearing values and practices, unfettered by Old World traditions or governmentally imposed edicts or contraints. Most English, Dutch, German, and Swedish settlers maintained rigid patriarchal families and applied strict Congregationalist, Presbyterian, or Quaker standards in raising their children. Anglican and Lutheran families, on the other hand, although also father-dominated, commonly were less restrictive with their young.

Colonists exulted in a new-found sense of independence, autonomy, and freedom. The journals of Puritans John Robinson and William Brewster expressed the attitude: "We are well weaned from the delicate milke of our mother countrie."[142]

New World children born into a politically and religiously liberated milieu were part of large families, in keeping with people's evaluation that family size was one of the components that marked compliance with Christian duty to God. It also is true that, in the colonies, land distributions were deeded according to family size.[143] It is reasonable to argue that families seized an opportunity to become substantial landowners by having a large number of children. Also, a "headright" or land allotment (generally 50 acres) was granted to those who indentured children, and it became common practice for landowners to pay transatlantic passages for indentured workers and thereby acquire both additional land and the laborers to cultivate it.[144] In 1665, John "King" Carter of Virginia paid for eighty indentured servants and subsequently was given four thousand acres by the colony.[145]

The zealously religious Puritans who settled in America in God's name procreated lustily and endowed their offspring with strong religious values as well as names synonmous with the virtues they wished to inculcate in their young: Faith, Hope, Charity, Mercy, and More Mercy. Names reflecting family values also were popular: Endurance, Increase, Supply, Reform, Restore, Comfort, and Tremble often were found in parish baptismal registers (unusually outlandish proper names, such as Kill-Sin and Fly-Fornication, also can be found in the registries). Another custom was to name children after the place where their birth occurred: Oceanus Hopkins, born on the *Mayflower*, and Seaborn Cotton, also born at sea during a later voyage,[146] are two examples.

Child-rearing practices among Puritans began with the premise that, at birth, children were blighted with original sin and life on earth was an endless process to earn salvation. Isaac Watts (1674–1748) reminded youthful readers, in *Divine and Moral Songs for the Use of Children* (1715),

> That I am led to see
> I can do nothing well
> And whither shall a sinner flee
> To save himself from Hell.[147]

Obedience to the will and authority of parents was a moral mandate in Puritan life. The biblical admonition to honor one's parents also was enacted into legislation—narrowing the distinctions between ecclesiastical and secular law. Although the law granted children the "free libertie to complaine to the Authoritie for redresse,"[148] the severest penalties were legislated for unjustifiable aggressive acts against a parent or parents:

If any Childe or Children above sixteen years old, and of competent Understanding, shall Curse or Smite their Natural Father or Mother; he or they shall be put to Death, unless it can be sufficiently testified that the Parents have been very Unchristianly negligent in the Education of such Children, or so provoked them by extreme and cruel Correction, that they have been forced thereunto, to preserve themselves from Death or Maiming. (*Body of Liberties* [1649], capital law 13)

In fact, the death penalty never was invoked for such an offense. The code, however, was cited at least once in 1679:

Edward Bumpus for stricking and abusing his parents, was whipt att the post; his punishment was alleviated in regard he was crasey brained, otherwise hee had bine put to death or otherwise sharply punished.[149]

The Church devised its own deterrents, terrifying children with threats of eternal damnation for offenses against parental authority, as Cotton Mather's (1663–1728) dire warning in "The Family Well Ordered or An Essay on Rendering Parents and Children Happy in One Another" (1699) illustrates:

Children, If by Undutifulness to your Parents, you incur the Curse of God, it won't be long before you go down into Obscure Darkness, even, into utter Darkness; God has Reserv'd for you the Blackness of Darkness forever.[150]

The gestational and accouchement customs of seventeenth-century Europe, familiar to mothers of colonial children, were incorporated by them into their own childbirth experiences, as were the accepted forms of neonatal care—bathing and swaddling and the like.[151] Young mothers were told to avoid vigorous exercise, dieting, the wearing of tight corsets, or being phlebotomized during the gestation period, thereby promoting healthy fetal growth and development. Despite these precautions, newborn mortality was high, occurring at the rate of 150 deaths per 1,000 live births. In the mother country, one English midwife, Elizabeth Cellier, attributed more than half of these deaths to improper midwifery:

. . . more than thirteen-thousand children have been abortive and about five-thousand chrysome infants have been buried within the weekly bills of mortality; above two-thirds of which, amounting to sixteen thousand souls, have in all probability perished, for want of the due skill and care, in those women who practice the art of midwivery.[152]

It is uncertain if early American midwives were subject to ecclesiastical licensing as was the requirement in England. There were, however, secular professional regulations much like those legislated in England: midwives were obliged to obtain information regarding the identities of infants' true fathers (e.g., their names), they had to baptize endangered newborns, and they were prohibited from using abortifacients or secretly disposing of stillborn infants. Midwifery remained an honorable profession in the colonies. The spouses of Puritan ministers Thomas Thatcher and John Eliot were midwives.

Colonial midwives cut umbilical cords at "four fingers breadth," the traditional length subscribed to in Europe. By the early seventeenth century, some midwives were ruled by a superstitious belief that may have had its origin in France. The cords were cut longer for boys to lengthen their tongues and penises. Occasionally, a baby was born with the amniotic membrane adhering to the scalp and face. This tissue was known as a "caul" and was believed to protect against drowning and conferring the gift of talk. Thus they were dried, preserved, and enclosed in silver cases as good-luck charms to be sold to sailors or lawyers. An advertisement in *The Morning Post* of 21 August 1779 read: "To Gentlemen of the Navy . . . to be disposed of, a child's Caul . . . the Price is 20 guineas." Belief in the protective nature of the caul persisted through the First World War.[153]

After newborns were washed, they were anointed with butter or oil and wrapped in linens. Bathing was infrequent and recommended only twice a week after the age of seven months. Diapers were changed with frequency to prevent dermatitis. *The Midwives Book* (1671) earthily explained the rational: "Shift the child's clouts often, for the Piss and Dung, if they lie long on it, will fetch off the skin."[154] In fact, it was an astute suggestion, since acid stools, or fecal acidorrhea, can burn the perianal area if left unattended.

Births in the Puritan community were commemorated by offering visitors a portion of "groaning cake,"[155] the ingredients of which were literally indigestible. This curiously named confection may have had its antecedents in the motherland, where there was a recipe for a so-called sickening cake, but no exact record can account for its formulation or purpose. Nor is it known why a form of sickening cake would have endured as part of a christening celebration rather than the more palatable Cornwall fuggan cake or the popular Edinburgh "christening bit" made from cheese and gingerbread and reserved for christening occasions.[156]

A christening often was the only birthday celebration a Puritan child would experience. A fifteen-year-old girl's diary entry, dated 1675, gave firsthand expression to what was the prevailing attitude in the Puritan community:

. . . My mother hath bid me this day put on a fresh kirtle and wimple, though it be not the Lord's day, and my Aunt Alice coming in did chide me and say that to pay attention to a birthday was putting myself with the world's people.[157]

In Europe, illegitimacy had not been considered shameful until the Reformation, and until that time there were no social stigmas regarding bastards. Reformation mores and attitudes promoted an increasingly puritanical and narrow outlook, with a more pronounced emphasis on chastity and the sanctity of marriage. Illegitimacy came to be viewed as a great offense against God. Once societal attitudes turned ugly and condemnatory, illegitimate children became victims at the hands of the mothers who bore them, who killed their offspring rather than endure society's scorn.

Legislation in Europe finally was passed to protect illegitimate children from harm. Mothers in the colonies, equally fearful of mean-spirited attitudes toward them and their illegitimate babies, also covertly disposed of their young, and penalties similar to those in Europe were written into law. The Act of 1623 "to prevent the Murthering of Bastard Children" addressed the problem and provided the state's solution:

Whereas many lewd women that have been delivered of Bastard Children do avoyd their shame and to escape punishment, doe secretlie bury or conceale the Death of their Children and after the Child be found dead the said Women doe alledge that the said Child was born dead, whereas it falleth out sometymes (although hardlie it is to be proved) that the said Child or Children were murdered by the said Women their Lewd Mothers, or by their assent or procurement. . . . [Any woman] be delivered of any issue of her Body Male or Female, which being born alive should by the Laws of the Realme be a Bastard, and that she endeavour privatelie either by drowning, or secrett burying thereof, or any other way, by herself or the procuring of others, soe conceale the Death thereof . . . the Mother soe offending shall suffer Death as in the case of Murther, except such Mother can make proofe by one witness at the leest, that the child . . . was borne dead.[158]

Justice John Marshall cited two examples of women executed in the colony of Massachusetts for murdering their bastards.[159] A gradual tolerance of illegitimate children, however, evolved in the new settlements by the end of the eighteenth century, probably in light of an accelerating rate of illegitimate births. There were estimates in some areas that nearly 40 percent of firstborns were of unwed mothers.[160]

A British act of 1617 granted permission to the lord mayor of London to ship poor, vagabond orphans to the colony of Virginia. Embellished with humanitarian phrases, a letter was sent by James I to the future governor of Virginia, John Smith, outlining his expectations for these children:

Whereas our Court hath been troubled with divers idle young people whoe although they have been twise punished still continewe to followe the same haveing noe ymploymente. Wee haveinge noeother course to cleere our court from them have thought fitt to send them unto you, desireing you att the next oportunitie to send them away to Virginia and to take such order that they may bee sett to worke there, wherein you shall onlie doe us good service, but also doe a deed of charitie by ymploying them whoe otherwise will never be reclaimed from the idle life of vagabonds.[161]

Later, in 1620, the king's Privy Council ordered another group of children transported: "We are informed that the City of London, by Act of Common Council, have appointed 100 children out of the Multitudes that swarm in that place, to be sent to Virginia."[162] It is estimated that by 1627 nearly 1,500 children[163] from London had been shipped to Viriginia for indentured work, many of them recipients of specific bequests made by London citizens for the voyage. In 1640, for example, Anthony Abdy, an alderman, had left money for "poore Boyes and Girles to be taken up out of the streets of London as Vagrants for the Cloathing and transporting of them to Virginia."[164] Without private support in England, the government's alternative to shipping out the homeless was to release children to the shelter of almshouses. Invariably, however, these children returned to their homeless existence in the streets of London, preferring it to the deplorable conditions in orphan asylums. Sending them to the colonies, therefore, was the preferred policy.

Transportation to the colonies, in fact, became a lucrative business, with purchasing centers or offices, formal contracts, shipping and arrival ports, and even a circulated price list. It was subtle, disguised barter in slavery. The port of Bristol, for example, shipped over ten thousand indentured servants between 1654 and 1686. For nearly 150 years, merchants shipped their convicts or indentured "free of charge," knowing the human cargo would fetch a good price or exchange at the other end or at the very least, a consignment of tobacco. A laborer fetched between ten and twenty-five pounds, depending on strength and skills. A Maryland census of 1755 counted 1,981 transportees, which broke down to 1,507 males, 386 women, 67 boys, and 21 girls.[165]

Scotland started transporting youth in 1766, employing local contractors to arrange voyages. A Glasgow merchant named Patrick Colquhoun served as a major organizer. The business became so profitable that his suppliers resorted to kidnapping children for transport to the colonies. The scandal of child snatching went unnoticed by the public until the revelations of Peter Williamson were published in Aberdeen in 1757. Williamson was kidnapped when eight years old, and in July 1743, together with sixty-nine other children, ages six to fifteen, he was put on board the *Planter* bound for Virginia. Williamson relates:

They conducted me between the decks to some others they had kidnapped [but] I had no sense of the fate that was destined for me and spent the time in childish amusements with my fellow sufferers in steerage, being never suffered to go up on deck while the vessel was in harbour, which was until such a time as they had got in their loading with a complement of unhappy youths. . . . When we arrived and landed in Philadelphia, that Captain soon had people enough who came to buy us . . .

sold us at about £16 a head. What became of my unhappy companions I never knew.[166]

Forced emigrations of children—and adults—continued to grow as a business, and between 1718 and 1775 most bartering remained in the hands of professional contractors. The mode of transport was undignified and the human cargo demeaned. Multiple tales of woe offer descriptions, such as this one from a William Green, who had been transported to Maryland aboard the *Sally* in 1762:

We were put ashore in couples chained together and driven in lots like oxen or sheep [to be inspected by purchasers who] search us there as the dealers in horses do these animals in the country, by looking at our teeth, viewing our limbs to see if they are sound and fit for their labour, and if they approve of us after asking our trades and names and what crimes we have been guilty of to bring us to that shame, the bargain is made.[167]

Attempted escapes were punished vigorously. In Virginia the penalty was thirty-nine lashes; in Maryland, ten days of service for every "free" day; and in South Carolina, for every day of escape the cost was an additional twenty-eight days of indenture.[168]

The numbers of transportees kept increasing, prompting some of the colonies to complain. In 1724, Hugh Jones, rector of Jamestown, Virginia, observed:

White servants are of three kinds: 1. such as come upon certain wages by Agreement for a certain Time; 2. such as come by indenture, commonly called *Kids*, who are usually to serve four or five years; and 3. those Convicts or Felons that are transported. . . . The Servants and inferior Sort of People, who have either been sent over to Virginia or have transported themselves thither, have been, and are, the poorest, idlest and worst of Mankind, the Refuse of Great Britain and Ireland, and the Outcast of the People.[169]

Transportation to America continued until the last ship, the *Jenny*, entered the James River in April 1776. This was the last ship to successfully disembark indentured convicts, vagrants, and orphans. Thereafter, England sent transportees to New South Wales, Australia.[170] Shipping children out of urban areas in attempts to solve problems associated with vagrancy was to be revised in the nineteenth century, when homeless children were sent from overcrowded slums in the east on "orphan trains" to the underpopulated west.

The English solution of shipping out orphans was not unique. The Portuguese shipped their homeless children to the African continent and later to the East Indies; the French sent children to colonies in the West Indies and later to Algeria and Louisiana; and between the years 1645 and 1660 the Dutch shipped orphans to New York, then known as New Amsterdam.[171]

As the numbers of vagrant immigrant children swelled and the number of indentured positions for children decreased, children were sent to almshouses.[172] With no authority to curtail the numbers of child vagrants sent from Europe, communities in the colonies began to experience the urban problems the motherland had long endured. It was not long before even almshouses became severely crowded and their young residents spilled out into the streets, much as they had done in the mother country.

The colonies, for the most part, however, welcomed the able-bodied to settle the country. Legislation was enacted detailing the conditions and terms for the immigration of new workers, clearly promoting such transactions. South Carolina's Act of 1698 illustrates the prevailing bias for white—"Irish only excepted"—servants, specifically between the ages of sixteen and forty:

. . . every merchant, owner or master of any ship or vessel, or any other person not intending to settle and plant here, which shall bring any white male servants, Irish only excepted, into Ashley river, above sixteen years of age and under forty, and the same shall deliver to the Receiver General, shall receive and be paid by the said Receiver.[173]

Young children, either indentured or members of families, began work on farms early in the morning, both to maximize their economic value to the family and to keep, as it was thought, idle hands away from the influence of Satan. Five- to six-year-olds were employed to sow seeds or weed the fields. As they grew, the chores increased in complexity. Girls were assigned to the spinning wheel to make fabric for the household and for farm use. Boys were given tasks of a more physical nature. A description of a typical life for a non-indentured boy in Connecticut was gleaned from the *Memoirs* of David and John Brainerd (c.1740):

The boy was taught that laziness was the worst form of original sin. Hence he must rise early and make himself useful before he went to school, must be diligent there in study, and promptly home to do "chores" at evening. His whole time out of school must be filled up with some service, such as bringing in fuel for the day, cutting potatoes for the sheep, feeding the swine, watering the horses, picking the berries, gathering the vegetables, spooling the yarn. He was expected never to be reluctant and not often tired.[174]

Girls began to interlace mastering the skills of sewing and embroidery with the learning of school and religious subjects. The sampler (figure 7.6) provided the medium with which writing skills were exhibited and could

Figure 7.6 A schoolgirl sampler (Edmonds, 1991).

express spirituality. Sampler sewing was a decorative art that dated to Elizabethan times, when maids of honor sewed eulogies in verse onto red silk pillow-size fabric in honor of their dead mistresses.[175]

The sampler was extensively used as an educational mechanism for girls in the early seventeenth century and reached its greatest popularity in the late eighteenth century. In principle, a sampler was like a hornbook executed in needlework, in that alphabet letters, numbers, prayers, crosses, and references to virtue and piety were standard elements incorporated into embroidered pieces. Samplers often ended with a verse honoring parents and country or with some form of doxology, as the following examples show:

This is my Sampler,
Here you see
What care my Mother
Took of me.

Mary Jackson is my name,
America my nation,
Boston is my dwelling place,
And Christ is my salvation.

Though life is fair
And pleasure young,
And Love on ev'ry
Shepherd's Tongue,
I turn my thoughts
To serious things,
Life is ever on the wing.[176]

Religion and the restraints of puritanism in colonial America were injected into all aspects of living, including child play. Children were punished if found laughing on the Sabbath day. Running, whistling, humming, whittling, or other similar activities were considered sinful any day of the week.

Colonial parents, however, seem to have recognized children's need for play and devised special "Sunday toys" that satisfied the impulse without breaching the Sabbath prohibition.[177] One of these was a board game, the "Game of Christian Endeavor," that reinforced the theme of Christian virtue. Players were penalized for landing in a box illustrating a vice and rewarded for landing in a box describing a virtue. Other Puritan Sunday toys included building blocks for making churches, Noah's ark with its menagerie of figures to move into position, and music boxes that played popular hymns.

The Puritan ethos that original sin tainted all, including children, influenced educational doctrine. Since the evil of original sin could be obliterted and redemption found only after a life of pious, righteous living, and—importantly—by a thorough knowledge of Scripture, there existed a Puritan requisite to master reading in order to learn Scripture. This standard and, in time, a population of immigrant yeoman who had been secularly educated at Oxford and Cambridge, together with their literate wives and children, contributed to a more generally literate society.

One very small measure of literacy is the abiity to write one's name. In 1660, 60 percent of men in the northeastern part of the Continent could sign. By 1710 this was true of 70 percent. By 1790 the figure was 90 percent, reflecting increased numbers of men with some education.[178]

Dame schools were a form of day-care that had originated in England. They were run by neighborhood women, to whom parents paid three pence a week to have their toddlers cared for while they worked. The earliest American dame school seems to have been founded in 1628 by Mrs. Mirick of Springfield, Massachusetts. Reference to this genre of school still was being made at the end of the eighteenth century, as George Crabbe's 1780 verse illustrates:

> When a deaf poor patient widow sits
> And awes some twenty infants as she knits
> Infants of humble busy wives who pay
> Some trifling price for freedom through the day.[179]

There were several impediments to education, despite the fact that, with the exception of Rhode Island, all of the northeastern colonies made attendance at public school a requirement under the law[180] and that these early northern colonial schools were free. They were not found in all settlements, and they seldom admitted girls or children from poor families. Farming chores, determined by growing cycles and weather, had the highest priority and often preempted attendance at schools. Parcels of land for school buildings, the buildings themselves, and schoolmasters all were scarce commodities. This was particularly so of money to pay teachers' salaries.

Girls in general were not educated by the state until the mid-nineteenth century. In colonial schools, girls were excluded from attendance, but the well-motivated acquired some instruction by eavesdropping outside the schoolhouse. The occasional community allowed girls to stand at the rear of a classroom, behind a "seriaglioesque" curtain.

In the South, the priority for fledgling colonies was the assistance of their young on farms, with little time allocated for formal education. Some people in the South, like the governor of Virginia, had distinctly antipathetical views on the matter:

I thank God there are in Virginia no free schools nor printing, and I hope we shall not have, for learning hath brought disobedience and heresy into the world. (Governor Berkeley, 1670) [181]

Most colonists, however, having brought with them from Europe religious precepts of Reformation reformists, considered the ability to read the Bible a necessary step in developing virtue that would contribute to a pious, godly life. Parents, therefore, encouraged all of their children to learn at least the rudiments of reading. Occasionally, farmers donated some land on which could be built a schoolhouse. Supportive governments in the Massachusetts and Connecticut colonies enacted laws stating that towns with fifty or more families had to have a school. In townships with more than one hundred families, a grammar school was mandated. Puritan ministers were appointed guardians of the schools. As the colonies grew in size and in diversity, the schools remained public but no longer were free. Taxation of parents provided operating expenses and salaries. Parental donations of firewood supplied warmth in the cold winters, and there were penalties for parents who failed to contribute their share of firewood—their children were banished from the classroom. The town of Windsor, Connecticut, decreed: "The committee be empowered to exclude any scholar that shall not carry his share of wood for the use of the said school"; and the town of West Hartford "barred from the fire" children of parents who were remiss in their obligation. [182]

At first only the basic subjects—reading, writing, and arithmatic—were taught, and as in Europe, teachers in the colonies were held in low esteem and received poor salaries. Consequently, it was not an occupation that always attracted qualified or even desirable candidates. Indentured servants sometimes functioned as teachers, as the following notice in the *Maryland Gazette* illustrates: "Ran away: A servant man who followed the occupation of a Schoolmaster, much given to drinking and gambling."[183] Alcoholism among teachers, incidentally, frequently was a complaint on the Continent, particularly in French and Dutch communities.[184] Those teachers with formal pedagogical training often assumed responsibilities beyond teaching arithmetic, penmanship, and reading. They often were expected to teach catechism and Sunday Bible classes.

The letter that follows, written by a colonial schoolboy to his father, shares, with epistles as far back as Roman, Greek, and Sumerian times, an apparently generic predisposition for aquisition of necessities as well as of treats. His requests for food, clothing, supplies, and money enlist him in the ranks of all those schoolboys who preceded him:

Honored Fethar,

These fiew Lines comes to let you know that I am in a good State of Health and I hope this may find you also. I have found all the things in my trunk but I must have a pare of Schuse. And mama please to send me some Ches Nutts and some Wall Nutts; you please to send a Slate, and som pensals, and please to send me some smok befe, and for bringing my trunk 3/9, and for a pare of Schuse 9 shillings. You please to send me a pare of indin's Schuse. You please to send me som dride corn. My Duty to Father and Mother and Sister and to all frinds.

> I am your Dutyfull Son,
> John Ten Broeck.[185]

In addition to the slate and pencils young John mentioned in his letter to his parents, school supplies in colonial American schools included writing paper, quills, knives for cutting the quills, ink, and wintertime candles. Students were expected to bring to school these and other supplies.[186]

In American schools the "battledore," modeled after the hornbook, was the learning tool most commonly available. The battledore listed the alphabet, arabic numbers, and reading phonemics on hard or stiff cardboard, with the ubiquitous cross and Pater Noster on occasion omitted. In time, the use of the battledore dwindled in favor of what became the most widely used book in American education—the *New England Primer*. The American version first was published in Boston by Benjamin Harris around 1690. It remained in circulation for almost two hundred years, selling more than five million copies. Based on religious precepts and called the "Little Bible of New England," the primer merits at least a footnote in history as the text in which first appears the universally known bedtime verse: "Now I lay myself to sleep, I pray the Lord my soul to keep." The primer incorporated biblical and general history into two sets of the alphabet. Beginning with *A*, which taught that "In Adam's fall, We sinned all," and ending with *Z*, which described how "Zaccheus he Did climb a tree, His Lord to see," the one set deftly employed biblical images as it taught the alphabet. It additionally justifies the use of the ferule* in education as an edifying instrument: The letter *F* describes how "The Idle Fool, Is Whipt at school," and *J* teaches that "Job feels the Rod, Yet blesses God."[187] The second alphabet set coalesced history and politics according to the sentiments of the times. In the early colonial primer the letter *K* exalted: "King Charles the Good, no man of blood"; in the postrevolutionary period, children learned that "Queens and Kings, are gaudy things."[188]

Colonial children learned mathematical word problems set to rhyme in *Crocker's Arithmetick*, as well as the similarly versified *Arte of Vulgar Arithmiteke*:

> The Partition of a Shilling into his Aliquot Partes.
>
> A farthing first finds forty-eight
> A Halfpeny hopes for twentiefoure
> Three farthings seeks out 16 streight
> A peny puls a dozen lower
> Dicke dandiprat drewe 8 out deade
> Twopence took 6 and went his way
> Tom trip a goe with 4 is fled
> But Goodman grote on 3 doth stay
> A testerne only 2 doth take
> Moe parts a Shilling cannot make.[189]

More concise versions of well-known English catechetical texts were published in the colonies. Faithful to the religious contents, the books were less repetitive, which suited the farming communities' abbreviated teaching periods, and cheaper to produce. The English text *The Careful Father and Pious Child*, containing 1,200 questions and answers, was edited down to 107. Appropriately, it was called the *Short Catechism*. It was Cotton Mather's favorite text.[190] An even shorter version of the catechism, with eighty-seven questions and answers, was called *Spiritual Milk for Babes*, by John Cotton (1584–1652).

The nonreligious curriculum emphasized penmanship, to the extent that teachers often were referred to as "Writing Masters." Entries into diaries and

---

*The word *ferule* is derived from *ferula*, or fennel. The stalks of the giant fennel from southern Europe were used by the Roman magisterium as disciplinary whips. In London, peddlers sold birch rods under the names of "Jemmies" or "London Tartars."

Today's London still opines that physical discipline may be necessary. A recent poll revealed that 88 percent thought it okay to occasionally smack a child, and 9 percent said a cane, belt, or slipper could be used. *Lancet* 2000; 356:1.

commonplace books—compilations of favorite passages and quotations—
were the most popular ways children practiced their writing skills, although
any handy surface sufficed. Rhyme was a favorite instructional device and
was used to teach proper methods and materials used for writing; in so
doing, it marked the supremacy of using the right hand to write:

> Ink alwais good store on right hand to stand
> Brown paper for great haste or else box of sand.
> Dip pen and shake pen and touch pen for haire
> Wax, quills and penknife see alwais ye beare.
>   *A New Book of Hands* (c.1650)[191]

Students, too, were fond of using rhyming couplets. The following expresses a view about education and reaches for posterity at the same time:

> When Land is Gone and Money Spent
> Then Larning is most Excellent.
>   If this you See
>   Remember Me.[192]

Students also wrote doggerel in the frontispieces of books to deliver warnings to those with thievery on their minds:

> Steal not this Book for if You Do
> The Devil will be after You.[193]

Finally, verse was used by educators to warn students of the disciplinary
consequences of inattention to studies[194]:

> My child and scholar take good heed
>   unto the words that here are set,
> And see thou do accordingly
>   or else be sure thou shalt be beat.
> *The English Schoolmaster*, Edward Coote (1680)

As in their European counterparts, discipline was corporal in colonial
schools and linked, in the public mind, with character building. Pilgrim John
Robinson, in his essay "Children and Their Education," wrote with passion:

Surely there is in all children (though not alike) a stubbernes and stoutness of minde
arising from naturall pride which must in the first place be broken and beaten down
that so the foundation of their education being layd in humilitie and tractableness
other virtues may in their time be built upon.[195]

Most punishment, with Deuteronomy, Proverbs, and parents to support it, was apportioned with a rod. The ferule arrived in America as an instrument invested with divine approbation, as was its replacement rods made with the more readily available birch. In time, other disciplinary devices, such as the flapper, were introduced. This was a piece of leather six inches across, with a hole cut out of the middle, attached to a wooden handle. When children were whipped with it, welts and blisters the size of the hole were raised. At times children were made to fetch a fresh green branch from a tree. Pinchers, which unfortunate children were forced to wear on their noses, were made from the severed, split ends. "Whispering sticks," wooden gags inserted into the mouth and tied around the back of the head like a horse's bit, were used to quell raucous behavior. Restless children had to balance themselves on a unipod, or one-legged stool, or kneel on a log as punishment. The Continent introduced to America the Ass of Shame, a carved-wood effigy upon which children had to sit while wearing a dunce's cap. Profane children were forced to wear a yoke. Punishment usually ended if tears fell, since the Puritans considered lacrimation a sign of remorse. Some aphorisms reflect this belief: "Better the child cries than its mother" and "Compulsion is necessary and crying is the music of children."[196]

John Eliot (1604–1690), in *The Harmony of the Gosple* (1678), appealed rhapsodically for a more tender, love-filled discipline reminiscent of that associated with the most ideal form of maternal care:

The gentle rod of the mother is a very soft and gentle thing; it will break neither bone nor skin; yet by the blessing of God with it, and upon the wise application of it, it would break the bond that bindeth up corruption in the heart.[197]

Other voices in the colonies expressed compassion for children and denounced the excesses of corporal punishment, but they were few. Curiously, Cotton Mather, the conservative Congregationalist, whose common image is that of a stern Puritan, was such a voice but only in his private family life. Publicly, the preacher Mather, the prosecutor of the Salem witch trials, earned a reputation for fanatically conservative religious views of the "fire and brimstone" variety. In one of his sermons he said, "Don't you know that your Children are the Children of Death, and the Children of Hell and the Children of Wrath, by Nature?"[198]

His son Samuel, writing after Mather's death, depicted an altogether different person, one who raised his children with quiet understanding and compassion:

The slavish way of education carried on with raving and kicking and scourging, in schools as well as in families, he looked on upon as a dreadful judgment of God on the world: he thought the practice abominable and expressed a mortal aversion to it.

The first chastisement which he would inflict for any ordinary fault, was to let the child see and hear him in an astonishment, and hardly able to believe that the child would do so base a thing. He would never come to give the child a blow, except in case of obstinacy, or something very criminal. To be chased for a while out of his presence he would make to be looked upon as the sorest punishment in his family.[199]

Popular European books of comportment found their way to the colonies. They were typically directives on topics that ranged from proper public deportment toward parents and company to behavior with peers and even correct conversation. The books reinforced parental efforts to acculturate the young. One such book published in London, *The School for Manners* (1715) by Eleazar Moody (d.1726), was a particular success in America.[200] Here is a sampling from the book—a veritable catalog of deferential manners that were expected of children:

> Approach near thy parents at no time without a bow.
> Dispute not, nor delay to obey thy parents commands.
> Among superiors speak not till thou art spoken to, and bid to speak.
> Boast not in discourse of thine own wit or doings.
> Laugh not in, or at thy own story, wit or jest.
> Look not over anyone while he is writing.
> Do not sing or hum while thou art in company.
>
> *The School for Manners*, chaps. 1–5

The Mirror of Compliments was printed in England in 1635 and reprinted in America by Isaiah Thomas (1749–1831) as late as 1795. It exemplifies the genre of book that listed on page after page decorous phrases and elegant expressions for young gentlemen and ladies to incorporate into their discourses:

Sir, you shall oblige me very much if you will do me the honour to take my poor dinner with me."

"Sir, you are too courteous and persuasive to be refused and therefore I shall trouble you."

"Truly, Sir, it has been very good, without any defect, and needs no excuse."[201]

The number of Puritan colonies in America inevitably produced a demand for books written specifically for children that emphasized redemption and moral behavior and condemned worldly vanities and sin. Some of the titles were deceptively engaging and simple, such as *The Plain Man's Pathway to Heaven* and James Janeway's (1636–1674) *The Looking Glass for Children*. Some books had exaggerated pedantic and gloomy narrative titles such as Janeway's (1672) *A Token for Children, being an Exact Account of the Conversion, Holy and Exemplary Lives and Joyful Deaths of Several Young Children. To which is added a Token for the Children of New England or Some Examples of Children in whom the Fear of God was remarkably Budding before they died; in several Parts of New England. Preserved and Published for the Encouragement of Piety in other Children.*[202] All preached a Calvinistic view that human beings, formed with original sin, were predestined to hell and that redemption was possible only through lifelong acts of atonement.

In Janeway's *The Looking Glass for Children*, subtle verses scorned worldly beauty with the reminder of universal damnation, a typical reflection of the Puritan view:

> When by Spectators I behold
>   What Beauty doth adorn me
> Or in a glass when I behold
>   How sweetly God did form me,
> Hath God such comeliness bestowed
>   And on me made to dwell
> What pity such a pretty maid
>   As I should go to Hell.[203]

One celebrated verse written in 1662 by Michael Wigglesworth (1631–1705) was entitled "The Day of Doom; or a Poetical Description of the Great and Last Judgement." Children had to memorize—and ministers liked to quote—stanza after stanza that condemned sinners to hell. Consistent with Puritan thinking, even infants were not exempt from eternal punishment, albeit they were given "the easiest room in hell":

> Will you demand Grace at my hand,
>   and challenge what is mine?
> Will you teach me whom to set free
>   and thus my Grace confine?
> You sinners are, and such a share
>   as sinners may expect;
> Such you shall have; for I do save
>   none but my own Elect.
> Yet to compare your sin with their's
>   who liv'd a longer time,
> I do confess yours is much less,
>   though every sin's a crime.

> A Crime it is, therefore in bliss
>   you may not hope to dwell;
> But unto you I shall allow
>   the easiest room in Hell.

Clerics, infused with Calvin's doctrine of original sin and predestination, naturally supposed newborns were equally tainted with at least the capacity for sin, and they believed maturation inevitably would see its manifestation in sinful behavior:

The very infants themselves, while they bring with them their owne damnation from their mothers wombe, are bound, not by anothers, but by their owne fault. For although they have not as yet brought foorth the fruits of their owne iniquitie, yet they have the seede thereof enclosed with them: yea, their whole nature is a certain seede of sinne: therefore it cannot be but hatefull and abominable to God. (John Calvin, *A Harmonie upon the Three Evangelistes . . .* [1610])[204]

Parents, anxious to ensure their children's redemption, eagerly sought advice from pedagogues such as John Brinsley (fl.1633). In 1612 his book *Ludus Literarius* or *Grammar Schoole*[205] was published, in which he promoted the view that education was necesssary as a tool to use in earning salvation. He advocated that children first learn the "abcies," then advance to primers and to the psalters in meter and, finally, to the Bible. He recommended edifying books of moral instruction to complement pedagogy:

Then if any other require any little booke meet to enter Children, the *Schoole of Virtue* is one of the Principall, and easiest for the first enterers being full of precept of civilitie. . . . And after the *Schoole of Good Manners*, leading the child as by the hand, in the way of all good manners.[206]

Finally, Puritan catechetical instruction by parents and teachers was guided by Herbert Palmer's (1601–1647) catechism, published in 1640, *On Endeavour of Making the Principles of Christian Religion namely the Creed, the ten Commandments, the Lords Praryer and the Sacraments plaine and easie*:

What is a man's greatest business in this world? Is it to follow the world, and live as he list? No. Or, is it to glorifie God, and save his own soule? Yes. So, what is a man's greatest business in this world:
   A man's greatest business in this world is to glorifie God, and save his own soule. How shall a man come to glorifie God and save his own soule? Can they do so that are ignorant? No.
   Or, they that do not believe in God? No.
   Or, do not serve him? No.

Or, must they not needs to learn to know God? and believe in him and serve him? Yes.[207]

By the end of the seventeenth century, the puritanical hold on the colonies began to weaken as the colonies grew, the numbers and diverse kinds of immigrants arrived on American shores, and trade routes prospered. American colonists began to develop an interest in and taste for *possessions* that endures in modern times and is widely imitated abroad when possible. The educated were for the most part the moneyed and privileged, and this group particularly welcomed the increasing exchange of goods between the colonies and Europe. The one grew rich on agricultural exports in order to purchase the furniture and fashion imported from Europe. There was an apparent snob appeal that led the colony of Massachusetts to legislate the preservation of the distinctions between gentry and commoner by dictating the garb each could wear.* Fancy dress was permitted only if the wearer was among the truly liberally educated class or had an annual income greater than two hundred pounds per year. A violation of this rule incurred a fine and punishment in the stocks. In the name of fashion, many risked the sanctions.[208]

In all of the colonies, trading ships were awaited impatiently for the arrival of new fabrics and other fashions the ships brought as cargo. It was not long before all strata of society aspired to ownership, and even Puritan families were beguiled by tempting concoctions—in dress, hairstyle, make-up, and furniture. Even European manners, gestures, and posture were copied avidly by the colonists, including the Puritans.

In keeping with the new trends in society, new kinds of schools were founded that were less motivated by the Puritan ethic and more complementary to the growing sophistication of the communities they served. In New England,† affluent colonists modeled private schools after the English

---

*This law was reminiscent of the sumptuary laws extant in 13th-century Venice and England, which controlled not only the value of clothing worn but also the quality and type of food consumed (Amt, 1993, pp. 74–78). The 15th-century Jewish communities of Forli, Italy, and Valladolid, Spain, also restricted opulent dress:

> In order also to humble our hearts, and to walk modestly before our God, and not to show off in the presence of the Gentiles, . . . no Jew or Jewess . . . shall be so arrogant as to wear a furlined jacket, unless, of course, it is black. (Amt, 1993, pp. 292–93)

†Genteel Southern families sent their daughters, when possible, to convent schools, where they were taught religion, needlwork, and basic reading. One prominent establishment in New Orleans was founded by Ursuline nuns in 1727. The school in time expanded to provide shelter for orphans and to teach African and Native American girls. Kendall, 1973, pp. 15–16.

urban-house schools. An advertisement that appeared in a Boston paper circa 1750 is descriptive of the growing secular tone:

All manner of instruments in Writing and Conveyances in the Law, now in Use and Practice, are carefully drawn and ingross'd. Also young Gentlemen and Ladies may be boarded and educated, and taught English, Writing and Arithmetick, both Vulgar and Decimal; with several other Branches of the Mathematics, after a very easy and concise Method.

by George Suckling

Also young Ladies may be taught plain Work, Dresden, Point (or Lace) Work for Child Bed Linnen, Crosstich, Tentstich, and all other sorts of Needle Work.

by Brigid Suckling[209]

In 1772, a twelve-year-old student in one of those schools wrote home imploringly to her mother regarding her old-fashioned clothing. Anna Winslow wrote: "Dear Momma, you don't know the fashion here—I beg to look like other folk." The sympathetic response to her entreaty prompted Miss Winslow to write again, blissfully:

My new cloak and bonnet on, my pompadour gloves, etcetera. And I would tell you, that for the first time, they all liked my dress very much.[210]

Lifestyles changed, along with elegant dresses, rich and luxurious fabrics, and social airs—and not just among the wealthy. Cotton Mather lamented: "I must weep and I now do it with a Loud Voice, for what I see."[211] Mather was referring not only to the growing attention to material values but also to the breakdown in courtship and marriage traditions. Although no changes in the laws had occurred, adolescents became bolder and engaged in open courtships. The laws against demonstrations of affection in public continued to be enforced, but penalities were relaxed. In Connecticut, for example, a young boy was fined for "smiling and larfing" in a church meeting during which he had been observed "pulling the heir of his naybor . . . playing with her Hand and fingers at her heir." In Mather's day he would have been flogged and put in the stockades.

As public mores changed, behavior in private experienced an even greater flux. Premarital cohabitation was regarded as mortally sinful, qualified only in the circumstance of an engagement or betrothal, in which case the degree of sin was lessened by half. Sin presumably was circumvented altogether, and chastity preserved, by the socially sanctioned custom of bundling (which the Dutch called "queesting"). This curious eighteenth-century custom was not without its perils:

Fully clothed, a young unmarried couple spent a cozy but chaste evening in bed together. For added security, a board was usually introduced between them, and the girl's mother was likely to tie or even sew her daughter into her clothing. But in spite of these precautions, bundling sometimes led to unplanned consequences. In 1781, a Groton minister, noting the number of confessions of fornication he had been hearing lately, urged the young people of Groton to give up bundling.[212]

The short-lived custom enjoyed a substantial notoriety, as two broadsides with "bundling" songs and multiple private diary references to bundling, published in Boston in 1787, suggest. By the early nineteenth century, the fad had all but disappeared.

In the midst of Puritan settlers in New England and Catholic settlers in Maryland and elsewhere, three unique groups, self-isolating then and in modern times, quietly established communities in the New World. The Anabaptist groups that appeared in Europe at the time of the Reformation had embraced a literal interpretation of Christ's edict: "Verily I say unto you, except ye be converted, and become as little children, ye shall not enter into the kingdom of heaven" (Matt. 18:3). Consequently, the behavior and mannerisms of children were aped to the extent that some adults played with toys, babbled like toddlers, and even ran about naked. The fundaments of Anabaptist beliefs eschewed infant baptism, since children were innocents. Baptism and repentance were adult obligations. In their communities, repetitive sinful behavior on the part of adults resulted in banishment.

These people also endeavored to keep themselves separate from the rules of government, which, being devised by men, were considered imperfect. They forbade the taking of oaths or serving in the military. The reaction from society at large was ridicule and persecution. Sensitive to society's jibes, church members began to dissent. This resulted in the splintering of the group, which fissioned into three distinct sects that are extant: the Mennonites, of Dutch and Prussian origin; Hutterians from Austria; and the Swiss followers of Jacob Amman—the Amish.

Sustained persecution in Europe had led to emigration of Anabaptist descendants to the colonies. By 1683 there was a Mennonite settlement in Germantown, Pennsylvania. Major migrations of the Amish occurred between 1727 and 1770, and from 1815 to 1860.[213] They carried with them an uncompromising code of behavior and of dress with which generations of their children were and continue to be acculturated.

To the Amish, infants were innocent beings—*res tabulae*—that gave joy to their families and were to be cherished. Exposure or abandonment were unheard of in their communities. The early years of childhood were unfettered and permissive, but beginning at about age two, group values and lifestyle began to be inculcated. As children grew older, they were introduced to household and farm chores appropriate to their age. Comportment and respect for elders, the matrix for life in the community, were concepts that were consistently reinforced.

Extensive education was discouraged and was limited to that which was necessary to learn Scripture. Intellectual curiosity was not rewarded or indulged. A reading knowledge of High German was encouraged because of its use in religious services, and English language and arithmetic studies were tolerated to the extent that they facilitated interaction, economic and otherwise, with neighboring communities. Child play was restricted to that among Amish children. Stories, such as fairy tales, were expressly forbidden.

Religious beliefs infused the group's approach to medical care for the sick adult or child. The Amish relied on a derivative form of faith healing, called *brauche*, composed of specific incantations for curing illness or avoiding harm. Children were taught these at an early age. A child confronting a strange dog, for example, was taught to say three times:

> Dog, hold thy nose to the ground;
> God has made me and thee, hound.[214]

Folk healing was a profession called upon for curative care. For a child infected with parasites, for example, a folk healer circled the patient three times, incanting:

> You are a little worm, not entirely grown.
> You plague me in marrow and bone.
> You may be white, black, or red,
> In a quarter of an hour you will be dead.[215]

Brauch-Doktors were relied on for diverse childhood ailments, from erysipelas, or streptococcal infections, and wasting or failure to thrive, to bedwetting. There was a curious entity called "livergrown" that, by its description, appears to have been nothing more than a form of colic.[216] A diagnosis was made if a prone infant's left arm and right foot could not be brought together (figure 7.7).

In the nineteenth century, the Amish began to accept traditional medicine, a reluctant and limited concession to mankind's societal progress. In matters of religion and culture, however, they remained an insular group that clung to its traditional values and teaching and, with a great deal of success, ingrained these into the minds and manners of their children. In the twentieth century further compromises in favor of modern living were made among the Amish groups, but, as a sect, they continue to be a society apart,

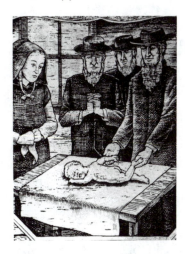

Figure 7.7
Elders attempting to diagnose "livergrown."

their traditions best recognized by the plain garb they wear and by the "hex" signs on their buildings.

ASPECTS OF REFORMATION CHILDHOOD

Royal Wards

Throughout the medieval period, noble titles, conveyed with large land grants, were the reward for exceptional military or political service to the state. In the event of a lord's death, there were provisions by the state to protect the assets of estates and legal minor heirs of the deceased. These lands in essence became fiefdoms of the Crown, and heirs were named royal wards. As early as 1185, Henry II of England had a census and registry, *Rotuli de Dominabus et Pueris et Puellis*, made of wards under his feudal controls.[217] Overlords were appointed as overseers, and all matters and persons that pertained to the property were subject to their authority. Male heirs could reclaim their inherited property at the age of twenty-one. The property of heiresses was part of their dowry, regardless of the age at which they married, and overlords had the jurisdiction to contract marriages of their rich female wards. There were handsome commissions and profits to be made from these arrangements, and the allure of money, combined with the power vested in overlords, inevitably led to corruption.

By the thirteenth century, trade in wardships and marriages of wards became a speculative commodity among the nobility. During the reigns of the Tudors, this last vestige of feudalism was a lucrative source of revenue for the Crown. In 1540, Henry VIII formalized the practice by establishing a Court of Wards, so that a cadre of the king's administrators controlled lands, successions, and marriages of all royal wards. Propertied orphans were immediately put on the selling block even as they were being named royal wards. The annual revenues to the Crown at this juncture was almost fifteen thousand pounds.[218] Prices of wardships were fixed according to the number of heirs, the ages of the heirs, and the extent of the land holdings. Female wards were the prized commodity, of course, since their assets were part of the marriage barter. Widowed mothers seldom had the means to buy back wardships, as their prices were usually high. In 1611 a legal gesture permitted families one month in which to raise the sums to make such purchases.[219]

Meanwhile, the educations of royal wards were notoriously neglected, leading several prominent statemen like Hugh Latimer (1485–1555), Nicholas Bacon (1509–1578), and Humphrey Gilbert (?1539–1583) to demand special schools for these children. In 1561, Bacon wrote to William Cecil (1520–1598), then Master of the Wards, with his recommendations on an appropriate instructional regime for wards. Beginning with morning services at 6 A.M., children were to study Latin until 11 A.M., be given a meal between 11 A.M. and noon, study music until 2 P.M., practice French until 3 P.M., then Latin again until 5 P.M. Evening prayers were expected, followed by supper. "Honest pastimes" were to be allowed from 8 to 9 P.M., before compulsory bedtime.[220]

Matrimonium per verba de futuro could be contracted by fathers when their children were as young as seven years old. By law these marriages were ratified when the children came of age—fourteen for boys, twelve for girls. A spate of child marriages in the sixteenth and seventeenth centuries were arranged by families hoping to secure their estates, merge assets, and certainly, to prevent the potential exploitation of wards by the Crown. Instead, the children were exploited by their own fathers. The common practice of contracting prepubescent daughters in marriage led reformer Hugh Latimer to protest:

There was never such marrying as in England as is now. I hear of stealing of wards to marry their children to. This is a strange kind of stealing: it is not the wards but the lands that they steal . . . and many parents constrain their sons and daughters to marry where they love not, and some are beaten and compulsed. And they that marry thus, marry in a forgetfulness and obliviousness of God's commandments.[221]

Playwright and author George Whetstone (1544–1587) also was outraged by these economically motivated transactions:

I crye out uppon forcement in Marriage, as the extreamest bondage that is: for that the raunsome of libertie is ye death of the one or ye other of the married. The father thinkes he hath a happy purchase, if he get a riche young Warde to match with his daughter: But God he knowes, and the unfortunate couple often feele, that he byeth sorrow to his Childe, slaunder to himselfe, and perchance, the ruine of an auncient Gentlemans house, by the riot of the sonne in Lawe, not loving his wife.[222]

The feudal regression of treating children as chattel, the abuse of wards, and pressure from the propertied aristocracy resulted in the dissolution of the Court of Wards in 1646. Childhood marriages continued to be arranged by families, but quietly, sub rosa. The natural claims to estates of widows and next of kin were legally reinstated. The large profits made by corrupt court representatives who abused their roles of in loco parentis abruptly ended.

Child Actors

Acting companies of children were found all over Europe and especially in England between about 1515 and 1616, reaching an apex of popularity in the Elizabethan court. The tradition evolved from language-dialogue exercises in schools that associated the development of language skills with such drills. The original purpose—to improve diction, posture, and poise and to develop eloquent rhetorical abilities—evolved into performance for the public. Troupes of boys began to be recruited from grammar schools, private chapels, and public institutions.[223]

Some of these recruits were choirboys. Choirboy troupes maintained by alms (*pueri eleemosynariae*) dated back to the medieval period. Their principal role had been to sing for church festivals. They participated in the processionals of the boy-bishop ceremonies and additionally assumed acting roles and gained experience in these revels. There was a strong emphasis on the study of music in their educational curriculum. Successful and well trained, they were highly regarded performers. Boys from the choir of St. Paul's Cathedral and the choir of the sovereign's private chapel were in particular highly regarded. The choirboys of Westminster Abbey and St. Paul's Cathedral enjoyed commercial success as well. They received an average of ten pounds for each performance at the Tudor court.[224]

Several of the acting companies evolved from these choirboy groups. Amateur actors primarily performed plays during festival times. Those that achieved professional status performed throughout the year. They relied on donations, audience receipts, and royal grants for support. Some groups were fortunate to have been specifically organized and endowed by royalty and the nobility to produce entertainments for the exclusive enjoyment of their patrons. The Blackfriar theater group, however, subsidized income by rehearsing for their court performances before paying spectators.

During the height of child actors' popularity there were two major companies and at least eight smaller troupes. The Blackfriars, called the Children of the Queen's Revels, performed for nearly a hundred years between 1516 and 1610. Their repertory included nearly seventy-five plays. Children of St. Paul's Cathedral performed from 1525 to 1606 and had a repertory of nearly fifty plays. Among the smaller companies were the Grammar School at Hitchens (1548–1556), St. Paul's Grammar School (1522–1586), Westminster Grammar School (1553–1566) and Westminster Choirboys (1551–1574), the Children of the Windsor Chapel (1571–1577), the Merchant Taylors' Boys (1573–1583), and the short-lived Whitefriars Children of the King's Revels (1607–1608).

Some groups specialized in performing morality plays and other edifying vehicles, a popular and long-standing tradition that had begun with the early passion plays, mystery plays, and the like. Jesuit scholastics wrote plays for children as part of the curriculum, for performance within the colleges. These dramas, the purpose of which was to teach and moralize, were so well received that communities began to request their performance outside the school setting. The impact and influence of such Jesuit works can be appreciated when it is remembered that Lope de Vega, Calderón, Gryphius, Bidermann, Corneille, and Molière all were products of Jesuit education.[225]

Parenthetically, one now obscure social drama that must have enjoyed general popularity with boy actors was an exposé of child abuse by schoolmasters in the schools. Thomas Ingeleland's *The Disobedient Child* (c.1570) attempted to shock his audience into awareness. In the play, a son informs his father:

> For as the Brute goeth by many a one,
> Their tender bodyes both nyght and day
> Are whypped and scourged, and beate lyke a stone
> That from tope to toe, the skin is awaye.

To which the incredulous father replies:

> But I am sure that this kynde of facion
> Is not shewed to children of honest condicion.

The boy convinces the father of the severity of the problem when he recounts an instance of a ward who died from a beating:

> . . . Beynge hanged up by the heeles togyther
> And bealy and buttocks grevously whipped.
> And last of all (which to speake I tremble)
> That his head to the wall he often crushed.[226]

For the most part, child-acting groups had major literary talents to draw on for their material. There were four types of drama: political, Greek and Roman heroine tragedies, derivative Roman comedies, and court comedies—the last a specialty of John Lyly (?1554–1606). Lyly's *Love's Metamorphosis* often was revived. Playwrights of the caliber of Ben Jonson (?1572–1637) wrote *Cynthia's Revels* and *Poetaster* for child actors. Nicholas Udall (1505–1556) wrote *Respublica, Jack Juggler*, and the ever-popular *Ralph Roister Doister* especially for children to perform. Francis Beaumont's (1584–1616) *The Knight of the Burning Pestle* was written for the Blackfriars company. There were, in fact, hundreds of these plays, written by George Chapman, John Marston, William Percy, Thomas Middleton, and others. William Shakespeare and Christopher Marlowe and all of their contemporaries depended, of course, on boy actors to assume female roles in their plays.

The demise of the child-actor groups began with the decline in their popularity at the court of James I (1603–1625). Economic pressures further contributed to their end. The Blackfriars' financial difficulties forced the child troupe to merge with that of the Whitefriars. Gradually, the company evolved into an all-adult group. The Elizabethan penchant for lawsuits rivals that of our own times. A plague of legal squabbles[227] about leases, costumes, patents, contracts, and venues took its financial toll. The few remaining companies were dissolved, and with them a unique aspect of sixteenth-century theater evaporated. Walter Raleigh was moved to remark: "With the disappearance of the boy-players the poetic drama died in England, and it has had no second life."[228]

The seventeeth century indeed was fatal to the life of drama written for children to perform. A wave of puritanical moralism suppressed dramatic creativity of all kinds, and for children, only spoken dialogues with ponderous messages related to virtue, character, or scholastic instruction were encouraged. These were read in small groups, usually without gestures or expression.

Ministers of many Protestant sects published little books of instruction, such as Samuel Shaw's (1635–1696) *Grammar* (1679) in which the protagonist is named King Syntax, and the dramatic conflict arises when elements of speech are used improperly. In Shaw's play, *Rhetoric*, Ellogus (rhetoric) and Ecologus (pronunciation) fight with each other.

Dramas that combined conflict with moral and religious overtones in terms understandable to children were particularly valued. Thomas Sherman, a Baptist preacher, wrote *Youth's Tragedy* (1671) and *Youth's Comedy* (1680). In both of these, the dramatis personnæ who drive home the moral lessons are Vanity, Wisdom, Death, Time, and the Devil. Another Baptist, Benjamin Keach, personified Youth, Truth, and Conscience in his dramalogues.

By far the most popular, truly enjoyed, and enduring of this genre was John Bunyan's (1628–1688) *The Pilgrim's Progress from this World to that Which Is to Come* (1678). There were fourteen editions of this work in five years. Allegorical characters named Obstinate, Pliable, or By-Ends (ulterior motives), Giant Despair and Slough of Despond are exposed by the protagonist, Christian, who reveals for all to despise the temptations of man and man's hypocrisies and deceits.[229]

The vogue of moral dialogues in the guise of drama waned by the end of the century, and the eighteenth century produced no new genre of entertainment specifically for children to perform. In the nineteenth century, virtually the only child actors to be found were performing on the streets. The 1861 census recorded thirty five- to nine-year-olds and one hundred ten- to fourteen-year-olds working on the streets as actors, dancers, and acrobats. It was estimated that as many as a thousand vagabond children in London were performing mime in the streets. In an attempt to force Parliament to act in behalf of these children, Lord Shaftesbury succeeded in having passed the Children's Dangerous Performance Act of 1879.[230] Lamentably, with the enforcement of this law, children did not cease to be urchins—only actors.

NOTES

1. Aries and Duby, 1989, 3:18.
2. Sommerville, 1992, p. 71.
3. Flandrin, 1976, pp. 54–59.
4. Ozment, 1983, p. 132.
5. Ibid.
6. Dunn, 1920, p. 76.
7. Ozment, 1983, p. 133.
8. Badinter, 1980, p. 33.
9. Ozment, 1983, p. 134.
10. Godfrey, 1907, pp. 90–95.
11. Sommerville, 1992, p. 95.
12. Durantini, 1983, p. 113.
13. Cairns, 1987, p. 39.
14. Sommerville, 1992, pp. 81–82.
15. Wooden, 1986, pp. xi–xv.
16. Rhodes, 1577 edition, p. 2 in Furnivall, 1868/1903.
17. Ascham, 1570/1977, p. 80.
18. Wooden, 1986, p. 134.
19. Godfrey, 1907, p. 95.
20. Erasmus, *De Pueris Instituendis*.
21. Ibid.
22. Erasmus, *De Civilitate*, "On Play."

23. Ibid., "On the Body."

24. Ibid., "On Banquets."

25. Sullivan, 1994, p. 95.

26. Ozment, 1983, p. 139.

27. Ibid., pp. 140–41.

28. Ibid., p. 170.

29. This poem is one of "nyne pageauntes" written by More on the topos Ages of Man. The others are entitled "Manhood, Venus and Cupid, Age, Death, Fame, Time, Eternity and Poet." Jones, 1853.

30. Ozment, 1983, p. 171.

31. Ibid., p. 151.

32. Marvick, 1988, p. 290.

33. Pinchbeck and Hewitt, 1969, pp. 18–19.

34. Ozment, 1983, p. 174.

35. Ibid., p. 176.

36. Wooden, 1986, pp. 77–78.

37. Ozment, 1983, pp. 166–67.

38. Ibid., p. 168.

39. Marshall, 1991, p. 57.

40. Josselin, 1648/1908.

41. Houlbrooke, 1988, p. 142.

42. Ibid., p. 128.

42. Ibid.

43. Foisil, 1989, p. 348.

44. Marshall, 1991, p. 56.

45. Ibid., 1991, p. 119. Mrs. Thornton apparently believed that spoiled breast milk caused fever and chills (ague), thereby producing prolonged and chronic rickets and tuberculosis. Rickets was a common disease in the 16th, 17th, and 18th centuries. Its study resulted in the publication of the first disease-specific pediatric text by Francis Glisson in 1650.

46. Durantini, 1983, p. 19. Personality traits may not be defined by the quality of milk, but recent evidence shows that taste preferences are. A controlled study showed that women who consumed carrot juice during their pregnancies cultivated a taste for carrots in their babies. Teleologically, therefore, breast feeding probably helps mammals teach their offspring which foods are safe and re-enforces cultural food preferences. *Science* 2000; 289:387.

47. Marshall, 1991, p. 56.

48. Houlbrooke, 1988, p. 141.

49. Ibid., p. 137.

50. Ibid., p. 153.

51. Ibid., p. 151.

52. Ibid., p. 138.

53. Durantini, 1983, p. 128.

54. Thompson, 1958, p. 16.

55. Ascham, 1570/1977, p. 29.

56. Thompson, 1958, p. 24.
57. Dunn, 1920, p. 300.
58. Thompson, 1958, p. 34.
59. Calvin, 1541/1975.
60. Luther, 1530.
61. Ibid.
62. Cairns, 1987, pp. 63–64.
63. Durantini, 1983, p. 165.
64. Ibid., p. 166.
65. Julius III, *Bull Ex Pacit Debitum*, 21 July 1550.
66. O'Malley, 1993, pp. 272–86.
67. Ibid., pp. 226–27.
68. Ulich, 1975, pp. 272–86.
69. "School of Grammar, Humanities and Christian Doctrine. Free." O'Malley, 1993, pp. 205–7.
70. Revel, 1989, p. 183.
71. Plutarch, "The Education of Children," in *Moralia*, 5.
72. Elyot, 1531/1970, p. 17.
73. Ibid., p. 28.
74. Ascham, 1570/1977, p. 31.
75. Ibid., p. 64.
76. Comenius, 1659.
77. Comenius, 1657/1968.
78. Ibid.
79. Still, 1931, pp. 311–14.
80. Petty, 1648/1911, pp. 315–16.
81. Locke, 1693/1989, pp. 84–101.
82. Ibid., pp. 262–63.
83. Ulich, 1975, p. 193.
84. Durantini, 1983, p. 170.
85. Ozment, 1990, pp. 105–9.
86. Among the posted rules of the school (c.1575) were (Ibid., p. 287):

> 2. [Students] must go to school daily.
> 6. [Students] shall dress honorably.
> 9. Bearing weapons is forbidden.
> 11. He who wounds a fellow student with a weapon shall be thrown into the city prison and expelled from school.
> 13. Inns and pubs are forbidden.

87. Aries and Duby, 1989, 3:112–15.
88. Durantini, 1983, p. 93.
89. Parker, 1979, p. 301.
90. Chartier, 1989, p. 123.
91. Dunn, 1920, p. 142.
92. Godfrey, 1907, p. 138.

93. A. W. Tuer, *History of the Horn Book* (New York: Arno Press, 1979).

94. Earle, 1899/1993, p. 124.

95. Pinchbeck and Hewitt, 1969, 1:95.

96. The acknowledgment of an inherent poverty and unemployment level has become one of the mainstays of economic law in Western civilization.

97. Pinchbeck and Hewitt, 1969, 1:97.

98. Manzione, 1995, pp. 16–20.

99. Pinchbeck and Hewitt, 1969, 1:127–41.

100. Manzione, 1995, p. 26.

101. Ibid., pp. 202–3.

102. Hanawalt, 1993, p. 43.

103. Pinchbeck and Hewitt, 1969, 1:129–34.

104. Marshall, 1991, p. 62.

105. Pinchbeck and Hewitt, 1969, 1:101–2.

106. Dunn, 1920, p. 314.

107. Laurence, 1960, p. 18.

108. Pinchbeck and Hewitt, 1969, 2:351–52.

109. Ibid.

110. Laurence, 1960, p. 18.

111. Schorsch, 1979, pp. 161–64.

112. Houlbrooke, 1988, p. 185.

113. Godfrey, 1907, p. 149.

114. King, 1991, p. 164.

115. Godfrey, 1907, p. 148.

116. King, 1991, pp. 168–70.

117. Pinchbeck and Hewitt, 1969, 1:13–14.

118. Brown, 1984, pp. 57–59.

119. Houlbrooke, 1988, p. 189.

120. Hanawalt, 1993, p. 179.

121. Pinchbeck and Hewitt, 1969, 1:22.

122. Amt, 1993, p. 73.

123. Fuchs, 1984, p. 8.

124. Payne, 1916, p. 309.

125. Fildes, 1986, p. 177.

126. Fuchs, 1984, pp. 15–16.

127. Badinter, 1980, pp. 42–44.

128. Sherwood, 1988, p. 99.

129. Ibid., p. 20.

130. Ibid., p. 11.

131. Ibid., p. 125.

132. Badinter, 1980, pp. 42–43.

133. Fildes, 1986, p. 177.

134. Badinter, 1980, pp. 94–95.

135. Fuchs, 1984, pp. 9–13.

136. Durantini, 1983, p. 18.

137. Flanderin, 1979, p. 160.

138. Mauriceau, c.1668, bk. 3, viii.

139. Durantini, 1983, p. 18.

140. Schama, 1988, p. 538.

141. Badinter, 1980, pp. 126–30.

142. Illick, 1988, p. 346.

143. Earle, 1899/1993, p. 13.

144. Kolchin, 1993, p. 9.

145. Ibid.

146. Illick, 1988, p. 324.

147. Wishy, 1968, p. 12.

148. *Body of Liberties*, 1649/1889, pt. 83.

149. Demos, 1970, p. 102.

150. Cable, 1972, p. 10.

151. Illick (1988) states: "There exists no evidence that infants were swaddled in the seventeenth century, although there can be no doubt that it was the practice later" (p. 325). Although the egalitarian family favored by English settlers was dissuaded from swaddling infants, it seems highly unlikely to this author that millennia of swaddling was abruptly abandoned only to be reinstituted just as unpredictably one hundred years later. The presumption here is that women continued to swaddle babies.

152. Ibid., pp. 305–6.

153. Ibid., p. 307; Kevill-Davies, 1991, pp. 24–25.

154. Ibid., p. 338.

155. Earle, 1899/1993, p. 17.

156. Dunn, 1920, pp. 68–69.

157. Illick, 1988, p. 346.

158. Pinchbeck and Hewitt, 1969, p. 209.

159. Illick, 1988, pp. 336–37.

160. A. Trafford, Unwed motherhood. *Washington Post*, 8 January 1991.

161. Pinchbeck and Hewitt, 1969, p. 107.

162. Coldham, 1992, p. 46.

163. Ibid., p. 106.

164. Schorsch, 1979, p. 161.

165. Coldham, 1992, p. 5.

166. Ibid., p. 91.

167. Ibid., p. 121.

168. Ibid., p. 125.

169. Ibid., pp. 63–64.

170. Ibid., p. 155.

171. Bremner, 1970–1971, pp. 23–24.

172. There were no actual orphanages in the colonies until one was established in 1739 by the divines John Zubly and George Whitefield. Schorsch, 1979, p. 164.

173. Bremner, 1970–1971, p. 13.

174. Earle, 1899/1993, pp. 307–8.

175. Ibid., p. 328.

176. Ibid., pp. 332–33.

177. Scheffel, 1993, p. 30.

178. Beales, 1985, p. 10.

179. Kendall, 1973, pp. 15–16.

180. Earle, 1899/1993, p. 64.

181. Hawke, 1988, p. 69.

182. Earle, 1899/1993, pp. 69–70.

183. Ibid., 1930, p. 72.

184. Durantini, 1983, p. 167.

185. Earle, 1899/1993, pp. 80–81.

186. Schorsch, 1979, p. 104.

187. Pinchbeck and Hewitt, 1969, 1:39.

188. Earle, 1899/1993, pp. 126–30.

189. Ibid., pp. 140–42.

190. Ibid., p. 131.

191. Ibid., p. 150.

192. Ibid., pp. 161–62.

193. Ibid.

194. Ibid., p. 191.

195. Ibid., p. 192.

196. Durantini, 1983, p. 92.

197. Illick, 1988, p. 328.

198. Ibid., p. 327.

199. Earle, 1899/1993, p. 209.

200. This book was copied from *Youth's Behavior or Decency in Conversation amongst Men*, a French text, circa 1650. Ibid., p. 221. An American version was printed in Boston by John Boyle in 1775. The first half of the book addressed comportment, the second half was a catechism. Rothman, 1972.

201. Earle, 1899/1993, p. 221.

202. Other favorite titles were *The Book of Martyrs, Narratives of Conversions, Pilgrim's Progress,* and *The Bible in Verse.* Earle, 1899/1993, pp. 248–50; Darton, 1982, pp. 52–53. Thomas White wrote *A Little Book for Little Children* (1674), which closely mimicked Janeway's book. Sommerville, 1992, p. 57.

203. Earle, 1899/1993, p. 252.

204. Wooden, 1986, p. 57.

205. Pinchbeck and Hewitt, 1969, p. 40.

206. Earle, 1899/1993, p. 222.

207. Sommerville, 1992, p. 139.

208. Cable, 1972, pp. 30–31.

209. Bremner, 1970–1971, p. 193.

210. Pollock, 1987, pp. 86–87.

211. Cable, 1972, p. 40.

212. Ibid., p. 42.
213. Hostetler, 1993, pp. 23–51.
214. Ibid.
215. Ibid.
216. Ibid., p. 338. An infant afflicted with livergrown exhibited crying and "discomfort not alleviated by food or physical care."
217. Amt, 1993, pp. 154–57.
218. Pinchbeck and Hewitt, 1969, p. 60.
219. Ibid., p. 62.
220. Ibid., pp. 35–36.
221. Ibid., p. 68.
222. Ibid., p. 70.
223. Shapiro, 1977, p. 2.
224. Ibid., p. 15.
225. O'Malley, 1993, pp. 223–25.
226. Durantini, 1983, p. 127.
227. Hillebrand, 1926, pp. 261–68.
228. Ibid., p. 253.
229. Sommerville, 1992, p. 20.
230. Rose, 1991, pp. 59–64.

Chapter 8

Revolutions: The Chimney Sweep

❏ ❏ ❏

T HE AGE OF ENLIGHTENMENT, as the eighteenth century has been called, was also the age of revolution, marked by two concomitant phenomena that had the cataclysmic magnitude and power to irrevocably alter societal structures throughout the Western world. The mechanical innovations of what we call the Industrial Revolution produced machinery and factories that forced a metamorphosis in the world's rural and urban landscapes and in the lives of the people who dwelled within them. The impact of the political revolutions in North America and in France on the world's philosophical and solonic temples of thought continues to reverberate the world over in our own times, as does the social and economic impact of industrialization.

It is axiomatic that these revolutions drastically and dramatically changed political systems and thought and economic and societal structures. The consequences of these changes for children were monumental. The private and governmental turmoil that pervaded Europe obliterated considerations about child nurture, both socially and medically. Although pediatric pedagogy and care continued to evolve, the morbidity and mortality of children changed little.

As shall be discussed, in France the political revolution was tumultuous and vengeful, and, along with the political and social institutions, most of the civil rules and regulations that inform a society collapsed. Amid the general suffering, children were more frequently abandoned or abused as the ranks of the poor swelled. It took several decades for the ideals of liberty and equality that had fomented the revolution to be incorporated into the new French society. Only when civility at last returned to France did schools reopen and social programs to alleviate the suffering of children become revitalized.

In England, children primarily had to contend with the consequences of the Industrial Revolution. It began principally with the weaving industry but quickly expanded to several other product-oriented economies. Machines were constructed that facilitated and increased rapid production, and as the size of the machines increased, so did the power needed to drive them. Mill factories were built near rivers to harness waterpower, coal-driven steam engine factories were constructed close to coal mines, and the residual land-scape was dotted with new urban milieus where the people who worked in the new industries had to live. Just as all aspects of living were forced to adjust to the requirements of industry, the means of livelihood experienced profound change.

CHILD LABOR

The international economy blossomed with new and extended trade routes and products. In all, domestic and international economies flour-ished—but at the expense of human life, which was more than ever reduced to a commodity. Most ominously, slave and child labor were essential to the radical economic expansion that was taking place.

An early casualty of the industrial age was the apprenticeship system. A tradition that had evolved during the Renaissance to a level of refinement and stability gradually became outmoded. The guild apprenticeships that had been so respected, that had been carefully contracted and monitored, and so prized by young boys aspiring to be skilled workers—craftsmen—in time became an anachronism. Some activities of production endured, of course, for which a degree of skill or least practice was a requisite. To fill this need, less-rigorous, less-lengthy training courses evolved; they were called fellowships or journeymanships, and adolescents were schooled in relatively short periods of time in trades such as carpentry, tanning, dyeing, and bas-ketry.[1] Since only one in ten journeymen attended school to learn reading and writing, journeymen could be productive immediately, even as they grew in experience. Although they received no wages during the training period, room and board were provided them. Often junior tradesmen trav-eled in fellowship, or *en compagnonnages*, with their mentors to exercise and refine their skills in other towns.[2] There was a code of behavior to be obeyed, but the shortened training period and the absence of an indentured period of pay back work made fellowships an attractive alternative to traditional apprenticeships.

Mostly, families and, pointedly, children had to turn to factory work and semiskilled labor, such as brick making, in order to survive. In the industrial age, work evolved into fragmented, segmented, and unrewarding units of labor. Factory work involved gathering and then feeding raw material into grinding machines to produce goods that were collected and prepared for shipment to buyers. A high level of training was not required to perform these functions. The unskilled could perform the repetitive and automatic operations that machine work required, and for the most part, the inexpert eventually replaced the highly trained, self-sufficient, skilled craftsmen. Pride and pleasure in craftsmanship were replaced by longer work hours and tedious, dangerous, monotonous, poorly paid, and generally unrewarding work.

With regard to children, industrialists soon capitalized on the realization that many of the newly mechanized tasks required no strength and that children, a tantalizing source of cheap labor, were ideally suited for work that could be accomplished by concentration on mindless repetitive actions, as well as for work in which small size was a considerable asset. Children were sent to work as weavers, feather cleaners, wool combers, glove makers, shoemakers, rope-makers, chair bearers, brick carriers, miners, linkboys, canal towers, vendors, domestics, and as we shall see, chimney sweeps. Child labor increased exponentially for over a century; in the census of 1861 it was noted that one-third of all boys between the ages of five and nine years, and 50 percent of young girls in the same age group, were working full time.[3] Poor girls in industrial areas, for whom there was no schooling and no future, who could not work productively at home or who could not be placed as domestic apprentices, were sent to do mill work, including, as they grew older, spinning and weaving.[4] They began as very young children who, typically, were forced to work twelve to fifteen hours a day. Daniel Defoe (1660–1731) early on had commented, "scarce anything above four years old, but its hand were sufficient to its own support."[5]

Children as young as three, in fact, were employed in mills to pick up cotton waste and, with their small bodies, creep under machinery.[6] Bobbin girls had to change empty bobbins to keep up with the weaving frames grinding out their cloth. They were flogged if they fell behind the workings of the machinery. Small boys worked in the mills as well. A Norbert Truquin of Rheims recorded his experiences as a wool comber. From the time he was seven years old he arose at three o'clock in the morning and worked a merciless eighteen-hour day, from four o'clock in the morning until ten o'clock at night, using his teeth and hands to remove impurities from the wool.[7]

The evolving industrial-urban manufacturing complexes that relished the increased profits that cheap labor allowed exhibited no scruples in ensuring the steady flow of this labor. Children were especially vulnerable to exploitation and were bought, "rented," or simply snatched and made to work. There were no laws to protect them from being kidnapped. Parliamentarian William Smith introduced legislation in the House of Commons in 1814 that would make kidnapping—by then a commonplace phenomenon—a crime. He argued that children were stolen for the clothing they wore, for substitution, or as objects to be sold. It was an abomination that existing law at that time recognized as a crime only the stealing of clothing.[8]

Despite scattered attempts at reform, the exploitation of children by industry continued. The coal mining industry employed boys to work the surface pits, to sort and load coal wagons until they reached the age of twelve, when they were considered strong enough to descend the shafts. Their bodies still small, they were given the fearsome responsibility of shearing up the shafts of ventilation systems. They were hitched to coal-filled tubs and made to pull the tubs along wooden runners in the narrow tunnels. Even after wheeled wagons were substituted, the work was grueling.[9] Some children pulled their loads in tunnels that had clearances of twenty to thirty inches for distances of four to six miles a day. An investigating Royal Commission of 1842 finally reported that children dragged these wagons

. . . chained, belted, and harnessed like dogs in a go-cart, black, saturated with wet, and more than half naked, crawling upon their hands and feet, and dragging their loads behind them—they present an appearance indescribably disgusting and unnatural.[10]

Many of the children working the mines were young girls, "pushing and hurrying" carts loaded with coal. Eliza Coats was one of those who testified to the 1842 commission: "I hurry with my brother. . . . It tires me a great deal, and tires my back and arms. . . . I can't read; I have never been to school."[11]

The arduous, debilitating, and even dangerous occupations and abuses described by child witnesses and reformers exposed the brutality of industrialization, but this is not to imply that child labor originated in the eighteenth century. Evidence of child miners exists from as early as the Bronze Age and in classical Rome. Rycharde Whyttyngton at least had the grace to be scandalized when he wrote the Ordinances of the Hurers in 1398:

. . . seeing that some persons in the said trade have of late sent their apprentices and journeymen as well as children of tender age and others, down to the water of the

Thames and other exposed places, and amid horrible tempests, frosts, and snows, to the very great scandal, as well of the good folks of the said trade.[12]

The Parliament of Henry VIII (1491–1547) bound all vagrant children to obligatory apprenticeships, empowering judges to indenture such children until well past their majority:

And be it further enacted that it shall be lawfull for the saide churchwardens and overseers, or the greater parte of them, by the assent of any two justices of the peace aforesaid, to binde any suche children as aforesaid to be apprentices, where they shall see convenient, till suche man child shall come to the age of fowre and twentie yeares, and such woman child to the age of one and twenty yeares, or the tyme of her mariage.[13]

Finally, just before the dawn of the industrial age, Charles II (1630–1685) of England sought to keep vagrant children out of charity houses. He issued authority to parishes to send paupers back to their places of origin, and to deny admission to a charity house those who might require a prolonged stay:

. . . everyone who by the existing law shall be deemed a rogue and a vagabond, or an idle and disorderly person, or shall not be able to give a satisfactory account of him or herself, is to be considered as actually chargeable and liable be removed, as is also every unmarried woman with child.[14]

One of the major by-products of the Industrial Revolution was the aggravation of the formidable social problems associated with the urban-dwelling poor. Samuel Johnson's (1709–1784) London illustrates the point. The city's dark and narrow streets were fraught with danger, as robber bandits stalked the city's populace like a plague. Linkboys provided oil lamps lighting the way for coaches and pedestrians traversing the menacing streets. Their compensation for a safe delivery home or to an inn was, typically, two pence.[15] This service was regarded as dangerous enough work for adults. The jeopardy for children, even those hardened by tough city life, was far greater.

The number of destitute families increased, and unable to cope, parents increasingly gave over their infants and children to charity workhouses. Illegitimate children of the poor and the well-to-do also were deposited and disposed of there. Those with means were asked to pay the parish a lump amount of ten pounds. Apparently the money seldom went to the care of children. One parishioner observed: "the custom of giving small sums seems to have induced an opinion that a parish child's life is worth no more than eight to ten month's purchase."[16] A sample weekly menu from St. Martin in the Fields workhouse of 1800 (table 8.1) indicates that insufficient funds

TABLE 8.1
MENU FROM A LONDON WORKHOUSE, CIRCA 1800

Day	Breakfast	Dinner
Sunday	Bread and butter	6-oz. meat with greens
Monday	Milk potage	Pease soup
Tuesday	Milk potage	Beef and greens
Wednesday	Milk potage	Pease soup
Thursday	Milk potage	Beef and greens
Friday	Sweet gruel	Barley gruel with milk
Saturday	Milk potage	1-lb. plum pudding

were spent on children's sustenance and care.[17] Even the quality of the milk served was questionable—and questioned. Investigations confirmed that milk was diluted with water, followed by scandalous attempts to reconstitute or thicken the liquid with the wheat paste called "lumpy Tom."[18]

The child committed to the workhouse had a short life expectancy. In 1767 the House of Commons issued a report revealing that toddlers had a two-year survival rate of 7 percent. This scandalous workhouse mortality prompted Parliament to pass legislation enabling infants and toddlers to be sent preferentially to foster homes. It is estimated that this legislation alone decreased London child mortality by two thousand per year.[19]

Infants abandoned in London were given shelter in the combination home and school known as the Foundling Hospital[20] (figure 8.1), established by Thomas Coram (1667–1751) in 1739 as a charitable institution.* Other homes were founded along the lines of Coram's model establishment, such as those in Bristol, Exeter, Plymouth, and Norwich. Coram's institution grew to an enrollment of almost 1,100; all but 80 were boys. A large basket always was kept on a step just outside the door as a discretion that protected the anonymity of the presumably pained and embarrassed parents abandoning their young.[21]

It became a custom to name foundlings after the day they were abandoned and the parish or site in which they were found. There are multiple

---

*A forerunner of the Foundling Hospital was Christ's Hospital, founded in 1552. Established to "take oute of the streates all the fatherless children, and other poor mens children, that were not able to kepe them," the facility was quickly inundated and overwhelmed by vast numbers of illegitimate infants. (See chapter 7.)

Figure 8.1 Foundling Hospital of London (Besant, 1902).

registry entries, for example, that refer to "Saturday Cripplegate."[22] Some foundlings were named after benefactors, such as Coram's friend and supporter, the painter and engraver William Hogarth (1697–1764), who was considerably active in the affairs of the Foundling Hospital and became a governor. He was an "inspector of children at nurse" and was instrumental in ensuring that abandoned infants were delivered to the hospital.[23]

Parliament provided funds to give infants under eight weeks access to the home; but for older children, government support and private funding were uneven at best. Poverty did not guarantee admission, since entry criteria had been designed to exclude problematic street urchins and beggars. Children could not be admitted who had

. . . any adequate means of being educated and maintained, or who are lame, crooked or deformed, so as not to be able to take care of themselves, or have any infection, distemper, as leprosy, scald head, itch, scab, evil or rupture.[24]

The school attached to the Foundling Hospital was supported by taxes collected specifically for that purpose from the commercial fees required of cart owners who transacted business on the streets of London. Children admitted to the school who, over the years, showed promise received timely contributions from city officials for a fund that accrued to offset expenses for their university study.

The Female Orphan Asylum was opened in Lambeth in 1758. A Bow Street magistrate, John Fielding, having successfully equipped a number of boys for maritime apprenticeships, had turned his attention and energies to the plight of vagabond girls. Established for girls between nine years and twelve years old, the asylum's goal was to train them for domestic service. Over a period of ten years, however, only 125 girls found employment.

Another Fielding project, established in the same year, was far more successful. The Magdalen Hospital was founded to provide shelter for sixteen- to seventeen-year-old prostitutes and to train them for productive and respectable occupations. After three years of training and rehabilitation, the girls were "released" to friends or placed in households as domestic servants. Over a period of nearly forty years the institution gave refuge to 2,851 girls and placed 1,874 of them in service. A follow-up study, conducted between 1786 and 1790, revealed that 60 percent of these girls had not reverted to prostitution.[25]

There were girls from manifestly different backgrounds, of course, in domestic service. Mostly, they were workhouse orphans in the cities who toiled as nurses, kitchen aides, laundresses, general cleaners, and servants. Charity houses and orphanages on the Continent also commonly sent girls into service when they were twelve years old.[26] One-quarter of the population of London in the eighteenth century eked out a living as domestics.[27] By the time of the English census of 1881 there were 1,200,000 female domestics, of which nearly 100,000 were under fifteen years of age. There were far fewer boys in domestic service; those who were, generally worked in the stables or the gardens or served as pageboys.[28]

There also were children who did what now is referred to as casual labor—workers hired on a day-to-day or weekly basis, as needed. There were established sites where one could find prospective child laborers. At the Spitafields market for children, a child could be hired to work for a mere fourteen pence per week.[29] Bethnal Green's White Street market gathered twice weekly to offer children for hire.[30] Children's parents generally initiated labor contracts at these markets and, in fact, were known to borrow against their children's future earnings from market bosses.[31]

The primary conduits for cheap, casual labor, however, were the overburdened charity workhouses and schools that had contracts with factory owners to deliver child laborers. The Statute of Artificers actually had a provision that allowed days to be set aside when children could be inspected and approved for factory work. Although euphemistically labeled "apprentices," the children were little more than chattels.* An occasional factory owner personally reviewed and selected prospective child laborers and conveyed them

---

*By this time the apprenticeship system as it had been known had disintegrated, along with the honorable meaning of the word. There were, however, children being committed to long-term apprenticeships—so called because, in the strictest sense, the children had to be trained to the job. The reference also minimized a sense that they were being exploited; in fact, they were not thought of as child laborers, but often they were just as abused. Samuel Johnson's London was bustling with so-called apprentices—boys indentured from age seven until they were, in the city, twenty-one and, in the country, twenty-four.

directly to the factory. More generally, agents were sent to round up groups of children and take them, by barge or wagon, to holding areas where, like livestock, they were held until factory owners arrived to select the number of them needed at worksites. Charity and parish-house officials, eager to reduce the number of mental incompetents in their care, forced factory owners to accept one imbecile for every twenty children selected. There was no follow-up on these retarded children, and most mysteriously disappeared.[32] The following is a succinct and graphic description of the tragic conditions all of those children had to endure:

The children who were apprenticed out to the mill owners were fed on the coarsest kind of food and in the most disgusting way. They slept by turns, in relays, in beds that were never aired, for one set of children were turned into the beds as soon as another set had been driven out to their long and filthy toil. Some tried to run away and after that they were worked with chains around their ankles; many died and little graves were unmarked in a desolate spot lest the number of the dead attract too much attention.[33]

Mortality rates soared to outrageous levels in Johnson's London. The living conditions were abominable, and poor nutrition and neglect were commonplace. The London General Bill[34] (mortality report) of 1741 observed that nearly 50 percent of all London deaths were children.* Thirty-three percent were children under the age of two years. The figure went up to 43 percent when children three years old to ten years old were counted, and an additional 3 percent when ten to twenty year olds were added to the statistic. "Consumption" or pneumonia was responsible for 25 percent of these deaths; "fevers" caused another 25 percent; 15 percent died of confirmed tuberculosis, and 5 percent from smallpox. "Overlaid" was the recorded cause of death of at least seventy infants. In England overall, from 1730 to 1749, 74.5 percent of child deaths struck children under five years of age. That figure dropped to 63 percent in the years 1750 to 1769, and further still, to 51.5 percent from 1770 to 1789.[35]

Sporadic reform bills probably contributed to the diminution of deaths in the statistic reports. One such legislative effort intended to reduce child mortality was the Hanway Act, approved by Parliament in 1767. It authorized children to be placed in foster homes out of the city. Two shillings sixpence

---

*During the same period, death records in Barcelona indicate that 60 percent were children; 45 percent of recorded deaths were children in Paris, and 40 percent in Florence and St. Petersburg. In Dublin, a shocking 88 percent of all deaths were children. It is supposed that the routine use of 5 percent opium in the "composing bottle," a soporific similar to the Godfrey's cordial, was in part responsible for the appalling statistic. Jordan, 1987, pp. 81–82, 97–100.

per week was paid to foster parents who sheltered these children; additionally, anyone who provided a home for a pauper was rewarded with a gratuity of 10 shillings. Statistical documents in parish registries suggest that this act reduced London child mortality by two thousand deaths per year.[36]

The statistics clearly indicated what a casual observer would have known, that social class and occupation were the determining factors regarding longevity. Among the poor, most children did not survive adolescence. In Manchester, average life expectancy was eighteen years; in Dublin, eighteen and a half; and in Bradford, sixteen years. In contrast, a member of the English gentry could expect to live to be forty-five or older.[37]

Expenses to bury the dead were beyond the means of the average laborer. Burial "clubs" were instituted, providing insurance that paid for funerals and internment. They charged exorbitant rates to workers—eighteen pence monthly that paid out a meager four pounds for a child's burial. Children also could join a burial club for one penny per week. Some children were registered in more than one club, and suspicion was aroused when it gradually became evident that there was a large discrepancy in death rates of children from one to five years old among members (68%) compared to nonclub members (36%). Once it was mandated that only parents could be beneficiaries and cash benefits were reduced, the death rate of the insured and noninsured, in time, became consistent.[38]

Urban Workers and Vagrants

Another social scourge in London was the swollen number of vagrants and beggars on the streets. By the time of an 1803 census there were an estimated 15,288 beggars, of which the majority (9,288) were children. Fully one-third were believed to have come from Ireland.[39] Female beggars hired small children at sixpence to 2 shillings a day to join them on the streets, as it was thought their presence in a diorama of familial poverty and homelessness increased the kitty. Deformed children commanded a larger fee (3 shillings a day), and deliberate maiming of children, a ploy that had been recorded in Roman times, was not uncommon.[40] Forced avulsion of teeth brought a "double" profit. A pitiful-looking edentulous child was an asset for begging, and the teeth could be sold as prosthetics for the mouths of the rich. A cartoon published by Thomas Rowlandson in 1790 shows a Georgian dentist transplanting "live" teeth into the mouth of a rich patron, while in the background can be seen children clasping their jaws following extractions.[41]

There is a record as far back as 1761 of a London woman convicted of putting out the eyes of several children to increase their "begging" value; she was given a mere two-year sentence.[42] In France, some infants were sold to witchcrafters, who mixed drugs and the blood of infants as an elixir for long life.[43] In Germany, the practice of intentional maiming was euphemistically termed "angel-making" in an 1849 newspaper feature:

In order to earn money by means of them and then get rid of them, children are mutilated intentionally and made sick, so that by their misery they will inspire pity on the arm of the female beggar and finally die . . . people just want a way to make some money, and because they know no other way of earning a living, they make angels.[44]

Beggars had no use for waifs beyond the toddler age, and having lost their appeal as mendicants, these children were forced into child labor. They found ready work at construction sites and factories where industrializing towns were expanding into cities. At one point in the late eighteenth century, more than thirty thousand children worked alongside their elders in brickyards.[45] From five o'clock in the morning until eight o'clock at night, children removed bricks from the kiln and stacked them. Or they labored as brick carriers, mold runners, or "puggers," who trod on clay to make it more malleable. A child could make four hundred to five hundred bricks a day, each weighing nine pounds. The compensation for this work was seven shillings per week.[46]

Despite the grueling work, child brick laborers at least escaped the exposure to infectious diseases endemic in most of the burgeoning industrial plants, where workers toiled in unsanitary, filthy environments in confined spaces. In cotton mills tuberculosis was widespread. By the time statistics were compiled by the Mulhouse Industrial Society in 1853, the epidemic conditions had become institutionalized. Twenty-nine percent of children between the ages of ten and nineteen died of tuberculosis. Of that number, half worked in the mill.[47] In textile factories, linens and calico were dried at 150 degrees Fahrenheit that produced ambient temperatures of 90 degrees. The oppressive heat and lack of ventilation exacerbated chronic respiratory infections.[48] Poor lighting and the carbon-laden air (from burning wax and oil) produced eye irritations and infections.

As might be expected, the health hazards attributable to squalid working conditions found in industrial England were commonplace in the industrial environment throughout Europe. In Madrid, *colicos saturnicos* was the term for glass- and metalwork-induced bronchitis. Glaziers and painters everywhere were poisoned with mercury. Tanners were infected with anthrax. Legions of afflicted laborers, debilitated by their illnesses, gave up their infants to foundling homes. These babies rarely survived there more than six months and can be counted, along with their parents, as victims of industrial hazards.[49]

This interpretation also applies to infants who were taken to the factories. In Russia, mothers breast-fed their young on the job. In Germany, the conditions in a glass factory were described by a fourteen-year-old: "I saw children of all ages in this dust-crammed place. Even new-born babies were there. . . . Most of the little ones lay in a cradle near the polishing boxes and screamed unbearably."[50] French mothers working the mills banded together to hire nurses to watch their infants. One mill in Tourcoing, during the 1850s, hired a *surveillant* to watch babies and toddlers.[51] Either left at home while family members were at work or taken to the factories, a large number succumbed to respiratory failure from opium cordials and treacles given to crying infants to quiet and sedate them[52]:

It is impossible to say how large a proportion of the unnatural deaths that now mow down our infant population is due to the habitual administration of poppies, of Godfrey's Cordial, and such narcotics. Their deaths are registered as due to the emaciation, the brain disease, the gastric fever, the tabes, the hydrocephalus, which are the slowly induced results of poisoning. Perhaps some notion of the extent to which the practice is still carried may be formed from the frequency of inquest in those cases where the safe limits of temporary narcotism have been exceeded, and an overdose has palpably resulted in death.[53]

The new breed of child worker spawned in the eighteenth and nineteenth centuries by the industrial age became victim to innovative forms of child cruelty and exploitation, and nowhere was this more pathetically visible than in cities. The well-documented plight of children who were urban chimney sweeps provides an excellent illustrative example. These sad tykes were an ubiquitous presence in every city. Their usefulness to the trade proved more compelling than the reports of their suffering, which were sporadically publicized, or the number of reform bills that were legislated in their behalf. It appears that the only relief English society gratuitously offered these children was a day of rest and merriment on May Day, when, showered with pennies, they marched together with milkmaids in an annual Jack-in-the-Green parade.[54]

Some child sweeps were pressed into service at four years old, while small enough to penetrate particularly narrow flues. These little boys generally were sold into the trade by their parents:

> When my mother died I was very young
> And my father sold me while yet my tongue
> Could scarcely cry, "weep!, weep!, weep!"
> So your chimney I sweep, and in soot I sleep.
>   William Blake (1757–1827)[55]

Other already indentured children were sold by workhouses as so-called apprentices to master sweepers. Some children were simply kidnapped. Children who specialized in extinguishing chimney fires earned more money than others, but they were at greater risk of suffocating.[56] There were recorded instances of fires deliberately started after a child entered a chimney flue to forestall any hesitation in proceeding forward. Asphyxiations resulted, many reported in France, where the children sweepers were referred to as *les petits ramoneurs*.[57] Charles Dickens's (1812–1870) Oliver Twist was sold by his workhouse keeper to a Mr. Gamfield who commented to officials:

Boys is wery obstinit, and wery lazy, gen'lmen, and there's nothink like a good hot blaze to make 'em come down vith a run. It's humane, too, gen'lmen, acause, even if they've stuck in the chimbley, roastin' their feet makes 'em struggle to hextricate theirselves.[58]

Chimney climbing required a thorough conditioning and hardening of the skin, a process described by a Mr. Ruff to an English investigating reform commission of 1863:

This is done by rubbing it, chiefly on the elbows and knees with the strongest brine, close by a hot fire. You must stand over them with a cane, or coax them by a promise of a halfpenny &c if they will stand a few more rubs. At first they will come back from their work looking as if the caps had been pulled off; then they must be rubbed with brine again.[59]

Chronic weeping dermatitis, anthracitic bronchitis, and often scrotal cancer were the legacies to these children in adulthood. In a world without workers' compensation, pensions, health insurance, or even care for these chronic, debilitating, and often fatal illnesses, chimney sweeps, along with countless other victims of the machine age, endured lives of hardship and faced early death.

There had been early manifestations of public outrage that materialized as early as 1817, when testimony was presented on 22 June of that year to a parliamentary hearing investigating the abuse of children working as chimney sweeps:

It is in evidence that they are stolen from their parents, and inveigled out of workhouses; that in order to conquer the natural repugnance of the infants to ascend the narrow and dangerous chimneys, to clean which their labour is required, blows are used; that pins are forced into their feet by the boy that follows them up the chimney, in order to compel them to ascend it, and that lighted straw has been applied for that purpose; that the children are subject to sores and bruises, and wounds and burns on their thighs, knees, and elbows; and that it will require many months before the extremities of the elbows and knees become sufficiently hard to resist the excoriations to which they are at first subject.[60]

Despite legislation intended to ban the use of children as sweeps and the reverberations of public outcry from outraged reformers, children continued to be victimized in a "profession" that was finally made redundant by the commercialization of coal gas and oil that curtailed greatly the burning of wood and coal in households.

This reference provides a convenient opportunity to comment further on the unremitting and catastrophic problems of city dwelling for poor children, where ignorance, disease, crime, and despair are the harsh consequences of the world's inability to provide for all of its inhabitants, let alone its most vulnerable souls. The pursuits of both family-connected and vagrant children in Third World countries today bear striking resemblance to the pitiful options available to their eighteenth- and nineteenth-century counterparts. Wherever survival is a day-to-day struggle, a vast number children, many of them vagrants, are left to fend for themselves with piecemeal service jobs, vending, and hiring themselves out as domestics, errand runners, street sweepers, and the like. Where these endeavors fail to sustain them, other approaches, some of them nefarious and criminal, are attempted. Most commonly, begging provides a means to meet the barest essentials to sustain life.

One category of child laborers—street entertainers—had been part of the urban street scene in Europe since the Middle Ages. During the nineteenth century, however, an influx of a new breed of street musician came from one particular country. Indentured Italian children began to appear on the streets of London and Paris around 1815. The children initially provided entertainment with cheap and easily transported trained white mice, to a musical accompaniment. For two to three years these children were expected to entertain passersby in the streets for coin donations. Each of them, threatened by severe penalties, was required to deliver a fixed amount of money to a *padrone* (a sardonic misuse of the Italian word meaning "father surrogate").[61] In Paris these children at first were called *les savoyards*, then, *les petits italiens*. Londoners referred to them as "Italian organ boys." Even New York in 1870 had a number of these children, called "little slaves of the harp." Worldwide, between 1860 and 1870, there were about three thousand to six thousand of these children working the streets.[62]

This system in itself was abusive of children, and many suffered further mistreatment at the hands of the *padroni*. As the public became more aware of the plight of these children, international reform measures were introduced. The London-based Italian Benevolent Society established a repatriation program to remove them from the streets and from their abusive operators and return them to their homelands. By 1874, France had passed a Children Labor Law prohibiting street trade among children under sixteen years of age. The intention of New York's "Padrone Act" of 1874 also was to protect these children. The Congress of the United States, in June 1874, passed legislation called "An Act to Protect Persons of Foreign Birth against Forcible Constraints or Involuntary Servitude." Unhappily, it was difficult to enforce this law, since a requirement of proof that a child had been inveigled to leave Italy was required, and this proof rarely was available.[63] The Society for the Prevention of Cruelty to Children was inspired to override this law's ineffectiveness by sponsoring a comprehensive bill, an "Act to Prevent and Punish Wrongs to Children," that prohibited the abuse of children by employing them as beggars, peddlers, or, specifically, entertainers:

. . . any person having the care, custody, or control of any child under the age of six-teen years, who shall exhibit, use, or employ, or who shall in any manner, or under any pretense, sell, apprentice, give away, let out, or otherwise dispose of any child to any person, in or for the vocation, occupation, service, or purpose of singing, play-ing on musical instruments, rope or wire-walking, dancing, begging, or peddling, or as a gymnast, contortionist, rider or acrobat . . . shall be guilty of a misdemeanor.[64]

Church choirs and schools were exempted from this law, and the city's mayor was authorized to grant an exemption for special situations. For example, exemption applications were approved by the mayor in 1888 for the world-renowned twelve-year-old Polish piano prodigy, Josef Hofmann (1876–1957) and for the great violinist and composer, Fritz Kreisler (1875–1962), who was then thirteen years old.

By 1873 the Italian government had itself become instrumental in pre-venting the emigration for work purposes of its children when it enacted the Law of 21 December 1873. The law in general prohibited the employment of children in itinerant trades and provided harsh penalties of fines and prison terms for those convicted of consigning children to Italian nationals or foreigners for purposes of *professioni girovaghe*.[65]

A mid–nineteenth-century newspaper reporter, Henry Mayhew (1812–1887), detailed the working lives of child vendors in his book *London Labour and the London Poor* (1851). Child hawkers of both sexes wandered the streets selling their wares of fruit, vegetables, flowers, firewood, buttons, and clothes-pins. Others sold services such as crossing sweeping (figure 8.2) or specialized in hailing cabs or running general errands. Some of these children were organized by philanthropic groups into specific "trade" brigades, or "juvenile guilds" if you like. Members of the shoeshine brigade belonging to the Shoe-black Society were provided uniforms and assigned to locations throughout the city. Some of the brigades amassed funds to establish hostels for the

Figure 8.2
Crossing sweeper, by W. R. Firth.
COLLECTION OF AUTHOR.

urchins, and for nearly fifty years thereafter a multitude of small newspaper boys, parcel carriers, and street sweepers—referred to as "broomers"—toiled long hours under the protection of these benevolent societies. When powerful legislation mandating school attendance was passed and youngsters left the streets, the brigades, their usefulness exhausted, were dissolved.[66]

Cottage Labor

Child labor in the home, to be sure, always had been part of the survival scheme of working families. As a consequence of the Industrial Revolution, homebound labor and its offshoots took on new and significant ramifications. Young girls, who traditionally had child care and general household chores, at this point were needed to assume full responsibility for the home so that the parents could work in the factories or in other people's homes or fields. Girls, moreover, were given these burdens at younger and younger ages.

There were opportunities for homebound occupations engaged in by entire families, such as canal towing for those who lived near the bustling waterways. There were approximately forty thousand canal-boat children who worked on the narrow barges that plied the English canal system. Unschooled, they worked long hours handling the horses that towed the barges and at times towed along with the animals. Children with less strength were assigned the task of cranking open and closing the locks.[67] Entire families lived and worked on these boats, and some families on barges that had become overcrowded sold or gave away children to other work boats.[68]

A cottage industry evolved that kept families together at home and out of the factories. Contract work, generally on spinning wheels, was engaged in by all of the members of a family, who toiled long hours at home for little wages. Usually, the father of the house controlled the workers and salaries, delivering finished goods to district managers who coordinated the work activities of several cottages. Luise Zietz, growing up in Germany during the 1870s, described what it was like:

We had to pluck apart and oil the raw wools . . . to be put through the carding machine two times. A pair of dogs, who switched off, drove this machine by a large treadwheel, and when one of the large dogs died on us, we ourselves had to get down in the wheel. . . . We crouched hour after hour on the low stool behind the spinning wheel at the horrible monotonous and exhausting work, just spinning, spinning, spinning.[69]

Prior to industrialization, poor farming families in rural areas always relied on child labor on their small, cooperatively worked parcels of common land. In family settings, children performed their assigned chores and tasks and shared meal times and respites. The industrialized mentality, greedy for cheap, collective labor, applied the psychology of industrial expansion to agriculture, recognizing an opportunity to use gang labor as "harvest machines." Entire families were contracted to work the fields for a set fee. In the industrializing world, the poverty was such that even the meager earnings of children were crucial to family survival. In 1843, for example, a single Norfolk farmer could earn twenty-five pounds per year; a team of man and wife added five pounds to that sum, and a family with four children could raise total earnings to nearly fifty-one pounds a year.[70]

Landed farmers contracted with gang masters to have crops harvested. After prices and the dates by which work was to be completed were agreed upon, gang masters selected work gangs, assigning them to farms. The presence of overseers guaranteed productivity. The men, women, and children often walked miles to the job sites and, after every working day, wearily walked back to their homes. Many of the children were only four and five years old when they were pressed into gang work. An investigating commission in 1843 heard this testimony from the father of an eleven-year-old girl:

[My daughter] has complained of pain in her side very often; they drive them along—force them along they make them work hard. Gathering stones has hurt my girl's back at times. Pulling turnips is the hardest work; they get such a hold of the ground with their roots; when the land's strong it's as much as we can do to get 'em out, pull as hard as we can pull. It blisters their hands so that they can hardly touch anything. . . . My girl went five miles yesterday to her work, turniping; she set off between seven and eight; she walked; had a piece of bread before she went; she did not stop work in the middle of the day; ate nothing till she left off; she came home between three and four o'clock. Their walks are worse than their work; she is sometimes so tired, she can't eat no victuals when she comes home.[71]

ADVOCATES OF REFORM

By 1867 the parliamentary Gang Act banned the hiring of English children under eight years of age. Moreover, in response to reports that young girls had been molested on occasion, the law mandated that they be protected by gang mistresses supervising on the job. Private gangs were not regulated, however, and the gang system flourished until 1876, when the Education Act of that year illegalized the employment on farms of children under ten years old. The system, however, did not disappear until modern machine technology—the reaper, binder, and harvester—replaced the children who harvested the fields.[72]

As the sporadic efforts of reform hitherto discussed indicate, there was a considerable body of enlightened and progressive thinkers in England who, mindful of the pain and suffering endured by small children in the workplace—indeed, by the working poor in general—were vocal advocates of reform. The influences on their thinking were several: John Locke's philosophy of reason and his theories of child nurture and education; the French moralist and romantic Jean-Jacques Rousseau's (1712–1778) passionately written theories on education, and the intellectual, moral, and emotional freedom and independence of children in *Émile* and, in *Du contrat social*, his views of an ideal society; Thomas Paine's (1737–1809) *The Rights of Man*, published in 1792, in which he set forth his theories on equality and personal liberty. Widely read, with views embraced by serious thinkers everywhere, Paine's treatise contributed to the foment of political reformation on two continents and to social reformation on at least one. In *The Rights of Man*, Paine proposed one social-reform program that had the markings of a form of child-welfare program. His idea was to provide financial support to poor families to enhance the quality of life for them and for their children. To this end he suggested heavy taxation of wealthy landowners—100 percent of all income above twenty-three thousand pounds per year. In Paine's view, the income from this money would provide every newly married couple a one pound stipend. At the birth of each infant, the parents would be given an additional pound, plus four pounds per year per child under fourteen years of age. Paine argued that such a program would keep children independent from parental dictates and that there would be sufficient income to the family that would obviate the economic dependency on child labor. Economic stability in the family, moreover, would prevent children from being turned out to the streets by their families as vagabonds. Paine also thought that there would be ample funds to set aside for children's educations. Finally, Paine's proposal offered a fifteen pound grant to every child as he or she reached majority.[73]

Writers such as the mature William Blake and the youthfully idealistic William Wordsworth (1770–1850) and Samuel Taylor Coleridge (1772–1834) initially supported Paine's ideas; but each in time disavowed the plan, believing it would undermine the traditional family unit and erode the work ethic, and from these would result a loss of fundamental Christian and human values.[74]

In varying degrees, then, the writers of the early, middle, and late nineteenth century were inspired by the ideas of Locke, Rousseau, and Paine in general and about children in particular. Their works were infused with their belief in the singular innocence and goodness of childhood and society's obligation to provide for their needs. Some writers used their influence as novelists, such as Charles Dickens, and poets, such as Elizabeth Barrett Browning (1806–1861), to expose societal ills. Consider Browning's anti–child-labor poem, an elegy that mourned the waste of children's childhood in factories[75]:

> Do ye hear the children weeping, O my brothers,
>   Ere the sorrow comes with years?
> They are leaning their young heads against their mothers,
>   And *that* cannot stop their tears.
> The young lambs are bleating in the meadows,
>   The young birds are chirping in the nest,
> The young fawns are playing with the shadows,
>   The young flowers are blowing towards the west—
> But the young, young children, O my brothers,
>   They are weeping bitterly!
> They are weeping in the playtime of the others,
>   In the country of the free.
>   "The Cry of the Children" (1843)

There was, additionally, a strong degree of pressure for reform from moralists, as much due to concern about children being corrupted by the lax and unprincipled environment of the workplace as it was concerned about the cruelty of their exploitation. The absence of education and the resultant ignorance of Scripture were thought appalling, and several individuals and groups pressured the government to enact educational reform laws. Promoting Christian values was a prominent theme in England, and this fervor was infused into much of the attempts at social reform to benefit the poor. The Society for Promoting Christian Knowledge had been founded in 1699. Believing that early indoctrination to the precepts of the Anglican church, Bible education, and anti-Catholic propaganda[76] were the key to producing good and virtuous Christian Englishmen, they established free schools throughout England. By 1740 there were over two thousand of these schools.[77]

Spurred by the abolition of slave trading in 1807 and of slavery in 1833, reform movements gained further momentum. The passionate interest and work of parliamentarian Lord Anthony Ashley Cooper Shaftesbury (1801–1885) spearheaded the movement. The Factory Act was enacted in the same year that slavery was abolished and in the same spirit—to eradicate conditions in which children were, in effect, treated as slaves.[78] Children under nine years old were barred from work in mills, and the law mandated that children between nine and thirteen years of age attend school for a minimum of two hours a day.[79] Health certificates were required of children hired to work in textile factories. Protection under the law for children ended when they were fourteen years old, the age considered by the Royal Commission as the end of childhood:

. . . the period of childhood, properly so called, ceases, and that of puberty is established, when the body becomes more capable of enduring protracted labor . . . in general at or about the fourteenth year young persons are no longer treated as children; they are not usually chastised by corporal punishment, and at the same time an important change takes place in what may be termed their domestic condition . . . they usually make their own contracts, and are, in the proper sense of the word, free agents.[80]

The Factory Act's exclusion of adolescents evoked a scathing critique from Richard Oastler in 1835:

That infamous Parliament, wept over the Black Slaves, and laughed at the sufferings of the poor Infant White Slaves! They could not afford to emancipate the Factory Children, because their killing labour was required to fill the King's Treasury; but they could afford to emancipate the Black Slaves, and to pay for it Twenty Million of Pounds, out of the Earnings of the Poor, over-worked Factory Children.[81]

Despite the Act's shortcomings, it was a catalytic force in helping to evolve the concept of universal education for children. In conjunction with pressure from social reformers, the Factory Act forced industrialists to ameliorate workplace conditions for children in several regards. One measure—the establishment of schools within industrial plants—was an apparent concession to reformers' demands for moral instruction of the young. As a cynical note, it may be said that industry intuitively understood that outcry over violations against humanity had little sway when society at large favored conditions that seemed integral to what was perceived as economic necessity. Industry also understood, however, that it was no match for the power of society's Second Estate when concerns about spiritual deprivation aroused moral indignation. Therefore, when puritanical views became incensed about children's exposure to moral and spiritual vapidity in factories, industry capitulated by establishing schools.

Industrial schools gave mere lip service to altruism, however. For the most part, the schools had two basic cores common to all: instruction in the manufacture of products to which was devoted longer hours and greater emphasis than the second core, instruction in reading. Other elements of education generally were ignored. The industrial schools adopted what was in fact an old tradition. The old occupational guilds had provisions in their own apprentice schools for special preapprentice programs expressly designed to train poor children. In the reign of Charles II, a school of mathematics was founded, endorsed by the king, to train England's future sailors. An apprentice program for the poor* that originally assigned ten boys a year to merchant ships had grown, by 1870, to number approximately eighteen thousand boys indentured as merchant-marine apprentices.[82] Goldsmiths, skinners, and fishmongers were among the trades that formed training schools for the poor. In France, stonemasons, joiners, and locksmiths established industrial schools.[83]

Some children of middle-class parents were excluded from these programs unless they paid for their training. Some parents borrowed tuition or applied to their "Box" clubs for funds. These were credit unions of a sort that provided assistance in times of need, stress, illness, or to help with schooling. Members paid subscriptions from one to five pence per week, and met monthly to decide the merits of loan petitions.[84]

---

*Well-to-do families also apprenticed their sons as seamen. Bayne-Powell, 1938, p. 267. John Stedman's short elegy of 1774 expressed grief over the loss to the sea of his son, a seventeen-year-old apprentice:

> O agonising pain! pain never felt before,
> My manly boy, my John, my sailor, is no more.
> Still let me mourn with hope,—and God adore,
> With hope to see my sailor once again,
> Floating on seas of bliss,—thro' the azure main,
> Till then, a short farewell, my lovely boy
> Thy shipmates' darling, and thy father's joy.

(Pollock, 1987, p. 126)

From 1840 to 1845 the City Mission Society opened schools, referred to as Ragged schools,[85] in the inner cities from Portsmouth to London "for children raggedly clothed." More than nine thousand children were enrolled in these schools, providing much-needed respite from streetlife. Some of the schools formed unions similar to the brigades of Mayhew and sent legally organized troops of street sweepers and bootblacks to work in the city without fear of intervention by police or, as street children called them, the "eslop."* The only means of support for these schools, financial and otherwise, derived from local patrons and residents who welcomed and approved of the aim to rid the streets of youthful vagabonds and renegades. The Ragged schools remained popular and active until the Forster Education Act of 1870 generated interest in schools for the education of the overall population and gradually replaced the earlier ones.[86] Meanwhile, education specifically for poor girls was sponsored by the Society for Promoting the Employment of Women, founded in 1859. Girls were taught letter writing, calculations, and ledgership to prepare them for administrative positions that would provide them with a decent living.[87]

❏   ❏   ❏

In Ireland they still refer to it as The Great Famine.† In the mid-nineteenth century, the scourges of poverty and disease and the cruelties associated with child labor were the common destiny of Ireland's children. But these tragedies became secondary considerations in the face of devastation to all of the population. When the country's major sustaining food source, the potato, became blighted (1845–1847) by a catastrophic epidemic of a parasitic fungus, *Phytophthora infestan*, famine ensued. Mass malnutrition and starvation engulfed the country, which in three years was reduced from 8.5 million to 6.5 million people. When possible, families escaped to other countries—mainly to America. Most families, without the means to emigrate, were forced to remain to suffer starvation. The Workhouse Union was one of several charitable organizations that made valiant attempts to distribute food donated by other countries to relieve the suffering. The effort, however, was sporadic and inadequate. Children under fifteen years were rationed

---

*Street children had an entire patois formed by letter reversal, of which "eslop," meaning "police," was an example. Jordan, 1987, p. 131.

†An outbreak of typhus occurred at about the same time, and therefore some call it the "Irish famine fever." *Lancet* 2000 (supplement iv); 354:37.

to up to one-half a pound of oatmeal a day—when the grain was available. Sadly, cornmeal from America served to compound problems associated with malnutrition. For families able to obtain it, the Indian meal, which was low in vitamin B complex and vitamin A, comprised almost 20 percent of their total food intake.[88] Pellagra and xerophthalmia (dry chronic conjunctivitis), especially for the children, were the consequence.

Ruled by England politically and economically for centuries, Ireland's people historically had been ignored by the sovereign nation. During the famine years, Irish political and civic leaders vainly petitioned the English Parliament to halt the exportation of Irish cattle and grain so that they might be used for famine relief. Concerned about principles of free trade and private enterprise, Parliament was deaf to humanitarian pleas, and exports continued while hundreds of thousands succumbed to starvation.[89] Throughout Ireland the "industrialized" cottages harbored sick and weakened children, found lying on the floors, without the energy to walk to a food collection center, much less work. They were edematous, bloated, or marasmic. A description of two children in an 1847 journal kept by Elihu Burritt (1810–1879) graphically chronicled the nature of the tragedy:

The cold, watery-faced child was entirely naked in front, from his neck down to his feet. His body was swollen to nearly three times its usual size, and had burst the ragged garment that covered him, and now dangled in shreds behind him. The woman of the other family, who was sitting at her end of the hovel, brought forward her little infant, a thin-faced baby of two years, with clear, sharp eyes that did not wink, but stared stock still at vacancy, as if a glimpse of another existence had eclipsed its vision. Its cold, naked arms were not much larger than pipe stems, while its body was swollen to the size of a full-grown person. Let the reader group these apparitions of death and disease into the spectacle of ten feet square, and then multiply it into three-fourths of the hovels in this region of Ireland, and he will arrive at a fair estimate of the extent or degree of its misery.[90]

In London, word of the cachexia and starvation of Irish children and their parents was widespread, but inexplicably, the English government did little to alleviate the wretched conditions, disdainfully attributing political agitation as a cause of the disaster. The famine in Ireland appears only to have given social agencies and Parliament in England the incentive to reexamine and improve the nutrition of the children in English workhouses. An impartial analysis might construe that socially concerned Englishmen were preoccupied, even immobilized, by the degree of poverty, economic depressions, and the cycles of starvation in its own population. The numbers of vagabonds, urchins, and abandoned children in the streets of London certainly exhausted relief resources. The 1851 English census numbered four million children three to twelve years of age, of which about eight hundred thousand were listed as urchins.[91] For more than a century, from this population of children emerged trained pickpockets, burglars, pimps, and prostitutes, providing thinly veiled fictional material for England's most prominent writers and novelists, from Joseph Addison (1672–1719) and Henry Fielding (1707–1754) to Charles Dickens. In 1745, for example, a Harry White of St. Bride's Parish operated a Fagin kitchen of child felons. In April of the same year, a member of the group, thirteen-year-old Sarah Bibby gave evidence against a fellow burglar, twelve-year-old Jack Price, for stealing razors. Price was sentenced and jailed. Bibby went on to give evidence against other thieves. Six were hanged.[92] Her motives for turning state's evidence were uncertain but probably were intended to thin out other gangs. Eight months later, however, Bibby herself was caught stealing and transported to the colonies.[93]

Early in the nineteenth century, increasing childhood crime prompted the establishment of the Society for Investigating the Causes of the Alarming Increase of Juvenile Delinquency in the Metropolis. A report was issued in 1816 that cited five factors as causes of delinquency:

The improper conduct of parents.

The want of education.

The want of suitable employment.

The violation of the Sabbath and gambling.

Poor governmental policies [including] the severity of the criminal code, defective policing, and police corruption.[94]

Believing that more humane penal enforcement would contribute to the reduction of juvenile delinquency, social progressives proposed that separate prisons be built for young offenders. In 1818, plans for a reformatory were presented to the home secretary by members of the Society for the Improvement of Prison Discipline and for the Reformation of Juvenile Offenders. Parliament was not persuaded that a brick-and-mortar solution would ameliorate the problem of delinquency, and the society's proposal was dismissed. The general principle, however, survived, and several years later, at the end of the Napoleonic wars, a plan was devised to isolate young delinquents on England's surplus warships. Vessels such as the *Fighting Temeraire* were decommissioned and reoutfitted as jails.[95] As existing structures, the ships could be adapted for incarceration at a fraction of the cost of building juvenile prisons.

In 1825 the *Euryalus*, berthed at Chatham, was pressed into service to house, initially, 320 convict boys under sixteen years of age in order to separate them from the company of hardened adult convicts. The boys' daily regimen appeared to be highly structured and purposeful:

Weekdays:

5:30 All hands called, ports opened, hammocks lowered.
6:00 To chapel and prayer.
6:30 Breakfast, $^1/_2$ daily allowance of oatmeal, $^1/_3$ allowance of bread, mess shift clean up.
7:00 On main deck for exercise.
7:30 Work, making of convict clothing.
9:30 Personal toiletry and bunk inspection.
11:30 Meal, $^1/_2$ oatmeal, $^1/_3$ bread, back to work.
5:30 School for two hours.
7:30 Evening hymn, $^1/_3$ bread.
8:30 Back to ward, secured for night, watch set.

Saturday:

Weekday regimen followed. Cheese given as dietary supplement;
time allocated for cleaning the ship and personal clothing.

Sunday:

Saturday regimen, plus morning church service and catechism lessons.[96]

An eyewitness report on shipboard conditions and the treatment of the boys, however, was condemnatory. Edward Brenton (1774–1839) was a retired navy captain and founder of the Children's Friend Society when he wrote a scathing indictment:

Who would have believed in the existence of such a ship, and for such a purpose, as the *Euryalus* at Chatham:—417 boys, between the ages of nine and sixteen, confined as convicts for seven years, each to cost from £70 to £100.—A floating Bastille;—children in iron cages, who should have been in a nursery garden;—children pining in misery, where the stench was intolerable. . . . And while unfortunate girls are starving for want of needlework, these boys are confined in dungeons, making shirts for convicts.[97]

Although, by 1827 more than one hundred boys had been taught to read and write,[98] the efficacy of the ship-based reform program continued to be questioned.[99] J. H. Capper, a clerk for the criminal division of the Secretary of State, was asked about the program's success at reform and responded: "I am sorry to say it has been very indifferent; for eight out of ten that have been liberated have returned to their old careers."[100] Despite the criticism, the *Euryalus* program survived until 1846.*

Ships in any case could accommodate only a limited number of boys, a mere percentage of those found delinquent by the courts. Prisons remained the primary corrective institution. The need for a separate facility for juvenile prisoners finally was acknowledged by the enactment of the Parkhurst Bill in 1838, which set the foundation for a prison designed for boys with terms ranging from two to fifteen years. The Summary Jurisdiction Act of 1847 further facilitated separate arraignment for children under fourteen years old. This law was followed, in 1854, by the Youth Offenders Act, which stipulated that children under sixteen years old had to be treated differently within the penal system. A boy sent to jail remained there only for fourteen days before being moved to a reformatory, where he was protected from the influences of hardened criminals and where, in the process, he could receive some education in reformatory classrooms.[101] There were three categories of prisoners in the Parkhurst reformatory: probationary boys, new arrivals who were watched and weighed; ordinary boys, compliant and not subject to punishment; and refractory boys, who received coarse discipline. As the prison population increased, so did the number of refractory boys. They were dealt with in three ways: they were put in solitary confinement, sent to adult prisons, or transported abroad. In 1843 a newly assigned warden reclassified the youthful prisoners into five categories: general ward boys, fourteen years and older; junior ward boys, under fourteen; probationary boys; refractory boys; and infirmary ward boys. A minimum schooling program for all of the boys was required, as were outdoor work and exercise. Multiple escape attempts by those working outdoors motivated the reinstatement of leg irons (not used since 1840). The flood of criticism that followed lasted for years.

In part a response to this criticism, authorities increased the transportation of prisoners to the colonies. Officialdom had viewed banishment from the homeland as the ultimate punishment, and had applied this measure only to the truly incorrigible. The youthful prisoners, ironically, welcomed such action, a fact not overlooked by prison authorities who, by 1846, used this attitude as an incentive for good behavior. The then-warden of Parkhurst wrote: "The desire to get their liberty by removal to the Colonies for good conduct has a very strong influence over the prisoners here."[102] As vagabond English children a century before had been shipped to the American colonies,

---

*A private philanthropic program sponsored by the Marine Society to train "poor distressed boys" as merchant marines began in 1828 on the ship *Solebay*. The fact that the program is ongoing is a mark of its success. As late as 1986 a ship, the *Jonas Hanway*, was commissioned by the founding society to continue training boys.

the Parkhurst boys now were sent to Tasmania, New South Wales, western Australia, and New Zealand. The French sent their undesirable children to Algeria. The Portuguese shipped out their delinquents to the East Indies.

EDUCATION

Dramatic contrasts form with any discussion of the lives of the well-to-do and their children in the dawn of the industrial age. Servants, governesses, private tutors were all a casually accepted part of growing up for girls and boys from families of means and/or title. The lives of these children were comfortable and sometimes filled with opulence and luxury. The rigors of life encountered by them generally were limited to socially agreed upon notions of discipline and how character was formed and developed.

Daughters in these families traditionally had governesses in the home to teach them social and domestic skills along with some of the academic subjects. Boys, too, often had private tutors, especially those boys who were destined to inherit titles and/or estates.[103]

By 1798 it had become somewhat *en vogue* to enroll young ladies of more modest means in boarding schools. A certain Mrs. Cross advertised her school near Finsbury Square in London in the *Times*:

Mrs. Cross respectfully informs the gentry, merchants and her friends in general that her school will recommence on Monday 22nd inst. and that she has accommodation for five more yearly ladies as boarders. She hopes that the flattering success she has met with these fourteen years in educating the daughters of some of the first families of the City (to whom references may be had) will be no small recommendation to those ladies and gentlemen who may honour her with their patronage. The house stands in a very airey and healthy situation, three doors from the Square, of which Mrs. Cross has a key and in which the young ladies will walk as often as convenience and the weather permit.[104]

Schools for girls ranged in cost from thirty to one hundred guineas per year, a considerable sum for the times but less than the cost of home tutoring.[105] The Queen's Square School, with an enrollment of over two hundred girls, commanded fees of a minimum one hundred pounds per year.[106]

Institutions of learning for boys from "good" families in "England's green and pleasant land" during the eighteenth century were the "public schools," where boys were sent to prepare for university life and to be formed into "gentlemen." Legendary institutions like Rugby, Westminster, and Eton had shockingly little adult supervision. Boys were boisterous, rowdy, and often overtly rebellious. Upper classmen notoriously extorted money and favors from younger boys and often abused them physically.

Joseph Addison's lament about the treatment of children in grammar schools applied to life in the public schools:

. . . I have very often with much sorrow bewailed the misfortune of the children of Great Britain, when I consider the ignorance and undiscerning of the generality of schoolmasters. The boasted liberty we talk of is but a mean reward for the long servitude, the many heartaches and terrors to which our childhood is exposed in going through a grammar school. Many of these stupid tyrants exercise their cruelty without any manner of distinction of the capacities of children or the intention of parents in their behalf. (*The Spectator*, 30 August 1711)

By the time Thomas Arnold (1795–1842) became headmaster of Rugby more than a century later, the abuses had become virtually institutionalized. Arnold announced on the day of his appointment: "My object will be, if possible, to form Christian men, for Christian boys I can scarcely hope to make."[107]

In place of positive efforts to engage students in constructive activity, rebellious patterns of behavior in these schools was handled with corporal punishment that increased in frequency and intensity. Flogging was a fact of life in eighteenth- and nineteenth-century England, and few boys were able to escape from punishing blows.[108]

In France, the *absence* of corporal punishment in the schools was a proud feature. Advertisements for boarding schools frequently boasted a no-flogging policy. The state committed itself to this position in 1834 and again in 1851 with declarations that primary school students were not to be struck. The law of 6 January 1881 was the most emphatic: "It is strictly forbidden to inflict corporal punishment of any kind."[109] In private homes, in contrast to public institutions, whipping continued to be a common form of discipline.

In England, although parents expressed concerns about corporeal punishment, they were concerned more about the introduction of their boys to the "sins of the flesh." Town prostitutes were readily available, and in the schools, homosexuality and masturbation were commonplace. The loss of "virtue and innocence" was a general anxiety. Collectively, parents insisted that, in order to "temper passions" and inculcate discipline, schoolmasters should keep students busy and active, with little idle time to fuel their passions. Samuel Knox (1785–1832) spoke of keeping students occupied "even to fatigue"[110]:

Irregular and intemperate passions indulged at a boyish age, will blast all the blossoms of the vernal season of life, and cut off all hope for future eminence.

Exercise and temperance are necessary both for the vigour of body and mind, and to these important ends ought even their recreation to be directed. With such they ought to have sufficient time to satisfy themselves even to fatigue, and such muscular exertions as should tend to promote growth, hardiness, and strengths of the body. (*Of Liberal Education*)

The fears of their children's sexual indoctrination in public schools were so strong for some families that their boys were sent to private, smaller institutions, where schoolmasters lived among the boys. The implied surveillance and vigilance against sexual corruption gave peace of mind. The curriculum was standard: schoolmasters taught French or Italian in addition to Latin, in preparation for a "Grand Tour" of the Continent, and a more humane discipline was practiced. However, schoolmasters in these institutions had uneven skills and varied in their pedagogical resolve. A public school education, therefore, remained the more desirable.

Several public schools, such as Rugby and Eton, began to solicit sons from mercantile and professional families to form a more heterogeneous mix with the aristocratic population it traditionally had educated. By the nineteenth century, therefore, these schools, while enduring as institutions primarily for the sons of the aristocracy, had a more diverse student body and were less provincial.[111]

Despite the reputations of public schools as "bastions of privilege," the opinion of many wealthy parents was that these schools conferred inadequate educations. Students, to be sure, became well versed in some of the classics and studied a little mathematics but little else. The common parental solution was to send the boys to the Continent, where, it was thought, they could broaden and cultivate their impressionable minds and gain worldly experience. The itinerary of the "Grand Tour," as it was called, could be as simple as a crossing of the English Channel to France or an extended traverse of much of the Continent, especially of Italy. Boys traveled from London to Dover to Calais and on to Paris for a prolonged stay; then Switzerland, Vienna, Baden-Baden, and finally, Italy—considered the jewel of the Grand Tour. Dr. Johnson is illuminating on the point: "A man who has not been in Italy is always conscious of an inferiority."[112] The Italian sojourn typically included languorous visits to Venice, Verona, Siena, Florence, Rome. Joseph Addison's admonition that such travel was a dubious educational experience for young school-age boys was largely unheeded:

Nothing is more frequent than to take a lad from the grammar and taw and under the tuition of some poor scholar, who is willing to be banished for £30 a year and a little victuals, send him crying and snivelling into foreign countries. Thus he spends his time as children do at puppet shows, and with much the same advantage in staring and gaping at an amazing variety of strange things, strange indeed to one, who is not prepared to comprehend the reasons and meaning to them; whilst he should be laying the solid foundations of knowledge in his mind, and furnishing it with just rules to direct his future progress in life, under some skillful master in the art of instruction.[113]

Older students, it may be supposed, profited from this prolonged, intense, and complex polycultural and polyglot experience. Certainly, John Locke (see chapter 7) recommended that the tour be taken between the ages of seven and fourteen.[114]

POSTREVOLUTION FRANCE

Social and political turmoil on an unprecedented scale in France, with reverberations and bloody civil and church anarchy throughout Europe, muted the voices of children's advocates as the nineteenth century dawned on the Continent. At the same time, at least one scholar credits the postrevolutionaries with vision and with concern about children and their futures:

Times of wars and political upheavals are always cruel for children. They suffer terrible hardships. But one must in all justice pay tribute to the concern of the Revolutionaries for the fate of young people, which always occupied their minds. At a period when so many problems demanded their attention, they never lost sight of educational questions; they were constantly concerned with children, not in order to pamper them but to prepare them for the parts they were to play in the future.[115]

The new republican order in France began by secularizing the then largely Roman Catholic country. With regard to marriage, the state rejected the 1579 Ordinance of Blois that had incorporated the Council of Trent's rules on marriage, requiring the announcement of wedding banns, the presence of a priest and of witnesses, and the registration of marriages.[116] Only the latter regulation was preserved, and marriages in the republic now were performed only by municipal officers. The attendance of a priest to serve as a witness to a marriage was allowed as a courtesy, but such presence was neither essential nor sanctioned by the state. The secularization extended to laws that forbade Christian names for children. In the heat of revolutionary fervor, families in any case turned to the revolution or to antiquity and literature in selecting names, and there were children called Brutus, Lykourgos, August the Tenth, and Constitution.[117] In the eleventh year of the republic, on 1 April 1803, the state relented, undoubtedly under pressure, with a proclamation that children could, after all, be given names of saints. Curiously, one aspect of the law persisted until 1993: local *mairie* could prohibit under the law names of personages and mythical figures predating the Middle Ages.[118]

The ninth-century B.C. Spartan, Lykourgos, influenced philosophical thought regarding child nurture. Louis Saint-Just (1767–1794), a zealous advocate and ideologue of the French Revolution, best expounded widely held principles on the subject:

The child belongs to the Patrie.
The child must be educated communally.
The child belongs to the mother until five, thereafter, to the State forever.[119]

Saint-Just posited his idyllic plan for a state-controlled Spartan pedagogy and Spartan philosophy. As children grew, any body contact, touching, or embracing was frowned upon, said Saint-Just. Children neither were to be flogged as punishment nor rewarded with hugs. He expected children to say little, thereby exercising a strict economy in the use of language. Saint-Just advised that the primary education of children should begin between the ages of five and ten years, to include reading, writing, and swimming.* He added agriculture and military science for students from ten to sixteen years, with required practical experience working in the fields and participating in infantry maneuvers. Since he believed that children belonged to the republic, he thought parents should be prohibited contact with their children until adolescence ended, lest youths be tainted by family influences. To achieve this end, he prescribed a state-run apprenticeship system for young men seventeen to twenty-one; at the latter age they could be emancipated. Saint-Just even had envisaged an emancipation ritual celebration called the Festival of Youth, in which young adults would prove their endurance by swimming across the River Seine.[120]

It was impossible for Saint-Just's pedagogical ideals to be widely adopted due to the severe budgetary constraints in the new regime. Favoring public education, the Law of December 1793 decreed mandatory attendance in free primary schools. The Law of November 1794, only one year later, was forced to remove the mandatory clause of the prior bill and permitted non-state-run schools. By October 1795 state coffers were so depleted that a new law was necessary; it required tuition fees of all who attended school so that desks and books could be bought and teachers could be paid.[121]

Rural children had few aspirations regarding education. By 1829 one-third of rural communities still lacked a primary school. Even in those

---

*It was an unusual combination of disciplines. Conspicuously missing was arithmetic. Perhaps swimming was Saint-Just's effort to conjoin the "cold-dippings" of the Stoics with the physical prowess of the Gauls.

places where the state had been able to fund and support schools, many farmers were opposed to sending their children to school. Farmers stubbornly insisted that children were needed at home, to sow, harvest, thresh, shepherd, and so on—all of which took precedence over education. In 1850, only 50 percent of French children between five and fourteen years old attended school.[122]

The cruelty and horror of violence in the young republic were especially visible in big cities, where postrevolutionary executions were celebrated by bloodthirsty crowds. It was not unusual for children to witness either executions or their aftermath—beheaded bodies transported in open carts across town. During the Reign of Terror, between May 1793 and June 1794, 1,255 were guillotined publicly in the Place de la Revolution. Over the next two months, an additional 1,270 lost their heads.[123] So inured were children to the events and so calloused the populace that miniature toy models of "La Sainte Guillotine" were sold shamelessly in the streets, together with living sparrows as victims.[124] But lack of funds with which to build the new political state was the dominant influence on a population newly liberated from the oppression and excesses of the old regime. Children were the most innocent of victims in a country filled with despair and poverty. Urban orphans of war and revolution, "street-wise" and precociously hardened children, often became street urchins and vagabonds, *gamins* who worked as messengers, street vendors, acrobats, and scavengers who collected wood, glass, rags—anything that could be sold. Metals picked from streams paid best, at five centimes per pound.[125] Many street urchins, perpetually hungry and ragged, resorted to forming gangs of petty thievery.

In the antireligious climate of the revolution, the country's infrastructure had been allowed to collapse. The religious and private charity houses had been nationalized or closed. These circumstances exacerbated a long-existing problem, as a new wave of abandoned infants flooded Paris. It was not until 1795 that the government was able to address the situation with a law enacted on June 28th, which, in the spirit of the new egalitarian republic, designated all children *enfants de la patrie* and mandated the "moral and physical education of *enfants trouves*."[126] These infants, moreover, were to henceforth be referred to as *orphenlins*, replacing the stigmatized term *enfants trouves* and its connotation of illegitimacy. Regardless of what the abandoned children were called, their numbers continued to overwhelm Paris.

In 1811 the French government, now administering an empire, required all hospices throughout the country to actively encourage the deposit of abandoned infants at local facilities in order to lessen the numbers reaching Paris. To this end, orphan *tours*, convent-like turntables resembling the Italian *routas*, were ordered installed.* The Napoleonic decree of 19 January 1811 reserved 4 million francs for asylum programs throughout France for the dual purpose of installing orphan *tours* and for providing care for the abandoned, defined as follows: "Article I. The children whose education is entrusted to public charity are: first, Foundlings; second, Abandoned children; third, Poor orphans."[127] The program may have had success, since, in fact, fewer abandoned infants arrived in Paris. Problematically, the instances of abandonment continued to increase all over the country. In 1809, 67,000 French infants were abandoned; by 1835 the number had nearly doubled to 121,000. Ironically, the *tours* were blamed for the increase, in the belief that, in facilitating anonymous abandonment, they encouraged immoral behavior![128] After several decades of debate on this point, by 1862 all of the *tours* were closed.

Abandonments now were by appointment: formal hours were established during which infants could be admitted to foundling homes. There was an office manned by a person known as the *garde du tour*, an official title and position until 1943. The *garde du tour* records indicate that approximately one-third of infants were delivered by the mother, 17 percent by police, 16 percent by priests, and 14 percent by midwives.[129]

The Office of Public Assistance during the 1850s and 1860s became the depository for orphaned and bastard children. These children thereafter generally were placed in rural homes or in vocational schools. Although officials frowned on admitting anonymously abandoned infants to hospices and asylums, the budgetary increases in welfare expenditures indicate that *l'assistance publique* was ineffective in curtailing the practice.

In the Second Empire, the age limit of eligibility for welfare benefits for children was adjusted from thirteen to twenty-one. The reasons were twofold: first, the government believed that money invested by the state should be repaid to the state with service from the adolescents who were being cared for; second, providing youths with employment at newly formed rural institutions, called the *colonies agricoles*, served to keep them out of urban environments, where, it was feared, there were smoldering insurrectionary influences.[130]

There was also, it would seem, an environment that bred criminal or at least intractable behavior, since Paris and its environs were replete with

---

*This remains an age-old problem of mankind. In March 1999 the German government passed legislation increasing the term of imprisonment to eight years for infanticide, and hospitals placed incubators outside their doors for unwanted babies—the modern *routas* or *tours* if you will (*Lancet* 1999; 353:570). In Hamburg, one hospital actually installed a modern *Drehlade*.

reform schools for boys.[131] Moreover, illegitimate, orphaned, and abandoned youths mingled in these "schools" and in detention homes with boys institutionalized by their fathers. Paternal power, reminiscent of the *patria potestas* of Roman times, had been absolute in the Bourbon regime. Louis XV's (1710–1774) ordinance of 15 July 1763, for instance, authorized fathers to petition for deportation to the Island of La Desirade in the French Antilles of any child "who has fallen into conduct that might endanger the honor and tranquility of the family."[132]

Despite postrevolutionary attempts to limit authority, paternal consent was required for virtually all endeavors. The most oppressive governance was the right of a father to send a son to a detention home or to jail. Under sixteen years of age, children could be held for one month, without review; over sixteen, they could be held for up to six months. In either situation, the state required no proof of charges. There were instances in which youths languished in institutions until reaching their majority.[133]

In nineteenth-century France, adolescence was viewed as a dangerous time of life, when youths were prone to develop antisocial behavior. Guillaume Duprat (1872–?) wrote a widely circulated book entitled *La Criminalité dans l'adolescence. Causes et remedes d'un mal social actuel,* in which adolescents were labeled intrinsically defiant, inclined toward obstructive behavior, and inherent vagabonds.[134] It is no wonder that the state did not challenge a father's wish to banish a son from the home. Like English families, upper-class French families worried about their progeny being indoctrinated on matters of sex, sexual perversities, and other vulgarities. English tutors or governesses often were employed for adolescents to thwart this eventuality. Out-of-control children were isolated and, when all else failed, sent to boarding schools.

There were few boarding-school establishments for girls. Traditionally, middle- and upper-class French girls were instructed by their mothers. The comments of Henriette Campan, a former lady-in-waiting to Marie Antoinette (1755–1793), reflected this belief:

There is no boarding school, however well-run, no grand national establishment, no convent, whatever its pious rules which can give an education comparable to that which a girl receives from her mother when the mother is well-informed and when she finds her sweetest occupation and her true glory in the education of her daughters.[135]

Mothers inculcated a mystique—a feminine mystique, if you like—at an early age. There were several manuals of comportment specifically for adolescent girls published in nineteenth-century France to complement mothers' teachings. The *Manuel de la Maitresse de Maison* (1821) and *La Jeune*

Maitresse de Maison (1836) are examples. In 1787, Mme. Gaçon-Dufour described the method and the results:

. . . having been taught by our mothers the difference of our sex from that of men—that is, understanding by being called a little girl or mademoiselle, that we were not at all little boys or men, we start to be reserved in our games, controlled in our walk, to lower our eyes, even to blush.[136]

Few girls had extensive schooling outside the home. Professional training for the commercial world of trade was available to girls, but those who decided on that course "stepped down" in public estimate.[137] Similar attitudes prevailed throughout the Continent, in Germany, Prussia, Spain, and Italy and was expressed in manuals and in literature. A cross-cultural sentiment about a proper lady was as follows: "What a sweet creature! She does not pretend to have opinions of her own."[138]

Repressed by society's ethos, many young girls throughout Europe took refuge in a private life of romantic and secret fantasy and penned their thoughts and feelings in florid script on perfumed pages, while the boys formed secret societies and clubs. Popular diaries were in the form of "birthday books." Birthday books generally had printed inspirational poetical excerpts interspersed with blank pages, so that special events and milestones could be recorded. It can be supposed that diary entries mainly were about fictional and imaginative romances, since the principal vocation considered seemly for young women of all classes was marriage. One aspect of a growing girl's duties was to complete a trousseau, including personal and household linens. Parents of girls had to accumulate dowries for them, for without one, spinsterhood was all but guaranteed.

Girls were considered mature women when they became engaged to be married. On the day of a formal engagement, a young lady was presented with a basket of gifts, called *la corbeille*.[139] Poor, country girls could expect the same ritual honor but on a more modest scale. The onus of raising dowries was, of course, problematical for the poor. Girls routinely were sent off to other households or farms to work and earn a small *pécule* to set aside for marriage. Prepubertal girls earned fifteen to twenty centimes a day, and at adolescence earned forty to sixty centimes a day. (The average wage for adult males was between 120 and 150 centimes a day.[140]) In Italy, the agricultural wage earners, called *braccianti*, sent their nubile children to work in their employers' houses as servants, or *garzoni*.[141]

As the Industrial Revolution on the Continent drastically changed the lives of agricultural workers, children's lives also were affected, and for most, detrimentally. In France, the textile industry, as in England and America, was the major employer of children. Overall, children under the age of sixteen

TABLE 8.2
CHILD LABOR IN SOME FRENCH INDUSTRIES (c.1850)

Industry	Percentage of Children Employed
Textiles	18.7
Mining	7.7
Foundries	8.7
Ceramics	12.2
Paper mills	11.5

comprised one-third of the country's workforce. Even after an attempt at reform in an 1839 state inquiry into child labor,[142] the numbers remained high (table 8.2). The figures for 1845 list nearly 145,000 children under sixteen working in French industry.[143]

French industrialists, along with their English counterparts, believed that children, with their small bodies and nimble fingers, were indispensable to industry production. One French factory inspector reported, referring to the *porters* who shuttled glass between the furnace and the glassblower, that:

A man would be unable to replace him; the child runs with his cane to the annealing furnace, and nearly always returns at the run to pick up another. His small stature and his agility permit him alone to perform this service. One can say that with its existing equipment, the glass industry cannot survive without children.[144]

More to the point, a child was paid approximately one-third the male adult salary.[145] About one-third of these children worked alongside their parents. Some, however, were placed in other factories, to protect a portion of the family income in the event of a plant closing.[146] Closings were particularly common between 1820 and 1850 due to market fluctuations.[147] Since shortages of child labor occurred periodically, industrialists in rural areas often arranged long-term contracts with poor families to ensure a steady and reliable supply of child workers. Shamelessly, these contracts, lasting four or more years, were called "ecole gratuité d'industrie."[148]

As in England, French foundling homes and orphanages in urban areas provided child labor for industry. One cotton spinner applied to the administrator of the Hospice Nationale in Amiens for one hundred children between the ages of ten and twelve. He informed the administrators that he was well practiced in handling children, since two hundred of them were already employed in his factory. Administrators *paid him* fifty francs per child for the purpose of feeding, clothing, and providing them with health care. Girls were cloistered in convents to do silk work under the supervision of nuns. Those twelve years and older were fed, clothed, and tutored in the catechism and silk weaving. In the year 1860, up to forty thousand girls lived and worked in these convents. By 1900 the number had grown to one hundred thousand.[149]

Reform efforts in France were ongoing after about 1828, the year in which Jean-Jacques Bourcart (1801–1855) wrote:

. . . It is noticeable that children employed for too long in the workshops have feeble bodies and feeble health, and that, not having time to look after their education, they cannot develop morally.[150]

As the earliest of French child-labor reformers, Bourcart emphasized his belief that reforms would not impinge on industrial production. He argued that shorter workdays would increase efficiency, and less fatigue would increase the quality of the work. He emphatically expressed the view that the welfare of children and that of the future of France were at stake in the matter.[151] A contemporary, Alban de Villeneuve-Bargemont (1784–1850), concurred on all points and further demanded that working children be given educational opportunities.

Louis Villermé (1782–1863), who investigated the textile industry first-hand between 1827 and 1840, was the most influential reformer in France. The vivid descriptions he gave of laboring children and their travails were seminal in persuading legislators to draft child-protection statutes.[152] Although Villermé realized that laws controlling child labor might impose financial hardships on some families, he concluded that the criminal treatment of children was an overriding consideration: "The remedy for the wasting of children in industry, for the homicidal abuse of which they are subjected, can be found only in a law."[153]

The state did not respond for a long time. Intuitive fear that industrialization and economic progress would suffer if meaningful remedial legislation were enacted made lawmakers reticent to effect change. Never was a laissez-faire approach so tantalizing: cheap child labor fueled one-third of industry; remove it, and prosperity itself would be at risk. Years of abuse were to transpire before there were serious efforts to meliorate conditions for children in the workplace and in the classroom. In small and gradual steps, after some improvements had met with compliance and acceptance, further reform was advanced. The strategy was to make child-labor reform part of education reform. To that end, a law was passed requiring proof of literacy for any child accepted for industrial work. The same bill set the minimum age for employment at eight years and prohibited night work before the age of twelve.[154]

The next step, the *loi sur le travail des enfants* in 1841, applied to industries employing twenty or more people. Attendance at school became mandatory for children under twelve. Eight- to twelve-year-old children could work only eight hours a day. The *loi* also limited the workday to no more than twelve hours for children twelve to sixteen years old.[155] One is left with the question: how many hours a day did these children work before the law was passed? It is, in any case, a moot point, since both industrialists and parents were noncompliant, disregarding the law on all points. In the prefect du Nord, a single factory inspector was hired to force industry compliance; but with one inspector responsible for major cities like Lille, Roubaix, Tourcoing, and Armentieres and their thousands of worksites, the move was largely a symbolic gesture.[156]

In 1851 an Apprenticeship Law was passed, in what seems an anachronism since apprenticeships were a tradition in Europe dating back to the Romans and had been institutionalized as the way in which craftsmen were trained since the Middle Ages. This new attempt to define the nature of a contract and obligations incurred by both master and apprentice probably reflects how completely the time-honored system in France had crumbled:

The master must conduct himself toward his apprentice as a good father of a family, oversee his conduct and his morals, both at home and outside . . . shall employ the apprentice only in labors and services that are connected to the practice of his profession . . . never employ him in those that would be unhealthy or beyond his physical capacity.

The duration of the actual work may not exceed ten hours a day for apprentices under the age of fourteen. . . . The apprentice owes his master fidelity, obedience, and respect; he must help with his labor.[157]

The *loi sur le travail des enfants et des filles mineures dan l'industrie* of 1874 prevented boys and girls sixteen to twenty-one from working in the manufacturing industries, and it raised the overall minimum work age from eight to twelve years old. Sunday was declared a holiday for all. Children under twelve years could not work the mines. A daily minimum of two hours of school was mandatory. There were significant fiscal penalties for violations of any part of the law:

Manufacturers, directors or managers of industrial establishments, and employers who have violated the stipulations of the present law . . . shall be prosecuted before the correctional tribunal and punished with fines of from sixteen to fifty francs.

The fine shall be assessed as many times as there were persons employed under conditions contrary to the law.[158]

Factory managers and foremen circumvented this law as well, finding ways to hide children from inspectors.

At the same time, the several legislative attempts at reform had had a cumulative and positive effect on public opinion. Private philanthropic measures such as Henri Rollet's Patronage de l'Enfance et de l'Adolescence, George Bonjean's Societé pour l'Enfance Abandonnée et Coupable, and Jules Simon's Union Française pour le Sauvetage de l'Enfance bolstered the society's growing conviction that the state had an obligation to protect and to provide for its children. Public approbation and support facilitated the passage of subsequent child-welfare laws. The *lois scolaires* in the 1880s guaranteed, at no cost, compulsory education for children between the ages of six and thirteen. Laws were passed granting L'Assistance Publique unprecedented authority to relocate abused children.[159] The law of 24 July 1889 safeguarded the *moralement abandonnés* by empowering the state to remove children abused by vice, drunkenness, or crime. The bill served to weaken the unchallenged privilege of *patria potestas* and, importantly, prescribed punishment for abusive parents who beat and/or starved their children.[160]

The society and institutions of France now were firmly committed to the protection of France's children. In 1886 the Third Republic lifted restrictions on admissions to the Hospice Enfants Trouvés and formalized social programs for unwed mothers.

The work of Le Sociéte Protectrice de l'Enfance, founded in 1865, and Le Societé d'Allaitement Maternelle had helped over the years to reduce infant mortality, but it was clear that far greater efforts had to be made. As the twentieth century approached, France became aware that its most precious resources were being lost by untimely and preventable deaths. In 1892, Pierre Budin (1846–1907) opened a center in Paris for routine postnatal care, where babies were examined and treated and mothers were given instruction in hygiene and nutrition. Budin's work contributed to a significant reduction in infant mortality—from 178 to 46 per 1,000 population in five years. In 1894, when milk stations, called *goutte de lait*, were established, there was a dramatic drop in child mortality from diarrheal diseases—51 percent to 3 percent.[161] The two programs' success in raising the rate of childhood survival was widely acclaimed, and other countries studied and adopted their format. Even governmental bureaus were impressed that such programs more than justified the national expenditures. Still, it seems clear that France had lagged behind other countries' child-welfare efforts to such a degree that, despite heroic attempts to reduce child mortality in France, the population from 1891 to 1910 increased less than one million, while Germany added over fourteen million to its population, and England grew by seven million.

❏ ❏ ❏

A glimpse into conditions in other European countries indicates that by the end of the nineteenth century, like France, the rest of Europe had begun to feel shame regarding the instances of child abuse. The progress made by child-welfare movements in England, America, and France catalyzed many countries to examine the quality of their children's lives. Sadly, all of Europe had allowed a millennium of abuse before efforts at reform were made.

The traditional use of child labor in agricultural and urban-industrial settings persisted, for example, in Scandinavia, despite a 1739 compulsory education law* that established a system of country-wide rural schools for the instruction of the fundaments—reading, writing, and arithmetic.[162] The law met with resistance by rich and poor, exemplified by parliamentary conservative August von Hartmansdorff's deprecating comments to the Swedish Riksdag[163]: "If peasant children are supposed to be in school . . . when will they learn to be peasants?"† Some towns grudgingly built proper schoolhouses, but many communities resented the imposition of forcing children to attend school, and schoolhouses conspicuously were not constructed. Mostly, communities were too poor to erect buildings, and itinerant teachers traveled the countryside to households that had been designated as classrooms. A hundred years later, in 1840, a government study reported that 15,000 students attended two hundred rural schools, and the bulk, 160,000

---

*In 1736 the Norwegian king, Christian VI, had mandated that all Christians be confirmed. This sacrament of the Lutheran Church, however, could be given only after schooling was completed. The 1739 legislation was a direct consequence of the king's decree.

†A similar sentiment was expressed by Isaac Watts (1674–1748) in *An Essay Towards the Encouragement of Charity Schools* (1728):

As the Children of the Rich in general, ought to enjoy such an Education as may fit them for the better Businesses of Life, so the Children of the Poor . . . should not be generally educated in such a Manner as may raise them above the services of a lower Station.

Also, in *A Discourse on the Education of Children and Youth* he said,

I limit these instructions, especially such as relate to this world, by the station and rank of life in which children are born and placed by the Providence of God. Persons of better circumstances in the world should give their sons and their daughters a much larger share of knowledge and a richer variety of instruction than meaner persons can or ought.

children, were being taught by itinerant teachers.[164] Of these, only 35,000, or about 22 percent, were literate and could write, evidence of sustained community indifference and resistance to education.*

Farm families, then, continued to rely on children for many farm operations, from planting and harvesting to the major occupation—herding animals. Children seven years old learned shepherding skills. As they grew older, they were sent off alone, from April until November, into mountain valleys to graze the animals. The youngsters had to stave off carnivore attacks on the herds, endure foul weather, resign themselves to monotonous diets, and cope with the lonely isolation. Several reports of bestiality shocked the Swedish clergy. An encyclical decree ordered preachers to instruct shepherds in morality and moral behavior and, whenever possible, to encourage them to seek different employment. The dependence on boy shepherds, however, was too ingrained in this predominantly agrarian culture for any serious attempt at change to occur.[165]

The oldest major industries in Scandinavia were mining and lumbering, and, to be sure, child labor formed part of the workforce. Children also were sent to work in match and textile factories, where girl workers were favored, and in tobacco and glass plants. Children who did not go to school worked in these factories ten hours a day, five hours if they attended school. None of the industries guaranteed long-term employment, with the exception of lumbering. Employment in lumbering mills was a kind of apprenticeship in which boys were trained to engage in all aspects of the trade. More than 50 percent of the boys continued to work in the mills as adults.[166]

In Spain, Ireland, and Italy the conditions were as bad, if not worse, than in the more powerful countries such as Germany, England, and France, and the problems—crop failures, industrial abuses, disease, and large destitute populations—were common to all. Resistance to and suspicions about change infected the exploited as well as the exploiters and all of the indifferent in between. Gradually, the necessity of commonly shared child-labor laws became evident in all of the industrialized nations. Although Germany had passed child-protection laws as early as 1853, it was not until 1878 that they were being uniformly enforced with consistent and mandatory factory inspections. A Europe-wide coalition for reform did not take place until 1890, when an International labor conference was held in Berlin. The rec-

---

*There is a certain irony in the fact that Sweden in the twentieth century has been a champion of child welfare and rights. Sweden led the field in institutionalizing sweeping child-welfare programs now found in countries such as Germany and France. Swedish maternal—and paternal—home leave, day-care programs, health programs, and even laws on car restraints for children, bicycle helmets, and laws against striking a child are all models for the world to study and emulate.

ommendations of the attendees were to raise the minimum working age to twelve, ban night work for children younger than fourteen, and fix the maximum workday at six hours.[167] The opposition this resolution received from industry was equal only to industry's power and political influence to thwart universal compassion and justice for children in the workplace. Germany, however, went further, and by 1891 more exacting laws raised the minimum working age: only children thirteen and older who had completed primary school could be employed.[168]

France initially lagged behind England in enacting legislation, but by mid-1880 well-established and enforced laws protecting children in the workforce were in place. In Japan, by the time the first factory laws that affected children were passed in 1911 and implemented in 1916—well after Japan had industrialized—98 percent of children between the ages of six and thirteen already were in school.[169]

The European consensus on the issue was not reached successfully until the first quarter of the twentieth century. Until then, increasing numbers of poor families were locked into exploitative labor contracts, endured foul working conditions in factories and cottage sweatshops, and suffered economic deprivation and debt, urban disease, and despair, much as they always had.

PEDAGOGUES

By the mid-eighteenth century, experiments in child-rearing practices, a continuum of late-seventeenth-century reexamination of how children should be nurtured,[170] became fashionable in upper-strata families throughout Europe and particularly in England. With a dash of aristocratic panache, the nobility and well-to-do women assumed egalitarian maternal roles with fervor,[171] and mothers from other classes soon followed suit. Wet nurses were dismissed and maternal nursing was resumed, supplemented by formula feedings. Swaddling was eschewed. Bathing infants in cold water became popular, as did inoculations against smallpox. Mothers elected to spend more time with their children. The French resisted adopting maternal nursing and continued to favor the *nourrice*, or wet nurse. They persisted in using *maillots*, or clouts, for their infants, swaddling their young for the first eight or nine months.

In England, John Locke had influenced the popularity of cold baths. He believed they prevented rickets and convulsions. Known practices of Stoics, Celts, and Vikings[172] and other, anecdotal evidence were the authorities on which he based his contention that cold bathing was salubrious.[173] His thinking appeared to be reasonable:

. . . everyone is now full of the miracles done by cold baths on decayed and weak constitutions for the recovery of health and strength, and therefore they cannot be impracticable or intolerable for the improving and hardening of bodies of those who are in better circumstances. (*Some Thoughts Concerning Education*)[174]

In any case, it was a popular, if frigid, part of household rituals. One household in Scotland in 1807 maintained a dipping tub full of cold water, as lamentably recalled by Elizabeth Grant:

In town, a large, long tub, stood in the kitchen court, the ice on the top of which had often to be broken before our horrid plunge into it; we were brought down from the very top of the house, four pairs of stairs, with only a cotton cloak over our night-gowns, just to chill us completely before the dreadful shock. How I screamed, begged, prayed, entreated to be saved, half the tender-hearted maids in tears besides me: all no use.[175]

John Locke apparently favored all physical measures, none of which he considered punitive, that promoted "hardening of bodies." He believed, for example, that children should have "[their] shooes so thin that they might leak and let water in whenever [they] come near it."[176] There were physicians contemporary with Locke who concurred with his idea that exposure to nature was an invigorating and positive influence on children's health. Christian Augustus Struve (1767–1807) opined in *Domestic Education of Children* (1802):

We cannot bestow greater benefits on our children, than exposing them frequently and daily to the enlivening influences of fresh air: health and sprightliness will be the immediate effects of so rational a practice.[177]

A similar philosophy of *retournez à la nature* was espoused by Jean-Jacques Rousseau for the edification of French mothers. In *Émile* (1762), Rousseau described the influence of nature even on infants:

We are born weak, we need strength; we are born destitute of everything, we need aid; we are born stupid, we need judgment. All that we are not possessed of at our birth, and which we require when grown up, is given us by education. This education we receive from nature, from men, from things. . . .

The education of a man commences at his birth: before he can speak, before he can understand, he is already learning. Experience anticipates lessons; the moment he knows the features of his nurse, he may be said to have acquired considerable knowledge. (*Émile*, bk. 1)

One aspect of the belief that nature should be an integral part of nurture led to a complete disavowal of the tradition of swaddling, which became much criticized as a form of negligence. It was thought that the inactivity of the bound infant was mind-dulling. The French naturalist Comte Georges Louis de Buffon (1707–1788) was representative of continental proponents of "natural" child rearing. In his *Histoire Naturelle de l'homme* he stated his case against the practice of swaddling:

Scarcely is the infant out of the womb of his mother, scarcely is he at liberty to move and to stretch his limbs, when he is given new bonds. He is swaddled, put to bed with his head fixed and his legs extended, his arms at his sides; he is wrapped in linen and bandages, to the extent that he cannot change position. He is lucky if he is not squeezed so hard that he is unable to breathe.[178]

Ultimately, common sense and practicality prevailed with the majority, who neither totally abandoned swaddling their infants nor submitted them to cold baths; and parenting practices continued to be a blend of the sensible, such as walking strings for toddlers beginning to amble, and the ignorant, not understanding the health risk of opiate sedation: "I buy a bottle of Godfrey's Cordial for making children sleep, since Geordy keeps all the house awake, also almost kills his poor mother" (John Stedman, 1785).[179]

Rousseau's influence extended to Germany, where his works were widely popular, and his pedagogical philosophy was espoused by two prominent writers, Johann Heinrich Pestalozzi (1746–1827) and Friedrich Froebel (1782–1852). Their influence was considerable, since they incorporated much of Rousseau's pedagogical philosophy into their thinking. Idealized images of children and family had a great impact on the romantic German psyche that until then had preserved an unshaken belief in absolute paternal power within the family. As a result of Rousseau and his followers, women reevaluated their maternal roles, especially their biological capacity to nourish as well as nurture, and educators pored over Rousseau's *Émile*, absorbing and adopting his thoughts on child nurture and education.[180] Pestalozzi was the first of these to win favor with his German audience and to influence fundamental change in attitudes about parenthood, the family, and education. He began with an appeal to maternal instincts and love:

The nursling, his hunger satisfied, learns in this way what his mother is to him; she develops in him love, the essence of gratitude, before the infant is able to utter the words of "duty" and "thank." (*Evening Hour of a Hermit*)[181]

In *Uber Gesezgebung und Kindermort* (On legislation and infanticide), Pestalozzi condemned infanticide and urged that it be criminalized. In his next work, a utopian novel published in 1781, *Lienhard und Gertrud* (Leonard and Gertrude), he created a village community in which child nurture was the supreme good, and the family and its work functioned under maternal moral and social influences. In 1802, in *Wie Gertrud ihre Kinder lehrt* (How Gertrude teaches her children), Pestalozzi emphasized the mother's central role as a pedagogue.[182] His romanticized belief in the emotional, moral, social, and pedagogical superiority of the maternal role had wide appeal—a view that directly challenged the notion of absolute power of the father and whittled away unquestioned paternal control of the family.

The combined influence of Rousseau and Pestalozzi contributed to an educational reform bill of 1802 in the Bavarian state. School attendance became compulsory for all children between six and twelve years. In 1804 a standardized curriculum was introduced, and, importantly, the German state established mandatory teacher-training schools to lend uniformity to teaching methodology. Friedrich Froebel (1782–1852) reinforced Pestalozzi's concepts and went further. Froebel believed that children would flourish best in a school environment that most closely reflected the warmth, comfort, and security of the mother and the home. In his first *kindergarten*, founded in 1839, he amalgamated homely principles of maternal love and family loyalty with play, nature, and instruction in one cozy composite. Only in such an atmosphere, he thought, were children free to develop independence and confidence. The influence of Froebel's idealized, nurturing and loving mother image later could be found in rhymes that were read to children:

> In the bushes, see the nest,
> Little eggs within it rest.
> When the babies break the shell,
> Mother feeds them very well.
> Little birdies sing together,
> "How we love you, dearest mother."
>
> *Mutter und Koselieder* (1883)[183]

Despite these trends in German society, most schools remained bastions of conservative moralism.

The schools in the German states between 1820 and 1850 also were predominantly religious schools, rooted in Bible study. They were called *Bewahranstalen*,[184] and all learning was by rote. School inspectors[185] functioned as truant officers, to ensure attendance at school. In rural Germany, however, school attendance predictably was especially poor during harvest and threshing times. A census conducted in 1803 revealed that many children did not go to school at all. Those that did not work the farm went off to work as domestics.[186]

A substantial aspect of Rousseau's "discipline" of returning to nature was the romantic image of childhood and its innocence. With so much attention and focus on children, indulgence and spoiling were inevitable. The middle and upper strata had the means to do it. Toy stores sprang up, vying with street toy vendors who had traditionally plied the streets of Europe. Toys made of inexpensive tin and lead were mass-produced, and almost every town catered to the demand for playthings. What had once been the sole domain of the rich, now was available to all but the poor: hobby horses, dolls, soldiers, cannons, hoops, musical instruments, and jigsaw puzzles (which had first appeared circa 1760 as a toy and as a geography teaching aid).[187]

Young Mary Sewell, in 1805, nostalgically recollected:

[In Norwich] not far from the inn where my father put up was a small shop where children's toys were sold. These were the high times of our baby-house, and in the shop-window we saw some little tin and lead plates, the very things for our baby house kitchen.[188]

There were critics—in England, France, the Netherlands, all over Europe, and in the new colonies in America—who regarded the indulgence of children as the cause of behavioral difficulties. Francois Bruys (1708–1738) wrote in 1729: "The Dutch have an exaggerated tenderness for their children. They do not know how to punish, nor refuse them their desires."[189] A letter from an Englishman appalled by the behavior of American children appeared in the *Virginia Gazette* in 1767:

On my arrival here I found a house full of children, who are humoured beyond measure, and indeed absolutely spoiled by the ridiculous indulgence of a fond mother.[190]

By the mid-nineteenth century it appeared that middle-class parents had all but relinquished their intuitions about child rearing, having developed an unquenchable thirst for advice. A new wave of "how to" books were published, with titles such as *The Book of Household Management* (1861), *Counsel to Parents on the Moral Education of Their Children* (1878), and *The Mother's Handbook* (1879). Advisory verses were published in serial form by the Ladies Sanitary Association, with laconic titles that intimated the text of the lesson—"Fresh Air," "Tidiness," "Clean Clothing," and "Vaccination" are examples. The instructive verses targeted parental emotions:

The Sick Child's Cry

Open the window, mother,
I can't breathe in this stifling room;

Open the window, mother,
and let out the weight and gloom!

It seemed like an angel breathing—
Now mother I've said my prayer—
I think I can sleep a little
Thank GOD for the blessed air.

The Neglected Child

See the neglected child,
He drags himself along,
Staring with dull and listless gaze
At the quick bustling throng.

In the still night or dawn
His father stumbles in,
In drunken rage or low abuse,
From his dark haunts of sin.

So days and nights pass on,
Yet life keeps strong within;
For God is caring for the child,
In his drear home of sin.[191]

Scientific advances marked the age, and although regular epidemics of plague, typhus, diphtheria, and whooping cough continued to occur, smallpox was still the single most-deadly killer. The urban mortality rate when smallpox erupted was 20 percent; in city children it killed one in three.[192]

Inoculation, in which smallpox serum from one infected person was etched into the skin tissue of a healthy person, was popularized for a time in the mid-eighteenth century. There were dangers of acquiring severe vaccinia reaction and actual smallpox using this method, however, and, in parts of America, inoculation was banned. Edward Jenner's (1749–1823) report in 1798 of his discovery that cows infected with cowpox produced a serum that prevented smallpox in humans, with few of the dangers of inoculation, was a milestone in medical history. Vaccination became well accepted by the turn of the nineteenth century, and now, two hundred years after Jenner's discovery, the smallpox virus has been obliterated worldwide. In the nineteenth century, epidemics of smallpox coming from the East already had waned. Although there were no major urban outbreaks, sporadic cases, with significant morbidity of facial disfigurement *and* the mortality associated with the pox, prompted many parents to vaccinate their children. It became the fashion in some circles, to tout the vaccination mark as a sign of gentry.

The return to maternal nursing was heralded by both physicians and moralists: some had considered wet nurses a potential disease vector, with poor-quality milk; nursing by the biological mother now was recognized as emotionally salubrious for both mother and infant and a contributing factor to healthy bonding. Archbishop Tillotson rhapsodized: "The pains of nursing as well as of bearing children doth insensibly create a strange tenderness of affection and care in the woman."[193] In reality, the demands of nursing on the cosmopolitan mother did to some degree intrude on her perceptions of the quality of life, evoking some maternal ambivalence. William Cadogan's (1711–1797) literary pronouncements in his "An Essay upon Nursing" (1748) gave the imprimatur to maternal nursing, declaring it most beneficial to the child. Cadogan generously recognized that, for a variety of reasons, some mothers could not nurse. In these instances he advocated wet nursing as a more favored substitute for "dry-nursing" and even recommended payment of twenty-five pounds a year for a good nurse.[194]

During the nineteenth century an interesting role-reversal occurred. As newly egalitarian aristocratic mothers moved away from employing wet nurses, poorer women began to hire them so that they could assume work outside the home. The practice was euphemistically referred to as "baby-farming."[195] In nineteenth-century Paris, the majority of wet nurses worked for poor mothers.[196] Since, however, the poor were unable, for the most part, to pay reasonable wages to wet nurses, a new wave of abandonment and infant mortality ensued. In a notorious case in England, a Brixton widow named Margaret Ellis Waters and her sister Sarah took in illegitimate babies, receiving ten pounds a year for each baby. The mortality rate was extremely high, and when a baby died, Waters abandoned the body in the streets. She was ultimately caught and executed in 1870, a year in which 276 dead infants were found in London streets.[197] In the winter of 1895 a baby farmer, Mrs. Dyer, was found guilty of strangling forty babies whose bodies had been found on Reading streets.[198] Infanticide at parturition was not uncommon. One midwife, Mrs. Martin of Soho, was hanged for the murder of more than five hundred newborns. There were several others who were convicted of killing newborns with opium cordials. They were jailed and forced to wear two red stars, an insignia of infanticide.[199]

POSTREVOLUTION AMERICA

Disruption to the *structure* of the family in America was minimal during and immediately after the momentous and unprecedented American Revolution which, as all know, had world-shaking political effects. Despite the tumultuous and uncertain years during the war for independence, the integrity of family life remained intact. Once the ties to the motherland had been severed and peace was restored, families in the newly formed independent states had the interest and opportunity to reflect on many aspects of their lives as Americans. Two important themes were child nurture and education, and in time a home-grown and identifiably American philosophy about both evolved.

Nurturing practices in the colonial settlements had been understandably variable, since the continent had attracted, from the first, Europeans from many countries. It has been said that to write about eighteenth-century American children necessitates the question:

"Which children?": Children of New England, or of the Chesapeake, or perhaps of Pennsylvania or the Carolinas? Farming youngsters of Dedham, Massachusetts, in 1700 or sons and daughters of Boston merchants in 1799? Irish apprentices in Philadelphia or German school children in Frederick, Maryland? Slave infants on a South Carolina plantation or youthful female converts at a Connecticut revival?[200]

The "American melting pot" had been a phenomenon from the time of the first settlers and for the most part was composed of groups of people who had brought legacies with them from Europe; namely, skills and education. There were late-sixteenth- and early seventeenth-century Spanish adventurers in the southern regions; English Puritans fleeing religious intolerance (and bringing a fair modicum of it with them) in the north. There were Huguenots escaping from the Spanish, German Protestants seeking economic and political freedoms, and Dutch merchants who established tidy and profitable communities in what was called New Netherlands. Only later, forcibly taken, uneducated but culturally rich Africans arrived in the New World to be used for slave labor, as did Scottish and Irish war prisoners sent by Oliver Cromwell. Additionally, it must be said, various English, Spanish, and French reprobates arrived, pressed into what was euphemistically termed indentured servitude but in fact was slave labor.

The settlers who chose to leave their homelands to build a new life on American shores looked, to a great extent, to their children to fulfill their many aspirations. From the beginning, North America was a child-centered society that emphasized education as a means to a better life. Even as this educational egalitarianism was invoked, Puritan theocracy remained a factor. This was reflected in the student hierarchy evident at Harvard and Yale, where sons of ministers were listed first, followed by sons of magistrates, lawyers, merchants, shopkeepers, master mariners, physicians, teachers, military officers, craftsmen, sailors, and servants.[201] It is noteworthy that in the theocracy of late–seventeenth-century America, craftsmen, sailors, and servants were educating their sons. This increasing equity of education gradually led Yale to give up a ranking system based on paternal prestige and position and adopt a simple alphabetical listing of students. Harvard followed soon thereafter.

The importance of literacy in colonial American life cannot be exaggerated. It was germane to the development of the American persona that eventually cultivated a revolutionary spirit. High instances of literacy reduced a dependence on scribes, businessmen, and even lawyers. The success that literate and even college-trained men had in dealing with their own affairs reinforced the colonists' sense of their own abilities and their independence. It was only a matter of time before an innate self-confidence seeded the desire for political independence. By the time the first shots of rebellion were heard at Lexington, America had nine institutions of higher learning: Harvard, Yale, Dartmouth, Princeton, William and Mary, University of Pennsylvania, Columbia, Brown, and Rutgers. Thomas Paine's *The Rights of Man*, moreover, had contributed not only to the colonists' egalitarian beliefs and revolutionary fervor to amend perceived injustices, but to a strongly held belief in the value of education. Postrevolutionary patriots and nationalists recognized that through education they could inculcate a national identity and purpose in their young. Legislation was passed to ensure that the education would be a homegrown variety. In 1785 the Georgia Assembly, for example, established penalties for young children sent abroad to study:

If any Person or persons under the age of sixteen Years shall after the passing of this Act be sent abroad without the limits of the United States and reside there three Years for the purpose of receiving an education under a foreign power, such person or persons after their return to this State shall for three Years be considered and treated as Aliens.[202]

In 1788, Noah Webster (1758–1843) argued:

. . . I beg leave to make some remarks on a practice which appears to be attended with important consequences; I mean that of sending boys to Europe for teachers. That this was right before the revolution will not be disputed; at least so far as national attachment were concerned; but the propriety of it ceased with our political relation to Great Britain.[203]

In reality, for the vast majority of American children, education was an unevenly distributed and haphazard commodity. Many, if not most, families depended on their children's share of the apportionment of labor at home and in the fields. For those families who were committed to having their children educated, there were only loosely organized village schools available. These, however, did not group pupils by level of development or grades but by the dates they were registered, leading Horace Mann (1796–1859) to comment that enrollment consisted of "infants but just out of their cradles . . . to men who had been enrolled . . . in the militia."[204] Village school records in Stow, Massachusetts, from 1810 to 1821, document children two and three years of age enrolled in what essentially was a day-care setting, supporting Mann's observation.[205] The end result was a nonuniform, irregular, and singular focus in these schools on reading—a useful tool in any case.

For the landed and wealthy, children's early education continued to be in the home with tutors or in small groups in the homes of other learned families. As they grew, children were sent to one of the growing number of "colleges" established for the education of young men. The government did not provide education for girls until the mid-nineteenth century, but private, typically religious establishments for girls had been instituted early on, such as the Georgetown Visitation College Preparatory School for girls founded in Maryland (later, the District of Columbia) in 1789. The more conservative New England communities immediately after the Revolution liberalized their attitudes about schooling for girls by permitting them to attend school during the summer when boys were doing field work. Dutch colonists in New York always had educated their daughters, albeit predominantly in reading and in segregated groups. Pennsylvania Quakers and Moravian schools traditionally were coeducational, and in Bethlehem, Pennsylviania, there was a Moravian boarding school for 120 girls.[206]

A movement toward a more formal education of girls began when Emma Willard (1787–1880) proposed a "Plan for the Improvement of Female Education" to the New York State Legislature in 1818. The legislative body debated the issue for several sessions, lasting years, before it was approved and the Willard Seminary was founded in Troy, New York, in 1822. In 1834, Mary Lyon (1797–1849) founded the Mount Holyoke Female Seminary in Massachusetts, but only after the crucial support of male colleagues had been enlisted. She had shrewdly assessed that:

It is desirable that the plans relating to the subject should not seem to originate with us but with benevolent *gentlemen*. If the object should excite attention there is danger that many good men will fear the effect on society of so much female influence and what they will call female greatness.[207]

In the new republic, the paternal role, so predominantly authoritative and autocratic in Europe, exhibited in the United States an eroded authority or, perhaps more to the point, a redefined authority. Alexis de Tocqueville's (1805–1859) observations in his famous book, *Democracy in America*, offered a kind tribute, describing relationships in which, clearly, respect for and obedience to fathers were accorded by sons but applied with a peculiarly American outlook that had its own idiom and norms of behavior and that was a very far cry from the old country's antiquated dictates of *pater potestas*:

In a democratic family the father exercises no other power than that which is granted to the affection and the experience of age; his orders would perhaps be disobeyed, but his advice is for the most part authoritative. Though he is not hedged in with
ceremonial respect, his sons at least accost him with confidence; they have no settled form of addressing him, but they speak to him constantly and are ready to consult him every day. The master and the constituted ruler have vanished; the father
remains.[208]

The status and importance of women's maternal roles also were imbued
with an original and unique American perspective. The primacy of their position as child nurturers even had legal recognition. A landmark court decision by the state supreme court of Pennsylvania in 1813 ceded the primary
custodial role to mothers (*Commonwealth v. Addicks and Wife*). In a statement to the court, the judge ruled:

. . . considering their tender age, [the children] stand in need of that kind of assistance, which can be afforded by none so well as a mother.[209]

In performing their maternal duties, American mothers employed many
child-rearing customs rooted in Europe and tapped a residue of superstitious
belief that also was a lingering legacy bequeathed by the Old World. For
example, a scarlet cloth was placed on a newborn's head as protection from
harm. After the first bath, the infant was symbolically brought upstairs
before being taken back downstairs so that it might "rise in the world." On
a first outing, those with means placed into a baby's small hand a silver and
gold item, so that position and wealth might be assured him. Swaddling was
rare. Salting was not done.

American mothers regarded engendering societal values in their children
an important aspect of their responsibility, stressing values such as self-sufficiency, confidence, and motivation. Mothers performed this duty with much
overt affection, holding, fondling, and soothing their babies, and with no
sense that such indulgence would spoil their infants. Consequently, some
saw spoiled children as the result of this approach, while others perceived
independent youths endowed with American optimism and a pioneer spirit,
Christian virtue, and a sense of civic duty. The ideal American child, it was
thought, confidently confronted and dealt with the challenges of a country
that had dazzling and vast resources and that promised opportunity and
wealth on an unprecedented scale.

American mothers also assumed the responsibility of inculcating religious
sentiments and piety in their children. They and their spouses rejected, however, the God-fearing Puritan and Calvinistic principles of inborn evil and

damnation in favor of a loving and joyful God who promised redemption and salvation. Children were introduced to church services in the first year of life so as to accustom them to Sabbath-day rituals.

Consistent with the nineteenth-century belief in nature and natural order, children were encouraged to look upon death as having a certain beauty. Funeral photographs of a child laid out in white were common mementos during the latter half of the century. Thomas Gallaudet (1787–1851), in *The Child's Book on the Soul*, published in 1831, even remarked that touching dead bodies at funeral wakes was an instructive measure that reinforced the lesson that death was a natural and necessary prelude to heavenly and eternal life.[210]

To aid them with their child-rearing responsibilities, American mothers avidly sought guidance from published authorities. Edifying books their children could read also were valued. Initially, literate America's thirst for books was quenched with publications from England, where dour Puritan dogma also had waned. Children's books continued to stress the moral and ethical, but the lessons were gently persuasive and noncondemnatory.

When the new republic began to produce its own literature for and about children, its flavor can be said to have been more permissive and indulgent than that of Europe. There was at least one exception to this caveat, a carry-over from the somber and damning Puritan fare of the past. The parable of *My Mother's Grave* (1830) illustrated the consequences of morally reprehensible behavior: in the book, a little girl refuses to take a glass of water to her sick mother. After a night disturbed by guilt and self-recrimination, the child goes to apologize, only to find her mother dead! The book apparently was very popular among mothers.[211]

Schoolbooks were obvious and popular vehicles for teaching ethical and moral lessons to young readers. The most famous examples are the "readers" published by college professor William McGuffey (1800–1873), that were used in American public schools well into the twentieth century. At least 120 million copies of these books found their way into children's hands and minds. They were filled with stories that promoted values like honesty, charity, and obedience, as in the following examples[212]:

The Little Heroes

Two little boys went to a birthday party at the home of one of their playmates. Their parents told them to come home at eight o'clock. . . .

In the midst of their play, some one came into the room and asked them to be seated. Just as some fruit and nuts were brought in, the clock struck eight.

The boys who had been asked to come home at that hour, looked at each other for a moment; then one of them said, "we must go."

The Kind Girl

The cows had come up to the barn, and Jane had milked them. As she came home, she saw bad boys and a dog that was worrying a cat . . . she put down her pail of milk and went to ask the boys not to let the dog hurt the cat. But the boys only laughed at her.

"I wonder how they can be so cruel!" thought Jane, as she walked sadly home. "I could not make them stop, but I am sure I did the right in speaking to them."

At another time, when her work was done, Jane went to visit a poor old lady who was ill. She boiled a bit of chicken for her, and made her a cup of tea.

Most books were genre books on child care addressed to mothers (and only on occasion to fathers) that emphasized loving and positive approaches to parenting. The poems written by the English sisters Jane and Anne Taylor about everyday home life were gentle and reassuring. They were also full of insight and wisdom that remain surprisingly fresh and applicable today. The verse they wrote on the subject of sibling rivalry is an example:

> O dear Mama, said little Fred
> Put baby down—take me instead
> Upon the carpet let her be
> Put baby down and take up me.
>
> No that my dear I cannot do
> You know I used to carry you
> But you are now grown strong and stout
> And you can run and play about.
>
> When Fanny is as old as you
> No doubt but what she'll do so too
> And when she grows a little stronger
> I mean to carry her no longer.[213]

Several authors advocated child-rearing theories that anticipated by more than a century the well-known book on child care by the twentieth century's Dr. Benjamin Spock. John Abbott (1805–1877), in *The Mother at Home* (1830), advocated a sparing use of the rod.[214] *The Mother's Book*, written by Lydia Maria Child (1802–1859) in 1831, was certain that "if you inspire [the child] with the right feelings, they will govern his actions." She further advised:

The first and most important step in management is, that whatever a mother says, always *must* be done. For this reason, do not require too much; and on no account allow your child to do at one time, what you have forbidden him at another.[215]

Theodore Dwight's (1796–1866) *The Father's Book* in 1834 counseled parents to avoid confronting and punishing children for engaging in normal child behavior. Instead, he said children should be distracted gently and firmly from situations that might result in undesirable consequences.[216]

Nature and nurture were the themes of two books that urged the understanding and forbearance of normal child behavior. George Ackerley's *On the Management of Children in Sickness and in Health*, written in 1836, pointed out the salubrious effects of energetic, youthful clamor on child development:

The noisy mirth of childhood ought never to be met with a frown for it ought always to be recollected, that it is not only natural to them, but actually necessary for the full and healthy development of every organ in the body. Every bounce and every shout adds vigor to their limbs and strength to their lungs.[217]

Of all of the child-advice books, T. S. Arthur (1809–1885), in *The Mother's Rule* (1856), best expressed the purpose of and relationship between child nurture and education:

The real object of education is to give children resources that will endure as long as life endures, habits that will ameliorate, not destroy; occupations that will render sickness tolerable, solitude pleasant, age venerable, life more dignified and useful, and death less terrible.[218]

In the second half of the nineteenth century, American child-care advice books moved even further away from the stern Protestant ethic of the past. Some were frankly permissive and sanctioned extremes of indulgence. The minister Jacob Abbott (1803–1879) in *Gentle Measures in the Management and Training of the Young* (1871) importuned mothers to be "unoppressive" in raising their children, lecturing that

. . . as a general rule, the more that children are gratified in respect to their childish fancies and impulses and even their caprices when no evil or danger is to be apprehended, the better.[219]

Abbott did believe, however, in parental authority, as he believed in a loving, unvengeful God. Parents, he pointed out, were God's surrogates and, as such, should govern with reason and affection. On disciplinary matters, Abbott advocated "manoevure and artifice" when exercising authority and believed that chastisements should be administered unthreateningly, devoid of anger and with nonpunitive motives. He especially encouraged parents to train their children "gently into action within the limits prescribed by the degree of maturity to which they have attained."[220] If all else failed, corporal punishment was countenanced, but it was to be delivered without anger.[221]

Mattie Trippe's *Home Treatment for Children* (1881), Hannah Smith's *The Science of Motherhood* (1894), and Elizabeth Glover's *Children's Wing* (1889)

all supported unlimited displays of parental affection toward children and a family atmosphere in which children were unimpeded by discipline and restraint. The view of F. McCready Harris in *Plain Talk with Young Homemakers* (1889) was that parents needed to exercise restraint. They were cautioned about interrogatives to their children, lest the children be pushed into lying. Parents were told to sanction unharmful activities of dubious value and to merely keep a watchful eye on their children, because, "if you forbid them, in nine cases out of ten you teach them to deceive."[222]

All of the above-mentioned books can be categorized as contributory works to the era that can justly be called the dawn of child psychology. This is especially true when the books written between 1880 and 1900 by John Dewey (1859–1952), William James (1842–1910), and G. Stanley Hall (1844–1924) are included. Hall's *The Study of the Child* (1883) prompted the establishment of popular child-study clubs in America. Specialty journals on child development and the understanding of cultural nurturing were published, ones such as *The Child Study Monthly* and *The Pedagogical Seminary.*

Kate Douglas Wiggin's (1856–1923)* *Children's Rights* (1892) entreated parents to teach by example, to retreat from self-righteous humiliation of children, and to make sacrifices for the good of their children; importantly, it urged fathers, the makers of male images, to be more directly involved with their sons: "Get down to the level of his boyhood, and bring him up to the level of your manhood."[223]

The environment that perceived children as intelligent, impressionable, and special *persona et anima* promoted an influx of childhood literature specifically produced for both the edification and the pleasure of the child. Long suppressed by the Protestant ethic, fantasy books became especially coveted, and the characters who were favored were supplied by English authors. Jim Hawkins, Mowgli, Robin Hood, King Arthur, and the sensate creatures in Beatrix Potter's (1866–1943) garden and the horse in Anna Sewell's (1820–1878) *Black Beauty* were among the most popular.[224]

Authors did attempt to balance permissive values, such as freedom, with advice about the proper public comportment and good manners children should demonstrate. There also was an entirely original genre of books on sex—that is to say, on how parents might deal with this delicate subject, characteristically taboo in Victorian times on both sides of the Atlantic. The repression and denial of sexual matters that permeated societal mores and demeanor began in the home. Strategies to obviate and/or bypass any youthful inquiries about sex abounded in books like Robert Tomes's (1817–1882)

---

*It was Wiggin, best known for *Rebecca of Sunnybrook Farm* (1903), who in 1878 opened the first free kindergarten in the West—in San Francisco.

The Bazar Book of Decorum (1870) that instructed mothers not to talk about pregnancy. If a reference could not be avoided, decorous terms, like the French *enceinte*, were offered by the author for use. Children, the book intoned, should be spirited away from home when parturition impended and allowed to return home only several weeks after the birth, when the infant that "angels" had delivered could be presented to the siblings. Birth announcements were not advised by the author, since they might be inclined to raise the question "Where did the baby come from?" Parents were counseled against adult displays of affection or intimacies (appropriate only in private) when children were present. The book supplied allegories about plants, oysters, and birds suitable as answers to queries about reproduction from older, more curious, and more persistent children.

The condemnation of masturbation throughout Europe by the moral leadership was vociferous and frequent. In America a strident, impassioned literature on the topic influenced parents, ministers, educators, and even doctors. It was voluminous and riddled with inaccuracies and what are now recognized as frank distortions. William Alcott (1798–1859), in *A Young Man's Guide* (1840), attributed insanity, St. Vitus dance, seizures, palsy, vermiculations, blindness, and strokes to masturbation. He warned that "unless the abominable practice which produced all the mischief is abandoned, death follows."[225] Seventy-three years later, in 1913, the American Medical Association published a pamphlet stating that masturbation produced "sissy young men . . . narrow-chested, flabby-muscled, mollycoddles."[226]

Admonitions of a different kind were given to girls. Emma Drake's (1849–?) *What a Young Wife Ought to Know* (1901) described passions as "due to some unnatural condition [which] should be considered a disease."[227]

ASPECTS OF CHILDREN'S LIVES IN AMERICA

The Westward Expansion and Slavery

The opening of the West by the Homesteading (1862) and Mining Acts (1866, 1872) began a process that remains one of the most remarkable, colorful, and referred-to aspects of American history. Families from the eastern United States began to populate the land west of the Mississippi,* gradually driving out the Native Americans who had thrived there for millennia. The peak years of the great overland westward migration were between 1841 and

---

*The Homesteading Act granted a land parcel of 640 acres to every male citizen over 18 years of age and 160 acres each to his wife and children.

1860. During this period there appeared guidebooks such as *The Emigrants Guide to Oregon* (1845), which provided advice on choosing and caring for stock, wagon repair, travel needs—clothing, food, tools, and medical kits—establishing camps, and contingencies experienced by earlier travelers.[228] A second wave of "melting pot" immigrants, between 1875 and 1890, joined already settled brethren in the move to populate the western territories. Along with American-born families were the hopeful from Scandinavia, Germany, Ireland, France, Russia, and Canada. They traveled in groups by cart and covered wagon—and later by rail—branching, fingering out, across the land. After the Civil War and Reconstruction, manumitted former slaves looked to the West as the "promised land" where they could build communities and work their farms in cooperative, friendly, and unfettered peace. Twenty-five thousand blacks settled in Kansas; in Nebraska, more than fifty thousand.[229] In all, more than 250,000 people crossed the country,[230] 35,000 of whom were children.*

Months of travel had to be endured by all. Parents, whose marriages were bound by cooperation and companionship as a working partnership more than by romance or passion, had little time or energy to give attention to their children, let alone for idle prattle or casual shows of affection toward either their children or themselves. Their hopes and dreams were vested in surviving the rigors and perils of the expedition, and their focus was to complete the trip. Day after day they crossed overland trails, exhausted by hard work, discomfort, and hunger, touched by sporadic and sometimes majestic natural beauty, challenged by adventure and threatened by danger. Constantly, they teetered on the brink of tragedy. For many, the trauma of the journey that had been experienced in childhood formed character and temperament traceable in generations to follow.

There were no schools or lessons, and there was little time for children to engage in recreational activities. Since they had few possessions and fewer toys, children most often played word games or competed in races and games of tag. They could be amusingly inventive. One anecdote recounts the adventure of

---

*The greatest American migration was to occur during the 1930s when the Oklahomans of the panhandle packed up their possessions and began a 2,000-mile trek to California. Forced into bankruptcy by five years of drought and dust storms, farmers in Texas, Oklahoma, and Arkansas lost their family farms to banks at a rate of 1,000 per week during 1932 alone. The "Okies," as they came to be called, moved west, 375,000 strong. Altogether, from these states between 1935 to 1940 over a million people, half of them children, set out for California. Although the migration was for the most part by automobile along the famous Route 66, these children ("maggies," for immigrants) faced hardships similar to those of their ancestors: starvation, dust pneumonia, dysentery, accidents, etc. They were all immortalized by John Steinbeck in *The Grapes of Wrath*.

several boys whose wagon train was camped near Fort Hall on the Snake River in Idaho. The boys found a dead ox baking in the sun. The carcass was bloated and tympanitic from postmortem fermentation. To the children's delight, it made a perfect trampoline, and the boys repeatedly dove at it and bounced off it. They formed a contest to determine which of them could bounce the farthest, but the game ended abruptly when a tall, lanky, and determined boy dove headfirst and burst through what was, after all, fetid, rotting carrion.[231]

There were unlimited kinds of chores for children, and they most often were meted out not by gender but to the strong who had stamina. There was work enough for all, in any case. Animals needed tending, cows and goats had to be milked, meals had to be prepared, clothing had to be cleaned and mended, wagons needed repair. Wood had to be gathered to make fires for warmth and for cooking. In the absence of available wood, sun-dried dung of buffalo was collected from the treeless plains. These "meadow muffins" as some called them produced a hot and odorless but smoky flame, which had the secondary advantage of acting as a mosquito repellant. In valley crossings, children foraged for wild berries that varied the staple diet of dried meat jerky and flour. When provisions ran out, children joined the men who searched for game in hunting parties. At times, children had to make desperate attempts to find food. Ellen Smith, a widow with nine children, described in a diary entry (1846) how children "would go out in the woods and smoke the Woud mice out of the Logs and Rost and Eat them."[232] A traveler near the Sierras in 1850 came across starving children who were sucking on pork rinds and rawhide.[233]

Small children encountered special hazards. Toddlers fell out of wagons, were abducted by Indians, or, in large and far-ranging wagon trains, became separated from their families, lost in an endless cavalcade of passing strangers. Exhausted children were sometimes tied to oxen by anxious parents who feared they would be lost and left behind. In addition to coping with traditional childhood ailments, measles epidemics, and scurvy, the consequences of fever, diarrhea, sunburns, blisters, insect bites, and accidents were major and constant concerns for families. The few medicines available often were not stable enough to maintain efficacy in the extreme cold, heat, wetness, or dryness to which they were exposed, but pioneer ingenuity contributed to the development of useful substitute remedies found on the trails. Mouth sores were treated with a mixture of sage, borax, alum, and sugar. Buttercup tea was brewed for asthmatics suffering attacks. Cough syrup was prepared from wild onions mashed in sugar. Fevers were treated with a rubdown of skunk grease and turpentine.[234]

One diary entry, by Jane Gould Tortillott on 11 July 1862, attests to the presence of physicians on occasional fortunate wagon trains: "There was a little child run over by a wagon. . . . They sent for a German physician that belongs to our train, to see the child that was injured."[235]

Some children never finished the crossing. Katherine Dunlap (1864) documented in her diaries the gravesites she saw along the trail. One pineboard marker reported: "Two children, killed by a stampede." One poignant diary entry, referring to an infant's grave, testifies to the sorrow that accompanied the ambitious trek west:

Oh, what a lonely, dark and desolate place to bury a sweet infant—We read the following inscription on the headboard of the death-sleeping infant: "Morelea Elizabeth Martess, died Aug. 9th, 1863, born July 7th, 1862. Friends nor physician could save her from the grave."[236]

At this particular gravesite a plea had been left for passersby to keep the grave in repair, and Dunlap noted in her diary that, indeed, "it was repaired and a pen of logs built around it."[237]

Tragedies on the trail were not limited to the deaths of children and infants. Often children suffered the loss of parents and were left both bereft and orphaned, as noted by Jane Gould Tortillott:

There was a woman died in this train yesterday. She left six children, one of them only two days old. Poor little thing, it had better have died with its mother. They made a good picket fence around the grave. (28 July 1862)

. . . We passed by the train I have just spoken of. They had just buried the babe of the woman who died days ago, and were just digging a grave for another woman that was run over by the cattle and wagons when they stampeded yesterday. She lived twenty-four hours, she gave birth to a child a short time before she died. The child was buried with her. She leaves a little two year old girl and a husband. They say he is nearly crazy with sorrow. (3 August 1862)[238]

One of every seventeen who crossed the Oregon Trail was buried by the roadside.[239]

The well-known and often romanticized westward migration has overshadowed the history of a southward passage resulting from land grant laws that facilitated homesteading. Families on these treks encountered fewer hazards and privations than their westbound equivalents, but they and their children nonetheless suffered similar illnesses and fatal accidents, and children similarly became permanently separated from their families. The weather for southbound homesteaders was not harsh, and wood and provisions generally were more plentiful. Overland wagons were not common or useful vehicles of travel in terrain that better accommodated packhorses.

Younger children, transported like supplies, were placed into hickory cages and baskets strapped to the sides of horses. Some families migrated on flatboats down major rivers. It was not uncommon to see several families and their livestock floating downriver in joint ventures.[240]

Southern homesteads were built with wood. Western homesteads typically were made from sod. Families settled into the work of homesteading with, commonly, six to twelve children to lend the helping hands necessary in the struggle to survive.[241] (In comparison, the mean English household of the period numbered 4.21.[242]) The chores were those to which children had become accustomed during the migration journey, with traditional gender roles restored, so gathering wood, fetching water, trapping animals, and gathering wild berries fell no longer merely to the ablest but to young males. Boys also learned how to plow and plant and to build and mend farm fences. Girls worked with their mothers, making candles and soap and tending to the unending domestic work of keeping house and an ample larder. When necessary, every member of the family was put to work in the fields.

Soap- and candle-making was complex and risky work and girls suffered multiple and sometimes severe accidental burns. Very young girls were taught to save the wood ashes from the household hearth, lard drippings, and the meat and fat scraps used to make tallow. Spring was the time programmed for soap-making, at which time the ashes were heaped into a perforated hopper, water was run through the ashes, and the leach was collected. This alkali suspension was added to a pot in which the scrap fats had been heating. The mixture was boiled down for hours, until the saponification resulted in a soft soap product; this was salted, placed in molds until dried and hardened, and then cut into pieces. Few young girls escaped without at least one fat-splatter burn, especially during the period when they were being trained to the task. Similar burn accidents were common when making candles, which involved repeated dippings of wicks into molten tallow or the pouring of hot paraffin into molds.[243]

General child care also was the responsibility of girls who, with sisterly affection, amused new babies and older toddlers with old potatoes, corncobs, and spools of thread that were pressed into service as toys or pacifiers.[244] They had to keep watchful eyes on sibling toddlers, to keep them out of harm's way from the ever-present dangers within the home—from hearthfires, boiling tallow and fat, burning candles—and from without. Toddlers could find many dangerous objects in barns and around houses, and, if they wandered off into fields, they were easy prey for both abductors and rattlesnakes. A Kansas pioneer named Bessie Wilson recalled a first childhood encounter with a poisonous snake:

Once when quite small, I crawled upon the roof of the cave to secure a board on which to place my mud pies. . . . I sat down and turned it over. There coiled around the hole was a very large rattle snake. It raised its head about five or six inches and began lolling its long red tongue at me. I was too young to be frightened but called, "Oh mamma! Come and see the snake." She came running, catching me by the arm and ruthlessly snatching me from my perilous position. By the time she had finished killing this snake with the garden hoe, she was ready to collapse.[245]

There was even danger for small children in the awesome and beckoning windblown "waves of grain." They could be lost from sight in these golden seas of grass, as happened in Lancaster City, Nebraska, in 1868, where two children, seven and eight years of age, were lost in the high grasses for days. The parents gave them up for dead, fearing wolves had attacked and killed them. Eleven days after their disappearance, they were found sleeping in the grass, weak and lethargic but alive.[246]

Parents were the educators on the frontier. Itinerant teachers were uncommon since the distances between land-claimed homesteads often were too great. Sometimes the government provided passive support for schooling by allowing forts near homesteads to serve as schooling centers, with literate soldiers and ranking officers inducted as teachers. There was a classroom in Fort Vancouver, for example, where homesteader Abigail Malick and her family lived alongside Oregon's Columbia River. Her children went to the fort's "school" where, Abigail wrote in her diary on 1 March 1854, "they lern very fast. They go to school to Asolder and he is Avery good teacher."[247]

Most frontier parents believed in the value of literacy and insisted that education sites be constructed. Settlers who lived in unorganized districts with no established government shared the cost of hiring teachers for their children and assumed the responsibility themselves for establishing makeshift schoolrooms. Classroom space occasionally was donated but usually was bare of furniture. Barrels, however, were used as desks; a few benches doubled as sitting and writing surfaces. Well-equipped facilities had slate blackboards, readers, or dictionaries, and some were fortunate to have all three. One pioneer woman commented about her childhood education: "I do not know how I learned to read. We had the English reader and the spelling book—Webster's great spelling book that saved the language of the country from being cut into little local dialects."[248]

Formal schoolhouses were erected only after local governments finally were organized. When the local school was built in Abigail Malick's district, she proudly wrote to her family, on 10 June 1855, about her own contribution: "It is a butiful school house And I had to help to build it. It was built by the District. I had to pay 10 dollars And A quarter for my share. It Cost 3 hundred dollars."[249]

Some districts levied education taxes on the community, but most simply charged parents small, affordable fees of about $1.50 per child per year. Teachers were paid up to fifty cents a day. In proportion to the number of children enrolled in school, each family was expected to contribute toward a teacher's room and board. Teacher turnover was high despite the short, five-month school year—three different teachers in a year was not unusual—and education remained haphazard.[250]

Even well-organized schools and dedicated teachers, however, had minimal scholastic impact in areas where students, overburdened and overworked, were at best part-time attendees. Prentice Mulford, a frontier teacher in California, expressed both frustration and awe. About a fifteen-year-old, he wrote:

He was not a regular scholar. He was sent to school only when it was an "off-day" on his father's ranch. In the scholastic sense, he learned nothing.

But that boy at the age of fifteen would drive his father's two-horse wagon, loaded with fruit and vegetables, 150 miles from California to Nevada over the rough mountain roads of the Sierras, sell the produce to the silver miners of Aurora and adjacent camps, and return safely home. He was obliged in places to camp out at night, cook for himself, look out for his stock, repair harness or wagon and keep an eye out for skulking Indians.[251]

In the South, schoolhouses were most commonly log cabins with split-log benches. Teachers in these schools were hired by the town. Customarily, goods were as good as cash for paying teachers their wages. Sam Huston, back in 1811 at Maryville, Tennessee, had a salary of eight dollars per student. He was paid in cash, corn, or cotton.[252]

An education report submitted by Richard Johnston (1822–1898) in 1894 described a typical middle-Georgia school:

A place was selected on the edge of a wood and a field turned out to fallow, sufficiently central, hard by a spring of purest water, a loghouse was put up, say 30 by 25 feet, with one door and a couple of windows and shelves, with benches along the unceiled walls, and the session began. Most families breakfasted about sunrise, and a brisk walk of three-quarters of an hour brought even the remotest dwellers to the early opening. The one who happened to reach the schoolhouse first on winter mornings kindled a fire. . . . At noon a recess of two hours was allowed for dinner and sports.[253]

Like others of its kind on the frontier, the one-room school had pupils of various ages. Antebellum plantations often had their own clerks-cum-teachers, but only for white boys, since education generally was not extended to either girls or slave children.

Eastern visionaries, however, recognized the need for teachers in the new territories and organized societies to raise funds to train teachers and pay their travel expenses to the frontier. These societies hoped to attract enthusiastic candidates—"educational missionaries"—dedicated to the challenge of teaching in new and uncertain circumstances. In 1847, Catherine Beecher (1800–1878) established the National Popular Education Board to direct the surplus of schoolteachers to head west. Between 1847 and 1858 the Board sent out about six hundred young women on a two-year commitment to teach.[254] Henry Ward Beecher (1813–1887), soliciting donations, said in an impassioned speech in 1859:

We have sent to the fairest fields that the sun ever lightened, or flowers enriched, our sons and daughters, who know nothing but to rear along the vast intervales and valleys of the West a civilization as deep, as wide . . . as that which hovers in their memory of dear old New England. . . .

Have you repined that your hand was not gifted with the pen of literature? Then let a hundred hands be created by your beneficence which would not have moved but for your wealth!

Have you repined that your tongue, like a dull and heavy ship, carried your thoughts with slow voyages? Then avenge yourself by chartering clipper-tongues of other men that shall go over the deep, free as the winds.[255]

There had been mission schools for Native Americans more than a hundred years before the federal government began to establish reservation schools, in which boys were taught new concepts of agriculture and were "Christianized." Few were for girls. In 1851, Oklahoma Territory Cherokees founded a female seminary, recruiting teachers from Mount Holyoke. In 1884 the Ursuline nuns traveled to Montana to establish the St. Labre mission school for the northern Cheyenne. This school instructed both boys and girls. Later, particularly amenable and industrious Indian students were sent east to boarding schools for more intensive catechismal study. The most outstanding of these was the Carlisle School of Pennsylvania, founded by Richard Pratt (1840–1924) in 1879 for the purpose of educating Native American children "in the ways of civilization."[256]

There was African slave labor in the Western Hemisphere as early as 1502, the year in which Spain authorized the exportation to Haiti of African men it had enslaved. By 1786 more than two million souls had been cruelly abducted from their villages, stripped of their human dignity, and transported in chains as chattel to Caribbean and American ports.[257]

On Caribbean plantations, or plantocracies,* slaves from Africa labored

---

*Plantations owned twenty or fewer slaves; plantocracies generally had over fifty slaves.

in mines, in sugarcane fields, and as servants.[258] They were occasionally joined by entire Native American Indian families and shipped as slaves to plantations in the West Indies. Authorities in the colonies found it convenient and more lucrative to transport captured Indians rather than imprison them.[259]

In time, Caribbean slaveholders became subject to multiple codices— English, French, and Spanish—enacted to protect Negro slaves from abuse. Several of these laws directly and indirectly affected children's lives. In 1695, for example, the French *Code Noir* punished a slaveholder who "debauched his slave" by confiscating both mother and child. The Spanish *Siete Partidas* enforced compulsory manumission for an abused slave.[260] None of the protective codes applied to Native American slaves.

By the late eighteenth century, when antislavery voices in England resounded with far-reaching reverberations, Caribbean planters, fearing that slave trading would be prohibited, began to purchase large family parcels, thereby significantly increasing the numbers of children being enslaved. As high-sea piracy made slave shipping more hazardous and prices for slaves rose, planters purchased greater numbers of families in anticipation of even higher prices. Meanwhile, the English slave laws in the Caribbean, until that point laxly enforced, became more consistently applied, and new laws were enacted to improve the quality of mothers' and children's lives. The Leeward Islands Act of 1798 ruled that only "light work" could be performed by female slaves in the second trimester of pregnancy, that hospitalization at parturition be mandatory, and "hard labor" for any mother with six children or more be prohibited. The Jamaica Law of 1826 ordered the penalty of death for anyone found guilty of abusing a slave girl under ten years of age.[261]

It was circulated in some quarters that slave mothers were uninterested in their children—and worse. If there was some basis to this scurrility, it would have emanated from the perceived behavior of despairing and despondent wretches whose humanity totally had been shattered. More likely, the accusation was a callow attempt to justify the heinous practices of the slave trade and the use of slaves. In the early 1700s, Hans Sloane (1660–1753) refuted the charge:

The Negroes are usually thought to be haters of their own children and therefore 'tis believed that they sell and dispose of them to strangers for money. But the Parents, here, although their Children are Slaves, for ever, yet have a great love for them, that no master dare sell or give away their little ones, unless they care not whether their Parents hang themselves or no.[262]

Sloane pointed out that mothers would not leave their babies unattended and went into fields to work with their babies on their backs. Attempts to encourage slave women to force-wean their babies, such as the Jamaican program of the early 1800s to enroll infants in "weaning homes," met with failure. Cash premiums for weaning their babies in twelve months generally were refused by the mothers.[263] The obstinacy and determination of these women are a striking contrast to the custom of urbanized industrial women workers in Europe, who often soporified infants and left them at home with little or no supervision.

Planters, quick to assess financial benefits, began to note a correlation between humane treatment and infant survival, and with economics the incentive, improved the treatment of women and their children. In 1780 the Barbados Committee had cited the statistics: of 288 slaves on one plantation, there were 15 births and 57 deaths over a three-year period. In the subsequent four years, after arbitrary punishments and whipping had been prohibited, there were 44 births and only 41 deaths.[264] In St. Lucia in 1815 the same observation was recorded by John Jeremie: "As births are increasing and deaths diminishing, so punishments have diminished by one half."[265]

Infant mortality remained high, however, due to ignorance and disease, malnutrition, and poor living conditions. In Jamaica the rate of mortality in the first fourteen days of life was 25 percent, mainly from infant tetanus. The tetanus neonatorum almost always came from omphalitis, or inflammation of the umbilical stump, which the slaves used to tie with a burned rag.[266] Smallpox, measles, yaws, and worms killed another 25 percent within the first two years.[267]

By 1800, Liverpool, England, trafficked in 90 percent of the world's African slave trade.[268] Members of Parliament, under the leadership of William Wilberforce (1759–1833), having pressed for the abolition of the slave trade, succeeded with a bill that passed on 5 February 1807. To the Royal Navy was given the difficult task of enforcing the law, since illegal trafficking continued. Captain James L. Yeo of HMS *Inconstant* was issued the following orders in 1816:

You are to repair in the first instance to Sierra Leone. . . . In proceeding down the coast you are diligently to look into the several bays and creeks on the same between Cape de Verd and Benguela, particularly on the Gold Coast, Whydah, the Bight of Benin, and Angola, in order to your seizing such ships or vessels as may be liable thereto, . . . and you are to use every other means in your power to prevent a continuance of the traffic in slaves and to give full effect to the Acts of Parliament in question.[269]

❑ ❑ ❑

The African-American experience began when English America first purchased slave cargo from a Dutch ship in 1619 at Jamestown. The subsequent
245-year timeline of the unique and tragic history of a whole race of people
did not end with the Emancipation Proclamation of 1864 that abolished
slavery, but nevertheless permits a framework within which a description of
their enslaved lives is made possible.

By 1700 there were twenty-six thousand African slaves in the colonies, 70
percent of whom were in Maryland and Virginia. "Seasoned slaves" were
shipped up from the Caribbean until 1740, after which they arrived directly from Africa.[270] When the American Revolution broke out, 80 percent of
blacks in the colonies were American-born.[271] After the English law of 1807
abolished the slave trade, slaves were smuggled into the United States, where
the demand for cotton slaves continued to be great enough to support what
became a prospering, thriving business. By 1861, about 450,000 Africans
had been sold to cotton plantation owners. The most active years of the slave
trade in America were between 1740 and 1780, and much of the trading
originated in New England and New York. In 1746, merchant and shipown-
er William Ellery, in his orders to Captain Hammond, first mentioned the
children:

You being Master of our Sloop Anstis and ready to Sail, our orders are that you
embrace the first opportunity and make the best of your way for the Coast of Africa
when please God you arrive there dispose of our Cargoe to the best advantage, make
us returns in Negroes, Gold Dust and whatever you think will answer. If you have a
good Trade for Negroes purchase forty or Fifty Negroes. Get most of them mere
Boys and Girl, some Men, let them be Young, No very small Children.[272]

Slave traders generally commanded better prices selling individuals, and
so motivated, dissolved family groups without compunction. One notable
exception described a remarkable series of coincidences that brought together a family that had been separated and a Caribbean slave trader who expressed a rare sympathy for their circumstances:

I also remember that I once, among my several runs along that coast, happened to
have aboard a whole family, man, wife, three young boys, and a girl, brought here
one after another at several places; and cannot but observe here what mighty satisfaction those poor creatures expressed to be so come together again, though in
bondage . . . and at Martinico, I sold them all together to a considerable planter, at
a cheaper rate than I might have expected had they been disposed of severally, being
informed of that gentleman's good nature, and having taken his word that he would
use that family as well as their circumstances would permit, and settle them in some
part by themselves. (John Barbot, South Guinea, 1682)[273]

The lowest prices for slaves were fetched by toddlers and babies, whose upkeep cost slaveholders time and money. That did not preclude babes in arms being enslaved along with their mothers. Edwin Stede wrote the Royal African Company in 1683:

And about one-third part of those he did bring were very small, most of them no better than sucking children, nay many of them did suck their mothers that were on board . . . some of [the] mothers we believe died on board of ship, and the most part of those small ones not worth about £5 per head.[274]

Children older than ten sold at the best price, since they were malleable, trainable, and had longer work lives. They also were easier to capture and transport, so raiding parties sought them out, some of whom were themselves members of African tribes. Thomas Clarkson, an early English abolitionist, wrote in 1789:

. . . the king of Barbasin has twice sent out his military to attack his own villages in the night. They have been very unsuccessful, having taken but three children. They had no better fortune last night, having brought in but one girl.[275]

In America, at the auction block, young, strong, and healthy boys were singled out by dealers, who separated them from their families. With anticipated long work lives, they were deemed most suitable for field work and commanded the highest prices. Harriett Jacobs* witnessed the sale of a ten-year-old boy who had been purchased at auction for an impressive $720.[276] One slave woman who suffered the loss of all seven of her children—all auctioned to different buyers—exemplified the experiences of many.[277]

With the abolition of the slave trade, obtaining new slaves became difficult, and American slave owners developed the strategy of the Caribbean plantocracies: slave-rearing. Georgia plantation owner John C. Reed remarked that "the greatest profit of all was what the master thought of and talked of all the day long—the natural increase of his slaves."[278] The plantations' trade journal, *The American Cotton Planter*, editorialized: "[The slave mothers,] . . . well treated and cared for, and moderately worked, their natural increase becomes a source of great profit to their owner. Whatever therefore tends to promote their health and render them prolific is worthy of . . . attention."[279] Moorehead Wright wrote to his brother about the deaths of some of his slaves and admitted:

---

*Harriett Jacobs was born in North Carolina in 1813. She escaped her masters in 1830 and had her autobiography published anonymously in 1861. She died in 1897.

. . . I should not complain for I have had a great deal of luck take it all around I have a very goodly number of Negro children coming and have paid a great deal of attention to that part of business. . . . [M]y rule is first plenty of corn and meat to be raised Negro children taken care of and cotton afterwards.[280]

On plantations, the death of the planter became a dreaded event, since his assets were counted and then distributed. The least respect was given to slave family units, who as property of an estate were regarded as numerical entities that could, with sangfroid, be divided and separated.

Although boys sometimes worked as domestics, girls nearly always did. It was common for children, independent of the parents, to be advertised as being available for domestic work. The notice of 28 January 1755 in the *Pennsylvania Gazette* was typical: "To be sold a Negro Girl of twelve Years old, that can be well recommended. Enquire of the Printer."[281]

Girls began their work as "servants" to slave-owners' young daughters and in this way acquired experience before qualifying for service to their mistresses. Girls were taught the proper way to comb "Missy's" hair, to fan her, to bring her slippers or tea.[282] Girls fortunate enough to have their natural mothers still working in the same households were kept under watchful eyes, for slave mothers knew, sometimes through terrible experiences of their own, that young girls could fall prey to the sexual whims of brutal masters. Harriett Jacobs bitterly noted the dehumanization "inflicted by fiends who bear the shape of men." Referring to her own experiences, she lamented, "I cannot tell how much I suffered in the presence of these wrongs, nor how I am still pained by the retrospect."[283] Since "deflowering" of young slave girls was a common danger, daughters were taught to use wild tansey, an excellent abortifacient, to forestall consequent pregnancies.[284]

African-American slaves always were addressed by their given names and rarely were dignified with surnames. Mindful of the fragility of family structures that easily and often were broken up, many adopted cognomens to facilitate tracing sold-off family members. Robert Smalls, who had been a slave, remarked in 1863 that "among themselves they use their titles (last names). . . . [B]efore their masters they do not speak of their titles at all."[285]

Like slaves, indentured children of European backgrounds also were sold: "To be sold by Thomas Overrend, at Drawbridge, Two white Boys and a Negro Lad; all about fourteen Years of Age."[286] Not all children were sold for field work. One man recollected how, as a boy, his master warmed him by the fire and then used him as a foot warmer at the bottom of the bed.[287]

Some children were bequeathed or sold to other children to serve as playmates.[288] In 1852, Peter Evans gave his granddaughter two slaves and wrote her:

You will recollect I told you if you learned well and stood well in the school I would make you a present & I have been as good as my word—I gave your father a deed of gift for Jane and Patience in your name; so they are your property—& at your uncle Hines's sale they would have sold for $1000 each—such negroes are now in great demand.[289]

In North Carolina, 15 percent of wills bequeathed slave children to grand-children.[290] One such child received an admonishment from his playmate's mother, his mistress: "I give your young master over to you and if you let him hurt himself I'll pull your ears, if you let him cry I'll pull your ears, and if he want anything and you don't let him have it, I'll pull your ears."[291]

Although children quickly understood the hierarchy of owner versus slave, the distinctions frequently became hazy in the glow of strong friend-ships. More often than not in such instances, parents stepped in to reassert their eminent domain and to reinforce in the mind of the slave his or her sta-tus as mere property.

By custom and sometimes by state law, slave children did not go to school, regardless of their status. A Mississippi law of 1823 banned any edu-cational gathering of five or more blacks:

All meetings or assemblies of slaves, or free negroes, or mulattoes, mixed and asso-ciating with such slaves above the number of five, at any place of public resort, or at any meeting-house or houses, in the night, or at any school or schools, for teaching them reading or writing, either in the day or night, under whatsoever pretext, shall be deemed and considered an unlawful assembly.[292]

The Commonwealth of Virginia had a similar law and, additionally, pun-ished anyone who facilitated the meeting:

. . . If any white person or persons assemble with free negroes or mulattoes, at any school-house, church, meeting-house, or other place for the purpose of instructing such free negroes or mulattoes to read or write, such person or persons shall, on con-viction thereof, be fined in a sum not exceeding fifty dollars, and moreover may be imprisoned at the discretion of a jury.[293]

The states of Alabama, South Carolina, and North Carolina also forbade the education of blacks, in statutes similar to the following from South Carolina:

If any person shall hereafter teach any slave to read or write, or shall aid or assist in teaching any slave to read or write, or cause or procure any slave to be taught to read or write, such person, if a free white person, upon conviction thereof, shall, for each and every offence against this Act, be fined . . . and imprisoned.[294]

As the American antislavery movement gained followers, influence, and power, euphemisms began to be used self-consciously among genteel Southern families who preferred to acknowledge ownership of "servants" rather than of slaves; and these, they said, were acquired from a "speculator," not a self-indicting slave trader. Slaves began to negotiate more legal "rights," and skilled slaves sought permission to work outside the plantation and to keep a portion of their earnings after a "working tax" was paid to their owners. Many of these slaves saved earnings to manumit their children.[295] Manumitted slave parents were able to have their children educated. In Washington, D.C., for example, a school for free black children advertised:

Founded by an association of free people of color of the city of Washington, called the "Resolute Beneficial Society," situate near the Eastern public school, and the dwelling of Mrs. Fenwick, is now open for the reception of children of free people of color, and others that ladies or gentlemen may think proper to send, to be instructed in reading, writing, arithmetic, English grammar, or other branches of education . . . it is presumed, that free colored families will embrace the advantages thus presented to them. (*National Intelligencer*, 29 August 1818)[296]

As the Civil War (1861–1865) became imminent, slavery as an institution was progressively being challenged, and an institutional breakdown widened. More and more slaves were emboldened to escape their oppressors, aided and abetted by the famous and successful "underground railroad." Children who had either escaped alone or who had experienced the disintegration of their families grew in number. Some, born out of wedlock and called "outside children," were pitied and taken in and supported by other black families.[297] Those orphaned by sale, death, or desertion also were absorbed into de facto kin groups. Their numbers increased dramatically during and after the Civil War—statistical displacements characteristic of the chaos of war. These children were adopted by others of the newly emancipated to share the warmth of a family and a common hardship. Accounts from refugee camps in Vicksburg described many black orphans, "hundreds of these little ones . . . being cared for by poor freedmen and freedwomen . . . [who are] barely able to take care of their own children."[298] The commonality of this phenomenon moved Thomas Conway, head of the Department of the Gulf's Bureau of Free Labor, to comment pragmatically: "I find the colored people themselves taking into their families the orphaned children of their former friends and neighbors thus saving us the necessity of bearing large expenses in caring for them."[299] A Quaker relief worker in Virginia wrote, with unbridled admiration:

It is remarkable to witness how much these poor people do for orphan children. We often find them with one, two, and three helpless children, not their own, but a deceased brother's, sister's, daughter's, son's, cousin's, and not infrequently a deceased friend's child.[300]

The final Proclamation of the Emancipation was issued on 1 January 1863, but the implementation was delayed in many juridictions. In the confusion of emancipation and the war's aftermath, former slaves found themselves adrift and without means to support themselves. Although thousands went west as homesteaders, hundreds of thousands more remained, with few resources or sponsors. Many jurisdictions sought ways to circumvent the good and bold intentions of the emancipation law and used the old laws of indentured servitude as one legal device to do so. Maryland invoked an antebellum apprenticeship law that empowered judges to indenture manumitted children when the court determined it "was better for the habits and comfort of the child that it should be bound as an apprentice to some white person."[301] Maryland implemented the Emancipation Proclamation on 1 November 1864. The next day, 2 November, a virtual stampede of ex-slave owners applied to orphanages to indenture apprentices. Nonorphans also were indentured by former owners, who petitioned the courts with claims of parental incompetence. The alarming number of children so newly and legally reshackled in the week following the Emancipation Proclamation elicited a military order on 9 November 1864, ensuring protection for all former slave families. The indenturing of children continued unabated, however, until 1867, when the Supreme Court struck down the antebellum laws as unconstitutional.[302]

The black manumitted child who remained in urban America generally joined the ranks of the child laborer caught in the industrial spindle of America. Like England, the United States suffered the abuses of child labor, and the response to the problem was just as tortuous and convoluted as society struggled with economic realities and the collective shame of child labor.

Child Labor

As in Europe, industrialization had begun with cotton mills. The first cotton factory, located in Beverly, Massachusetts, justified child labor as a benefit to society. In 1789 a town official reasoned that the factory offered "employment to a great number of women and children many of whom [would] be otherwise useless, if not burdensome to society."[303] Alexander Hamilton (1757–1804) expressed an identical argument about mill work to Congress in 1791: ". . . in general women and children are rendered more useful, and the latter more early useful, by manufacturing establishments, than they would otherwise be."[304]

As late as 1866, factory owners rationalized the employment of children, maintaining that their small torsos were essential to productivity in some industries. A report to the Massachusetts legislature documented that children specifically were sought out, because of their size, to work the factory equipment: "Small help is scarce; a great deal of machinery has been stopped for want of small help, so that the overseers have been going around to draw the small children from schools into the mill; the same as a draft in the army."[305]

Manufacturers of machinery routinely evaluated and sold equipment in terms of children's ages. One claimed that six-spindle machines could be operated by five- to ten-year-olds, whereas twelve-spindle machines required older operators—girls ten to twenty years of age.[306] Factory owners preferred children because they were cheaper to hire, more tractable, reliable, faster, nimbler, and less likely to strike. Small children's wages also kept the overall wage scale artificially low for adults.

In Massachusetts, the Samuel Slater (1768–1835) factory consolidated all stages of manufacturing into one system, from picked cotton to polished yarn. Slater knew that the diversified jobs and the digital finesse required for the machinery were particularly suited to children. In 1801 his factory employed one hundred children from four to ten years of age. By 1810 the Slater system had expanded all across New England, with twenty-seven mills in operation that employed more than 3,500 women and children. By 1820, 43 percent of textile workers in Massachusetts were children, 47 percent in Connecticut, and 55 percent in Rhode Island.[307] State governments approved of child labor in factories, since work there kept potentially idle hands busy, thereby preventing mischief, and most important for the national economy, child labor provided the means by which men could continue their work on farms and thus allow the urban labor market a controlled expansion.

A semi-indentured system had evolved in the United States in which children working in mills were given low wages and compensatory food and shelter. Farm girls in particular were attracted to this system by the protective aspects of this type of employment. After several years of work they were able to accumulate small dowries that made them more eligible candidates for marriage. In time, however, owners stopped providing room and board, while keeping wages low. In Paterson, New Jersey, in 1835, for example, six hundred children employed in a mill earned from $0.50 to $1.75 per week for fourteen-hour workdays—from six o'clock in the morning to eight o'clock at night.[308] The wages were the national norm. Children under ten years generally earned only $0.50 a week. The buying power of such wages was very limited. The Slater Company, like many factories, had a company store in which, in 1810, flour cost $0.09 a pound; sugar, $0.23. Soap cost $0.16 a pound; candles, $0.20. Corn was $1.34 a bushel, and potatoes were $0.16 a bushel. Although these commodities seem incredibly cheap by today's standards, their purchase soon depleted the pitifully small salaries of most wage earners. Even with all of the children working, account ledgers show that families usually had credit balances owed to the store.[309]

Mining, glass, and cotton industries were the most notoriously exploitive of children.[310] In Pennsylvania the number of children employed in coal mines equaled the combined number of children working in New York, Illinois, and Massachusetts. Just before the turn of the century, fourteen thousand children were "legally" working the mines and an additional ten thousand were illegal. They were mule drivers, runners, gate tenders, and "breakers," who separated slate from coal. The glass industry, which by 1890 employed more than 7,500 boys, worked them at night when the temperatures of the day had cooled. Children worked in furnace rooms where the heat kept molds malleable and where temperatures ranged from 100 to 130 degrees Fahrenheit. They sweltered twelve hours a day for sixty-five cents.

Social legislation enacted in England occasioned empathetic reactions in America that resulted in some early nineteenth-century legal reforms. Initially, although these reform laws did not prohibit child labor, they did mandate education. Connecticut passed a law in 1813 requiring that all children who worked in factories be instructed in reading, writing, and arithmetic. Massachusetts passed a similar law in 1836, and by 1850 both Rhode Island and Pennsylvania had followed suit. These laws were the precursors of public education in the United States.

Organized labor had been active as early as the 1840s in supporting child-labor reform by demanding that children's work hours be decreased. Massachusetts responded in 1842 by decreasing children's workdays from twelve to ten hours. In 1848, Pennsylvania, for the first time in history, set a minimum working age. Children had to be twelve years old before they could legally be employed. The legislation, sadly, was largely ignored, and young children, as always, were sent to work in coal mines. Connecticut established a minimum working age as well—nine years and older. In Massachusetts it was ten years old.

In the South, the efforts of Alabama's Rev. Edgar Murphy (1869–1913) resulted in child-labor legislation but not until 1903. The other Southern states remained steadfastly resistant to abolishing or ameliorating child-labor practices. It was not until the late 1920s that national labor laws forced reforms, even in the South.

Prior to national labor standards, poor, itinerant worker families had little or no protection as they moved from state to state seeking work. Poor children and immigrant families often sought refuge in almshouses. There were few specific shelters for children. In 1825 there were four; by 1865, sixty.* The New York House of Refuge, which had been established in 1825, accommodated only sixteen children[311] and was, in any case, more a house of correction than a shelter.

Reformatories were thought to be a solution for a growing national problem. One such school, opened in 1854 in Massachusetts, exclusively housed wayward girls. By 1885 there were forty-five reform schools scattered across America, in large urban areas, supported mainly by public funds. Some of these received support from contractors who set up and supervised shops on the premises, where children were put to work. Otherwise, the asylums had supervisors who administered the hard work with strict regimentation and punishments. The children could anticipate few school hours, despite prevailing laws. Most reformatories admitted only boy offenders who had been caught stealing. Girls were sent to the reformatories for sexual behavior.[312] Reformatories were criticized for their prison-like environments by several concerned bodies. European-type family reform schools were proposed, in which small groups of children living in cottages were supervised by surrogate parents. The aforementioned Massachusetts State Industrial School for Girls adopted this concept, as did institutions in Ohio and New Jersey. Institutions called protectories also were founded, for children who were thought to be too old for orphanages and too young to be sent to houses of correction. The intention was to remove children from corruptive urban environments and to favorably mold their characters with compassion in a lenient atmosphere. The New York Catholic Protectory, with more than two thousand children in residence by 1875, became the largest of these.[313] Critics of these arrangements either favored gender segregation for the protectories or insisted that a fabricated family setting was salubrious and necessary.

In 1848, New York City counted ten thousand vagrant children. Communities in all of America's urban areas were hard-pressed to deal with the increasing numbers of the poor, orphaned, and destitute who were to be found in the streets. Charles Loring Brace (1826–1890), a graduate of the

---

*At the beginning of the nineteenth century there were only four orphanages in the country—in Boston, Philadelphia, Georgia, and in French New Orleans. The Georgia orphanage had been founded by George Whitefield in 1739. The New Orleans orphanage had been founded by Ursuline nuns in 1728 to care for orphaned children of the company of the Indies. The Natchez uprising increased the number of orphans, and in 1732 the French government subsidized the institution with 4,500 livres. The Ursulines also had a school for black and Native children in the confines of the convent school, which taught girls from 1:00 to 2:30 every afternoon (Bremner, 1970, pp. 60–61, 271). By 1877 there were 208 orphanages nationwide.

Yale Divinity School and the Union Theological Seminary, vividly explained the phenomenon:

. . . [Great] numbers of human beings are crowded together. From this massing together of families and the drunken habits prevailing it results very naturally that the children prefer outdoor life to their wretched tenements . . . picking up a livelihood by petty thieving and peddling.[314]

In 1854 he founded the Children's Aid Society in New York to deal with the problem. Brace borrowed an old idea of removing children from the urban squalor and relocating them in rural areas. Between 1854 and 1929 the Children's Aid Society sent west 150,000 children from New York slums.* Orphans were organized into "little companies" of five to thirty children and, accompanied by adult leaders, were sent via train and by prearrangement to waiting communities. In adulthood, one man recalled the experience:

We boarded the . . . train somewhere close to New York City. The train had four coaches with about forty orphans each. In St. Louis, Missouri, the train was divided and the coaches went to four different states, Kansas, Missouri, Oklahoma, and Arkansas. My coach went to Berryville, Arkansas.[315]

Ninety percent of the children placed were American-born of German or Irish ancestry. Less than 1 percent were from Italian, Jewish, or Russian backgrounds.[316] Brace favored "western European" cultures for his experiment, believing they would interact better. There were no shortages of vagrant children. The Civil War exaggerated the number of vagrant children, and as a result, Boston had six thousand and New York City over thirty thousand on their streets.[317] Overwhelmed cities welcomed placing out as a coping maneuver. Municipalities were willing to contribute to the cost of the program, which became progressively more expensive. In 1880 the program was estimated to cost fifteen dollars per child, which included clothing, food en route, and train fare. By 1892 over eighty-four thousand children had found country homes,[318] but by 1900 the cost of sponsorship had increased to thirty-eight dollars, and Brace was forced to make wide appeals for funds.[319]

The children arrived at a local church, city hall, school, or county courthouse, where townsfolk and farmers gathered and waited to select the child they were going to "adopt." One boy arriving in Arkansas related:

---

*Brace's program of "placing out" was adopted by several other organizations, such as the New York Foundling Hospital (1869), Boston's Children's Mission (1850), the New York Five Point Mission (1852), and the Philadelphia Women's Industrial Aid Association (1857). In all, two hundred thousand women and children were relocated. Holt, 1992, pp. 2–4, 82–110.

We were taken from the train to the Methodist Church. Speeches were made and folks were asked to take an orphan home for dinner. Later that afternoon we were brought back for the selection process. . . . I felt sorry for the others because some of them were not chosen. I know now how it must have hurt them to feel that no one wanted them.[320]

The Society was not naive. It recognized that some children might be abused, and it had a mandate for follow-up visits. However, the number of children and the distances involved were so great that not every child was followed up. There were no contracts for placements, only verbal agreements,[321] but the Society agreed to remove any child if the new employer was unhappy. Some complaints began to filter down, and the Society was accused of sending out juvenile delinquents and other undesirables. Brace and his administrators, however, were not always at fault. Some children, particularly boys, simply packed up and ran away. Additionally, it became obvious that not all the children were orphans—many were handed over by families too poor to care for their children. The complaints began to take their toll, and conjoined with the evolving child-labor laws, new foster-care programs, and a National Children's Bureau, the "orphan trains" and placing out came to an end.

The new discipline of social work[322] and the widespread establishment of kindergartens also played a part in the end of the placing-out programs. American kindergartens in particular became popular as efficient and cost-saving containment centers. Large cities began to develop these preschool settings in growing numbers, not so much for teaching as to remove slum children from the streets and to prevent them, as early as possible, from developing criminal habits.[323]

Charles Loring Brace and the Children's Aid Society also were active in the educational effort and founded many industrial schools among the tenements of the urban sprawl. In New York City alone, by 1890 the society had twenty-one schools, and a sister institution, the American Female Guardian Society, had an additional twelve. Among the thirty-three schools, enrollment was fifteen thousand. Only poor slum children were accepted, following a credo written by the board of the Children's Aid Society expressing the purpose of the schools:

. . . to receive and educate children who cannot be accepted by the public schools either by reason of their ragged and dirty condition, or owing to the fact that they can attend but part of the time, because they are obliged to sell papers or to stay at home to help their parents. The children at our schools belong to the lowest and poorest class of people in the city.[324]

Anonymous donors and benefactors sponsored the school meal that was served daily to the children. For many, it was the only meal of the day. The school halls resounded with Italian, Bohemian, Yiddish, Irish, and German accents as children from a variety of ethnic and racial backgrounds, including manumitted children, casually mingled and interacted.[325] The multiethnic socialization among the children at school strikingly differed from the behavior of the typically self-isolating clusters of individual ethnic groups that comprised the neighborhoods in which the children lived.

A second wave of immigrants from Europe, conjoined with increasing industrialization, kept the population of working children high. Between 1860 and 1900, 14 million immigrants settled mostly in the urban-industrial Northeast. A census in 1870, the first to classify occupations, initiated a tally of working children. The 1880 census recorded over a million child workers between the ages of ten and fifteen, and by 1890, the number had increased to 1.5 million—almost 20 percent of all American children between the ages of ten and fifteen years. The American Federation of Labor (AFL) reacted to the statistic by adopting a resolution encouraging all states to ban from factory work children younger than fourteen years. Although the resolution lacked legal might, the political power of the AFL could be detected in the 1892 platform of the Democratic Party Convention: "We are in favor of the enactment by the States of laws for abolishing the notorious sweating system, for abolishing contract convict labor, and for prohibiting the employment in factories of children under fifteen years of age."[326]

❑ ❑ ❑

Not just in America but all over the world, the social scientist and worker as legitimate agents of change proposing solutions in the struggle for children's rights, were gaining recognition.[327] In England in 1883, Samuel Smith, MP, founded in Liverpool the Society for the Prevention of Cruelty to Children. In 1889, Lord Shaftebury organized a similar society in London. In France, Paul Nourisson and Ernest Nusse founded a society with the same goal. In Germany, von Pelet-Narbonne chaired the Verein zum Schutz der Kinder vor Ausmutzung und Misshandlung. In Austria, Lydia von Wolfring organized the Wiener Kinder Schutz und Rettungs Verein, and in Italy, Count Boromeo inaugurated the Milan Society to Protect Children. The American equivalent, the Children's Protective Society, was founded by Henry Bergh.

Twenty years after Brace had started his program, the Society for the Prevention of Cruelty to Animals (SPCA), his attention turned to the plight of children trapped in urban poverty and abuse. The former head of the SPCA, Henry Bergh (1811–1888) joined him in founding the Society for the Prevention of Cruelty to Children. In 1875, Bergh inaugurated the Society with the startling statement that "the child is an animal . . . if there is no justice for it as a human being, it shall at least have the rights of the stray cur in the streets."[328] Thereafter, the SPCC worked independently but alongside the Children's Aid Society. The SPCC defined as cruelty the following[329]:

All treatment or conduct by which physical pain is wrongfully, needlessly, or excessively inflicted, or by which life or limb or health is wrongfully endangered or sacrificed, or neglect to provide such reasonable food, clothing, shelter, protection, and care as the life and well-being of the child require; the exposure of children during unreasonable hours of inclement weather, as peddlers, hawkers, or otherwise; their employment in unwholesome, degrading, or unlawful callings; or any employment by which the powers of children are over-taxed or their hours of labor unreasonably prolonged; and the employment of children as mendicants, or the failure to restrain them from vagrancy or begging. (Brooklyn SPCC, 1884)

The SPCC prosecuted abusive parents and gained custody of the children, placing them in asylums or referring them to the Children's Aid Society.

The printed media was used effectively by child advocates. Several exposés and analyses were published, including Franklin Briggs's *Boys as They Are Made and How to Remake Them* (1894), Jacob Riis's (1849–1914) *The Children of the Poor* (1892), Stanley Hall's *Adolescence*, and Jane Addams's (1860–1935) *The Spirit of Youth*. All agreed that the pitiful lives of neglected and abused children were the root cause of juvenile crime.[330]

In 1889, Jane Addams and Ellen Starr (1859–1940) founded Hull House in Chicago as a social-settlement institution that explored labor conditions in factories and provided families in the community with extensive social services, including housing and day-care. The following year the National Consumers League was founded. By the turn of the century the League was the most powerful anti–child-labor force in America. The league organized campaigns against sweatshops, long working hours, low wages, and child labor in general. The general secretary, Florence Kelley (1859–1932), a resident of Hull House, was an attorney and chief factory inspector for the state of Illinois. Her vivid descriptions of working conditions in factories prompted the passage of legislation that limited children's workload,[331] and in conjunction with the efforts of other social reformers, by the 1900s protective legislation passed in the Northern states had reduced the number of children in the workforce by 50 percent.

No such legislation altered the factory-labor population in the South. Despite the legislative gains in the North, the 1900 census registered two million working children, a reflection of an overall increase in the region's population.[332] This led the National Child Labor Committee, in conjunction with the Consumers League to agitate for national legislation to uniformly prohibit these child abuses.

ASPECTS OF EIGHTEENTH-CENTURY CHILDHOOD

Changelings Endure

From primitive to classical cultures and onward, inexplicable congenital infant malformations were ascribed to mysterious forces beyond human control. Empedokles (490–430 B.C.) posited the theory that maternal sensory input—*phantasiai*—determined infants' phenotype. He believed that "women who have fallen in love with statues and pictures frequently give birth to children who resemble them."[333] Six hundred years later the Roman physician Soranus cited examples of women who gave birth to monkeys after having seen monkeys during coitus.[334] Primitive cultures also believed in transmutations that occurred during intercourse. As late as 1820, Edwin James recorded the stories of American Plains Natives who described instances of anomalous births of newborns with animal features if their mothers had seen just such animals during coitus.[335]

Throughout the Christian era, churchmen blamed sinful behavior or heresy for congenital anomalies. In 1570 the French bishop Arnaud Sorbin (1532–?) wrote an entire book on the topic, called *Tractus de Monstris*. In one example, he blamed the birth of Muhammad in 570 for the occurrence in 578 of a child born with sirenomelia, or fused lower extremities without

Figure 8.3a Illustrations from Sorbin's book *Tractus de Monstris*: a sirenomelus.
REPRINTED BY PERMISSION OF OXFORD UNIVERSITY PRESS.

Figure 8.3b
Illustrations from Sorbin's book *Tractus de Monstris*: a boy with a hare-head.
REPRINTED BY PERMISSION OF OXFORD UNIVERSITY PRESS.

feet (figure 8.3a). In another instance of a child who resembled a rabbit (figure 8.3b), he maintained that its birth coincided with that of the Roman Catholic heretic Martin Luther.[336]

By the eighteenth century, Christian Europe no longer necessarily considered sin to be the cause of malformations. The more general belief was that mutations occurred by sensory transmissions catalyzed by a mother's chance experience—casual or dreadful. Such reports published by figures of authority authenticated their credibility and fueled the common and enduring belief that mystical forces caused birth defects. For example, Daniel Turner's (1667–1741) *Treatise of Diseases Incident to the Skin*, published in 1714, described several examples of anomalous births and how, purportedly, they occurred:

. . . At Leyden in the year 1638 a Woman of the meaner Sort who lived near the Church of St. Peter was delivered of a Child well shaped in every respect but had the Head of a Cat: Imagination was that which had given Occasion for this Monster, for being big with Child she was frighten'd exceedingly by a Cat gotten into her Bed. . . .

. . . A Niece of Pope Nich. 3., of the Family of the Ursini, had a monstrous Birth all over hairy, armed as it were with Bears Claws instead of Toes and Fingers, which she ascribed to her looking on the Picture of the Creature everywhere hung up in the Dwellings of the said Family. . . .

. . . In the year of 1517 a Child was born with the Shape in its Face exactly like that of a Frog, which was brought to pass by the Mother's holding that Creature in her Hand to allay the Heat of a Fever about the Time of her Conception. . . .

. . . She stayed a good while in the Water and fixed her eyes on some red Pebbles which lay at the bottom of the water and a While after, growing big, she was delivered of a Child whose white Skin was copiously speckled with Spots of the Colour and Bigness of those Stones.[337]

J. A. Blondel ridiculed Turner's logic as well as his tales in two scathing books (1729 and 1730).[338] His rational views apparently did not influence thinking among either the populace or scientists. In 1726, Sarah Toft of Godalming astonished all of England with her claim that she had given birth to seventeen rabbits. This remarkable feat had been attested to by no less a personage than Mr. St. Andre, surgeon to King George I, in *A Short Narrative of an Extraordinary Delivery of Rabbets Perform'd by Mr. John Howard Surgeon at Guilford*.[339] St. Andre's skeptical colleague, Sir Richard Manningham, ultimately extracted a confession of fraud from the woman. That this extraordinary episode of fraud managed to embroil not only the *accoucheurs* and doctors but also the king of England and England's citizenry illustrates how persistent was the belief in changelings. A treatise published in 1787 by Karl Christian Krause (1781–1832), *Von der Wirkung und dem Einflusse der Einbildungskraft der Mutter auf die Frucht . . .,*[340] once more reinforced ancient concepts that, in fact, prevailed until late in the nineteenth century, when teratogenesis was scientifically studied and explained.

Pap, Gin, and Opium

Simon de Vallambert (?–1565) was the first to publish, in 1565, a treatise on nourishing weaning foods for children. *De la maniere de nourrir et gouverner les enfans de levr naissance* contained recipes for pap and panada, a nutritious preparation used for a quarter of a century. Pap consisted of flour or bread crumbs cooked in water or milk, and in panada meat broth and eggs were added to the basic ingredients. In the two hundred years that followed, multiple recipes were developed and published, but the simple and most commonly affordable recipes were those of Vallambert:

[Pap]
The flour of which it is made nowadays the greater part of the nurses pass simply through a sieve without other preparation. Others cook it in the oven. . . . The milk mixed with the flour is commonly from the goat or cow, that of the goat is better. When one intends to add more nourishment one adds finally an egg yolk, when one wishes to guard against constipation one adds honey.

[Panada]
One grates a crumb of bread very small, then one puts it in a bouillon of good flesh in a small glazed earthen pot and puts it to cook on a small charcoal fire without smoke. Sometimes it is cooked in a bouillon of peas or other legumes, with oil or

butter and more often it is cooked with goats or cows milk or milk of sweet almonds. Others mix with the panada an egg yolk or the entire egg.[341]

Adults also chewed food thoroughly and offered the mass on a spoon to their toddlers, an ancient custom that is practiced today in many parts of the world.* At a glance, it seems unaesthetic and unhealthy, but, in fact, infants can be successfully weaned on prechewed foods that, surprisingly, have some health benefits. Saliva contains amylase that initiates starch digestion, as well as lysozymes and other proteolytic proteins that function as antibacterials.

Questions regarding nutrition and weaning became controversial as the twentieth century approached. Evidence of nutritional values in food was, for the most part, anecdotal and unproven, but authorities were doctrinaire in the diets they developed and supported. The American Emmett Holt (1855–1924) advocated in his 1896 text that nothing but mother's milk be given infants until the age of ten months, when beef juice and a gruel of oats, wheat, and barley could be supplemented. At twelve months, nothing but a pap, three times daily, was recommended. It consisted of milk, five ounces; cream, one ounce; water, two ounces; and cereal gruel, two ounces per feeding.[342]

Ernst Moro (1874–1951), the Heidelberg professor, suggested that his *karotten suppe* (1902) be fed as a weaning food; in France, Antonin Marfan (1858–1942) prohibited the introduction of meat to the diet until eighteen months of age, yet August Steffen (1825–1909), in Germany, recommended that children be fed twenty-five grams of meat and one egg daily from the age of nine months.[343] Thomas Rotch (1849–1914) of Philadelphia insisted that tightly controlled percentages of protein, carbohydrate, and fats be fed to the young, and he developed formulas for lowering casein and increasing fat and sugar in the diet (c.1900). His recipe was water, five ounces; cream, two ounces; and milk, one ounce, combined with lactose, limewater, and cereal.[344]

A soy formula (c.1909) first was used by John Ruhräh (1872–1935), and in 1928 when canned baby food first arrived on the American grocery shelf, *beikost* was commercialized. The topic of what, when, and how to feed babies stimulated great controversy and debate, inspiring a poet—strongly suspected to be John Ruhräh himself—to compose the following:

---

*Weaning with prechewed foods has been recommended through a long continuum by no lesser figures than Galen, Soranus, Trotula, and Wurtz, to name but a few. Some cultures, in imitation of birds, pass masticated food, mouth to mouth, directly to the infant, in a process called "food-kissing."

Soranus, he of ancient Rome,
He had a simple trick
To see if milk was fit for sale,
He merely dropped it on his nail
To see if it would stick;
Yet spite of this the babies grew
As any school boy'll tell to you.

Good Metlinger in ages dark
Just called milk good or bad
No acid milk could vex his soul
He gave it good, he gave it whole
A method very sad;
Yet babies grew to man's estate
A fact quite curious to relate.

Time sped and science came along
To help the human race,
Percentages were brought to fame
By dear old Rotch, of honored name,
We miss his kindly face;
Percentages were fed to all
Yet babies grew both broad and tall.

The calorie now helped us know
The food that is required
Before the baby now could feed
We figured out his daily need
A factor much desired;
Again we see with great surprise
The babies grow in weight and size.

The vitamin helps clarify
Why infants fail to gain,
We feed the baby leafy food
Which for the guinea pig is good
A reason very plain;
And still we watch the human race
Go madly at its usual pace.

We have the baby weighed today
The nursing time is set,
At last we find we are so wise
We can begin to standardize
No baby now need fret;
In spite of this the baby grows
But why it does God only knows.

Away with all such childish stuff
Bring chemists to the fore,
The ion now is all the rage
We listen to the modern sage
With all his latest lore;
And if the baby fret or cry
We'll see just how the ions lie.

A hundred years will soon go by
Our places will be filled
By others who will theorize
And talk as long and look as wise
Until they too are stilled;
And I predict no one will know
What makes the baby gain and grow.[345]

Opioid elixirs were used with regularity during the seventeenth, eighteenth, and nineteenth centuries. Only in the early twentieth century did their use diminish. Many nineteenth-century physicians considered opium a *donum Dei* for children. It was used liberally as a soporific and was sold therapeutically for a number of childhood ailments—teething, diarrhea, colic, and parasites. Concentrated opioids were prescribed by physicians and were also available in proprietary products such as Godfrey's Cordial, which had an opium concentration of 1 mg/ml, and Dalby's Carminative, which had an 0.25 mg/ml opium concentration.[346]

Unaware of its depressive and addictive nature, opium was a popular soporific used casually by wet nurses and haggard mothers. The readily available product was facile to administer to an infant or toddler, for whom a dose of five milliliters sufficed to induce sleep. Many infants were overdosed with opium unwittingly and died of respiratory depression. Cocaine, a weaker narcotic, also was available over the counter. It was an ingredient in many compounds.

Gin also was given to children as a soporific, and its consumption by adults and children was a significant public-health issue in England during the eighteenth century. In the seventeenth century, gin had been an expensive libation imported from the Netherlands. The British government encouraged its domestic distillation and production through a series of legislative acts that provided large tax incentives. Gin then became locally produced and a very cheap source of liquor; a penny's worth was sufficient to intoxicate the average adult. Consumption of gin in England[347] rose from 527,000 gallons in 1685 to 11,000,000 gallons in 1750. Alcoholism became an addition to the already extensive list of risk factors associated with infant mortality.

Figure 8.4 *The Drunkard's Children*, by George Cruickshank (1848).
COLLECTION OF DR. AND MRS. BRUCE RITSON.

Infants of a chronically drunken parent or parents suffered from total neglect as well as from stuporous abuse. Also, parents gave their infants and children as much as sixty milliliters of gin on a routine basis to sedate them. The administration of alcohol to children was a problem throughout Europe and America. The abuses and consequences of alcohol were studied and publicized throughout the Western world by many figures. The abuse in England was depicted in the etchings of William Hogarth and Thomas Rowlandson (1757–1827) and the illustrations of George Cruickshank (1792–1878) (figure 8.4), as well as in the writings of Henry Fielding, John Wesley (1703–1791), and Thomas Trotter (1760–1832). In Austria, F. W. Lippich (1799–1845) and, in France, Rosch (1808–1866) wrote extensively on alcohol abuse. In America, Anthony Benezet (1713–1784) warned about alcohol habituation, and Benjamin Rush (1747–1813), a distinguished physician and signer of the Declaration of Independence, focused attention on the harmful use of alcohol by children in the fledgling nation. The term *alcoholism* was not used in any country until it appeared in a study titled *Alcoholismus Chronicus* and written by Magnus Hall, a Swedish physician, in 1849. The book was an authoritative work that described both the organic and psychiatric detriments of alcohol use.[348]

Subsequent data were accumulating in the medical literature regarding the chronic use of alcohol. This was sufficient to cause many physicians to question its use medically. Alcohol as therapy continued, however, to be advocated even as late as the 1916 edition of *Diseases of Infancy and Childhood* by Emmett Holt:

An infant one year old for whom alcohol is indicated should not be given to begin with more than one-fourth of an ounce of brandy or whisky during the twenty-four hours, and even in bad conditions it is rarely advisable to give more than twice this quantity, except for a very short period. In children four years old double the amount may be employed in the corresponding conditions. Little good and much harm is likely to follow such amounts as four or five ounces daily. . . . There certainly is a strong tendency at the present time to use less and less alcohol in therapeutics and many would abandon it altogether.[349]

Future studies of alcohol use and its effect on children in utero took the modern world full circle, backward in time to the biblical wisdom of Judges (13:7) that advised, "Behold thou shalt conceive and bear a son: now drink no wine or strong drink," predating the scientific description of the etiology of fetal alcohol syndrome by more than two thousand years.

NOTES

1. Schwartz, 1983, pp. 42–44.
2. Heywood, 1988, pp. 195–98.
3. Rose, 1991, p. 3.
4. Anderson and Zinsser, 1988, vol. 2, pp. 254–58.
5. Turberville, 1926, p. 156.
6. Pinchbeck and Hewitt, 1973, vol. 2, p. 354.
7. Heywood, 1988, pp. 130–31.
8. Pinchbeck and Hewitt, 1973, vol. 2, p. 360.
9. Ibid., pp. 141–42.
10. Ibid., p. 401.
11. Anderson and Zinsser, 1988, vol. 2, p. 262.
12. Payne, 1916, pp. 313–14.
13. Ibid., pp. 317–18.
14. Bayne-Powell, 1938, p. 91.
15. Schwartz, 1983, p. 15.
16. Ibid., p. 88.
17. Bayne-Powell, 1938, p. 90.
18. Jordan, 1987, p. 31.
19. Coldham, 1992, p. 16.
20. Pinchbeck and Hewitt, 1969, vol. 1, pp. 127–41.
21. Johnson, 1991, pp. 26–27.
22. Besant, 1902, p. 156.
23. J. H. Baron. Hogarth and hospitals, *Lancet* 1987; 2:1512–14.
24. Bayne-Powell, 1938, pp. 267–68.
25. Pinchbeck and Hewitt, 1969, vol. 1, pp. 117–21.
26. Anderson and Zinsser, 1988, vol. 2, pp. 254–58.

27. Johnson, 1991, p. 4.
28. Rose, 1991, pp. 36–37.
29. Pinchbeck and Hewitt, 1973, vol. 2, p. 403.
30. Rose, 1991, p. 20.
31. Jordan, 1987, p. 35.
32. Payne, 1916, pp. 319–24.
33. Ibid.
34. Caulfield, 1931, pp. 8–9.
35. Ibid.
36. Bayne-Powell, 1938, p. 89.
37. Jordan, 1987, pp. 84–85.
38. Ibid., pp. 83–84.
39. Pinchbeck and Hewitt, 1973, vol. 2, pp. 497–98.
40. Schwartz, 1983, p. 40.
41. Schorsch, 1979, p. 143.
42. Ibid.
43. Fuchs, 1984, p. 5.
44. Anderson and Zinsser, 1988, vol. 2, p. 246.
45. Rose, 1991, pp. 51–52.
46. Jordan, 1987, p. 37.
47. Heywood, 1988, pp. 171–73.
48. Jordan, 1987, p. 22.
49. Sherwood, 1988, pp. 134–35.
50. Anderson and Zinsser, 1988, vol. 2, p. 262.
51. Reddy, 1984, p. 165.
52. Pinchbeck and Hewitt, 1973, vol. 2, p. 406.
53. *London Lancet*, 1859; 1:247–48.
54. Bayne-Powell, 1938, pp. 303–4.
55. W. Blake, *Essays of Elia* (New York: Macmillan, 1931), p. 153.
56. Schwartz, 1983, p. 41.
57. Heywood, 1988, p. 58.
58. C. Dickens, *Oliver Twist* (Oxford: Oxford University Press, 1966), p. 14.
59. Rose, 1991, pp. 56–57.
60. Besant, 1902, p. 387.
61. The padrone system predominantly was used to exploit children as "entertainers," but other enterprises adopted the tactic. In southern European cities, itinerant padroni and their Polish and Bohemian children went from farm to farm in the summers, picking berries, and moving to Gulfport cannerys in oyster and shrimp seasons. Kemp, 1986, p. 20.
62. Zucchi, 1992, pp. 18–40.
63. Ibid., pp. 138–42.
64. Ibid., p. 128.
65. Ibid., pp. 175–77.
66. Mayhew, 1861/1985, pp. 524–40.
67. Rose, 1991, p. 53.

68. Jordan, 1987, pp. 68–70.

69. Anderson and Zinsser, 1988, vol. 2, p. 250.

70. Pinchbeck and Hewitt, 1973, vol. 2, p. 391.

71. Ibid., pp. 392–93.

72. Rose, 1991, pp. 32–33.

73. Paine, 1792, pp. 66–81.

74. Sommerville, 1992, pp. 166–70.

75. E. B. Browning, *The Poetical Works* (Boston: Houghton Mifflin, 1974), p. 156. As a child advocate, Charles Dickens was instrumental not only in social reforms but also in moving public consciousness in support of a children's hospital. Writing in *Household Words*, he brought attention to the Hospital for Sick Children on Great Ormond Street and in the process let the public know that the differences between the adult and the child patient constituted the discipline of pediatrics:

> It does not at all follow that the intelligent physician who has learnt how to treat successfully the illnesses of adults, has only to modify his plans a little, to diminish the proportions of his doses, for the application of his knowledge to our little sons and daughters. Some of their diseases are peculiar to themselves; other diseases, common to us all, take a form in children varying as much from their familiar form with us as a child varies from a man. (*Lancet* 1999; 354:673–75)

76. The Society's avowed aim was to make every charity school "a Fortress and a Frontier Garrison against Popery" (Cunningham, 1992, p. 33).

77. Bayne-Powell, 1938, p. 277.

78. Cunningham, 1992, pp. 72–78.

79. Pinchbeck and Hewitt, 1973, vol. 2, pp. 404–5.

80. Cunningham, 1992, p. 94.

81. Ibid., p. 77.

82. Rose, 1991, p. 35.

83. Heywood, 1988, p. 203.

84. Besant, 1902, p. 155.

85. Lord Shaftesbury's relentless reform work contributed greatly to the Ragged school movement, and he was president of the Ragged School Union for forty years. Additionally, he was a principal founder of reformatory and refuge unions, Young Men's Christian Associations, and working men's institutes. Hammond, 1958.

86. Jordan, 1987, pp. 168–69.

87. Anderson and Zinsser, 1988, vol. 2, p. 185.

88. Jordan, 1987, p. 14.

89. Gwynn, 1958, p. 612.

90. Jordan, 1987, p. 15.

91. Rose, 1991, p. 80.

92. Most executions of children were for the felony of stealing. In 1808, Michael Hammond, aged eleven, and his sister, aged seven, were hanged for stealing, and as late as 1831 a nine-year-old boy was hanged at Chelmsford for setting a fire. Laurence, 1960, p. 18.

93. Coldham, 1992, p. 14.
94. Pinchbeck and Hewitt, 1973, vol. 2, pp. 433–35.
95. Jordan, 1987, p. 277.
96. Pinchbeck and Hewitt, 1973, vol. 2, pp. 447–49.
97. Ibid., p. 455.
98. Jordan, 1987, pp. 278–79.
99. Pinchbeck and Hewitt, 1973, vol. 2, pp. 447–49.
100. Jordan, 1987, pp. 277–80.
101. Ibid., pp. 288–90.
102. Pinchbeck and Hewitt, 1973, vol. 2, p. 547.
103. Trumbach, 1978, p. 255.
104. Bayne-Powell, 1938, pp. 68–69.
105. Jordan, 1987, p. 151.
106. Bayne-Powell, 1938, pp. 273–74.
107. Colón, 1987, p. 11.
108. Trumbach, 1978, pp. 257–60.
109. Perrot, 1990, p. 210.
110. Knox, 1799, p. 134.
111. Trumbach, 1978, pp. 264–65.
112. Pickles, 1990, pp. 8–10.
113. Bayne-Powell, 1938, p. 273.
114. Locke, 1693/1989, pp. 262–63.
115. Robiquet, 1965, p. 81.
116. Hunt, 1970, pp. 61–62.
117. Ibid., pp. 63–64.
118. *Economist*, 31 July 1993, p. 46.
119. Robiquet, 1965, p. 83.
120. Ibid., pp. 82–84.
121. Ibid.
122. Heywood, 1988, pp. 62–63.
123. Laurence, 1960, p. 74.
124. Ibid., p. 73.
125. Heywood, 1988, p. 128.
126. Fuchs, 1984, p. 18.
127. Payne, 1916, p. 341.
128. Perrot, 1990, pp. 143–44.
129. Fuchs, 1984, pp. 111–14.
130. Ibid., pp. 46–48.
131. Ibid., pp. 157–58.
132. Badinter, 1980, p. 22.
133. Perrot, 1990, pp. 168–70.
134. Badinter, 1980, pp. 213–14.
135. Anderson and Zinsser, 1988, vol. 2, p. 156.
136. Ibid.

137. Perrot, 1990, p. 314.

138. Ibid., p. 157.

139. Ibid., p. 226.

140. Heywood, 1988, pp. 21–35.

141. D. I. Kertzer, *Family Life in Central Italy, 1880–1910* (New Brunswick, NJ: Rutgers University Press, 1984).

142. Heywood, 1988, pp. 102–5.

143. Weissbach, 1989, p. 16.

144. Heywood, 1988, p. 113.

145. Reddy, 1984, p. 162.

146. Weissbach, 1989, pp. 12–13.

147. Reddy, 1984, p. 166.

148. Ibid.

149. Heywood, 1988, pp. 121–23.

150. Ibid., p. 146.

151. Weissbach, 1989, pp. 23–26.

152. Ibid., pp. 31–36.

153. Ibid., p. 49.

154. Heywood, 1988, pp. 220–24.

155. Ibid., p. 229.

156. Reddy, 1984, p. 236.

157. Weissbach, 1989, pp. 236–37.

158. Ibid., pp. 245–46.

159. Heywood, 1988, pp. 256–65.

160. Fuchs, 1984, p. 59.

161. Cone, 1979, pp. 155–56.

162. Martinson, 1992, pp. 89–92.

163. Ibid., p. 112.

164. Ibid., pp. 112–19.

165. Ibid., pp. 81–82.

166. Ibid., pp. 89–93.

167. Rose, 1991, p. 15.

168. Nardinelli, 1990, pp. 127–28.

169. Ibid., p. 147.

170. Fildes, 1986, p. 288.

171. Trumbach, 1978, pp. 3–4.

172. Locke most likely did not know that Eskimo, American Northern Plains, and Tierra del Fuego cultures also practiced cold-water dipping of newborns.

173. In the twentieth century, "Polar Bear Clubs" and Eleanor Roosevelt promoted cold bathing; the Scottish Gordonstoun School and America's "Outward Bound" programs are advocates of the practice.

174. Locke, 1693/1989, pp. 84–101.

175. Pollock, 1987, p. 105.

176. Locke also was a strong proponent of regimenting bowel elimination and

advised that plentiful portions of dried fruit, apples, and berries be part of children's diets to stimulate postcibal breakfast defecations. Candy in the diet was forbidden. Locke, 1693/1989, pp. 84–101.

177. Struve, 1801, p. 331.
178. Hunt, 1970, p. 131.
179. Pollock, 1987, p. 74.
180. Allen, 1991, pp. 15–21.
181. Ulich, 1975, p. 481.
182. Allen, 1991, pp. 22–26.
183. Ibid., p. 37.
184. Ibid., pp. 59–60.
185. Evans and Lee, 1981, pp. 86–87.
186. Ibid., pp. 96–99.
187. Pollock, 1987, pp. 135–36.
188. Ibid., p. 145.
189. Durantini, 1983, p. 73.
190. Schorsch, 1979, p. 85.
191. Jordan, 1987, pp. 58–63.
192. Colón and Colón, 1999, pp. 184–239.
193. Trumbach, 1978, p. 203.
194. Cadogan, 1773, p. 25.
195. Anderson and Zinsser, 1988, vol. 2, p. 245.
196. Ibid.
197. Jordan, 1987, p. 91.
198. Ibid., p. 92.
199. Ibid., pp. 267–68. The egalitarian spirits of the times even assigned paupers to baby farms. They fared equally poorly. In 1848, a Mr. Peter Drouet was assigned 1,400 children at his Tooting Baby Farm. He was paid 4s, 6d a week for each child. Cholera killed 150 of them, and the rest fared miserably, sleeping four to a bed, eating rotten potatoes. Their state of ill health was discovered, and Drouet was indicted for manslaugher but escaped on a technicality. Parliament responded by amending the Poor Law Act to prohibit baby farming. *Lancet* 1999; 354:1214.
200. Schulz, 1985, p. 58.
201. Cable, 1972, p. 30.
202. Bremner, 1970–1971, p. 211.
203. Ibid.
204. Larkin, 1987, p. 28.
205. Ibid., p. 30.
206. Earle, 1899/1983, p. 114.
207. Kendall, 1973, pp. 76–77.
208. de Tocqueville, 1862, vol. 2, bk. 3, chap. 8.
209. Bremner, 1970–1971, pp. 370–73.
210. Wishy, 1968, p. 30.
211. Cable, 1972, pp. 70–91.

212. McGuffey, 1887, pp. 12–13, 41–42.
213. Cable, 1972, p. 69.
214. Abbott, 1834, pp. 24–40.
215. Bremner, 1970–1971, p. 354.
216. Ibid., pp. 70–91.
217. Ackerley, 1836, p. 61.
218. Ibid., p. 31.
219. Cable, 1972, pp. 100–12.
220. Wishy, 1968, p. 97.
221. Ibid., p. 100.
222. Cable, 1972, pp. 100–102.
223. Wishy, 1968, p. 123.
224. Ibid., pp. 170–71. In the nineteenth century, the phenomenon of the "expurgator" appeared. Authors such as Thomas and Harriet Bowdler and Charles and Mary Lamb published versions of classics from which "everything that can raise a blush on the cheek of modesty" had been expurgated. The works of Shakespeare in particular were rewritten, with ribald situations and dialogue removed. Sommerville, 1990, p. 169.
225. Alcott, 1844, pp. 337–41.
226. Cable, 1972, pp. 116–17.
227. Ibid., pp. 100–103.
228. Peavy and Smith, 1996, p. 17.
229. Barnard, 1977, p. 307.
230. West, 1985, pp. 90–91.
231. Schlissel, 1982, p. 48.
232. West, 1985, p. 93.
233. Ibid., p. 95.
234. Freedman, 1983, p. 77.
235. Schlissel, 1982, p. 222.
236. Ibid., p. 135.
237. Ibid.
238. Ibid., p. 223.
239. Freedman, 1985, p. 23.
240. Dick, 1948, pp. 17–20.
241. Stratton, 1981, p. 144.
242. Pollock, 1987, p. 12.
243. Woestemeyer, 1939, pp. 294–98.
244. Stratton, 1981, p. 149.
245. Ibid., p. 153.
246. Woestemeyer, 1939, p. 293.
247. Schlissel et al., 1989, pp. 26–37.
248. Stratton, 1981, p. 160.
249. Schlissel et al., 1989, p. 43.
250. Barnard, 1977, p. 320.

251. Freedman, 1983, p. 71.
252. Dick, 1948, p. 170.
253. Woestemeyer, 1939, pp. 439–40.
254. Peavy and Smith, 1966, pp. 120–22.
255. Woestemeyer, 1939, pp. 444–45.
256. Freedman, 1983, p. 52.
257. Ingram, 1958, p. 779.
258. Censer, 1984, p. xiv.
259. Kolchin, 1993, p. 8.
260. Bush, 1990, p. 28.
261. Bremner, 1970–1971, p. 29.
262. Bush, 1990, p. 103.
263. Ibid., p. 127.
264. Bush, 1990, p. 127.
265. Ibid., p. 128.
266. Some cultures used cow dung for hemostasis, ironically providing both the spores and an ideal growing medium for *Clostridium tetani.*
267. Bush, 1990, p. 143.
268. Plimmer and Plimmer, 1975, p. 83.
269. Ibid., pp. 86–87.
270. Gutman, 1976, pp. 328–29.
271. Kolchin, 1993, p. 49.
272. Bremner, 1970–1971, p. 22.
273. Ibid., p. 15.
274. Ibid.
275. Ibid.
276. Jacobs, 1861, p. 6.
277. Ibid., p. 16.
278. Gutman, 1976, p. 76.
279. Ibid.
280. Censer, 1984, p. 137.
281. Bremner, 1970–1971, p. 154.
282. Cable, 1972, p. 81.
283. Jacobs, 1861, pp. 27–28.
284. Bush, 1990, pp. 141–42.
285. Kolchin, 1993, p. 140.
286. Bremner, 1970–1971, p. 154.
287. Cable, 1972, p. 81.
288. Jacobs, 1861, p. 8.
289. Censer, 1984, p. 148.
290. Ibid., p. 140.
291. Cable, 1972, p. 81.
292. Bremner, 1970–1971, p. 513.
293. Ibid.

294. Ibid., p. 514.

295. Jacobs, 1861, p. 5.

296. Bremner, 1970–1971, p. 329. Just after the Civil War, the M Street School was founded in 1866 to educate the newly emancipated children in Washington.

297. Gutman, 1976, p. 73.

298. Ibid., pp. 226–27.

299. Ibid.

300. Ibid., p. 228.

301. Ibid., p. 402.

302. Ibid., pp. 406–12.

303. Payne, 1916, p. 333.

304. Cable, 1972, p. 127.

305. Payne, 1916, p. 333.

306. Bremner, 1970–1971, p. 148.

307. Trattner, 1970, p. 27.

308. Cable, 1972, p. 128.

309. Bremner, 1970–1971, pp. 145–47.

310. Trattner, 1970, pp. 32–42.

311. Cable, 1972, pp. 126–27.

312. Clement, 1985, pp. 255–57.

313. Ibid., pp. 258–59.

314. Ibid., p. 235.

315. Holt, 1992, p. 39.

316. Ibid., pp. 70–71.

317. Ibid., p. 74.

318. Riis, 1970, p. 248.

319. Holt, 1992, p. 68.

320. Ibid., p. 49.

321. Ibid., p. 62.

322. Ibid., pp. 162–69.

323. Clement, 1985, pp. 245–46.

324. Riis, 1970, p. 189.

325. Ibid., pp. 187–95.

326. Trattner, 1970, p. 33.

327. Payne, 1916, pp. 334–35.

328. Ibid., p. 335.

329. Hawes, 1991, pp. 21–22.

330. Davis, 1972, pp. xi–xiii.

331. Ibid., pp. xv–xvii.

332. Trattner, 1970, pp. 32–42.

333. Garland, 1990, p. 34.

334. Ibid.

335. Bremner, 1970–1971, p. 393.

336. Still, 1931, pp. 343–48.

337. D. Turner, 1736, vol. 12, pp. 60, 61, 75, 82.

338. Still, 1931, pp. 342–43.

339. Ibid., p. 339.

340. Ibid., p. 345.

341. Fildes, 1986, pp. 224–30.

342. Cone, 1979, p. 146.

343. Ballabriga, 1991, p. 16.

344. Rotch, 1903, pp. 112–45.

345. Veeder, 1957, p. 154.

346. Cone, 1979, pp. 94–95. Other brand names were McMunn's Elixir, Bartley's Sedative, and Mother Bailey's Quieting Syrup.

347. Sournia, 1990, p. 20.

348. Ibid., pp. 23–46.

349. Holt and Howland, 1916, pp. 54–55.

Chapter 9

Modern Times:
The Adolescent

❏ ❏ ❏

THE TWENTIETH CENTURY BEGAN with shining new promise for children's status and treatment. In the words of author Ellen Key (1849–1926), it was to be "The Century of the Child."[1] In Europe and in North America, philosophers, physicians, educators, and social workers separately and in united forces advanced children's causes both in the legislature and in the forums of public opinion and concern and promoted parental bonding and nurturing. Although the century began tainted by ongoing child-labor and -domestic abuses, inadequate education, and social services, there was, nevertheless, at least a foundation of reforms regarding all of these: in the legislatures, child-protection laws had been enacted; in institutions of learning there were early-education kindergartens and mandatory primary school programs; there were many day-care programs. The medical community had established clinics where infants could be examined and inoculated and their growth and development monitored by physicians.

There remained, however, formidable obstacles to real progress in all of these areas. Child-labor abuses, for example, were an ongoing and seemingly interminable issue of concern.

Three features common to the evolution of child-protection laws in industrialized nations cited in a 1990 study of the history of child labor—

timing, motivation, and long-term effects—elucidate the dynamics that are involved but do little to record the human tragedy experienced by so many.[2] The *timing* of child-protection legislation rarely occurred during the formative period of new industries, when the employment of cheap labor benefited business growth. Felix Adler (1851–1933), American educator and ethicist, addressing his fellow members of the National Child Labor Committee, described the phenomenon as early as 4 April 1904, at the Committee's inaugural meeting:

What we have witnessed is that one state after another, as it swings into line in the introduction of the factory system, repeats the experience of the older states, allows its children to be sacrificed, and learns only after bitter experience that protective legislation is required. If this danger is met at its very inception, the continuance of such needless sacrifices may be prevented. The existence of a National Child Labor Committee acting promptly and aiding to form public sentiment at the critical moment will prevent the repetition of this experience in communities which have not yet passed through it.[3]

Motivation to support child-protection legislation emerged only when enterprises stabilized and flourished. Then, driven by business interests and only secondarily by humanitarian concerns, secure and thriving industries made gestures to embrace opportunities to support labor-reform movements. This support was and is vital, since legislation never has been successful without tacit approval from industrial lobbyists. Historically, powerful industries also have lobbied for *repeal* of legislation found to be detrimental to profits and business practices.

Finally, the *long-term effects* of reform laws affecting children were not as substantial as the improvements in factories and industrial plants due to technological advances. As new and more complex machinery required mature, skilled operators, child workers—and women—became detriments to productivity and were replaced.

In England in 1901 there were more than three hundred thousand school-age children working, mostly on farms and in factories and shops. Nutritional deprivation, inconsistent schooling, insufficient rest, and inadequate living conditions supplied a steady agenda at governmental hearings and inquests. The public was especially appalled by the degree of malnutrition that was reported and agitated for reform. The labor movement, curiously, outdistanced reformers in leading the campaign to legislate a mandatory meal per day for all schoolchildren. In 1906 such a bill was enacted, but it remained unimplemented until 1912, and even then, less than 10 percent of eligible children profited from the measure.[4] A major catalyst of reform in England had been the National Society of the Prevention of Cruelty to

Children (NSPCC), whose work had increased public awareness and compassion and had enlisted the public's support for reform. One of the results of the Society's efforts was a 1908 Children's Act that addressed several problem issues pertaining to children, including baby farming, industrial and domestic abuses, education, and the work of the juvenile-offenders court. In 1913, a Children's Branch of the Home Office Bureau was formed to monitor and intervene in instances of child neglect and assaults on children. By 1923 the Bureau had accumulated data that demonstrated significant improvements in child welfare.[5]

At the turn of the century the United States was engaged in ongoing industrial expansion. Manufacturers were employing increasing numbers of children and hordes of immigrants. Individuals and organizations united to form a national reform campaign whose goal was to galvanize public sympathy and support. The weight of public pressure to prohibit child labor was an effective means to bring about legislative reform, despite industry's resistance to such measures. The National Child Labor Committee (NCLC)[6] was founded in 1904 for these purposes by a number of civic leaders from around the country. Among them were Edgar Murphy (1869–1913), a Montgomery, Alabama, minister; Alexander McKelway (1866–1918), a newspaper editor from North Carolina; Owen Reed Lovejoy (1866–1961), a Michigan minister; Jane Addams (1860–1935) of Hull House; Ben Lindsey (1869–1943), a Denver juvenile court judge; Adolf Ochs (1858–1935), publisher of the *New York Times*; James Kirkland (1859–1939), chancellor of Vanderbilt University; and Charles Eliot (1834–1926), president of Harvard University.

NCLC's Felix Adler emphasized the necessity of a coordinated national effort to achieve uniform and enforceable legislation against child labor on a state-by-state basis. Recognizing that federally imposed legislation would be vulnerable to challenges based on constitutional law, the NCLC withheld support for a child-labor bill introduced in the U.S. Senate in 1906 by the Indiana senator, Albert Beveridge (1862–1927). The Southern states also opposed the bill—and any bill that would curtail child labor. Since Reconstruction, the Southern states believed that only industrialization could achieve economic viability in the region, and cheap labor was necessary for that effort. Northern manufacturers exploited the opportunity to expand their profit base, and between 1880 and 1904 branches and subsidiary factories were established all over the South. In 1900 the number of children working in Northern mills decreased by 50 percent, forming 7.7 percent of the workforce, while in the South the numbers of children working in factories increased to 25 percent of the workforce.[7]

Despite Southern resistance, the NCLC aimed to establish a national

Figure 9.1 Pennsylvania breakers, circa 1908. PHOTOGRAPH BY LEWIS HINE.

standard that all of the states could consider and, they hoped, adopt. The
Committee wanted to prohibit work in factories of children under fourteen
years of age, and in mines under sixteen years of age, and to establish an
eight-hour workday, with no night work of any kind. As its first task the
NCLC elected to examine existing legislation in the various states throughout the country, hoping both to arrive at a consensus that would serve as
model guidelines for all of the states and to strengthen existing legislation as
they went along. The work was begun in 1904 in the mining state of Pennsylvania, where as many children were employed as in the combined states
of New York, Illinois, and Massachusetts. Fourteen thousand children
worked legally in the mines, and an additional ten thousand children, under
twelve years, worked illegally as mule drivers, gate tenders or breakers, working conveyor belts, and separating coal from slate. Through public hearings,
publication of its conferences, and the inauguration and commemoration of
National Child Labor Day, the NCLC maintained pressure on the Pennsylvania legislature to enact protective laws. Public outrage increased with every
inquest of a mining accident and publication of a postmortem report. By
1909, after five years of persistent efforts, the NCLC, together with concerned Pennsylvania lawmakers, produced a successful bill that required a
minimum working age of sixteen years and proof of age before hiring.
    It should be noted that not all Pennsylvania industrialists adopted legisla-
tive mandates grudgingly. The prominent chocolate magnate, Milton Her-
shey (1857–1945), in 1909 established a vocational school that combined
altruistic benevolence with pragmatic foresight. His intention to generate a

Figure 9.2 North Carolina doffers, circa 1908. PHOTOGRAPH BY LEWIS HINE.

cadre of future loyal workers—all boys—was successful and largely due to his progressive principles. By 1930 more than one thousand boys had been educated as a result of his largesse.[8]

As part of a propaganda campaign to influence public opinion, the NCLC hired photographer Lewis Hine (1874–1940) in 1907 to document the vicissitudes of life for working children. For the ensuing eleven years Hine crossed the country producing portfolios of photographs that graphically illustrated the impoverished and demeaning conditions of child laborers and their families (figures 9.1 and 9.2). The arresting visual impact had the desired effect on the public imagination, and strong public demands for legislative action resulted. The passage of reform laws, however, continued to be resisted by legislators and industrialists.

In 1906 the proposal of Florence Kelley (1859–1932) and Lillian Wald (1867–1940), of the Henry Street Settlement in New York, to establish a federal agency that exclusively addressed children's issues, received the support of the NCLC and, significantly, President William Howard Taft (1857–1930). A nationwide lobbying campaign to garner support for the creation of a federal Children's Bureau was launched by the NCLC. The Children's Bureau contrasted its proposed budget of $50,000 with the annual $1.5 million budget of the U.S. Bureau of Animal Husbandry. Legislation for the U.S. Children's Bureau was passed on 9 April 1912.[9] It had taken six years for the legislation to pass. Julia Lathrop (1858–1932), an associate of Jane Addams, was appointed director of the new bureau, to which Congress had appropriated a mere $25,640—half the amount requested.[10]

In consultation with the individuals and organizations that had conceived and fought for the bureau, a priority list of the bureau's work was established. The first order of business was to determine the annual number of children born, and by 1915 a national registry was established to maintain a vital statistics databank. Parent-education programs to reduce child morbidity and mortality were allocated a top priority, and a series of pamphlets and booklets were printed by the government, ushering in a new era of government involvement with the country's social issues. On a regular basis, the U.S. Children's Bureau published and distributed parental guides, gratis, to the public. *Prenatal Care* was written by Max West[11] in 1913. The same author wrote *Infant Care* in 1914, followed by *Child Care: The Preschool Child* and *Your Children from 6 to 12.*[12]

In the meantime, the work of the NCLC and the Children's Bureau had firmly engaged public support for anti–child-labor laws. The Keating-Owen Bill, which set the minimum age for employment at fourteen, was passed in 1916. The Supreme Court overturned the law in 1918 as an unconstitutional invasion of states' rights, bearing out President Woodrow Wilson's (1856–1924) contention that a federal law would not survive a constitutional challenge. A subsequent congressional attempt to curtail child labor was a rider to a revenue bill that exacted a 10 percent surcharge tax on the profits of any company that employed children. This 1919 law, which resulted in a more than 50 percent decrease in the numbers of children employed, was overturned in 1922 by a Supreme Court decision that declared taxation as a control mechanism was an unconstitutional abuse of congressional power.[13] The Court made clear for the record, however, that child labor and abusive child-labor practices were abhorrent, and the Court would support any measures that did not violate constitutional law.

The NCLC's faith in grass-roots campaigns on the state level to effect change resulted, by 1929, in a fourteen-year-old minimum age law in all of the states, a ban on night work in three-quarters of the states, and a maximum eight-hour work day.[14]

The agitation for reform was not limited to child-labor issues. Progressives lobbied as well for prenatal and postnatal care, day-care centers, compulsory education and improved curricula in schools for children, shelters for "wayward" girls, apprenticeships for delinquent boys, and milk purity. New York City led the country in providing its community with these services. By 1892 New York City had established twenty-eight day-care centers, forty kindergartens, thirty-five permanent and temporary foundling homes, and fourteen children's hospitals.[15] By 1910 there were eighty-five nurseries in New York, serving five thousand children daily—18.5 percent of the country's total number of facilities.[16] The subject of day-care evoked heated controversy. Detractors argued that placing infants in day-care programs weakened family ties and maternal bonding and nurturing and encouraged mothers to work outside the home, thereby abandoning their maternal responsibility as well as eroding job opportunities and wages for men. Ignored were the factors that typically marked the placement of infants and children in day-care facilities. A 1913 survey taken by the Association of Day Nurseries in New York City indicated that 17 percent of working mothers were widows; 20 percent had been deserted by their husbands; 27 percent had husbands who were sick and unable to work; and 36 percent claimed that, with only one breadwinner in the family, incomes were insufficient to support family necessities.[17]

The Association of Day Nurseries acted as a forum of information and guidance on virtually all aspects of child care and well-being. They published and disseminated articles on general health care—even information about tonsillectomies—and enriched the day-care experience by promoting the educational principles of Friedrich Froebel (1782–1852) and especially Maria Montessori (1870–1952). In 1917 the Association established and published a set of recommended standards for all of the nation's day-care nurseries to follow:

> Hygienic plumbing, washable floors, ceilings, walls
>
> Medical examination upon enrollment
>
> Social worker case surveillance
>
> Two meals daily for each child
>
> Nursery apron and clothing
>
> Separate towels and spoons
>
> Limit of eight infants or sixteen toddlers per attendant
>
> Written records for each child[18]

Across the country, nurseries did not receive consistent monetary support from state or city governments, and certainly, the population being served could not afford to pay for all services. By the end of the 1920s, many nurseries, critically strapped for funds, were maintaining deteriorating physical plants and were understaffed. The situation worsened with the onset of the Great Depression and was not to be relieved until Franklin Delano Roosevelt's (1882–1945) 1933 Works Progress Administration (WPA), which, among other measures, provided needed funding to day-care nurseries. The primary motivation of the federal government in allocating funds to the nurseries, however, was to create employment. Families and children were secondary beneficiaries. Nonetheless, with the advent of the WPA, nurseries became equipped on an unprecedented scale. Day-care centers employed teachers, nurses, nutritionists, and maintenance workers. By 1937 there were nearly two thousand day-care programs nationwide that cared for forty thousand children. The Lanham Act of 1942 provided uninterrupted day-care funding for the duration of World War II. By the end of 1945, fifty million dollars had been invested in 2,800 day-care centers that cared for 1.5 million children.[19]

The Sheppard-Towner Act of 1921, with a federal appropriation of seven million dollars, aimed to reduce infant and child mortality by providing state-planned and -administered health clinics for prenatal and preventive pediatric care and public-health nurses to instruct mothers on nutrition and child care. Senator James Reed (1861–1944) of Missouri considered the Act a harbinger of socialized medicine and was one of many dissenting voices regarding the legislation, claiming that "the fundamental doctrines on which the bill is founded were drawn chiefly from the radical, socialistic, and bolshevistic philosophy of Germany and Russia."[20] In 1922, at its annual association meeting, however, the pediatric branch of the American Medical Association (AMA) supported the Sheppard-Towner Act. Before the day was over, the AMA House of Delegates condemned the Act. After intense lobbying by various groups, including the AMA, the law was repealed in 1929. A year later, no longer able to tolerate fundamental philosophic differences, a schism group of AMA members, strong advocates of children's rights, established the American Academy of Pediatrics (AAP).[21]

Institutionalization was a late-nineteenth and early twentieth-century solution to many problems emanating from the poverty in America's urban slums. Orphanages, reform schools for boys, and homes for "wayward" girls were the repositories for the country's poor children who, it was thought, were being removed from their degrading and dangerous lives on the street. An exemplar of the laws governing these matters was an 1886 statute applicable in New York City that recommended commitment to reform homes of any girl twelve years old and older who had been "found in a reputed house of prostitution or assignation; or [who] is willfully disobedient to parent or guardian and is found in danger of becoming morally depraved."[22]

A similar statewide statute, called the Wayward Minor Act, was passed in 1923. The law could convict a girl brought into court solely on the testimony of a guardian, and it gave parents the option to elect between a probationary commitment at home or an institutional placement. Similar legislation was supported in other states and prevailed until the Depression, when funding for special shelters and programs disappeared.

Federal government interest in education had been acknowledged with the establishment, in 1867, of the Office of Education, a branch of the Federal Security Agency. Individual states, however, funded their public schools, with increasing per-capita expenditures; from 1870 to 1920, the per-capita amount of $1.64 for schools rose to $9.80.[23] Schooling at all levels also steadily increased nationwide. At the turn of the century there were 225,394 kindergartens in the United States.[24] In 1890, 200,000 students were enrolled in 2,500 high schools. By 1920 there were nearly 2 million students in 14,000 high schools.[25]

Educational philosophies of progressives Friedrich Froebel, sociologist Lester Ward (1841–1913), William James (1842–1910), G. Stanley Hall (1844–1924), and especially John Dewey (1859–1952), emphasizing the learning process rather than *materia*, had a steadily increasing influence on curriculum changes. By the 1930s, progressive theories were being tested in many mainstream schools. Metropolitan-area classrooms were transformed into "real life" minicommunities, the formality of the classroom was greatly relaxed, and barriers between teachers and pupils were narrowed.

Inadequacies in educational standards that had plagued schools throughout the United States perhaps first surfaced most glaringly at the onset of World War I, when large numbers of draftees and volunteers were rejected for service because of illiteracy. The congressional response at the federal level was immediate. Senator Hoke Smith (1855–1931) of Georgia and Representative Horace Towner (1855–1937) of Iowa introduced a bill that proposed federal aid to education and the establishment of a cabinet-level Department of Education:

. . . that there is hereby created an executive department in the Government to be called the Department of Education, with a Secretary of Education, who shall be the head thereof, appointed by the President. . . . It shall be the duty of the Department of Education to conduct studies and investigations in the field of education and to report thereon. Research shall be undertaken in (a) illiteracy; (b) immigrant education; (c) public school education, and especially rural education; (d) physical education, including health education, recreation, and sanitation; (e) preparation and supply of competent teachers.[26]

The Smith-Towner proposal of 1918 was defeated. It was not until 11 April 1953 that a cabinet position responsible for national education issues was created as a part of the newly formed Department of Health, Education and Welfare, and a distinct cabinet-level Department of Education was not established until 1979 by President Jimmy Carter (b.1924).

As mandatory public-school education had become an assumed feature of American life, there had been a notable increase in the number of denominational schools (Roman Catholic, Lutheran, Hebrew, etc.) throughout the United States. These tended to maintain traditional philosophical principles on education and focused, additionally, on parochial subjects in the class-room. The Third Plenary Roman Catholic Council, meeting in Baltimore in 1884, issued a decree that each parish church erect a parochial school. Attendance for Catholic children was made mandatory unless exempted by the local bishopric. Teaching orders such as the Sisters of Notre Dame, Sisters of Charity, Sisters of Mercy, Xaverian Brothers, and the Marists were strongly supported and subsidized as a consequence of this decree, and Catholic publishing firms emerged that specialized in producing textbooks and pamphlets approved by the bishopric.[27] Hebraic studies generally were offered to students as weekend courses and commonly were held in synagogues and community centers. Many private schools promoted a philosophy, rather than a religious belief, representing a spectrum of ideology ranging from most conservative to ultra-progressive and innovative. Socialist schools, operating on weekends as ancillary to traditional schools and their curricula, sprang up throughout the country between 1900 and 1920. Most were in New York and, curiously, Milwaukee. Ten thousand children attended these Social Sunday Schools, instructed in socialist principles expounded in socialist "catechisms." John Spargo (1876–1966) of the Socialist Party wrote one of these, in which children in the schools were taught to recite in a rote manner appropriate responses to posed questions:

We are socialist because we believe the state that is called socialism is the next step in human progress. . . . Because there is a great deal of poverty, sorrow, and pain in the world. . . . [Because] the laws and customs of capitalism make it possible for a few to own the things that all depend upon for life—the things that socialists want to make social property.[28]

These ideas were overwhelmingly rejected by the majority of Americans, and public sentiment often was openly hostile to socialist philosophy and socialist schools, which, by the late 1920s, faded into obscurity.

During the period when progressives on both sides of the ocean were articulating their views, an eminent physician, L. Emmett Holt (1855–1924), published in 1894 the first of seven editions of a widely acclaimed book called *The Care and Feeding of Children: A Catechism for the Use of Mothers and Children's Nurses.* Holt's advice to American middle-class mothers spanned the first-quarter of the new century and returned child-rearing practices to non-permissive, spartan principles. Crying, even screaming babies were not to be embraced and soothed; infants were not to be rocked, played with, or kissed. Holt expounded his theories in his medical textbook* for physicians:

---

*This pediatric text is the longest in continuous publication. It was first published in 1896 and has evolved into *Rudolph's Pediatrics,* currently in its twentieth edition.

Playing with young children, stimulating to laughter and exciting them by sights, sounds, or movements until they shriek with apparent delight, may be a source of amusement to fond parents and admiring spectators, but is almost invariably an injury to the child. This is especially harmful when done in the evening. It is the plain duty of the physician to enlighten parents upon this point, and insist that the infant shall be kept quiet, and that all such playing and romping as has been referred to shall, during the first year at least, be absolutely prohibited.[29]

Neither pacifiers nor self-gratifying thumb sucking were permitted. Holt insisted on this point and suggested that elbow splints be applied during the day and arms tied down at night. Toddlers were not to play with food. Habits, Holt maintained, were formed early, and therefore advocated that proper training be started in infancy:

Training in proper habits of sleep should be begun at birth. From the outset an infant should be accustomed to being put into his crib while awake and to go to sleep of his own accord. Rocking and all other habits of this sort are useless and may even be harmful. An infant should not be allowed to sleep on the breasts of the nurse, nor with the nipple of the bottle in his mouth. Other devices for putting infants to sleep, such as allowing the child to suck a rubber nipple or anything else, are positively injurious.[30]

Two new descriptive nouns evocative of new concepts were introduced into the lexicons of Europe and America—adolescence and the adolescent. Ancient cultures recognized and understood this age group as one experiencing a time of passage into adulthood and devised elaborate and specific initiation rites passed down from one generation to the other as a method of ensuring the continuity of the culture. In the twentieth century the phenomenon of these years was couched in psychodynamic language and theory that led to revolutionary change in the attitudes toward and treatment of young people emerging from childhood. In 1904, G. Stanley Hall's book, *Adolescence: Its Psychology and Its Relation to Physiology, Anthropology, Sociology, Sex, Crime, Religion and Education*, characterized this period of life, between the ages of thirteen and twenty-one, as a turbulent one. The time, he noted, is marked by acute self-consciousness, an opinionated stance, the arousal of sexual instincts, and what Hall ominously considered to be an inherent criminality.[31] Hall's belief that youth of this age required a distinct discipline and education influenced America's moral and educational leadership. By 1910 educators formally established the eighth grade as a transitional year in a junior high school. They developed vocationalguidance programs for the schools and welcomed extracurricular programs that were perceived as safe and morally acceptable, such as those provided by the YMCA, the YWCA,[32] and the Boy and Girl Scouts of America.*

Later, in 1928, the psychologist John B. Watson (1878–1958) published his own spartan and conservative views, which outpaced those of Holt. A behaviorist who worked primarily with animals, Watson wrote *The Psychological Care of Infants and Children* in which he pontificated that "no one today knows enough to raise a child" and arrogantly dedicated the book to "the first mother who brings up a happy child."[33] His attitudes were echoes of those propounded throughout the centuries from Plato[†] to the French revolutionist Saint-Just:

It is a serious question in my mind whether there should be individual homes for children—or even whether children should know their own parents. There are undoubtedly much more scientific ways of bringing up children which will probably mean finer and happier children.[34]

Like Otto Brunfels, he favored little physical contact with the child: "Never hug and kiss them, never let them sit in your lap. If you must, kiss them once on the forehead when they say goodnight. Shake hands with them in the morning."[35]

In 1933 the prominent pediatrician John Ruhräh (1872–1935) teased his professional colleagues' extremist viewpoints[36]:

The Times Have Changed

In ancient days long since gone by
    When Solomon was king,
The erring child who strayed from God
Was straightway brought back by a rod
    It seemed the proper thing,
And sanctioned by the Holy Writ
The psyche was not hurt a bit.

---

*The American Boy Scouts, modeled after the English scouting system of Robert Baden-Powell, took hold around 1911. It succeeded where the Sons of Daniel Boone and the Woodcraft Indians failed, mainly because of adult supervision, organization into troops and patrols, uniforms, and a handbook laying out a clear track for achievement and advancement. Earned "merit badges" provided for a sense of pride and promotions. West, 1996, pp. 17–19.

†In Book 5 of the *Republic*, Plato proposed that all children be made wards of the state, that cadres of wet nurses be contracted by the state to provide nourishment, and that no mother be allowed to recognize her own child. Plato envisaged a eugenic society that manipulated the gene pool, reminiscent of the *Lykurgos*:

. . . there should be as many unions of the best sexes, and as few of the inferior, as possible, and . . . only the offspring of the better unions should be kept. (*Republic* bk. 5, 459d)

One hesitates to cast a doubt
    Upon the tale as voiced,
The child to elders showed respect
His conduct was most circumspect
    The heavenly hosts rejoiced.
They could not pass such angels by
Which made the death rate very high.

Those days were really wondrous days
    It scarcely seems 'twas true.
Whate'er the parents chanced to say
The child was taught he must obey
    Or else the hour he'd rue.
The ego, in between the id
And superego, smoothly slid.

Behaviorism was unknown
    In those old simple days,
No child e'er dared to answer back
For if he did he got a crack
    Where now we give him praise.
The child was seen and never heard
Psychologists said not a word.

But times have changed, as proverb says,
    Old things are obsolete,
We stress the feeding of the child
Which rouses ire and make him wild,
    And now he will not eat.
The more we talk, the more we fret,
The worse the youngster seems to get.

Psychologists now come to aid
    With psychiatrists wise
Before the parent dares to chide
The wise guys take the child aside
    And psychoanalyze.
They probe his every hope and fear
And wonder why the child is queer.

The clinic doors are open wide
    Professors sit within
The more they strive with their advice
To make the wee one mild and nice
    The more the young ones sin.
They wonder what it's all about
And so do I, which lets me out.

The eminent playwright and self-proclaimed social reformer George Bernard Shaw (1856–1950) expounded his own child-rearing philosophy in the preface essay of his play *Misalliance* (1910). Shaw believed that all of Western societal structures and stratagems conspired to suppress childhood spontaneity, gaiety, and curiosity and that parents in particular were culpable, since they condoned and facilitated state and church imposition on children's minds and behavior in schools, catechisms, and discipline:

. . . there is, on the whole, nothing on earth intended for innocent people so horrible as a school. To begin with, it is a prison. But it is in some respects more cruel than a prison. In a prison, for instance, you are not forced to read books written by the warders and the governor . . . and beaten or otherwise tormented if you cannot remember their utterly unmemorable contents.[37]

Shaw's advice to parents was characteristically blunt:

If you must hold yourself up to your children as an object lesson . . . hold yourself up as a warning and not an example. But you had better let the child's character alone. If you once allow yourself to regard a child as so much material for you to manufacture into any shape that happens to suit your fancy you are defeating the experiment of the Life Force [Will of God].[38]

Shaw blended his cynicism with social satire and his renowned barbed wit to denounce family life, particularly the paternal figure:

The Roman father was a despot: the Chinese father is an object of worship: the sentimental modern western father is often a playfellow looked to for toys and pocket-money. The farmer sees his children constantly: the squire sees them only during the holidays, and not then oftener than he can help: the tram conductor, when employed by a joint stock company, sometimes never sees them at all.[39]

The father character in *Misalliance*, John Tarleton, expresses Shaw's own alliance with the beliefs of Plato, Saint-Just, and Watson that the family should be eliminated: "Parents and children! No man should know his own child. No child should know its own father. Let the family be rooted out of civilization! Let the human race be brought up in institutions!"[40]

Progressive ideas and thinking, then, were debated by experts in an inexhaustible number of disciplines. There also was considerable focus on the physical needs of children to promote good health. The leadership ensured that milk was certified and free of disease, developed general maternal–child health-care-education programs, and distributed wholesome dietary plans for the edification of the citizenry. They fostered a new image of hospitals as institutions of science and progress, not just places where sick and/or dying people sought refuge and care. Moreover, new sanitized hospital procedures eradicated infectious diseases and the impression that hospitals were incubators of disease. By 1938 hospitals commanded communities' respect, reflected in the surge of in-hospital parturitions, which had increased to nearly 50 percent of all births in the country.[41] Impulses to be modern and sophisticated on occasion led to the adoption of scientifically dubious assumptions, namely, that "scientifically designed" infant formulas were superior to mother's milk. There was an edge of intellectual and social superiority and intolerance in the prevailing attitudes:

Formula feeding was so closely linked to the power of science and the Progressive's drive for better health, sanitation, and overall social and economic efficiency that breast-feeding was easily linked to the "old-fashioned," poverty-stricken, immigrant, and other "inferior" types.[42]

Science did not begin to reevaluate and promote breast feeding as the preferred and superior nutritional source for infants until after World War II.

It has been theorized that the progressive reform movement was motivated by the fear of radical revolt by America's poorest and most oppressed and the belief that promoting, manipulating, and controlling a middle class with a strong work ethic reduced the danger of social unrest by radical forces. Whatever the merits of the argument, clearly, progressives and industrialists interacted with mutual support of social legislation.[43] Subsequent restrictions of child and woman labor did increase job prospects for adult males, retiring women and children to the home, ever more dependent on male providers. The American Federation of Labor (AFL), for example, supported child-labor laws solely to keep children out of the workforce in order to protect the interests of adult laborers. The unintended beneficiaries were children.

When the stock market crashed in 1929, social progress was abruptly halted. As business after business failed the unemployment rate increased, and at the peak of the Depression 25 percent of the work force could not find a job. Widespread hunger during the Great Depression became a daily aspect of life for a newly formed impoverished class. A Children's Bureau pamphlet for 1931, entitled *Emergency Food Relief and Child Health*, reflected the prevailing stark social conditions. The government pamphlet, omitting references to expensive sources of protein such as meat, eggs, or fish, described instead the minimum nutritional requirements established for children. Even these modest standards, however, had become beyond the ability of millions to provide them: "For every child everyday at least one pint of milk . . . two teaspoonfuls of cod liver oil . . . one vegetable or fruit . . . and also plenty of breads, cereals, and other energy and body-building foods."[44]

Social agencies in New York City noted a 42 percent increase in child malnutrition; from 18 percent malnourished, the figure rose to 60 percent. Pennsylvania recorded an increase in malnutrition of 15 percent.[45]

Families during the Depression years were destitute and desperate to work at any level. In many cases, in order to survive, children had to work. Cheap child labor enabled manufacturers to undercut competitors in cost and prices, further unbalancing the state of the economy. States, in the interest of stabilizing the economy, created restrictive codes to control the employment of children.

On the federal level, beginning in 1932, the administration of Franklin Delano Roosevelt revived interest in and support for social programs on an unprecedented scale. The National Recovery Act (NRA) of 1933 established a national code of fair competition in the labor market, which placed some constraints on child labor. Programs were developed that directly benefited children and their mothers. The Sheppard-Towner Act, enacted in 1921 to provide prenatal and preventive pediatric-care health clinics, was repealed in 1929. With its demise, maternal- and child-health legislation at the federal level also had vanished until, in 1935, the Social Security Act and Aid to Dependent Children included extensive maternal–child initiatives. This was followed, in 1941, by the Community Facilities Act (the Lanham Act) that included day-care provisions to meet the needs of children with working parents. Until that time, day-care had remained an inconsistently available service, except, as has been noted, in large metropolitan areas like New York City, where well-organized and safe day-care facilities had long been established. Then, in 1938, the Fair Labor Standards Act (FLSA) was passed, making it illegal to employ children under sixteen while school was in session. Exempted from this ruling were newspaper vendors, farm workers, and restaurant, retail store, and laundry workers. Despite its weaknesses, the FLSA was the first *national* child-labor law, and the number of working children significantly decreased until the outbreak of World War II.

A powerful, strong, centralized government issuing federal laws and regulations on social issues was a novelty to the American public, prompting the celebrated humorist, Will Rogers (1879–1935), to comment:

I am mighty glad so many people in America are taking up the children work. Being a ranchman and a farmer, and also a child owner, I have often wished that when one of my children got sick I could wire or call some Government expert and have him look after them, like I can do if one of my cows or pigs get some disease. If your fertilizer is not agreeing with your land, the Government will send a specialist, but if the food is not agreeing with the baby, why, we have to find out what's the matter ourselves, and lots of times parents mean well but they don't know much. It's not a bad idea whoever thought of doing something for the children. If it works and you improve them, I will send you mine.[46]

At the outbreak of World War II, in a spirit of patriotic fervor, women and children joined the workforce, thus easing the severe shortage of manpower. The contribution of children's labor to the war effort was rewarded by vigilant attention to their well-being. Abuses in the workplace were no longer tolerated. Gone were children in sweatshops, in mines, and in glass factories. Young children were obliged to attend school. Older children proudly took the places of men who went off to battle, in the workplace and at home. Work permits were strictly controlled, granted only if a job complied with national standards with regard to age, type of work, and number of hours of employment. These regulations are the nexus to today's tightly controlled teenage job market.

CHINA

Looking to the East, long-standing traditions, reinforced by religious philosophies, strengthened the people of China and their children as they endured the ever-present poverty, natural and man-made calamities, and the complex demands that the twentieth century imposed on them. A mostly peasant population of 430 million people in 1850 grew to 500 million in the early twentieth century. Hunger and starvation, infestations of locusts, earthquakes, floods, and epidemics of pox and plague were pervasive facts of life for these people. Plundering soldiers, rebellions, and revolutions added to the general suffering. Against these destructive forces were pitted the familiar and reassuring customs and traditions of an ancient culture whose adaptation was consciously slow and unyielding.

Parents held onto traditional lore, legend, and religion as stabilizing and sustaining elements in their lives, passing on their beliefs to new generations of children whom they would protect from harm. One protective ritual guarded against a "spirit sadism"—the belief that the souls of children, particularly treasured children, are desired by the devil.[47] Parents engaged in a ruse to dupe the evil force with a pretense of indifference, behaving as if the child was not much valued, so that a covetous demon would reject the progeny. In addition to feigned lack of interest or even disdain, parents publicly and ceremoniously gave their prized infant boys degrading names such as "Dog" or "Pig," or dressed them in girl's clothing, or staged a sham adoption.

Menacing spirits of unmarried female ghosts, called t'ou-sheng kuei, were thought to return from the netherworld to search out the souls of young boys so that they could be reincarnated as males. Parents thwarted these spirits by burning worn, odoriferous shoes or by hanging a fishing net smeared in pig's blood over their infant sons' cradles. These "spiritual" exercises were performed with the same degree of attentiveness that was given to infants' physical needs in rituals virtually identical to those practiced a millennium before.

On the third day of life, infants were bathed, and an old coin or red thread was tied around each wrist. Mother and infant did not leave the home until one month after the birth. Boys, at this time, were given their names, and a head-shaving ceremony was held. Tufts of hair usually were left over the fontanel, at the back of the neck, and over the ears, or hair was braided on the side of the head.[48]

Apart from maneuvers to protect infants from harm, the behavior of parents in China toward their infants was that of doting and loving parents. Crying infants elicited immediate attention from parents and, in fact, from all members of the family. Infant mortality was appallingly great, reflected in the aphorism "One son is no son, two sons are an undependable son, and only three sons can be counted as a real son."[49] Children were raised with much care and attention, therefore, and as they grew, their play was closely supervised to prevent injurious accidents. Family loyalty was the supreme virtue parents constantly inculcated in their young, with frequent reminders of the filial duty to honor and serve parents and forebears. In the West, this custom has long been referred to as "ancestor worship," and indeed there were religious rituals in which incantations to ancestors were made.

Several Chinese children's nursery rhymes are markedly similar to those familiar to English-speaking children.[50] The translation of the Chinese rhyme "Little Brown Mouse," for example, resembles the tale of "Jack and Jill":

> He climbed up the candle-stick,
>   The little mousey brown,
> To steal and eat tallow,
>   And he couldn't get down.
>
> He called for his grandma,
>   But his grandma was in town,
> So he doubled up into a wheel,
>   And rolled himself down.

Played on infant toes like "This Little Piggy," China's "This Little Cow" delivers a cultural value lesson:

> This little cow eats grass,
> This little cow eats hay,
> This little cow drinks water,

This little cow runs away,
This little cow does nothing,
Except lie down all day.
    We'll whip her.

At seven, children experienced a transition in nurturing within the family. Considered ready to strive for *ch'eng ien*, the cycle of self-disciplining behavior to achieve maturity and develop into a complete human being, they were weaned away from the dependent state of childhood.[51] Parental behavior toward children assumed an aura of detached discipline. Mindful that the child was moving into a behavioral stage of preadolescence known as *t'ao-ch'i*, variably translated as being disobedient, willful, obstinate, or assertive,[52] parents steeled themselves for the inevitable with expressionless interactions and reserved emotions devoid of joy or anger, laughter or tears. Affectionate displays and intimacies were eschewed in the belief that they ultimately engendered resentment and weakened family harmony. The 1893 diary of an adolescent who was studying at Yale University, courtesy of the Chinese Educational Mission, illustrates the societal behavior and expectations of Chinese family life:

... obedience and respect, rather than affection, are required of the Chinese child. His homelife ... is constrained, sober, and dull. The boy attains to the ideal character only when he habitually checks his affectionate impulses, suppresses his emotions, and is uniformly dignified with his inferiors. Therefore the child is early taught to walk respectfully behind his superiors, to sit only when he is bidden, to speak only when questions are asked him, and to salute his superiors by the correct designations. It would be the height of impropriety for him to mention his father's name, or call his uncles and elder brothers by their names.[53]

More than a chronicler of his culture, the student at Yale exemplified how Chinese intellectuals, having been sent to the West for study by mission schools and influenced by Western culture and education, technological advances, and economic development, kindled a spirit of reform in their country. In the ancient (705–1905) system of civil-service examinations, the literacy rate in China was about 20 percent.[54] The government in China, clinging tenaciously to its traditions, focused on improving that statistic. After the Boxer Rebellion of 1900, with the assistance of the U.S. government China embarked on liberalizing the process of education and making education accessible to all. The government of the United States established a $22.4 million indemnity fund for education, and by 1915 there were over 1,500 Chinese students in American universities on travel scholarships, in addition to the numbers of students who were beneficiaries of church-mission scholarships. A cadre of returning students, hired as teachers in mission schools, developed new curricula adapted from the Western world that blended with the contemplative, traditional philosophies China had sustained for millennia.

Following a 4 May 1919 demonstration* of nationalistic unity by all of the elements of Chinese society—students, merchants, peasants, and intellectuals—an intensified fervor for increased literacy through education swept the country. New schools were built, enrollments were increased, curricula were revised and updated. The 1912 record listed 83,000 elementary schools teaching 2.8 million children, and 373 middle schools with a student body of merely 52,000 students. By 1937 these numbers had swelled to 260,000 elementary schools with 11.7 million pupils, and 3,000 middle schools with 500,000 students.[55,56]

In 1918 James Yen compiled a list of the most commonly used ideograms in vernacular writing and speech, greatly facilitating what had been a complex feature in Chinese education. Further simplification in the 1940s was achieved by reducing the number of ideogram strokes. The simplification of written language, conjoined with increased schooling, resulted in a rise in China's literacy rate from 20 percent to 85 percent in 1975.[57]

The emphasis in China on the value of male children derived from the Confucian philosophy of filial loyalty and perpetuation of the family name and the insurance and security provided by males for parents in their old age. This tradition made children vulnerable and subject to many dangers. Females in families that had too many were commonly discarded. Boys were abducted and sold to families eager to pay the price to have a boy. In the modern world, population control in a country with more than a billion people is in conflict with the traditional values that endure, and ongoing child abuse of the nature described is the result of this clash. The Chinese state at first mandated birth control, limiting families to two children. After 1980 the number allowed was reduced to one child per family. In 1991 the Chinese Security Bureau rescued 3,500 kidnapped boys, acknowledging that the number represented a small fraction of males who were missing.[58] There are strict laws against kidnapping, but filial loyalty and the concept of continuing the family name are so ingrained that the impulse for clandestine purchase of a child is as irresistible as the illegal profits.

Despite the endurance in China of its rich culture and elements of a her-

---

*The Versailles Conference of April 1919 had adjudicated the rights and leases of territory granted Germany by the province of Shantung. Instead of reverting to China, the claim to the area was given to Japan. The impassioned nationalistic protest by the Chinese on 4 May 1919 resulted.

itage of an ancient civilization, the country remains a vast and heavily populated agrarian one, with social issues, in many respects, found in developing nations in the so-called Third World.

JAPAN

Like China, Japan entered the twentieth century clinging to its cultural heritage and ancient traditions, certainly so with respect to its children. Japanese newborns remained unswaddled and unnamed until the occasion of the temple naming ceremony—for girls on the thirteenth day after their birth, for boys on the thirty-first day. Following the temple event, fathers took their infants to their nearest kinsmen, who presented newborns with a bundle of hemp symbolic of a long life that would be spun. Boys were given two fans representing a sword and courage, and girls were given shells filled with paint representing beauty. No constraints on behavior, other than to protect them from bodily harm, were imposed on children during the early, formative years. Life centered around the mother, the nutritor and protector of her young. A Shôwa-era haiku (c.1927) honored the relationship and illustrated the intensity of the bond[59]:

> When the mother is scolded,
>   The child also
> Boo-hoos.
>
>   Shirô

The death of a child was considered to be an omen from an angry Heaven, and it was believed that the next child also would be in mortal danger from divine wrath. Therefore, in a family that had experienced a childhood death, there was particular vigilance about a subsequent birth to ensure that no harm fell to the infant. In a feigned abandonment to appease the gods, a newborn was hastily taken to a bamboo grove, where a waiting relative or friend could serendipitously "stumble" upon the infant and claim it. Thereafter, the infant would be presented to "grieving" parents as a surrogate for them to nurture and raise. Infants who had in this way appeased the gods were given names that reflected their condition: new babies were co-named *sute* (abandoned), *sutejiro* (abandoned second-born), or *sutesaburo* (abandoned third-born), and so on.[60]

Prayer was taught to children over three, at which time a girdle was given to a child. Annually, on the fifth day of the fifth month, Boys Day was celebrated. Every home with a boy or boys hoisted carp windsocks on a pole, symbolizing perseverance and strength. The size and number of carp indicated the ages and number of boys in the family. For girls, 3 March was the day of honor. It was called the Festival of Dolls because girls traditionally were given special dolls to add to their collections.[61]

For all Japanese children, school started when they were seven years old. Education generally ended with the completion of primary school. Children of the nobility and higher orders proceeded to "superior" school, where, in addition to arithmetic, calligraphy, and astrology, they were taught comportment, ritual, ceremony, and an intricate etiquette that was applied to individuals according to their rank and station.

At the completion of his studies, a boy's head was shaved; he was given a new name and was considered mature and ready for a contracted marriage. Boys also were taught *hara-kiri** (the happy dispatch), the solemnity and methodology of suicide to protect the honor of the country.[62] The equivalent duty for girls was called *jigai*, piercing the throat to sever the arteries.[63] Culturally and philosophically, death in Japan was viewed as sacred, as a continuity of life; in this context, suicide was not necessarily anathema. There was no punishment in death, only peace. Children who grew up with these concepts had no negative attitudes about suicide, and even among children, suicide was not rare in Japan.[†]

Girls' educations traditionally had been limited to domestic work and needlework. Few learned reading and writing, and at the age of fifteen, formal lessons of any kind were completed. As the twentieth century approached, Japan embraced the prevailing spirit of the age and fostered a more liberal and egalitarian educational curriculum and enrollment that included girls. In 1878, three-quarters of students in higher education were from families of the nobility or the military; by 1885 they represented half of the total students,[64] as the enrollment of middle-class children dramatically increased. Japan remained an agrarian nation, however, and many children of both the middle class and the lower classes still worked on farms.

---

*The act of self-evisceration was carried out with a knife called *seppuku*, considered a more polite term to use than *hara-kiri*. Boys and girls in the twentieth century were taught the ritual; in 1916, for example, out of nearly 12,000 suicides, about 4 percent were by *seppuku*. Scott, 1922, p. 55.

Although the ritual of *seppuku* has nearly disappeared, the spirit of its meaning endured. In the aviation age of World War II, bombers suicidally dove into fleets of ships as a final gesture of honor to their country.

†In 1977, a total of 784 childhood suicides was recorded in Japan, mostly in despair over academic performance. Courdy, 1984, pp. 145–54.

Suicide among young people, however, is not merely an occurrence rooted in an aspect of traditional Japanese culture. In America in 1990 there were more than 3,000 suicides among children; nearly 50 percent of them were committed with handguns. Center for Health Statistics, 23 March 1993; Colón and Colón, 1989, pp. 52–53.

Children in urban areas worked in factories, in such numbers that by 1911, as has been noted, child-labor laws had been instituted in Japan.

The influence of the West began to appear even in the countryside. Robertson Scott, touring Japan in 1915, noted one local school with portraits of local leaders plus Peter the Great, Benjamin Franklin, Abraham Lincoln, and Commodore Matthew Perry. Another school had large wall maps of Southeast Asia and Australia and portraits of Florence Nightingale, Abraham Lincoln, and Napoleon Bonaparte.[65] In their schools, the Japanese tradition was sustained by teaching the "Twelve Counsels," which were read every morning in every school:

Do your own work and don't rely on others to do it.

Be ardent when you learn and play. Endeavor to do away with your bad habits and cultivate good ones.

Never tell a lie and be careful when you speak.

Do what you think right in your heart and at the same time have good manners.

Overcome difficulties and never hold back from hard work.

Do not make appointments which you are uncertain to keep.

Do not carelessly lend or borrow.

Do not pass by another's difficulties and do not give another much trouble.

Be careful about things belonging to the public as well as about things belonging to yourself.

Keep the outside and inside of the school clean and also take care of waste paper.

Never play with a grumbling spirit.[66]

In the home, children studied the *Hyakunin Isshu*, a collection of one hundred poems written in old Yamato dialect. A compendium of traditional beliefs and form, it instructed children about the elements necessary for a model life and for interpersonal skills. It recounted household lore and taught astrology, and every daughter was expected to read and reread the work until the traditions were committed to memory.[67]

By the early twentieth century, Japan's population was fifty-six million people. One-and-a-quarter million boys and one million girls attended school in Japan, and more than one thousand students were studying abroad.[68]

Despite the many aspects of values and educational methodologies from the West that the Japanese were exposed to and in some cases were adopting, many traditional aspects of the Japanese culture endured. Children, for example, continued to be endowed with a *jizo*—that special spirit, like a guardian angel, that guards and protects children—a tradition that could be traced back to the medieval period.

In the haiku of the Taishô era (1912–1925), the traditional Japanese regard, even reverence, for children was expressed. Several, however, revealed attitudes and life experiences of a darker nature suffered by children in all cultures in all periods of the world's history.[69] Children were desirable but difficult:

> The children;
> "What a nuisance they are!"
> But she wants them all.
>
> Yanami

Some children were rejected and abandoned:

> "Mama gave it me,"
> Says the abandoned child,
> Holding up the letter.
>
> Hisabô

Or simply unloved:

> She does not dare
> Lift her hand against the step-child,
> But he gets thinner and thinner.
>
> Jirakujin

Some women abandoned their husbands and infants:

> The man goes for milk,
> Is asked again by the wet-nurse,
> "You still don't know where she is?"
>
> Masao

Some were forcibly removed by the father from the mother:

> The child actor
> Just comes on the stage,
> And the divorcée melts into tears.
>
> Keinan

Whatever vicissitudes suffered by children in Japan and the world over in the first half of the twentieth century, they paled in comparison to that which was to befall them when World War II erupted.

PEDIATRICS

Scientific and medical discoveries in the twentieth century advanced the knowledge and practice of medicine to a degree beyond that which collectively had taken place in the prior two millennia. The breakthroughs in anesthesia and drugs, the understanding of disease modalities, and the development of cures for illnesses that in the past almost always led to death progressed steadily and rapidly. Pediatrics, a firm new discipline, benefited as much as adult medicine.

From the perspective of social and domestic dynamics of child care, a book, without a doubt the most important of its kind in the twentieth century, was published in the United States in 1946. Called *Baby and Child Care*, it was written by Benjamin Spock (1903–1998). The book has been reprinted more than two hundred times, and over forty million copies have been sold. Parents in a radically changed and more child-centered world were ready for a "how to" book that was thorough yet concise, facile to read, and urged a common-sense approach to nurturing. More than anything else, Dr. Spock gave reassurance and confidence to mothers everywhere. In supporting the appropriateness of maternal concerns and instincts, with a thorough review of illnesses and symptomatology and the milestones of normal, expected behavior of children, Dr. Spock, in effect, bestowed on mothers the status of expert caregivers nonpareil:

Don't be overawed by what the experts say. Don't be afraid to trust your own common sense. . . . Every time you pick your baby up . . . even if you do it a little awkwardly at first, everytime you change her, bathe her, feed her, smile at her, she is getting a feeling that she belongs to you and that you belong to her. Nobody else in the world, no matter how skillful, can give that to her.[70]

The name Spock, however clichéd a thought, became a household word, known to all. His influence on child care and on the proliferation of child-care literature that inundated the last half of the century cannot be overestimated. Dr. Spock has been a leading member of those pediatricians whose texts can rightfully be said to have made the twentieth century into the "medical century of the child."

Of the many contributors to the pediatric literature, some merit special mention from both a scientific and a public-health perspective.

Kwashiorkor, or protein malnutrition, throughout history has affected and still does affect tens of millions of children. An estimated ten million toddlers still die from kwashiorkor yearly. Not until 1933 was the first careful study of kwashiorkor published, by Cecily Williams (1893–1992). Dr. Williams wrote:

The syndrome consists of oedema, chiefly of the hands and feet, followed by wasting; diarrhoea; irritability; sores, chiefly of the mucous membranes; and desquamation of areas of the skin in a manner and distribution which is constant and unique.[71]

The scientific recognition of kwashiorkor as a distinct syndrome, more complex than just a lack of calories, constituted a major milestone in pediatrics. Williams's initial observations facilitated the research of Derrick Jelliffe (b.1921), whose insights led him to devise protocols for the effective field treatment of this form of childhood malnutrition.[72]

Pierre Budin (1846–1907), in France (c.1905), promoted milk sanitation and formula vitamin enhancement.[73] Around 1910 in Germany, Heinrich Finkelstein (1865–1942) produced *Eiweissmilch*, a casein-fortified milk developed to restore malnourished children to health. In 1912 nutritional anemia was first described by Adalbert Czerny (1863–1941).[74] Arvo Ylppö (c.1916), in Finland, focused attention on the clinical needs of infants, especially premature infants. Mortality rates in his country dropped from 22 percent to 10 percent by 1920.[75] Ernst Moro (1874–1951), professor at Heidelberg University, described in 1919 what since has been called the Moro reflex—the autonomic stretch response of newborns to startle, a reaction that can aid in the prognostication of neurological health. John Thomson's (1856–1926) study of 950 children offered the first well-researched and long-term follow-up on childhood mental retardation.

Henry Dwight Chapin (1857–1942) was a pioneer in articulating, around 1915, a concept of the medical condition in infants called "failure to thrive"[76] and, moreover, made the association of the condition with institutional care. His work was enhanced and enlarged by Rene Spitz (1887–1974), who described failure to thrive secondary to anaclitic depression in the institutionalized child (c.1938). Spitz, citing emotional deprivation as the central cause of this type of failure to thrive, popularized the syndrome as "hospitalism."* Around 1947, Nathan Talbot followed with further elucidation of the syndrome, noting the common elements in all failure to thrive—calorie and energy loss. The aforementioned Heinrich Finkelstein, a

---

*The chronicler of thirteenth-century German Emperor Frederick II related what may be the earliest description of "hospitalism." In trying to learn the origins of language, Frederick "bade foster mothers and nurses to suckle the children, to bathe and wash them, but in no way to prattle with them or to speak to them, for he wanted to learn whether they would speak the Hebrew language, which was the oldest, or Greek, or Latin, or Arabic, or perhaps the language of their parents, of whom they had been born. But he labored in vain, because all the children died. For they could not live without the petting and the joyful faces and loving words of their foster mothers." Sommerville, 1990, p. 83.

German Jew, had resettled in Chile, where he researched failure to thrive. He also referred to the condition as hospitalism. Around 1935, Finkelstein described "alimentary fever," pointing to bowel infections as a major contributory factor in malabsorption and malnutrition.[77] This valuable observation further facilitated the care of the malnourished child by calling attention to the immune system. In 1949, Harry Bakwin (1894–1972) classically described the involutionary marasmic child:

The hospitalized infant is thin and pale . . . the facial expression is unhappy and gives an impression of misery. Muscle tone is poor and it is impossible to extend the legs fully at the knees . . . the infant shows no interest in his environment, lying quietly in bed, rarely crying, and moving very little. Such movements he makes are slow and deliberate.[78]

Great strides were made in the early part of the twentieth century to combat epidemics. The work of Theodor Escherich (1857–1911) made monumental contributions to the study of intestinal bacterial flora. Diphtheria—el garrotillo, or morbis stangulatorius—killed tens of thousands annually. The loss in Germany in 1892 of fifty thousand children in a epidemic of this disease exemplifies how quickly infection ravaged the young organism.[79] A vaccine (c.1925) developed by Gaston Ramon (1886–1963) caused mortality to drop immediately, from 73 percent to 14 percent.

The diagnosis and prevention of tuberculosis, an insidious killer, were facilitated by the development of an intradermal test (c.1908) by Charles Mantoux (1877–1947) and the Calmiette-Guérin bacille vaccine (c.1921). The so-called BCG vaccination of newborns against tuberculosis became a mandatory public-health measure in many countries.[80]

These examples of the medical revolution occurring in the study, prevention, and treatment of infectious diseases were the vanguard of the conceptualization and development of future vaccines against measles, mumps, rubella, polio, and others. Preventive medicine in public health began with the infant child and its physician. The study of disease in children—pediatrics—had become a mature and respected medical discipline. A migratory route tracing the movement in Europe of physicians who focused on the medical needs of children can be plotted: from Austria to Germany to France and to England and, crossing the ocean, to the Americas, where the first full-time department of pediatrics was headed by John Howland (1873–1926) at Johns Hopkins University in 1911. John Hall Mason Knox (1872–1951) presided over the merger of the American Child Hygiene Association with the American Child Health Association in 1922. The resulting partnership became a strong and powerful adjunct to the work of the country's Children's Bureau.[81]

Pediatric medicine and child health worldwide had become major features of governmental agendas and public concern and permanently influenced greatly both public thinking and legislative bodies.

CHILDREN IN WORLD WAR II

In February 1939 the *Times* of London editorialized about mass disruptions spreading epidemically across Europe. About the children it noted:

One of Finland's most serious problems is that of the evacuated civilians, and especially the children, who number probably one-third of a total of half a million. The death-rate among these children has risen considerably. . . . The interruption of all normal existence caused by the bombing of the towns and villages is undoubtedly a cause of danger not to be measured by the relatively small number of casualties.

Last winter these were Spanish children.

This winter—Finland's.

This summer will they be our own?[82]

The editorial was perspicacious, but England, already alerted to the danger, had been doggedly preparing for conflict, after only two decades since it had celebrated the end of "the war to end all wars." In 1938 the British government distributed thirty-eight million gas masks to its citizens. An incubator-like canister was developed for infants, and "Mickey Mouse" masks were devised for the toddlers as a stratagem to dispel the anxiety or alarm the children might otherwise have felt wearing the contraptions.

The courage, good cheer, and determined optimism of the British *anima* won the admiration of the free world. Most important, adult examples supported British children's ability to cope during the precarious and treacherous years of the war. There were helping hands tangibly extended to the children: hundreds of thousands of families who lived in rural areas volunteered to lodge children evacuated from urban areas that were vulnerable to enemy bombers. At the end of the war the government acknowledged the bravery of the children with certificates of merit.

The first evacuation of children occurred in the first days of September 1939, when 734,883 unaccompanied children traveled to homes in the English countryside.[83] Most left their parents and their London homes with few belongings by train for a sojourn they were told would last the duration of the war. When possible, they traveled with brothers and sisters as a family unit, but commonly, children were separated from siblings and thus totally distanced from every member of their families. Many volunteer hosts requested children with specified characteristics, such as a particular age or gender, overall size or stature. Compliance with stated preferences generally did not materialize:

I had asked for and been promised a helper, no boys, and six girls of about nine "plus." . . . out tumbled eight little beings, none of them more than knee-high and half of them boys . . . a tangle of gas-masks, knapsacks, tiny great coats, tumbled all over the floor of the hall, and tins of condensed milk. . . .

The children were absurdly small. It turned out that the two oldest, both boys, were only eight, while a little elfin being with big eyes was found to be only five.[84]

The children arrived with apparently heavy kits issued by the government, containing items deemed useful and essential for the circumstances. A nine-year-old described the experience: "I paraded with the other children from Tollington School outside Hornsey station as heavily loaded as a soldier in full marching kit. A gas mask in a white tin box stuffed with sticky plaster, anti-burn cream and iodine pulled me down on one side."[85]

In addition to providing for children's physical needs and comforts, host families had the awesome task of quieting children's fears. Initially, the frequent questions were: "Why have we been evacuated?" "If it isn't safe for us, why is it safe for Mummie and Daddie?"[86] When bombings did not occur immediately, the question commonly changed to "Why are we here?" The answer would not be forthcoming until July of the following year, when the bombing of British cities by the Germans began in earnest. By that time the numbers of children in the major cities had swelled, as "vackies," lured back by the inaction of the "phoney war" to their urban roots and to their families, had returned to the cities. Their arrival coincided with the inauguration of the blitzkrieg (the bombing war) that had been threatened. In all, more than two-thirds of those evacuated had returned to the cities to endure the frightening air raids and destructive bombing, to suffer hunger from food shortages, and worse, to numbly witness the loss or maiming of parents and siblings.

There was little left in the cities for able-bodied children to do. Most schools were closed, and only weekend church schools functioned.[87] Many children became scavengers, combing the ruins for wartime souvenirs or some foodstuff. In the early part of 1940 the British census bureau had counted five million elementary-school-age children. In the confusion of the war, eight hundred thousand children could not be accounted for; they were not among those evacuated, nor were they attending rural schools. The supposition is that many had resorted to street life. Gertrude Willoughby, of the Union of Girls' Schools Settlement, commented at the time: "The fact that children are running wild is incontrovertible. We have not had so much trouble with organized gangs of children since we started here ten years ago."[88]

There was another evacuation in August 1940, when approximately 1.25 million women and children were given billets in rural areas. One hundred forty thousand were unaccompanied children.[89] This time the evacuees stayed the course, grateful to be safe from the devastation wrought by the unrelenting bombing raids on London, Liverpool, and other industrial cities. Some of the evacuated children went overseas. Four thousand children were sent to the United States, Australia, South Africa, and New Zealand. The majority, about 1,500, went to Canada. Not all of them survived the trip. In 1940, within the span of seventeen days, the evacuation ships *Volendam* and *City of Benares* were sunk by German U-boats. Two children on the *Volendam* and seventy-seven children on the *City of Benares* died.[90]

A total of 7,736 children died during the blitz years in the United Kingdom.[91] Compared to the children across the Channel, however, the mortal danger to British children was minimal. Hundreds of thousands, even millions, of the sad children of the Continent tragically disappeared; some were victims of bombing raids by Allied forces. Others were cruelly vaporized in terrifying chambers of death.

In the United States there were evacuations of a different character. Now an admittedly shameful and illegal episode in the nation's history, the forced evacuation from their homes of 25,000 Japanese-American families—over 120,000 individuals—was ordered by the War Relocation Authority established by President Franklin D. Roosevelt and enacted on 18 March 1942. The then-governor of California, Earl Warren (1891–1974), a future Chief Justice of the United States, was empowered to administer the enforced encampment of these people, seventy-seven thousand of whom were *nisei*, first-generation American-born citizens. The rest, the *issei*, had been denied naturalization, but most had been resident aliens[92] in the United States for more than twenty years, and some were residents dating back to at least 1924, when immigration from Japan had been curtailed.[93] A retrospective examination of what occurred exposes a frank racism toward Americans of Japanese descent, especially in view of the fact that only ten thousand Italian and German aliens were relocated in California during the war and then only for a brief time, from February to June 1942.[94] It took the U.S. government nearly fifty years to offer both profound apologies to the Japanese-American community and monetary compensation for their material losses during the period of relocation.

Young Japanese-American males took advantage of a government exemption from detention for those who joined the armed services. Grouped together in units, these young men won every distinction for valor and service in the European theater of the war.

By 7 August 1942, almost all Japanese-American families and orphaned children in the United States had been interned in detention camps (table 9.1). Most suffered the loss of property and personal belongings, but care was taken to keep families together in the ten different camps that had been prepared for them for the two to four years they were detained.[95] Living in

TABLE 9.1
JAPANESE-AMERICAN DETENTION CAMPS, 1942–1946

Camp	State	No. Internees
Tule Lake	California	18,789
Manzanar	California	10,046
Minidoka	Idaho	9,397
Topaz	Utah	8,350
Heart Mountain	Wyoming	10,764
Granada	Colorado	7,318
Poston	Arizona	17,814
Gila River	Arizona	13,348
Rohwar	Arkansas	9,475
Jerome	Arkansas	8,497

guarded areas, waiting out the war in the Pacific, the detainees sustained their traditional family values—American and Japanese—and their faith in and commitment to the United States of America.

The last of the Japanese-American families waited until March 1946 before being released and relocated to their homes.[96]

The Nazi[97] vision of youth and a new world order had been thoroughly articulated by Adolf Hitler (1889–1945) as early as 1933:

In my new *Ordensburgen* a youth will grow up before which the world will shrink back. A violently active, dominating, intrepid, brutal youth—that is what I am after. Youth must be all those things. It must be indifferent to pain. There must be no weakness or tenderness in it. I want to see once more in its eyes the gleam of pride and independence of the beast of prey.[98]

Surrounding himself with zealots and, on a national scale, appealing to the patriotism of a vanquished nation, Hitler applied an instinctive genius for mass manipulation and fashioned the image of a future Germany, inhabited by a cultural elite led by Aryan youth who could restore the country to glory.

The mold of the new German citizen was to be formed by a series of sequential steps organized through the National Youth Movement, the Staatsjugend. First, an introduction to Nazism: boys ten to fourteen were recruited into the Jungvolk and girls into the Jungmädelbund. After fourteen years of age, the adolescent boy joined the Hitlerjugend, and the girl joined the Bund Deutscher Mädel and after eighteen or twenty years of age, the Reichsarbeitsdienst. For boys, a compulsory enlistment in the Wehrmacht ended the indoctrination. Those who showed promise went to special Adolf Hitler Schulen and then to the Ordensburg.

Girls were indoctrinated to evolve a sense of duty as future mothers of German citizens. In socialization sessions and summer camps, they learned folk songs, dances, and stories that conveyed and perpetuated a German "culture." Eugenic attitudes were emphasized, and girls were discouraged from association with "inferiors." This large body of uniformed young women also served as a support resource, and as the war progressed, more than nine million of them were enlisted to work in agricultural programs and in aiding wounded German soldiers during their recoveries.[99]

Boys were openly indoctrinated into the war effort, and their uniformed organizations mimicked troop activities. Military discipline and marches produced homogeneous and well-oiled machines, as Hermann Rauschning commented: "Marching kills thought and destroys individuality. It is a magic and irreplaceable ritual, a medium to mould the community of the nation down to its subconsciousness."[100] New textbooks were written glorifying and aggrandizing the *Herrenvolk*, or master race. One book, *Giftpiltz*, reinforced anti-Semitism, comparing Jews to poisonous mushrooms. A mother instructs her son:

. . . people of this world are very much like mushrooms in a forest. There are good mushrooms as there are good people. There are poisonous, evil mushrooms as there are evil people . . . and do you know who are these evil people, these poisonous mushrooms of mankind? . . .

Yes, Mummy, I know it—they are Jews. Our teacher has often told us about them in school.[101]

The new German order produced disciplined, hardened, fanatically loyal children saturated in propaganda and racism, who were known to betray to authorities their own family members who rejected der Führer's philosophy. They were taught that Jews and Jewish children were the primary targets of venom; but other inferiors also were singled out, and the children were encouraged to support and help to implement the new hatred laws directed at these people. Poles and Slavs, like Jewish children, were prohibited from riding bicycles and visiting museums, theaters, libraries, or parks. In 1942 three Polish girls who went to a ballet at the Poznan Opera House were jailed for four months.[102] These groups were forbidden to possess cameras or radios. They suffered stiff penalties for disobedience.

The Nazi government forced children and their families into walled-off urban pocket zones called ghettos. These guarded areas were cheerless and undesirable industrial parts of cities with deteriorating infrastructures. They were places of abandonment as well as of isolation. The ghetto streets, with a backdrop of neglected buildings, crumbling rubble, and gray smoke-filled skies, became littered with corpses, many of them children. Chaim Kaplan wrote from Warsaw, "Every morning you will see little bodies frozen to death in the ghetto streets. It has become a customary sight."[103] Thousands of children died, directly by execution or, facilitatively, from the cold, from starvation, and from disease. By the end of the war, 73 percent of the children in the Warsaw Ghetto had lost at least one close relative—either in a camp (23%), by execution (24%), from war injuries (14%), or from malnutrition (39%).[104]

The ghettos were intended, moreover, to enhance prisoners' sense of psychic deprivation, even from the pleasure derived from nature's bounty. One mother in the Warsaw Ghetto wrote that "with intentional foresight, not one park, not one playground or public garden was included in the area."[105] Hungry, cold, frightened children, some of whose families either disappeared or died, yearned for mental and emotional escapes—any respite from reality. An examination of ghetto children documented, for example, many instances of children expressing the desire to see natural foliage and flowers. Warsaw Ghetto teacher Genia Silkes related:

But there was no green. One little girl, she was dying, told her sister she would like to see a leaf, to hold something green. Her sister went out, under the wall. . . . The children would pick away bricks and go under the wall. If there was a kind Jewish policeman, they would bring in food. This little girl went to the Aryan side, to a park, and picked a little leaf. That was all. She came back through the hole and put it in a glass by her sister's bed. The other little girl lay there, sucking her thumb, smiling. And then she died.[106]

The only schooling in the ghettos was clandestine, since teaching was forbidden. Games were permitted, so children were posted as "look-outs," and at the approach of the dreaded SS men,* any semblance of a classroom was camouflaged and the area was transformed into a playroom. Small classes often were conducted in apartments. Scarce textbooks were smuggled about with great caution. A teacher from Lublin recalled: "With beating hearts we conducted the lessons, simultaneously on the alert for the barking voices of the SS, who frequently raided Jewish homes."[107]

---

*The SS were the Schutzstaffel elite guards. Initially established as a bodyguard unit for Hitler, their role expanded into security, intelligence, policing, and extermination.

In several countries annexed by Germany—Belgium, France, Luxembourg, Czechoslovakia, Yugoslavia, Poland, and Greece—teachers were expelled and schools were eliminated. In other occupied lands, school curricula were altered. Revised textbooks were issued in Holland, and in Norway and Denmark, school buildings were appropriated and used as military administration headquarters. They all were maneuvers devised by Hitler to destroy systems of education and render ignorant the subjugated masses of people:

... instruction should at best be restricted to the understanding of road signs. Geography should be roughly limited to the teaching that Berlin is the capital of the *Reich* and that everybody should visit it at least once in his lifetime. Apart from that, it will be quite enough if the non-German population learns a little how to read and write in German. The teaching of arithmetic, etc., is superfluous.[108]

Some children were singled out as worthy Aryan types, and Slavic, Russian, Czech, Rumanian, Norwegian, Dutch, and, predominantly, Polish children were wrested from their protesting parents and "expropriated" by the German state for indoctrination in Nazi philosophy. These children were forbidden to use their native languages and costumes, and their names often were changed. Heinrich Himmler (1900–1945), the SS Reichsführer, stated the German case in 1943: "Obviously in such a mixture of peoples there will always be some racially very good types. In these cases I think it is our duty to take their children with us to remove them from their environment, if necessary by robbing or stealing them."[109]

In the many ghettos, most notoriously in Warsaw and Cracow in Poland and in Vilna, Lithuania, conditions facilitating and inexorably leading to death systematically had been devised by the Nazi government. Lack of clothing, lack of shelter from the cold, starvation, and the absence of medical care took their inevitable toll. There were decrees forcing abortions; the penalty for ignoring the regulation was the execution of the infant and of the mother. The Sialaui ghetto in Lithuania had an SS poster that read:

... The 15th of August is not far! Remember Jewish women, after that time no births will be allowed in the ghetto hospital ... even in private homes. A strict examination of private dwellings will be conducted. Physicians, midwives, and nurses will be forbidden to assist Jewish women. In case of insubordination, all will be punished with utmost severity.[110]

As the war escalated, the number of deaths from "facilitated executions" and overt extermination sweeps by the Nazis in the ghettos also increased. Ghettos had become elimination camps, and children and entire families went into hiding in sewers, living there to escape detection by Nazi troops. One little girl related her fear as she saw "big, gray rats scurrying about."[111] Kind strangers, friendly policemen, and sympathetic lookouts exhibited isolated but generous impulses toward many of these children, who were able at times to emerge from hiding to search for food only as a result of such kindnesses.

In Marysin, a suburb of the ghetto in Lodz, Poland, day-care camps had been established. In the fall of 1942, one camp for four- to seven-year-olds was surrounded and all of its members were taken to the Chelmno extermination center. That same year, the kindergartens, orphanages, and private homes of Marysin were raided until no child under ten years of age remained.[112] These periodic raids and sweeps were called *Kinderaktion*.[113]

As the war intensified, the infamous "final solution" was designed and death camps were constructed to which millions were shipped to be ignominiously slaughtered. All unborn, infants, toddlers, and unproductive children were subject to *Die Sonderunterbringung*,[114] one of the euphemisms for execution.*

The number of children who died in the camps is not exact. Testimony at the Nuremberg trials indicates one of the reasons:

. . . We, the internees, often tried to ascertain the number of people who perished in gas chambers, but our estimates of the number of children executed could only be based on the number of children's prams which were brought to the storerooms. Sometimes there were hundreds of these carriages, but sometimes they sent thousands.[115]

Official documents from the Auschwitz death camp indicate that 99,922 sets of children's clothing were shipped from the camp during a forty-seven-day period between December 1944 and January 1945. Similar numbers were recorded at the camp in Majdanek.

Hundreds of babies were born in the camps. Most were immediately

---

*This was nothing new. The policy was essentially a continuation and extension of the *Behandlung* program of the *Kinderfachabteilungen* (special care wards) designed to euthanize unwanted German children. In 1939, Hitler's government implemented a program based on eugenic *Rassenhygiene* philosophy. The Reichsausschuss zur wissenschaftlichen Erfassung von erb- und anlagebedingter schwerer Leiden (Reich Committee for the Scientific Treatment of Severe Genetically Determined Illness) was a paper umbrella granting authenticity and sheltering the bureaucracy involved. Children with Down's syndrome, microcephaly, hydrocephaly, limb deformities, spina bifida, spastic diplegia—any obvious congenital anomaly (*missgebildetes*) were referred to one of 22 *Kinderfachabteilungen* for treatment. The treatment was a lethal dose of chloral hydrate. Five thousand children are estimated to have died in these wards. Parent and Shevell, 1998, pp. 79–83.

placed in drowning buckets.[116] Overall estimates are that 1.2 million Jewish children were executed.[117] Not all were gassed or burned. Some were used by physicians for medical experiments. At the Lubliniec hospital in Silesia, the neurophysiological effects of large doses of sodium phenobarbital in children were recorded. Of 235 children in this experimental "protocol," 221 died.[118]

Between 1943 and 1944, three thousand sets of twins were abused as experimental subjects in the "laboratories" of Josef Mengele (1911–1979) at Auschwitz. All nontwins in the camp were executed. As one twin served as the "research" subject, the other served as an experimental control. Mengele's deluded goal was to establish a eugenic stage for the perfect Nordic strain. A preliminary step was to sterilize those with undesirable genetic traits. Horst Schumann, Mengele's aide, assisted him as both exposed thousands of children to massive doses of sterilizing radiation.[119]

Mengele's first experiment—to encode for genetic transference—involved mutilating children, despite known scientific data that acquired or inflicted lesions were not mutations and therefore not inheritable. He stained children's eyes chemically by injecting their eyes (antechamber and iris) with pigment, to "induce" blue eyes. Resulting blindness was common.[120] In the name of science he conducted experiments for the sole purpose of observing, comparing, and recording data. He transfused blood from one twin to another; isolated subjects for psychological endurance testing; injected children with microbes, including tuberculosis and typhus; attempted sex changes. Finally, to instantly kill his subjects and thereby preserve their organs, Mengele gave them intracardiac injections of phenol.[121]

One hundred of these children survived.[122]

Countless children were victims of Nazi terror. Sometimes entire communities were massacred, as in June 1944, when most of the inhabitants in the Italian village of Civitella were shot or burned to death in their homes. Half the victims were children. That same month, 104 children of Lidice were snatched from their village; only 17 ultimately returned.[123]

In the midst of horror, children's natural impulses to play meshed with their instincts to survive. Play was restorative and sustaining and allowed an emotional escape from realities otherwise too brutal to endure. Poignantly, their games in another age would have been artistically immortalized by Breughel—children raced and chased, they played hide-and-seek, and they had childish scuffles.

In the Ravensbrueck concentration camp for women, children sometimes were permitted incarceration with their mothers. Emma Gluck-LaGuardia wrote in her memoirs of 1944 that there were about five hundred children in the camp: "They looked like skeletons wearing rugs; some had no hair on their heads. Nevertheless, they behaved like children, running around and

Figure 9.3 Two confused and forlorn Hungarian boys standing on the train platform in Auschwitz. COURTESY OF THE SIMON WIESENTHAL CENTER BEIT HASHOAH MUSEUM OF TOLERANCE LIBRARY AND ARCHIVES, LOS ANGELES.

begging things from their elders. They even played games."[124] Hungry and surrounded by pain, suffering, and the stench of death, children pushed aside grim realities through play. Sometimes they invented games that served as soothing psychological balm to assaulted sensibilities. One game, called *Appel*, was modeled after the camps' daily roll; in another, *Klepsi*, a blindfolded participant, having been struck by a playmate, had to identify the culprit after the blindfold was removed. Often play imitated life down to the smallest detail: one little girl in the Lodz ghetto had two yellow stars stitched to her doll's dress.[125]

Playgrounds were fabricated wherever an open space was found—in bombed-out ghetto lots; along train platforms where carloads of people were herded, destined for the death camps of Auschwitz (figure 9.3) and Majdanek; and in the camps, adjacent to the smokestacks of the death chambers. One eyewitness, overwhelmed by the inhuman conditions the Nazis had created, rejected the use of the term *play*. Jan Karsi, whose mission was to secretly inspect the Warsaw Ghetto, wrote back to authorities in London:

We passed a miserable replica of a park—a little square of comparatively clear ground in which a half-dozen nearly leafless trees and a patch of grass had somehow managed to survive. It was fearfully crowded. Mothers huddled close together on benches nursing withered infants. Children, every bone in their skeletons showing through their taut skins, played in heaps and swarms.

"They play before they die," I heard my companion on the left say. . . .

Without thinking—the words escaping even before the thought had crystal-lized—I said: "But these children are not playing—they only make believe it is play."[126]

Among nations, some outstanding heroic and charitable policies saved thousands of children's lives. Appalled by the destruction of Jewish quarters by incensed mobs on *Kristallnacht*, the Netherlands immediately acted to admit more than 1,700 refugee children. Belgium took in several hundred and England, nine thousand. In France, members of the underground resistance sheltered thousands of children and provided identity cards, birth certificates, and even baptismal papers. Similar deeds happened in Spain, Slovakia, Switzerland, and Turkey. In Norway and Sweden, rescue boats were used to smuggle children to safety.[127] Even islands in the Caribbean offered refuge.

The United States remained insular. Senator Robert F. Wagner (1877–1953) of New York and Representative Edith Rogers (1881–1960) of Massachusetts did propose legislation in January 1939, called the Child Refugee Act, that authorized the American Friends Service Committee to supervise the arrival and placement of twenty thousand refugee children. Within six months, a negative lobbying effort by the American Legion, Veterans of Foreign Wars, Daughters of the American Revolution, and the Allied Patriot Societies succeeded in having the bill defeated.[128]

In the annals of the history of Nazi victims, hundreds of individual acts of heroism and charity have been recorded anecdotally and historically documented. During 1940 and 1941, nearly one million Poles were arrested, herded into boxcars, and sent into Soviet Russia. In 1942 some forty-five thousand of them were allowed to leave for Iran. Of that number, three thousand were children under fourteen years of age. They went to the ancient Persian city of Isfahan,[129] where they were entrusted to the care of a consortium of religious and lay workers, which provided for the welfare of these children until the war's end. Twenty-one schools housed, boarded, and educated these orphans of war, most of them Catholics who were within hearing distance of muezzins chanting from minarets. Although they lived humbly, the children lived with hope and without fears, waiting for the end of a vicious war that had wrenched them from their families and their friends. Their dream of returning to Poland was shattered by the divisions of territory made by Roosevelt, Winston Churchill (1874–1965), and Josef Stalin (1879–1953) at the Yalta Conference. Poland, its files and records destroyed, was politically unstable and under Communist rule once the war ended. Return to Poland was no longer possible for the children of Isfahan. They went instead to Lebanon and other parts of the world, a great diaspora that lasted for years.[130]

Of other children in the war, the numbers of those who died are not exact, but at war's end some three million children were known dead. Common wisdom has it, however, that nearly twenty-five million civilians died during the conflict, and if that is the case, the number of dead children comes closer to ten million.

❑ ❑ ❑

I chose to end this history at this juncture in time. It seems to me that the events of the second half of the twentieth century have not seasoned enough for unprejudiced interpretation and analysis. Passions still run high about many events that seem very fresh, and therefore, objective study is difficult. Occurrences and decisions that shape history often are chiseled slowly and deliberately. There are, nevertheless, some observations I wish to make, not in a historical context but simply as an observer with a historical interest.

There is an overwhelming amount of statistical data that represent the tragedies of tens of millions of children, for whom life has been a series of unspeakable suffering and dangerous experiences. During the decade of 1980 alone, 1.5 million children died in wars, both declared and undeclared. Four million were permanently disabled. During the Iran–Iraq war, there were ten- and eleven-year-old boy soldiers, ninety-five thousand of whom died. In Mozambique, a policy of destabilization produced nearly five hundred thousand deaths of children. Currently, five million children live in refugee camps; twelve million more are homeless.[131] In Chernobyl and its environs, radiation-contaminated and untreated children suffer with cancer. In the favelas of Brazil, children grow up untutored and unschooled. Homeless street children are "regularly murdered and tortured" in Brazil, Guatemala, and Colombia.[132] In Somalia, marasmic and kwashiorkor children stare vacantly at the future that offers no hope. Waifs in Romania, child prostitutes in Thailand and elsewhere, the dead and maimed victims of hate wars in Bosnia and Northern Ireland, and the gang dead in America all point to the failure of our species globally to provide a safe haven for our young or even for ourselves.

Illegal child labor persists throughout the world. At least 250 million children under fourteen years of age are employed worldwide, and in some countries 15 percent to 25 percent of the workforce is made up of children. India has 20–50 million; Bangladesh, 6.6; Peru, 4; Pakistan, 3.3; Brazil, 2.5; Egypt, 2; Philippines, 1.8; Turkey, 1.5; Mexico, 1.1; Kenya, 1—the vast majority of all these children, some 70 percent, working in agriculture.[133]

In the United States alone there are thirty thousand injuries and over a hundred deaths yearly due to child-labor accidents. There are losses of limbs and eyes, burns, and electrocutions that mostly occur on farms. Eighty-six percent of deaths occur in illegal, unsupervised, and unregulated employment.[134]

As of December 1999 there were 1.3 million children under 15 years of age living with HIV/AIDS, some two hundred thousand in South Asia and one million in sub-Saharan Africa. Thirteen million, two hundred thousand children already have been orphaned by the disease.[135]

The ancient shame of abandonment continues. The *columna lactaria* and the *ruota* are gone, but in our "modern civilization" the conditions and consequences of poverty and despair persist, and there are instances of babies abandoned behind stoops or in rubbish bins. Documented cases of abandonment come from hospitals. In America's sanitized hospital nurseries, 60 percent of abandoned babies are low-birth-weight or premature infants, and 80 percent of these were delivered of drug-addicted mothers. More than 12,650 infants annually are abandoned in hospitals. They live as "boarder babies" until they either are adopted or, for the majority (96%) of them, foster homes are found.[136]

At the end of the twentieth century, three-quarters of the world's entire population and nearly 85 percent of the world's children reside in developing countries. In 1985 there were approximately 1.458 billion children in these poorest countries.[137] They mostly are medically, nutritionally, and educationally deprived. Death from preventable diseases is commonplace—in 1986 fourteen million children under five years of age died (table 9.2).

The Pacific Ocean El Niño phenomenon occurs in two- to seven-year cycles and has been associated with increased incidences of malaria, cholera,

TABLE 9.2
1986 CAUSES OF DEATHS OF CHILDREN UNDER 5 YEARS[138]

Disease	No. of Deaths (millions)	Percentages
Diarrhea	5.0	35
Malaria	3.0	21
Measles	2.1	15
Other	1.3	10
Respiratory tract infections	1.3	9
Tetanus	0.8	6
Pertussis	0.6	4

and dengue. Now, increases in noncholera diarrheas have been documented, and deaths from diarrheal dehydrations may increase by the millions with each degree of increase in ambient temperatures. The 1997–1998 El Niño raised ambient temperatures in Peru by five degrees Celsius and diarrhea incidence by 200 percent.[139]

The statistics of deaths due to wars and famine, both preventable conditions, are still being compiled.

NOTES

1. Cable, 1972, p. 163; Cunningham, 1992, p. 163.
2. Nardinelli, 1990, pp. 123–52.
3. Trattner, 1970, pp. 58–59.
4. Cunningham, 1992, pp. 188–208.
5. Ibid., p. 219.
6. Offenhartz-Greene, 1992, p. 37.
7. Kemp, 1986, p. 8.
8. Bongartz, 1973, pp. 95–96.
9. Trattner, 1970, pp. 96–119.
10. Hutchins, 1994, p. 695.
11. Bremner, 1970–1971, p. 1067.
12. These publications were among the most enduring of the bureau's efforts. As late as 1943, a revision of *Infant Care* by Dr. Dorothy V. Whipple (1900–1995) was published.
13. Offenhartz-Greene, 1992, p. 65.
14. Trattner, 1970, p. 184.
15. Riis, 1970, pp. 291–300.
16. In 1910 there were 450 day-care facilities in the United States that were registered by the Association of Day Nurseries. Steinfels, 1973, p. 34.
17. Ibid., pp. 49–52.
18. Ibid., p. 34.
19. Ibid., pp. 66–69.
20. Hawes, 1991, p. 56.
21. J. G. Hughes, *Pediatrics* 1993; 92:469–70.
22. Alexander, 1992, p. 283.
23. Morison and Commager, 1962, p. 390.
24. Schlereth, 1991, p. 246.
25. Ibid., p. 247.
26. Bremner, 1970–1971, p. 1270.
27. Ibid., p. 246.
28. Teitelbaum, 1993, pp. 1–10.
29. Holt and Howland, 1916, p. 5.
30. Ibid., p. 6.
31. Hall, 1904/1969, pp. 325–410.

32. Schlereth, 1991, pp. 277–79.

33. Watson, 1928, p. ii.

34. Ibid., p. 12.

35. Ibid., pp. 81–82.

36. *Journal of Pediatrics* 1933; 2:391–92.

37. Shaw, 1930, pp. 19–20. Shaw, it may be remembered, left school when he was fourteen years old.

38. Ibid., p. 11.

39. Ibid., p. 86.

40. Ibid., p. 199.

41. Green, 1992, p. 121.

42. Ibid., p. 123.

43. Nardinelli, 1990, pp. 140–42.

44. Bremner, 1971, pp. 1083–85.

45. Ibid., p. 1089.

46. Hutchins, 1994, p. 696.

47. Saari, 1990, pp. 13–14.

48. Chrisman, 1920, p. 112.

49. Saari, 1990, p. 82.

50. Chrisman, 1920, pp. 113–14.

51. Saari, 1990, p. 2.

52. Ibid., p. 86.

53. Ibid., p. 90.

54. Tom, 1989, pp. 139–43.

55. Ibid., pp. 143–47.

56. A State Statistical Bureau in Peking reported in 1990 that 30 million children between the ages of six and twelve did not attend school. *China News Analysis*, no. 1495 (15 October 1993): 2.

57. Tom, 1989, pp. 143–47.

58. Tofani, 1993, pp. 1–13.

59. Blyth, 1960, p. 193.

60. Chrisman, 1920, pp. 143–44.

61. Courdey, 1984, pp. 132–34.

62. Von Siebold, 1973, pp. 124–26.

63. Chrisman, 1920, p. 156.

64. Courdey, 1984, p. 155.

65. Scott, 1922, pp. 124–27.

66. Ibid.

67. Chrisman, 1920, pp. 158–59.

68. Scott, 1922, pp. 391–404.

69. Blyth, 1960, pp. 182–86.

70. Spock, 1976, pp. 1–2.

71. C. D. Williams, *Lancet* 1935; 2:1151–52.

72. Jelliffe, 1968.

73. LaPlane, 1991, p. 41.

74. Braun, 1991, p. 226.

75. Ballabriga, 1991, pp. 9–10.

76. Goldbloom, 1982, p. 151.

77. Ballabriga, 1991, p. 15.

78. Goldbloom, 1982, p. 153.

79. Ibid., p. 13.

80. LaPlane, 1991, pp. 43–44.

81. Veeder, 1957, p. 157.

82. Strachey, 1940, p. 120.

83. Ibid., p. ix.

84. Ibid., pp. 3–4.

85. Inglis, 1989, p. 8.

86. Ibid., p. 47.

87. Westall, 1985, p. 55.

88. Strachey, 1940, pp. 108–11.

89. Inglis, 1989, pp. 1–2.

90. Ibid., pp. 105–24.

91. Ibid., pp. 4–5.

92. Tateishi, 1984, p. xiii.

93. Bosworth, 1967, pp. 36–37.

94. Fox, 1990, pp. xii–xiv.

95. Tateishi, 1984, p. 2.

96. Bosworth, 1967, pp. 254–57.

97. The term *Nazi* comes from the pronunciation of the first two syllables of Hitler's Nationalsozialistische Deutsche Arbeiterpartei (National Socialist German Workingmen's Party).

98. Sosnowski, 1983, p. 12.

99. Pine, 1999, pp. 24–29. In America, during the early twentieth century, many prominent citizens supported the concept of eugenics. They believed that family planning, improved public health, and reproduction only among the "fit" would solve the many complex problems facing American society. They promulgated the concept that the mentally retarded, addicted, criminal, and vagabond elements of society should not be allowed to reproduce. There was an American Eugenics Party with an official platform, and colleges offered courses on eugenics. The movement survived into the 1940s.

100. Sosnowski, 1983, p. 18.

101. Ibid., pp. 17–18.

102. Ibid., p. 46.

103. Eisen, 1988, p. 20.

104. Sosnowski, 1983, pp. 56–58.

105. Ibid.

106. Eisen, 1988, p. 60.

107. Ibid., p. 85.

108. Sosnowski, 1983, pp. 158–59.

109. Ibid., pp. 56–58.

110. Eisen, 1988, p. 15.

111. Ibid., p. 91.

112. Ibid., pp. 37–38.

113. Ibid., p. 16.

114. Sosnowski, 1983, p. 71.

115. Ibid., p. 72.

116. Ibid., pp. 100–101.

117. Ibid., p. 73.

118. Ibid.

119. Lagnado and Dekel, 1991, p. 51.

120. Ibid., pp. 65–66.

121. Ibid., pp. 67–70.

122. Ibid., p. 7.

123. Ibid., pp. 81–92. This action was reminiscent of the Buitrago village massacre in the Guadarrama mountains during the Spanish Civil War. Eighty children found hiding in a church were dragged out, lined up, and shot (*Time*, 24 August 1936, p. 19). Such massacres of children have been common in history, but the Nazi actions of World War II happened with numbing frequency, repetition, and cruelty.

124. Eisen, 1988, pp. 79–80.

125. Ibid., p. 107.

126. Ibid.

127. Morse, 1983, pp. 252–69.

128. Ibid., pp. 313–49.

129. Stankiewicz et al., 1989, p. xvi.

130. Ibid., pp. 124–25.

131. Schaller and Nightingale, 1992, pp. 642–44.

132. *Lancet* 1998; 351:1955.

133. P. J. Landrigan et al., Child labor, *Pediatr Ann* 1995; 24:657–62; *Washington Post*, 16 March 2000, p. A20.

134. Landrigan and Belville, 1993, p. 1029.

135. <www.unaids.org>.

136. U.S. Department of Health and Human Services, 1991.

137. MacPherson, 1987, p. 18.

138. Ibid., p. 79.

139. *Lancet* 2000; 355:442.

PART TWO

❏ ❏ ❏

summary and conclusions

Throughout history, recorded data have ignored children. We are reminded that "the sources used for the history of childhood are overwhelmingly secondary: [they are] moral and medical tracts, religious sermons and the views of contemporary 'experts.'"[1] Furthermore, "because boys and girls left little behind in the places historians have looked for evidence, they have often been shunted to the shadowy margins of history, barely visible to those who write or study our past."[2] Still, the examination of parish registers, plague journals, private diaries, *hausbuchs*, incunabula, and paintings contributes a general understanding of the evolution of children's places in societies as well as how the societies in which they lived regarded and treated them.

A thousand years marks the timeline from late antiquity to the Golden Age of Kings, at the zenith of which foundling homes and schools had become common features in the West, and the quality of children's lives had become greatly enhanced as a result of a gradual but progressive interest in children rooted in Christian philosophy. More than any other factor, canonical decrees, which often became de facto civil law, altered society's views that children could be used as chattel and insurance to preserve property. Catholic doctrine reinforced the idea of the deity's special love for children and the divinely ordered obligation of parents to nurture and protect their children. From these concepts, pediatric care and child-protection laws evolved as extensions of parental nurturing. Infanticide, abandonment, and child abuse became grave sins, punishable by excommunication from the church and condemnation to hellfire, and became subject to civil punishment by secular authorities.

Children learned about divine will and their spiritual destiny from Protestant catechists who, after the Reformation, infused these ideas into secular education. In the East, child nurture stemmed from the perceived duty to raise filial, unquestioningly loyal sons to honor parents and ancestors, an objective unchanged until the advent of the twentieth century.

Some social historians have detected a waning interest in children's well-being during the Middle Ages, based on interpretations of the absence of child depictions in art, the nature of children's clothing, the naming of children, the practices of swaddling infants and farming out children to wet nurses, the customs of oblations and apprenticeships, and the escalating numbers of street urchins.[3] The text of this book argues otherwise. Children, at best featureless afterthoughts in scattered works of art, were, to the medieval mind, God's innocents, and the Western art world aimed to deliver a spiritual message to adults in pursuit of salvation. The rendering of adults in art, therefore, reflects the interest in illuminating the soul's yearning for salvation through Christ. The grace, beauty, and proportion of the human body that distinguishes the art of the Greeks were replaced by flat, bidimensional images, outlined like leaded stained glass, that indicated nothing more than an inattention to art form in favor of a theocratic vision of man's purpose on earth. In the Islamic cultures, it was considered sinful pride and arrogance to reproduce the human image. Stylized miniatures were the only acceptable moral concession to this view.

Under the age of seven years, children were dressed in tunics that opened down the front, with no distinction according to sex or age. It was argued that this represented children dressed as small adults, with a disregard of childhood. Yet we have seen that, through the ages, children have always been dressed in tunics that opened down the front, probably to facilitate toiletry. Until the completion of toilet training, diapers of some genre were worn, and an open tunic facilitated their changing. Thereafter, a gown that opened readily was welcomed for coping with the typically sudden and last minute micturation urgencies of children. Additionally, using a common pattern cut for childhood gowns was probably economic and facile. To argue that an open tunic represented medieval indifference to children is at the very least forced.

It has been argued that the medieval child had no individual identity, based on the common custom of giving a newborn the name of a prior sibling who had died. The counterargument is that acknowledging individuality with a singular given name in the Western world is a modern phenomenon. In the classical Roman world, children commonly were named numerically (Primus, Secundus, Tertius, etc.). Eastern and New World cultures thought to honor their children by naming them after ancestors. Driven by religious ferver rather than by lack of interest in their children, parents in the Renaissance were influenced by hagiography in naming their children, and after the Reformation, "imaginative," sometimes outlandish names, with spiritual or ethical references, became popular.

Swaddling as a societal indicator of indifference to the child lacks plausibility, since it has been a ubiquitous feature of societies worldwide for millennia and continues to be practiced in many cultures. It would have been an uncaring mother who did not swaddle her child. Swaddling is known to be a calming and heat-conserving measure advocated by physicians for centuries.[4] Only recently has swaddling been questioned as a possible contributor to infant apnea.

Egyptian, Hebrew, Etruscan, Greek, and Roman monuments and inscriptions indicate that wet nursing was a common ancient practice. From medieval and Renaissance diaries we have learned that the "balias" often were loved and treasured by the children they suckled. There is some validity to the idea, however, that farming out children to wet nurses, commonly initiated to accommodate an aristocratic woman's lifestyle or to satisfy a husband's claim to conjugal rights,* was a form of abandonment, since the maternal obligation to first provide infants' needs was abrogated.

The significant mortality among wet-nursed infants during plague years lends credence to a charge that this practice was a form of infanticide. For overtly abandoned infants being nursed in foundling homes, death was a

---

*The eighteenth-century *Dictionnaire des cas de conscience*, by Fromageau, poses the question: "Jeanne, having had a first child by her husband, wishes to feed it herself; but since her husband wishes to demand of her his conjugal rights, she asked whether she is obliged to satisfy him." He answers, "The wife should, if she can, put her child out to nurse." Flandrin, 1976, p. 206.

predictable outcome. In the Rouen hospice, 90 percent of infants died in the first year of life. At the Hotel-Dieu in Paris, between 62 percent and 75 percent of infants died.[5]

Infanticide and abandonment were distinctly ancient practices that most cultures condemned. Instances decreased significantly from the late antiquity and patristic periods, yielding to oblique but sanctioned forms of abandonment—oblation and apprenticeship. The rationale for oblating children to monasteries as offerings to God obfuscated motivations to prevent the dilution of estates from multiple heirs. Likewise, apprenticeships, particularly those initiated when the child was seven years old, were in too many instances abandonment to abusive indenture and child labor that could end in the death of the child. With the Renaissance, oblation disappeared, and the rules of apprenticeship were codified and made humane, predominantly from the self-regulation of guilds.

The establishment of foundling homes is cited as symptomatic of an uncaring society that abandoned its children to the streets. To the contrary, the increase in the numbers of orphans and street urchins is easily attributable to the tolls exacted by poverty, plague, and wars, none of which were inventions of the Middle Ages or thereafter. The compassionate response to these societal ills was the establishment of the foundling home and, in the Renaissance, laws introduced to provide foundlings with education, apprenticeships, and even dowries. Orphans fared somewhat better than did street urchins. The latter frequently were rounded up and either contracted out for child labor or shipped abroad to colonies or workhouses.

The medieval and Renaissance Western world can be regarded as periods in which humanistic concern for the needs of children was initiated; in the closing centuries of the second millennium, this concern has evolved to include stringent child-labor laws and an acknowledgment of the legal rights of children.

With the Reformation, pedagogy became a respected interest and a distinct discipline, a *negotium cum Deum*. For reformists, education was the key to spiritual enlightenment, and catechismal doxology was emphasized in education. Influenced by Locke and Rousseau and ideas of egalitarianism, the aim of education shifted, and broad humanitarian and secular training of children became the norm. Guilt associated with industrialization and institutional abuses of children resulted in universal education. Sunday schools, then settlement schools, industrial schools, foundling schools, and finally public or state schools mark the sequence of progression that culminated with state recognition that children are society's resources for a sound future and therefore must be educated.

Abuses to children spawned by industrial greed inspired a new age of professional reformers, social workers, and psychologists—champions of childhood who exposed the miseries of poverty, disease, and neglect and the plight of children decompensated physically by long hours of work in the factories of Europe and America. The list of child advocates and physicians who advanced the rights, needs, and health of children is long but well annotated:

Our beadroll of benefactors of child-life includes . . . Vincent de Paul, the patron of friendless children, whose charitable endeavors led to the foundation of the *Hospice des enfants trouvés* (1640); George Armstrong, who founded the first dispensary for children (1769); Johann Peter Frank, the pioneer of school hygiene (1779); Count Rumford, who originated school lunches for children (1792); John Bunnell Davis, who adumbrated the modern methods of lowering mortality of infants (1817); Morel de Villiers, Benjamin Broadbent, and S. G. H. Moore, of Huddersfield, and Sir Arthur Newsholme, who made them accomplished facts; Semmelveis and Credé, who made the prevention of puerperal septicemia and infantile conjunctivitis viable; Théophile Roussel, the physician-legislator whose beneficent laws for the protection of children have been our models; O'Dwyer, the inventor of intubation; Roux and von Behring, the discoverers of antitoxin; Grancher, the originator of isolation cubicles and of surgical cleanliness in children's wards in hospitals; Soxhlet, Rotch, Coit, Schlossmann and others who have made "clean milk" possible; the many investigators of infant nutrition and metabolism; and the great humanistic pediatrists, like Charles West, Jacobi, and J. Lewis Smith, who have practiced this branch of medicine, not merely as scientific specialty, but from genuine love of the children themselves.[6]

Throughout the nineteenth century the Western world was ushering in an Age of the Child. Life expectancy and the quality of life improved. Developmental milestones were marked and celebrated, specialized shops for children—toy stores, clothing stores—proliferated, a literature written specifically for children emerged, some of which was overladen with Victorian sentimentality, as in Coventry Patmore's (1823–1896) poem, "The Toys," which exemplifies the romantic image of childhood that predominated:

> My little Son, who look'd from thoughtful eyes
> And moved and spoke in quiet grown-up wise,
> Having my law the seventh time disobey'd,
> I struck him, and dismiss'd
> With hard words and unkiss'd,
> His Mother, who was patient, being dead.
> Then, fearing lest his grief should hinder sleep,
> I visited his bed,
> But found him slumbering deep,

With darken'd eyelids, and their lashes yet
From his late sobbing wet.
And I, with moan,
Kissing away his tears, left others of my own;
For, on a table drawn beside his head,
He had put, within his reach,
A box of counters and a red-vein'd stone,
A piece of glass abraded by the beach
And six or seven shells,
A bottle with bluebells
And two French copper coins, ranged there with careful art,
To comfort his sad heart.
So when that night I pray'd
To God, I wept, and said;
Ah, when at last we lie with tranced breath,
Not vexing Thee in death,
And Thou rememberest of what toys
We made our joys,
How weakly understood,
Thy great commanded good,
Then fatherly not less
Than I whom Thou hast moulded from the clay,
Thou'lt leave Thy wrath, and say,
"I will be sorry for their childishness."[7]

Since Patmore wrote "The Toys," the world's children have experienced paradoxes that, more than any single truth, perhaps best represent the human condition. We can commend the establishment of children's rights in the workplace until we think of ongoing industrial child abuse in many parts of the world; we can commend scientific advances that have saved tens of millions of children's lives, until we remember the tens of millions of children who died in wars in the twentieth century; we can commend society's willingness to allocate hundreds of thousands of dollars to save a single premature infant's life, until we remember our passivity to reports that, in other parts of the world, street urchins are gathered up from the streets and executed; we can commend ourselves for nurturing, educating, and indulging our children, until we think of the consequences of racism to our minority children, of our indifference to Romanian foundlings who wither with iatrogenic viremias, to five hundred thousand children dying as a consequence of exposure to Chernobyl's radiation, or acknowledge our indifference to the hundreds of thousands of Iraqi children who have died as a consequence of a politically imposed embargo, or to one million cachectic, fly-ridden, marasmic children who stare vacantly at death in the eastern horn of Africa.

NOTES

1. Pollock, 1983, p. 22.
2. Hiner and Hawes, 1985, p. 167.
3. Pollock, 1983, pp. 23–27.
4. E. L. Lipton et al., Swaddling: a child care practice. *Pediatrics* 1965; 35:519–67.
5. Flandrin, 1976, p. 204.
6. Garrison, 1923, pp. 168–69.
7. F. Page, *The Poems of Coventry Patmore* (London: Oxford University Press, 1949), pp. 365–66.

Epilogue

❏ ❏ ❏

I N 1959 THE GENERAL ASSEMBLY of the United Nations produced a document called *The Rights of the Child*.* Governments acknowledged for the
first time in the history of mankind the necessity to nurture and protect the
world's children. The document endorsed the conditions that support the
growth and development of healthy, happy, and productive human beings.
It merits being restated in these pages:

Whereas mankind owes to the child the best it has to give Now therefore, The General Assembly proclaims this Declaration of the Rights of the Child to the end that
he may have a happy childhood and enjoy for his own good and for the good of society the rights and freedoms herein set forth, and calls upon parents, upon men and
women as individuals and upon voluntary organizations, local authorities and
national Governments to recognize these rights and strive for their observance by
legislative and other measures progressively taken in accordance with the following
principles.

---

*Resolution 1386 xiv, 20 November 1959. An earlier version, called *The Declaration of the
Rights of the Child*, was generated by a committee led by Eglantyne Jebb, founder of Save the
Children Fund. It was adopted in 1924 by the League of Nations. MacPherson, 1987, pp.
4–5.

Principle 1

The child shall enjoy all the rights set forth in this Declaration. Every child, without any exception whatsoever, shall be entitled to these rights, without distinction or discrimination on account of race, color, sex, language, religion, political or other opinion, national or social origin, property, birth or other status, whether of himself or of his family.

Principle 2

The child shall enjoy special protection, and shall be given opportunities and facilities, by law and by other means, to enable them to develop physically, mentally, morally, spiritually and socially in a healthy and normal manner and in conditions of freedom and dignity. In the enactment of laws for this purpose, the best interests of the child shall be the paramount consideration.

Principle 3

The child shall be entitled from his birth to a name and a nationality.

Principle 4

The child shall enjoy the benefits of social security. He shall be entitled to grow and develop in health; to this end, special care and protection shall be provided both to him and to his mother, including adequate pre-natal and post-natal care. The child shall have the right to adequate nutrition, housing, recreation and medical services.

Principle 5

The child who is physically, mentally or socially handicapped shall be given the special treatment, education and care required by his particular condition.

Principle 6

The child, for the full and harmonious development of his personality, needs love and understanding. He shall, wherever possible, grow up in the care and under the responsibility of his parents, and, in any case, in an atmosphere of affection and of moral and material security; a child of tender years shall not, save in exceptional circumstances, be separated from his mother. Society and the public authorities shall have the duty to extend particular care to children without a family and to those without adequate means of support. Payment of State and other assistance towards the maintenance of children of large families is desirable.

Principle 7

The child is entitled to receive education, which shall be free and compulsory, at least in the elementary stages. He shall be given an education which will promote his general culture, and enable him, on a basis of equal opportunity, to develop his abilities, his individual judgement, and his sense of moral and social responsibility, and to become a useful member of society. The best interests of the child shall be the guiding principle of those responsible for his education and guidance; that responsibility lies in the first place with the parents. The child shall have full opportunity for play and recreation, which should be directed to the same purposes as education; society and the public authorities shall endeavour to promote the enjoyment of this right.

Principle 8

The child shall in all circumstances be among the first to receive protection and relief.

Principle 9

The child shall be protected against all forms of neglect, cruelty and exploitation. He shall not be the subject of traffic, in any form. The child shall not be admitted to employment before an appropriate minimum age; he shall in no case be caused or permitted to engage in any occupation or employment which would prejudice his health or education, or interfere with his physical, mental and moral development.

Principle 10

The child shall be protected from practices which may foster racial, religious and any other forms of discrimination. He shall be brought up in a spirit of understanding, tolerance, friendship among peoples, peace and universal brotherhood, and in full consciousness that his energy and talents should be devoted to the service of his fellow men.

At this writing it has been forty-one years since the rights of the child were proclaimed by members of the United Nations.* As an epilogue to this book, this long-ignored document, its aspirations and principles violated repeatedly, often to the point of genocide, is hereby resurrected as a manifesto for the future. For the love of children and of mankind, the future depends on it.

---

*In 1994, American ambassador to the UN Madeleine Albright signed the Convention on the Rights of Children. To this date only two countries have not ratified it—Somalia and the United States.

Bibliography

❑ ❑ ❑

PRIMARY SOURCES

Abbott, J. S. C. 1834. *The Mother at Home.* Boston: Crocker and Brewster.

Ackerley, G. 1836. *On the Management of Children in Sickness and Health.* New York: Bancroft & Holley.

Addison, J. 1970. *Selections from the Tatler and the Spectator.* Annotated by R. J. Allen. New York: Holt, Rinehart & Winston.

Aeschines. 1919. *The Speeches.* Translated by C. D. Adams. London: William Heinemann.

Albertus Magnus. 1987. *Man and the Beast.* Translated by J. J. Scanlan. Binghamton, NY: Medieval and Renaissance Texts.

Alcott, W. A. 1844. *The Young Man's Guide.* Boston: T. R. Marvin.

———. 1846. *The Boy's Guide.* Boston: Waite, Peirce & Company.

Ascham, R. 1570/1977. *The Scholemaster.* London: John Day. Norwood Edition reprint.

Athenagoras. 1956. *Embassy.* Translated by J. H. Crehan. London: Newman Press.

Augustine, Saint. 1964. *On Free Choice of the Will.* Translated by A. S. Benjamin and L. H. Hackstuff. New York: Macmillan.

———. 1972. *City of God.* Translated by W. M. Green. London: William Heinemann.

Benedict, Saint. 1948. *St. Benedict's Rule for the Monasteries.* Translated by L. S. Doyle. Collegeville, MN: St. John's Abbey Press.

Body of Liberties, Colonial Laws of Massachusetts. 1660/1889. Boston: Rockwell and Churchill.

Brinsley, J. 1612. *Ludus Literarius or the Grammar Schoole.* London: Thomas Man.

Cadogan, W. 1773. *An Essay Upon Nursing, and Management of Children, from Their Birth to Three Years of Age.* London: William and Thomas Bradford.

Calvin, J. 1975. *Ecclesiastical Ordinances 1541.* Translated by J. Dillenberger. Missoula, MT: Scholar Press.

Catullus. 1913. *The Poems.* Translated by F. W. Cornish. London: William Heinemann.

Celsus. 1935. *De Medicina.* Translated by W. G. Spencer. London: William Heinemann.

Codex Mendoza. 1978. Annotated by K. Ross. Fribourg: Liber, S.A.

Comenius, J. A. 1657/1968. *Magna Didactica.* Farnborough, UK: Gregg International Publishers.

———. 1659. *Orbis Sensualium Pictus.* Translated by C. Hoole. London: F. Kirton.

Dewees, W. P. 1829. *A Treatise on the Physical and Medical Treatment of Children.* Philadelphia: Carey, Lea and Carey.

Diodorus Siculus. 1933. *The Histories.* Translated by C. H. Oldfather. Cambridge, MA: Harvard University Press.

Dominici, G. 1927. *Regola del Governo di Cura Familiare.* Translated by A. B. Coté Washington, DC: Catholic University Press.

Elyot, T. 1531/1970. *The Boke Named the Governour.* Menston, UK: Scholar Press.

Epictetus. 1926. *Discourses.* London: William Heinemann.

Erasmus, D. 1990. *De Pueris statim ac Liberaliter Instituendis Declamatio* (translated by B. C. Verstraete) and *De Civilitate Morum Puerilium* (translated by B. McGregor). In *The Erasmus Reader.* Edited by E. Rummel. Toronto: University of Toronto Press.

Foxe, J. 1810. *Book of Martyrs.* New York: Samuel Wood.

Fuller, T. 1642. *The Holy State.* Cambridge: Roger Daniel.

Furnivall, F. J. 1868/1969. *The Babee's Boke.* London: N. Trübner. Reprint, Westport, CT: Greenwood Press.

Hall, G. S. 1904/1969. *Adolescence.* Reprint, New York: Arno Press.

Herodotus. 1954. *The Histories.* Translated by A. Selincourt. Harmondsworth, UK: Penguin Books.

Hesiod. 1990. *Works and Days.* Translated by S. Lombardo. Cambridge: Hackett Publishing Company.

Hippocrates. 1886. *The Corpus.* Translated by F. Adams. London: Sydenham Society.

———. 1995. *The Fleshes.* Translated by P. Potter. Cambridge, MA: Harvard University Press.

Holt, L. E., and J. Howland. 1916. *The Diseases of Infancy and Children.* New York: Appleton and Company.

Isokrates. 1928. *Panathenaicus.* Translated by G. Norlin. London: William Heinemann.

Jacobs, H. A. 1861/1987. *Incidents in the Life of a Slave Girl.* Cambridge, MA: Harvard University Press.

Josselin, R. 1908. *Diaries 1616–1683.* Edited by E. Hockliffe. London: Royal Historical Society.

Justin Martyr. 1948. *Apology I.* Translated by T. B. Falls. New York: Christian Heritage Press.

Juvenal. 1967. *The Satires.* Translated by P. Green. Harmondsworth, UK: Penguin Books.

Knox, S. 1799. *Of Liberal Education.* Baltimore: Warner and Hanna.

Locke, J. 1693/1989. *Some Thoughts Concerning Education.* London: Clarendon Press.

Luther, M. 1530/1955. "Sermon on Keeping Children in School." Translated by C. M. Jacobs in *Luther's Works,* vol. 46. Philadelphia: Fortress Press.

Marco Polo. 1926. *The Travels of Marco Polo.* Translated by W. Marsden, 1818. New York: Horace Liveright.

Mauriceau, F. 1668. *Des maladies des femmes grosses et accouchees.* Paris: Jean Henault.

Mayhew, H. 1861/1985. *London Labour and the London Poor.* Annotated by V. Neuberg. London: Penguin Books.

McGuffey, W. 1887. *Second Reader.* New York: American Book Company.

Montaigne, M. de. 1957. *Essays.* Translated by D. M. Frame. Stanford, CA: Stanford University Press.

Moody, E. 1793. *The School for Good Manners.* Norwich, UK: Winsdor.

Mulcaster, R. 1582. *The First Part of the Elementarie.* London: Thomas Vautroullier.

Oribasius. 1876. *Synopsis.* In Oeuveres d'Oribase. Translated by U. C. Bussemaker and C. V. Daremberg. Paris: J. B. Brailliere.

Paine, T. 1792. *The Rights of Man.* London: H. D. Symonds.

Papyrus Carlsburg No. VIII. 1939. Annotated by E. K. Iverson. Munksgaard, Denmark: Benharn.

Papyrus Ebers. 1931. Annotated by C. P. Bryan: New York: Appleton.

Paul of Aegina. 1846. *The Seven Books.* London: Sydenham Society.

Petty, W. 1648/1931. "Advice to Mr. Samuel Hartlib for the Advancement of Some Particular Parts of Learning." In *The History of Pediatrics,* by G. F. Still. London: Oxford University Press.

Plato. 1930. *Republic.* Translated by P. Shorey. Cambridge, MA: Harvard University Press.

———. 1937. *Theaetetus.* Translated by B. Jowett. New York: Random House.

Pliny. 1938. *Natural History.* Translated by W. H. S. Jones. Cambridge, MA: Harvard University Press.

Plutarch. 1927. *Moralia.* Translated by F. C. Babbitt. London: William Heinemann.

———. 1950. "The Lycurgus." In *Lives.* New York: Mentor Classics.

Polybius. 1922. *The Histories.* Translated by W. R. Paton. London: William Heinemann.

Quintilian. 1921. *Institutio Oratoriae.* Translated by H. E. Butler. London: William Heinemann.

The Quran. 1981. Translated by M. Z. Khan. London: Cruzon Press.

Rhodes, H. 1577/1868. *Boke of Nurture.* In *The Babee's Boke*, by F. J. Furnivall. London: N. Trubner.

Rotch, T. M. 1903. *Pediatrics: The Hygienic and Medical Treatment of Children.* Philadelphia: J. B. Lippincott.

Rousseau, J.-J. 1762/1979. *Émile.* Translated by A. Bloom. New York: Basic Books.

Soranus. 1956. *Gynaecology.* Translated by O. Temkin. Baltimore: Johns Hopkins University Press.

Stevenson, R. L. 1919. *The South Seas.* New York: Charles Scribner's Sons.

Strabo. 1854. *The Geography.* Translated by H. C. Hamilton. London: Henry G. Bohn.

Struve, C. A. 1801. *The Domestic Education of Children.* London: Murray and Highley.

Tacitus. 1914. *Dialogues and Germania.* Translated by W. Peterson. London: William Heinemann.

Tacuinum Sanitatis. 1537/1976. Compiled by L. C. Arano. New York: George Braziller.

Talmud. 1989. Translated by Ben Zion Bokser. New York: Paulist Press.

Tennent, J. 1736. *Every Man His Own Doctor.* Williamsburg, VA: Wil Parks.

Thomas Aquinas. 1952. *Summa Theologica.* Dominican translation. London: Encyclopedia Britannica Press.

Tocqueville, A. de. 1862. *Democracy in America.* Translated by H. Reeve. London: Longman, Green and Roberts.

Turner, D. 1736. *De Morbis Cutaneis.* London: R. Wilkins.

Watson, J. B. 1928. *Psychological Care of Infants and Children.* New York: W. W. Norton and Company.

Watts, I. 1810. *Complete Works,* vol. 5. London: John Barfield.

Wigglesworth, M. 1777. *The Day of Doom.* Norwich, UK: Green and Spooner.

Wordsworth, W. 1924. *Poetry and Prose.* Oxford: Clarendon Press.

Xenophon. 1849. *On the Lacedemonian Republic.* London: Henry Bohn.

SECONDARY SOURCES

Abt, A. F. 1965. *Abt-Garrison History of Pediatrics.* Philadelphia: W. B. Saunders.

Aldred, C. 1961. *The Egyptians.* London: Thames & Hudson.

Alexander, R. M. 1992. "Wayward Girls in New York." In *Small Worlds.* Edited by E. West and P. Petrik. Kansas City: University Press of Kansas.

Allen, A. T. 1991. *Feminism and Motherhood in Germany, 1800–1914.* New Brunswick, NJ: Rutgers University Press.

Amt, E. 1993. *Women's Lives in Medieval Europe.* New York: Routledge.

Anderson, B. S., and J. P. Zinsser. 1988. *A History of Their Own,* vols. 1 and 2. New York: Harper & Row.

Andrieux, M. 1972. *Daily Life in Venice.* New York: Praeger.

Aries, P. 1965. *Centuries of Childhood.* New York: Vintage.

Aries, P., and G. Duby. 1989. *A History of Private Lives,* vols. 1–5. Cambridge, MA: Belknap Press.

Aston, W. G. 1972. *Nihongi.* Rutland, VT: Charles Tuttle.

Babcock, B. A. 1991. *Pueblo Mothers and Children.* Santa Fe, NM: Ancient-City Press.

Badinter, E. 1980. *Mother Love.* New York: Macmillan.

Bagley, J. 1960. *Life in Medieval England.* London: Batsford.

Bahadur, K. P. 1979. *A History of Indian Civilization.* New Delhi: Ess Ess Publications.

Baker, J. P. 1991. The incubator controversy. *Pediatrics* 87:654–62.

Baldson, J. P. 1962. *Roman Women.* Westport, CT: Greenwood Press.

Ballabriga, A. 1991. "One Century of Pediatrics in Europe." In *History of Pediatrics 1850–1950.* Edited by B. Nichols, A. Ballabriga, and N. Kretchmer. New York: Raven Press.

Bancroft-Hunt, N., and W. Forman. 1981. *The Indians of the Great Plains.* London: Orbis.

Barnard, E. S. 1977. *Great American West.* Pleasantville, NY: Reader's Digest Association.

Basham, A. L. 1954. *The Wonder That Was India.* New York: Grove Press.

Baumslag, N. 1986. *Primary Health Care Pioneer.* Washington, DC: American Public Health Association.

Baumslag, N., and D. Michels. 1995. *Milk, Money, and Madness.* Westport, CT: Bergin & Garvey.

Baxby, D. 1999. The end of smallpox. *History Today* 493:14–16.

Bayne-Powell, R. 1938. *Eighteenth-Century London Life.* New York: E. P. Dutton.

Beales, R. W. 1985. "The Child in Seventeenth-Century America." In *American Childhood.* Edited by J. M. Hawes and N. R. Hiner. Westport, CT: Greenwood Press.

Bellwood, P. 1987. *The Polynesians.* London: Thames & Hudson.

Besant, W. 1902. *London in the Eighteenth Century.* London: Adam and Charles Black.

Beynon, A. D., and M. C. Dean. 1988. Distinct dental-development patterns in early fossil hominids. *Nature* 335:509–14.

Bhagvat Sinh Jee, H. H. 1927. *Aryan Medical Science.* Gondal, India: Electric Printing Press.

Billings, M. 1987. *The Cross and the Crescent.* London: BBC Publications.

Bloch, R. 1958. *The Etruscans.* New York: Frederick Praeger.

Blumenfeld-Kosinski, R. 1990. *Not of Woman Born.* Ithaca, NY: Cornell University Press.

Blumner, H. 1914. *The Home Life of the Ancient Greeks.* New York: Funk & Wagnalls.

Blyth, R. H. 1960. *Japanese Life and Character in Senryu.* Tokyo: Hokuseido Press.

Bonfante, L. 1986. *Etruscan Life and Afterlife.* Detroit: Wayne State University Press.

Bongartz, R. 1973. The chocolate Camelot. *American Heritage* 24(4): 95–96.

Boswell, J. 1988. *The Kindness of Strangers.* New York: Pantheon Books.

———. 1995. *Same-Sex Unions.* New York: Vintage Books.

Bosworth, A. R. 1967. *America's Concentration Camps.* New York: Norton.

Boyle, L. 1989. *St. Clement's.* Milan: Kina Italia.

Bradley, K. R. 1991. *Discovering the Roman Family.* Oxford: Oxford University Press.

Braun, W. 1991. "German Pediatrics." In *History of Pediatrics 1850–1950.* Edited by B. L. Nichols, A. Ballabriga, and N. Kretchmer. New York: Raven Press.

Bremner, R. H. 1970–1971. *Children and Youth in America*, vols. 1 and 2. Cambridge, MA: Harvard University Press.

Briggs, L. C. 1960. *Tribes of the Sahara.* Cambridge, MA: Harvard University Press.

Brondsted, J. 1960. *The Vikings.* Baltimore: Penguin.

Brown, C. 1984. *Scenes from Everyday Life.* London: Faber & Faber.

Brown, F., et al. 1985. Early *Homo erectus* skeleton from west Lake Turkana, Kenya. *Nature* 316:788–92.

Bryson, B. 1990. *The Mother Tongue.* New York: William Morrow.

Bullis, D. July 2000. The longest hajj. *Aramaco World* 3–38.

Burridge, K. 1969. *Tangu Tradition.* Oxford: Clarendon Press.

Burrows, E. G., and M. E. Spiro. 1957. *An Atoll Culture.* Westport, CT: Greenwood Press.

Bush, B. 1990. *Slave Women in Caribbean Society.* London: James Currey.

Cable, M. 1972. *The Little Darlings.* New York: Charles Scribner's Sons.

Cairns, T. 1987. *Renaissance and Reformation.* Cambridge: Cambridge University Press.

Campbell, B. 1985. *Human Evolution.* New York: Aldine Publishing.

Cann, R. L., et al. 1987. Mitochondrial DNA and human evolution. *Nature* 325: 31–36.

Carcopino, J. 1940. *Daily Life in Ancient Rome.* New Haven, CT: Yale University Press.

Cardini, F. 1989. *Europe 1492.* New York: Facts on File.

Carmichael, A. G. 1986. *Plague and the Poor in Renaissance Florence.* Cambridge: Cambridge University Press.

Carrington, R. 1971. *The Mediterranean.* New York: Viking Press.

Casson, L. 1975. *Daily Life in Ancient Egypt*. New York: American Heritage.

———. 1975. *Daily Life in Ancient Rome*. New York: American Heritage.

Caulfield, E. 1931. *The Infant Welfare Movement in the Eighteenth Century*. New York: P. B. Hoeber.

Censer, J. T. 1984. *North Carolina Planters and Their Children*. Baton Rouge: Louisiana State University Press.

Cervantes, M. A. 1978. *Treasures of Ancient Mexico*. New York: Crescent Books.

Chadwick, J. 1976. *The Mycenaean World*. Cambridge: Cambridge University Press.

Chamberlain, B. H. 1971. *Japanese Things*. Rutland, VT: Charles Tuttle.

Chamberlin, E. R. 1966. *Everyday Life in Renaissance Times*. London: Batsford.

Champollion, J. 1971. *The World of the Egyptians*. Geneva: Minerva.

Chartier, R. 1989. "The Practical Impact of Writing." In *A History of Private Lives*, by P. Aries and G. Duby. Cambridge, MA: Belknap Press.

Cheng, T. 1980. *The World of the Chinese*. Hong Kong: Chinese University Press.

Chrisman, O. 1920. *The Historical Child*. Boston: Richard G. Badger.

Christ, K. 1984. *The Romans*. Berkeley: University of California Press.

Clement, P. R. 1985. "The City and the Child." In *American Childhood*. Edited by J. M. Hawes and N. R. Hiner. Westport, CT: Greenwood Press.

Clendening, L. 1942. *Source Book of Medical History*. New York: Henry Schuman.

Coates, S. May 1999. Scissors or sword? *History Today* 7–13.

Cockburn, A., and E. Cockburn. 1985. *Mummies, Diseases, and Ancient Cultures*. Cambridge: Cambridge University Press.

Codrington, R. H. 1981. *The Melanesians*. Oxford: Oxford University Press.

Coldham, P. W. 1992. *Emigrants in Chains*. Gloustershire, UK: Alan Smith.

Colón, A. R. 1987. *The Boke of Children*. Columbus, OH: Ross.

Colón, A. R., and P. A. Colón. 1999. *Nurturing Children: A History of Pediatrics*. Westport, CT: Greenwood Press.

Colón, A. R., and M. Ziai. 1985. "Growth and Aging." In *Pediatric Pathophysiology*. Boston: Little, Brown and Company.

Colón, P. A., and A. R. Colón. 1989. "The Health of America's Children." In *Caring for America's Children*. Edited by F. J. Macchiarola and A. Gartner. New York: Proceedings of the Academy of Political Sciences.

Cone, T. E. 1961. De pondere infantum recens natorum. *Pediatrics* 27:490–98.

———. 1979. *History of American Pediatrics*. Boston: Little, Brown and Company.

Constantelos, D. J. 1968. *Byzantine Philanthropy and Social Welfare*. New Brunswick, NJ: Rutgers University Press.

Contenau, G. 1966. *Everyday Life in Babylonia and Assyria*. New York: W. W. Norton.

Cooper, M. 1965. *They Came to Japan*. Berkeley: University of California Press.

Corlett, W. T. 1935. *The Medicine Man of the American Indian*. Baltimore: C. C. Thomas.

Cotterell, A. 1979. *The Minoan World*. New York: Charles Scribner's Sons.

Cottrell, L. 1965. *The Quest for Sumer.* New York: G. P. Putnam.

Courdey, J. C. 1984. *The Japanese.* New York: Harper & Row.

Cravens, H. 1985. "Child-Saving in the Age of Professionalism, 1915 to 1930." In *American Childhood.* Edited by J. M. Hawes and N. R. Hiner. Westport, CT: Greenwood Press.

Crawford, S. 1999. *Childhood in Anglo-Saxon England.* Phoenix Mill, UK: Sutton Publishing.

Cunningham, H. 1992. *The Children of the Poor.* Oxford: Blackwell.

Dardess, J. 1991. "Children in Premodern China." In *Children in Historical and Comparative Perspective.* Edited by J. M. Hawes and N. R. Hiner. Westport, CT: Greenwood Press.

Darlington, H. S. 1931. Ceremonial behaviorism. *Psychoanalytic Review* 18:180–328.

Darton, F. J. H. 1982. *Children's Books in England.* Cambridge: Cambridge University Press.

Davidson, B. 1966. *African Kingdoms.* New York: Time-Life.

Davies, W. V. 1987. *Egyptian Hieroglyphs.* London: British Museum Publications.

Davis, A. F. 1972. In *The Spirit of Youth and the City Streets,* by Jane Addams. Urbana: University of Illinois Press.

Dawes, J. D., and J. R. Magilton. 1984. *The Cemetery of St. Helen-on-the-Walls, Aldwark.* London: Council of British Archeology.

Day, G. A. 1964. *They Peopled the Pacific.* New York: Duell, Sloan and Pearce.

Defourneaux, M. 1979. *Daily Life in Spain.* Stanford, CA: Stanford University Press.

Delcort, R. 1972. *Le Moyen Age.* Lausanne: Edita Lausanne.

Delson, E. 1985. *Ancestors: The Hard Evidence.* New York: Alan R. Liss.

De Mause, L. 1974. *The History of Childhood.* New York: Psychohistory Press.

Demos, J. 1970. *A Little Commonwealth.* New York: Oxford University Press.

DeOliveira Marques, A. H. 1971. *Daily Life in Portugal in the Later Middle Ages.* Madison: University of Wisconsin Press.

Diakonoff, I. M. 1985. "Elam." In *The Cambridge History of Iran.* Edited by I. Gershevitch. Cambridge: Cambridge University Press.

Dick, E. 1948. *The Dixie Frontier.* New York: Alfred A. Knopf.

Diesner, H. J. 1978. *The Great Migration.* Leipzig: Hippocrene Books.

Distasi, L. 1981. *Mal Occhio.* San Francisco: North Point Press.

Dixon, S. 1988. *The Roman Mother.* London: Croom Helm.

Driver, H. E. 1961. *Indians of North America.* Chicago: University of Chicago Press.

DuBoulay, F. 1970. *An Age of Ambition.* New York: Viking Press.

Duby, G. 1983. *The Knight, the Lady and the Priest.* New York: Pantheon.

Du Chaillu, P. B. 1889. *The Viking Age.* New York: Charles Scribner's Sons.

Duffy, J. 1953. *Epidemics in Colonial America.* Baton Rouge: Louisiana State University Press.

Dundes, A. 1992. *The Evil Eye.* Madison: University of Wisconsin Press.

Dunn, C. 1920. *The Natural History of the Child.* New York: John Lane Company.

Durantini, M. F. 1983. *The Child in Seventeenth-Century Dutch Painting.* Ann Arbor, MI: UMI Research Press.

Earle, A. M. 1899/1993. *Child Life in Colonial Days.* New York: Macmillan. Reprint, New York: Berkeshire House.

Eastman, C. A. 1971. *Indian Boyhood.* New York: Dover.

Eisen, G. 1988. *Children and Play in the Holocaust.* Amherst: University of Massachusetts Press.

Elkins, A. P. 1938. *The Australian Aborigines.* Sydney: Angus and Roberston.

Elton, G. R. 1963. *Reformation Europe.* London: Fontana Press.

Epstein, L. M. 1948. *Sex Laws and Customs in Judism.* New York: KTAV Publishing House.

Erikson, E. 1950. *Childhood and Society.* New York: W. W. Norton and Co.

Evans, J. 1925. *Life in Medieval France.* New York: Phaidon.

Evans, J. K. 1991. *War, Women, and Children in Ancient Rome.* London: Routledge.

Evans, R. J., and W. R. Lee. 1981. *The German Family.* London: Croom Helm; New York: Barnes and Noble.

Fagan, B. M. 1984. *The Aztecs.* New York: W. H. Freeman.

———. 1989. *People of the Earth.* Glenview, IL: Scott, Foresman, and Company.

Fildes, V. 1986. *Breast, Bottles, and Babies.* Edinburgh: Edinburgh University Press.

Finucane, R. C. 2000. *The Rescue of the Innocents.* New York: St. Martin's Press.

Fitzhugh, W. W., and A. Crowell. 1988. *Crossroads of Continents.* Washington, DC: Smithsonian Institution Press.

Fitzhugh, W. W., and S. A. Kaplan. 1982. *Inua.* Washington, DC: Smithsonian Institution Press.

Flandrin, J. L. 1976. *Families in Former Times.* Cambridge: Cambridge University Press.

Foisil, M. 1989. "The Literature of Intimacy." In *A History of Private Life,* vol. 3. Edited by P. Aries and G. Duby. Cambridge, MA: Belknap Press.

Foley, R. A., and P. C. Lee. 1989. Finite social space, evolutionary pathways, and reconstructing hominid behavior. *Science* 243:901–6.

Fox, S. 1985. *The Medieval Woman.* Boston: Little, Brown and Company.

———. 1990. *The Unknown Internment.* Boston: Twayne Publishers.

Frazier, J. 1951. *The Golden Bough.* New York: Macmillan.

Frederic, L. 1972. *Daily Life in Japan at the Time of the Samurai.* New York: Prager.

Freedman, R. 1983. *Children of the Wild West.* New York: Clarian Books.

Fremantle, A. 1965. *Age of Faith.* New York: Time-Life.

Fuchs, R. G. 1984. *Abandoned Children.* Albany: State University of New York Press.

Furst, P. T., and J. L. Furst. 1982. *North American Indian Art.* New York: Rizzoli.

Garland, R. 1990. *The Greek Way of Life.* Ithaca, NY: Cornell University Press.

Garrison, F. H. 1923/1965. "History of Pediatrics." In *Abt-Garrison History of Pediatrics.* Edited by A. F. Abt. Philadelphia: W. B. Saunders.

Gernet, J. 1962. *Daily Life in China.* New York: Macmillan.

Gibbs, J. L. 1965. *Peoples of Africa.* Prospect Heights, IL: Waveland Press.

Gies, F., and J. Gies. 1987. *Marriage and the Family in the Middle Ages.* New York: Harper & Row.

Gil'adi, Auner. 1992. *Children of Islam.* New York: St. Martin's Press.

Glass, H. 1762. *The Servants Directory.* Dublin: J. Potts.

Glob, P. V. 1969. *The Bog People.* London: Faber & Faber.

Godfrey, E. 1907. *English Children in Olden Times.* New York: E. P. Dutton.

Goldbloom, R. B. 1982. Failure to thrive. *Pediatr Clin North Am* 29:151–66.

Golden, M. 1990. *Childhood in Classical Athens.* Baltimore: Johns Hopkins University Press.

Gordon, E. C. 1991. Accidents among medieval children as seen from the miracles of six English saints and martyrs. *Medical History* 35:145–63.

Gottfried, R. S. 1983. *The Black Death.* London: Free Press.

Gottlieb, B. 1993. *The Family in the Western World.* Oxford: Oxford University Press.

Gowlett, J. A. 1984. *Ascent to Civilization.* New York: Alfred A. Knopf.

Grant, M. 1969. *The Ancient Mediterranean.* New York: Charles Scribner's Sons.

Gray, G. 1872. *The Children's Crusade.* New York: Hurd & Houghton.

Green, H. 1992. *The Uncertainty of Everyday Life.* New York: HarperCollins.

Greenberg, J. H., et al. 1986. The settlement of the Americas. *Current Anthropology* 27:477–88.

Guidoni, E., and R. Magni. 1977. *The Andes.* New York: Grosset & Dunlop.

Gurney, O. R. 1972. *The Hittites.* London: Allen Lane.

Gutman, H. G. 1976. *The Black Family in Slavery and Freedom.* New York: Vintage Books.

Gwynn, D. R. 1958. "Ireland." In *Encyclopedia Britannica.*

Hale, P. 1909. *Great Portraits of Children.* Boston: Bates & Guild.

Hammond, J. B. 1958. "Shaftesbury, Anthony Ashley Cooper." In *Encyclopedia Britannica.*

Hampsten, E. 1991. *Settler's Children.* Norman: University of Oklahoma Press.

Hanawalt, B. A. 1986. *The Ties That Bind.* Oxford: Oxford University Press.

———. 1993. *Growing Up in Medieval London.* Oxford: Oxford University Press.

Hand, W. D. 1974. That the child may rise in the world. *Trans Stud Coll Physicians Phila* 42:77–80.

Harden, D. 1962. *The Phoenicians.* London: Thames & Hudson.

Harper, R. F. 1904. *The Code of Hammurabi, King of Babylon.* Chicago: University of Chicago Press.

Harris, D. R. 1981. "The Prehistory of Human Subsistence." In *Food, Nutrition, and Evolution*. Edited by P. Walker, N. Kretchmer, and N. Masson. New York: Masson.

Hausfater, G., and S. B. Hrdy. 1984. *Infanticide*. New York: Aldine.

Hawes, J. M. 1991. *The Children's Rights Movement*. Boston: Twayne Publishers.

Hawes, J. M., and N. R. Hiner. 1985. *American Childhood*. Westport, CT: Greenwood Press.

Hawes, J. M., and N. R. Hiner, eds. 1991. *Children in Historical and Comparative Perspective: An International Handbook and Research Guide*. Westport, CT: Greenwood Press.

Hawke, D. F. 1988. *Everyday Life in Early America*. New York: Harper & Row.

Hay, D. 1967. *The Age of the Renaissance*. London: Thames & Hudson.

Heaton, E. W. 1956. *Everyday Life in Old Testament Times*. New York: Charles Scribner's Sons.

Heichelheim, F. M., et al. 1962. *A History of the Roman People*. Englewood Cliffs, NJ: Prentice-Hall.

Herlihy, D. 1978. *Medieval Children*. Walter Prescott Webb Memorial Lectures. Austin: University of Texas Press.

———. 1985. *Medieval Households*. Cambridge, MA: Harvard University Press.

Herm, G. 1975. *The Celts*. New York: St. Martin's Press.

Heurgon, J. 1964. *Daily Life of the Etruscans*. New York: Macmillan.

Heywood, C. 1988. *Childhood in Nineteenth-Century France*. Cambridge: Cambridge University Press.

Hicks, J. 1974. *The Empire Builders*. New York: Time-Life.

Highwater, J. 1984. *Ritual of the Wind*. New York: Alfred van der Marck.

Hillebrand, H. M. 1926. *The Child Actors*. Urbana: University of Illinois Press.

Hinckeldey, C. 1985. *Pictures from the Crime Museum*. Rothenburg, Germany: Druckerei Schulist.

Hiner, N. R., and J. M. Hawes. 1985. *Growing Up in America*. Chicago: University of Illinois Press.

Hollister, C. 1982. *Medieval Europe*. New York: Knopf.

Holmes, G. 1988. *The Oxford Illustrated History of Medieval Europe*. Oxford: Oxford University Press.

Holt, M. I. 1992. *The Orphan Trains*. Lincoln: University of Nebraska Press.

Hood, S. 1971. *The Minoans*. New York: Praeger.

Hostetler, J. A. 1993. *Amish Society*. Baltimore: Johns Hopkins University Press.

Houlbrooke, R. 1988. *English Family Life, 1576–1716*. Oxford: Blackwell.

Hsu, C. H., and A. H. Ward. 1984. *Ancient Chinese Society*. San Francisco: Yee Wen Publishing.

Huard, P., and R. LaPlane. 1981. *Histoire Illustre de la Pediatrie*. Paris: Roger da Costa.

Huizinga, J. 1924. *The Waning of the Middle Ages.* London: Edward Arnold.

Hunt, D. 1970. *Parents and Children in History.* New York: Basic Books.

Hutchins, V. L. 1994. Maternal and Child Health Bureau *Pediatrics* 94:695–99.

Hyatte, R. 1984. *Laughter for the Devil.* Rutherford, NJ: Associated University Presses.

Illick, J. E. 1974. "Child Rearing in Seventeenth Century England and America." In *The History of Childhood,* by L. de Mause. New York: Psychohistory Press.

Inglis, R. 1985. *The Children's War.* London: Collins.

Ingram, J. K. 1958. "Modern Slavery." In *Encyclopedia Britannica.*

Iversen, E. 1939. *Papyrus Carlsberg No. 8.* Copenhagen: Carlsbergfondet.

Jacobs, D. 1969. *Constantinople.* New York: American Heritage.

Jaggi, O. P. 1977. *Medicine in Medieval India.* Delhi: Atma Ram and Sons.

Jastrow, M. 1914. *Babylonian–Assyrian Birth Omens and Their Cultural Significance.* Opelmann: Giessen.

Jelliffe, D. B. 1968. *Child Nutrition in Developing Countries.* Washington, DC: U.S. Department of Health, Education and Welfare.

Jenness, D. 1960. *Indians of Canada.* Ottawa: National Museum of Canada Press.

Jesch, J. 1991. *Women in the Viking Age.* New York: Boydell.

Johanson, D., and M. Edey. 1981. *Lucy.* New York: Simon & Schuster.

Johnson, N. 1991. *Eighteenth-Century London.* London: Museum of London Press.

Jones, J. W. 1893. Observations on the origin of the division of man's life into stages. *Archaeologia* 35:167–89.

Jordan, T. E. 1987. *Victorian Childhood.* Albany: State University of New York Press.

Josephy, A. M. 1968. *The Indian Heritage of America.* New York: Bantam.

Karageorghis, V. 1981. *Ancient Cyprus.* Baton Rouge: Louisiana State University.

Kemp, J. R. 1986. *Lewis Hine.* Jackson: University Press of Mississippi.

Kendall, A. 1973. *Everyday Life of the Incas.* New York: Dorsett.

Kendall, E. 1973. Beyond mother's knee. *American Heritage* 244:12–16.

Kevill-Davies, S. 1991. *Yesterday's Children.* Suffolk: Antique Collector's Club.

King, M. L. 1991. *Women of the Renaissance.* Chicago: University of Chicago Press.

Klein, A. 1932. *Child Life in Greek Art.* New York: Columbia University Press.

Kleinbaum, A. W. 1983. *The War against the Amazons.* New York: McGraw-Hill.

Knaak, M. 1988. *The Forgotten Artist.* Benego Springs, CA: Anza-Borrego Association.

Kolchin, P. 1993. *American Slavery, 1619–1877.* New York: Hill & Wang.

Kottak, C. P. 1987. *Anthropology.* New York: Random House.

Kramer, S. N. 1967. *Cradle of Civilization.* New York: Time-Life.

———. 1981. *History Begins at Sumer.* Philadelphia: University of Pennsylvania Press.

Kutumbiah, P. 1962. *Ancient Indian Medicine.* Bombay: Orient Longmans.

Lacey, W. K. 1984. *The Family in Classical Greece.* Ithaca, NY: Cornell University Press.

Lagnado, L. M., and S. C. Dekel. 1991. *Children of the Flames*. New York: William Morrow.

Landrigan, P. J., and R. Belville. 1993. The dangers of illegal child labor. *Am J Dis Child* 147:1029.

LaPlane, R. "French Pediatrics." In *History of Pediatrics 1850–1950*. Edited by B. Nichols, A. Ballabriga, and N. Kretchmer. New York: Raven Press.

Larkin, J. 1987. *Children Everywhere*. Sturbridge, MA: Old Sturbridge Village.

Latham, R. 1982. *The Travels of Marco Polo*. New York: Arabis Books.

Laurence, J. 1960. *A History of Capital Punishment*. New York: Citadel Press.

Leakey, R. E. 1981. *The Making of Mankind*. New York: Dutton.

Leakey, R. E., and R. Lewin. 1978. *People of the Lake*. New York: Anchor Press.

Leibowitz, J. O., and S. Marcus. 1984. *Sefer Hanisyonot*. Jerusalem: Magnes Press.

Leonard, J. N. 1967. *Ancient America*. New York: Time-Life.

———. 1968. *Early Japan*. New York: Time-Life.

Levy, H. S. 1966. *Chinese Footbinding*. New York: Rawls.

Lewin, R. 1987. *Bones of Contention*. New York: Simon & Schuster.

Lewis, N. 1983. *Life in Egypt Under Roman Rule*. Oxford: Clarendon Press.

Lipkin, L. 1996. The child I've left behind. *New York Times Magazine* (19 May):44–45.

Lopez, A. A. 1988. *The Human Body and Ideology: Concepts of the Ancient Nahuas*. Salt Lake City: University of Utah Press.

Loth, H. 1987. *Woman in Ancient Africa*. Westport, CT: Lawrence Hill.

Loverance, R. 1988. *Byzantium*. London: British Museum Publications.

Lowie, R. H. 1954. *Indians of the Plains*. New York: Natural History Press.

Lucas-Dubreton, J. 1961. *Daily Life in Florence*. New York: Macmillan.

Luzbetak, L. J. 1951. *Marriage and Family in Caucasia*. Vienna: St. Gabriel's Mission Press.

MacDowell, D. M. 1986. *Spartan Law*. Edinburgh: Scottish Academic Press.

MacPherson, S. 1987. *Five Hundred Million Children*. Sussex, UK: Wheatsheaf Books.

Macqueen, J. G. 1986. *The Hittites*. London: Thames & Hudson.

Macquoid, P. 1923. *Four Hundred Years of Children's Costumes*. London: Medici Society.

Majno, G. 1975. *The Healing Hand*. Cambridge, MA: Harvard University Press.

Makris, M. L. 1985. *The Human Story*. London: Commonwealth Institute.

Manzione, C. K. 1995. *Christ's Hospital of London*. London: Associated University Presses.

Marcus, I. G. 1996. *Rituals of Childhood*. New Haven, CT: Yale University Press.

Markale, J. 1975. *Women of the Celts*. London: Gordon Cremonesi.

Marshall, S. 1991. "Childhood in Early Modern Europe." In *Children in Historical and Comparative Perspective*. Edited by J. M. Hawes and N. R. Hiner. Westport, CT: Greenwood Press.

Martinson, F. M. 1992. *Growing Up in Norway, 800 to 1990.* Carbondale: Southern Illinois University Press.

Marvick, E. W. 1974. "Nature versus Nurture." In *The History of Childhood,* by L. de Mause. New York: Psychohistory Press.

Mason, J. A. 1966. *The Ancient Civilizations of Peru.* Harmondsworth, UK: Penguin.

Maspero, H. 1978. *China in Antiquity.* Kent, UK: Dawson and Sons.

Masson-Oursel, P., et al. 1934. *Ancient India and Indian Civilization.* London: Kegan Paul.

Maxwell, J. A. 1978. *America's Fascinating Indian Heritage.* Pleasantville, NY: Reader's Digest Association.

McLaughlin, M. 1974. "Survivors and Surrogates," In *The History of Childhood,* by L. de Mause. New York: Psychohistory Press.

McMillen, S. G. 1990. *Motherhood in the Old South.* Baton Rouge: Louisiana State University.

Mead, M. 1953. *Growing Up in New Guinea.* New York: Mentor Books.

Means, P. A. 1964. *Ancient Civilizations of the Andes.* New York: Gordian Press.

Mee, C. L. 1975. *Daily Life in Renaissance Italy.* New York: American Heritage.

Meyerhof, M. 1984. *Studies in Medieval Arabic Medicine.* London: Variorum.

Montanari, F. 1990. *The Roman Forum.* Rome: Nuova Tourifon.

Morison, S. E., and H. S. Commager. 1962. *The Growth of the American Republic.* New York: Oxford University Press.

Morley, S. G. 1946. *The Ancient Maya.* Stanford, CA: Stanford University Press.

Morse, A. D. 1983. *While Six Million Died.* Woodstock, NY: Overlook Press.

Murdock, G. P. 1959. *Africa: Its People and Their Cultural History.* New York: McGraw-Hill.

Murthy, K. K. 1982. *Social and Cultural Life in Ancient India.* Delhi: Sundeep.

Musil, A. 1928. *The Names and Customs of the Rwala Bedouins.* New York: American Geographic Society.

Nardinelli, C. 1990. *Child Labor and the Industrial Revolution.* Bloomington: Indiana University Press.

Nicholas, D. 1985. *The Domestic Life of a Medieval City.* Lincoln: University of Nebraska Press.

———. 1991. "Childhood in Medieval Europe." In *Children in Historical and Comparative Perspective.* Edited by J. M. Hawes and N. R. Hiner. Westport, CT: Greenwood Press.

Norton-Taylor, D. 1974. *The Celts.* New York: Time-Life.

Oates, J. 1979. *Babylon.* London: Thames & Hudson.

Offenhartz-Greene, L. 1992. *Child Labor: Then and Now.* New York: Franklin Watts.

O'Malley, J. 1993. *The First Jesuits.* Cambridge, MA: Harvard University Press.

Oppenheim, A. L. 1964. *Ancient Mesopotamia.* Chicago: University of Chicago Press.

Origo, I. 1957. *The Merchant of Prato.* New York: Alfred A. Knopf.

Ozment, S. 1983. *When Fathers Ruled.* Cambridge, MA: Harvard University Press.

———. 1990. *Three Behaim Boys.* New Haven, CT: Yale University Press.

Parent, S., and M. Shevell. 1998. The "first to perish." *Arch Pediatr Adolesc Med* 152: 79–86.

Parker, G. 1979. *Europe in Crisis, 1598–1648.* Ithaca, NY: Cornell University Press.

Parsons, C. D. 1985. *Healing Practices in the South Pacific.* Honolulu: University of Hawaii Press.

Payne, G. H. 1916. *The Child in Human Progress.* New York: G. P. Putnam's Sons.

Payne, R. 1984. *The Dream and the Tomb.* New York: Stein & Day.

Peavy, L., and U. Smith. 1996. *Pioneer Women.* New York: Smithmark.

Perrot, M. 1990. *A History of Private Life,* vol. 4. Cambridge, MA: Belknap Press.

Pheiffer, J. E. 1977. *The Emergence of Society.* New York: McGraw-Hill.

Pickles, S. 1990. *The Grand Tour.* New York: Harmony Books.

Pinchbeck, I., and M. Hewitt. 1969. *Children in English Society,* vols. 1 and 2. London: Routledge and Kegan Paul.

Pine, L. 1999. Girls in uniform. *History Today* 493:24–29.

Plimmer, C., and D. Plimmer. 1975. *Slavery: The Anglo-American Involvement.* New York: Barnes and Noble Books.

Poland, F., et al. 1926. *The Culture of Ancient Greece and Rome.* Boston: Little, Brown and Company.

Pollock, L. A. 1983. *Forgotten Children.* Cambridge: Cambridge University Press.

———. 1987. *A Lasting Relationship.* Hanover, NH: University Press of New England.

Precope, J. 1954. *Medicine, Magic, and Mythology.* London: William Heinmann.

Preston, S. H., and M. R. Haines. 1991. *Fatal Years.* Princeton, NJ: Princeton University Press.

Quennell, M. 1959. *Everyday Life in Roman and Anglo-Saxon Times.* London: Batsford.

Rawson, B. 1986. *The Family in Ancient Rome.* Ithaca, NY: Cornell University Press.

———. 1991. *Marriage, Divorce, and Children in Ancient Rome.* Oxford: Oxford University Press.

Razi, Z. 1980. *Life, Marriage, and Death in a Medieval Parish.* Cambridge: Cambridge University Press.

Read, M. 1960. *Children of Their Fathers.* New Haven, CT: Yale University Press.

Reddy, W. M. 1984. *The Rise of Market Culture.* Cambridge: Cambridge University Press.

Reiss, R. E., and A. D. Ash. 1988. The eighth-month fetus. *Obstet Gynecol* 71:270–73.

Revel, J. 1989. "The Uses of Civility." In *A History of Private Lives,* by P. Aries and G. Duby. Cambridge, MA: Belknap Press.

Rhodes, E. H. 1979. *An Army of Children.* London: Granda Publishing.

Rice, T. T. 1967. *Everyday Life in Byzantium.* New York: G. P. Putnam's Sons.

Riedel, E., et al. 1979. *The Book of the Bible.* New York: William Morrow.

Riis, J. A. 1892/1970. *The Children of the Poor.* New York: Johnson Reprint Corporation.

Roberts, R. 1925. *The Social Laws of the Quran.* London: Williams & Norgate.

Robiquet, J. 1965. *Daily Life in the French Revolution.* New York: Macmillan.

Romer, J. 1982. *People of the Nile.* New York: Crown.

Rose, L. 1991. *The Erosion of Childhood.* London: Routledge.

Ross, J. B. 1974. "The Middle-Class Child in Urban Italy, Fourteenth to Sixteenth Century." In *The History of Childhood,* by L. de Mause. New York: Psychohistory Press.

Ross, K. 1978. *Codex Mendoza.* Fribourg: Miller Graphics. Liber S.A.

Rothman, D. J., and S. M. Rothman. 1972. *The Colonial American Family.* New York: Arno Press.

Rountree, H. C. 1989. *The Powhatan Indians of Virginia.* Norman: University of Oklahoma Press.

Rowland, B. 1981. *Medieval Woman's Guide to Health.* Kent, OH: Kent State University Press.

Rowling, M. 1968. *Everyday Life in Medieval Times.* New York: G. P. Putnam's Sons.

Ruhräh, J. 1925. *Pediatrics of the Past.* New York: Paul Hoeber.

Saari, J. L. 1990. *Legacies of Childhood.* Cambridge, MA: Harvard University Press.

Safway el-Alfy, A. 1981. *Childhood and Egyptian Civilization.* Cairo: Egyptian Antiquities Organization Press.

Salzman, L. 1926. *English Life in the Middle Ages.* Oxford: Oxford University Press.

Sansom, G. 1958. *A History of Japan to 1334.* Stanford, CA: Stanford University Press.

Scarborough, J. 1969. *Roman Medicine.* London: Thames & Hudson.

Schaller, J. G., and E. O. Nightingale. 1992. Children and childhoods. *JAMA* 268: 642–44.

Schama, S. 1988. *The Embarrassment of Riches.* New York: A. A. Knopf.

Scheffel, R. L. 1993. *Discovering America's Past.* Pleasantville, NY: Reader's Digest Association.

Schendel, G. 1968. *Medicine in Mexico.* Austin: University of Texas Press.

Schlereth, T. J. 1991. *Victorian America.* New York: HarperCollins.

Schlissel, L. 1982. *Women's Diaries of the Westward Journey.* New York: Schocken Books.

Schlissel, L., et al. 1989. *Far from Home.* New York: Schocken Books.

Schorsch, A. 1979. *Images of Childhood.* New York: Mayflower Books.

Schulz, C. B. 1985. "Children and Childhood in the Eighteenth Century." In *American Childhood.* Edited by J. M. Hawes and N. R. Hiner. Westport, CT: Greenwood Press.

Schwartz, M. 1985. "The Old Eastern Iranian World View According to the Avesta." In *The Cambridge History of Iran*. Edited by I. Gershevitch. Cambridge: Cambridge University Press.

Schwartz, R. B. 1983. *Daily Life in Johnson's London*. Madison: University of Wisconsin Press.

Scott, J. W. R. 1922. *The Foundations of Japan*. New York: Appleton and Company.

Scudder, H. E. 1895. *Childhood in Literature and Art*. Boston: Houghton Mifflin and Company.

Seidler, E. 1989. "A Historical Survey of Children's Hospitals." In *The Hospital in History*. Edited by L. Granshaw and L. Porter. London: Routledge.

Sena, N. 1901. *The Ayurvedic System of Medicine*. Calcutta: Chatterjee.

Severy, M. 1968. *Greece and Rome*. Washington, DC: National Geographic Society.

Shahar, S. 1983. *The Fourth Estate*. London: Methuen.

———. 1990. *Childhood in the Middle Ages*. London: Routledge.

Shapiro, M. 1977. *Children of the Revels*. New York: Columbia University Press.

Shaw, G. B. 1930. *Plays,* vol. 13. New York: W. H. Wise and Company.

Shein, M. 1992. *The Precolumbian Child*. Culver City, CA: Labyrinthos.

Sherrard, P. 1966. *Byzantium*. New York: Time-Life.

Sherwood, J. 1988. *Poverty in Eighteenth-Century Spain*. Toronto: University of Toronto Press.

Shore, H. 2000. The idea of juvenile crime in nineteenth-century England. *History Today* 50(6):21–28.

Shostak, M. 1983. *Nisa*. New York: Vintage.

Showerman, G. 1931. *Rome and the Romans*. New York: Macmillan.

Sik, E. 1966. *The History of Black Africa*. Budapest: Academy Kiado.

Simons, E. L. 1989. Human origins. *Science* 245:1343–50.

Singh, M. P. 1981. *Life in Ancient India*. Varanasi, India: Vishwanidyalaya.

Slater, M. 1984. *Family Life in the Seventeenth Century*. London: Routledge and Kegan Paul.

Smith, B. 1968. *Mexico: A History in Art*. New York: Doubleday.

Smith, B., and W. Weng. 1972. *China: A History in Art*. New York: Doubleday.

Sommerville, C. J. 1990. *The Rise and Fall of Childhood*. New York: Vintage Books.

———. 1992. *The Discovery of Childhood in Puritan England*. Athens: University of Georgia Press.

Sosnowski, K. 1983. *The Tragedy of Children under Nazi Rule*. New York: Howard Fertig.

Sournia, J. C. 1990. *A History of Alcoholism*. Oxford: Basil Blackwell.

Spencer, R. F., et al. 1977. *The Native American*. New York: Harper & Row.

Spitz, L. W. 1985. *The Protestant Reformation*. New York: Harper & Row.

Spock, B. 1976. *Baby and Child Care*. New York: Pocket Books.

Stankiewicz, I. B., D. W. Kamieniecka, and J. L. Howells. 1989. *Isfahan: City of Polish Children*. Lebanon: Association of Former Pupils of Polish Schools.

Steinfels, M. O. 1973. *Who's Minding the Children?* New York: Touchstone Books.

Stenning, D. J. 1959. *Savannah Nomads.* London: Oxford University Press.

Steuer, R. O., and J. B. de Cusance. 1959. *Ancient Egyptian and Cnidian Medicine.* Berkeley: University of California Press.

Stevens, D. 2000. Orphans and musicians in Venice. *History Today* 50(5):21–28.

Steward, J. C. 1995. *The New Child.* Berkeley: University of California Press.

Still, G. F. 1931. *The History of Pediatrics.* London: Oxford University Press.

Stockel, H. H. 1991. *Women of the Apache Nation.* Reno: University of Nevada Press.

Strachey, A. 1940. *Borrowed Children.* New York: The Commonwealth Fund.

Stratton, J. L. 1981. *Pioneer Women.* New York: Simon & Schuster.

Strong, D. 1968. *The Early Etruscans.* New York: G. P. Putnam's Sons.

Stuart, D. M. 1926. *The Boy Through the Ages.* London: Harrap and Company.

Stuart, G. E., et al. 1969. *Man's Past in the Americas.* Washington, DC: National Geographic Society.

Sullivan, M. A. 1994. *Brueghel's Peasants.* Cambridge: Cambridge University Press.

Taddei, M. 1970. *India.* London: Barrie & Jenkins.

Tateishi, J. 1984. *And Justice for All.* New York: Random House.

Teitelbaum, K. 1993. *Schooling for "Good Rebels."* Philadelphia: Temple University Press.

Thompson, C. R. 1958. *Schools in Tudor England.* Charlottesville: University of Virginia Press.

Thomson, G. 1965. *Studies in Ancient Greek Society.* New York: Citadel Press.

Tigner Holmes, U. 1952. *Daily Living in the Twelfth Century.* Madison: University of Wisconsin Press.

Todd, M. 1972. *The Barbarians.* New York: G. P. Putnam's Sons.

Tofani, L. 1993. *Philadelphia Inquirer* 327(101):1–13.

Tom, K. S. 1989. *Echoes from Old China.* Honolulu: University of Hawaii Press.

Trattner, W. I. 1970. *Crusade for the Children.* Chicago: Quadrangle Books.

Trepp, L. 1973. *A History of the Jewish Experience.* West Orange, NJ: Berhman House.

Trumbach, R. 1978. *The Rise of the Egalitarian Family.* New York: Academic Press.

Tuchman, B. 1978. *A Distant Mirror.* New York: Ballantine.

Tucker, M. J. 1974. "The Child as Beginning and End." In *The History of Childhood,* by L. de Mause. New York: Psychohistory Press.

Tuer, A. W. 1887/1979. *History of the Horn Book.* New York: Arno Press.

Tunis, E. 1959. *Indians.* New York: Thomas Crowell.

Turberville, A. S. 1926. *English Men and Manners in the Eighteenth Century.* Oxford: Oxford University Press.

Turnbull, C. M. 1965. *Wayward Servants.* Westport, CT: Greenwood Press.

Turner, E. S. 1957. *Call the Doctor.* New York: St. Martin's Press.

Tyrrell, B., and P. Jurgens. 1983. *African Heritage.* Johannesburg: Macmillan South Africa.

Ulich, R. 1975. *Three Thousand Years of Educational Wisdom.* Cambridge, MA: Harvard University Press.

Uno, K. S. 1991. "Japan." In *The Children's Rights Movement,* by J. M. Hawes. Boston: Twayne Publishers.

U.S. Department of Health and Human Services. 1991. *Annual Report.* Washington, DC: Government Printing Office.

Vahlquist, B., and A. Wallgreen. 1964. *Nils Rosen von Rosenstein.* Uppsala: Almquist & Wiksells.

Veeder, B. 1957. *Pediatric Profiles.* St. Louis: C. V. Mosby.

Verut, D. D. 1973. *Precolumbian Dermatology and Cosmetology.* New York: Schering.

Veyne, P. 1987. *A History of Private Lives.* Cambridge, MA: Belknap Press.

Viets, H. R. 1977. *Smallpox in Colonial America.* New York: Arno Press.

Von Hagen, V. W. 1961. *The Ancient Sun Kingdoms of the Americas.* Cleveland: World Publishing Company.

Von Siebold, P. F. 1841/1973. *Manner and Customs of the Japanese.* Rutland, VT: Charles Tuttle.

Walker, C. B. 1987. *Cuneiform.* London: British Museum Publications.

Weissbach, L. S. 1989. *Child Labor Reform in Nineteenth-Century France.* Baton Rouge: Louisiana State University Press.

Wensinck, A. J. 1932. *The Muslim Creed.* Cambridge: Cambridge University Press.

West, E. 1985. The youngest pioneers. *American Heritage* 371:90–96.

Westall, R. 1985. *Children of the Blitz.* New York: Viking.

Wheeler, M. 1966. *Civilization of the Indus Valley and Beyond.* London: Thames & Hudson.

White, J. M. 1979. *Everyday Life of the North American Indian.* New York: Holmes & Meier.

White, R. 1986. *Dark Caves, Bright Visions.* New York: W. W. Norton.

Whitlock, R. 1976. *Everyday Life of the Maya.* New York: Dorset.

Whymant, A. N. J. 1958. "Polynesian Languages." In *Encyclopedia Britannica.*

Wiedemann, T. 1989. *Adults and Children in the Roman Empire.* London: Routledge.

Willetts, R. F. 1977. *Civilization of Ancient Crete.* Berkeley: University of California Press.

Williams, J. A. 1962. *Islam.* New York: George Braziller.

Wilson, E. B. 1963. *Early America at Work.* New York: Barnes and Company.

Winston, C., and R. Winston. 1975. *Daily Life in the Middle Ages.* New York: American Heritage.

Wishy, B. 1968. *The Child and the Republic.* Philadelphia: University of Pennsylvania Press.

Wissler, C. 1940. *Indians of the United States.* New York: Doubleday.

Woestemeyer, I. F. 1939. *The Westward Movement.* New York: Appleton-Century.

Wong, C. 1936. *A History of Chinese Medicine.* Shanghai: National Quarantine Service.

Wood, C. T. 1970. *The Quest for Eternity.* Hanover, NH: University Press of New England.

Wooden, W. W. 1986. *Children's Literature of the English Renaissance.* Lexington: University Press of Kentucky.

Zinkin, J. 1965. *India.* London: Thames & Hudson.

Zucchi, J. 1992. *The Little Slaves of the Harp.* Montreal: McGill-Queens University Press.

Name Index

❑ ❑ ❑

Subject Index

❏   ❏   ❏

About the Authors

A. R. Colón is Professor Emeritus of Pediatrics at Georgetown University School of Medicine. His career in academic medicine spans over thirty years, during which time he taught pediatrics and lectured nationally and internationally on pediatric diseases and child development and health. He has authored several books on pediatric topics, including one on pediatric aphorisms, *The Boke of Children*, and, with P. A. Colón, *Nurturing Children: A History of Pediatrics* (Greenwood Press, 1999).

P. A. Colón is a freelance writer who has collaborated with A. R. Colón on several publications of pediatric interest.

Hamlet